Reviews for
Integral Development

A tour de force in relation to the notion of social innovation, the authors take us through an energizing new understanding of development. The task is irresistible. The review is far-reaching. The proposals are inspirational. A must-read.

> Pilar Alvarez-Laso, Assistant Director-General for Social and Human Sciences, UNESCO, France

In Integral Development, *Alexander Schieffer and Ronnie Lessem communicate their passion for economic and social transformation by introducing a new, holistic development framework. Rather than top-down, this approach supports mutuality and creative co-creation. Interspersed with first-hand illustrative cases, this is both a visionary and practical book designed to actualize the potential of individuals, organizations, and societies through much-needed partnership and caring.*

> Riane Eisler, author of *The Chalice and the Blade* and *The Real Wealth of Nations*, USA

Integral Development *is outstanding on many levels. Like no other contribution to the field of development it shows the crucial role of culture and spirituality in development processes. Schieffer & Lessem illustrate how community, culture, technology and economics need to interact co-creatively for authentic, sustainable development to happen. The theoretical concepts and practical roadmaps provided in* Integral Development *will enable today's agents of transformation to bring about a much needed, more holistic development paradigm. I rejoice to see how the authors convincingly illustrate how new approaches to education and research, and to the university as a whole, can indeed enable all of us, individually and collectively, to become Integral Developers.*

> Dr. A.T. Ariyaratne, founder and chairman, Sarvodaya Shramadana Movement, Sri Lanka

Integral Development *contains a unique fusion of personal, organisational and societal development. It clearly shows the next evolutionary step for corporate enterprise, taking it beyond Corporate Social Responsibility.* Integral Development *is hugely relevant for anyone concerned with identifying the future role of business in society.*

Birgit Klesper, Senior Vice President, Group Transformational Change & Corporate Responsibility, Deutsche Telekom Group, Germany

Integral Development *by Alexander Schieffer and Ronnie Lessem offers a wonderful opportunity for us to understand the past, the present and the future of development. We often think about development as 'economic development'. Development indeed cannot be dissociated from our human and civilisational evolution. The authors use the term 'integral development' and offer theoretical frameworks and comparative analysis that help us understand what development really means at this important historical junction. It helps us see the choices we have ahead of us. As a social entrepreneur and innovator, I found the book extremely useful and inspiring. I would define it as a road map. It helps strengthen one's vision in order to better contextualise actions. The book is very well written and I recommend it for anyone interested in contributing to our balanced and peaceful co-evolution as humanity.*

Thais Corral, Social Entrepreneur and Innovator, Founder of Network of Human Development and of the social enterprise SINAL do VALE, Brazil

With Integral Development, *Schieffer and Lessem have built a much-needed bridge between individual, organisational and societal development. Organisational developers and transformation agents from all sectors of society will find in this book the knowledge and processes to respond holistically to the multiple crises we face today. It will show them how they can construct creatively on the particular contribution that each context and culture has to make. This eminent work is compulsory reading for everybody engaged in constructive societal change.*

Martin Hilb, Professor and Director, Institute for Leadership and Human Resource Management, University of St. Gallen, Switzerland

From Alexander,
to his cherished son Arjuna.

From Ronnie,
to his angelic granddaughter Saana.

From both of us,
to all agents of transformation
committed to co-creating positive futures
for humanity and the planet.

Integral Development

Transformation and Innovation Series

Series Editors:
Ronnie Lessem, Trans4m Center for Integral Development, Switzerland
Alexander Schieffer, Trans4m Center for Integral Development, Switzerland

The world's economic and socio-political landscape has changed dramatically and created a now-or-never momentum for transformation and innovation. "Business as usual" no longer works. The time has come to fundamentally rethink enterprise, economics and development.

The Gower "Transformation and Innovation Series", with contributions by leading thinkers-and-doers from diverse cultures across the globe, combines theory and practice, informing both decision makers and scholars. It provides cutting-edge, viable approaches to the unprecedented challenges faced by business leaders, management consultants, economic policy makers and development agents.

The pioneering Integral Worlds approach, developed by Lessem and Schieffer, provides a unique and coherent orientation to the wide-ranging volumes in the series. This approach combines individual, organizational and socio-economic development. Drawing on the particularities of each and every culture, it enhances local identity while contributing to global integrity. It activates the potential for a holistic realignment of enterprise and economics with other major dimensions of society, such as nature and community; culture and spirituality; as well as science, systems and technology.

Latest titles in the series

Integral Dynamics
Political Economy, Cultural Dynamics and the Future of the University
Ronnie Lessem with Alexander Schieffer, Junie T. Tong and Samuel D. Rima
ISBN 978-1-4094-5103-7

Integral Community
Political Economy to Social Commons
Ronnie Lessem, Paul Chidara Muchineripi and Steve Kada
ISBN 978-1-4094-4679-8

Integral Economics
Releasing the Economic Genius of Your Society
Ronnie Lessem and Alexander Schieffer
ISBN 978-0-566-09247-3

Integral Research and Innovation
Transforming Enterprise and Society
Ronnie Lessem and Alexander Schieffer
ISBN 978-0-566-08918-3

Integral Development

Realising the Transformative Potential of Individuals, Organisations and Societies

ALEXANDER SCHIEFFER and
RONNIE LESSEM

GOWER

Gower Applied Business Research
Our programme provides leaders, practitioners, scholars and researchers with thought provoking, cutting edge books that combine conceptual insights, interdisciplinary rigour and practical relevance in key areas of business and management.

Published by
Gower Publishing Limited
Wey Court East
Union Road
Farnham
Surrey
GU9 7PT
England

Gower Publishing Company
110 Cherry Street
Suite 3-1
Burlington
VT 05401-3818
USA

www.gowerpublishing.com

British Library Cataloguing in Publication Data
A catalogue record for this book is available from the British Library.

ISBN: 978-1-4094-2353-9 (hbk)
ISBN: 978-1-4094-2354-6 (ebk – ePDF)
ISBN: 978-1-4094-6040-4 (ebk – ePUB)

The Library of Congress has cataloged the printed edition as follows:
Schieffer, Alexander.
 Integral development : realising the transformative potential of individuals, organisations and societies / by Alexander Schieffer and Ronnie Lessem.
     pages cm. -- (Transformation and innovation)
 Includes bibliographical references and index.
 ISBN 978-1-4094-2353-9 (hbk) -- ISBN 978-1-4094-2354-6 (ebk) -- ISBN 978-1-4094-6040-4 (epub) 1. Economic development--Social aspects. 2. Political development--Social aspects. 3. Social systems. I. Lessem, Ronnie. II. Title.
HD75.S34 2014
338.9--dc23
2013035196

Printed in the United Kingdom by Henry Ling Limited,
at the Dorset Press, Dorchester, DT1 1HD

Contents

List of Figures

List of Tables

About the Authors

Professor Alexander Schieffer, Co-Founder, Trans4m Center for Integral Development, Geneva, Switzerland

Born in Germany, Alexander Schieffer studied economics, business and social sciences at the University of St. Gallen, Switzerland. His Doctoral thesis, also at St. Gallen, addressed new styles of organizational leadership ("Führungspersönlichkeit"). He initially worked as an executive in International Investment Banking, and then in Media and Communication with the media giant Bertelsmann. He then moved to Singapore where he founded and built up First Asia Publishing, a leading special-interest publishing house, which he sold in 2002 to a Chinese media conglomerate. From this point onwards, Schieffer pursued his passion of bringing about transformation in the economic, social and cultural sphere. Together with his colleague Ronnie Lessem, he established TRANS4M Center for Integral Development (www.trans-4-m.com), headquartered in Geneva. The center focuses on "transformational education" and "research for innovation". At the heart of TRANS4M's work is its integral approach – one of the most innovative and globally applicable approaches to individual, organisational and societal transformation in the field. All of Trans4m's cutting edge programs are geared towards addressing, in a culturally resonant way, burning socio-economic issues on the ground. The programs are spread across Africa (from South Africa to Zimbabwe to Nigeria), in the Middle East (Egypt and Jordan), in Asia (Sri Lanka, India) and Europe (Switzerland, Germany, UK). In parallel, Schieffer is an engaged and dynamic professor, and teaches management, economics and development at universities around the world. He is co-editor (together with Ronnie Lessem) of two Gower–Ashgate book series: the 'Transformation and Innovation Series' and the 'Series on Integral Green Economy and Society'.

Email: schieffer@trans-4-m.com

Professor Ronnie Lessem, Co-Founder, Trans4m Center for Integral Development, Geneva, Switzerland

Ronnie Lessem, born in Zimbabwe of central European parentage, and a graduate of Harvard Business School and the London School of Economics, while a Reader in International Management at City University in the UK, co-founded New Work Ventures, which focused enterprise development, through action learning, within inner cities, and on women finding their niche. At the same time he launched projects on European Management, with IMD in Switzerland, European-ness and Innovation, with Roland Berger Foundation in Germany, African management, with Wits Graduate Business School in South Africa, and Arab as well as Islamic Management, with TEAM International in Cairo and Jordan, before co-founding TRANS4M in Geneva. Lessem studied economics at the University of Zimbabwe, the economics of industry at the London School of Economics, Corporate Planning at Harvard Business School, and he completed his doctorate in Action Learning for Enterprise Development at Cass Business School in London. Ronnie Lessem has written some 30 books, the last six together with Alexander Schieffer, on self, organizational and societal development from a transcultural, transformational perspective. He has also been an international management consultant in Europe and America, India and Africa for some three decades.

Email: lessem@trans-4-m.com

Acknowledgements

In writing this book, we have been fortunate in having wonderful collaborators from across the world. All of them have contributed generously. To all of them we wish to express our heartfelt gratitude.

- From Africa we thank Basheer Oshodi from Nigeria; Debbie Tarr, Bennie Anderson and Barbara Nussbaum from South Africa; as well as Paul Chidara Muchineripi, Steve Kada, Mai Mlambo and Sam Kundishora from Zimbabwe.
- From the Middle East we thank Shaykh Fadhlalla Haeri, originally from Iraq; as well as Ibrahim Abouleish, Helmy Abouleish, Maximilian Abouleish-Boes and Bianca Fliss, all from Egypt.
- From Asia we thank Vinya Ariyaratne from Sri Lanka; as well as Radhike Khanna, Rishab Khanna and S.V. Mani from India.
- From Australia we thank Mohan Bhagwandas.
- From Europe we thank Cornelio Sommaruga from Switzerland; Geanina Nae from Rumania; Reza Moussavian from Germany; Darja Piciga from Slovenia; Tony Bradley from the UK; Unai Elorza from Spain; Robin Alfred from Scotland; and Tatiana Sokolova from Russia.
- From the Americas we thank Ashok Gangadean, Erin Meezan, Lindsay Stoda, Sam Rima, Neva Morrison and Rebecca Adamson from the USA; as well as Juan Carlos Kaiten from Mexico.

In addition to individual contributions, we wish to acknowledge all the participants from our research, educational and Development programmes who, as co-creators with us, shape new Integral landscape, in theory and in practice. Working together with all of you has greatly influenced this book and has been highly rewarding for us.

We are also deeply grateful to the entire team of our publisher Gower, who supported the writing of this book greatly, from beginning to end.

Finally, Alexander wishes to thank Rama, his wife and companion in life, for her trust in this book and in our work and for her rich input, inspirations and ongoing help in birthing *Integral Development*. Ronnie would like to thank his son Gabriel, for helping his father reach more deeply into his own heritage, and thereby extending his reach into Integral Development.

Prologue

Integral Development: A Journey for All of Us

ABOUT THE BOOK

Integral Development offers a framework and processes that enable us to realise our full transformative potential – as individuals, organisations and societies. It is geared towards four overarching objectives that are of concern to humanity at large: healthy and participatory coexistence; balanced and peaceful co-evolution; open and transparent knowledge creation; as well as equitable and sustainable livelihoods.

To achieve these goals, *Integral Development* departs from the notion of development as we know it. It is not primarily oriented towards the development of so-called 'developing' societies. Rather, *Integral Development* is written for each one of us and for all societies – from the South, East, North, West and centre of our World. Hence, Integral Development is not about 'developing' others. Rather, Integral Development is a process of continuous co-evolution, where Development agents, as individuals and as institutions, learn from each other, rather than telling each other how to develop.

Integral Development includes but goes beyond the notion of economic and technological development, to incorporate also natural and communal, as well as cultural and spiritual dimensions of development.

Integral Development places the responsibility for development not on some distant development agencies or departments, but on each one of us, both individually and also collectively. It does so, by linking individual, organisational, communal and societal development. Thereby, each individual, each organisation and enterprise, as well as each community, is a potential development actor within society. In that sense, Integral Development is a process to renew ourselves, our organisations, communities and societies – in integral fashion.

Integral Development purposefully builds on the most innovative development Theory and practice from the four corners of the globe, as well as the world's centre. It is framed to enable you to co-engage with others in bringing about integral human systems – each one of them contributing to an integral society and an integral world.

While standing on the shoulders of many past and current integral thinkers, the integral approach underlying Integral Development is unique in various respects. First, it invokes the active participation of the Integral Developer. Second, it actively includes diverse worldviews, drawn from all corners of the globe. Third it provides a circular developmental rhythm that draws interactively on each one of these diverse grounds, as opposed to pursuing purely linear development. Thereby, Integral Development seeks to contribute to an integral world of unity in diversity.

Finally, in order to fully realise our collective, transformative potential, Integral Development incorporates processes that lead to new educational-development entities. Such entities – we call them Uni-Versities – are designed to bring forth locally unique Development Theory and practice that contribute, altogether, to a world of unity in diversity (hence Uni-Versity). As we shall show in this book, such Uni-Versities fundamentally challenge our conventional understanding of a university. They bring education, research and development right into the centre of individual life, community and society, making them relevant for and resonant with particular cultural and societal contexts.

Development thereby is no longer delegated to often-distant experts, but lodged in the very centre of a particular person, organisation, community or whole society, concerning and engaging all of us.

ABOUT YOU – THE READER

This book has been written for anyone who is concerned with a more healthy, participatory, balanced, peaceful, open, transparent, equitable and sustainable future and who is keen to bring it about, together with others. Whether you are a concerned business or political leader, organisational developer, societal development practitioner, community leader, transformatively oriented schoolteacher or faculty at a university – or simply an individual with a passion for development – this book is for you.

Integral Development is specifically oriented toward the particular development context you, your community, organisation and society are in: in terms of your individual background and situation, your organisational environment, as well as your societal and cultural background. Ultimately, any successful form of development needs to grow out of, fit into, and serve to evolve the particular context that it seeks to enhance.

Therefore, *your* particular development concern and calling, as an individual, as an institution and as a community or society, is the starting point of the Integral Development journey. Your calling and challenge is related to who you are, where you are based, where you belong. Taking your own individual and collective callings and challenges seriously, you get in touch with the needs and capacities within yourselves and within your contexts. From there the Integral Development journey unfolds through the levels of individual, organisational, communal and societal development.

It is this journey that the book invites you to embark on.

ABOUT US – THE AUTHORS

Integral Development is the fruit of many decades of integral work. It builds on our overarching '*Integral Worlds*' approach and the many articulations of it that we have presented over the past years – from Integral Enterprise to Integral Economics, from Integral Community to Integral Dynamics and Integral Research. All of these articulations have been captured in separate volumes published in this Transformation and Innovation Series. Integral Development can be seen as the culmination of our work so far.

As you will notice throughout the book, *Integral Development* is not about theory alone. From the very outset it interlinks theory and practice. In many of the practical case stories that are introduced, we – through Trans4m, our Geneva-based Center for Integral Development – are intimately involved.

Indeed, we see ourselves not as distant experts, but as involved co-creators. From a rural community in Zimbabwe, to a country-wide development initiative in Sri Lanka, from integral research centres in Nigeria and Zimbabwe to a prospective new university in and for Africa, from an Indian social enterprise for mentally challenged women to a new Egyptian university for Sustainable Development, from a global conference initiative to Germany's largest Telkom company – in all of these cases we are co-engaged in Integral Development processes. Each of these is geared in its own way to bring about healthy and participatory coexistence with nature and humankind, balanced and peaceful co-evolution between peoples, open and transparent knowledge creation and equitable and sustainable livelihoods. In each case, we work towards the full actualisation and institutionalisation of the Integral Development process through a new educational-developmental entity that we term Uni-Versity.

Altogether, the integrated combination of the diverse types of Uni-Versities that we shall introduce in this book is called an Integral University. Together, with our global network of co-creators, we work towards bringing about such Integral Universities. We invite you to join us.

A FEW SUGGESTIONS ON HOW TO READ INTEGRAL DEVELOPMENT

To counteract the necessary 'linearity' of this book, where each chapter follows sequentially from another, we provide you with 'multiple entry points' into Integral Development.

- *Orientation and Integration:* Each chapter begins with a short orientation and ends with an integrative conclusion. Through these introductions and conclusions you are provided not only with quick access into each chapter, but also with a storyline interconnecting all chapters.
- *Guiding Questions:* Each chapter responds to a guiding question. At the end of each chapter (except for the concluding Part VII of the book), highlights drawn from the chapter are summarised in a short table.
- *Reflection and Action:* Each concluding table offers a set of poignant questions to reflect upon. We thereby invite you to formulate your own responses and proposed respective actions.
- *Maps and Compass:* Part I of the book challenges the existing perspective on 'Economic' Development and provides first intimations of an integral perspective. Such a new perspective is then fleshed out in Part II, which includes a detailed overview of the full terrain of Integral Development. At the end of Part II (⇨6) we equip you with a compass, so to speak, and a set of maps, providing you with orientation for the terrain. That includes guiding questions, as well as the theory and practice introduced in the book. With the help of compass and maps, you can navigate easily and freely.
- *Cross-References:* In order to create maximum 'interaction' between the various Development perspectives introduced, we continuously cross-reference between chapters. To keep that short, we use the symbol '⇨' followed by the chapter number.

We wish you an interesting and inspiring journey through Integral Development – alone and with others, in theory and in practice. May it be useful for your own development journey, and that of your organisation, community and society!

May it help to realise the transformative potential in all of us.

Alexander Schieffer and Ronnie Lessem

PART

Divided World: The Need for Renewing Human Development

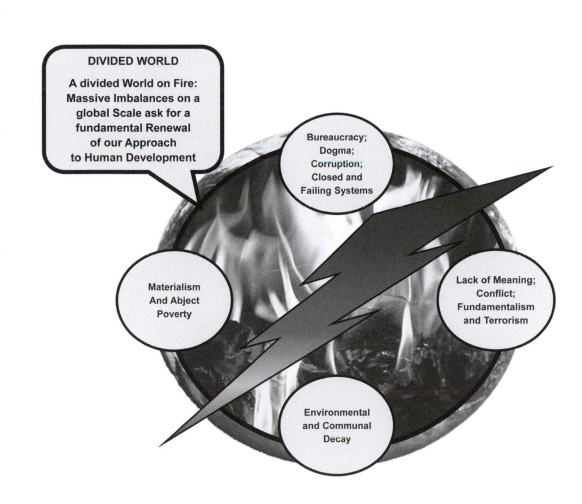

DIVIDED WORLD

A divided World on Fire: Massive Imbalances on a global Scale ask for a fundamental Renewal of our Approach to Human Development

Bureaucracy;
Dogma;
Corruption;
Closed and
Failing Systems

Materialism
And Abject
Poverty

Lack of Meaning;
Conflict;
Fundamentalism
and Terrorism

Environmental
and Communal
Decay

CHAPTER 1

Development – Quo Vadis?: Turning Point in Human Development

Guiding Question: Why is there a need to fundamentally renew Human Development and what is the direction to take?

1.1 Orientation: What Integral Development is About

IS DEVELOPMENT DEAD?

Is development dead? Many renowned commentators from within the development field have claimed that development has reached a 'dead end', declaring that over five decades of development have been 'lost'. As a consequence they have requested an end to all 'authoritarian engineering' into other people's lives and societies. Despite the occasionally successful project or initiative here and there, for these critics development is bankrupt and any attempts to revive it should be abandoned.

We shall explore later (⇨2) in more detail the nature of these critiques. For now, we want to give our preliminary response to the question 'Is development dead?': 'Yes and No'. We reply 'yes' because we think that the conventional approach towards development is ultimately futile, and does not serve us well any longer. We reply 'no', because we shall propose in this book an alternative, fundamentally new and (for us) more authentic approach to development.

We call it Integral Development.

INTEGRAL DEVELOPMENT

This book is about Integral Development. It is about its theory, and it is about its practice. It builds on our lifelong research, educational and practical experiences, and it is an evolution of the body of integral theory[1] that we presented over the past years and that we shall later introduce in some more detail (⇨4).

Integral Development aspires to make development fully relevant to human life – to your life, my life, our lives. To live up to this goal, it is concerned with all aspects of human life and hence looks at development, in holistic fashion, from multiple perspectives. That makes our approach integral, as you will see.

This book is about 'you' and your society. It brings development to your doorstep, takes it out of the closet of mere academic theory, or of sheer socioeconomic policy – both, all too often too alien, too distant from the person on the ground eager to develop him- or herself and the surrounding context. This book is not about 'foreign development aid', nor is it about a simple set of success factors. It is about a journey that empowers you to bring development, in a holistic and sustainable manner, right into your own context. It is a journey that integrates your personal development, with the development of your organisation and community and from there with the development of your society. That is the other reason why this approach is integral.

But it is not just an integral approach to development that we propose in this book. It is also a 'human' approach that we offer. It anchors both the freedom and the responsibility to develop within human beings – as individuals, and as members of organisations, communities and societies. It takes development out of the exclusive hands of national, regional and international, often self-declared development agencies, and invites every individual, organisation or community to become an agent for conscious development – or, in our terms, an Integral Developer. The book shows you possible paths to actualise Integral Development. It accompanies you, and your organisation and society– step by step. These are the reasons that make this approach human – it is lodged in and related to 'human life', your particular life.

Furthermore, Integral Development allows you to choose your own path, in relation to your development issues at hand, as well as your own particular gifts and capacities, in relation to your context. Whether you are working in the so-called 'development field', say for example in community development in Southern Africa, or whether you are active in organisational development in North America – this approach supports you in becoming – together with your organisation – an agent for Integral Development. It invites you to reflect and act, as you – together with others – move forward, coming up with a development approach, that authentically mirrors your individual and collective journeys. This is what makes our orientation not only 'human', but also 'humane'. Such 'humaneness' however, requires each of us to start the development journey with ourselves, understanding and engaging with our true development needs, desires and tasks. Integral Development works 'inside-out', not – as most of conventional development does – 'outside-in'.

Let us start by examining the question: Why is Integral Development needed?

RESPONDING TO THE CIVILISATIONAL CRISIS OF OUR TIME

Integral Development addresses the profound civilisational crisis humanity is facing at this time, and shows new pathways of development that enable us to build sustainable futures, collectively.

This crisis affects many scientific disciplines in theory and almost all countries in practice. It is a universal crisis with many facets. The most visible and dramatic facets are economic, political, environmental, social, cultural and spiritual in nature.

It is not only the sheer scale of the crisis that makes us argue that we are living through a major civilisational moment that cries out for transformation. It is becoming increasingly obvious that the deep-rooted assumptions underlying the very understanding of ourselves, our societies, and humanity as a whole have become increasingly dysfunctional. We literally need a new foundation to co-engage with each other – economically, politically, culturally, environmentally.

We have come to the conclusion that if we do not fundamentally renew these underlying assumptions, we will not be able to respond adequately to the crisis at hand. In other words, we won't be able to renew the very foundations on which we are standing. If we are unable to do that, we have no chance to face a sustainable future.

Conventional development is in the midst of this civilisational crisis. As an interdisciplinary field it is not only, simultaneously, affected by all the crises alluded to above, it also deals with a large percentage of the world's population. Furthermore, given that quite a number of so-called developed economies in Western Europe – from Greece to Ireland, from Portugal to Spain – seem to be (at the time of writing) at the brink of economic collapse while the USA has again faced a so-called fiscal cliff, development, as we conventionally know it, now reaches across the proverbial north–south divide. It concerns all of us.

You might be surprised by our statement that the civilisational crisis we are facing, is also a crisis of the university as we know it. Indeed, universities are even vitally concerned, given that much of the development theories that have been adopted until now have been conceived of by university scholars. In dealing with the crisis, humanity will be required to critically revisit its approaches to learning, research and education. Our collective capacity to renew these key developmental functions is, in our view, one of the crucial factors for a positive, collective future. It is for that reason that Integral Development is primarily an understanding-learning-research-and-education journey, resulting in action. It requires you to continuously reflect *and* act. And in the process, as you will see, we shall develop new developmental-educational spaces that become authentic catalysts for the sustainable development of individuals, organisations and society. Such spaces (we shall call them Uni-Versities) have little to do with the conventional educational experiences most of us underwent at university. If that sounds too tall an order, be surprised by the practical cases that we introduce in this book. They show us the way.

We begin our examination with a critical appraisal of the academic field of development – and hence with related development theory and practice. But ultimately, this book seeks to transcend the disciplinary perspective by liberating it from its relatively narrowly defined box with its predominant focus on socioeconomic development.

Where do we start?

BUILDING THE FOUNDATIONS FOR THE INTEGRAL DEVELOPMENT JOURNEY

In this book we are not concerned with tweaking existing development theories and models. Yes, we will revisit the existing theory and practice, as conventionally defined – because we are keen to learn from the past. But, ultimately, we shall offer a dramatically new perspective that builds on the best that humanity's development knowledge and practice has to offer, from all around the world.

We shall present an approach to human development that enables you and your organisation to engage with this knowledge and practice in a systematic manner, thereby addressing the development issues you are dealing with within your particular context – in theory and action. Integral Development does not offer ready-made formulae for the particular development issue you are concerned with. What it offers, though, is a 'software' that can guide and accompany you in shaping your own solutions. It is comprised of thought-provoking content, inspiring practice and a catalytic development process – that supports you in your journey towards finding locally adequate and authentic solutions to your particular issue.

Having set the overall scene for Integral Development, the next question we are going to explore is whether the overall failure of development is just a failure of a particular set of theories and practices. Or, is its failure a symptom of a much larger phenomenon?

1.2   Global, Outer Shift: Dealing with the Profound Civilisational Crisis of Our Time

THE CRISIS OF OUR TIME

We are living in a time of confusion. Many of the social and economic systems of our time seem to be either dysfunctional or ripe for transformation.

We therefore ask the question whether our very understanding of how we design and develop our lives, our organisations and our societies requires a fundamentally new perspective. The answer is yes. Clear as it may look, this is not an easy answer. We need to explore deeper, with the help of leading thinkers, what this crisis is about. We begin with Immanuel Wallerstein, seen as one of the world's most eminent sociologists and particularly well-known for his approach to World Systems Analysis.[2]

THE END OF THE WORLD AS WE KNOW IT

Wallerstein, whose work also contributed immensely to modern development theory (⇨17), argues that the modern-world system has entered a terminal crisis and is unlikely to survive the next 50 years. That includes, first and foremost, the current economic system that, for Wallerstein, will be overturned in the years to come by a new economic system.

In his book entitled *The End of the World as We Know It*, he makes the point that 'we do not know whether the resulting system will be better or worse than the one we are living in, but we do know that the period of transition will be a time of terrible troubles, since the stakes of the transition are so high, the outcome so uncertain, and the ability of small inputs to affect the outcome so great'.[3]

It is widely believed that the collapse of Communism in 1989 marks a great triumph of liberalism. However, Wallerstein sees the event rather as marking the definitive collapse of liberalism as the defining geo-culture of our world system. For him, liberalism essentially promised that gradual reform would ameliorate the inequalities of the world system and reduce acute polarisation. It apparently did not. The collapse of Communism, along with the disintegration of the national liberation movements in the Third World, and the collapse of the faith in the Keynesian model in the Western world were all simultaneous reflections of popular disillusionment with the validity and reality of the reformist movements each had propagated. But this disillusionment, however merited, challenges the popular legitimacy of the states and undoes any reasons why their populations should tolerate the continuous and increasing polarisation of the world system. The world, for Wallerstein, has not morally advanced in the last several thousand years, but it could. We could move in the direction of what Max Weber called 'substantive rationality', that is rational values and ends, arrived at collectively and intelligently.

Another conclusion Wallerstein arrives at is that the belief in certainties, a fundamental premise of modernity, is blinding and crippling us. Modern science (read: Cartesian-Newtonian science) has been based in the 'certainty of certainty'. The basic assumption is that there exist objective universal laws governing all natural phenomena, that these laws can be ascertained by scientific inquiry, and that once such laws are known, we can, starting from any set of initial conditions, predict perfectly the future and the past. Furthermore, the belief in certainty is increasingly under severe attack within natural science itself, prominent examples being Nobel Laureate Ilya Prigogine's book on *La Fin des Certitudes*[4] and American complexity scientist Sally Goerner's work on a *New Science of Sustainability*.[5] These new views are called the science of complexity, partly because they argue that Newtonian certitudes hold true only in very constrained, simple systems, but also because, they maintain, the universe manifests the evolutionary development of complexity, and the majority of situations cannot be explained by assumptions of linear equilibria and time-reversibility.

Wallerstein sees humanity wrestling with the current transition for many more years. For him, the human social systems are the most complex systems in the universe, therefore the hardest to analyse. Hence, the struggle for the good society is a continuing one. He argues that despite these difficulties it is precisely in periods of transition from one historical system to another one – whose nature we cannot know in advance – that human struggle takes on most meaning. Or to put it another way, it is only in such times of transition that what human beings call free will outweighs the pressures of the existing system to return to equilibria. Thus fundamental change is possible, albeit never certain, and this, for Wallerstein, makes claim on our moral responsibility to act rationally, in good faith, and with courage to seek a better world system.

A CRISIS OF CONSCIOUSNESS

The late and great German-Spanish philosopher Jean Gebser, in his analysis of the current civilisational crisis, goes a step further. For him, such 'substantive rationality' is not a sufficient answer.

According to Jean Gebser, to whom we shall return later in more depth (⇨13), we are currently living through a time that seeks to bring forth a new 'consciousness'.[6] For him, the so-called modernist time, beginning with Europe's Renaissance in the sixteenth century, has given rise to the liberation of the human intellect, resulting in unprecedented scientific and technological progress. This victory of the rational mind over the preceding more irrational, emotional-mystical orientation of Medieval Europe, also had its downside, affirms Gebser. By totally disconnecting from prior forms of being in and interpreting the world (wordviews), that very rationalism gradually became footloose. An isolated means in itself, rationalism was deprived of meaning and purpose. For Gebser, this describes the situation much of humanity finds itself in for the past few decades. He further argues that in particular towards the end of any one evolutionary era of humankind (in this case the rationalist era), the very defining strength (in this case the rational mind) turns into its negative aspect, resulting in an overly rationalistic perspective on life. The originally gained strength, so Gebser, then turns into an impediment for further evolution. The challenge for humanity, he says, is to transcend such overemphasis of rationalism through what he terms an 'integral' perspective as the next 'port of call' in human consciousness. On such a new integral level, prior modes of being in the world – such as the mystical or rational mode – would be integrated in a balanced manner, without giving pride of place to any singular one of the human modes. Arriving at this new level is the great evolutionary challenge – the dramatic shift of consciousness – that, Gebser says, is required to liberate ourselves from the deadlock of a rationalistic perspective. The difficulty, however, is that the rational perspective has become so all-pervasive, that it does not acknowledge itself as the root of the problem. Hence, and 'logically', humanity continues trying to resolve the current crisis with ever more sophisticated models, systems, regulations and technologies. But, as Albert Einstein famously stated: 'No problem can be solved from the same level of consciousness that created it'. To Einstein, considered by many as the greatest natural scientist and intellectual of the past century, also the following expression is attributed: 'The intuitive mind is a sacred gift and the rational mind is a faithful servant. We have created a society that honors the servant and has forgotten the gift'.

Gebser makes the point that the time has come for humanity to move beyond such a rationalist, modernist society. Is postmodernity the answer? We believe it is not. Postmodernism can be described as the breakdown of the singular rhetoric of one dominant (modernist) worldview, into an ever-growing myriad of parallel discourses. We see it as an interim period, a period of reorientation, of necessary collapse of the so-called 'dominant discourse'. It is a time of active search for new answers. But most postmodernist discourses still remain overly intellectual and rationalistic. A synthesising, new perspective that integrates the multiplicity of perspectives has not yet been reached. But nevertheless, Gebser and many integral thinkers claim that a new integral paradigm is in the making. Among them are the most influential integral thinkers of our time, such as Ken Wilber and Don Beck (⇨4). Such a new integral viewpoint will give space for the myriad of local perspectives, and yet, it will offer also an interconnecting, synthesising, integrating perspective – linking multiple local perspectives to one shared global perspective.

Then, in Gebser's term, we would reconnect to our 'ever present origin', to the original state of consciousness in humankind's evolution, where the human being felt 'one' with creation. While the original state was, however, one of 'unconscious unity' with creation, the integral state, so Gebser, is one of 'conscious unity' with all life – a conscious awareness of the interconnectedness of all life that natural science increasingly confirms. Our colleague and integral enterprise philosopher Tony Bradley from Liverpool's Hope University calls this new state 'Integrality' (⇨4).

While all this seems to be on the emergent horizon, until now, such integral perspectives have not yet reached mainstream thought. They exist in sizable pockets, though, but it seems, to align ourselves with Gebser, that the great evolutionary shift is still to come.

HUMANITY: STUCK IN ADOLESCENCE – URGE FOR MATURITY

Gebser is echoed by Farzam Arbab, the renowned Iranian development economist, now with a particular focus on the role of development in this evolutionary shift.

For Arbab who has founded a successful development programme in Columbia (⇨14), the current crisis has its roots in rampant materialism and in the spiritual void of our time. He offers perhaps the most articulate plea from within the developing world to reconfigure development in a way that it becomes a catalytic force for a new civilisation that equally embraces material and spiritual values.

Arbab stresses that:

> *Development programs will continue to be relevant to the life of society only to the extent that they are formulated and carried out in the context of an emerging world civilisation'.[7] He argues that 'to achieve the required vitality, systematic effort to bring about the social and economic development of nations must be conceived in the context of a greater process that will carry humanity into the next stage of evolution … No matter how cursory, a survey of the historic forces that are shaping the structure of society … should convince even the staunch defenders of today's global policies that unchecked material progress is not what is needed. A dual cry can everywhere be heard rising from the heart of the great masses of humanity. It demands the extension of the fruits of material progress to all peoples, and, at the same time, it calls out for the values of spiritual civilisation … True prosperity has both a material and a spiritual dimension.[8]*

Arbab asks the question whether humanity's journey as a whole is not analogous to the life cycle of an individual human being from youth to adulthood, and later from midlife to maturity. Humanity, he says, has come to a stage where it needs to transit from youth to adulthood.

> *If humanity is indeed approaching adulthood, the revolutionary changes occurring with bewildering swiftness in every department of its collective life assume the character of two parallel processes, one integrative and the other of ruinous disintegration.[9]*

Supporting the process of integration is indeed, for Arbab, a crucial task for everyone engaged in the field of development. However, he demands that the developer needs to deeply understand the transitive nature of our current time. For this understanding 'can help us free ourselves from excessive attachment to the standards of the past and move on to find new and viable paths of development. If old conventions are allowed to persist, the fate of humankind will be a global society ruled by the interest of a relative few and held in the grip of political and economic forces'.[10]

For Arbab, such a society will be unacceptable to a human race that overcomes the habits of adolescence. We also would need to let go of an understanding of development as something that is handed over by the 'developed' to the 'underdeveloped'. Nor can it be merely imitation of the conventional pattern of industrialisation. Equally inadequate, Arbab argues, 'is a vision of development as a haphazard process whose aims emerge from its own dynamics'. He concludes his passionate quest for a new form of development with the anticipation that humanity as a whole attains a whole new level of consciousness:

> *As this increasingly occurs, the only acceptable development strategies will be those that centre on people and their institutions that legitimately serve its interests. If development is to be defined at all, then it will have to be in terms of the building of capacity in individuals,*

communities and institutions to participate effectively in weaving the fabric of a materially and spiritually prosperous world civilisation.[11]

We conclude this brief exposition about the global crisis with a short analysis of the transformative challenges that business and economics are faced with.

THE POST-CAPITALIST TRANSFORMATION: TOTAL REARRANGEMENT REQUIRED

For Austro-American Peter Drucker, the management guru of the twentieth century, every few hundred years in history there occurs a sharp transformation.[12] Then, within a few short decades, society – its worldview, its basic values, its social and political structures, its arts, its key institutions – rearranges itself.

Already in the 1990s, Peter Drucker proclaimed that humanity is faced with what he termed a 'post-capitalist transformation':

> *We are far enough advanced into the new post-capitalist society to review and revise the social, political and economic history of the Age of Capitalism and the nation state … The one thing we can be sure of is that the world that will emerge from the present rearrangement of values, beliefs, social and economic structures, of political concepts and systems, indeed of worldviews, will be different from anything anyone imagines.*[13]

Drucker goes on to say:

> *That knowledge has become the resource rather than a resource is what makes our society post-capitalist. This fact changes fundamentally the structure of society. It creates new social and economic dynamics, and politics.*[14]

Today, that seems to be coming to pass. The Belgian futurist Marc Luyckx Ghisi claims in his recent book, *The Knowledge Society: The Breakthrough toward Genuine Sustainability*,[15] that the industrial economic system, based on the concepts of quantitative growth and tangible assets, is incapable of leading us toward a genuine sustainable future.

Yet, for Luyckx Ghisi, we have at our disposal right now the tools we need to shift our economies and our politics (and therefore our world) toward genuine sustainability and toward a positive human footprint on earth. He argues that such a shift is possible for two reasons: one, because the world business community has already begun to shift into a new economic logic based on the idea of a 'knowledge society' and two, because the collective mind of the world is changing and ushering humanity into a new level of consciousness.

According to Luyckx Ghisi, we are currently in a process of 'dematerialising' the value creation process itself, steering away from measuring according to tangible (material) assets and more toward intangible (nonmaterial) ones. And among these intangible assets, 'sustainability' and 'social inclusion' are becoming increasingly important. At the same time, we are at a point in history in which humankind is confronted with the danger of extinction if it does not change the way it manages its relationship to the environment and to the economy in general.

For Luyckx Ghisi, modernity is incapable of helping humankind in the face of the survival urgency, owing to its overemphasis on analysis. Rather, we must now look for holistic, synthetic, and global solutions that concern our collective survival, thereby rethinking:

- the global economy;
- our relationship with nature and the environment;
- our relationship to the sacred;
- our political systems, which are not even capable of engaging in a fundamental debate.

Modernity then, for Luyckx Ghisi, is in effect dead, or at least dying, but most citizens of the world are unaware of the fact. Everything is happening in the background. A world is dying, he says, but in an astonishing silence.

AND NOW?

Each great change produces a new system of society, organised around what American philosopher Stephen Pepper[16] calls a new 'world hypothesis', a vision of 'how the world works', which is itself woven around a 'root metaphor'. Medieval European society, for example, built itself around the metaphor of 'God's design', a hidden, organising master plan guiding all things. Its successor, modern society, saw the rise of the 'machine' metaphor, a logical system of material parts connected by mechanical cause and effect.

Yet nowadays, integral reformers, such as Sally Goerner, Ken Wilber, James Lovelock and ourselves are reweaving civilisation around the image of an 'ecosystem', or web, symbolic of our interconnected age. The way knowledge is generated and flows through such a web will become a crucial feature of this new civilisation.

So what?

Ervin Laszlo, the Hungarian integral philosopher and author of *World Shift 2012*[17] has often stated, that the current time of transition is characterised by two parallel processes. On the one hand, the still prevailing mainstream – led by modernist capitalism – is once more flexing all its muscles, as it sees its underlying assumptions massively challenged. On the other hand, a plethora of initiatives, movements, new forms of enterprises and lifestyle experiments is gradually emerging – invisibly connected in their shared attempt to bring about a different, more sustainable future. All these impulses, for him, have not yet formed a new integrated pattern, but they are on the way towards it. For him, as for Wallerstein and for us, what now counts is that each one of us takes the initiative to engage in bringing about alternative, positive futures. It is in the continuous co-weaving of such a new web, that the interconnectedness, the 'integrality' of humankind will become not only ever more visible, but also a unifying force. Integral Development see itself as a 'software' to increasingly bring about such integrality.

The first step is to be sensitised to the larger dimension of our shared work, being aware of the global shift that we are collectively part of. The second step is to recognise the core personal shift that each one of us is challenged to undertake, in order to contribute meaningfully to an integral perspective. This is the personal shift from duality to integrality.

1.3   Personal, Inner Shift: Transcending Duality, Evolving Integrality

WITH AND WITHIN OURSELVES: WHERE DEVELOPMENT NEEDS TO START

Etymologically, the term development refers to 'an unfolding', to the 'bringing out of latent possibilities'. Linking that to the civilisational challenge of our time, we interpret such 'unfolding' as a movement towards a new world system, towards a new level of consciousness, towards a more sustainable, life-affirming future. On a personal and collective level, such 'bringing out of our latent possibilities' involves a purposeful effort to evolve our worldview in a way that it corresponds with our best possible understanding of what such a sustainable, life-affirming future can look like.

Development begins with a personal, inner shift.

Isn't it obvious that we can only engage in human development, if we can grasp, at first hand, what such human development involves? If our understanding of human nature is limited, on what basis then do we ground our development intervention, an intervention into other humans' lives?

Hence, if you intend to become an agent for authentic development, you have to start by developing yourself. There is no shortcut. Indeed this is a well-accepted norm for those becoming counselling psychologists, dealing with the development of individual people, so why should this be different for development writ large? The first principle is: You have to *become* what you want to bring to the world. In Gandhi's terms: 'Be the change'.

Hyperactivity and the common habit of 'thinking big' from the outside takes us away from the first true task of the developer: to develop ourselves. Also, new development theory and policies won't help, if our collective understanding of 'who we are' remains the same. The common argument that such self-reflection is selfish and that 'there is no time for navel gazing, given the dramatic state the world is in', for us, does not count. Our point is that nothing will fundamentally change from the outside, if it is not preceded by a fundamental change within.

By starting with ourselves as individual transformation agents, we thereby take development out of the closet of a narrowly defined societal development discourse, involving primarily so-called development experts, practitioners as well as consultants and academics. We also take responsibility into our own hands – for our lives, and for the development of the planet. We can't leave the development field any longer to a limited group of actors, given the desolate state humanity is in and the immense evolutionary task that is ahead of us.

Including ourselves in the development process is also the first step of transcending dualism. What do we mean by that?

BEYOND DUALISM

A defining feature of a rationalist view on the world is its dualistic perspective. We are used to seeing everything as pairs of opposites: good or bad, black or white, rich or poor, developed or underdeveloped. And so on.

It is closely linked with a scientific perspective of continuously analysing, evaluating, rating, comparing, measuring things and events – an attitude that most of us have deeply internalised. Many people continuously rate and compare themselves. While there is nothing wrong with these traits in general, they can become destructive if overemphasised. But it is not just an individual phenomenon. It equally happens between economic and political systems (capitalism versus Communism), between worldviews, religions or academic disciplines. And so on.

The danger of an overemphasised dualistic perspective is that one does not see the whole. Individually or collectively, we continuously decide for one side of the polar-opposite spectrum (the one we prefer), often ignoring if not denying the other side (the one we dislike).

The problem that comes with duality is that it is likely to lead to one side oppressing the other, causing split personalities (we only want to see the good side within us), split societies (we ignore those we do not like or that disturb us), and ultimately a highly split world (into the haves and the have nots). That can creative massive imbalance, within ourselves, within our societies and within the world. This is exactly what we experience in today's world.

Arguing with Einstein's quote that a problem can't be solved on the same level of consciousness on which it has been created, we can see, that a dualistic perspective can't lead us out of that dilemma. Why? Because the dualistic view always favours one way of resolving the problem over the other, resulting in a continuous battle between polar-opposite perspectives. The result: a deadlock. While opposite opinions and perspectives, in general, can be very useful, each perspective can only develop its particular potential, if it can evolve and co-evolve with others. To make that happen, we need to step out of a dualistic view of the world – and that includes a dualistic perspective of ourselves. That requires us to face – in the terms of the renowned Swiss psychoanalyst Carl Gustav Jung – our shadow.

FACING OUR SHADOW: FROM EITHER-OR TO BOTH-AND-MORE

The inclination to think in dualities has its roots in our mind and psyche. The work of Jung and in particular his concept of the 'shadow' allows us to understand this very human inclination.

The shadow represents the unconscious part of the human psyche that often largely remains unknown to the individual. Engaging with previously unconscious material of the psyche is a difficult process, as it requires the 'stepping into the unknown'. Such a process of engaging with one's unconsciousness is difficult and at times painful, as Jung illustrates powerfully through text and images in his remarkable *Red Book*.[18] It forces the individual to let go of a previous state of consciousness and to move on to a new level. However, as we shall learn from mythologist Joseph Campbell[19] (⇨11) and many others, such transformation journeys are highly personal, with no ready-made paths to follow. The combination of difficulty and pain that characterise such individual development trajectories, lead most people to settle for the 'known' or 'conscious' part of themselves.

Consequently, we base our lives, organisations and societies on a limited (conscious) understanding of who we are. This organising pattern works as follows: what is conscious or known is comfortable and is used to interpret reality; what is unconscious or unknown is uncomfortable and feared. What is feared is to be avoided or fought, be it in concepts or through action. In that sense, dualistic thinking is a survival pattern (friend or foe, developed or developing, modern or traditional) and it helped humankind throughout millennia to distinguish quickly within dangerous situations, how to respond. As such, dualistic thinking was highly useful in specific contexts.

In fact, it was neither good nor bad, as consciousness evolved gradually according to the inner and outer needs of humanity. When a particular response pattern did not provide any more for the desired results, it resulted in the search for a new understanding and thereby gradually led to a rise in human consciousness.

The real problem comes though, when a large number of response patterns fail the individual and society, and human systems become significantly imbalanced. In such a situation a major shift in consciousness is necessary, leading to a fundamentally new perspective on human systems. We have argued that the time we are living in, is such a transformational period, where the hitherto dualistic interpretation of the world has become limited and limiting to such a degree that humanity as a whole is in danger.

The major enhancement of consciousness we require then, for Jung, can only occur, when we are willing to engage with our shadow, to make conscious what previously was unknown. This, however, is not primarily an intellectual act, but a psychological process. It usually begins with a period of suffering, caused by an insufficient understanding of ourselves, individually, institutionally or societally. Furthermore, our conscious understanding represses other unconscious parts, which would allow for a larger understanding of reality, thereby failing to 'put light on the shadow'.

Such repression, says Jung, comes out of fear – fear of the unknown. Two possible reactions to such fear can be observed in human systems, from self to organisation to society. The first and perhaps most common response is the retreat to so-called 'safe ground', to the perceived base of one's limited, and limiting, existence. While this can be helpful for a certain time to re-establish a certain sense of orientation, it is not a sustainable position, if the imbalance persists. The second and more rare response is the search for a new, more meaningful understanding of one's world, upon which new life patterns can be developed. The latter response requires a 'stepping into the unknown', to gain an expanded understanding into the complexity of life, in other words: to make conscious what hitherto has been in the shadows.

That is why every individual's development journey counts!

Indeed, for Jung, the entire purpose of human life is a gradual progression to make unknown parts of the psyche known and thereby integrate them into consciousness. Jung calls this lifelong process 'individuation'. For him, it is successful individuation processes that are catalytic of the evolution of humankind towards higher states of consciousness.

Through this process, we transcend the earlier dualistic approach to life and society, each in our own particular way. We learn that life manifests itself in the endless variety of 'both and', and that a dualistic response of 'either-or' limits our understanding and our action so that we fail to live and act in accordance with life's principles. That makes our own life and, simultaneously, life on the planet, unsustainable. In fact, we even argue for, as you will soon see, a 'both-and-more' perspective, as we evolve the dualistic (two opposite poles) perspective into an integral (four poles, circling around a centre) perspective.

Moving from a dualistic 'either-or' to an integral 'both-and-more' approach to life, we are jointly 'stepping into the unknown'. We become explorers, challenging old response patterns and seeking new, more relevant ways, of human development. Development, now, is 'over to us' – all of us!

1.4   Integration: Development – Over to All of Us!

In this opening chapter we began by illustrating what Integral Development, in a nutshell, is about, why it is needed and whom it addresses. We also introduce you to the structure of this opening part of the book, comprised of the first four chapters, jointly building the foundation for the then following Integral Development journey.

We maintain that with Integral Development we are not aspiring to tweak existing development theories, but rather to offer a new catalytic approach, that enables each of us to engage meaningfully in development processes that contribute to sustainable, positive futures.

Integral Development is thereby responding to the profound civilisational crisis of our time. This crisis marks the global shift we are collectively experiencing. In the midst of this dramatic transition, Integral Development serves as an understanding-learning-research-education-action-journey, supporting our evolution towards a more integrated paradigm.

We then highlight that the global shift that we experience on an outer level, needs to be accompanied by an inner shift on a personal level. Indeed, we argued, that Integral Development starts not only with each of us, but also *within* each of us. The inner shift required is one from the hitherto dualistic (either-or) perspective on the world and ourselves, to an integral (both-and-more) perspective.

In conclusion, development for us is not about finding remedies for so-called developing countries, often subsumed as the 'Global South'. It is not about developing others. In line with a newly emergent worldview, characterised by interdependence and interconnectedness, we are, at the very best, co-developing with others. The emphasis on co-development is thereby not primarily a moral statement, but a necessity relevant for all engaging parties. The image of one person, institution or country developing another, belongs to Newtonian physics, where the scientist is outside the experiment, observing the effects of his intervention. Integral Development then is about creating a new image of development that makes all of us equal, interdependent actors in the one large project of human development.

In the concluding Table 1.1 we invite you to reflect on the central question and guiding thoughts of this opening chapter. You shall find such a table at the end of each chapter, helping you to distil the core development tasks that emerge along the journey, and to engage with them – through reflection and action.

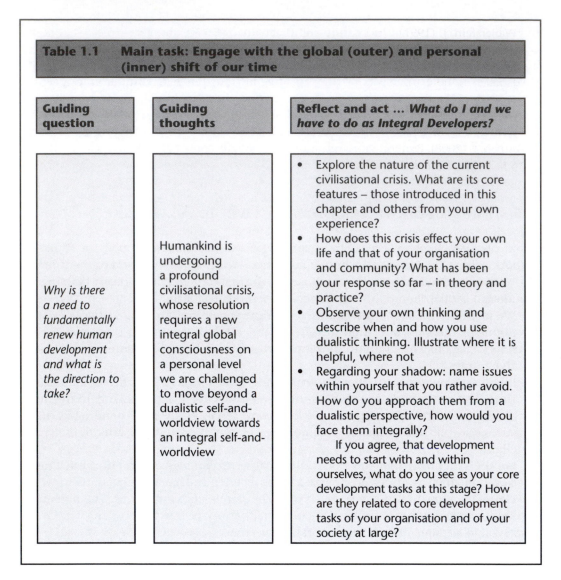

Table 1.1   Main task: Engage with the global (outer) and personal (inner) shift of our time

Guiding question	Guiding thoughts	Reflect and act ... *What do I and we have to do as Integral Developers?*
Why is there a need to fundamentally renew human development and what is the direction to take?	Humankind is undergoing a profound civilisational crisis, whose resolution requires a new integral global consciousness on a personal level we are challenged to move beyond a dualistic self-and-worldview towards an integral self-and-worldview	• Explore the nature of the current civilisational crisis. What are its core features – those introduced in this chapter and others from your own experience? • How does this crisis effect your own life and that of your organisation and community? What has been your response so far – in theory and practice? • Observe your own thinking and describe when and how you use dualistic thinking. Illustrate where it is helpful, where not • Regarding your shadow: name issues within yourself that you rather avoid. How do you approach them from a dualistic perspective, how would you face them integrally? If you agree, that development needs to start with and within ourselves, what do you see as your core development tasks at this stage? How are they related to core development tasks of your organisation and of your society at large?

To further strengthen our foundation, we shall now, in the following chapter, critically review past approaches to development as well as current trends.

References

1   Lessem, R. and Schieffer, A. (2009 ongoing). Transformation and Innovation Series. Farnham: Gower. The series includes, among others: Lessem, R. and Schieffer, A. (2009). *Transformation Management: Towards the Integral Enterprise*; Lessem, R. and Schieffer, A. (2010). *Integral Research and Innovation: Transforming Enterprise and Society*; Lessem, R. and Schieffer, A. (2010). *Integral Economics: Releasing the Economic Genius of Your Society*.

2   Wallerstein, I. (2004). *World Systems Analysis: An Introduction*. Durham, NC: Duke University Press.

3   Wallerstein, I. (1997). Uncertainty and Creativity. Talk given at: Forum 2000 – Concerns and Hope on the Threshold of the New Millennium, Prague, 3–6 September, 1997.

4   Prigogine, I. (2010). *La Fin des Certitudes: Temps, Chaos et les Lois de la Nature*. Paris: Odile Jacob.

5   Goerner, S. et al. (2008). *The New Science of Sustainability: Building Foundations for Great Change*. Chapel Hill, NC: Triangle Centre for Complex Systems.

6   Gebser, J. (1985). *The Ever-Present Origin*. Athens, OH: Ohio University Press.

7   Arbab, F. (2000). Promoting a Discourse on Science, Religion and Development. In: Harper, S.M.P (ed.), *The Lab, the Temple and the Market: Reflections at the Intersections of Science, Religion and Development*. Ottawa. ON: International Development Research Center, p. 195.

8   Arbab, F. (2000). Promoting a Discourse on Science, Religion and Development. In: Harper, S.M.P (ed.), *The Lab, the Temple and the Market: Reflections at the Intersections of Science, Religion and Development*. Ottawa, ON: International Development Research Center, p. 196.

9   Arbab, F. (2000). Promoting a Discourse on Science, Religion and Development. In: Harper, S.M.P (ed.), *The Lab, the Temple and the Market: Reflections at the Intersections of Science, Religion and Development*. Ottawa, ON: International Development Research Center, p. 196.

10 Arbab, F. (2000). Promoting a Discourse on Science, Religion and Development. In: Harper, S.M.P (ed.), *The Lab, the Temple and the Market: Reflections at the Intersections of Science, Religion and Development*. Ottawa, ON: International Development Research Center, p. 197.

11 Arbab, F. (2000). Promoting a Discourse on Science, Religion and Development. In: Harper, S.M.P (ed.), *The Lab, the Temple and the Market: Reflections at the Intersections of Science, Religion and Development*. Ottawa, ON: International Development Research Center, p. 198.

12 Drucker, P. (1992). *The Age of Discontinuity*. Piscataway, NJ: Transaction Books.

13 Drucker, P. (1992). *A Functioning Society: Community, Society, and Polity in the 20th Century*. Piscataway, NJ: Transaction Books, p. 157.

14 Drucker, P. (1993). *The Post-Capitalist Society*. New York: Harper Collins, p. 45.

15 Luyckx Ghisi, M. (2009). *The Knowledge Society: The Breakthrough toward Genuine Sustainability*. Cochin, India: Arunachala Press.

16 Pepper, S. (1992). *World Hypotheses: A Study in Evidence*. Berkeley, CA: University of California Press.

17 Laszlo, E. (2009). *World Shift 2012: Making Green Business, New Politics and Global Consciousness Work Together*. Rochester, VT: Inner Traditions Bear and Company.

18 Jung, C.G. (2009). *The Red Book: Liber Novus*. New York: Norton.

19 Campbell, J. (1973). *The Hero with a Thousand Faces*. Bollingen Series. Princeton, NJ: Princeton University Press.

2 *Looking Back and Current Trends: A Critical Review of Human Development*

Guiding Questions: How did development develop over time? What major damaging patterns can we identify? And what signposts do we have for the future of development?

2.1 Orientation: Or Rather Disorientation?

In the opening scene-setting chapter we shared what we interpret to be the multiple crises that humanity is currently facing. These we believe to be not merely the result of temporary flaws in our political and economic systems. Rather, we see these crises as symptoms for massive systemic failures and signs of a fundamental, paradigmatic shift towards a new way of looking at the world.

We maintain then that the crisis of development that has been diagnosed by a wide range of critics is not merely a crisis of this particular field, but we see it as part of a major civilisational transition.

We believe that more viable approaches to development are crucially needed to support humanity in mastering this transition phase towards a positive, sustainable future for our species and the planet. With Integral Development we seek to contribute to this challenge.

A new development perspective, though, requires us to understand past and current approaches to development to allow us to identify helpful as well as destructive patterns. We need to understand what we can learn from past development, and what it is that we need to leave behind us. It is for that reason that we begin with a critical review of the field of development as conventionally understood, primarily focusing on socioeconomic development of so-called developing countries. In this review we are guided by the following questions:

- How did the field of development develop over time – in particular during the so-called Age of Development – from early stages to Post-Development?
- To what degree can we identify within these various 'developments' helpful clues why existing theory and practice by and large failed? How are these clues related to the larger crisis of our time?

- What 'signposts' do we find that help us understand how a future, more viable approach to human development needs to be modelled – an approach that would support humanity in mastering the civilisational transition to a new paradigm, beyond modernity and postmodernity, and that would enable life-affirming future development work?

Given the wide range of development theory and practice, we shall not attempt to provide a comprehensive overview of the entire field. Rather, we focus purposefully on selected, highly relevant themes, impulses and conflictual areas within the field – and explore them critically with the help of our guiding questions.

We have refrained from the temptation of starting with a definition of development. Why? A definition may have set or narrowed our minds at a too early stage of our explorations, may have hampered our attempts to deconstruct and reconstruct the field of development.

Furthermore, we were affirmed by Swedish anthropologist Gudrun Dahl and Ethiopian cultural researcher Gemetchu Megeressa who expressed the futility of attempting to arrive at a common understanding of the term:

> Development is an abstract notion, the use of which is ambiguous even in the industrialised and urbanised West. Translations between the expressions used in the dominant Western European languages is difficult enough. The aim of comparing different notions of 'development' between cultures and languages, which are distant in terms of space, origin and social context is thus futile. When do we find the notions similar enough to merit comparison at all? When do we classify a concept as corresponding to that of development? Would we include all ideas of a directed historical change in the state of society and its resources? Or do we only refer to concepts relating to the content of that direction in Western thinking – industrialisation, rationalisation, technological improvement, the acquisition of a Western political and administrative system, literacy, or whatever else 'development' may contain?[1]

Hence, we decided to postpone the task of defining development until later in this book and to start, without further ado, with our explorations of the historical evolution of the field and its major approaches, as well as of selected major discourses and practices that have marked it. We first return to the early days of the so-called Development Age.

2.2   The Development Age: How it Began …

WESTERN ORIGINS OF DEVELOPMENT

For Gilbert Rist, Emeritus Professor at the Graduate Institute of Development Studies in Geneva, the backdrop to 'development' was the League of Nations. According to his *History of Development*,[2] if colonisation threw up an array of arguments justifying intervention outside Europe to serve the national interest, the League of Nations legitimated the internationalisation of this intervention in the name of civilisation itself. It becomes clear, however, that civilisation was understood as the common heritage of the European countries. In 1919, the newly founded League of Nations articulated the following, as per Covenant 22:

- To those colonies which as a consequence of the late war have ceased to be under the sovereignty of the States which formerly governed them and which are inhabited by peoples not yet able to stand by themselves under the conditions of the modern world, there should be applied the principle that the well-being and development of such people form a sacred trust of civilisation.
- The best method of giving practical effect to this principle is that the tutelage of such peoples should be entrusted to advanced nations.
- The character of the mandate must differ according to the stage of development of the people, the geographical situation of the territory, its economic conditions and other similar circumstances.

For Rist, the above three points are interesting in a number of respects. First, they introduce the concept of 'stages of development' into the literature of international organisations, according to which there were 'developed' nations at the top of the ladder, and thereby exempt from the need for 'development'. At the same time, there were supposed to be universal values – 'civilisation', 'material and moral wellbeing', 'social progress' – that could be legitimately invoked to justify intervening in the existence of other peoples. Finally, this universalism was itself underwritten by an international authority, the League of Nations, that played the role of a kind of family counsellor, mediating between a 'minor' native population and 'adult' mandatory power. Furthermore, 'development' was cast from the outset to have a primary focus on economics, technology and politics.

The 'international community' now seemed to embrace most of the peoples of the world, and its belief – or its good conscience – looked as if it rested on a general consensus, albeit it was merely a 'consensus' of the European nations. Meanwhile there was still one actor missing from it: the United States. With the USA coming to the scene, it became even clearer, that the Global South had no say whatsoever.

DEVELOPMENT IMPERIALISM

Rist argues that it was the Second World War that turned everything upside down. The discovery of the Nazi concentration camps had shown the atrocities that followed when one race dominates others. By the end of 1948, at a time of American foreign policy ferment, three ideas had won unanimous support: the United States would continue to back the new United Nations; it would keep up the European reconstruction effort by means of the Marshall plan; and it would create a joint defence force (NATO) to meet the Soviet threat. A civil servant suggested adding a fourth clause that the technical assistance already given to parts of Latin America would be extended to the poorer countries of the world. This fourth clause, something of an afterthought, inaugurated the 'Development Age', proclaimed by former US President Harry Truman in January 1949:

> we must embark on a bold new program for making the benefits of our scientific advances and industrial progress available for the improvement and growth of underdeveloped areas. More than half of the people of the world are living in conditions approaching misery. For the first time in history, humanity possesses the knowledge and skill to relieve the suffering of these people. Our main aim, then, should be to help the free peoples of the world, through their own efforts, to produce more food, clothing, materials for housing, and mechanical power to lighten their burdens. The old imperialism – exploitation for foreign profit – has no place in our plans.[3]

However, freeing people through their own efforts was inevitably seen in Western guise. There was no recognition of the rich diversity that the world's cultures embodied, and 'sustainable development' was not yet on the global agenda.

'THEY' COULD ALWAYS HOPE TO CATCH UP

At the end of the opening paragraph of Truman's declaration appears the adjective 'underdeveloped'. This was the first time it had been used in a text intended for such wide circulation. The term evoked not only the unilateral idea of change in the direction of a final state but, above all, the possibility of bringing about such change. No longer was it just a question of things developing by themselves; now it was possible to 'develop' a region from the outside-in. Thus development took on a transitive meaning, albeit one defined by the West.

Until then, North–South relations had been organised largely in terms of coloniser and colonised. The new developed-underdeveloped dichotomy proposed a different relationship, in keeping with the new Universal Declaration of Human Rights and the progressive globalisation of the system of states. Now, underdeveloped and developed were members of a single family: the one might be lagging a little behind the other, but they could always hope to catch up, so long as both continued to play the same game. 'Underdevelopment' was seen not as the opposite of 'development', only as its incomplete, or embryonic, form. This is how development came to be framed in linear stages.

Another core issue, for us, is that development was defined in technocratic-economic terms, ignoring local natural and communal grounds, as much as regional perspectives on culture and spirituality. In other words, there was only a singular 'North-Western' European-American perspective that was general rather than particular.

To the extent, that the Global South was not willing to 'play the same North-Western game', it had not much choice, though there were, as we shall see now, some variations of the development theme over time.

2.3   And How it Continued: A Brief Overview of Core Development Approaches

PERSPECTIVES AND MEANINGS OF DEVELOPMENT OVER TIME

The leading Dutch development economist Jan Nederveen Pieterse provided in his work on Development Theory a comprehensive overview of trends in societal development thinking[4] that we have adapted in the following Table 2.1.

The overview shows that the field of development has been in constant flux. However, approaches don't just come and go, but rather stay, overlap, fuse, and evolve over time – and, they are heavily influenced, by historical events.

The initial and perhaps the most influential perspective to date has been the one on development economics, with its focus on economic growth – closely aligned with the economic and political hegemony of the USA following World War II. Though diverse parallel discourses and approaches have emerged over time, development economics certainly has been the most impactful force within development, and it has found its

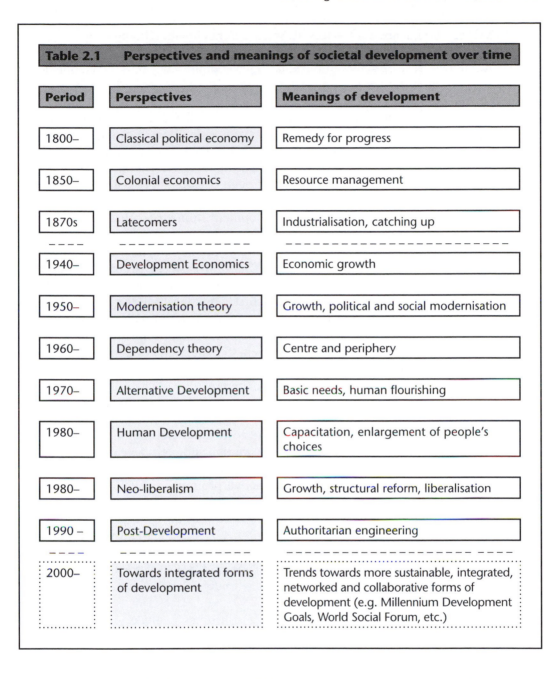

Table 2.1   Perspectives and meanings of societal development over time

Period	Perspectives	Meanings of development
1800–	Classical political economy	Remedy for progress
1850–	Colonial economics	Resource management
1870s	Latecomers	Industrialisation, catching up
1940–	Development Economics	Economic growth
1950–	Modernisation theory	Growth, political and social modernisation
1960–	Dependency theory	Centre and periphery
1970–	Alternative Development	Basic needs, human flourishing
1980–	Human Development	Capacitation, enlargement of people's choices
1980–	Neo-liberalism	Growth, structural reform, liberalisation
1990 –	Post-Development	Authoritarian engineering
2000–	Towards integrated forms of development	Trends towards more sustainable, integrated, networked and collaborative forms of development (e.g. Millennium Development Goals, World Social Forum, etc.)

most untamed articulation from the 1980s onwards with the rise of neo-liberalism – politically mirrored by the decline of Communism. It is for this reason that we shall have a particularly close look at the evolution of development economics (in theory and in practice) in the following sub-chapter.

The other major development theory, that has, in its various guises, survived till today, is modernisation theory – a theory that found fierce opposition in dependency theory, emerging out of the decolonisation processes of Latin America in the 1960s and 1970s. We shall equally analyse this dialectic in more detail later in this chapter.

ALTERNATIVE DEVELOPMENT AND HUMAN DEVELOPMENT

With Alternative Development and Human Development we find two approaches attempting to transcend prior, overly mechanistic and financial-economic perspectives on development by, instead, putting people in the centre of development work. Alternative Development with its orientation on 'basic needs' was introduced for the first time in the mid 1970s by the International Labour Organisation (ILO). Consequently it has become one of the major measurements of so-called 'absolute poverty', initially defined as minimum consumption requirement to afford minimal standards of food, shelter and clothing. Its primary focus on consumption, though, was replaced within the Human Development Approach by 'human capacities', or better, by 'capacitation' as an enabling process.[5] Core protagonists of the Human Development Approach – that was to become up till now the guiding theory of the UNDP United Nations Development Program – were the Pakistani Development Economist Mahbub Ul Haq (dubbed as 'The Father of People-Centric Development')[6] and the Indian Economist and Nobel Laureate Amartya Sen. Together they were the core architects of the '*Human Development Index*' – annually analysed in the Human Development Report, first launched in 1990. This influential report, published annually by the UNDP, reflects for former UN Secretary-General Kofi Annan 'Mahbub's profound conviction that what matters in development is not quantity but the quality of life lived by human beings'.[7] Sen, in particular, developed the idea that such increased quality of life is to be achieved by the enlargement of peoples' choices – in short: 'Development as Freedom',[8] expanding thereby his earlier thinking on 'human capacities'.

Compared with development economics, modernisation and dependency theories, the approaches to Alternative Development and to Human Development have shifted the perspective from outside-in-development towards inside-out-development, at least to some degree. However, despite the relative influence in particular of the Human Development approach today and despite its active promotion via the UNDP, its real impact on development work worldwide remains relatively small. That may have to do with its 'contradictory embeddedness' in the prevailing modernist economic paradigm, that limits its effectiveness. In this context it is notable, that the UN supported Human Development approach often stood in clear opposition to the most dominant international development institutions: World Bank and IMF. It is for that reason, that alternative approaches, so far, at best represented a mildly balancing force with regards to the imbalances that we experience worldwide.

While the dominance of World Bank and IMF continues, changes seem to be on the way. The ratification of the eight Millennium Development Goals at the UN Millennium Summit in 2000 by all the world's countries and accepted by major development institutions around the world is a clear sign that a broader, more interconnected, integrated and collaborative approach to development is not only asked for but on its way. It is for that reason that we added – in dotted lines – at the end of the above table a field, intimating the emergence of more integrated forms of development. We see Integral Development in that light.

Until now, however, it has remained unclear what a more integrated approach will look like. The argument of protagonists of the post-development era (that we shall introduce later in this chapter) is that such an approach lies beyond the existing Western, modernist paradigm, in which all prior approaches, including the Millennium Goals are rooted. Unless a major, paradigmatic shift has been achieved, so they claim, we are faced with ineffective global development work with its lack of understanding of true human needs. Such an understanding, they maintain, can, however, only be found through a deeper understanding of ourselves as human beings. Here, in post-development thinking, we see mirrored what we argued for in the opening chapter: the need for a simultaneous shift within the outer-directed paradigm (on a local and global level) and the inner directed, consciousness oriented one (on an individual and collective level). Both inner and outer 'shifts', as we see it, are intertwined. As a step towards this necessary move, so leading post-development thinkers maintain, we need to declare 'the end of development as we know it'.

SUSTAINABLE DEVELOPMENT

Is 'sustainable development' the answer? We think not – but it is an important step in the right direction. The debate on sustainable development has undoubtedly been and still is a major catalyst for sensitising humanity for environmental requirements, for re-searching our relationship to nature, and for acknowledging the 'limits to growth' based on non-renewable natural resources.

The *Limits to Growth*[9] published by the Club of Rome, and the so-called 'Brundtland Report' on 'Our Common Future', commissioned by the World Commission on the Environment and Development (WCED) were just two major milestone for the sustainable development movement, both serving as wake up calls to the world. Published in 1983, the Brundtland Report resumed:

> *many present development trends leave increasing numbers of people poor and vulnerable, while at the same time degrading the environment. How can such development serve next century's world of twice as many people relying on the same environment? This realisation broadened our view of development. We came to see it not in the restricted context of growth in developing countries ... rather that a new development path was required, one that sustained human progress not just in a few places for a few years, but for the entire planet into the distant future.*[10]

Since then, sustainable development thinking has strongly influenced the more generic development agenda, and continues to do so. However, the mainstream notion of sustainable development is heavily focused on ecology and environmental concerns, and on considerations of social economic justice. In other words, the conventional wisdom on 'sustainable development' is strongly underpinned by the 'hard' environmental, political and economic 'sciences', and hardly at all by the humanities, or by the 'soft' social sciences – a characteristic that we notice, up to today, in almost all 'official' approaches to sustainable development. Most discourses on sustainable development evolve around new technologies, standards and regulations. The minority of discourses are about the role of culture in sustainability thinking, new consciousness or new ways of living on and with the earth, and with each other. Rarely do such discourses serve to integrate such multiple perspectives. In that respect, also the approach to sustainable development is often caught up in the dualistic worldview of our time.

We shall see how this wordview played out in development theory and practice, as we turn now to examine various facets of it in more detail. We begin with a critical review of economic development theory and practice.

2.4   Reviewing Economic Development Theory and Practice: The West (Mis-)Leading the Rest

ECONOMIC DEVELOPMENT THEORY: AN INTRODUCTION TO MAJOR THINKERS

Overview

The single most influential force of development has been economics. Indeed, modernity with its focus on 'material life' has been a nurturing ground for unprecedented economic growth. With Truman officially inaugurating the 'development era' in 1949, it was obvious that development was primarily understood in economic and technological terms. And, it was understood, that the answers to such economic and technological development lay with the US and Europe. Finally, it was clear, that such 'development' had to be 'brought' in an 'outside-in' manner to the so-called developing countries.

While the following short analysis of the most influential economic theories and practices over the past six decades only provides snapshots, it at least serves to illustrate these core points. We have been guided in our analysis very much by the work of James Cypher, Research Professor at the Universidad Autonoma de Zacatecas in Mexico, and James Dietz, Professor of Development Studies in the Department of Economics at California State University in Fullerton. Their work on *The Process of Economic Development*[11] provides an excellent overview on the subject. With their help we shall now revisit the wide array of economic development theory and practice. We begin with theory. The point of departure, for Cypher and Dietz, is no other than Adam Smith.

Adam Smith – A theory of competitive capitalism and growth

Smith, in the late eighteenth century, provided one of the earliest and most enduring metaphors for the operation of the capitalist system: the 'invisible hand'. In his view, self-interested behaviour is functional and virtuous, since it leads an economy to the highest levels of economic welfare. Yet eighteenth- and nineteenth-century industrial Britain hardly bore this notion out. Only a tiny minority seemed to be benefiting. So Robert Malthus attempted to explain this state of affairs by claiming that the poor were responsible for their own misery, because of their 'animal nature'.[12]

David Ricardo, Robert Malthus and the law of diminishing returns

Following Smith, Robert Malthus and David Ricardo concocted between them the law of ultimately diminishing returns. Every economy has a maximum level of income per person that can be produced, though free trade and an 'open economy' may serve to counteract such. That led Ricardo onto his famous theory of comparative advantage, which underlies international trade theory to this very day. This theory argues that each country should produce where it has a relative advantage over others. In recent times this claim has become increasingly contested. Marx, in the nineteenth century, built on the 'labour theory of value', developed in the first place by Ricardo.[13]

Karl Marx's analysis of capitalist development – a brief digression!

Cypher and Dietz regarded Karl Marx as a digression. For unlike Smith, Malthus, Ricardo and most other classical economists, Marx did not assume capitalism to be immutable or to be the natural order of society. He believed it to be a stage of society's historical development, which began with primitive Communism and then evolved toward slavery, feudalism and eventually to capitalism – which would eventually break down and from which would be created a socialist economic system. As we learned from Immanuel Wallerstein, Peter Drucker (⇨1) and others – proclaiming the current era as the age of post-capitalism – Marx, to whom we shall once more return (⇨21), may well be proven right. Perhaps, in reviewing economic development theory in a century from now, capitalism will be described as a digression.

Ragnar Nurkse to Walt Whitman Rostow

After the Second World War – with the 'official beginning' of the 'development age' and particularly after the quick success of the US financed Marshall plan in helping to rebuild the European economies – several economists turned their attention to the question of the economic development of the less-developed regions, in particular in Africa, Asia and Latin America, thereby not only dealing with growth issues but also with structural transformation. Among these pioneers were the Finnish economist Ragnar Nurkse, the Austrian economist Paul Rosenstein-Rodan, German-born Albert Hirschman, the West Indian Sir Arthur Lewis, and American economic historian Walt Whitman Rostow. In a broad sense, the ideas of these early development economists were mutually supportive. We shall briefly introduce all of these thinkers and their main theories.

Paul Rosenstein-Rodan's theory of the big push

Much of Rosenstein-Rodan's work centred on taking advantage of the increasing returns that would be realised from large-scale planned industrialisation projects that encompassed several major sectors of the economy simultaneously. This was termed 'big push-push'.[14] In terms of the sequencing of investment decisions, Rosenstein-Rodan prioritised social overhead capital as an essential initial endowment, albeit one that nations have to actually create.

Ragnar Nurkse's theory of balanced growth

Like Rosenstein-Rodan, Ragnar Nurkse emphasised above all the need for a coordinated increase in the amount of capital utilised in a wide range of industries if the critical threshold level of industrialisation was to have a chance of being achieved. Nurkse agreed that a massive injection of new technology, new machines, and new production processes spread across a broad range of industrial sectors held the key to igniting the development process in less-developed nations.[15]

Albert Hirschman's backward and forward linkages

Albert Otto Hirschman was an influential economist with major contributions to development economics. One of Hirschman's best-known ideas was that of 'industrial linkages'.[16] When one industry expands, it needs inputs from other industries to be able to produce. These are called 'backward linkages'. For example, coal mining is a backward linkage from steel. On the other hand, when an industry sells and transports its production to other firms and sectors, these are 'forward linkages' of the original producer, toward the final consumer.

Arthur Lewis' surplus labour model

Arthur Lewis, a Caribbean from St Lucia was the first black person to receive the Nobel Prize for Economics in 1979. Lewis presumed that the typical less-developed nation was dualistic, not only in having two key sectors, formal and informal, but in the sense that these had very little interconnection. As labour leaves agriculture, the marginal and average product of labour must eventually rise as the labour surplus is exhausted. To keep the 'virtuous circle' of labour transfer going once started, there would have to be more and more capital formation in manufacturing capacity.[17]

Walt Whitman Rostow's stages of growth theory

Rostow became the most renowned development theorist, and the most avowedly anti-communist, being a strong believer in capitalism and free enterprise. He thereby eclipsed Marx's more thoroughgoing, developmental orientation. Like Marx before him, Rostow sought a universal interpretation of history, and he provided this in his stage model. He argued that all nations pass through five stages: traditional society, preconditions for take-off, the take-off, the drive to maturity, and the age of mass consumption.[18] He built his theory on the history of Britain, as had Marx. Rostow, though, failed to entertain the likelihood that the process of destruction of traditional society will be so thorough, that the colonised society will be set on a path that does not lead to take-off, but to stagnation. Also, he did not explain the process involved in moving from one stage to another. For many development economists, his 'stages' do not concur with the history of most nations that have taken off into sustained growth.

Robert Solow's theory of economic growth and the Solow-residual

The empirical research on growth undertaken by the American economist and Nobel Laureate Robert Solow using the neoclassical framework, seemed to validate the policy recommendations of early development economists and their policy-oriented theories, such as the 'big push', 'balanced growth', and 'unbalanced growth' strategies. The primacy of physical capital accumulation, in Solow's production function, has been a focus for development economists since the time of Adam Smith. In this view, countries need to save and invest sufficiently so as to augment their total physical capital stock if they are to reach higher income levels. However, Solow found also that a significant proportion of the growth rate of a country – over 50 per cent – could not be accounted for by physical capital and labour. That resulted in the so-called 'Solow Residual'.[19] Increases in income per person were assumed to be the result of exogenous technology, but the Solow model had no theory of how or why technology changed. Something was missing from the story that the neoclassical model had to tell. All the diverse factors and influences that might reasonably be attributed to generating the Solow Residual – education, technology, culture, business organisation, research and development, international trade – invited much speculation. 'Something in the air' was responsible.

Endogenous growth models

Then, in the late 1980s, so-called endogenous growth models began to emerge in the economics literature. According to them, growth can become a permanent feature of an economy's history. In other words, the more you learn, the faster you learn. Research and development and the creation of knowledge becomes key. Education, institutionalisation and knowledge creation becomes central to endogenous growth models. From the perspective of endogenous growth, the ability to use technology, to develop new knowledge and new products, and the skills of the labour force which complement knowledge creation and its application, are formed and shaped by each particular economy. In other words, growth is an endogenous process, coming from within each particular economy. Each economy had a different production function reflecting different qualities and quantities of inputs and their ability to adapt, develop and use knowledge about how to produce within that economy. For American development economist Paul Romer goes $Y = F(R,K,H)$, whereby Y is total output, R is research and development done by all firms in the economy, K is the accumulated physical capital stock, and H is the accumulated stock of human capital. In a very general way, endogenous growth models focus on how capitalist economies expand over time.[20] They show how new knowledge, new products, and a finer division of labour within and between firms can contribute to both income growth and higher income, as has been the case in East Asia.

What then are key learnings from this introduction into the most influential economic development theories?

The history of economic development theory so far: Focus on capital formation, savings, investments and growth

The brief overview of selected core thinkers of economic development theory illustrated that all of them, at least to some degree, followed in the footsteps of Adam Smith, with whom we began this excursion. All of them focused on capital formation, savings, investments and growth. The one major exception is Karl Marx, whose thinking has been seen rather as a digression, and who only recently has once again re-entered the mainstream economic discussion (⇨21), as the prevailing capitalist system reveals its flaws. Core international institutions promoting development, such as the World Bank and the IMF, however, continue to build on the major economic development thinkers introduced earlier, remaining by and large on the capitalist track. In the more recent history, increased consideration has been given to endogenous growth, with a stronger emphasis on knowledge creation and human capital. Cypher and Dietz claim, however, that all of these theories of economic development have been faltering and ultimately proven insufficient or unsuccessful. A number of leading World Bank economists have outwardly critiqued the World Bank and its sister organisation IMF over the past decades. Among the most outspoken critics are former World Bank chief economist and Nobel Laureate Joseph Stiglitz[21] and former World Bank senior consultant Thomas Dichter.[22] That leads us to have a closer look at the dominant practice of the official economic development agenda pursued by the West.

ECONOMIC DEVELOPMENT PRACTICE: DOMINANT RECENT PRACTICE AS EXPRESSED BY THE WASHINGTON CONSENSUS

Turning to the dominant development practice in recent decades, we shall deal primarily with the most influential carrier of international development policies: the so-called 'Washington Consensus'. The term describes the kind of standard reform package that the so-called developed world had put together for faltering so-called developing countries.[23] This standard package comprised of policies with regards to macroeconomic stabilisation, strengthening of market forces within the local economy, and opening of local markets to international trade and investment. The main actors in this neoclassical play were the three Washington based institutions: World Bank, International Monetary Fund (IMF) and the US Treasury Department. Though the term 'Washington Consensus' was only invented in the late 1980s (by the US Economist John Williamson), the alliance between these three core players has its institutional beginnings within World War II.

The conception of IMF and World Bank at Bretton Woods

The classical and neoclassical approach to economic development, whereby the market mechanism was king, began to be institutionalised across the world stage at the tail end of the Second World War. Both the IMF and the World Bank – at that time called the International Bank for Reconstruction and Development (IBRD), which is now integrated into the World Bank – were conceived at the Bretton Woods conference in New Hampshire in 1944, bringing together representatives of 44 nations to think through and plan a new international financial and trade system. Participants of the conference were united by a shared belief in capitalism. The new system needed to be both stable enough to maintain confidence and able to avoid the international chaos of the 1920s and 1930s, and yet be flexible enough to be able to accommodate changing circumstances. It is somewhat ironic that while John Maynard Keynes was the major influence at the conference, the IMF and World Bank have never demonstrated a major affinity for Keynesian-type approaches on economic issues, and over the past 30 years neo-liberalism has triumphed.

The reactive IMF: Lender of last resort – from bridge financing, conditionality and surveillance to structural adjustments

Typically, today, resort to IMF financing reflects an inability on the part of a country to access more normal channels of international financing. In other words, going to the IMF is tacit recognition of currently unstable economic policies, either due to internal policy failures or to external changes in the international economy that adversely affect an economy – such as a sudden shift in the terms of trade or collapse of a major export commodity. In principle, the Fund's loans are short-term and conceived as 'bridges' for resolving short-term balance of payment and exchange rate difficulties. The approach is therefore reactive rather than proactive.

So-called 'conditionality' seeks to ensure that members using IMF resources will adopt the policy measures the IMF believes are needed to improve balance of payments positions and resolve exchange rate difficulties. It is also important that the country is able to repay its debts in a timely manner. Yet, as befits the unsettled nature of Fund policies in recent years, the IMF has decided that its policies on conditionality have contributed to economic turmoil. In 2002, the Fund discussed the 'growing intrusiveness' of conditionality, concluding that the countries should 'own' their restructuring programmes. The new conditionality guidelines were to be 'more of a cooperative venture' with borrowing nations.

From the IMF perspective, countries are forced to make appeals to the Fund because they have mismanaged their finances, most specifically their exchange rate and balance of payments position. According to the IMF, to begin to solve the problem of such an imbalance, a stabilisation programme must be introduced in the country that typically results in compression of the economy. Excess demand and spending by consumers and government must be wrung out of the system, and therefore a short-term economic downturn must be imposed. Once the so-called economic fundamentals are stabilised and brought into equilibrium, the Fund believes the economy will bounce back.

Such a structural adjustment involves:

- *Devaluation of the Currency:* To stimulate exports and downplay imports.
- *Control of the Money Supply:* To stem inflation.
- *Reduction of Government Spending:* To control the fiscal deficit.
- *Reduction in Real Wages:* To mitigate internal aggregate demand.

As a result, austerity programmes often impose an inordinate burden on those in society who can least afford the effects of income and spending compression. According to Cypher and Dietz, if the IMF demands a cut in spending without some fundamental analysis of the structural and institutional transformations desired for that particular society, it can further inhibit progress. According to the Fund's own self-evaluation, the externally instigated structural adjustment programmes have proved to be largely unsuccessful, at least in stimulating growth and investment.

We now turn from the IMF to its twin, the World Bank.

The proactive World Bank?

Like the IMF, the World Bank commenced lending on a very modest scale, in its initial 20 years. While the IMF lent short-term, the Bank lent long-term. Another distinction between the Fund and the Bank in the early years was that the latter offered project loans and technical expertise to promote large-scale capital-intensive mega-investment projects in less-developed nations, mostly water related projects. Its emphasis on large-scale infrastructure projects has, however, often been of dubious value to the host nation.

In addition to its general role in long-term finance, the Bank formed in 1956 the International Finance Corporation (IFC) and in 1960 the International Development Association (IDA). Whereas the IFC supports as a co-investor private sector development with an emphasis on small and medium-sized business, the IDA focuses exclusively on the world's poorest countries; in other words, it lends to nations that cannot qualify for World Bank loans. Finally, the Multilateral Investment Guarantee Agency (MIGA) organises international conferences to promote investment opportunities in developing nations, and also gives policy advice to investors. Since its inception, the Bank has only had US citizens for its presidents, whereas in the IMF case such presidents have been European – a 'tradition' that is increasingly contested by other countries. The US is also the largest financial shareholder in both institutions.

Emerging institutionalisation of development: The McNamara era and the basic needs approach

As an institution, the World Bank rapidly changed under the leadership of Robert McNamara (1968 to 1981), thereby moving to the centre of the development dialogue. He built up a cadre of highly trained economists. The World Bank's funding rapidly expanded and its mission was radically overhauled to the basic needs approach. Now the central focus of the Bank was on alleviating world poverty, hunger and misery. In that sense it leapt from its hitherto modest goals to addressing the most intractable of development issues: with a new emphasis, now more oriented towards promoting endogenous growth, through housing, water sanitation, the Green Revolution, schooling and related matters.

Between 1967 and 1993 the World Bank lent $224 billion, and the IDA an additional $76 billion. Just as important was the co-financing that developed in parallel, through international banks. At the same time, however, beginning in the 1970s, increasing environmental and social concerns were raised regarding World Bank sponsored activities.

The rise of structural adjustment lending: 1979 to 2007

By the late 1970s, McNamara's vision had gone beyond that of meeting basic human needs. He now believed that the World Bank had to get directly involved in guidance and implementation of development programmes. Again, the emphasis was on shared implementation. The new style loans were termed 'structural and sectoral adjustment loans' (SAL). By 1986, about one-third of all World Bank loans were under the guise of structural adjustment. By 2002 such SAL's amounted to 64 per cent. In essence, an SAL is not geared to building anything in particular, but rather to changing national economic policies in some desired direction. Most commonly addressed were the improvement of export incentives, the reform of the government's budget, improving the financial performance of public enterprises, improving agricultural policies, and strengthening the capacity to formulate and implement public investment policies.

The central thrust of the SAL's was the paring back of the role of the state – rather than promoting endogenous growth – through sell-offs or privatisation funded by the Bank. According to Cypher and Dietz, in every instance, the Bank sought to remould the society and economy to create an environment it believed would be more encouraging to the private sector, including international corporations. Furthermore, under so-called '*cross-conditionality*', countries could only receive SAL's if they had stand-by arrangements with the IMF. And they could only receive such stand-by loans if they had SAL agreements with the Bank. What a turnaround from the original intention to cater for basic needs.

A survey of the effectiveness of World Bank SAL's was conducted in 33 African nations, between 1980 and 1989. Results showed that per capita income declined 1.1 per cent in these nations, while per capita food production declined overall. The purchasing power of the minimum wage fell by 25 per cent. Government expenditure on education fell by 35 per cent.

Critiques of World Bank and IMF structural adjustment loans

World Bank and IMF came increasingly under pressure from civil society groups. The critique was on two fronts: interfering with national sovereignty and pursuing a relentlessly neo-liberal path. As a consequence, an internal review into the overall effects of the SALs was conducted in 2002. It arrived at the following results:

- Trade liberalisation had been pushed through, destroying domestic firms.
- There was a lack of meaningful participation of local stakeholders.
- Financial assets had become more concentrated.
- Financial reforms had promoted short-term financial speculation.
- Employment levels had worsened and wage levels deteriorated.
- Women had suffered most of all.
- The elimination of food subsidies had affected the poorest most.

In other words, externally imposed regulations by the World Bank had bypassed if not suppressed endogenously based enterprise and growth.

Strategy Change: Sustainable Development + Comprehensive Development Framework + Social Capital + Knowledge Bank

Another internal World Bank report – commissioned in the 1990s, after evidence of the weakness of the SAL approach had mounted – served to conclude that loan performance in the early 1990s was far worse than it had been a decade before. The then Bank president, Lewis Preston, quickly brought the concept of 'sustainability' into the foreground, in the same way as McNamara had focused on basic needs. Under James Wolfensohn who took over between 1995 and 2005, the emphasis was now on 'sustainability + comprehensive development framework + social capital + knowledge bank'. The argument from critics was that such a plethora of goals had been established to deflect from the underlying criticism of the institution. To put it another way, many still regarded the World Bank as a case of a 'neo-liberal wolf in integral sheep's clothing'.

The poverty reduction approach

The widespread critique of the World Bank structural adjustment policy led to one further change that subsumed policy-based lending under the heading of the Poverty Reduction Strategy Papers (PRSP's). The PRSP's programme – sometimes labelled the 'new aid model' – came into effect in 2000, becoming the centrepiece of the IMF, the World Bank, bilateral agencies and NGO's involved with development policy. By 2007, 64 nations had become involved, spanning 2 billion people.

Under the terms of the new PRSP's, not only were both the Bank and the IMF involved simultaneously, but the host nation was a 'co-owner' of the programme from the outset. Development Assistance – the official term for financial aid given by governments and other agencies for the development of so-called developing countries – was now set within a long-term framework. This framework was supposed to be consistent with the capabilities and objectives of the borrowing nation – a conceptual break from prior foreign aid practices that have been vertical in nature, uncoordinated with the Bretton Woods institutions and often ad hoc in manner.

The PRSP's are national development programmes, based on the hypothesis that foreign trade and investment are the engines of economic growth, and that economic growth is the only way to address poverty. There are four essential elements:

- Stabilisation of the macroeconomy through IMF conditionality.
- Implementation of structural adjustment.
- Focus on economic growth as the underlying means to reduce poverty.
- Domestic participation in formulation and ownership of the programme.

We argue that PRSP's programmes have been very narrow in both their substance and their participation. Also Cypher and Dietz see these recent changes in a very critical light. For them, they have served to camouflage the IMF and to shroud World Bank leverage in a fog of participatory rhetoric. Actually, PRSP's are seen as a means to 'engineer consent'. There was little to back up the claim that emphasis was now on sustainability + comprehensive development framework + social capital + knowledge bank.

Tangible changes underway?

As we write this book the era of Robert Zoellig as the World Bank's President from 2007 to 2012 has come to an end. Under his leadership the World Bank has significantly increased its efforts for the poorest countries and gained recognition for massive steps towards openness and transparency, for example through its Open Data Initiative. Also, the Bank's leadership has been considerably restructured in the past five years. By now almost 50 per cent of the senior officials are women; and almost 50 per cent of the senior staff are representatives from so-called developing countries. So, yes, we can see signs of change. What has not been changed though is the Bank's unilateral focus on boosting growth in order to alleviate poverty. Doing so, the world remains with an image of poverty being solely defined in economic and material terms – perhaps increasingly linked to environmental degradation. Recently, in October 2012, the new World Bank President Jim Yong Kim has announced fighting climate change as one of the Bank's new core aims, acknowledging the close link between environmental decay, hunger and poverty.

Review of mainstream development practice

We have based our analysis of the theory and practice of economic development strongly on the excellent research undertaken by Cypher and Dietz. Doing so, we have purposefully selected two critical voices with regards to the Washington Consensus and the overall unhealthy dialectic between a reactive IMF and a supposedly more proactive World Bank. Their arguments though are sound, and – other than much of the critique of these both institutions – relatively free of polemic. The failures of decades of development work have also been acknowledged by internal World Bank studies. And we can see, change seems to be underway. Yet, the Washington Consensus – to our Integral Development eye – is still promoting not only a one-sided purely economic approach to development, but also the underlying economic model and its sustainability remains largely unquestioned. Despite their rhetoric about participation, most of the approximately 9,000 World Bank staff are far removed from the contexts they seek to develop; and even if stationed within the so-called developing country, an intense immersion and bottom-up co-evolution with local contexts, as we propose in this book, is not in sight.

We are fully aware that our critique of mainstream economics may be countered by the demand to offer something better instead. We have taken on this challenge and it is with this challenge in mind that we have recently come up with *Integral Economics*,[24] an approach that we shall briefly introduce later in this book (⇨21).

At this stage we regard it as important to see that the world's most influential development institutions, IMF and World Bank, define and seek to address poverty purely in economic and financial terms. Thereby they continue to reduce the human being to a primarily economic entity. Furthermore, they also continue to define development 'outside-in'.

Such an economic 'outside-in in' perspective has had its early ally in so-called 'modernisation theory' which itself got later a fierce opponent in so-called 'dependency theory'. This brings us to a highly influential, often-furious development dialectic between the West and the Rest.

2.5 Modernisation versus Dependency: The Rest Opposing the West

OVERVIEW

We now introduce two major, though conflicting development theories: modernisation theory and dependency theory. While the former has been conceived of and driven by the USA, the latter had its origins in Latin America and has turned increasingly into a position representing much of the so-called 'Global South'. Together they form a polar-opposite dialectic within the development discourse of the past 50 years. Modernisation Theory originated in the time after World War II and took the lead as a major philosophical underpinning of early development economics. Dependency Theory followed as an antithesis, as a reaction of the so-called developing world to being forced on a development path defined and imposed by the West. Both theories have undergone considerable 'development' within and among themselves, as the following overview demonstrates. Therein we shall be drawing on many sources, but in particular on Hong Kong-based sociologist Alan So's in-depth research on *Social Change and Development*.[25]

We begin with modernisation theory.

THE MODERNISATION PERSPECTIVE

Structural functionalism as key to define the functionality of a society

The late Talcott Parsons, a distinguished sociologist from Harvard University, was a major influence on modernisation theory in development. In particular he became known for his 'functionalist perspective'. Though he never liked to see his body of theory labelled as structural functionalism, he nevertheless saw it as an important sociological method, which he himself employed. Structural functionalism is an approach within sociology that views society from a perspective of the functioning of its different parts that altogether make up its structure. For Parsons, human society is like a biological organism and can be studied as such. He identified four critical functions that every society as a social system must perform, or else it will die. These four functions constitute the scheme known as AGIL:[26]

* *Adaptation:* Adaptation to the environment – performed by the economy.
* *Goal Attainment:* Achievements of goals – performed by the government.
* *Integration:* Integration via linking institutions together – performed by legal institutions and religion.
* *Latency:* Latency promoting pattern maintenance of values from generation to generation – performed by family and education.

Evolving from traditional to modern society – an either-or process

Strongly influential on development theory was also Parson's concept of 'pattern variables' to distinguish traditional (from his perspective: less evolved) from modern (more evolved) societies. According to him, these differentiations took place on five scales:

* *Affective versus Affective-Neutral Relationships:* In traditional societies social relationships tend to have an affective component: personal, emotional and face-to-face. In modern societies social relationships have an affective-neutral component: impersonal, detached and indirect.
* *Particularistic versus Universalistic Relationships:* In traditional societies people tend to associate with the same social circle. In modern ones, where there is a high density

of population, people are forced to interact with strangers frequently, and to interact using universalistic norms.

- *Collective versus Self-Orientation:* In traditional societies loyalty is often owed to the collectivity, such as the family, community or tribe. In modern societies self-orientation is stressed, encouragement to be yourself, to develop your own talent, and to build up your own career.
- *Ascription versus Achievement*: In traditional societies a person is evaluated by his or her ascribed status. In modern ones evaluation has to be carried out on an achievement basis due to market competition.
- *Functionally Diffused versus Functionally Specific Relationships*: Traditional societies tend toward the diffused, modern societies toward the specific articulation of functions.

According to this scheme, by moving between the poles towards so-called higher levels of development, societies are bound to disintegrate, rather than integrate these opposites. It is an either-or decision between community and individuality, between being affective and being emotionally neutral, between personal and impersonal, between local and universal.

In summary, for Parsons, as well as for many conventional modernisers, modernisation is an either-or, rather than an integrating process. This is the tragedy that Jean Gebser (⇨1, 13) saw as a main reason for the stuckness of the modern world. This either-or thinking, as we argued already earlier, had a profound influence on development thinking, in particular in the 1950s, but it remains so until today.

Modernisation theory: Inspired by classical evolutionary theory – developing countries condemned as 'backward followers'

We notice here also the strong influence of classical evolutionary theory on modernisation theory. Classical evolutionary theory had the following features. First, it assumed that social change is linear, standardised and unidirectional; that is, all human societies invariably move in one direction, from a primitive (primary) to an advanced (secondary) state, the one precluding rather than building upon the other. Secondly, evolutionary theory imposed a value judgment on the development process. The movement toward the secondary phase is considered good because it represents generalised progress, humanity and civilisation, irrespective of the particularities of a specific community. Thirdly, it assumed that the rate of social change is slow, gradual and piecemeal – evolutionary, not revolutionary. The departure from a simple, primitive society to a complex, modern one will take centuries to complete. Such a viewpoint saw the so-called developing world almost forever in the role of 'backward followers' of a set development track.

Perceived characteristics of modernisation: Systematic, transformative and immanent

Following Parsons, modernisation researchers have implicitly formulated their theories with the following traits, whereby modernisation is a:

- *Phased Process:* Societies begin with the primitive, simple, undifferentiated traditional stage and end with the advanced, complex, differentiated modern stage, one being set apart from the other.
- *Homogenising Process:* It produces tendencies towards convergence between societies, rather than each one having its own specific 'genius'.
- *Progressive Process:* The modernised political system has a much better capacity to handle the functions of national identity, legitimacy, penetration, participation and distribution than the traditional one.
- *Lengthy Process:* An evolutionary rather than a revolutionary process of change prevails.

Furthermore, modernisation is commonly seen as a:

- *Systematic Process:* It involves generalised changes in virtually all aspects of behaviour, including industrialisation, urbanisation, differentiation, secularisation, participation and centralisation.
- *Transformative Process:* In order for society to move into modernity its traditional structures and values must be totally replaced by modern ones.
- *Immanent Process:* Once a change has started in one sphere of activity it will necessarily produce comparative changes in all other spheres.

Critique of classic modernisation studies – a homogenising, universal lens

The overall policy implication of such a modernisation approach is that the First World is modern and advanced and the Third World is traditional and backward. As an inevitable result, the latter should look to the former for guidance. Then, if Third World countries are to modernise, they should be moving along the path that North America and Western Europe, as well as by now countries like Japan, South Korea or Taiwan have travelled.[27]

If what is needed is more exposure to modern values and more productive investment, then the so-called developed countries can help by sending advisers, by encouraging First World business to invest abroad, making loans, and rendering other services to the so-called underdeveloped Third World.

Many of the classic modernisation studies help to illustrate this point. Notable are for example the 'achievement motivation theory'[28] of David McClelland, a psychology theorist based at Harvard University in the 1950s and 1960s, and the research of Alex Inkeles, Professor of Sociology at Stanford University in the 1960s, on *'Pattern of Modern Men'*.[29]

In both studies – and in many other modernisation studies of that time – one recognises that a homogenising, universal lens (which basically means: a Western lens) had been applied. Research subjects were primarily men, cultural idiosyncrasies were neglected, and the research focus was on achievement – which for us is a core value in Western cultures, in particular in relation to economics. Many critics argued that concepts such as 'advanced', 'modern' and 'traditional' as well as 'primitive', are merely ideological labels to justify Western superiority. Indeed, most of the core protagonists are so-called Ivy League Professors, from Talcott Parsons and David McClelland from Harvard, to Alex Inkeles from Stanford. Furthermore, critics assert that the belief in unidirectional development has resulted in modernisation researchers overlooking alternative paths of development for Third World countries.

It becomes clear that such an understanding of modernisation disconnects a society from its traditional grounds; in its striving towards homogenisation it is devoid of transcultural co-evolution, whereby each culture remains in touch with its own particularities.

We now move on to explore a field that is called 'new modernisation studies'. We shall notice an evolution, as recent approaches to modernisation are more anthropologically religiously based, and more context-and-case-sensitive.

The new modernisation studies: Reconnecting to tradition

The *'new'* modernisation studies are somewhat more balanced in nature and scope than their classical predecessors. In what way? Firstly, they avoid treating tradition and modernity as a set of mutually exclusive concepts. Further, tradition and modernity could not only coexist, but could penetrate and intermingle with each other. Secondly, the new modernisation studies tend to focus on concrete cases. History is often brought back in to show the specific pattern of development in a particular country. Thirdly, as a result of paying more attention to history and concrete cases, the new modernisation studies do not assume a unidirectional path as per the Western model.

An example is Siu Lun Wong's work on 'Entrepreneurial Familism' in China. Classical modernisation researchers advocated discarding traditional Chinese family values in order to promote economic growth in China. In his study, *Emigrant Entrepreneurs in Hong Kong*,[30] Wong criticises this viewpoint for overlooking the dynamic role of the Chinese family in promoting economic development. The tendency to see only the sharp dichotomy between European universalism and Chinese particularism resulted in the 'old moderniser's' inability to understand the Chinese family's role. Wong believed that the European experience of capitalist development was not likely to be replicated in China. However, China's different patterns of social structure would necessarily result in different patterns of modernisation. Similar arguments were advanced by a number of scholars who focused on the role of religion in modernisation.

Modernisation revisited – beyond catching up?

Modernisation theory has dominated the development discourse powerfully, in particular in the 1950s and 1960s and was the guiding theory for much of development practice. We have criticised its highly detrimental underlying assumption that development was all about the so-called developing countries 'catching up' with the so-called developed world, thereby banished to a course of imitation and followership. Local particularities – in form of, for example, culture, tradition, religion – were overlooked. Indeed, most of the classical modernisation studies were conducted in a way that they seemed to affirm a universal (= 'Westernwestern') pattern. New modernisation studies have added value in that they have taken a much closer look at what tradition is, how it interacts with Western forces, and what role it has played in modernisation, thereby adopting a more balanced approach.

The push to look at development differently came very much from the developing countries themselves, in particular from the Dependency School from Latin America. We shall explore now, to what degree the dependency perspective served to advance development thinking.

DEPENDENCY THEORY: A REACTION TO MODERNISATION

The 'dependentistas' – offering a Third World perspective on development

The so-called South American *dependentistas* came into existence in the 1970s as a reaction against the Western approach to modernisation. According to Swedish development economist Björn Hettne,[31] the Dependency School represents 'the voices of the periphery' that challenge the intellectual hegemony of the American Modernisation School. Alvin So commented that, just as the classical version of the Modernisation School can be said to examine development from a First World point of view, the Dependency School adopted a Third World perspective.[32] What are its origins?

A critique of the one-sided international division of labour and diminishing terms of trade

Initially, the Dependency School arose in South America in response to the bankruptcy of the programme of the UN Commission for Latin America (ECLA) in the early 1960s. Raúl Prebisch who can be seen as a predecessor to the Dependency School, had been the head of ECLA in the 1960s. He criticised strongly the outdated international division of labour. The flaw, for him, was that Latin America was asked to produce food and raw materials for the great industrial centres, and, in return, it would receive industrial goods from these. It was Prebisch's contention that this scheme was at the roots of the developmental problems of Latin America.[33] Reliance on the export of food and raw material would inevitably lead to a deterioration of Latin America's terms of trade, which would further affect its accumulation of capital. Prebisch came to this conclusion in his research approximately at the same time as the German Jewish development economist Hans Singer arrived at similar results.[34] It is for that reason that their mutual discoveries became internationally known as the 'Singer-Prebisch-Thesis'.

Prebisch's strategy for Latin American development called for the one-sided international division of labour to be stopped, and for Latin America to undergo industrialisation. He suggested that governments should actively participate as coordinators, to break the chains of underdevelopment. Unfortunately, the ECLA programme did not succeed. Purchasing power was restricted to certain social strata, and the domestic market showed no tendency to expand after its needs had been fulfilled. Brief expansion turned to economic stagnation.

Providing an external explanation of underdevelopment

The Dependency School was also a response to the crisis of orthodox Marxism in Latin America in the 1960s, which had by then lost most of its original appeal. Dependency theory then spread from South to North America. German Jewish American historian and sociologist Andre Gunder Frank happened to be in South America in the early 1960s, and was instrumental in disseminating dependency theory to the English-speaking world. For him, imperialism, not backwardness and lack of modernity, was the enemy.[35]

As a founder member of the Dependency School, Frank strongly rejected the prevailing assumption made by modernisers that Third World countries were at an early stage of their development – according to the experience of Western countries – and therefore needed to follow the same path to reach modernity. For him, the colonial experience had completely restructured Third World countries and thereby drastically altered the potential trajectory of their path.

As a reaction to the 'internal' explanation of the Modernisation School for the Third World's state of development, Frank offered an 'external' explanation. According to him, backwardness cannot be explained by feudalism or traditionalism. For many countries, such as China and India, were quite advanced before imposed by colonisers. For him, a core reason lay in a sophisticated system for extracting economic surplus from the developing world. Just as national cities in colonised countries had become satellites of Western metropolises, so these satellites immediately have become the colonial metropolises with respect to provincial cities, which in turn have local cities with satellites surrounding them. Hence, a whole chain of constellations of satellites is established to extract economic surplus.

Distinguishing different forms of dependence

In spelling out the classical definition of dependence, Brazil's sociologist Theotonio Dos Santos stated that the relationship between two or more countries assumes the form of dependence when some countries (the dominant ones) can expand and be self-starting, while others (the dependent ones) can do this only as a reflection of that expansion.[36]

Dos Santos distinguished three forms of historical dependence. In the first form of colonial dependence the commercial and financial capital of the dominant country monopolised the control of land, mines and human resources (serf or slave) and the export of raw materials from the colonised country. However, by the end of the nineteenth century, financial-industrial dependence emerged as the second form. Although still dominated by the big capital of the European centres, the economies of the dependent countries were then centred on the export sector, with rigid specialisation and mono-cultivation.

In the third and latest form of technological-industrial dependence, the unequal capitalist development at the international level is reproduced internally, with the productive structure of the underdeveloped countries torn between a traditional agrarian export sector and a modern sector of technological and economic-financial concentration. This unequal production structure has imposed limits on the growth of internal markets in so-called underdeveloped countries. The growth of consumer-goods markets is limited by the low purchasing power of the labour force and by the small number of jobs created by the capital-intensive sector. In addition, the growth of capital-goods markets is limited by the remittance of profits to foreign countries, which carries away part of the economic surplus generated in the domestic economy.

Dos Santos concludes that it is the monopolistic control of foreign capital, finance and technology at national and international levels that prevents underdeveloped countries from reaching an advantageous position, resulting in the reproduction of backwardness, misery and social marginalisation within their borders.

Shared assumptions of the Dependency School amidst high heterogeneity

As we have seen, the Dependency School was – like the Modernisation School it critiqued – highly heterogeneous. However, its members nevertheless shared the following group of assumptions.[37] Dependency is:

- Seen as a very general process, applicable to all so-called Third World countries.
- Understood to be an external condition, imposed from outside.
- Analysed mainly as an economic condition.
- Treated as a component of a regional polarisation of the global economy.

Proponents felt, that there was a need to redefine development. Development should mean more than just more industry, more output, and rising productivity. Instead it should be redefined as involving the improving of the living standards for all the people on the periphery. Since the era of colonialism, the political economy of the periphery had been totally restructured to meet the needs of the core, thereby leading, in terms of the *dependentistas*, to the 'development of underdevelopment'.[38] Consequently the Dependency School suggested that peripheral countries should sever their ties with core countries. Instead of relying on foreign aid and technology, peripheral countries should adopt a self-reliance model.

An example of classical dependency study: Paul Baran on India

As in the Modernisation School, we also find in the Dependency School a distinction between classical and new studies. A famous example of a classical dependency study is the exposition on colonialism in India by Paul Baran, a Russian-born American development economist.[39] In his study, Baran argued that the transfer of economic surplus from India to Britain, the de-industrialisation of Indian industries, the flooding of Indian society with British manufactured goods, and the pauperisation of the Indian countryside led to the underdevelopment of India on the one hand, and capital accumulation for Britain on the other. British colonialism, however, had more than economic impact on India. It also had profound impacts on the country's political and cultural spheres as well. As an overall result, India moved backward, from a relatively advanced industrial nation to a backward one in the nineteenth century.

Classical dependency theory – A critique

The dependency perspective is said to have committed the major error of treating all peripheral areas as if they were the same, without any respect to specific community contexts and cultural particularities. As a result, *dependentistas* were inclined to take a deductive approach to national studies, making them conform to what is logically expected on the basis of the dependency model. According to Alvin So, dependency studies seldom made a serious attempt to bring out the historical specificity, or the cultural and spiritual uniqueness of each particular Third World country.[40] Moreover, argued the critics, dependency and development may actually coexist. For example, South Korea and Taiwan were once colonies of Japan, yet these two countries have attained rapid economic development since World War II. How does the Dependency School answer such criticisms? For answers, we turn to the new dependency studies, which, like the new modernisation studies, were more country and context specific.

The new dependency studies: New horizons through associated-dependent development and dynamic dependency

Henrique Cardoso, Brazilian sociologist and thirty-fourth president of Brazil (1995 to 2003) is often singled out as the main protagonist of the new dependency studies. His goal was to delineate historically specific situations of dependency in the search for differences and diversities. Consequently, his key research questions were as follows: how can the researcher bring out the historical uniqueness of a particular dependency situation? How do the existing dependency structures themselves generate possibilities for transformation?[41]

Unlike the researchers of the classical Dependency School, who emphasise the structural determination of dependency, Cardoso regarded such structures as an open-ended process. Given similar structures of dependency, there is a range of possible responses depending on internal political alliances and movements.

New was his argument that dependency and development can coexist. Cardoso deliberately used the phrase 'associated-dependent development' because it combines two notions that generally have appeared as separate and contradictory – dependency and development. Classical modernisation theories focus on only modernisation and development, while classical dependency theories view the basic relationship between a dependent capitalist country and an underdeveloped one as one of extractive exploitation that perpetuates stagnation.

But Cardoso asserts that a new phase has emerged as a result of the rise of multinational corporations, the immersion of industrial capital into peripheral economies, and a new international division of labour. He argues that to some extent the interests of the foreign corporations become compatible with the internal prosperity of dependent countries. Thereby, they help to promote development. From this angle, development implies a definite articulation with technological, financial, organisational and market connections that only multinational corporations can ensure.

At the same time, not being willing to go all the way to join the Modernisation School, Cardoso immediately stresses the costs of associated-dependent development. For example, he points out that the Brazilian economic boom was based on a regressive profile of income distribution, emphasising luxury consumer durables as opposed to basic necessities, generating increasing foreign indebtedness, contributing to social marginality and the underutilisation and exploitation of manpower resources, and thereby leading to an increase of relative misery.

Another well-known example of the new dependency studies is so-called 'dynamic dependency'.

Thomas Gold, Professor of Sociology at the University of California, has taken Cardoso's argument further by distinguishing between classic dependence, dependent development and dynamic dependency. For him each represents a different phase of development and degree of dependence. He illustrates his argument with the case of Taiwan. According to Gold, Taiwan had been restructured by its former dependent relation with Japan in colonial times, not underdeveloped. This occurred in the first phase of classical dependence. Then, in 1950, Gold sees Taiwan entering the second phase of dependent development. After Taiwan became 'Free China' and an ally of the United Sates, it depended heavily on military and economic aid from the US. In the then following 30 years, Taiwan's political and economic sector got reformed and rapidly developed – in particular the textile and electronics industry grew dramatically, in the case of electronics very much through the triple alliance amongst the state, local capital and Transnational Corporations. From the early 1980s onwards, Gold argues, Taiwan entered the third state of dynamic dependency, during which industrialisation was deepened through upgrading industries and their vertical integration. By the mid 1980s, Taiwan, as a whole, had left the problems of economic underdevelopment behind it.[42]

REVIEWING MODERNISATION AND DEPENDENCY THEORY: MULTIFACETTED DUALISM

Comparing and contrasting these two major theories we came across an intense, however seemingly unconscious, dualism.

The Dependency School emerged as a reaction to the prior Modernisation School. It provided an external perspective on development, from the point of view of the so-called developing countries. The Dependency School holds that underdevelopment is a state imposed from outside, primarily through colonialism and its long-term effects. Modernisation Theory, on the contrary, saw the main reasons of so-called underdevelopment in internal reasons, specifically in the backwardness of the developing countries – pointing to such traits as traditional culture, lack of productive investment and absence of achievement motivation.

While the Dependency School clearly reversed the direction of the development discourse, it remained, like modernisation, a very abstract theory. Both theories strongly generalise and fail to be connected to particular development contexts. In its reactive response to modernisation, the Dependency School equally neglected the cultural particularities of each specific context. In other words, it claimed to speak for the Global South, but the local, indigenous voices of the people concerned were not heard.

As with modernisation theory, the dependency theorists are still primarily interested in economic and technological development, while environmental concerns, communal development, or the culture and spirituality of the developing countries were not of concern. That also did not really change with the new dependency studies, out of which came, for example, the theory of associated-dependent development and dynamic dependency.

The development dialectic between both theories remained throughout one about systems and frameworks on an overall societal level. The roles of development processes on an individual level, or of development requirements on an organisational and community level, were not discussed.

The dualistic attitude inherent within and in between both perspectives becomes further evident in relation to the particular theoretical framework in which each operates: modernisation theory works with the rivalling poles of tradition versus modernity, while dependency theory works largely with the opposite poles of core (former coloniser, metropolis) versus periphery (formerly colonised country, satellite).

This dualism in and between both theoretical approaches to development continues up to this date. However, as we could see, latest evolutions of both theories display much more balanced perspectives. Then, from the 1980s onwards, a new, more synthesising theory emerged, that increasingly gains influence in the world: World Systems Analysis. We shall return to it later (⇨17) in detail as an important element in our overall Integral Development framework. For now, we comment on the immense dualism that has been played on the stage of the world's 'development theatre' in between the two influential theories presented here.

Such dualism is mirrored, as shown earlier, within the more specific theories and practices on economic development worldwide. For Columbian anthropologist Arturo Escobar, development thereby turned ultimately into a destructive force. As one of the most prolific voices in today's development discourses, his critique of development crystallises many of the former arguments made, but also intimates potential future directions. He begins with questioning the very concept of 'underdevelopment' as has been promoted for decades by the West.

2.6   Development = A Destructive Force?: Is Another World Possible?

DEVELOPMENT AS A DESTRUCTIVE FORCE: TOP VERSUS DOWN; WHITE VERSUS BLACK; POWERFUL VERSUS POWERLESS; GLOBAL VERSUS LOCAL, ETC.

According to Arturo Escobar, a prominent figure in the post-development discourse, the dominant, 'westernised' orientation towards development deals with surface phenomena. It is often quantitatively oriented, rather than entering in depth into the life worlds of the people involved. Engaging with such life worlds requires a degree of empathy and immersion that is seldom seen.[43]

Massive underdevelopment and impoverishment, untold exploitation and oppression has resulted, so Escobar, from this 'top-down-outside-in' approach. For him, the debt crisis, the Sahelian famine, increasing poverty, malnutrition, and violence are only the most pathetic signs of the failure of past decades of development.

Escobar confirms that when Western experts and politicians started to see certain conditions in Asia, Africa and Latin America as representing a problem – mostly what was perceived as poverty and backwardness – development as a new domain of thought and experience came into being. This resulted in a new development strategy, as originally suggested by President Truman, for dealing with the alleged problems.

In that context, there emerged a perception of 'under-development', characterised by features such as powerlessness, passivity, poverty and ignorance. The 'subjects to be developed' were usually dark and lacking in historical agency, as if waiting for the (white)

Western hand to help subjects. Not infrequently, they were hungry, illiterate, needy and oppressed by their own characterised stubbornness, lack of initiative and disabling traditions. This image also universalised and homogenised Third World cultures in the eyes of the Western spectator.

Yet, Escobar argues, such poverty in its modern sense appeared only when colonialism and the spread of the market economy broke down community ties and deprived millions of people of access to land, water and other resources. Ignoring this fact, the conviction that the essential trait of the Third World was poverty and that the solution was economic growth and development, one interchangeable with the other, became self-evident, necessary and a universal truth.

Development then proceeded by creating 'abnormalities' – such as the 'illiterate' and the 'underdeveloped' – which it would later treat and reform. Development thereby became (and continues to be for the most part) a top down, ethnocentric, and technocratic approach that treated people and cultures as abstract concepts, statistical figures to be moved up and down in the 'charts of progress'.

Development was conceived not as a cultural process – culture was a residual variable, to disappear with the advance of modernisation – but instead as a system of more or less universally applicable technical interventions intended to deliver some 'badly' needed 'goods' to a 'target' population. In other words, it was 'scientifically' oriented, in a narrowly based, outer-directed sense, rather than broadly humanistic in orientation. For Escobar, it comes as no surprise that development became a force utterly destructive to Third World cultures and natures, ironically in the name of people's interests.

What is required, for Escobar, is a 'liberation' from the dominant Western worldview, or, in other words, a pluralisation of the modernist perspective. What does that mean?

BEYOND THE 'ONE- SIZE- FITS- ALL' WESTERN APPROACH TO DEVELOPMENT: THE ARGUMENT FOR THE PLURALISATION OF MODERNITY

For Escobar, contemporary debates on development are subsidiary to discussions on globalisation and on modernity. The widely accepted thesis that globalisation entails the universalisation of modernity, where modernity is understood as a distinct mode of sociocultural organisation that originated in Europe, leads to the conclusion that there is no outside to modernity, that from now on it is modernity all the way. What is possible, though, in this first perspective, is what has been coined 'Alternative Development', with its focus on 'basic needs' – understandably, within the current modernist paradigm.

A second perspective is contributed largely by anthropologists who advocate for the pluralisation of modernity toward a conception of alternative modernities, a more self- and-inner-directed form of modernity.

A third approach involves the possible reconstruction of local and regional worlds on different logics, which, if strongly networked, may get to constitute narratives of alternatives to modernity.

Escobar proposes that social movements, and the academics and policy makers studying these, must hold in tension these three coexisting processes and political projects:[44]

1. Alternative Development: focused on food security and the satisfaction of basic needs, as well as the overall well-being of the population.

2. Alternative Modernities: building on the countertendencies effected through development interventions by local groups, contesting global designs.
3. Alternatives to Modernity: as a more radical and visionary project of redefining and reconstructing local and regional worlds from the perspective of practices of cultural, economic and ecological difference.

Based on our analysis in the opening chapter that the world is undergoing a profound civilisational crisis in an attempt to outgrow the existing, modernist worldview and forming a new, more sustainable paradigm, our approach to Integral Development sees itself clearly contributing to the third project of building an 'alternative to modernity'. We thereby see our approach also aligned with the attempt of the World Social Forum that indeed believes that 'Another World is Possible'.

ANOTHER WORLD IS POSSIBLE: THE WORLD SOCIAL FORUM

The World Social Forum, established in Porto Alegre in Brazil in 2001, represents the radical critique of present-day reality and the aspiration to a better society.

Boaventura De Sousa Santos, a Portuguese Professor of Sociology, who has been involved with the WSF since its outset, argues for its vision that 'Another World is Possible' – thereby creating an alternative to modernity. He believes that if there is unemployment and social exclusion, if there is starvation and death on the periphery of the world system, then it is not generally perceived as being the consequence of the deficiencies of the laws of the market. One rather finds the opposite standpoint, articulating that these deficiencies result from the fact, that such laws have not yet been applied. The horizon of such a conservative worldview is thus a closed one, an end to history, or, in Escobar's terms, a clinging to modernity. The World Social Forum, however, sees itself as a force promoting a new beginning of history.[45]

The idea for the WSF was struck, originally, amongst a group of Brazilians, who wished to oppose neo-liberalism's single way of thinking, and to give symbolic expression to the start of a new period. Francisco 'Chico' Whitaker, a Roman Catholic activist, and Oded Grajew, a Brazilian businessman with social concerns, presented the idea to Bernard Cassen, editor of *Le Monde Diplomatique*. In 2001, a Brazilian Organising Committee was formed, and thereafter an International Council to support the Forum was created in Porto Alegre in Brazil. From the very beginning the WSF understood itself also as a counterweight to the World Economic Forum (WEF) in Davos, Switzerland. According to the WSF Charter:

*   The WSF is an open meeting place for reflective thinking, democratic debate of ideas, formulation of proposals, free exchange of experiences and interlinking of effective action, by groups and movements of civil society opposed to neo-liberalism, and committed to building a planetary society directed towards fruitful relationships among humankind and between it and the Earth.
*   The alternatives proposed at the WSF stand in opposition to a process of globalisation commanded by the large multinationals and by governments and international institutions at the service of these. These alternatives are designed to ensure that globalisation in solidarity will prevail as a new stage in world history.

- The WSF is a plural, diversified, non-confessional, non-party and non-governmental context that, in a decentralised fashion, integrates organisations and movements engaged in concrete action at levels from the local to the international to build another world.
- It upholds respect for human rights, the practices of real democracy, participatory democracy, peaceful relations, in equality and solidarity, among people, ethnicities, genders and peoples, and condemns all forms of domination and all subjection of one person over another.
- As a forum for debate, the WSF is a movement of ideas that prompts reflection, and the transparent circulation of the results of that reflection, on the mechanisms and instruments of domination by capital, on the means and actions to overcome that domination, and on the alternatives proposed to solve the problems of exclusion and social inequality.
- As a framework for the exchange of experiences, the WSF encourages understanding and mutual recognition amongst its individual and institutional participants, and places special value on exchange between them, particularly on all that society is building to centre economic activity and political action on meeting the needs of people and respecting nature, in the present and for future generations.

The original World Social Forum was not an organisation per se, nor an institution led by a powerful individual, nor indeed a close-knit community, but a local and global movement. It is worthwhile to mention that the World Social Forum itself was preceded by a multitude of affirmations of local identities all over the world – via particular communities or ethnicities resisting being subsumed under one modernist Western development perspective.

By now the World Social Forum has grown into a major global movement, redefining development bottom-up. As opposed to the dominance of economic and sociological voices, as per all prior approaches to development, we now enter much stronger into anthropological and culturally oriented thinking. For the first time, we encounter large-scale assertion of cultural identity around the world, within an interconnected, concerted framework. Though still seen by many as a polarising rather than integrating force (standing in opposition to the World Economic Forum) it has displayed a remarkable capacity to accommodate a wide range of alternative perspectives. Surely, it can be seen, together with a myriad of other local and global movements engaging in the search of new perspective of Human Development, as an indicator for the breakdown of a monocultural modernist worldview and of a 'one-size-fits-all size fits all' Western approach to development. Is that the end of development, as we know it?

2.7   The End of Development? The Claim for a New Aesthetic Order of Development

THE AGE OF POST-DEVELOPMENT: DECONSTRUCTING THE MISLEADING ASSUMPTIONS AND PREMISES OF PAST DEVELOPMENT

Several decades of development work have not measured up to expectations. This is especially the case in Africa and parts of Latin America and South Asia. The universalist claims of classical economics and structural adjustment policies, have undermined the foundations of many developing countries.

Majid Rahnema – a former Iranian Minister of Education, Executive Council Member of the UNESCO, Senior UN Diplomat and Representative of the UN in Mali – is perhaps one of the most outspoken development critics. A true insider of the development field, he concludes the compelling *Post-Development Reader* that he has edited together with Victoria Bawtree – and which features around 40 diverse viewpoints of prominent development thinkers:

> *The facts and testimonies gathered in this Reader show that development did not prove to be the panacea those elites believed it to be. Despite the new governments of the 'Third World' according it absolute priority for fifty years, at least in their official discourse, the great majority of them soon realised that the objectives they had set for themselves were unrealistic and impossible to achieve. As it stands now, they have also to admit that not only did development fail to resolve the old problems it was supposed to address, but it brought new ones of incomparably greater magnitude. Not only did development prove to be simply a myth for the millions it was destined to serve; the very premises and assumptions on which it was founded were misleading.*[46]

Rahnema stresses that it is short-sighted to attribute the failures of development merely to the governments, institutions and people in charge:

> *In fact, had they been successful in fulfilling all the promises made to their peoples, and had there been enough money and resources to bring about the development of all the so-called underdeveloped countries of the world to the level of the 'most advanced', the resulting deadlocks and tensions would perhaps have taken an even more dramatic turn.*[47]

As has now become common knowledge, the natural resources of the planet simply won't suffice to sustain such an endeavour.

He emphasises that it is not any more about tweaking the existing approach to development. For him, it is not that development strategies or projects should be better planned and delivered. Rather, it:

> *is that development, as it imposed itself on its 'target populations', was basically the wrong answer to the true needs and aspirations. It was an ideology that was born and refined in the North, mainly to meet the needs of the dominant powers in search for a more 'appropriate' tool for their economic and geopolitical expansion. As such it could, at best, transfer on to the new nation-states the contradictions of their own socio-economic systems.*[48]

In his analysis, Rahnema also rejects the common belief of the inability of so-called underdeveloped countries to develop themselves. On the contrary, he reverses the argument and calls on the so-called developed world to learn from the so-called developing world. For him:

> *many modern societies still have much to learn from them. This is not to say that they were 'better', or that we should go back to a 'state of Nature' – a prospect that would be neither desirable nor feasible. Nevertheless, a deeper and unbiased knowledge of how different cultures*

have solved their problems and of what they learned to cherish or dislike through the ages
would be instructive for all those in search of alternatives to our own dilemmas.[49]

IN THE END OF DEVELOPMENT LIES THE SEARCH FOR A NEW BEGINNING: TOWARDS A NEW AESTHETIC ORDER

For Rahnema, we have come to an end of development, as we know it. This view, as we have seen, is shared by many prominent development thinkers. Talking about development, Susan George, well-known Franco-American political scientist, talks for example of 'decades of brainwashing about development, aid progress and other mortal dangers of the twentieth century'.[50] As early as 1992 Wolfgang Sachs, a leading German social ecologist, declared 'the idea of development stands today like a ruin in the intellectual landscape'. Together with a group of influential development thinkers, he called 'for bidding farewell to the whole Eurocentric development idea. This is urgently needed … in order to liberate people's mind – in both North and South – for bold responses to the environmental and ethical challenges now challenging humanity'.[51] Even earlier, in 1971, Peter Bauer, former Professor of Economics at the London School of Economics, issued his acclaimed collection of essays entitled *Dissent on Development*. More recently, Oswaldo de Rivero, former Ambassador of Peru to the World Trade Organisation, wrote his influential pamphlet *The Myth of Development*;[52] Thomas Dichter, former consultant to USAID, UNDP and World Bank, published his experience-based analysis *Despite Good Intentions: Why Development Assistance to the Third World has failed*;[53] and one of the more recent critiques of conventional development is *Dead Aid*[54] by Dambisa Moyo, Zambian Economist and former consultant to the World Bank. These are just few examples of prominent critics, announcing the doom of development.

Their critical evaluation of past development work has led many post-development thinkers to stigmatise all development work as 'authoritarian engineering' and consequently to the claim of rather ending all development work.

Renowned development economist Björn Hettne affirms the post-development analysis but only partly agrees with its conclusion:

> *A rather widespread view today is that the very meaning of development is an imposition of institutions and values by the West on areas deemed to be in need of development, guided by an over-ambitious, all explanatory development theory. Thereby the people in these areas have been seen as legitimate objects for development intervention, more often than not of a harmful kind. Hence, according to the current "post-development' view, the less development the better. This harsh assessment is not completely groundless, but nevertheless somewhat exaggerated.*[55]

But reading Rahnema – and his *Reader* – as a kind of 'distilling voice' of current post-development thinking carefully, we notice, that in the claim for an end of development is the seed for a new beginning. Rahnema emphasises that the:

> *end of development should not be seen as an end to the search for new possibilities of change, for a relational world of friendship, or for genuine processes of regeneration able to give birth to new forms of solidarity. It should only mean that the binary, the mechanistic, the reductionist, the inhumane and the ultimately self-destructive approach to change is over.*[56]

He requests 'replacing the present dis-order' by an 'aesthetic order' based on respect for differences and the uniqueness of every single person or culture.

It is out of this impulse for a new 'aesthetic order', respecting differences and the uniqueness of every single person or culture that Integral Development has been written. You will notice when we introduce this approach in more detail (⇨4), that it has indeed a strong aesthetic appeal, as its visual representation is resonant with many balanced and integrated designs in most world cultures.

BUILDING A NEW ORDER: DEEPENED SELF-KNOWLEDGE AS STARTING POINT

What then is the starting point for such a new aesthetic order of development? Rahnema introduces the same premise that we postulated in the opening chapter. The fundamental revision of the existing development paradigm has to start with a fundamental deepening of our self-knowledge. Rahnema demands of any person engaged in development intervention:

exceptional personal qualities ... needed to prevent 'well-intentioned' interventions producing results contrary to those planned – as has been the case in most 'developmental' and many 'humanitarian' instances. Before intervening in other people's lives, one should first intervene in one's own; 'polishing' oneself to ensure that all precautions have been taken to avoid harming the objects of intervention.[57]

The development agent should engage in a process of self-examination:

What prompts me to intervene? Is it friendship, compassion, the 'mask of love', or an unconscious attempt to increase my powers of seduction? Have I done everything I could to assess the usefulness of my intervention? And if things do not proceed as I expect them, am I ready to face the full consequences of my intervention? To what extent, that is, am I seriously committed to the intervention?[58]

Based on such serious self-examination and self-polishing, the individual should then expand his or her radius, by linking and exchanging with like-minded others who are engaged in similar developmental work. Rahnema calls it the building of 'circle of friends' that gradually expands. 'What these expanding circles of friends might do now is see whether and how their action can pave the way for the emergence of a different, an aesthetic, order arising from the grassroots'.[59] For Rahnema, for such an aesthetic order to emerge many assumptions that govern our understanding of today's reality have to be challenged and outgrown. 'Among these will be the nation-state as the protector of the people placed under its jurisdiction; progress and development – both clinging to the sub-paradigms of continuity and linearity; scarcity – as the basis and justification of modern economy'.[60]

Overall, a tremendous task awaits us. Rahnema builds on the Chinese philosopher Confucius' notion of 'the good people' – for Confucius those people able and willing to lead a society forward. Rahnema maintains that this task:

should represent a call to the 'good people' everywhere to think and work together. It should prompt everyone to begin the genuine work of self-knowledge and 'self-polishing' ... an exercise that enables us to listen more carefully to each other, in particular to friends who are ready to do the same thing.[61]

What Rahnema ultimately proposes is a new 'bottom-up-inside-out' transformation of Human Development – leading to a new aesthetic order. According to Rahnema, all we have for now with regards to such a new order are signposts but not yet a clear picture. Integral Development seeks to contribute to making this emergent picture visible. Part of such a new picture, as we see it, is also Nederveen Pieterse's claim towards a 'balanced approach' to development that embraces 'paradox as a natural feature' of development processes.

2.8   The Tao of Development: Overcoming Dualism and the Call for Balanced Development

For the prominent Dutch development economist Jan Neverdeen Pieterse, overcoming the dichotomy conventional development is caught in, is the major challenge to reinvent development.

For him, the core problem of development is 'its pretentiousness, the insurmountable arrogance of intervening in other people's lives. This may be balanced by an equal but entirely different kind of pretension – the Tao of Development'.[62]

He rejects joining the rising choir of voices singing the song of the end of development. Instead he claims that:

setting a high goal for development may be better than setting no goal at all or, worse still, declaring development over and done with while in the meantime development business goes on as usual. Setting an elusive goal may be better than carrying on with development as a positivist politics of measurement.[63]

Nederveen Pieterse builds on the Tao te Ching – an ancient Chinese wisdom book attributed to the legendary sage Lao Tse and presented in often paradoxical philosophical chapters. He means by the Tao of Development:

acknowledging paradox as part of development realities; such as the antinomies between measurement and meaning, between intervention and autonomy, or the field of tension between the local and the global.[64]

Neverdeen Pieterse sees these antinomies as part of the perplexities of human nature, and hence also of development (as a human product).

With balanced development, however, he asserts, he does not refer to balance as it is often used in conventional development, where it alludes to a balance of economic growth and redistribution, and between growth across different societal sectors. Rather he means balance in a wider and deeper sense, and lists the following ingredients of balanced development:

- *Balance between the Horizontal and Vertical Development Spheres:* Nederveen Pieterse calls for a multidimensional approach, or balance between the horizontal (the outer, worldly and social spheres) and vertical (inner and deeper spheres of subjectivities and meanings) dimensions of collective existence.

- *Balanced Cross-Sectoral Perspective:* A multifaceted approach or a *'diamond'* social science is vital to reflect light upon relations and dynamics across sectors (economic, political, social, cultural, etc., sectors).
- *Balanced Social Science:* A *chiaroscuro* (light-dark) social science, which abandons the assumption that society is fully transparent (which is a balance between what is known and unknown, conscious and unconscious, light and dark), is a further prerequisite for balanced development.
- *Balance between Development Thinking and Practice:* Development thinking, for Neverdeen Pieterse, is now increasingly anchored in people's subjectivities rather than in overarching institutions – the state or international institutions. Development thinking has become more participatory and insider-oriented. However, development practice, particularly when it comes to macroeconomic management, has not been democratised, so there is a growing friction between development thinking and practice.
- *Balance between Diverse Development Actors:* There is a recognisable trend in local (and increasingly also large-scale) development towards social partnerships across sectors, or synergies between different development actors. This is a marked departure from times when development was seen as either state-led, or market-led, or civil-society led.
- *Balance between Multiple Time Frames:* A more complex awareness of time in development is required. That includes combining multiple time frames and a balance between 'slow knowledge' and the 'fast knowledge' of instant problem-solving. Since development is concerned with the measurement of desirable change over time it is chronocentric. The conventional time horizon of development policy (often around five years) has changed, however, with sustainable development and the implied notion of intergenerational equity, and 'co-evolutionary development' to much longer periods.

Nederveen Pieterse's call for balanced development provides us with further clues for a new aesthetic order of development. With the voice of this prominent development expert, we conclude our – necessarily selective – review of past development theory and practice, including current trends. We are now ready to conclude this chapter.

2.9   Integration: Or Rather Disintegration?

THE DEVELOPMENT OF DEVELOPMENT OVER TIME

Writing this chapter has been a challenging task for us. After a critical introduction to the origins of the Development Age (from World War II until now), and an equally critical synopsis of past and current development approaches (from development economics to post-development), we dealt, in some detail, with a number of key development positions of our time, and shed light on dominant development practice. Understandably, we could not and did not aim for a comprehensive overview of the entire field (if such an overview at all exists). The purpose was rather to focus on selected key viewpoints on development that had been particularly influential with regards to the dominant development theory and practice.

We hence provided a condensation of the field, allowing us to identify key patterns in conventional development thinking and practice, seeking to understand why development, by and large, has failed and what insights we may gain for a new approach to development. In the following we shall briefly summarise our core findings. For now, we distinguish, as per the guiding questions of this chapter, between rather damaging and rather helpful patterns.

DIVIDED WORLD: DAMAGING, DISINTEGRATING PATTERNS OF PAST DEVELOPMENT

We identified a number of damaging, if not destructive patterns that, to our view, can be seen as root causes of the major imbalances caused by development. They are:

- *Division of the World into Developed and Developing Countries:* It became obvious that the field of development has been and is still rooted in the dualistic mindset dominant in the modernist worldview (⇨1). It has been instrumental in dividing the world into 'developed' and 'developing' countries thereby establishing linear development tracks whereby the so-called developing world is supposed to imitate the development path of the so-called developed countries – a conviction that is held by many until today, despite the obvious systemic disfunctionalities in the 'Western' model. Such a dividing pattern – articulated through one aspect dominating another – leads to dramatic imbalances and can equally be seen in the following issues.
- *Monocultural Dominance:* Most of conventional development – consciously or unconsciously – is an articulation of the dominant 'Western', modernist worldview, with a strong orientation on private enterprise and capitalist economics. Also, much of the theory of economic development evolved almost exclusively in the USA and Europe. Few South American approaches are the only partial exception to this rule. The 'Western' perspective has become so all-pervasive that it is often not noticed as a cultural expression, or better as monocultural oppression, inhibiting co-evolution between cultures and culturally diverse viewpoints on development.
- *Economically and Technologically Driven Approaches:* Most of development practice looks at development primarily from an economic and technological perspective – to the exclusion of, for example, community-driven or culture-based approaches. However, it is increasingly recognised that development is a multi-issue terrain, and issues have to be dealt with in an interconnected, parallel and interdisciplinary manner.
- *An Outside-In Pre-Orientation:* Most of past development work has operated 'outside-in', whereby development was brought from so-called developed countries to so-called developing countries. 'Inside-out' perspectives of development, whereby the particular development context takes the lead – and whereby (e.g.) local capacities, local knowledge systems, and locally validated culturally rooted value bases are in the foreground – have been largely neglected.
- *Dominance of a Few Disciplines:* Much of the mainstream development thinking has been provided by economists (e.g. most of development economics) and sociologists (e.g. modernisation and dependency theories), often with an overtly rationalistic-pragmatist orientation. It was conceived in the fact-driven 'hard' social sciences rather than in the humanities and more interpretatively oriented 'soft' social sciences. Other, very relevant disciplines for development issues, such as anthropology, cultural

studies or psychology, are increasingly raising their 'development voice', but remain relatively disconnected from mainstream development discourses and hence have little impact on development practice. We shall argue later, that such disconnected disciplinary perspectives don't do justice to the transdisciplinary complexity of most development contexts and challenges. The result is a lack of true innovation in the development field, as well as a disconnect from local contexts.

* *Dominance of Global and Societal Perspectives on Development:* Most development discourses focus in particular on either global or national perspectives. Local, community-based perspectives are rarely taken into account, ignoring the development potential from within local development contexts.

We can conclude that much of development – over the past, and indeed until today – is trapped by a cultural distortion. In a nutshell, we can see a 'Western' economic and enterprise perspective and a 'Northern' political, scientific and technological perspective, dominating the global development scene. While much of the geographic East of the world is on the rise – for example from China to India to South Korea to Taiwan – we don't find much by way of an authentic 'Eastern' approach to development, with the exception, at least until now, of Japan. And, of course, there is hardly any explicitly and functionally 'Southern' approach – though almost all of the so-called developing countries of the world are located in the 'Global South'. It seems, for us then, that the world is

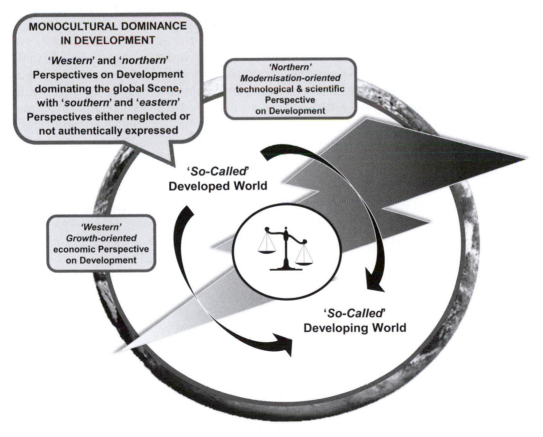

Figure 2.1   Monocultural dominance in development

one-sidedly following a monocultural 'Western' (or at best 'North-Western') development track. However, as we continually maintain, such a modernist-universalist 'one-size-fits-all' development perspective, widens the division that we encounter in today's world ever more. Figure 2.1, on the previous page, attempts to illustrate this predicament of the divided world in which we live.

All in all, we notice intense imbalances within the field of development. They are, as we argue, a reflection of a worldview that seems unable to integrate diverse perspectives. Nederveen Pieterse's *Tao of Development* is calling for exactly such integration, which includes accommodating opposing and even paradoxical perspectives. That brings us to newly emerging patterns that provide insights for a less divided development future.

MOVING FORWARD: INSIGHTS IN EMERGING HELPFUL PATTERNS THAT MAY GUIDE FUTURE DEVELOPMENT PRACTICE

Perhaps the most visible transformation within the development field that took place within the past two decades, is that critical and diverse development thinking has moved much more to the centre of attention. The current stream of post-development thinking with its radical rejection of conventional development seems to find increasing validation with ever more mainstream systems being affected by significant turbulences.

At the same time, significant movements and initiatives have mushroomed worldwide that engage in new bottom-up and inside-out development practices. Many of these movements seem to have their starting point in an assertion of local and cultural identity, claiming the right for self-defined development processes. The most notable movement of that character is the World Social Forum. Its highly networked almost organic design can be seen as an early expression of an emergent new worldview, embodying interconnectedness, interdependence and co-evolution as major design principles. Its slogan 'Another World is Possible' is articulating WSF's acknowledgement that the existing paradigm – including Western neo-liberal economics – is not the one, their participants (local and global communities, networks, initiatives, movements) seek to live by any longer. As for now, the World Social Forum can be seen as a countermovement to the predominant Western development practice, with no integration in sight. Their struggle is uneven, the outcome unclear.

We also encountered new thinking from within the established development institutions, including the World Bank and the IMF. Sustainable Development, for example, has become a constant part in the mainstream development vocabulary, though, as we have critiqued, primarily from a technological (natural science) perspective.

Also the Human Development approach, originally conceived of by Mahbub Ul Haq and Amartya Sen and translated into global practice by the UNDP, is – in its people-centredness – a valuable step towards a more integrated perspective on development. Furthermore, the unequivocal acceptance of the UN-driven Millennium Development Goals can be regarded as another important sign from the international community, acknowledging that a number of interdependent goals have to be addressed simultaneously through much better coordinated and much more collaborative development work, including all nations and major development institutions. However, so our argument, even the MDG's are still, to a large degree, a reflection of a modernist worldview, analytically distinguishing a set of goals, to be achieved in primarily linear processes, evaluated in primarily quantitative (statistical) terms.

Using the argument of many post-development thinkers, these changes may be regarded as positive, but remain ineffective until we have more fundamentally evolved the underlying assumptions that define development and that we shall review in more depth in the following chapter. Within the existing divisive rather than integrative systems they can hardly unfold their potential. As for us, they provide us with useful clues for a new approach to development: they are hopeful signposts but not yet anywhere near the fundamental shift of perspective required.

WHAT DO YOU THINK?

As with every chapter ending, we invite you to critically review this chapter and its core findings. In particular, we encourage you, to enrich it with your own discoveries, to link your reflection and subsequent action to the development context you yourself are lodged in.

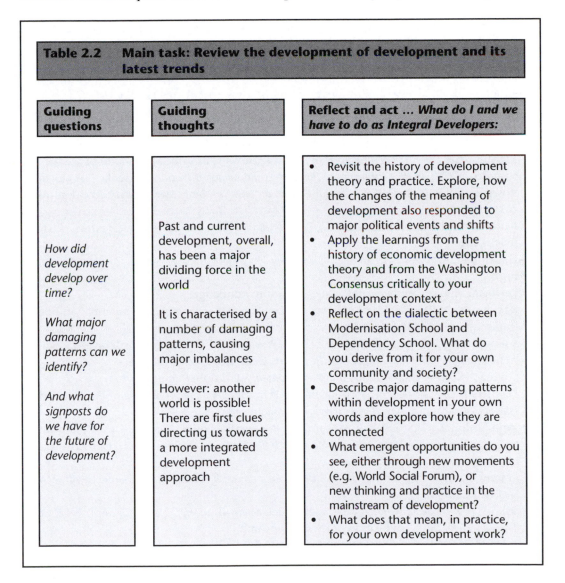

Table 2.2	Main task: Review the development of development and its latest trends	
Guiding questions	**Guiding thoughts**	**Reflect and act ... *What do I and we have to do as Integral Developers:***
How did development develop over time? *What major damaging patterns can we identify?* *And what signposts do we have for the future of development?*	Past and current development, overall, has been a major dividing force in the world It is characterised by a number of damaging patterns, causing major imbalances However: another world is possible! There are first clues directing us towards a more integrated development approach	• Revisit the history of development theory and practice. Explore, how the changes of the meaning of development also responded to major political events and shifts • Apply the learnings from the history of economic development theory and from the Washington Consensus critically to your development context • Reflect on the dialectic between Modernisation School and Dependency School. What do you derive from it for your own community and society? • Describe major damaging patterns within development in your own words and explore how they are connected • What emergent opportunities do you see, either through new movements (e.g. World Social Forum), or new thinking and practice in the mainstream of development? • What does that mean, in practice, for your own development work?

References

1   Dahl, G. and Megeressa, G. (1992). The Spiral of the Ram's Horn: Boran Concepts of Development. In: Dahl, G. and Rabo, A. (eds), *Kamp-Ap or Take-Off: Local Notions of Development*. Stockholm: Stockholm Studies in Social Anthropology, 1992.

2   Rist, G. (2008). *The History of Development: From Western Origins to Global Faith*. London: Zed Books.

3   Truman, H.S (1949). *Inaugural Address*. 20 January 1949 (www.presidency.ucsb.edu).

4   Nederveen Pieterse, J. (2008). *Development Theory: Deconstructions/Reconstrutions*. 2nd Edition. London: Sage, p. 10.

5   Sen, A. (2005). Human Rights and Capabilities. In: *Journal of Human Development*, Vol. 6, Issue 2.

6   Haq, K. and Ponzio, R. (eds) (2008) *Pioneering the Human Development Revolution: An Intellectual Biography of Mahbub Ul Haq*. Oxford: Oxford University Press.

7   Annan, K. (2008). In: Haq, K. and Ponzio, R. (eds), *Pioneering the Human Development Revolution: An Intellectual Biography of Mahbub Ul Haq*. Oxford: Oxford University Press, Backcover.

8   Sen, A. (1999). *Development as Freedom*. New York: Anchor Books.

9   Meadows, D. et al. (1972). *The Limits to Growth*. New York: Universe Books.

10 Brundtland, G. (1987). *Our Common Future: The World Commission on Environment and Development*. Oxford: Oxford University Press.

11 Cypher, J. and Dietz, J. (2008). *The Process of Economic Development*. London: Routledge.

12 Malthus, T.R. (2001). *The Principles of Political Economy*. Boston, MA: Adamant Media.

13 Ricardo, D. (2004). *The Principles of Political Economy and Taxation*. Mineola, NY: Dover.

14 Rosenstein-Rodan, P. (1964). *Capital Formation and Economic Development*. London: Allen & Unwin.

15 Nurkse, R. (1953). *Problems of Capital Formation in Underdeveloped Countries*. Oxford: Blackwell.

16 Hirschman, A. (1964). *The Strategy of Economic Development*. New Haven, CT: Yale University Press.

17 Lewis, A. (2003). *Development Planning*. London: Routledge.

18 Rostow, W. (1991). *The Stages of Economic Growth: A Non-Communist Manifesto*. Cambridge: Cambridge University Press.

19 Solow, R. (2003). *Explaining Growth: A Global Research Project*. New York: Palgrave Macmillan.

20 Aghion, P. (1998). *Endogenous Growth Theory*. Cambridge, MA: MIT Press.

21 Stiglitz, J. (2009). *Globalization and its Discontents*. London: Penguin.

22 Dichter, T. (2003). *Despite Good Intentions: Why Development Assistance to the Third World Has Failed*. Amherst, MA: University of Massachusetts.

23 Williamson, J. (1989). What Washington Means by Policy Reform. In: Williamson, J. (ed.), *Latin American Readjustment: How Much has Happened*? Washington, DC: Institute for International Economics.

24 Lessem, R. and Schieffer, A. (2010). *Integral Economics: Releasing the Economic Genius of Your Society*. Farnham: Gower.

25 So, A.Y. (1990). *Social Change and Development: Modernisation, Dependency and World System Theories*. New York: Sage Library of Social Research.

26 Talcott, P. (1964). *The Social System*. New York: Macmillan.

27 So, A.Y. (1990). *Social Change and Development: Modernisation, Dependency and World System Theories*. New York: Sage Library of Social Research.

28 McClelland, D. (1988). *Human Motivation*. Cambridge: Cambridge University Press.

29 Inkeles, A. et al. (1976). *Becoming Modern: Individual Change in Six Developing Countries*. Cambridge, MA: Harvard University Press.

30 Wong, S.L. (1988). *Emigrant Entrepreneurs: Shanghai Industrialists in Hong Kong*. Oxford: Oxford University Press·

31 Hettne, B. (1995). *Development Theory and the Three Worlds: Towards an International Political Theory of Development*. Harlow: Longman-Pearson.

32 So, A.Y. (1990). *Social Change and Development: Modernisation, Dependency and World System Theories*. New York: Sage Library of Social Research.

33 Prebisch, R. (1950). *The Economic Development of Latin America and its Principal Problems*. New York: United Nations.

34 Shaw, J.D. (2002). *Sir Hans Singer: The Life and Work of a Development Economist*. New York: Palgrave Macmillan.

35 Frank, A.G. (1998). *Reorient: Global Economy in the Asian Age*. Berkeley, CA: University of California Press.

36 Apter, D.E. (1975). *Political Change: A Collection of Essays*. London: Frank Class.

37 So, A.Y. (1990). *Social Change and Development: Modernisation, Dependency and World System Theories*. New York: Sage Library of Social Research, pp. 104f.

38 Chew, S.C. and Denemark, R.A. (1966). *The Underdevelopment of Development: Essays in Honour of Andre Gunder Frank*. London: Sage.

39 Baran, P. (1989). *The Political Economy of Growth*. New York: Monthly Review Press.

40 So, A.Y. (1990). *Social Change and Development: Modernisation, Dependency and World System Theories*. New York: Sage Library of Social Research, pp. 131f.

41 Cardoso, F. (1992). *Dependency and Development in Latin America*. Berkeley, CA: University of California Press.

42 Gold, T.B. (1986). *State and Society in the Taiwan Miracle*. Armonk, NY: Sharpe.

43 Escobar, A. (1995). *Encountering Development: The Making and Unmaking of the Third World*. Princeton, NJ: Princeton University Press.

44 Escobar, A. (2003). The Latin American Modernity/Coloniality Research Program: Worlds and Knowledges Otherwise. In: *Curzando Fronteras en America Latina*. Amsterdam: Center for Latin American Research and Documentation.

45 De Sousa Santos, B. (2006). *The Rise and Fall of the Left: The World Social Forum and Beyond*. London: Zed Books.

46 Rahnema, M. (1997). Towards Post-Development: Searching for Signposts, a New Language and New Paradigms. In: Rahnema, M. and Bawtree, V. (eds), *The Post-Development Reader*. London: Zed, p. 378.

47 Rahnema, M. (1997). Towards Post-Development: Searching for Signposts, a New Language and New Paradigms. In: Rahnema, M. and Bawtree, V. (eds), *The Post-Development Reader*. London: Zed, p. 378.

48 Rahnema, M. (1997). Towards Post-Development: Searching for Signposts, a New Language and New Paradigms. In: Rahnema, M. and Bawtree, V. (eds), *The Post-Development Reader*. London: Zed, p. 379.

49 Rahnema, M. (1997). Towards Post-Development: Searching for Signposts, a New Language and New Paradigms. In: Rahnema, M. and Bawtree, V. (eds), *The Post-Development Reader*. London: Zed, p. 381.

50 George, S. (1992). In: Sachs, W. (1992) (ed.), *The Development Reader: A Guide to Knowledge and Power*. London: Zed, Backcover.

51 Sachs, W. (1992) (ed.), *The Development Reader: A Guide to Knowledge and Power*. London: Zed.

52 De Rivero, O. (2003). *The Myth of Development: The Non-Viable Economics of the 21st Century*. London: Zed.

53 Dichter, T. (2003). *Despite Good Intentions: Why Development Assistance to the Third World Has Failed*. Amherst, MA: University of Massachusetts Press.

54 Moyo, D. (2009). *Dead Aid: Why Aid is Not Working and How there is a Better Way for Africa*. New York: Farrar, Straus and Giroux.

55 Hettne, B. (2009). *Thinking about Development: Development Matters*. London: Zed. p. 2.

56 Rahnema, M. (1997). Towards Post-Development: Searching for Signposts, a New Language and New Paradigms. In: Rahnema, M. and Bawtree, V. (eds), *The Post-Development Reader*. London: Zed, pp. 391f.

57 Rahnema, M. (1997). Towards Post-Development: Searching for Signposts, a New Language and New Paradigms. In: Rahnema, M. and Bawtree, V. (eds), *The Post-Development Reader*. London: Zed, p. 399.

58 Rahnema, M. (1997). Towards Post-Development: Searching for Signposts, a New Language and New Paradigms. In: Rahnema, M. and Bawtree, V. (eds), *The Post-Development Reader*. London: Zed, p. 399.

59 Rahnema, M. (1997). Towards Post-Development: Searching for Signposts, a New Language and New Paradigms. In: Rahnema, M. and Bawtree, V. (eds), *The Post-Development Reader*. London: Zed, p. 399.

60 Rahnema, M. (1997). Towards Post-Development: Searching for Signposts, a New Language and New Paradigms. In: Rahnema, M. and Bawtree, V. (eds), *The Post-Development Reader*. London: Zed, p. 400.

61 Rahnema, M. (1997). Towards Post-Development: Searching for Signposts, a New Language and New Paradigms. In: Rahnema, M. and Bawtree, V. (eds), *The Post-Development Reader*. London: Zed, pp. 391f.

62 Nederveen Pieterse, J. (1999). Critical Holism and the Tao of Development. In: Munck, R. and O'Hearn, D. (eds), *Critical Development Theory: Contributions to a New Paradigm*. London: Zed. p. 79.

63 Nederveen Pieterse, J. (1999). Critical Holism and the Tao of Development. In: Munck, R. and O'Hearn, D. (eds), *Critical Development Theory: Contributions to a New Paradigm*. London: Zed. p. 79.

64 Nederveen Pieterse, J. (1999). Critical Holism and the Tao of Development. In: Munck, R. and O'Hearn, D. (eds), *Critical Development Theory: Contributions to a New Paradigm*. London: Zed. p. 79.

3 *Deconstruction – Reconstruction: Steps towards Renewing Human Development*

Guiding Question: How do we move beyond the prevailing, disintegrating and imbalanced approach towards a new, integrating and balanced understanding of development?

3.1 Orientation

In the previous chapter we critically reviewed major theory and practice throughout the Development Age, from early stages after World War II to the current notion of post-development. We concluded the chapter by identifying major disintegrating patterns within development, which, to our mind, can be seen as root causes for the overall failure of conventional development. We have also distilled significant integration trends that emerged within theory and practice of development.

We shall now deepen our understanding of the major disintegrating patterns. In the process, we undergo a deconstructive exercise, necessary to outgrow these patterns. In facing these disintegrating and dividing patterns 'head on', we seek to gradually transcend them.

Such deconstruction then prepares us to engage in a reconstructive exercise towards the end of this chapter. Here we shall formulate core design principles of a new integrating approach to human development.

3.2 Deconstruction: Facing the Disintegrating Patterns of Past Development

OVERVIEW

We shall now explore in more depth the disintegrating patterns we have already identified in the previous chapter, and shall enrich and broaden our analysis with a number of perhaps less obvious patterns. As we are ultimately concerned with human development from multiple perspectives, our overall deconstructive critique will also draw on input from new fields, such as, for example, individual and organisational development. We thereby intend to embed the topic in a much richer field. This allows us also to apply insights from disciplines that conventionally have been either sidelined or omitted in development theory and practice – but that will ultimately play an important role in the reconstruction of development in a more integrated guise.

We have highlighted in the identified patterns the disintegrative tension between opposing poles that all of them showcase. It is this dualistic tendency that we indeed experience whenever we operate in development contexts. It is easily observable in the prevailing concepts and language that continuously force the mind into taking a stance in favour of either the one or the other. Perhaps the most striking distinction in this regard, as we pointed out, is the – to our mind, obsolete – differentiation between developing and developed countries.

In the following Table 3.1 we offer a selection of such opposing terms; countless further examples could be added.

Table 3.1   The development language: A language laden with dualities

Developed countries	⇔	Developing countries
North (rich)	⇔	South (poor)
West (USA/Europe)	⇔	Rest (rest of world)
Capitalism	⇔	Communism/socialism
Global knowledge	⇔	Indigenous wisdom
Global	⇔	Local
Private	⇔	Public
Private enterprise	⇔	Social business
Technology and modernity	⇔	Culture and tradition
Action	⇔	Research
Quantitative approaches to development	⇔	Qualitative approaches to development
Development of society	⇔	Development of self
Top-down approach	⇔	Bottom-up approach
...	⇔	...

Many conversations on development get stuck, because individuals or organisations are overly inclined toward one end of the continuum, to the exclusion of the other. This is one reason why development has reached a cul-de-sac, in that 'duality' rather than 'dialectic' or 'dialogue' is the order of the development day.

However, if a new approach to development is to accommodate such polar opposites within a more holistic and dynamic development framework, we need to understand the deeper origins of such dualistic thinking and how it can be overcome.

Altogether we distinguish 10 major disintegrating patterns (see Table 3.2) that we shall discuss in the following in some detail. Though listed in a sequential manner, they are deeply intertwined with each other.

Table 3.2	Ten major disintegrating patterns in development – an overview	
①	**Domination *versus* partnership**	⇨ Development is embedded in the predominant cultural myth of domination
②	**We *versus* them**	⇨ Development focuses unilaterally on 'developing underdeveloped' countries
③	**Monocultural domination *versus* transcultural co-evolution**	⇨ Lack of appreciation of diverse worldviews and subordination to one worldview
④	**Linearity *versus* process**	⇨ Development often misunderstood as linear progress
⑤	**Outward focus *versus* inward focus**	⇨ Development is overly outward-focused on enterprise, economics, systems and technology
⑥	**Outside-in *versus* inside-out**	⇨ Most of development work neglects the inner dimensions of development
⑦	**Society *versus* self**	⇨ Development lacks integration of individual, organisational and societal development
⑧	**Imitation *versus* innovation**	⇨ Development often inhibits dynamic knowledge creation and innovation, and perpetuates repetition
⑨	**Generalisation *versus* contextualisation** Globalisation *versus* localisation Top-down versus bottom-up	⇨ Most development efforts lack deep understanding of the local societal and cultural context
⑩	**Competition *versus* collaboration**	⇨ Lack of cooperation between different development actors, each pursuing their own agenda in relative isolation

① DOMINATION VERSUS PARTNERSHIP: DEVELOPMENT IS EMBEDDED IN THE PREDOMINANT CULTURAL MYTH OF DOMINATION

All social systems that we humans have brought forward are influenced by our underlying belief systems. To understand the dysfunctional attributes of development, we need to begin by looking at the deeper cultural myth or story, in which our collective thinking is embedded. For the renowned US social scientist Riane Eisler, development does not spring up in a vacuum, but is embedded in a larger social, cultural and technological context. In her groundbreaking work on *The Chalice and the Blade*,[1] she compares and contrasts, over millennia, feminine or matriarchal 'partnership' societies with masculine or patriarchal 'dominator' societies. In the domination system, development policies and practices are designed to benefit those at the top at the expense of those at the bottom. Trust is scarce and tension is high, as the whole system, for Eisler, is held together by fear and force. The partnership system, conversely, supports mutually respectful and caring relations. There are still hierarchies, as there must be to get things done. But in these hierarchies, which Eisler calls 'hierarchies of actualisation' rather than 'hierarchies of domination', accountability and respect flow both ways rather than just from the bottom-up. Social structures are set up so that there is input from all levels. In comparing dominator and partnership systems, Eisler comes up with the following features:

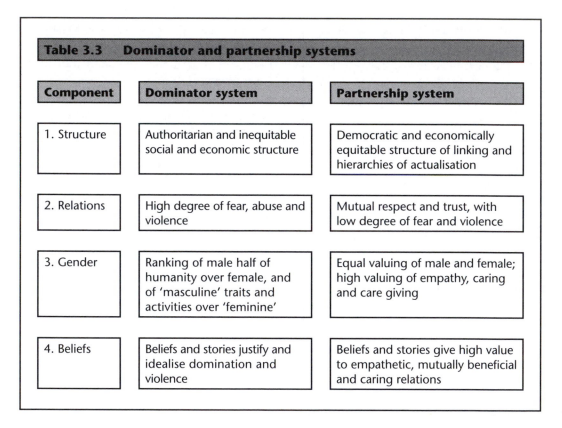

Table 3.3	Dominator and partnership systems	
Component	**Dominator system**	**Partnership system**
1. Structure	Authoritarian and inequitable social and economic structure	Democratic and economically equitable structure of linking and hierarchies of actualisation
2. Relations	High degree of fear, abuse and violence	Mutual respect and trust, with low degree of fear and violence
3. Gender	Ranking of male half of humanity over female, and of 'masculine' traits and activities over 'feminine'	Equal valuing of male and female; high valuing of empathy, caring and care giving
4. Beliefs	Beliefs and stories justify and idealise domination and violence	Beliefs and stories give high value to empathetic, mutually beneficial and caring relations

We have a choice, according to Eisler, to shape the story by which we live. History shows, that societies have lived according to different guiding myths and stories, and though our prevailing domination story seems to be 'all we know', there is, she affirms, an alternative. Indeed, we need an alternative, given that our existing social and economic structures are not adequately meeting the material needs of humanity, much less our needs for meaning and dignity. Leading advocate of *Non-Violent Communication*,[2] Marshall Rosenberg, builds on Eisler in his pamphlet on *The Heart of Social Change*.[3] For him, there are four key dimensions for social change: story, gangs, education and human development. These four dimensions build on each other. With 'story', Rosenberg alludes to the guiding myth a society lives by. Based on that, social structures – he uses the term 'gangs' – are designed to realise the story: from families to communities, from enterprises to social systems. Education, then, prepares the individual to function well within these 'gangs', and equips individuals with the mindset and language needed for that. And finally, based on the guiding story, the social structures and the education system, human development happens. Hence, for Rosenberg, human development is primarily a derivative of the first three prerequisites of social change, with the story being the most important one. For him, as for Eisler, we need to challenge this story, in order to create a new foundation for a different kind of social structures, education and development.

A new perspective on development, therefore, needs to allow for diverse perspectives and storylines to co-engage in partnership. Such a perspective, and set of alternative stories, would profoundly challenge our predominant value basis: how we distinguish between good and bad, superior and inferior, masculine and feminine, and seek for a transcendence of such dividing dualities within a new integrative partnership oriented paradigm.

② WE VERSUS THEM: DEVELOPMENT FOCUSES UNILATERALLY ON 'DEVELOPING UNDER-DEVELOPED' COUNTRIES

Development Studies are conventionally described as a multidisciplinary branch of the social sciences that addresses issues of concern to so-called 'developing countries'. However, this particular focus on the developing world does not make much sense, not only because of its patriarchal, domineering undertone but also given that the current economic paradigm within the developed world is deeply flawed.

Current examples of the systemic crisis in the developed world – from Greece to Portugal, from Spain, Ireland and Italy – illustrate that 're-development' has become a necessity for virtually every country. The question of course is which kind of redevelopment are we talking about?

Furthermore, we have become increasingly aware that the plethora of global crises – from climate change to food security, from financial meltdown to poverty, from global terrorism to regional conflicts, etc. – are strongly interconnected. Hence, we simply can't afford to continue with a 'we versus them' development practice, but are bound to come up with a unifying development frame that encourages and enables co-development.

A new perspective on development needs to be equally relevant for developing as well as developed countries. Hence, the developing as well as the developed world need to work together to establish a new development framework that works for all, on a local and on a global level, and that allows for the co-creation of locally relevant, innovative solutions.

③ MONOCULTURAL DOMINATION VERSUS TRANSCULTURAL CO-EVOLUTION: LACK OF APPRECIATION OF DIVERSE WORLDVIEWS

With major thinkers on societal development having come from North America and Western Europe or having been educated at universities of these two World regions, and with the developed countries strongly influencing the existing development agenda, there is an inherent – often subtle, sometimes overt – dominance of one or two (North American/Western European) worldviews over other ontological perspectives. This is reinforced by research methodologies and methods – employed by universities and research centres as approaches to the acquisition of knowledge – as they, too, are reflections of such worldviews. Such methods and methodologies thereby have an enormous influence on how we see the world, and how such views on the world are perpetuated or changed. As we illustrated in our work *Integral Research and Innovation*[4] (⇨13), the vast majority of research methods and methodologies have been invented in Europe and the US, thereby reinforcing their particular ontological outlooks on the world. Take for example, empiricism, which rules the roost in today's natural and social sciences, and also strongly influenced development as a discipline. Empiricism is a reflection of a primarily Western worldview. Such a worldview focuses on the tangible, material, so-called objective dimensions of reality, and dismisses the intangible, immaterial, subjective and indeed inter-subjective dimensions, that for example play a much more important role in large parts of Asia and Africa.

The notion of research methods and methodologies as an instrument of monocultural domination – whether conscious or unconscious – is a very subtle one, and often overlooked. It is, however, an extremely important one, as the very way of development theory is developed defines, naturally, also its outcome. In today's knowledge-driven world, the ability of diverse wordviews (and their respective approaches to knowledge generation) to coexist and co-evolve will be a major indicator of whether or not humanity is able to tap into the creative source that lies within its cultural diversity.

For Ali Mazrui, the reputed African Muslim scholar, any civilisation, in the course of its evolution, can be characterised as a creative synthesis of different cultures and worldviews.[5] History is full of examples where civilisations went through periods of enormous creativity when they were open to other civilisations (e.g. the Arab period on the Iberic Peninsula), and equally full of examples where civilisations declined when they oppressed or were oppressed by others. In other words: oppression, in the long run, ultimately leads to the decline of the oppressor himself, as he deprives himself of an evolutionary counterpart.

A new approach to development would need to allow for integration of the rich diversity of existing ontological perspectives. Thereby, creative interaction between diverse worldviews needs to be stimulated. The close interrelatedness of ontological perspectives and research methodologies has to be taken into account. That requires that knowledge creation processes need to be authentic to the worldview of a particular context and place, in order to lead to the creation of relevant knowledge that can meaningfully contribute to a particular social problem addressed. Such an authentic knowledge creation process could then also draw meaningfully on the local capacities and skills of a specific society, allowing it to purposefully build on what has been created and developed in its own history rather than being one-sidedly 'trained' in skills that have been developed outside the developing country, responding to problems that have equally been analysed and specified outside it.

④ LINEARITY VERSUS PROCESS: DEVELOPMENT OFTEN MISUNDERSTOOD AS LINEAR PROGRESS

Many development thinkers have complained about the linearity that still underlies much of development theory and practice. Given the complexity of development, further underlined by the critique articulated in this and the previous chapter, the fact that the field is still widely approached in a predominantly linear cause-effect fashion is puzzling. Based on the all-pervasive Eurocentric emphasis in development – thereby building on a long-standing tradition of progress-oriented thinking since the time of European Enlightenment – one might be led to think that there is a uniform, relatively linear trajectory from underdevelopment to development. However, it is surprising to see, that despite overwhelming evidence arising from research in social systems – for example via complexity theory, social ecology and group psychology – and despite the massive failures in development over the past decades, this kind of thinking still holds its ground. One reason for this attitude may be found in the strong influence that the natural sciences have had on the social sciences, in transferring its approach to empiricist thinking onto the latter. Such empiricist thinking often artificially eliminates complexity within a system to observe the particular relationship between two factors, thereby ignoring the influence of others.

A new approach to development needs to purposefully challenge such linear cause-effect thinking, by introducing complimentary development processes, suitable to address the full complexity of the social system in question. We begin to notice increasingly, how the issues raised here, are strongly interconnected.

⑤ OUTWARD FOCUS VERSUS INWARD FOCUS: DEVELOPMENT IS OVERLY OUTWARD-FOCUSED ON ENTERPRISE, ECONOMICS, SYSTEMS AND TECHNOLOGY

We suggest then distinguishing in development between the outer and inner development of a society. With outer development we mean predominantly tangible and explicit forms of development, such as support in the design and implementation of new trade or tax policies, of political systems and institutions and the transfer of technology and knowledge. Broadly speaking, this is the world of economics and politics, science, systems and technology.

With inner development we allude predominantly to intangible and implicit forms of development, such as working with and purposefully building on the particular cultural context of a developing country, which would, for example, include the tapping into its indigenous knowledge systems. Inner development also draws upon the particular spirituality of the developing society, engages with historical and communal ways of living, and includes the particular local perspectives on nature and the relationship between wo/man and nature.

Table 3.4, on the next page, illustrates some of the many facets of this outer-inner divide in human development.

Table 3.4 The outer-inner divide in human development		
OUTER	⇔	**INNER**
Society		
Economics/enterprise	⇔	Culture/spirituality
Science/systems/technology	⇔	Nature/community
Private sector/public sector	⇔	Civic sector/environmental sector
Self		
Action	⇔	Reflection
Knowledge	⇔	Wisdom
Public persona	⇔	Authentic self
General notions/relatively ...		
more explicit	⇔	more implicit (tacit)
more linear	⇔	more circular
more masculine	⇔	more feminine
more loud and fast	⇔	more still and slow
more public	⇔	more private
more general/impersonal	⇔	more particular/personal
more material/tangible	⇔	more immaterial/intangible
more analytic	⇔	more synthetic
more goal oriented		ore process oriented
more objective	⇔	more subjective
more quantitative/measurable	⇔	more qualitative/immeasurable
more global	⇔	more local

⑥ OUTSIDE-IN VERSUS INSIDE-OUT: MOST OF DEVELOPMENT WORK NEGLECTS THE INNER DIMENSIONS OF DEVELOPMENT

Most approaches to societal development are not only outer-directed, but also operate in an outside-in manner, typically coined as 'intervention'. Such outer-directed and outside-in interventions are primarily focused on changing the structural frameworks within the economic or political system of a society, using universalised criteria for societal development. It is only a minority of approaches that focuses on the inner development of a particular society. However, so our argument goes, outer development needs to build on inner development, in order to root economic, political, scientific and technological development measures in the cultural, spiritual, communal and natural context of a particular society. Overall, that demands an integrative perspective on development that unites a society's outer constituencies (enterprise, economics, science, systems and technology) with its inner constituencies (nature and community, culture and spirituality).

Within this book, we shall explore the extent to which the inner-directed form of development needs to lead the developmental process – in particular in times like the current ones, that calls for renewal of development. Development then has to be grounded anew within local contexts, and as such needs to come as an inside-out impulse.

Indeed, development – be it on an individual, organisational or societal level – has to be initiated from within. That requires, as we have shown in the first two chapters, that each one of us, engaging in development processes, is challenged to seek for ways to integrate the inner dimension within the development task at hand. That includes, first and foremost, a purposeful articulation and gradual integration of our own inner (reflective, intuitive, spiritual, cultural, etc.) dimensions. As Andrew Harvey states in his work on 'Sacred Activism',[6] we can simply not afford any longer to disconnect our own inner spiritual journeys with the transformation of outer society. Indeed, given the inertia in which he sees most of the world's population despite the growing acknowledgement of the massive issues we are facing, he comes to the conclusion, that without such a reawakened inner world, we simply do not have the insight, clarity and strength to bring about outer change in a significant and meaningful way. In that sense, development needs to be seen – in particular in this transition time – as an 'inside-out process'. Naturally, it needs to be both: inside-out as much as outside-in, with inner and outer dimensions in co-evolutionary interaction. However, until we have developed newly functional institutions and societal systems, one may well argue that a crucial responsibility lies with individual pioneers, able to intimate, through their own journeys – from individual to societal development – how newly integrated development practice may look like. That brings us to another disintegrated pattern, the conventional disconnectedness of individual, organisational and societal development.

⑦ SOCIETY VERSUS SELF: DEVELOPMENT LACKS INTEGRATION OF INDIVIDUAL, ORGANISATIONAL AND SOCIETAL DEVELOPMENT

The conventional field of development studies and development practice focuses on society in isolation of individual and organisation. However, not only does working with a local context require us to engage with individuals and institutions, but important developmental insights can be derived from individual and organisational psychology and culture. As described earlier, the development of such local individuals and institutions needs to be first and foremost informed by local and inner-directed development impulses, rather than by global and outer-directed prescriptions. This, however, is in most cases not taking place. As a result many development programmes are not responding to the real needs nor do they build on the innate capacities of local people. One disastrous effect is that many institutions in developing countries are merely imitations of institutional forms in developed countries, thereby often carbon copies of former colonial powers.

Furthermore, the isolation of self, organisational and societal development is apparent not only in so-called developing countries. It is interesting to witness, that the self-development movement, which is very prominent in the developed world, is by and large disconnected from the sustainable development ethos that has reached the corporate world. This, in turn, is primarily focused on environmental sustainability, which in itself is disconnected from the development of sustainable political and economic institutions, for example. Needless to say, that these developmental discourses on both self and also sustainable development, are primarily taking place in the developed world, and are by and large disconnected from development as a discipline.

With respect to a new approach to development, authentically working with local contexts implies engaging with individuals and local institutions. Indeed, so our argument goes, the development of society needs to be aligned with self and organisational development. We will illustrate with cases from Asia, Africa, Europe and the Middle East, that an integrated approach to development needs to align all levels – self, organisational and societal development.

Furthermore, if development aspires to become innovative as a field, it needs to include the knowledge base of individual and organisational development. But that alone is not enough, as we shall illustrate with the next issue.

⑧ IMITATION VERSUS INNOVATION: DEVELOPMENT OFTEN INHIBITS DYNAMIC KNOWLEDGE CREATION AND INNOVATION

The general emphasis on the outer development of society is also the reason why economics, political science and sociology are the academic disciplines that dominate the development discourse. An authentic interdisciplinary discourse is thereby inhibited, even if those disciplines, that are more involved with the inner realm of a society – anthropology, social psychology, social ecology, religious studies, philosophy – do strongly shape alternative development discourses. Furthermore, studies of individual and organisational development, which would include disciplines such as, for example, depth psychology and organisational psychology, are completely separated from the realms of development studies.

In addition, the social sciences have largely failed to develop research processes that serve to align research with development, thereby leading to social innovation. While in the natural sciences, fundamental and applied research and development are closely aligned, thereby leading to technological innovation, the social sciences have failed to develop an analogous process. It is in this guise that we shall be revisiting the role of the university through the course of our book, in both theory and in practice. That includes the role universities can and should play in catalysing individual, organisational and societal development processes. For now, the overwhelming majority of universities and university programmes focus on educating individuals, rather than catalyse development processes that respond to the development needs of their societies.

By the same token, while in the natural sciences, large innovation laboratories are the norm, with often hundreds and even thousands of natural scientists working together to resolve technological problems, we do not find anything like it within the social sciences.

And finally, equally damaging, is the lack of theory building within developing countries. The vast majority of institutional theory building is still done in the US and Europe. Paulin Hountondji, Benin's philosopher and former minister for culture and education, sees herein a core reason for the failure of development in Africa.[7]

What does all that mean for a new approach to development? Firstly, development needs to be understood in much wider transdisciplinary terms, allowing for creative interaction between diverse disciplinary perspectives. Secondly, we need to urgently look into research processes that link research and development, so that social innovation can occur. Social innovation implies a combination of knowledge creation and transformative impact: thereby research generates new relevant knowledge addressing a serious developmental problem in a particular context, and the subsequent application of this new knowledge results in a successful contribution to overcoming that problem. Institutionally, that requires also new development institutions that are fully embedded in the developing society, and that pursue theory building and application on the ground. This addresses also our earlier claim of a development that operates 'from the inside out' – and from an individual level to the societal level. Such local centres for development then need to be purposefully connected to transdisciplinary and transcultural networks and institutional environments in which interaction between diverse individuals, institutions and communities can flourish. Altogether that also includes a different kind of university environment, to which we will come later in this book. Altogether, such new developing institutions will have to put much more emphasis on local context.

⑨ GENERALISATION VERSUS CONTEXTUALISATION: MOST DEVELOPMENT EFFORTS LACK DEEP UNDERSTANDING OF THE LOCAL SOCIETAL AND CULTURAL CONTEXT

Most of development concepts and policies are developed and applied top down (world to nation, nation to local community, community to individual), rather than the other way round. That's why they are often not only irrelevant for a particular context, but they fail to draw on the rich, more 'bottom-up-insights' into development that come from fully understanding and engaging with a local context. Authentic contextualisation, however, includes not only understanding the particular burning needs, but also the unique capacities and aspirations of particular individuals, community or society.

The often underestimated but necessary starting point for any successful development process is the need to tap into the 'local identity' of the people involved. For a deep understanding of a particular place, though, it is important that we draw on the wisdom of those disciplines that engage most profoundly with understanding a particular context, e.g. anthropology, philosophy and religion. Furthermore, such deep understanding of a particular place requires that one works concretely with individuals and institutions.

Rahnema critiques:

> The decisive factors and motivations that have prompted the governments and aid-providing institutions of the North to support development activities have, to date, had little or nothing to do with the desires or needs of their so-called 'target populations'. To use the term coined by James Scott, the humanitarian and 'helping' arguments used ... are the 'public transcript' of the development deal. Its 'hidden transcript' is quite different. The wishes of the people in need are a myth, well maintained by foreign and national authorities for their political, economic, military and sometimes geopolitical objectives. It is a fact that all requests for development assistance are made, as a rule, by national governments or organisations that are controlled by them. Similarly, at the donor end of the line, it is up to the official authorities to agree to such requests. The 'target population' rarely have any say in these agreements.[8]

Even if individual developers are sensitive to context, the structures in international development often inhibit a direct and intensive engagement with the local culture. A colleague of ours, working as an official in a Geneva based UN agency, described to us his experiences on one of his recent (2012) trips to Darfur in Africa:

> By now there are so many layers in between the development worker and the people he or she intends to work with. Arriving from Geneva in Sudan's capital Khartum, we went on to Darfur in a UN airplane. A UN convoy then brought us from Nyala to our hotel, which primarily hosted UN officials and was heavily guarded. For every trip outside the hotel you take a UN car and one of the drivers employed by the UN. We needed lots of determination to break out of this system, and to get into a TucTuc that brought us to a local market. We were lucky to have a local interpreter with us, so we could finally start talking to 'real' people ....

Of course, we are aware that the process of really engaging with a local context has thereby only started for our colleague. How much more is needed to really understand language and culture, and to get a sense for the particularity of local life worlds.

Considering context, we shall also explore to what extent each cultural context has a particular inherent developmental path. For example, the Sri Lankan case of Sarvodaya (⇨14), deeply rooted in Buddhist and Ghandian philosophy, has, so our analysis shows, a different development path than we identified in the Spanish case of Mondragon (⇨18), an organisation that is deeply steeped in a combination of Basque traditions, Christian philosophies and secular cooperative theories.

But by emphasising local contextualisation, one should equally not make the mistake of ignoring a global perspective. A new approach to development needs to integrate both, the local and global perspective. It would have to be simultaneously relevant on a local and global level, whereby the local context is the starting not the end point of development. If the point of departure is inside-out and bottom-up, we are also less likely to recreate the following disintegrating pattern so common in today's development work.

⑩ COMPETITION VERSUS COLLABORATION: LACK OF COOPERATION BETWEEN DIFFERENT DEVELOPMENT ACTORS

Initially, development has been very much in the hands of such supranational institutions as the World Bank, the IMF and the WTO, with the United States invariably setting the agenda. In addition, influential national agencies like USAID (USA), CIDA (Canada), JICA (Japan), DFID (UK), AFD (France), GIZ (Germany), etc. were important actors in the development field, the latter primarily representing national interests coupled with development spending. Overtime, there was a shift from development aid to development cooperation, involving to a stronger degree the development objectives of the developing countries themselves. The past 30 years have furthermore seen a massive expansion within the civic sector, with thousands of NGOs – in addition to religiously inspired organisations that have exerted long-standing influence – engaging in development. In the last decade we witnessed, furthermore, a strongly increasing engagement of the corporate sector in the field of development, with countless examples of inspiring development projects initiated by private enterprises. Many of these activities, however, happen in isolation. They are not aligned. Even worse, quite regularly we can observe competition of such development actors about particular topics or regions, given that national interests play a major role in the allocation of development monies. But also corporations are often primarily guided by uniquely positioning themselves within a development field of high public visibility, in order to be clearly recognised by their current and potential customers as a so-called 'force for good'. To some degree, we conclude, such personal interests, be it on the level of a state agency or corporate or NGO, inhibit agents of development in acting in the interest of the larger common good and to align development efforts in a way, that the collective efforts could exceed the sum of individual parts. Such an interest driven development engagement ultimately cements a one-sided, hierarchical orientation toward development preventing the development actors from co-evolving with the developing country or community. Notable are the efforts around the Millennium Development Goals initiative to foster collaboration among development actors on a global scale, but it is still a long way towards co-evolution.

A new approach to development would need to illustrate the mutual advantage of a co-evolutionary perspective in a way, that the prevailing distinction between 'developed' and 'developing' is transcended.

Where do we go from here?

3.3 Reconstruction: Building Integrating Patterns into Future Development

OVERVIEW

Identifying and understanding the major disintegrating patterns in past development work, has taken us many years. Indeed, our own journey through this deconstruction and reconstruction process, that we share here with you in a distilled manner, was preceded by a long immersion in development theory and practice from all over the world – thereby including those theories and cases that often do not form part of the mainstream development discourse. Simultaneously, our close affiliation and cooperation with leading development practitioners in the four corners of the globe helped us further to identify core integrating patterns that would need to be built purposefully into a new approach to human development. Both, the most relevant theory and the most advanced practice in terms of integrated approaches to development, will be introduced later in this book (⇨7 to 22). Together, they will be introduced to you in travel maps (⇨6), designed to guide you on your own journey to contribute to more sustainable development work in the future.

Our integral analysis resulted in four core design principles that, as an interrelated composite, enable us to overcome the disintegrating patterns past and current development is faced with.

FOUR CORE DESIGN PRINCIPLES FOR A NEW INTEGRATIVE APPROACH TO DEVELOPMENT

The first design principle = differentiating and integrating realms:
All developmental realms need to be looked at simultaneously and interactively

Over time, development has been increasingly interpreted as 'economic and technological advancement', and with that came terms like 'progress', 'industrialisation' and 'modernity'. Politics (and policies) are closely aligned with economics, and partly also with technology; and science, in turn, is primarily focused on technological, less so on social, advancement and innovation. As a consequence, we overemphasise a limited number of developmental perspectives that are relevant for society in general: enterprise and economics, systems (e.g. political systems), science and technology. What remains relatively marginalised are natural and communal, spiritual and cultural perspectives on development. While the former perspectives are more outward oriented, universalist and quantifiable, the latter are relatively more inward oriented, particular and qualitative.

Based on our earlier integral work, on which we build from Chapter 4 onwards in great detail, we distinguish four major, interconnected realms, each of them holding a set of perspectives:

- *The Realm of Action:* Enterprise and economics.
- *The Realm of Knowledge:* Science, systems and technology.
- *The Realm of Inspiration:* Culture and spirituality.
- *The Realm of Relationship:* Nature and community.

By now it has become clear that most of today's development work is focused on the first two realms: Looking closer at the history of development, we learn that the common linear orientation to development and the accompanying orientation to entrepreneurial, economic, scientific, and technological evolution are rooted in the European Renaissance. The outer success of Europe's development since its Enlightenment era, given its economic growth as well as technological and scientific advancement, and the subsequent colonisation of the world by European powers and thought, has made the 'European Way' (or indeed by now the 'Euro-American Way') the all-pervasive norm for societal progress. By the same token, many view Euro-American style democracy as the most advanced political system, setting the global benchmark for the political development of each society. The American Japanese social philosopher Francis Fukuyama even coined the expression of 'the end of history', which would have been reached once all countries had adopted free markets and liberal democracy, Western style of course, both positioned at the very end of the (relatively linear) development ladder.[9]

As we have illustrated, the dominance of one worldview is also reflected in the ontological perspectives that pervade the development discourse. As ontology or theory of reality is at the very heart of research methodologies, the process of scientific knowledge creation that feeds into development as a scientific discipline becomes equally one-sided. Indeed, it perpetuates and reinforces this problem on an ongoing basis, as the way in which knowledge is to be created is set from one particular perspective. This is a highly oppressive, limiting, and ultimately dangerous situation, as it totally blocks the knowledge creation potential of humanity as a whole.

Development, then, needs to be embedded in a social system as a whole, thereby equally engaged with the inner dimensions of nature and community, culture and spirituality of a social system, as well as focusing on the outer aspects of science, systems and technology, enterprise and economics. Fully interdependent and interconnected, they mirror jointly the full complexity of a social system.

Through a full engagement with all of these perspectives, we break the pattern of only asking outer-directed questions such as 'What do we need to know?' in terms of new scientific knowledge, relevant systems and advanced technologies or 'What do we need to do?' in terms of new enterprises and economic activities. For us, development starts with the inner-directed quest of 'Who are we?' in terms of understanding of our (human) nature and acknowledging our human relations (community); and it begins with exploring 'Who are we becoming?' in terms of cultural and spiritual interpretations of our existence. These two questions have a profound influence on the overall direction of the development path in which one chooses to engage. We take them as the starting point of development, as we need to be clear about the direction of our development work before we engage in it.

Based on this backdrop, we can see that the first integral design principle addresses simultaneously a number of the earlier mentioned disintegrating patterns:

- By bringing the 'inner' perspectives of a development context (its nature and community, culture and spirituality) to the fore, local development actors have something to bring to the development table, the following disintegrating patterns are challenged: 'us versus them', 'domination versus partnership' and 'outward focus versus inner orientation'.
- By beginning with the inner aspects of development, we add the inner quest to the outer exploration, thereby addressing the disintegrating patterns of 'outside in versus inside out' as well as 'generalisation versus contextualisation'.
- As each perspective is underpinned by particular scientific disciplines, we create spaces for transdisciplinary interaction, a crucial prerequisite for authentic social innovation to take place. We thereby address the pattern of 'imitation versus innovation'.
- Finally, as the wide range of perspectives can't be held together by one development actor alone, it is also an invitation to collaboration and co-evolution, thereby addressing the disintegrating pattern of 'isolation versus collaboration'.

The second design principle = differentiating and integrating rounds: All development levels – self, organisation, society, world – need to be holistically and interactively included ('fully rounded')

We have argued that the discourse on development is primarily held at a societal level, as well as, partly, on a community level. Usually not included are the levels of individual and organisational, development. Thereby, we overlook not only that individuals and organisations (as well as their development!) are an essential ingredient in any given development context, but also neglect much of the wealth of knowledge that underpins these two developmental levels.

In other words, the knowledge fields of self-development, organisational development, community development and societal development are disconnected from each other. This is mirrored by the fragmentation of human knowledge in scientific disciplines, institutionalised in university faculties that often operate in complete isolation from each other. As argued earlier, this disconnection of development levels and their respective knowledge fields is another important reason why human development as a whole seems to fail us. Consequently, we see a closer alignment of these diverse levels to be a vital part of a new approach to development.

We propose, as part of this second design principle, to distinguish the following four interconnected levels, and to look at them within any given development context:

- *Level 1/Round 1:* Self-development (self and other).
- *Level 2/Round 2:* Organisational development (group and organisation).
- *Level 3/Round 3:* Societal development (community and society).
- *Level 4/Round 4:* Global development.

Not only would the first three levels have to be closely aligned with each other, but it is also required that they find, in level 4, an overall integration in a relevant practise – whereby theory is embodied in practice, and practice gives rise to new theory – that addresses the development issue at hand and that contributes to global development.

Besides recognition of all levels – from self to world – it is also important to look at each level in a holistic or 'rounded' way. In this respect, we need to become aware that the described overemphasis of outer perspectives on the level of societal development has also pervaded the levels of self and organisational development. These two levels often focus primarily on 'what do I need to know?' and, subsequently, on 'what do I need to do?' in order to advance from one development stage to another. These two questions correspond with the realm of knowledge (science, systems and technology) and with the realm of action (enterprise and economics). What often moves into the background of self- and organisational development are questions like 'who am I?' and 'what am I becoming?' These two questions correspond with the realm of relationship (nature and community), addressing our multiple relationships (to our own self, to others, to our community, to nature and so on) and with the realm of inspiration (culture and spirituality). What is required then, is a holistic consideration of each level, including the four human modes of being, becoming, knowing, and doing – that are in turn reflected in the four realms.

Such an alignment of all levels does not seek to establish a standardised understanding of the development of each level. On the contrary, it seeks to open the knowledge field underlying each of them to all others, fostering a more transcultural perspective on each level. It also does not see development happening in a linear way through the levels. On the contrary, the levels are in constant intense interaction with each other. What we are saying, however, that, in order to consciously rebuild development, we require an alignment of the diverse levels – and that alignment cannot be imposed but need to be initiated on the level of the individual. We maintain then that the starting point for a new authentic development is 'inside out', beginning with individual development: understanding and developing oneself necessarily precedes the understanding and development of others. In so doing, the individual however needs to continuously respond and engage with organisational and societal realities and development processes.

With the inclusion of all levels in a holistic and interconnected manner, this second, integral design principle contributes to addressing a number of the disintegrating development patterns we have been exposed to:

- By opening the field of development from a societal to the individual and organisational perspective of development, we address the disintegrating pattern of 'society versus self'.
- Then, by seeing development as a gradual, interconnected process from individual to organisational to societal development – altogether aligned in integrated practice – we address patterns such as 'inside out versus outside in'.

- Also, by bringing the knowledge fields of individual and organisational development to the fold, we foster transdisciplinary perspectives, contributing to overcoming 'imitation versus innovation'.
- Starting on an individual and group level within a particular development context also contributes to transcend the harmful patterns of 'generalisation versus contextualisation' as well as 'monocultural domination versus transcultural evolution'.

The third design principle = differentiating and integrating rhythm: Development is to be primarily understood as a rhythmical, dynamic interactive process, with linear action components

Often, there is the underlying belief that development is linear, and to be achieved through 'progressive stages', through which a system unfolds on a given trajectory from a less desired to a more desired state. Good examples of linear thinking are, on the one macro hand, our fixation – via the prevailing economic system – on 'linear growth', and, on the other micro hand, a need to organise life (not only economic life) in to-do-lists, action plans and strategies. Similarly politics is increasingly geared towards pragmatic, linear responses to current day issues.

Evidently, this emphasis on linearity is linked to the emphasis on the two realms of knowledge and action, as discussed earlier. Together, they promote a fast track of a more linear and pointed approach to development, while the two realms of inspiration and relationship rather promote a slow, nonlinear development process, suggesting a rather back and forth, cyclical and spiralling form of development.

That is resonant with findings from the natural sciences that indicate that the evolution of living systems does not at all follow purely linear patterns. Rather we see here life cycles, and life always includes growth and decline, departure and return, the one building on the other. Indeed, living systems, once they die and transform into in-organic matter, become the very foundation of new life, thereby born out of the old. Such cyclical perspective, hence, needs to be accommodated in an integrated approach to development.

It is notable that we also find cyclical orientations within the world's diverse cultural and spiritual interpretations of human development. The great myths and religions served as inner guides for civilisations for many centuries, and sometimes even for millennia, always offered understandings into the dynamic-rhythmical relationship between life and death. They also provided an interpretation of how individual and society could 'develop a good life' – in between the polarities of life and death. The interpretation, of course, of what was to be understood by a good life, varied in each culture, and within any given culture over time; and that is the case up to our current day and age.

As we shall illustrate in this book, an open dialogue between diverse cultural perspectives and knowledge fields on 'a good life' as a direction and 'result' of development, is an important prerequisite for successful development itself. Such a dialogical process allows for the continuous evolution of the development concept base with a long-term focus, thereby taking us out of an overly linear perspective, which is generally short-term oriented.

With a dynamic, rhythmical, interactive, processal approach to development moving to the foreground – inclusive, of course, of the ability of short-term pointed action –the disintegrating pattern of 'linearity versus process' is most directly addressed. Indirectly, however, it contributes also to the overcoming of many others of damaging patterns of past development. Why? Such a new design principle would stimulate interaction between opposing terms, seeing them altogether as integral components of a larger, holistic perspective, in which dualities are genuinely transcended. We then move from an 'either/or' to a 'both/and', or, as we have suggested in the opening chapter: 'from either/or to both and more'.

The fourth design principle = local-global differentiation and integration: Development has to be relevant to particular local worldviews and contexts as well as to a global perspective

A new approach to development would need to enable us to work with the particular understanding of a 'good life' that any specific development context holds. However, as we seek to integrate also the diverse levels from self to organisation to society, and ultimately the world, each context needs to see itself not only in the light of its own particularity and through the lens of its own worldview, but also in the light of how its own development path contributes to the development of the planet at large.

One of the great challenges of our time will be to come up with designs and framework in all sectors of society, that genuinely honour local particularities and surface local capacities on the one hand, but that also include a planetary perspective to which the myriads of local contexts – in co-evolutionary manner – contribute.

The primary crisis of our time, as outlined in the opening chapter, is one of global dimensions, and we are hence challenged to develop in each local context enough of a planetary consciousness that enables us to design and drive development processes that equally promote a local and a global perspective.

It is important, though, that a combined local-global perspective is not merely seen as a question of moral responsibility. Rather, it is one of necessity. Both, the local and global perspective require each other to fully actualise. It is precisely in the interaction between local capacities, value bases, and development intentionality on the one hand and global knowledge, creative resources and development initiatives and needs on the other hand, that the most impactful development processes have taken place. The Grameen Bank in Bangladesh is a good example. Its profound understanding of local context and capacities on the one hand and the global economic understanding of Muhamad Yunus and other on the other hand, enabled Grameen not only to come up with a new development instrument – Micro Finance – with enormous impact on the local society, but it could thereby also make a profound contribution to the world at large.

With equal consideration of the local and global perspective, we address, as in the case of the third design principle, almost all disintegrating patterns simultaneously. This is possible, because the four design principles are to be seen as highly interdependent, interconnected and integrated ingredients of a new development approach. That brings us to a holistic criteria framework.

Table 3.5   Towards Integral Development: The four core integrating design principles

First principle: INTEGRATING REALMS Inclusive recognition and creative interaction between all development perspectives		Second principle: INTEGRATING ROUNDS Dynamic interweaving of holistic, 'well-rounded' individual, organisational, communal, societal, and ultimately global development	Third principle: INTEGRATING RHYTHMS Actualising development through rhythmical, dynamic processes
Realm of relationship: nature and community	*Inner-directed being and becoming reflective*	Guiding questions: *Who am I?/Who are we?* Focus: continuously deepening our understanding of who we are as humans, in relation to each other (in community) and as part of nature and natural life	Development processes and rhythms that: • foster the interweaving of all levels (rounds) • support the dynamic Interaction between the core development perspectives (realms) • are applicable to any given local context, addressing its burning needs and building on its particular qualities • have a more processal research and a more linear action component • and ultimately lead to social innovation and transformation on the ground
Realm of inspiration: culture and spirituality		Guiding questions: *What am I becoming?* *What are we becoming?* Focus: continuously reinterpreting and renewing (together with others) our understanding of the deeper meaning of human existence and on what truly constitutes the 'good life'	
Realm of knowledge: science, systems and technology	*Outer-directed knowing and doing active*	Guiding questions: *What do I need to know?* *What do we need to know?* Focus: developing new knowledge, new systems and new technologies to strengthen the 'good life'	
Realm of action: enterprise and economics		Guiding questions: What do I need to do? What do we need to do? Focus: designing and co-creating institutions, enterprises and economic systems to be able to live the 'good life'	

Fourth principle:
LOCAL-GLOBAL INTEGRATION
Development to be relevant to local contexts and worldviews as well as to global well-being

HOLISTIC CRITERIA FRAMEWORK FOR A NEW APPROACH TO DEVELOPMENT

These four design principles can only be understood as an ensemble, illustrated by the following integrative framework. In a way, this framework also summarises the 'job profile' of an Integral Developer, inviting him or her to accommodate all four integrating principles. Each of the principles requires differentiation prior to integration. For example, the criteria of 'local-global integration' requires to differentiate, that means for us to be aware of and understand distinctly different local contexts, including their arts, worldviews, knowledge systems and personal-interpersonal attributes; equally, the criteria of 'integrating realms' requires us to differentiate, that means to recognise and explore the different development perspectives. Indeed, it is such in-depth exploration in differences and variations, that allows to gradually shedding more light into the very nature of human development.

TOWARDS A TRULY INTEGRAL PERSPECTIVE

The framework presented above illustrated the core design principles of an integrated approach to development in a systematic manner. However, breaking out of the perceived stuckness between disintegrating polar opposites, includes for us also a new form of visual representation – one that transcends the representation of content in boxes and matrixes. Based on the integral model we have developed over time (and on which we shall build in detail from the following chapter onwards), we have translated this framework in

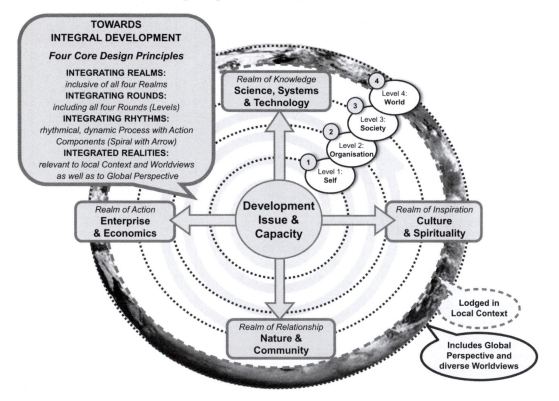

Figure 3.1   Towards Integral Development: A first overview

a more 'life-like', circular, flowing and dynamic perspective (see Figure 3.1). The circle thereby encompasses the integrated totality, the spiral the inherent dynamics of life – and thereby also development. A deeper introduction into our integral model (⇨4, 5, 6) will demonstrate that the design principles articulated in this chapter are deeply rooted in healthy living systems – over time and across the globe. For now, we let Figure 3.1 (on the previous page) which includes all four integrating principles and puts the development issue at hand as well a particular local development capacity in its very centre, speak for itself.

In the following chapters, we shall explain and evolve our approach to Integral Development in detail, providing you not only with an in-depth understanding of the general model underlying it, but also with its concrete application.

3.4   Integration

In this chapter we have highlighted the major disintegrating patterns inhibiting successful development from taking place. We were thereby confronted with a combination of highly complex issues, the dealing with anyone of them providing us with immense challenges. A new understanding of development needs to engage with these challenges and offer pathways to resolve them in the future.

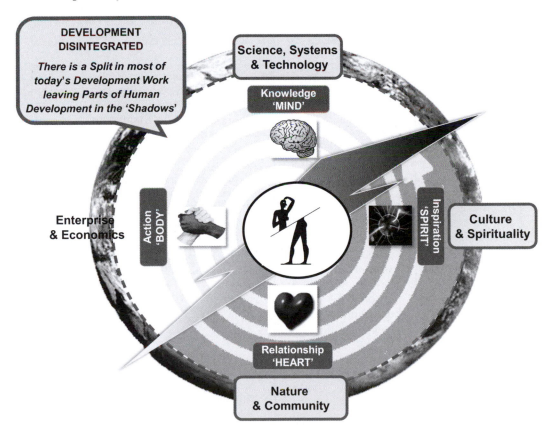

Figure 3.2   Development disintegrated: The split in human development

The nature of the 10 major issues that we have identified was highly dualistic, in a sense, that unresolved tensions had been created between opposing terms, such as, for example, 'linearity versus process', 'outward focus versus inward focus' or 'generalisation versus contextualisation'. In all of these cases, we noticed not only unresolved tensions, but thoroughgoing domination of one side of the spectrum over the other. The most obvious domination is visible in that one 'Western' monocultural worldview is still, by and large, controlling the development stage, whereby 'Western' perspectives on enterprise and economics, together with its science, systems and technology drive the development agenda. Other cultural worldviews and perspectives (such as community based approaches) are thereby literally pushed into the development shadow.

Using the integral perspective that we have introduced in the latter part of this chapter – including a set of integrating design principles that are required for a future oriented development approach aiming to overcome these disintegrating patterns – we can intimate the status quo of today's development with the help of Figure 3.2 (see the previous page).

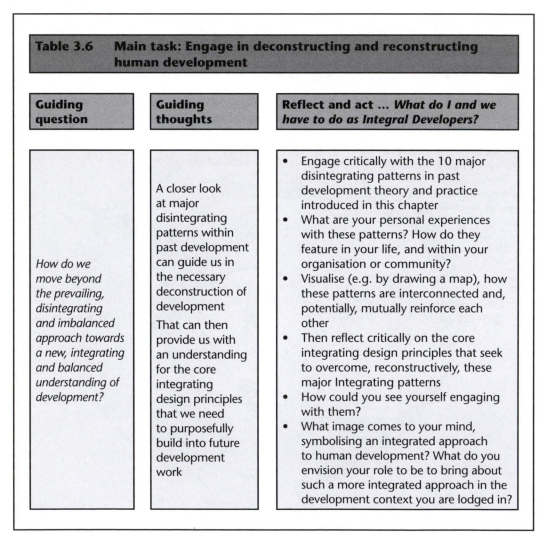

Table 3.6   Main task: Engage in deconstructing and reconstructing human development

Guiding question	Guiding thoughts	Reflect and act … *What do I and we have to do as Integral Developers?*
How do we move beyond the prevailing, disintegrating and imbalanced approach towards a new, integrating and balanced understanding of development?	A closer look at major disintegrating patterns within past development can guide us in the necessary deconstruction of development That can then provide us with an understanding for the core integrating design principles that we need to purposefully build into future development work	• Engage critically with the 10 major disintegrating patterns in past development theory and practice introduced in this chapter • What are your personal experiences with these patterns? How do they feature in your life, and within your organisation or community? • Visualise (e.g. by drawing a map), how these patterns are interconnected and, potentially, mutually reinforce each other • Then reflect critically on the core integrating design principles that seek to overcome, reconstructively, these major Integrating patterns • How could you see yourself engaging with them? • What image comes to your mind, symbolising an integrated approach to human development? What do you envision your role to be to bring about such a more integrated approach in the development context you are lodged in?

In the figure we align the core realms of human systems introduced in this chapter (Relationship, Inspiration, Knowledge and Action) and their respective perspectives (e.g. Nature and Community) with the individual heart, spirit, mind and body. The realms of heart and spirit are positioned in shadow land. The arrow illustrates the outer-inner split that divides the world of human development. The arrow also interrupts the dynamic spiral with the pointed arrow at its end, illustrating that creative interaction between all parts of the totality and effective action resulting thereof is massively inhibited. Overcoming this split will be the core task for a new, integral approach to development, to which we shall now turn in detail.

We shall conclude this chapter with a brief reflection on the guiding question and thoughts presented in this chapter (see Table 3.6 opposite). What does this chapter make you think? How does it inform your action as an agent for more integrated forms of human development?

References

1 Eisler, R. (1998). *The Chalice and the Blade: Our History, Our Future*. New York: Harper Collins.
2 Rosenberg, M.B. (2003). *Nonviolent Communication: A Language of Life*. Encinitas, CA: Puddle Dancer.
3 Rosenberg, M.B. (2003). *The Heart of Social Change: How to Make a Difference in Your World*. Encinitas, CA: Puddle Dancer.
4 Lessem, R. and Schieffer, A. (2010). *Integral Research and Innovation: Transforming Enterprise and Society*. Farnham: Gower.
5 Mazrui, A. (1987). *The Africans: A Triple Heritage*. London: Little, Brown.
6 Harvey, A. (2009). *The Hope: A Guide to Sacred Activism*. Carlsbad, CA: Hay House.
7 Hountondji, P.J. (2002). *The Struggle for Meaning: Reflections on Philosophy, Culture and Democracy in Africa*. Athens, OH: Ohio University Press.
8 Rahnema, M. (1997). Towards Post-Development: Searching for Signposts, a New Language and New Paradigms. In: Rahnema, M. and Bawtree, V. (eds), *The Post-Development Reader*. London: Zed, pp. 385ff.
9 Fukuyama, F. (1996). *The End of History and the Last Man*. New York: Harper Perennial.

PART II

Integral Worlds: A New Integral Perspective on Human Development

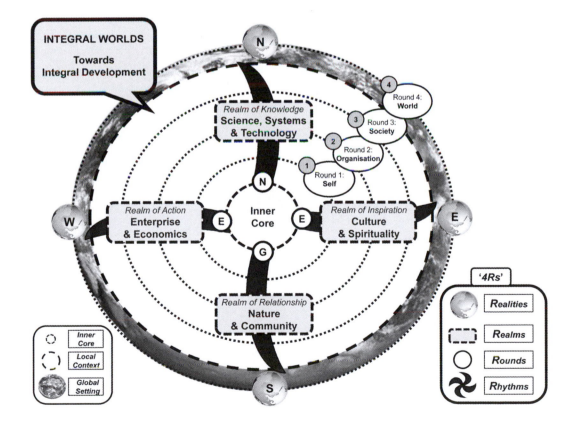

4 *The Integral Perspective: Holistically Renewing Development*

Guiding Question: What kind of integral perspective can serve to fundamentally renew human development?

4.1 Orientation

In the previous chapter, concluding Part I of the book, we have developed new design principles required in the necessary reconstruction of development and development studies, as we seek to overcome its hitherto overwhelmingly destructive dualistic overtone. We ended by introducing a new integral framework.

Entering the second part of the book, we shall now leave the dualistic, divided world (Part I) behind us, and enter – with a significant evolutionary step – into the integral world.

We begin by setting this new scene by exposing you briefly to the major protagonists of the coming 'Integral Age' – an emergent era of integral thinking and practice that is gradually rising on humanity's horizon. In that context we shall also share our own integral work to date, during which we developed a particular Integral Worlds approach and various applications of it. This approach, in its most recent and most refined form, will then serve as the guiding framework for the Integral Development approach, which is at the heart of this book.

In other words, this chapter will give you the necessary general context (Integral Age) and specific backdrop (Integral Worlds) that is required to understand the relevance and significance, as well as the history and potential future of an integral approach to human development. We begin by reviewing the rise of the Integral Age.

4.2 The Rise of the Integral Age

OVERVIEW

Everything emerges in context. Before we lay out the full architecture of Integral Development it is important to relate it to the overall integral movement of our time and to our personal life stories. The latter led us to co-evolve, over the past decade, our own Integral Worlds approach that serves as the guiding frame for Integral Development. Our own approach – in true integral manner – has been influenced by many thinkers and practitioners from all over the world. It has not been conceived of in isolation, but we see it as a contribution within the emergent field of integral thought and practice. What then is the larger integral movement about?

THE RISE OF THE INTEGRAL AGE

The voices that demand integrated, holistic, whole-systems perspectives are on the rise – all over the world, throughout all disciplines and fields, in theory and practice. Terms like 'holistic', 'integrated' or 'integral' have, together with many similar terms, almost become inflationary. While we regard this urge for integration as truly important, as we have illustrated in the previous chapters, we see it as equally crucial to overcome an often over-simplistic, generalising tenor that all too often dominates.

It is for that reason, that we need to identify those approaches that do have the potential to help humanity in this civilisational crisis to understand the deeper meaning of 'integrality' and to enter, full-fledged, the Integral Age.

There are a number of highly respectable integral approaches that have indeed helped shift our global perspective towards a more integral viewpoint over the past 200 years. All of them are, again, not to be seen in isolation, but in their specific historical context and in the interconnected light of a slow process that gradually led to the rise of the Integral Age.

The contemporary US integral philosopher and evolutionary activist Steve McIntosh offers with his work on Integral Consciousness[1] a very useful historic account of the evolution of integral thinking itself. In a fascinating journey, he traces the beginnings of an integral perspective back to the German philosopher Georg Wilhelm Friedrich Hegel (1770 to 1831) and his theory of history unfolding in a dialectical process towards higher forms of evolution. He then moves on to French Jewish philosopher Henri Bergson (1859 to 1941) who emphasised the importance of intuition, or unmediated knowledge of the inner nature of things. Other important 'torchholders' of the integral flame were, for McIntosh, the English philosopher Alfred North Whitehead (1861 to 1947), the French Jesuit Pierre Teilhard de Chardin (1881 to 1995), as well as Jean Gebser (1905 to 1973) and Jürgen Habermas (born 1929).

Perhaps the best-known integral approach of our time is that of the American social philosopher Ken Wilber – widely known through his AQUAL 'All Quadrants All Levels' model (⇨19). It was in particular Wilber's work that served as a catalyst to bring integral thinking in a more systematic way to today's global stage. It is for this reason, that we shall introduce Wilber's work later in this book in some more detail (⇨19). His work, in turn, inspired countless further variations of the integral theme, including the excellent work *The Radiance of Being*[2] by Allan Combs. Other prominent integral thinkers of our time are the Hungarian philosopher Ervin Laszlo[3] (⇨22), US philosopher Ashok Gangadean,[4] and US integral theorists Michael Zimmermann and Sean Esbjörn-Hargens and their work *Integral Ecology*.[5]

Wilber, almost single-handedly, managed to penetrate much of the human knowledge base structuring it in his fourfold AQUAL scheme. It enabled us to understand human systems and their evolution over time from an individual and collective, as well as from a subjective and objective perspective.[67] His own integral approach has been strongly nurtured by the prior work of German Spanish philosopher Jean Gebser (⇨13) and Indian Sage Sri Aurobindo (⇨13), among others. It has also been influenced by contemporary thinkers such as the German philosopher Jürgen Habermas and the American organisational and societal consultants Don Beck and Chris Cowan and their work *Spiral Dynamics*.[8]

With Spiral Dynamics, a comprehensive theory on human development along major civilisational stages culminating – for now – in an integrative, holistic stage was introduced. Its originators, Beck and Cowan, had borrowed and then further evolved the evolutionary spiral from the earlier work of US psychologist Clare W. Graves.

Spiral Dynamics depicts a dialectic, spiralling, upwards-oriented movement that all societies appear to go through. On its particular civilisational journey, any given society, according to this model, is called to overcome evolutionary hurdles that each transition from one stage to another imposes. Spiral Dynamics is a highly useful illustration of the evolutionary challenge of our time. According to this approach, human consciousness – reflected in different modes of societal organisation, such as tribes, feudal societies and nation states – gradually moves towards more integrated, holistic forms of organisation and consciousness. Spiral Dynamics differentiates eight different stages, from archaic consciousness to a post-integral consciousness, with the eighth stage merely indicating that the theory is open-ended, embracing the potential for further, not yet known, evolutionary phases. Figure 4.1 illustrates the core stages of human evolution as per Spiral Dynamics:[9]

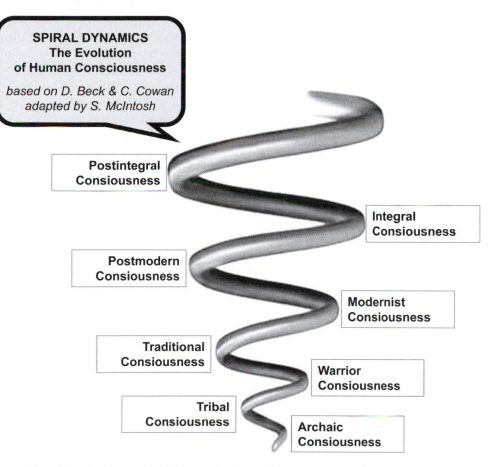

Figure 4.1   Spiral dynamics: The evolution of human consciousness over time

Though each stage of consciousness or 'time world' is distinct in its evolutionary context, it is notable that Beck and Cowan have a very 'generalising touch' to it, making no real distinction between particular places or cultural context, be it Belgium or Benin, Senegal or Singapore. In cooperation with Ken Wilber, Don Beck fused his spiral theory with Wilber's integral four-quadrant theory, calling it 'Spiral Dynamics Integral'.[10]

In his latest book, *Evolution's Purpose: An Integral Appreciation of the Scientific Story of Our Origins*, McIntosh stresses that the resolution of the problems humanity is facing can only be achieved through the further evolution of consciousness and culture. According to McIntosh, all forms of evolution – cosmological, biological and cultural – are part of the same overarching process, despite their significant differences and discontinuities.[11] McIntosh, building on the evolutionary spiral in Figure 4.1, recognises the sequential emergence of value-based stages of human cultural development. In a sense, he translates the individual stage-theory of cognitive development of the renowned Swiss child psychologist Jean Piaget, for whom 'there is no development that lacks structure', for societal and global scale.[12]

For McIntosh, the three main value-based stages that we find today across humanity, subsequent to the premodern stage, are what he calls traditional, modernist and postmodernist consciousness. In addition there is an emergent integral consciousness. These worldviews or levels of consciousness coexist in many societies. For example, McIntosh maintains that even in the so-called developed world the traditional worldview remains the centre of gravity for significant minorities who give more importance to scripture than to science. Humanity's challenge, for him, is to gradually transcend prior stages and move altogether towards an integral appreciation of our world.

Such a transcendence to a holistic perspective, affirms integral psychologist Vera Schiller de Kohn, Jewish Ecuadorian founder of the Centre of Integral Development in Quito, is, though immanent, by no means an easy process. Quite the contrary, it is a rather painful transition that breaks all existing boundaries of consciousness.[13]

Table 4.1 shares the defining features of the main historical stages of consciousness, recognising the presence of indigenous societies holding a premodern worldview. Again the difference between McIntosh's approach (like Wilber and Beck) from our own Integral Worlds approach is that theirs are entirely time-based, in an evolutionary respect, and there is no particularity of place, except in that evolutionary respect. In other words, there is nothing, for example, 'African' about Africa, except for where it stands in the evolutionary spiral. So if both the Igbo in Nigeria and the Maori in New Zealand constitute, say, a mix of premodern, traditional and modern, there is no difference between them!

What all of the integral thinkers introduced so far have in common is an attempt to integrate diverse value orientations that emerged over time and space – such as traditional, modern, postmodern – into an integral perspective. The key feature across all approaches is the propagation of a new evolutionary level of human consciousness, enabling humanity to transcend fragmented, isolated perspectives into a holistic, integrative one. Our own *Integral Worlds* approach equally seeks to contribute to a new integrated perspective, but takes a slightly different – complementary – angle.

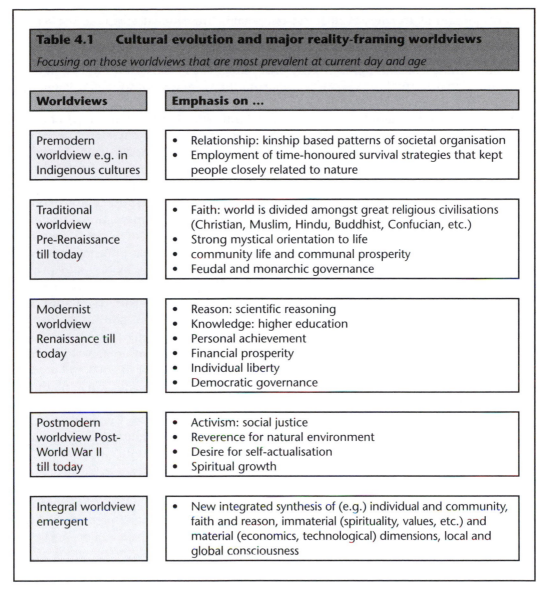

Table 4.1   Cultural evolution and major reality-framing worldviews

Focusing on those worldviews that are most prevalent at current day and age

Worldviews	Emphasis on ...
Premodern worldview e.g. in Indigenous cultures	• Relationship: kinship based patterns of societal organisation • Employment of time-honoured survival strategies that kept people closely related to nature
Traditional worldview Pre-Renaissance till today	• Faith: world is divided amongst great religious civilisations (Christian, Muslim, Hindu, Buddhist, Confucian, etc.) • Strong mystical orientation to life • community life and communal prosperity • Feudal and monarchic governance
Modernist worldview Renaissance till today	• Reason: scientific reasoning • Knowledge: higher education • Personal achievement • Financial prosperity • Individual liberty • Democratic governance
Postmodern worldview Post-World War II till today	• Activism: social justice • Reverence for natural environment • Desire for self-actualisation • Spiritual growth
Integral worldview emergent	• New integrated synthesis of (e.g.) individual and community, faith and reason, immaterial (spirituality, values, etc.) and material (economics, technological) dimensions, local and global consciousness

OUR OWN STORY: THE BACKDROP TO OUR FOUR-DIMENSIONAL INTEGRAL APPROACH

Our own integral approach has long standing roots. For both of us authors, the origin of our integral journey is in the fields of economics and enterprise.

For one of us, Ronnie Lessem, the journey began in his country of birth and upbringing: Zimbabwe. Having studied economics and management at the University of Rhodesia (in the 1960s pre-independence Zimbabwe was still called Rhodesia), London School of Economics and Harvard Business School, he found it impossible to relate his hard-won learnings back to a local Zimbabwean context. Furthermore, he saw his home continent Africa falling ever more down the economic wayside. Colonialism, though ending politically, was still economically and educationally continuing. It was then, when his personal journey of discovery explicitly started, that he was led to develop the first version of an integral approach, with a particular focus on management practices in Europe.[14]

For the other one of us, Alexander Schieffer, the journey began during his studies of economics and business at the University of St Gallen at Switzerland. It was at that time, when he started to think of a more holistic educational approach to management and economics, having been deeply affected primarily by three issues: firstly, the increasingly destructive effect business (as well as mass consumption) had on the environment; secondly, a growing awareness of the disfunctionality of the 'Western' economic paradigm coupled with the ever increasing wealth-poverty gap within many countries and in between so-called developed and so-called developing countries: and thirdly, his exposure to a so-called elite education that did not feed the soul, but only the mind – without relating to the core problems of our time to which enterprise and economics were massively contributing. After many years of working in the international corporate world – from Investment Banking in Germany, to a Global Media Conglomerate in London, from his own publishing company in Singapore to a large number of consulting and teaching assignments around the world – that the 'integral' penny began to drop.

With both of us having our original professional roots in economics and business – having worked in various sectors and in various continents for many years – we then returned, at different stages of our lives to research and education. Both of us felt that the very knowledge foundation on which business and economics stood had to be fundamentally revised, as well as the educational and research process that went along with them. Many years further down our individual roads, we met in 2003 and decided to work together to further develop the integral knowledge base and transformational education alongside it, to both of which Ronnie Lessem had laid the foundation. This cooperation led to the co-foundation of the Geneva based Trans4m Center for Integral Development in 2006. Together we have designed and run master's and doctoral programmes on Social and Economic Transformation as well as on Integral Innovation in the Middle East, in the US, Europe, as well as in South Africa and Zimbabwe. On an ongoing basis we have developed the integral knowledge basis that serves as the core curriculum in our programmes. This resulted also in an entire book series on Transformation and Innovation with the UK/US publisher Gower, of which this book is part. Within this series we introduced the following integral concepts – each developed to a degree that it can provide a new integral basis for the discipline it dealt with:

- *Integral Enterprise:*[15] A micro-economic blueprint for a new organisational design – and the transformational process underlying it – with a combined environmental-civic-public–private dimension.
- *Integral Economics:*[16] A macroeconomic overview of major innovative economic approaches from all over the world, in theory and practice – designed within a dynamic framework for a new integral economy.
- *Integral Community:*[17] Introducing a framework for an integral community, focusing on two Zimbabwean social innovators, their rural community and Zimbabwe as a whole – thereby conceptually connecting political economy and social commons in the overall context of an Integral Development programme and process.
- *Integral Research and Innovation:*[18] A transcultural research framework, drawing in a new way on major research methods and methodologies, in order to enable locally

relevant and culturally resonant knowledge creation that leads to social innovation on the ground.

- *Integral Dynamics:*[19] Focuses, on the one hand, on dynamic integral rhythms, articulated as individuation, transformation, and acculturation, and, on the other hand, on an integral worldview, expressed in the realms of nature, culture, science and economics.

These integral concepts were further complemented by colleagues from Africa, Australasia and South America, the Middle East, the Indian subcontinent, the Far East, Europe and America, all of them contributing to a growing integral knowledge basis. All of them employed, in some form, our particular Integral Worlds approach, to which we shall now come.

4.3   Integral Worlds Approach: The Guiding Frame for Integral Development

OVERVIEW

Integral Worlds is a holistic approach to understanding and consciously evolving human systems. It serves to address imbalances – within an individual, organisation, community and or society, but also within specific fields, such as economics, enterprise,

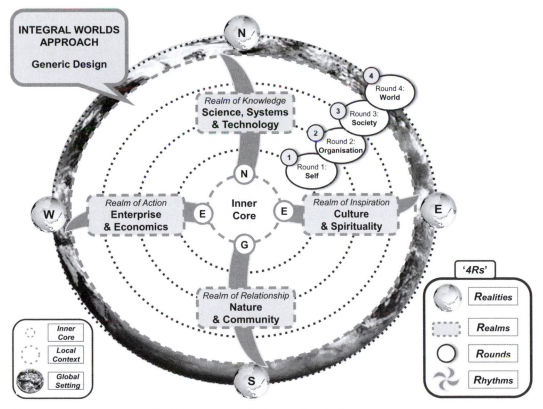

Figure 4.2   Integral Worlds approach: Generic design

or, as in this book, human development at large. We shall now introduce core aspects of this approach, beginning, through Figure 4.2 (see the previous page), with a visual overview. Later in this chapter, when we outline the specific application of the Integral Worlds approach to human development, we shall deepen and expand much of what we introduce now rather briefly. As this approach continuously evolves, it is important to say, that this version of Integral Worlds is the latest, most refined, up-to-date version. You will find small variations in earlier works of ours, though the basic design principles have remained relatively stable.

INTEGRAL WORLDS: AN INITIATING INNER CORE AT THE CENTRE OF A CIRCULAR HOLISTIC FRAMEWORK

The underlying circular design is derived out of intense exploration over four decades, across the four corners of the globe, acknowledging that since time immemorial the circular shape has been a symbol for the totality. It also symbolises the cycle of life that each living system undergoes. In Integral Worlds, the outer globe marks a worldly, holistic perspective. Embedded in the outer global circle is the local context (see Figure 4.2), which is where we part company from our fellow integral philosophers like Wilber, McIntosh, Beck and Cowan. At the very centre of such a globally embedded context is, what we call, the inner core. It is here, at the core of an individual, organisation, community, or society, that the impulse for transformation or development is initiated – be it through a perceived imbalance of the overall system, that becomes your objective concern, be it through a particular, subjective evolutionary calling. This inner personal core and the outer, global circle are then connected through the '4Rs' of Integral Worlds: Realities, Realms, Rhythms and Rounds. We shall now introduce each one of them, starting with Integral Realities.

INTEGRAL WORLDS: FOUR INTEGRAL REALITIES

Over the course of historical time, and spread across geographical space, humanity has developed diverse reality perspectives – different interpretations of the world through different individual and collective lenses. Culture, thereby, has always played an immensely important role in shaping such individual and collective worldviews or realities. In our explorations of world philosophies, cultures and religions we discovered that many holistic interpretations of human systems and of the cosmos, throughout history and across all cultures used fourfold patterns to indicate this diversity in wholeness – often represented within a circular outer design. The differentiation into four poles represents differentiated human consciousness, which is able to self-reflectively understand that, within the overall world (the circle) it is lodged in, there are diverse individual and collective positions – each of them sharing a part of the totality. This diversity is also reflected within ourselves, as different aspects of our individual personality.

Some of the core cultural symbols that mirror this fourfoldness within a circular design are representations of the Tibetan Mandala, the Christian Cross, Native American Medicine Wheels, the (double fourfolded) Buddhist Wheel of Life, some of Arab Calligraphy as well as some of the African Cosmologies, such as the Cosmograms of the Yorubas in Nigeria and the BaKongo in Kongo (⇨7). Such integrated fourfoldness is also represented in the four directions, four seasons, four temperaments, and the four elements.

'Fourfold integrality' is also the inspiration behind the work of the anthropologist Margaret Mead, the analytical psychologist Carl Gustav Jung (⇨7, 11) and the learning theorist David Kolb (⇨15). It surfaces in many commonly used human development tools, such as Honey and Mumford's Learning Styles,[20] the Myers-Briggs Personality Type Indicator[21] and David Keirsey's Temperament Sorter.[22] The research of integral thinker Tony Bradley from Liverpool's Hope University affirms these ancient and newly emerging fourfold patterns. For him, such integrality represents a specific renewal of the inner consciousness that situates each human person within a fourfold constructed world, searching for individuation or wholeness, by bringing together each quadrant. He calls this the 'integral spirit'. He acknowledges that it is found in most, if not all, indigenous and ancient civilisations. It is represented in Sumerian, Greek, Judeo-Christian, medieval Western, Celtic, Buddhist, Hopi Indian and many other cultures.

Through Integral Worlds we have chosen the four directions (South, East, North, West) to illustrate the diversity of cultural lenses. In very general terms, these four directions represent the following Reality perspectives:

- *The 'Southern' Reality Perspective:* Views the world primarily through relationships; that includes our relationship to nature (including our inner nature) and to other human beings and the community we are building with them.
- *The 'Eastern' Reality Perspective:* Views the world primarily from an inner, interpretive, cultural and spiritual perspective, seeking to understand the deeper meaning of human existence, and our holistic relationship with the world and the cosmos.
- *The 'Northern' Reality Perspective:* Views the world primarily through a scientific, rational perspective, seeking to distinguish patterns and structures within reality and to translate them into viable concepts and systems.
- *The 'Western' Reality Perspective:* Seeks to understand the world primarily through active experimentation and practical treatment of things, emphasising the application of ideas through action.

We put terms like 'Southern', 'Eastern' and the like consistently into quotation marks. We do that to highlight their metaphorical meaning and to avoid a simplistic, geographic association. However, one can't help observe the resonance between these diverse reality views and aspects of global geography. Travelling through Africa, for example, we can experience a strong sense for human community and the capacity to relate to and live with nature. The East of the World – represented, for example, by India, Japan and China – has without doubt developed a profound understanding of the inner spirituality of the human being and its relationship with the world at large and the cosmos. The North – perhaps best represented by many middle and northern European countries – has developed a particular affinity for developing systems, methods, structure, logic and philosophies. And the West – well represented by the USA – has developed a gift in translating knowledge into action, in particular through private enterprise.

With a world growing ever closer together and with cultural identities increasingly fusing, these distinctions may become less clear. But that, in any case, does not matter. What matters is that we are able to recognise, that each one of us, and to a degree also each particular society and culture, employs a particular lens or combination of lenses that is different from others. As we evolve further, within ourselves and in relationship with others, we are called, as individuals, organisations, communities and societies, to be aware of our particular lens (or combination of lenses), and to acknowledge that each lens holds only a part of the understanding of the totality. For understanding the integral totality, we are required to explore the lenses – in our terms realities – of others, be they individual beings or entire societies. Being aware and being able to engage with the rich diversity of reality perspectives is a crucial component of our integral model.

In our work across the globe, and in many different cultures, we learned that our particular fourfold differentiation into distinctive Reality viewpoints also helps to bring the different 'time worlds' that we introduced earlier (⇨4.2) into an interactive, creative relationship. To some degree, there is a clear resonance of the 'Southern' Reality viewpoint with the premodern stage of consciousness, and its emphasis on kinship and nature. The 'Eastern' Reality viewpoint corresponds with the more faith-based traditional stage and its emphasis on religion, the 'Northern' Reality viewpoint communicates well with the modernist stage and its emphasis on reason and knowledge and, finally, the 'Western' Reality viewpoint resonates, in some way, with a postmodern Perspective with its more activist orientation.

However, where we differ from our integral counterparts is that such a 'Southern' reality has one flavour in Zimbabwe and another flavour in Nigeria, one orientation in Africa and another in South-East Asia – and that has as much to do with the particularity of place as it has to do with its evolution over time. For example, both African *Ubuntu* and Chinese *Guanxi* may have premodern origins and both concern social relationships, but each one is ultimately very different in nature and scope.

There is another important reason why Integral Worlds puts so much emphasis on recognising and consciously co-evolving with diverse reality perspectives, and this lies in the way knowledge (and thereby reality perspectives) is generated. We have illustrated in our work *Integral Research and Innovation*[23] that most of the research methods and methodologies currently employed have been developed in Europe and the USA, and hence tend to strengthen a European-American reality perspective – leveraged through countless educational institutions worldwide, all transmitting the knowledge derived out of such a monocultural perspective. Indeed, our critique is that this 'North-Western' bias occurs throughout the natural and social sciences.

INTEGRAL WORLDS: FOUR INTEGRAL REALMS

Out of these diverse reality perspectives grew, over time, highly differentiated perspectives on the world. Each perspective got translated into knowledge fields or disciplines that deepened the understanding of the world (or, as differentiation continued ever further: of a small part of it). Again, by individual and collective predisposition, we tend to favour particular knowledge fields or disciplines over others, as we interpret the world. Over time, that has led to dramatic compartmentalisation of knowledge, with most knowledge fields or disciplines totally disconnected from each other – through professions, terminologies and mental models. That has contributed to a highly fragmented world – including highly fragmented university worlds. Integral Worlds is designed to bring the rich diversity of knowledge and disciplines, through four different realms, to our attention and to generate interaction between them. The four realms are closely aligned with the four realities. Each realm is comprised of a core perspective, illustrating the main tenor for this realm. In the course of the book, we shall relate the four major perspectives to respective knowledge fields and disciplines. For now, we focus on the four realms and their major knowledge perspectives. They are:

- 'Southern' Realm of Relationship: Nature and Community.
- 'Eastern' Realm of Inspiration: Culture and Spirituality.
- 'Northern' Realm of Knowledge: Science, Systems and Technology.
- 'Western' Realm of Action: Enterprise and Economics.

What we are arguing in Integral Worlds is that we need to engage – interactively – with all four realms, for any given transformational issue that we are engaging with through this approach. It becomes quickly evident, that in order to do that, we require competent others to work closely with. Integral solutions to the complex issues we are facing in today's world can't be dealt with through individual researchers. The natural sciences, in which research teams proliferate, have long understood this; the social sciences still need to develop the equivalent to the multitude of laboratories around the world, employing, tens, hundreds, sometimes even thousands of natural scientists to develop technological solutions. The same is required for the 'social technologies', the social innovation that the world needs to bring about a more positive future. How then does our Integral Worlds approach invite such interaction?

INTEGRAL WORLDS: FOURFOLD INTEGRAL RHYTHMS

With every human system being in continuous evolution, so does Integral Worlds incorporate an inbuilt transformational rhythm, which makes the entire approach dynamic. It is a rhythm that we could equally trace back to natural cultural systems and their respective evolution. We call this rhythm the GENE (grounding, emerging, navigating, effecting), representing a fourfold spiralling force, activating the entire Integral Worlds model. The GENE rhythm is embedded in the diverse reality views and realms, thereby serving to tap into the dynamic aspect of each reality view and realm, bringing them altogether in transformative interaction. While we see the GENE as a spiralling, iterative, ever-unfolding force, we nevertheless start the conscious transformational process in the South, thereby beginning with a conscious grounding in a given context and issue, before we then engage in its transformation. The fourfold GENE rhythm flows as follows:

- *'Southern' Grounding:* The issue at hand and the people involved are grounded in a particular nature and community, which need to be fully understood. For any living system, the Southern grounds represent its 'local identity' and its connection to a common source of life. Southern grounding is about 'being' in as well as feeling and 'experiencing' a particular life world. It is seeking to activate the relational 'feeling' or 'heart'-level of a human system as well as participation and engagement. This is the 'formative' part of the transformation process.

- *'Eastern' Emergence:* Moving to 'Eastern' emergence 'lifts' the issue and the people involved to deeper insights into the unfolding nature of the issue. Here the people and issue engage in dialectic processes with others, thereby co-evolving to new insights. Such a process always includes a 'stepping into the unknown' and 'letting go' of some of the previous assumptions. It therefore requires us to consciously transcend our prior life world. New insights – often in forms or images and visions – emerge, that provide clues for the transformative process. 'Eastern' emergence is hence about 'becoming'. It deals with 'intuiting' and 'imagining' the new form that is emerging. Here the 'local' perspective of the Southern grounds evolves to 'local global' viewpoints. This is the 'reformative' part of the transformation process. Here, we seek to activate 'inspiration' or the 'spirit'-level of a human system.

- *'Northern' Navigation:* The move to 'Northern' navigation requires that the new insights (images, visions) gained are translated – in a structured and systematic manner – into new concepts, new knowledge. 'Northern' navigation is hence about 'knowing' and about 'making explicit' what hitherto had been rather implicit. Now, the 'local global' viewpoint is turned into a more general, abstract 'global' viewpoint. New 'norms', related to the issue at hand, are developed. Northern 'navigation' is about activating the 'mind'-level, the conceptualising prowess of the human system at hand. This is the 'normative' part of the transformation process.

- *'Western' Effect:* Moving to 'Western' effect is now requiring us to put all prior three levels into integrated action. It is about pragmatically applying the new knowledge that has been developed, thereby actualising the innovation that it contains. 'Western' effect is hence about 'doing' and about 'making it happen'. Now the 'global' viewpoint is turned into a 'global local' standpoint, whereby what has been globally developed is locally implemented. We call it 'global local', as the local application is taking place with the larger 'global' perspective in mind. This is the ultimate 'transformative' level of the GENE-process, activating, metaphorically, the 'body' or 'hand'. However, the process does not stop here. Rather, it continuously moves on. Any transformative, active effect has to be continuously revisited, exploring whether it remains resonant with the 'Southern' grounds it seeks to serve. Any solution is considered a temporary one. Evolution is infinite.

By continuously engaging in the GENE rhythm, thereby addressing imbalances within the larger system on an ongoing basis, we can consciously contribute to the evolution of ourselves and of the human systems (from organisations to society, from economics to development) that we bring forth. We thereby release the 'GENE-i-us' of a system: individual gene-ius ('i') and collective gene-ius ('us').

In conclusion, we have now introduced not only the GENE rhythm but also a series of accompanying fourfold rhythms thereby drawing on a number of approaches to individual and collective transformation. The following Table 4.2 summarise the core fourfold patterns introduced, as well as their originators.

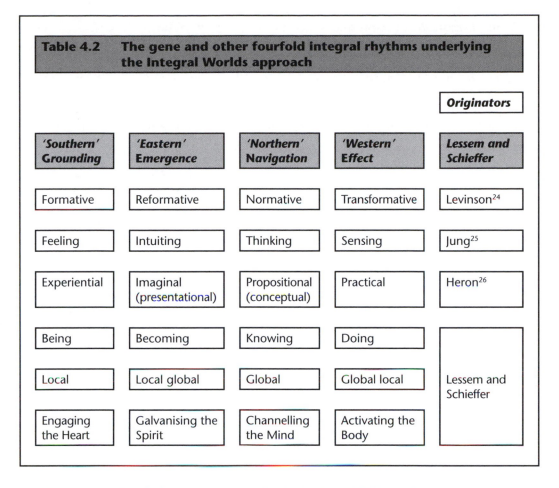

Table 4.2   The gene and other fourfold integral rhythms underlying the Integral Worlds approach

				Originators
'Southern' Grounding	**'Eastern' Emergence**	**'Northern' Navigation**	**'Western' Effect**	**Lessem and Schieffer**
Formative	Reformative	Normative	Transformative	Levinson[24]
Feeling	Intuiting	Thinking	Sensing	Jung[25]
Experiential	Imaginal (presentational)	Propositional (conceptual)	Practical	Heron[26]
Being	Becoming	Knowing	Doing	
Local	Local global	Global	Global local	Lessem and Schieffer
Engaging the Heart	Galvanising the Spirit	Channelling the Mind	Activating the Body	

The multitude of these rhythms, of which the GENE can be seen as a generic distillation, underlines their wide applicability. Within the Integral Worlds approach, this rhythm represents the dynamic part of the model, affecting, in its interlinked way, all other core aspects of the model. It is linking the inner core circle and the outer circle, and it is moving dynamically, through the diverse reality views, realms and rounds, which we shall now introduce.

INTEGRAL WORLDS: FOUR INTEGRAL ROUNDS

The evolution that each human system continuously undergoes does not occur in isolation, but in interdependence with all other human systems, as well as with the world's natural ecosystem which humanity is part of and embedded in. Every holistic perspective needs to simultaneously involve these multiple systems.

Within this approach, we distinguish between four interconnecting levels, which we describe here as 'rounds'. These four 'rounds' – which Figure 4.2 depicts as concentric circles – are:

- *Round 1:* Individual perspective.
- *Round 2:* Organisational perspective.
- *Round 3:* Societal perspective.
- *Round 4:* Global perspective.

Why did we call these levels 'rounds'? It is not just because of the harmonious 'ring' of having '4Rs' – realities, realms, rhythms and rounds. More importantly, we seek to illustrate with this term three aspects: firstly, we are looking at each level in a fully 'rounded', holistic manner. Secondly, the circular 'rounded' understanding of self, organisation, society, world, alludes to their being living, moving, interconnected systems. Thirdly, more poetically, as we are rebuilding human development bottom-up and inside out, we also see that all levels of development (from self to world) ripple like concentric circles on a water surface, once the rock of 'concern and calling' has fallen into the 'development ocean'. We call the totality of the rounds 'transpersonal', as any given development impulse cannot be limited to an individual 'personal' level, but needs to straddle all rounds to become fully actualised.

Finally, a 'round' is a term for 'a musical composition in which two or more voices sing exactly the same melody (and may continue repeating it indefinitely), but with each voice beginning at different times so that different parts of the melody coincide in the different voices, but nevertheless fit harmoniously together'.[27] This insight provides us with a beautiful guiding metaphor in our attempt to align the various development rounds more purposefully with each other. We shall make this attempt in each of the four realms, as the four rounds are equally applied to each of them.

Of course, reducing the rounds to four is a simplification as there are many more rounds or levels that one could distinguish: groups, families, communities, networks and so on. We found this differentiation, however, particularly useful.

We shall close this overview of the Integral Worlds approach with a brief analysis of the differentiation of this model compared with other integral approaches.

4.4   Comparing Integral Worlds with Other Integral Approaches: Key Distinguishing Elements

Our own long journey in bringing forth a new integral approach started when we recognised that existing approaches were still lacking few fundamentally important aspects, that a fully integral approach would need to offer.

Many of the existing integral designs – in particular the ones of Gebser, Wilber, Beck and McIntosh – offer great insight when it comes to explaining the overall individual and collective evolutionary journey of humankind. That includes the developmental stages that each society has to pass through, in some form or shape, to reach a more integrated and holistic civilisational stage. Our own work has been greatly inspired by all of them.

Our Integral Worlds approach stands purposefully on the shoulders of these giants. However, it adds the following hitherto missing elements:

- *Enabling Active Participation:* Our dynamic framework allows you not only to understand the world integrally, but also to engage actively with it in contributing to bringing about an integral world. It is about activating our co-evolutionary potential.

- *Within a Given Particular Context:* The Integral Worlds approach is designed to be locally applied in a given context, but not through a 'one-size-fits-all' design, but rather by recognising and dynamically engaging with specific local needs and capacities. It allows thereby for any local context ('for each world') to be valued for its particularity and to make a locally authentic contribution to the evolution of the global whole.
- *Via the Recognition of and Interaction between Diverse Reality Perspectives:* The approach allows for the dynamic interaction between these diverse local realities to promote an altogether integral *'unity in diversity'* reality view.
- *Via the Inclusion of Individual and Collective Levels:* Most integral approaches focus either on the individual or the societal perspective. This approach seeks for an interconnected inclusion of all levels (or 'rounds'), from self, to organisation, to community, to society, ultimately embracing a global perspective.
- *Altogether 'Activated' by an Embedded Rhythm:* Integral Worlds is underpinned by an embedded rhythm, engaging all worldviews (realities), knowledge fields (realms) and all levels (rounds) dynamically – thereby allowing conscious co-evolution towards more integral designs to take place.

We are now ready to conclude.

4.5 Integration

There is an increasingly growing global movement, seeking more integrated, balanced approaches to how we look at the world and how we live in the world.

More concretely, we witness a rising body of integral approaches that has its roots in major integral philosophies and thinkers that have emerged over the past two centuries, paving the way for the current rise of the Integral Age. We position our own Integral Worlds approach as part of this globally emergent integral movement.

Core features of our approach are the dynamic interaction between:

- Integral Realities (Worldviews).
- Integral Realms (Knowledge fields).
- Integral Rounds (different levels, from self to world).
- Integral Rhythms (transformational rhythms), applied to all of them.

Integral Worlds, much more so than the other integral approaches cited, is designed to work with the particularity of any given context it is applied to, bringing about locally integral solutions, altogether contributing to an integral world.

Integral Worlds and its various applications that we developed over time, provides – together with general backdrop of the Integral Age – the overall setting for Integral Development, to which we shall now turn in the following chapter.

Before we move on, we shall pause for a moment, reflecting on the guiding question for this chapter.

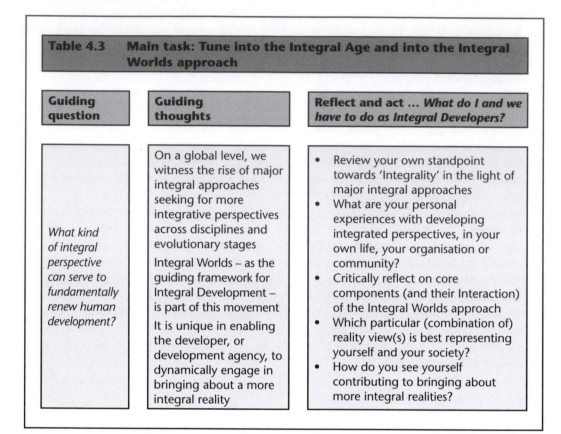

Table 4.3   Main task: Tune into the Integral Age and into the Integral Worlds approach

Guiding question	Guiding thoughts	Reflect and act ... *What do I and we have to do as Integral Developers?*
What kind of integral perspective can serve to fundamentally renew human development?	On a global level, we witness the rise of major integral approaches seeking for more integrative perspectives across disciplines and evolutionary stages Integral Worlds – as the guiding framework for Integral Development – is part of this movement It is unique in enabling the developer, or development agency, to dynamically engage in bringing about a more integral reality	• Review your own standpoint towards 'Integrality' in the light of major integral approaches • What are your personal experiences with developing integrated perspectives, in your own life, your organisation or community? • Critically reflect on core components (and their interaction) of the Integral Worlds approach • Which particular (combination of) reality view(s) is best representing yourself and your society? • How do you see yourself contributing to bringing about more integral realities?

References

1   McIntosh, S. (2007). *Integral Consciousness and the Future of Evolution*. St. Paul, MN: Paragon. Available at: www.integralworld.net/mcintosh2.html.

2   Combs, A. (2002). *The Radiance of Being: Understanding the Grand Integral Vision; Living the Integral Life*. St. Paul, MN: Paragon House.

3   Laszlo, E. (2007). *Science and the Akashic Field: An Integral Theory of Everything*. Rochester, VT: Inner Traditions Bear & Company.

4   Gangadean, A. (2008). *Meditations of Global First Philosophy: Quest for the Missing Grammar of Logos*. Albany, NY: State University of New York Press.

5   Esbjörn-Hargens, S. and Zimmermann, M. (2009). *Integral Ecology: Uniting Natural Perspectives on the Natural World*. Boston, MA: Integral Books.

6   Wilber, K. (2001). *Sex, Ecology, Spirituality: The Spirit of Evolution*. Second Edition. Boston, MA: Shambhala.

7   Wilber, K. (2001). *A Theory of Everything: An Integral Vision for Business, Politics, Science and Spirituality*. Boston, MA: Shambhala.

8   Beck, D.E. and Cowan, C.C. (2002). *Spiral Dynamics: Mastering Values, Leadership and Change*. Hoboken, NJ: Wiley Blackwell.

9   Spiral Dynamics Integral Website. Available at: www.spiraldynamics.net / Accessed: 19 October 2012.

10   McIntosh, S. (2007). *Integral Consciousness and the Future of Evolution*. St. Paul, MN: Paragon.

11 McIntosh, S. (2012). *Evolution's Purpose: An Integral Appreciation of the Scientific Story of Our Origins*. New York: Select Books.

12 Piaget, J. (1929). *The Child's Conception of the World*. Lanham, MD: Littlefield Adams.

13 Schiller de Kohn, V. (2006). *Terapia Iniciática: Hacia el Núcleo Sagrado*. Quito: Centro de Desarrollo Integral, p. 35.

14 Lessem, R. and Palsule, S. (1997). *Managing in Four Worlds: From Competition to Co-Creation*. Oxford: Blackwell.

15 Lessem, R. and Schieffer, A. (2009). *Transformation Management: Towards the Integral Enterprise*. Farnham: Gower.

16 Lessem, R. and Schieffer, A. (2010). *Integral Economics: Releasing the Economic Genius of Your Society*. Farnham: Gower.

17 Lessem, R., Muchineripi, P. and Kada, S. (2012). *Integral Community: Political Economy to Social Commons*. Farnham: Gower.

18 Lessem, R. and Schieffer, A. (2010). *Integral Research and Innovation: Transforming Enterprise and Society*. Farnham: Gower.

19 Lessem, R., Schieffer, A., Tong, J. and Rima, S (2013). *Integral Dynamics: Political Economy, Cultural Dynamics and the Future of the University*. Farnham: Gower.

20 Honey, P. and Mumford, A. (2006). *Learning Styles Questionnaire 2006: 80 Item Version*. Oxford: Pearson.

21 Briggs Myers, I. and Briggs, P.B. (1995). *Gifts Differing: Understanding Personality Types*. Palo Alto, CA: Davies-Black.

22 Keirsey, D. and Bates, M. (1984). *Please Understand Me: Character and Temperament Types*. San Diego, CA: Prometheus Nemesis.

23 Lessem, R. and Schieffer, A. (2010). *Integral Research and Innovation: Transforming Enterprise and Society*. Farnham: Gower.

24 Levinson, D.J. et al. (1979). *The Seasons of a Man's Life*. New York: Knopf.

25 Jung, C.G. (2009). *Psychological Types*. London: Routledge.

26 Heron, J. (1992). *Feeling and Personhood: Psychology in Another Key*. London: Sage.

27 Available at Wikipedia on 'Round'. Accessed: 19 October 2012.

CHAPTER 5

A New Approach: The Integral Development Framework

Guiding Question: What are the main components of the Integral Development approach?

5.1 Orientation

We shall now lay out the full architecture of Integral Development. Thereby we are strongly guided by the Integral Worlds approach that was introduced in the previous chapter. The Integral Worlds model represents, if you like, the foundation for Integral Development.

Both frameworks – Integral Worlds and Integral Development – are to be seen within the larger context of the global push towards more integrative and balanced perspectives, across knowledge fields, societal sectors and national perspectives.

In the process of coming up with an integral approach to human development, we have not merely applied a generic approach (Integral Worlds) to a specific field (development). Quite the contrary. Coming up with Integral Development – through reviewing and engaging with major theory and practice in the field of human development – has also helped to significantly evolve further the Integral Worlds approach.

As a result, you shall find all the main design components of Integral Worlds – in particular the '4Rs' of Realities, Realms, Rounds and Rhythms – incorporated also in Integral Development.

Each of the four realms, or knowledge fields, has a guiding theme relevant to human development: Restoring Life; Regenerating Meaning; Reframing Knowledge; and Rebuilding Infrastructure and Institutions. These themes set the overall tone for what Integral Development seeks to achieve. Figure 5.1 presents an overview of the approach and its four main themes.

In the following we shall 'unpack' the model. We begin in the very centre, where we see the development process initiated by a particular calling and challenge.

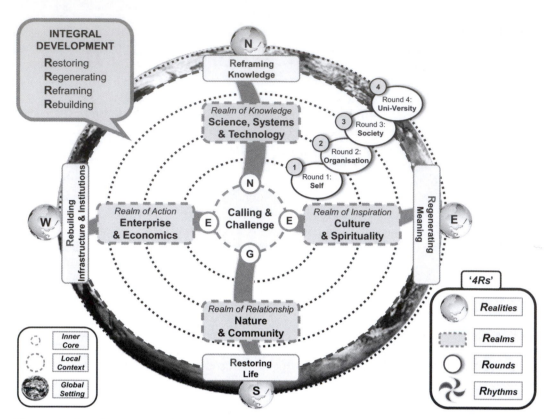

Figure 5.1   The Integral Development model

5.2   Initiation: Initiating Integral Development via the Inner Core

We start with the inner core. For us, each particular development process begins with what we termed a 'calling' and a 'challenge'. Usually such calling originates within an individual actor, at times also within an organisation, a community, or even entire society. A 'challenge' is linked to a perceived imbalance (inwardly or outwardly) and matched by the 'calling' to respond and a sense of being 'response – able' (having the capacity) to address this imbalance. Sometimes, a person or group of people may also feel simply 'called' to develop something new that advances society, without necessarily being aware of a particular imbalance.

In any case, such calling and challenge arise in relation to a particular local context. Each development context – be it rural Zimbabwe, metropolitan Rio de Janeiro, a traditional First Nation tribal settlement, or a Swiss mountain village – is profoundly different, and has its very own particular features, as well as its specific development capacities (gifts) and development needs (issues). This is indeed why we refer, from the outset, to Integral Worlds, rather than just one world, as there is no presumption of homogeneity. Hence, we wish to understand, simultaneously and interactively, both: the development calling of a particular development agent or agency, and the development challenge within the particular development context at hand.

This is enabled by the Integral Development approach being highly sensitive and adjustable to any given local development context. For a development process to be sustainably successful, it needs to be firmly rooted in the particular situation it addresses. We shall demonstrate that through numerous examples in the course of this book.

The Integral Development approach integrates in its design and processes the development context. Visually, the local context is represented by the outer dashed circle in the model, just inside the globe (see Figure 5.1). This local context itself is embedded within a global setting represented by the globe spanning the entire model.

In many development processes, the inner core (calling and challenge), local context and global setting are often disconnected – or, at best, considered in a linear, static way. Looking at Figure 5.1, you can fathom such a disconnect if the model would only consist of the inner circle of 'calling and challenge' and the outer circle of 'development context', as well as the global setting. All of them need to be interconnected – and that is exactly what happens by applying our 'transcultural Realities', 'transdisciplinary Realms', 'transpersonal Rounds' and 'transformative Rhythms', altogether coined the '4Rs'.

Realities, Realms, Rounds and Rhythms allow for the conscious and dynamic interaction between inner core, local context and global setting. While the inner core provides the initiating impulse (calling and challenge) for the Integral Development journey – it is through the purposeful engagement with all '4Rs' that the journey can lead to successfully and sustainably addressing the development issues at hand. We shall now introduce these '4Rs' of Integral Development in some detail.

5.3   Realities: Engaging with Four Transcultural Reality Viewpoints

The more dynamic process begins as we go under the surface of each particular local context. Here we notice particular predispositions that each one of us – as well as each organisation, community or society – holds to some degree. As described earlier (⇨4), we tend to develop distinct worldviews, individually and collectively.

Most development work involves a large number of diverse stakeholders. These stakeholders often represent, as individuals and through their organisation, a wide range of diverse backgrounds: from different societal sectors (local communities, conventional development institutions, donors, private sector enterprises, civic sector organisations and so on), to diverse cultural backgrounds (European, African, Asian and so forth); different educational backgrounds (academics and non-academics, wide range of disciplines), as well as people with a more urban or more rural background, traditionalist and modernist etc.

Each one of those stakeholders represents a different view on reality, derived and developed as an amalgam of the diverse experiences and learnings, as well as social and cultural conditioning that got imprinted onto individual and collective minds. If one observes closely – and without being labelled as either an 'essentialist' or 'stereotypist' – one notices relatively easily that there are commonalities in the reality viewpoints within particular cultures, organisation types, disciplines.

In itself, such a particular reality is nothing good or bad. However, not only do certain viewpoints – in human development specifically – get short shrift in relation to others, each reality viewpoint is also invariably incomplete. Every person's or every culture's reality includes or excludes certain aspects.

As development processes always happen in interaction and through communication, the awareness of the diversity of reality viewpoints is crucial for co-development to take place. Unfortunately, as we have illustrated earlier (⇨2, 3), what usually happens, is that one reality viewpoint dominates others. When that occurs, constructive communication becomes massively inhibited. This is an experience we all have had in situations when, for example, one party monopolises while another is silenced or refuses to engage.

Because of the importance of understanding and trusting each other in development processes, and because of the negative experiences we have had in the past with regards to the domination of many worldviews by one predominantly 'Western' perspective, we believe that the proactive engagement with the rich diversity in reality viewpoints that any given development context holds, is absolutely crucial. Our colleague and integral philosopher, Ashok Gangadean from Haverford College in the US – in his book entitled *Between Worlds*[1] as well as in his 'Awakening Mind'-portal – underlines the need for us to have a 'global lens'. He argues that an acute sensitivity toward our own particular worldview-lens and that of the other being is required to 'graduate' to a more integral lens.[2]

To enable the development of such 'lensitivity' – as Gangadean coins this quality – we have integrated diverse reality viewpoints into the Integral Development model. Therein each of the four 'Southern', 'Eastern', 'Northern' and 'Western' poles represents a particular perspective:

- *Southern Reality:* Nature and community perspective.
- *Eastern Reality:* Culture and spirituality perspective.
- *Northern Reality:* Science, systems and technology perspective.
- *Western Reality:* Enterprise and economics perspective.

Naturally, there are many more reality viewpoints than just these four. To be precise, there are probably as many realities as people on the planet. And yet, usually we are unaware of using a lens at all. Often we are convinced of having a most complete, balanced and differentiated view of the world, and it is rather the other whose lens is too narrow.

The distinction in these four generic lenses should help us, as Integral Developers, to become as a first step simply more aware, in any given development context, of the multiplicity of worldviews in action. In the second step, we are called to engage with the diversity of worldviews at hand, and in the process broaden our own and that of other development agents involved. Thereby, we discover increasingly the large number of individual and collective predispositions to look at reality. Some of these predispositions are so deeply culturally rooted, that they are not seen as a 'relative bias' but rather as an 'absolute fact'. Then communication gets difficult, and artful developmental skills are required.

As we now move on to the four different realms that each human system consists of, take a moment to notice in which of the realms you feel most comfortable. That will give you an initial indication of the composition of your own reality viewpoint, as well as that of your organisation and society.

Whatever your particular calling and challenge, we see you gradually engaging with all four realms of Integral Development.

5.4 Realms: Understanding the Four Transdisciplinary Realms

OVERVIEW: FOUR REALMS WITH FOUR MAIN THEMES AND FOUR CORE VALUES

Each of the four realms is underpinned by a main theme, illustrating the developmental significance of each realm. Furthermore, each realm is oriented towards a core developmental value. Table 5.1 below indicates the main themes and core values.

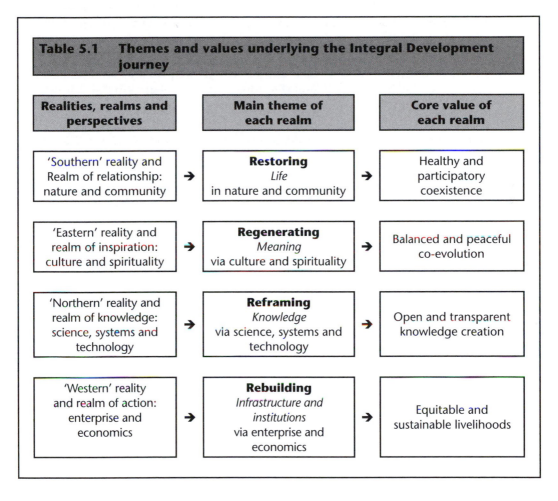

Table 5.1   Themes and values underlying the Integral Development journey

Realities, realms and perspectives	Main theme of each realm	Core value of each realm
'Southern' reality and Realm of relationship: nature and community	**Restoring** *Life* in nature and community	Healthy and participatory coexistence
'Eastern' reality and realm of inspiration: culture and spirituality	**Regenerating** *Meaning* via culture and spirituality	Balanced and peaceful co-evolution
'Northern' reality and realm of knowledge: science, systems and technology	**Reframing** *Knowledge* via science, systems and technology	Open and transparent knowledge creation
'Western' reality and realm of action: enterprise and economics	**Rebuilding** *Infrastructure and institutions* via enterprise and economics	Equitable and sustainable livelihoods

We shall now describe the nature of each realm from a developmental perspective. As we move through the four realms, we not only illustrate how they are transdisciplinary interconnected, but also, how they build on each other.

THE SOUTHERN REALM OF RELATIONSHIP: RESTORING LIFE IN NATURE AND COMMUNITY

For us, the 'Southern' existential grounds of nature and community offer the 'natural' starting point of Integral Development. This is for two reasons. Firstly, the Southern development theme is about 'restoring life in nature and community'. Such prior restoration is required, at least to some degree, at the beginning of the development journey, in order to activate the local transformational energy that is required in the process. Secondly, the 'Southern' grounds represent the concrete context of development to which the concluding development action is supposed to be applied. Hence, we as Integral Developers need to start with acquiring a profound understanding of the development context. We need to connect to it, and thereby get in touch with the interconnectedness of all creation, a core principle of an ecological nature-rooted orientation.

The term 'ecology' includes environmental ecology, as much as human and social ecology. The human species is part of nature, not outside of it. The visual symbol of the 'Southern' realm is the 'web of life'. The human organ is the heart. The corresponding inner capacities that are particularly needed now, are captured by what Daniel Goleman calls 'emotional intelligence'[3] and Howard Gardner terms interpersonal and intrapersonal intelligence.[4] If we translated the Integral Developer's – or Development Agency's – tasks in this 'Southern' realm into music, we think of strong earthy rhythms that we often find in indigenous music. The instruments that come to mind are drums, and indeed, the entire human body, dancing in and with creation, inspired by the rhythm of life.

Table 5.2 Characteristics of the 'Southern' realm of relationship
• *Core Value*: Healthy and participatory coexistence • *Symbol*: Web of life within a circle – representing life and the interdependency of all life, framed in one huge web/the circle alludes to the original oneness of all life, underlying all of creation • *Human Organism/Attribute*: Heart/emotional intelligence/interpersonal and intrapersonal intelligences • *Sound/Music*: Heartbeat/strong earthy rhythms/Indigenous music • *Instrument*: Drums/human body

Usually – and this we see as a fundamental error – the 'Southern' realm of nature and community is not the starting point for most development work. That mirrors a typical human phenomenon: for answers to our personal development needs, we tend to look first at our outer environment rather than within ourselves. Both approaches, inward and outward looking, have their validity and need to be balanced with each other. A temporary emphasis on one may be fine for a short period. The problem starts if one approach dominates the other. From an Integral Development perspective, not accepting any input from outside can be as detrimental as only depending on inside support. In time, the entire human system falls into imbalance. That is the situation we are currently facing in development. Too much of existing development work comes from the outside in. Furthermore, it often arrives by far too early and too forcefully, before an inside-out movement of development has begun, and then gets drowned out. Beginning with the 'Southern' realm means that we firstly seek to activate the local inside-out orientation to development, starting thus with local nature and community.

By starting with the 'Southern' realm of nature and community, we also avoid a common pattern that many of us unconsciously follow, as it is part of our social conditioning of the all-pervasive 'Western way of life'. The pattern is that theories and concepts of development (knowing) and a need to act (doing) come all too often too soon, before we are fully familiarised with the context (being). While knowing and doing provide us with a sense of security (we think we know what we are doing) as well as a sense of progress (let's get going), these habitual responses have caused much harm in development work, and indeed have inhibited individual and collective becoming. Ultimately, these impulses, if not preceded by a thorough exploration of the local context, are self-centred, putting the needs of the external development expert (for knowing better, for measurable results, etc.) in the centre, rather than the needs of the context and people that he or she is supposed to serve.

We are aware that each of us has a natural predisposition to dealing with life's issues. Some of us engage with problems relationally through our network of friends and colleagues. Others begin with reflection, others conceptualise and seek for scientific responses. And others naturally plunge straight into action. There is nothing wrong with any of these response patterns.

However, our suggestion is that we consciously transcend any predisposition, and start with revisiting the grounds of the development context. It is one of the most common mistakes in development, that the development agent (as an individual or as an organisation) misses out on profound and purposeful grounding within the development context. As we as Integral Developers regard ourselves as part of the development context, it implies that we not only revisit our own cultural and societal grounds but also deepen our understanding about ourselves, our motives and motivations with regard to the development work.

The experience of Majid Rahnema strongly supports this starting point as a fresh take on development. For him, a first condition for a new approach to development is to understand the true nature of things, which includes the true nature of ourselves and our own motives. For him, we need 'to look at things as they are, rather than as we want them to be'. It is crucial, Rahnema argues, that 'instead of claiming to be able to change the world and to save "humanity", we rather need to save ourselves from our own compelling need for comforting illusions'. For him:

> the hubris of the modern individual has led him or her to believe that the existential powerlessness of humankind can usefully be replaced with compulsive 'actomania'. This illusion is similar to the modern obsession with fighting death at all costs. Both compulsions tend, in fact, to undermine, disfigure and eventually destroy the only form of power that defines true life. Paradoxically, it is through fully experiencing our powerlessness, as painful as that may be, that it becomes possible for us to be in tune with human suffering, in all its manifestations; to understand the 'power of the powerless' ... and to rediscover our oneness will all those in pain.[5]

Rahnema offers a strong critique of much of today's development work, which he sees as 'wearing the mask of love'. For him it is a mask because:

development incarnated a false love for an abstract humanity, so that it ended up by upsetting the lives of millions of living human beings. For half a century its 'target populations' suffered the intrusion in their lives of an army of development teachers and experts, including well-intentioned field workers and activists, who spoke big words – from conscientisation to learning from and living with the people. Often they had studied Marx, Gramsci, Freire and the latest research about empowerment and participation. However, their lives (and often careers) seldom allowed them to enter the intimate world of their 'target populations'. They were good at giving people passionate lectures about their rights, their entitlements, the class struggle and land reform. Yet few asked themselves about the deeper motivations prompting them to do what they were doing. Often they knew neither the people they were working with, nor themselves. And they were so busy achieving what they thought that had to do for the people, that they could not learn enough from them about how actually to 'care' for them, as they would for their closest relatives and friends whom they knew and loved.[6]

Rahnema's critique affirms us that 'seeing what is' is our starting point. And because of that the 'Southern' realm is the first we engage with.

Table 5.3 below gives an overview on the qualities that are required from the Integral Developer, and, subsequently, from his or her organisation, for engaging with the 'Southern' realm.

Table 5.3 Key qualities required of the Integral Development agent and agency in the 'Southern' realm of relationship
• Ability to observe, empathise and care • Ability to face reality: to describe things as they are, not as one wants them to be • Ability to deeply immerse oneself in a particular natural and communal context • Ability to relate to other human beings/ability to tune into the relational level of existence (including relationship to yourself; relationship with others, in groups, organisations and communities) • Ability to strongly relate to and care for nature and to see relationship and interrelatedness as a core principle in nature • Ability to 'look deep' and to see the generative grounds of a particular context • Trust and love (thus transcending the 'mask of love')

THE EASTERN REALM OF INSPIRATION: REGENERATING MEANING VIA CULTURE AND SPIRITUALITY

Having engaged in rediscovering and restoring the relationship with inner and outer nature and with community, we have created a foundation for further development. We now deal with cultural and spiritual perspectives on development, focusing in particular on the regenerative potential of this realm.

Putting culture and spirituality as an equally relevant realm on the Integral Development map emphasises its significance for all other realms. Nobel laureate in Economics, Amartya Sen stresses that 'cultural liberty is important not only in the cultural sphere, but in the successes and failures in social, political and economic spheres. The different dimensions of human life have strong interrelations. Even poverty, a central economic idea, cannot be adequately understood without bringing in cultural considerations'.[7]

From our experience, this realm is the most neglected and misunderstood in general development work. One may argue, it is also the most intricate, as this realm includes not only an enormous complexity, but is also the most qualitative, inexplicit and intangible, while development so far, like economics, principally relies on tangible, explicit and measurable, quantitative indicators.

The modern social scientist prefers to deal with empirically verifiable data, and hence with countable and measurable phenomena. The rather immeasurable and unquantifiable realm of culture and spirituality is often excluded from empirical studies. Yet it is this realm which is the most personal to every human being, to every organisation, to every community, to every society. Culture is the glue that links people together, the web of meaning that provides interpretation of life and afterlife. It is the pool of shared stories that enables us to relate to each other on a deeper level. The realm of culture and spirituality is a reflection of the level of consciousness of a society and its members.

It does not matter whether you as development actor feel particularly drawn to cultural and spiritual issues. You may even be completely averse to any form of religion and spirituality. But we need to consider that every human being is at least to some degree concerned with the issues that give meaning to his or her life. For most people it is indeed one of the most important questions, if not the most important question, guiding and orienting their lives. Consequently, we need to be able to tune in to the very same question in dialogue with the people, organisations and communities our development work affects. Moreover, a whole society that loses its overall sense of meaning and purpose will ultimately be doomed.

The core value of the 'Eastern' realm of Integral Development is 'balanced and peaceful co-evolution'. The 'Eastern' realm's symbol is the 'spiral of conscious co-evolution'. The human element and inner attributes that are particularly needed now, are the spirit, our inner spiritual force – or, in the terms of Zohar Danar and Ian Marshall: our 'spiritual intelligence'.[8]

If we translated the Integral Developer's task in this 'Eastern' realm into music, we think of very delicate, almost spherical, contemplative tunes, with long periods of silence interspersed with occasionally emergent sounds. The instruments that come to mind are harps, flutes, perhaps even bells, able to transport us into new inner spaces where we can discover ourselves and others anew. Table 5.4 summarises these core characteristics.

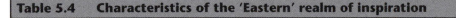

Table 5.4 Characteristics of the 'Eastern' realm of inspiration

- *Core Value*: Balanced and peaceful co-evolution
- *Symbol*: Spiral of conscious co-evolution – represents regeneration and renewal of the cultural and spiritual dimension in humans and society
- *Human Organism/Attribute*: Spirit (supported by heart)/spiritual intelligence
- *Sound/Music*: Stillness or spherical sounds/sounds of emergence/contemplative music
- *Instrument*: Harp/flute/bell

In this 'Eastern' realm we understand culture and spirituality as a living fabric providing shared meaning for those it interconnects. The cultural fabric lives by being continuously renewed by individuals, organisations and communities revisiting its validity and regenerating new meaning adequate for each period.

Here, we recognise the dual potential of culture. As a constructive force, it functions as an evolutionary, developmental agent, providing a space for rich interaction, introspection, imagination and renewal. As a destructive force it functions as an ossifying agent, stifling the development of society, by being reduced to superficial and meaningless rituals, repetition and dogma, while avoiding and even prohibiting any critical interaction with it, from the inside and outside.

Every culture ossifies when its evolution is suspended. And it stops evolving, when critical and creative impulses of renewal from within and without are inhibited. We can easily recognise this phenomenon in our personal context. When we experience a person insisting on his or her own interpretation of a particular matter, without allowing others to challenge his or her thinking, the creative flow within human interaction comes to a halt.

The same happens on a societal level. When a whole culture, religion, philosophical or spiritual system regards itself as superior, and as a consequence shuts itself off from other cultural influences, or even seeks to oppress other cultures considered inferior, the process of co-evolution between cultures comes to a halt, or never even begins. So too, if a culture is oppressed and comes to see itself as inferior to other cultures, as often happened during colonialism, it can also lead to ossification and alienation. In the long run, we argue, this is to the detriment of both, the oppressed and the oppressing culture.

Hence in this realm, we are not only seeking to identify and reactivate the meaning giving reservoir that culture and spirituality provide to the individual, organisation, community or society, but, even more importantly, we seek to articulate the creative potential that lies in the interaction between individuals, between organisations, between communities and between one society and another, when these diverse cultures and spiritualities meet and communicate with each other.

In our current day and age the principle of co-evolution will be of rising importance. Living in a 'globalised world', our human fate will depend on whether we are able to peacefully co-evolve with each other, giving each individual, and each society its particular place among equals. The principle of co-evolution emphasises the uniqueness of every individual and his or her path, as well as of each society and its culture and spiritual values. We have dealt with the societal-cultural level intensely in *Integral Dynamics*.[9] Only if these unique creative sources are kept alive through a process of mutual respect and purposeful co-evolution, can our collective potential to renew ourselves as a species, be released.

It is for this reason that we are sceptical of the image of a 'global village' as it tends to gloss over the rich cultural and spiritual diversity of our planet. Instead of 'unity in conformity' we need to foster 'unity in diversity', where each individual, each village, each society contributes through its own creativity and uniqueness, through its own culture and spirituality to the peaceful co-evolution of all.

It is also for that reason that we like to think of our time as a trans-modern time, transcending earlier notions of modernity and postmodernity. The 'trans' puts the emphasis on 'the space in between': between you and me, between organisations, between societies. Given the deadlock human civilisation as a whole seems to be in, the 'in between' is the unknown space that we need to enter to make the required evolutionary steps. Entering the 'trans' requires us to let go of some of the old, in order to renew ourselves.

The 'Eastern' cultural and spiritual realm is probably the most challenging for us as Integral Developers, as we are likely to be confronted with a letting go of some of our initial development beliefs.

We conclude by indicating the key qualities that are required of any Integral Development agent or agency in this 'Eastern' integral realm.

Table 5.5 Key qualities required of the Integral Development agent and agency in the 'Eastern' realm of inspiration
• Listening (picking up the implicit, behind the explicit messages) • Reflective, intuitive and pattern-seeking mind • Will and ability to grow in consciousness • Ability to enter unknown, unfamiliar spaces • Ability to engage with the cultural and spiritual dynamics of a particular place • Ability to question and to let go of some of one's own convictions and beliefs • Openness for surprising Insights, and emerging patterns of culture • Ability to co-evolve with others, and to be a catalyst for the evolution of others • Ability to envision and to imagine the new, emerging dialectically out of the old • Faith in oneself and others

THE NORTHERN REALM OF KNOWLEDGE: REFRAMING KNOWLEDGE VIA SCIENCE, SYSTEMS AND TECHNOLOGY

We now enter the 'Northern' realm and its core perspectives of science, systems and technology.

The sheer quantity of development literature that has been published in this 'Northern' realm also reflects the emphasis that is given to the intellect and mind, to science and technology in dealing with development. This is not only true for societal development, but equally for individual and organisational development. Typically, if we face development problems, we lean towards getting a fast expert opinion, an established roadmap, or a tool that has already been created and applied elsewhere.

How detrimental this one-sided focus on science, systems and technology has been for development at large is expressed by Jan Nederveen Pieterse, Professor for Globalisation and Sociology at the University of California in Santa Barbara:

> *Modern development has suffered from a severe case of 'psychological modernism', placing technological progress over human development. In Latin America, the work of the cientificos is not yet complete. In Asia, 'laboratory states' have used science as an instrument of power and reason of state ... Even critical Marxist development thinking has been 'scientist' in temperament. As 'science became the integrating myth of industrial society' ... so it became the guiding light of development policy. Rationalisation became the key to modernisation, so it became the master key to development.*[10]

From our integral perspective we argue that much of those over-rationalistic, one-sidedly 'Northern' perspectives miss the link to the 'Southern' and 'Eastern' realms. Isolated from particular contexts, these theories tend toward a high level of abstraction, with often little concrete relevance for people and community on the ground. It is for that reason that this 'Northern' realm sets out to reconnect science, systems and technology driven approaches to development with the other three vectors of our integral model. In touch with 'Southern' nature and community as well as with 'Eastern' culture and spirituality, such reconnected 'North' is invaluable, as we shall see, for individual, organisational, and societal learning and knowledge creation.

One of the challenges of this 'Northern' realm is to create an environment for 'open and transparent knowledge creation', the principle value of this realm. Thereby, narrow and abstract disciplinary perspectives can be transcended into useful transdisciplinary knowledge, relevant for the enormous complexity inherent to most development contexts.

The symbol of the 'Northern' realm is a 'grid of knowledge'. The human organism and inner attributes that are particularly relevant now, are the mind and our analytical intelligence, though in close connection with our emotional and spiritual intelligence. If we translated the Integral Developer's – or development agency's – tasks in this 'Northern' realm into music, we think of complex, solid structures, like that of an entire symphony. Also, we now envision a full ensemble, an orchestra, that gives space to the talent and distinctiveness of each instrument and musician, and that is able to integrate them all into coherent rhythms and melodies. Table 5.6 summarises the key characteristics of the 'Northern' realm.

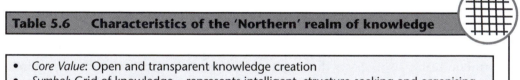

Table 5.6   Characteristics of the 'Northern' realm of knowledge

- *Core Value*: Open and transparent knowledge creation
- *Symbol*: Grid of knowledge – represents intelligent, structure-seeking and organising processes of knowledge creation
- *Human Organism/Attribute*: Mind/intelligence (supported by spirit and heart)
- *Sound/Music*: Symphony/complex, highly structured music
- *Core Instruments*: Symphony orchestra

We conclude by indicating the key qualities that are required of the Integral Development agent and agency in this 'Northern' realm.

Table 5.7	Key qualities required of the Integral Development agent and agency in the 'Northern' realm of knowledge

- Conceptual and analytical strength
- Ability to share knowledge in the context of teamwork
- Ability to translate strong cultural Images into concepts and theories
- Ability to deal with complexity
- Some playfulness/ability to let go of useless thoughts
- Intellectual explorer, adventurer of the mind
- Ability to articulate and communicate new thoughts

THE WESTERN REALM OF ACTION: REBUILDING INFRASTRUCTURE AND INSTITUTIONS VIA ENTERPRISE AND ECONOMICS

By engaging in developmental practice, our ultimate objective in this 'Western' realm is to contribute to 'equitable and sustainable livelihoods'. Having travelled through the 'Southern', 'Eastern', and 'Northern' realms, our very understanding of life has almost certainly changed. It has grown and expanded. Certainly, the 'Western' realm is not about livelihoods from a merely economic perspective. While enterprise and economics are the practical outlets, into which our new developmental practice is inserted, it has nevertheless become by now a fully integral realm, that is infused with nature and community, culture and spirituality, as well as science, systems and technology.

The orientation of the 'West' is that of building and renewing infrastructure and institutions. It is important to revisit the terms of 'infrastructure' and 'institutions' in an integral manner. Infrastructure is not merely to be understood as new physical infrastructure, in terms of, for example, transport systems, ICT equipment or energy grids. Nor are institutions just to be understood as outer institutions, such as organisations in brick-and-mortar buildings. Again, it would need to equally embrace the natural, communal (or social), cultural, spiritual, scientific and technological infrastructure and institutions – each not in isolation, but as design patterns, as 'intra-structure' (internal structures) and inner institutional base. The inner and outer design patterns then mutually inform and strengthen each other. To some degree, the new material designs – physical infrastructures and institutions – are then something like a natural derivative of a profound developmental process that has come before. Furthermore, such an inner and outer process towards new infrastructure and institutions will have to straddle the individual, organisational and societal levels, altogether. On an individual level, for example, we would need to find out what kind of inner and outer infrastructure and institutional base provides the living platform for the active development of individuals – again, integrating all three prior realms, thereby providing for a fully 'rounded' life.

This is a radical departure from today's practice, where community based and cultural infrastructure and institutions are often left behind. In addition, most of the technological, political, and economic infrastructure and institutions within so-called developing countries are often imitated or imported from the so-called 'developed' West. Much of these infrastructure and institutions are highly dysfunctional, lacking any traces of originality. The latter we can notice most poignantly on our travels – when airports, banks, malls, supermarkets, hotels and even restaurants in foreign countries often look homogenised and lack any local flavour. One could be anywhere. Even the language used – English – has become 'globalised', often in a highly abbreviated, almost mutilated way – only the accents vary. Despite outer busyness, activity and liveliness, we feel somehow alienated. Something is missing, and it is not easy to articulate what this is.

From our integral perspective, we would say, that we can't see any more the original nature and social fabric of the people, their particular culture and spirituality, their own knowledge sources and wisdom shining through the outer layer of a life, that has been absorbed by intense, but one-sided economic activities, with often dysfunctional enterprises, economic and political systems benefiting an 'elite' that is enjoying the material fruits of unequally distributed economic wealth.

Integral Development seeks to look at enterprise and economics anew, in a way that the other realms do richly shine through, so that the outer manifestations of a community or society is comprised of the whole diversity of human life. We see such an approach also as key to genuine sustainability. All integral realms profoundly need each other for their own evolution, and for the ability of each to contribute to the whole.

As we travel through the 'Western' realm (⇨19 to 22), we need to have such an expanded perspective of life in mind, so that we can build new infrastructure and institutions that are able to support and serve to transform all aspects of life.

The symbol for the Western realm is the 'arrow of integrated action'. The human 'organ' and inner attributes that are particularly required now, are our active and practical hand, guided by focused determination to actively contribute to the development context what we are lodged in. If we tried to translate the Integral Developer's – and development agency's – tasks in this 'Western' realm into music, we would compare it with that of a group of jazz musicians, who, together explore new rhythms, discover new patterns and co-create new structures. Instruments that come to mind are, for example, saxophones and clarinets: expressive and articulate they weave together new musical patterns and structures. We now summarise the characteristics of the 'Western' realm of action.

Table 5.8 Characteristics of the 'Western' realm of action
• *Core Value*: Equitable and sustainable livelihoods • *Symbol*: Arrow of integrated action – represents focus, goal-oriented, co-creative realisation of a new Development Impulse through actively building new infrastructure and institutions • *Human Organism/Attributes*: Hand (supported by mind, spirit and heart) • *Sound/Music*: Jazz (exploring new patterns; co-creating new structures) • *Instrument*: Jazz combo (clarinet, saxophone, cello, etc.)

We conclude this sub-chapter on realms by indicating the key qualities that are required of the Integral Developer and Development Agency in this 'Western' integral realm.

Table 5.9   Key qualities required of the Integral Development agent and agency in the 'Western' realm of action

- Ability to co-create and to team up with others
- Ability to translate knowledge into capacities, and capacities into action
- Strong project management skills
- Ability to construct an appropriate form to fulfil a specified function
- Focus and determination to make a tangible contribution
- Stamina and willingness to face and overcome obstacles on the way
- Strong communication skills
- Humility to see one's own work share as a contribution to a larger project

---

POLITICS WITHIN INTEGRAL DEVELOPMENT

You may have been wondering, why we have not identified 'politics' as a separate realm. After all, it is an important function within society, and, together with business, undoubtedly the most powerful societal sector. Furthermore, the political caste forms the government, and governments issue development strategies and policies – for their own countries, and, in the case of so-called developed countries also for others. If that was not enough of an argument, just observe how strongly politicised development agendas are, and so are the most influential development institutions of the world, such as the World Bank and the IMF. So why have we not articulated this important function as yet?

We have thought long and hard about it. The deeper we went into this question, the more we understood politics as an 'embedded function' permeating all realms. In other words, in our attempt to rebuilding human development, bottom-up, we have located politics – as a design and governing function – in all developmental realms. Our approach to development, that potentially sees everyone and every organisation as an Integral Development agent or agency, can't possibly delegate the political function to one realm alone.

As we begin our journey through the realms in the 'Southern' realm of 'Nature and Community', we can't possibly ignore the political dimension within communities. Equally, 'Northern' science, technology and systems, are strongly affected by politics, and so are frameworks for 'Western' enterprise and economics. And even the 'Eastern' cultural and spiritual realm is strongly influenced by politics, though often more on an implicit rather than explicit level.

While we acknowledge the presence of politics in all realms, we equally invite it – as a function – on all levels (or rounds) of society. As we work ourselves through the rounds of individual, organisation, community and society development, we gradually strengthen the ability to 'self-govern' – on all levels. Thereby, we see ourselves altogether contributing to more mature political systems, where responsibility for 'engaged governance' is not delegated to a few individuals, but rather carried by a large part of society in a participatory manner.

In the overview to the four realms we introduced their main themes and core values. Returning to them, we can now understand politics *anew* as a function integrated in all realms that simultaneously 'enables, catalyses, governs and institutionalises' the realisation of the four core values. These core values can equally be understood as political principles that together cover all realms of society and constitute essential pillars of a healthy society. One may well call such an integrated approach to politics 'Integral Politics'. The concluding table is highlighting this point.

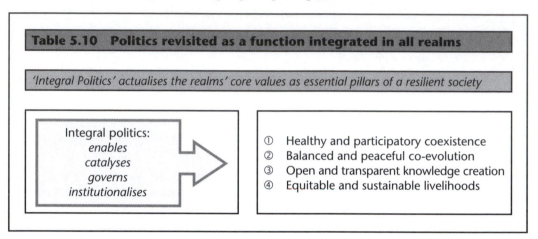

Table 5.10   Politics revisited as a function integrated in all realms

'Integral Politics' actualises the realms' core values as essential pillars of a resilient society

Integral politics:
enables
catalyses
governs
institutionalises

① Healthy and participatory coexistence
② Balanced and peaceful co-evolution
③ Open and transparent knowledge creation
④ Equitable and sustainable livelihoods

5.5   Rounds: Straddling All Four Transpersonal Rounds

OVERVIEW

Having deepened our understanding of the four realms we now move to the four levels of self, organisation, society and world. As we explained earlier (⇨4), we call these four levels 'rounds'. We now introduce all four rounds, though only briefly, as they are self-explanatory.

ROUND 1: SELF DEVELOPMENT

In Round 1 we explore the individual development perspective. This, we assert, is the fundamental starting point. We concur with Rahnema that the development agent needs to first have a thoroughgoing understanding of his or her own development process, before engaging with the outer development task at hand. However, as no development process occurs in isolation, but always in interaction with context and people, we already reach out to the 'other', thereby creating an opening towards Round 2.

ROUND 2: ORGANISATIONAL DEVELOPMENT

Once firmly grounded in individual development processes, we explore in this second round the relevance of the integral realm's core theme on an organisational level. Thereby we not only 'collect' valuable learnings and refined developmental approaches that exist on that level, we also expand our own sphere of influence. This second round forms the bridge between Round 1 and Round 3, enabling us as Integral Developers to carry forward our own development work into the organisational sphere, as our radius of understanding and action grows.

ROUND 3: SOCIETAL DEVELOPMENT

It is only in Round 3 that we actually deal with community and society, the general focus of conventional development theory and practice. By now we have built up our development understanding and capacities with the help of the two prior rounds. Each round includes the prior round(s); thus as Integral Developers we are from the very beginning an intimate particle of the development process and context. That reemphasises our understanding of development as 'co-development'. Rather than development 'of' others, 'for' others or 'by' others, we are committed to co-develop in close interaction 'with' others. The development process is always also developing the developer. Development within the integral framework is always co-evolution.

ROUND 4: GLOBAL, UNIVERSAL PERSPECTIVE – DEVELOPMENT THROUGH A UNI-VERSITY

Round 4 requires some more explanation. On the one hand, the global perspective follows naturally from the societal perspective. On the other hand, the 'global' comes all too often too quickly to our lips. However, dealing with the totality is not only an impossible task (as we have seen in the past), it is also, in most cases, an imposing one. A global perspective can only be developed by all participants of the 'global choir'.

It is for that reason that we see the global, universal contribution of this fourth round in a perhaps surprising new light. We propose to 'universalise' our Integral Development through what we call 'Uni-Versities'. Concretely, the Integral Development journey leads to the set-up of new educational-developmental spaces that enable individual-organisational-societal development, locally and globally. By doing so, newly conceived and integrated development theory and practice becomes 'universalised'. That can happen, so our argument, because such new theory and practice grew out of and remain relevant for one's own 'universe', personally, institutionally, communally, and can as well contribute to global knowledge and practice. On that global, universal level, however, this contribution becomes one of many integral voices, each born out of locally relevant and resonant new theory and practice. Thereby, we evoke the rich diversity of an integral 'choir of societies', rather than falling back into the old trap of promoting merely one global view. How then do we activate such a 'universal' process?

5.6   Rhythms: Activating Fourfold Transformational Rhythms

A TRANSFORMATIVE RHYTHM WITHIN EACH REALM

The fourfold developmental rhythms underlying our integral approach serve to activate the Integral Development process. This takes place in the following ways *within* each realm:

- The GENE rhythm (⇨4) functions as our core rhythm, with its core elements of grounding, emerging, navigating and effecting.

- It is underpinned by a cyclical rhythm, supporting transformative developmental processes in human systems, including the four stages of formative, reformative, newly normative and transformative development.
- Altogether, these rhythms are aligned with the four rounds of development: self, organisation, society, Uni-Versity.

That leads to the following rhythmical perspective (see Table 5.11 below):

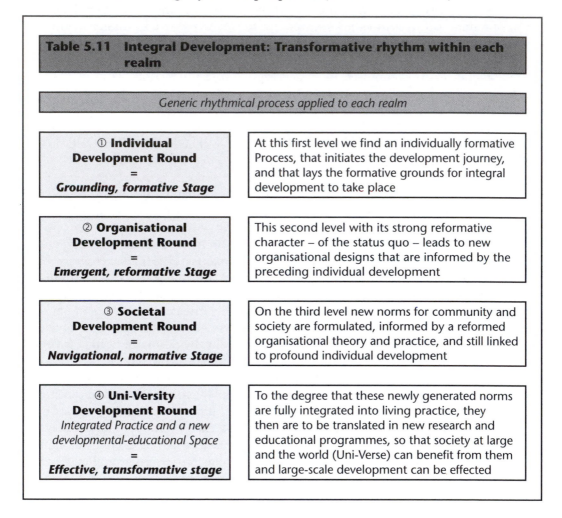

Table 5.11 Integral Development: Transformative rhythm within each realm

Generic rhythmical process applied to each realm

① **Individual Development Round** = *Grounding, formative Stage*	At this first level we find an individually formative Process, that initiates the development journey, and that lays the formative grounds for integral development to take place
② **Organisational Development Round** = *Emergent, reformative Stage*	This second level with its strong reformative character – of the status quo – leads to new organisational designs that are informed by the preceding individual development
③ **Societal Development Round** = *Navigational, normative Stage*	On the third level new norms for community and society are formulated, informed by a reformed organisational theory and practice, and still linked to profound individual development
④ **Uni-Versity Development Round** *Integrated Practice and a new developmental-educational Space* = *Effective, transformative stage*	To the degree that these newly generated norms are fully integrated into living practice, they then are to be translated in new research and educational programmes, so that society at large and the world (Uni-Verse) can benefit from them and large-scale development can be effected

A TRANSFORMATIVE RHYTHM CONNECTING ALL REALMS

The transformative rhythm within each realm is mirrored by a transformative rhythm connecting all four realms. Such inter-realm rhythm straddles all four realms, aligned with the four reality viewpoints (worldviews). Again the GENE is applied:

- *Grounding:* Within the realm of relationship and its perspectives of nature and community, aligned with a 'Southern' view on reality.

- *Emergence:* Through the realm of inspiration and its perspectives of culture and spirituality, aligned with an 'Eastern' view on reality.
- *Navigation:* Via the realm of knowledge and its perspectives of science, systems and technology, aligned with a 'Northern' view on reality.
- *Effect:* In the realm of action and its perspectives of enterprise and economics, aligned with a 'Western' view on reality.

Table 5.12 Integral Development: Inter-realm-and-reality-rhythm			
Generic rhythmical processes applied in between all realms			
Realities			
Southern	Eastern	Northern	Western
Realms and perspectives			
Realm of relationship: nature and community	Realm of inspiration: culture and spirituality	Realm of knowledge: science, systems and technology	Realm of action: enterprise and economics
Inter-realm-and-reality-rhythm			
Grounding	*Emerging*	*Navigating*	*Effecting*

Altogether the Intra-Realm Rhythms and the Inter-Realm-and-Reality Rhythms 'activate' the Integral Development model. When we come to providing orientation maps for your journey through the integral territory in the following chapter, you will notice that the Intra-Realm Rhythms will 'activate' the vertical axis of the map, whereby the Inter-Realm-and-Reality Rhythm 'activate' its horizontal axis.

Altogether the rhythms activate not only each of the other three '*Rs*' – realities, realms and rounds – they thereby also connect dynamically (transformatively, transculturally, transdisciplinarily, transpersonally) the inner core (your calling and challenge) with the local context and global setting. Having looked now at all components of Integral Development in details, we are ready to conclude.

5.7   Integration

In this chapter we introduced you to the core components of Integral Development, which are all dynamically interconnected.

The initiation of the Integral Development process is to be found in a particular individual or collective calling and challenge, lodged within a specific local context and framed by an overall global setting. To come up with an integrated, sustainable response to such calling and challenge, the Integral Developer is required to engage with the so-called '4Rs': transcultural realities (worldviews), transdisciplinary realms (knowledge fields), transpersonal rounds (levels) and transformational rhythms.

All '4Rs' relate to the development issue at hand, which is evoked by the inner core of our circular model. In this inner core we find the particular 'calling and challenge' of the Integral Developer. It is articulated as a deep concern for a profoundly perceived and highly challenging imbalance, and as an inner calling to respond to that challenge. Such calling and challenge are then exposed to diverse reality viewpoints and to all four realms, as well as taken through all four levels (rounds). That takes place in a rhythmic and spiralling manner, following the composite GENE-rhythms – with a view to releasing individual and collective Gene-ius. This we believe is real, authentic development – Integral Development.

Following an evolutionary understanding of life and world, the development process never ends. Certain imbalances will continue to occur naturally, and equally naturally they are continuously readdressed. In an ever-changing, ever-unfolding world, where actors and issues change as much as the local contexts in which they are lodged we have no other choice, but to see this process as one of individual and collective responsibility. The global view, in our case a combination of all worlds, is of equal importance as the local perspective in a sense, that each local context is dependent on its interaction with other contexts for its own evolution. Furthermore, each local context sees itself as an integral and contributing part of the global reality all contexts share.

At the end of this chapter, we reflect again on the guiding question and thoughts presented in this chapter. What did the overall framework make you think? And to what degree do you see it guiding your action as an Integral Developer?

Table 5.13   Main task: Discover the Integral Development framework

Guiding question	Guiding thoughts	Reflect and act ... What do I and we have to do as Integral Developers?
What are the main components of the Integral Development approach and how does it work?	Integral Development builds on the overarching Integral Worlds framework The inner core of the model with a particular calling and challenge within a specific context initiates the process Then, the Integral Developer is required to engage with the '4Rs': Realities, Realms, Rounds and Rhythms – to bring about Integral Development	• What is your particular development 'calling' and 'challenge'? What are those of your organisation, your community and potentially even your society? How are they interrelated? • Describe your specific local context and the overall global setting in which your calling and challenge is lodged • Describe the '4Rs' of Integral Development in your own words and illustrate how they are interconnected • With regards to your development calling and challenge, which of the '4Rs' have been overlooked hitherto, and within the realms, which of the realms have been rather neglected in the past?

We shall now take on the necessary processes that help you navigate the Integral Development terrain.

References

1   Gangadean, A. (1998). *Between Worlds: The Emergence of Global Reason*. New York: Peter Lang.

2   Gangadean, A. (12 October 2004). *Note on Educational Policy Regarding South Asian Studies*. Awakening Mind Portal. Available at: www.awakeningmind.org.

3   Goleman, D. (1996). *Emotional Intelligence: Why it Can Matter More than IQ*. London: Bloomsbury.

4   Gardner, H. (2011). *Frames of Mind: The Theory of Multiple Intelligences*. New York: Basic Books.

5   Rahnema, M. (1997). Towards Post-Development: Searching for Signposts, a New Language and New Paradigms. In: Rahnema, M. and Bawtree, V. (eds), *The Post-Development Reader*. London: Zed, p. 392.

6   Rahnema, M. (1997). Towards Post-Development: Searching for Signposts, a New Language and New Paradigms. In: Rahnema, M. and Bawtree, V. (eds), *The Post-Development Reader*. London: Zed, p. 392.

7   Sen, A. (2004). Cultural Liberty and Human Development. In: *Human Development Report 2004*. New York: UNDP, p. 13.

8   Danar, Z. and Marshall, I. (2001). *Spiritual Intelligence: The Ultimate Intelligence*. London: Bloomsbury.

9   Lessem, R., Schieffer, A., Tong, J. and Rima, S. (2013). *Integral Dynamics: Political Economy, Cultural Dynamics and the Future of the University*. Farnham: Gower.

10 Nederveen Pieterse, J. (1999). Critical Holism and the Tao of Development. In: Munck, R. and O'Hearn, D. *Critical Development Theory: Contributions to a New Paradigm*. London: Zed, p. 72. Note: Nederveen Pieterse refers in his quotation also to other authors, namely Shiv Visvanathan and Morris Berman.

6 Compass and Map: The Integral Development Journey

Guiding Question: How does Integral Development work?

6.1 Orientation

As you embark on the Integral Development journey you will engage with all its interactive components. Depending on your very particular 'calling and challenge', you will naturally put more emphasis on certain elements as opposed to others. Yet, operating within an overall integral framework, you are continuously and dynamically invited to integrate diverse viewpoints and knowledge fields. Furthermore, as our approach has a strong holographic character whereby its integral realities, realms, rhythms and rounds mirror each other throughout, you almost automatically engage with the integral perspective, even if you have decided to zoom in, say, into one particular knowledge field.

In other words, whatever your particular calling and challenge, any given development issue is to be looked at integrally. While a particular issue may have its primary home in one of the four main realms – say, for example, currency instability may be primarily seen as an economic issue – the Integral Development framework would require you to deal with the issue: (a) from a particular reality; (b) via all four key realms; (c) adopting a fully integral rhythm; and (d) adopting individual, organisational and societal rounds, ultimately contributing to new global perspectives.

We understand the Integral Development journey primarily as an inside out process. As we jointly reconfigure development, you yourself, and the developmental issues you identify and seek to address, are the starting point. However, you will not stay on that individual level, but gradually broaden your perspective, from self-knowledge, to organisational knowledge, to a deeper understanding of the community and society, in which you are lodged, and to which your development work is supposed to contribute.

Integral Development further proposes that you begin your travels with the 'Southern' and 'Eastern' realms, as both realms represent the more implicit, more inner (and if you want: more local) dimensions of a human system. The reconfiguration of development work is thereby firmly lodged in a deep understanding of a particular natural, community-based, cultural and spiritual real-life context, before we move to more abstract scientific, systems-oriented, technological, and economic responses to the context at hand.

Progressing inside out and beginning in the 'South' and 'East' also helps us to deal step by step with the full complexity of Integral Development. Also, to keep focus, we root each particular development impulse firmly in a particular individual and his/her specific organisational-communal-societal context.

This implies a dramatic shift of responsibility. The responsibility in an Integral Development paradigm lies not any longer primarily with abstract political systems, economics, science and technology. Rather the responsibility for development lies with the people living within a particular context who see a need or follow a desire for development. The process, we are proposing, increases the 'response-ability' of each individual development agent.

For your journey through the complex terrain of Integral Development you will need a compass and a couple of key maps. The compass will help you not to lose sight of the destination while the maps will strengthen your orientation as you travel the territory.

Once you are equipped with compass and maps you are almost 'ready to go'! Before you 'take off', though, we introduce you at the end of this chapter to what we call a 'Uni-Versity'. Here we briefly intimate the transformative educational space that we see as the major institutionalised vehicle for the Integral Development process. With the 'Uni-Versity' we depart fully from the conventional notion of a university – and have put in its place new forms of collective learning, research and innovation of local relevance, global resonance, that is transcultural, transdisciplinary, transformational and transpersonal. The 'universal significance' of the 'Uni-Versity' lies in its 'unity-in-variety', not in its mere universalism. In this chapter, we shall only provide a first taste of such 'Uni-Versities', which you will then experience, in theory and practice, in the chapters that follow.

We now turn to compass and maps.

6.2　The Compass: Journeying with a Fourfold Purpose

The core values indicate – in broad yet inspiring terms – the 'destination', if you like. It is not, of course, a final destination, as there are no finite states, in an ever unfolding, living world. However, these values strengthen our sense of purpose and provide us with a firm goal to contribute to their actualisation within ourselves, our organisations, our communities, our societies, our world.

Figure 6.1, opposite, translates the main themes and core values into the integral model, equipping us with a veritable compass.

6.3　Key Maps: Charting the Integral Development Terrain

INTRODUCTION: THE MAPS ARE NOT THE TERRITORY

The maps that we introduce here are designed to support your orientation in the Integral Development terrain. They present our very best effort to provide insights on every step on your journey. They guide you towards stimulating theory and practice. But these maps are not static. While the underlying integral design of the maps has profound roots, the surface theories and practice introduced change much faster over time. Hence, one thing is important to keep in mind: the maps *are* not the territory. They provide signposts,

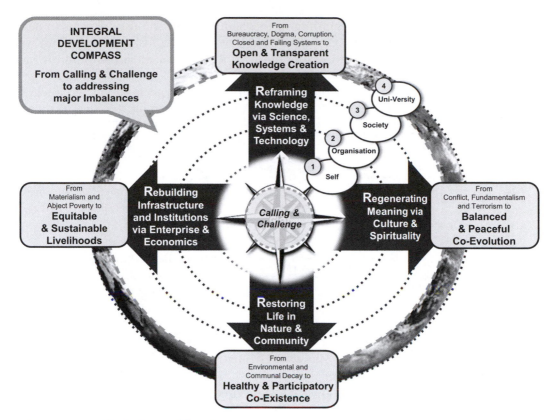

Figure 6.1   The Integral Development compass

though, towards dealing with the multiple challenges that you will encounter on your journey. To deal with these challenges, your own knowledge, experiences and reflections are as important, as well as new theories and practices that you discover on the way.

MAP 1: OVERVIEW OF CORE CHAPTERS UNDERLYING THE INTEGRAL DEVELOPMENT JOURNEY

Each of the four following parts of this book is dedicated to one realm. Each realm-part is then divided in four chapters, following simultaneously the four rounds (self, organisation, society, Uni-Versity) and the major rhythms of the book (formative grounding, reformative emergence, newly normative navigation and transformative effect). That sums up to a total of 16 chapters that together provide orientation in the integral terrain. Map 1 (Figure 6.2), on the next page, illustrates the structure of the integral terrain.

MAP 2: THE ENGAGEMENT MAP WITH GUIDING QUESTIONS

Each of the four levels of each realm is guided by a question or a set of questions. The theory pieces that follow are not to be seen as definite answers to the questions, but as inspirations on the development journey. The ensemble of all questions can be seen as an 'Engagement Map' for us as Integral Developers.

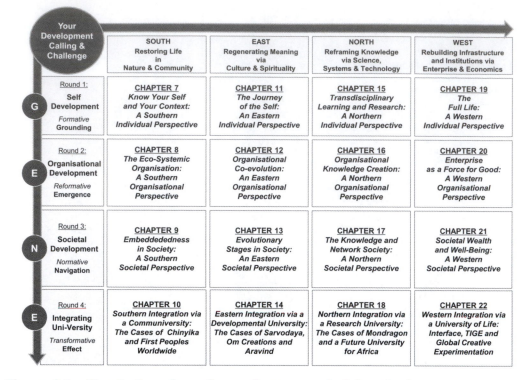

Your Development Calling & Challenge	SOUTH Restoring Life in Nature & Community	EAST Regenerating Meaning via Culture & Spirituality	NORTH Reframing Knowledge via Science, Systems & Technology	WEST Rebuilding Infrastructure and Institutions via Enterprise & Economics
Round 1: **G** Self Development *Formative Grounding*	**CHAPTER 7** *Know Your Self and Your Context: A Southern Individual Perspective*	**CHAPTER 11** *The Journey of the Self: An Eastern Individual Perspective*	**CHAPTER 15** *Transdisciplinary Learning and Research: A Northern Individual Perspective*	**CHAPTER 19** *The Full Life: A Western Individual Perspective*
Round 2: **E** Organisational Development *Reformative Emergence*	**CHAPTER 8** *The Eco-Systemic Organisation: A Southern Organisational Perspective*	**CHAPTER 12** *Organisational Co-evolution: An Eastern Organisational Perspective*	**CHAPTER 16** *Organisational Knowledge Creation: A Northern Organisational Perspective*	**CHAPTER 20** *Enterprise as a Force for Good: A Western Organisational Perspective*
Round 3: **N** Societal Development *Normative Navigation*	**CHAPTER 9** *Embeddededness in Society: A Southern Societal Perspective*	**CHAPTER 13** *Evolutionary Stages in Society: An Eastern Societal Perspective*	**CHAPTER 17** *The Knowledge and Network Society: A Northern Societal Perspective*	**CHAPTER 21** *Societal Wealth and Well-Being: A Western Societal Perspective*
Round 4: **E** Integrating Uni-Versity *Transformative Effect*	**CHAPTER 10** *Southern Integration via a Communiversity: The Cases of Chinyika and First Peoples Worldwide*	**CHAPTER 14** *Eastern Integration via a Developmental University: The Cases of Sarvodaya, Om Creations and Aravind*	**CHAPTER 18** *Northern Integration via a Research University: The Cases of Mondragon and a Future University for Africa*	**CHAPTER 22** *Western Integration via a University of Life: Interface, TIGE and Global Creative Experimentation*

Figure 6.2   Map 1: Overview of core chapters underlying the journey

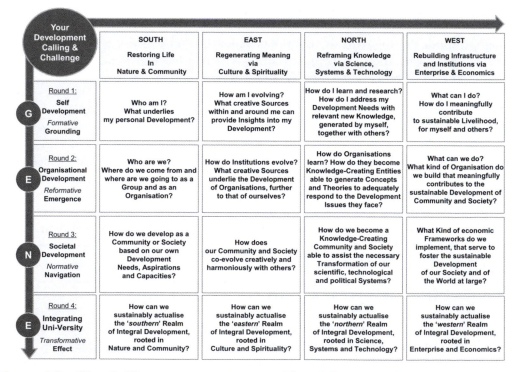

Your Development Calling & Challenge	SOUTH Restoring Life In Nature & Community	EAST Regenerating Meaning via Culture & Spirituality	NORTH Reframing Knowledge via Science, Systems & Technology	WEST Rebuilding Infrastructure and Institutions via Enterprise & Economics
Round 1: **G** Self Development *Formative Grounding*	Who am I? What underlies my personal Development?	How am I evolving? What creative Sources within and around me can provide Insights into my Development?	How do I learn and research? How do I address my Development Needs with relevant new Knowledge, generated by myself, together with others?	What can I do? How do I meaningfully contribute to sustainable Livelihood, for myself and others?
Round 2: **E** Organisational Development *Reformative Emergence*	Who are we? Where do we come from and where are we going to as a Group and as an Organisation?	How do Institutions evolve? What creative Sources underlie the Development of Organisations, further to that of ourselves?	How do Organisations learn? How do they become Knowledge-Creating Entities able to generate Concepts and Theories to adequately respond to the Development Issues they face?	What can we do? What kind of Organisation do we build that meaningfully contributes to the sustainable Development of Community and Society?
Round 3: **N** Societal Development *Normative Navigation*	How do we develop as a Community or Society based on our own Development Needs, Aspirations and Capacities?	How does our Community and Society co-evolve creatively and harmoniously with others?	How do we become a Knowledge-Creating Community and Society able to assist the necessary Transformation of our scientific, technological and political Systems?	What Kind of economic Frameworks do we implement, that serve to foster the sustainable Development of our Society and of the World at large?
Round 4: **E** Integrating Uni-Versity *Transformative Effect*	How can we sustainably actualise the 'southern' Realm of Integral Development, rooted in Nature and Community?	How can we sustainably actualise the 'eastern' Realm of Integral Development, rooted in Culture and Spirituality?	How can we sustainably actualise the 'northern' Realm of Integral Development, rooted in Science, Systems and Technology?	How can we sustainably actualise the 'western' Realm of Integral Development, rooted in Enterprise and Economics?

Figure 6.3   Map 2: The engagement map with guiding questions

The questions asked are opening queries to spur exploration and initiate the respective development process on each level. Each of you is invited to add questions, to broaden the scope of exploration. This is crucial as each of you not only brings a knowledge base and practical experience, as well as cultural and societal conditioning – but also, even more important, every development context is different and its specific constellation varies in space and time.

The engagement map with guiding questions can be seen in Figure 6.3).

MAP 3: THE THOUGHT-AND-ACTION MAP WITH GUIDING THEORY AND PRACTICE

Throughout the 16 chapters, we offer perspectives for all of the guiding questions with the help of a wide range of respected thinkers and innovative practitioners. Again, these theories and practical cases are to be regarded as starting points, road signs, pointers, inspirations, and 'challengers' of our own development thinking and they have to be individually assimilated and adapted to each of our specific development contexts. Further, as the body of theory evolves and grows over time, the space that the Integral Development framework offers, is to be seen as an open space, not only to be shaped, flexed, and widened by all of us collectively, thereby making the framework and underlying process ever more resilient and reliable.

In each realm, we present respected thinkers dealing with the development of self, organisation, community and society, all of them innovators in their field. We have carefully selected those thinkers from the vast field of human development who recognise the interdependency of those levels or rounds, and who also reach beyond the particular realm in which we positioned them. In other words: most of the thinkers and theories introduced already have some kind of integral edge to them. Move have transcended their own discipline and positioned themselves in transdisciplinary guise. Therefore, the overlapping of theories is intentional. They form the necessary bridges within and between the four integral realms.

It is for that reason that the reader will find many cross connections between the diverse theories and between theory and practice, across all realms. Within the rich diversity of the presented approaches, we found fascinating 'integral resonance'. In each of the four realms you will encounter reverberations of all other realms. That refers to a core thread of the emergent integral paradigm: the whole can be found in each individual part. Wherever you start, you will be able to reach out – in some form or shape – to all other elements of the integral whole.

Some of the practical cases we used have become international icons of an integrated form of development. They help us to see how much courageous individuals and their organisations can achieve, whenever they are willing and able to leave the conventional development track. All of them are pioneers and provide powerful inspiration into a new development practice. They also demonstrate how such new practice can inform new types of 'Uni-Versities' – educational and developmental frameworks and institutions that enable the large-scale dissemination of newly conceived development theory and practice. That includes, as you will see, an articulation of the underlying development processes, important to avoid imitation and rather stimulate origination, authentically befitted to diverse contexts.

Figure 6.4   Map 3: Thought-and-action map with guiding theory and practice

We were lucky that we have worked directly with most case study organisations, interacted closely with their founding fathers and mothers, and observed them for a long period, enabling us to gain insights into the strengths but also weaknesses of each case. In the process, we have witnessed that almost all of them – despite their outstanding achievements and international status – regularly face internal crises that sometimes even endanger the entire organisation or initiative. It is important for us that we approach each case with a certain degree of humanity and humility. None of the cases is presented as 'perfect', in order for others to imitate it. Rather, they serve to further awaken our own originality as Integral Developers.

We seek to present balanced pictures of the cases, but for the sake of illustration – and also due to the natural restriction of space – we decided to focus relatively more on achievements than on failures. The cases presented usually do not cover a particular realm entirely, but are powerful practical expressions of core aspects of the realm. Most cases introduced cover more than one realm; some of them – the most integral cases – could easily be used as a showcase for each realm. However, as you will notice, each case has specific emphases and natural strengths and serves to illustrate one of the realms particularly well.

Figure 6.4, above, provides a full overview on the theory and practice selected for the four integral realms. It is the third map for the journey: a thought-and-action map with guiding theory and practice helping us to find answers to our development questions.

Equipped with compass and maps we are now almost ready to start the Integral Development journey. Before we do that, though, we would like to shed some further light on the fourth and final round of each realm, in particular on, what we coined, a 'Uni-Versity'.

6.4   Build as You Travel: Co-Creating New Uni-Versities

Perhaps to your surprise, we have proposed that the final transformative effect in Round 4 of each realm needs to go beyond even a fully integrated practice. Rather, out of such integrated practice a developmental-educational space has to be created, that allows for a continuous and widespread local-global dissemination of the new theory and practice. That is what we mean by the creation of new kinds of 'Uni-Versities'.

Whenever we witnessed full-fledged developmental processes in practice, they invariably built up to an innovative educational initiative. It is exactly in such educational initiatives where we see the biggest potential for large-scale societal transformation. We experienced that educational programmes, processes and institutions that grow organically and authentically out of the three individual-organisational-societal levels, have a much larger chance to of actualising sustainable development than conventional, top-down orchestrated development policies and programmes. Such organically grown programmes, processes and institutions are likely to be deeply 'embedded' in a particular society, connected to that society's core capacities and issues, linked to living local role models, able to tap into the developmental potential of that community or society, and thereby to contribute to the restoration of its vitality.

Hence, the final and crucial task in each realm is the translation of a home-grown developmental theory and practice (evolved through the Rounds 1, 2 and 3) into a relevant research and educational programme and institution (Round 4). These, however, are not meant to codify the prior three rounds in order to merely facilitate imitation, but rather to design authentic transformational processes and spaces, for individual, organisation and community, that enable original innovations in a particular context. We coined these spaces Uni-Versities, whereby each one of them is:

- a 'uni-que' educational-developmental expression of an actualised developmental journey;
- 'uni-ting' individual, organisational and societal development;
- 'uni-versalising' new development theory and practice through making it institutionally accessible for the world – though remaining in 'uni-on' with its particular local and societal ground out of which it emerged;
- responding in a locally relevant and resonant way to particular developmental callings and challenges, while simultaneously contributing to global development – thereby nurturing a world of 'uni-ty' in 'di-versity'.

In other words, the fourth round – the fourth concentric cycle in our integral approach – needs to translate newly generated theory and practice into research-and-education programmes, processes and institutions, that stimulate widespread innovation in and beyond the particular society in which the original development impulse was lodged.

Following this organic logic, we can gradually – bottom-up – replace or renew established research and educational processes and institutions, that hitherto failed to contribute to the holistic development of a particular individual, organisation and community, or even society.

You can imagine that the full actualisation of each realm results in a different type of renewed educational and developmental spaces. Indeed, in the course of this book you will meet a rich variety of learning, research and education – all the way from community-based learning in rural community to action-learning-action-research processes in modern enterprises. Learning, education and research is thereby literally taken into all realms of society – in process, in which we shall completely revisit the conventional notion of a university.

You notice already, that in order to achieve this objective, we are required to think beyond individual educational programmes. Much of today's individualised education programmes are dramatically 'out of touch' with the core developmental challenges, societies are facing – and equally disconnected from the true learning and innovation needs and capacities of the individual learners they are supposed to cater for. Furthermore, important as individual programmes are, they are bound to be constrained by existing education and research formats and standards. We have personally experienced, again and again, that in particular educational programmes with a highly transformative and innovative character do not fit the conventional university bill and are pushed either to the margins or completely out of the university.

Hence, what is ultimately required is a fundamental revision of the very design of our universities. That includes a re-evaluation of existing universities based on their actual contribution to the sustainable evolution of particular individuals, organisations, communities and society. And it also includes that the conventional notion of a university is enriched and complemented by new types of universities. Such new types of 'Uni-Versities' have not much in common with a university, as we know it. They mark creative and innovative spaces for learning and development, that can (and that do already, as you will see!) emerge literally anywhere – within a community, within large network of communities, within enterprises, etc.

In our own journey of developing and experimenting with educational and research formats that can indeed make a difference to a specific society, we experienced that each of the four realms has, through its distinct orientation and theme, a substantial contribution to make in building such new educational-developmental spaces and in designing new educational programmes, processes and institutions. In Table 6.1 opposite we provide an overview of the transformative educational institutions that we see in each realm, when fully actualised, bringing about. The Table also introduces the main focus and key defining terms of each institution. To each institution we shall return in detail in the course of this book. In the culminating chapters of each realm (⇨10, 14, 18, 22), we provide examples of how such new developmental-educational institutions – each serving to renew self-organisation-society-world – can be built up.

The ultimate institutional form we envision is an 'Integral University' that serves to integrate the characteristics of all four proposed university types, thereby becoming an all-round catalyst for Integral Development. We shall return to the Integral University in the final two chapters of this book.

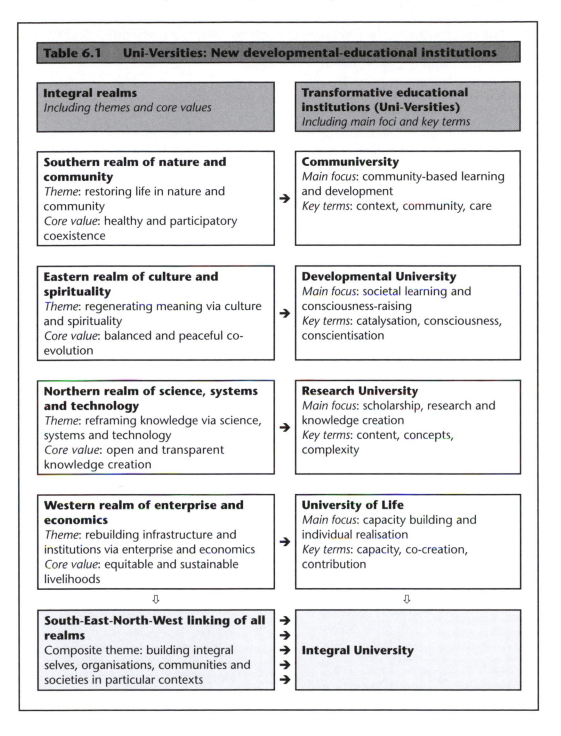

Table 6.1   Uni-Versities: New developmental-educational institutions

Integral realms *Including themes and core values*	Transformative educational institutions (Uni-Versities) *Including main foci and key terms*
Southern realm of nature and community *Theme*: restoring life in nature and community *Core value*: healthy and participatory coexistence	**Communiversity** *Main focus*: community-based learning and development *Key terms*: context, community, care
Eastern realm of culture and spirituality *Theme*: regenerating meaning via culture and spirituality *Core value*: balanced and peaceful co-evolution	**Developmental University** *Main focus*: societal learning and consciousness-raising *Key terms*: catalysation, consciousness, conscientisation
Northern realm of science, systems and technology *Theme*: reframing knowledge via science, systems and technology *Core value*: open and transparent knowledge creation	**Research University** *Main focus*: scholarship, research and knowledge creation *Key terms*: content, concepts, complexity
Western realm of enterprise and economics *Theme*: rebuilding infrastructure and institutions via enterprise and economics *Core value*: equitable and sustainable livelihoods	**University of Life** *Main focus*: capacity building and individual realisation *Key terms*: capacity, co-creation, contribution
South-East-North-West linking of all realms Composite theme: building integral selves, organisations, communities and societies in particular contexts	**Integral University**

6.5 Integration

This chapter served to prepare you for the Integral Development journey that we shall now begin. This journey spans the following 16 chapters, framed in four parts during which you progressively travel through the 'Southern' realm of relationship (Part III), the 'Eastern' realm of inspiration (Part IV), the 'Northern' realm of knowledge (Part V) and the 'Western' realm of action (Part VI).

You are equipped with a compass and maps for your travels. You also got a first sense for the important outcome: the co-creation of new developmental-educational spaces (so-called 'Uni-Versities') that serve to implement sustainably the holistic process underlying Integral Development. As we indicated, the journey-process leads to the co-creation of such 'Uni-Versities' – as you travel in each realm through the four rounds of self-development, organisational development, societal development and, ultimately, integrated practice. It is in this fourth and final round of integrated practice that you also establish a duly differentiated and ultimately integrating 'Uni-Versity', serving to actualise development theory and practice.

Before the journey starts, let us reflect for a moment on the guiding question and thoughts presented in this chapter. Having assimilated the compass and maps informing your journey, do you feel ready for the journey ahead?

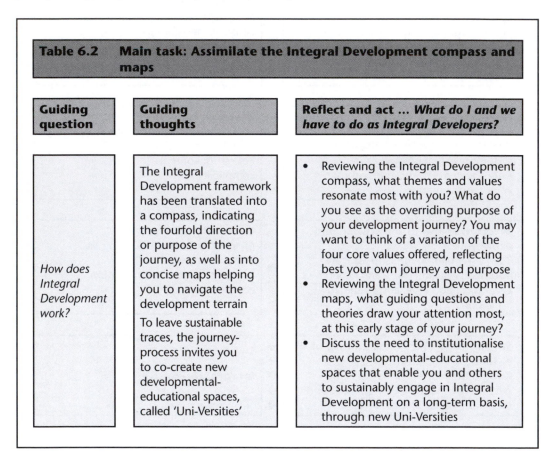

Table 6.2　Main task: Assimilate the Integral Development compass and maps

Guiding question	Guiding thoughts	Reflect and act ... *What do I and we have to do as Integral Developers?*
How does Integral Development work?	The Integral Development framework has been translated into a compass, indicating the fourfold direction or purpose of the journey, as well as into concise maps helping you to navigate the development terrain To leave sustainable traces, the journey-process invites you to co-create new developmental-educational spaces, called 'Uni-Versities'	• Reviewing the Integral Development compass, what themes and values resonate most with you? What do you see as the overriding purpose of your development journey? You may want to think of a variation of the four core values offered, reflecting best your own journey and purpose • Reviewing the Integral Development maps, what guiding questions and theories draw your attention most, at this early stage of your journey? • Discuss the need to institutionalise new developmental-educational spaces that enable you and others to sustainably engage in Integral Development on a long-term basis, through new Uni-Versities

The Southern Realm of Integral Development: Restoring Life in Nature and Community

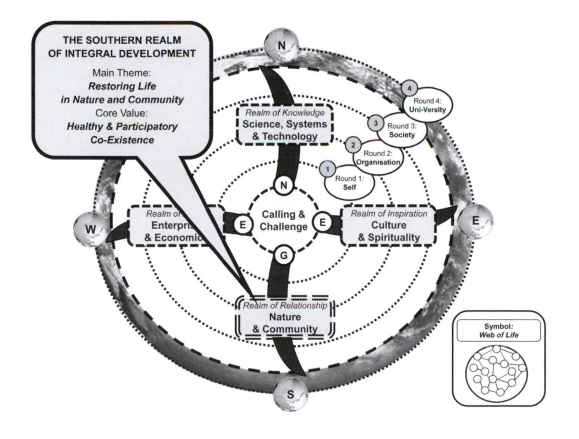

THE SOUTHERN REALM
OF INTEGRAL DEVELOPMENT

Main Theme:
**Restoring Life
in Nature and Community**
Core Value:
**Healthy & Participatory
Co-Existence**

N

4
Round 4:
Uni-Versity

3
Round 3:
Society

Realm of Knowledge
**Science, Systems
& Technology**

2
Round 2:
Organisation

1
Round 1:
Self

N

Realm of
**Enterpr
& Economi**

E
Calling &
Challenge
E

Realm of Inspiration
**Culture
& Spirituality**

W

E

G

Realm of Relationship
**Nature
& Community**

Symbol:
Web of Life

S

CHAPTER 7

Know Your Self and Your Context: A Southern Individual Perspective

Guiding Questions: Who am I? What underlies my personal development?

7.1 Orientation

Gnothi seauton! Know thyself! This is one of the most famous mottos of the oracle of Delphi. Delphi was the most important site of pilgrimage and worship in classical Greece. It was seen as the centre of the known world. Though the temple of Delphi became later attributed to Apollo, the sun god, it was originally dedicated to Gaia, the Greek goddess of the Earth, of nature. In fact, the name Delphi is likely to be derived from the term *delph* (hollow) or *delphus* (womb) and alludes to the original veneration of nature by our human ancestors around the globe. The famous oracle, embodied by a priestess, once declared Socrates the wisest man of all Greece, because he alone was aware of his ignorance.

This extract of ancient Greek history and mythology takes us back to the development drawing board. As we evolve our thinking on self, organisational and societal development over the coming chapters, we start each time with our individual grounding, that is understanding ourselves alongside others.

We are not saying that one should not engage in any outer development work before we have settled all of our inner development issues. That would be absurd – for self-knowledge is an iteratively inner and outer directed process, not something we can fix once and for all and be done with. But what we do say is that it is important, that we make thorough headway on this journey to 'know thyself' before we engage with the purposeful development of the outer world. We need to be sufficiently sensitised to ourselves to be able to be truly empathetic with others. We need to understand our own self before we can understand the inner world of another person, let alone of an entire group, organisation or community. Such an understanding involves the probing into the following questions:

*   Who am I?
*   Who am I in relation to others and to the world?
*   What is my relationship to nature, in particular to my inner nature?
*   What does the circle of my life look like and where within it do I stand?
*   What are my own inner development issues, needs, aptitudes and desires?

- How do they relate to the outer development issues in which I am interested?
- How do my personal development needs and capacities inform the group, organisation, community and/or society of which I am a part and how am I, in turn, shaped by them?

We start our individual and societal exploration in Africa, for it is the cradle of humankind. With the help of African American scholar Clyde Ford, we explore remarkable African approaches to development. Subsequently, we tap into ancient wisdom of the world's indigenous people – those who live, to this day, closest to nature and who cherish the importance of living in nature and community. The American cultural anthropologist Angeles Arrien will guide us into the fourfold way of indigenous people. After that we shall turn to two of the most eminent psychologists of the twentieth century, C.G. Jung and Daniel Levinson. As you journey through this chapter, have in mind, that although we start here with your 'self', such a self is to be seen contextualised within a learning community and within a particular development context.

7.2   Answers from Africa: Development Views from the Cradle of Humankind

INCLUDING AFRICA: BUILDING A SHARED SPACE FOR HUMANITY'S CHOIR OF CULTURES

In starting the development journey we first want to reflect on it from the perspective of those people to whom much development work has been 'applied' in vain and who are still suffering from being materially excluded from many of the riches of our time: the Africans. How do Africans think about human development? Home to one-sixth of the world population but contributing only about a fortieth of global GDP, Africa is often dubbed 'the lost continent'. Reduced to economics, Africa is thus seen as a 'basket case'. For us, such metaphors merely serve to reinforce a hopelessly negative judgement, and thereby overshadow the true wealth and potential of Africa and its people. We have seen this cultural and social wealth in our work, and we are ever more convinced, that Africa has profound contributions to make to the remaking of the world as whole.

In this respect, Integral Development seeks not only to contribute to the overall renewal of today's approach to 'economic' development, but in particular to the renewal of those world regions and societies on which the world 'looks down' – interestingly enough many of the so-called 'developing' countries are located in the geographic South of the world. Hence, we propose an approach to development that not only measures the performance of those countries based on their economic productivity, but rather serves to build up a shared human perspective whereby the multifaceted contribution of each world region and society forms a vital and inclusive part. Hence, Integral Development is altogether inclusive in two major respects: firstly it is inclusive 'of all worlds' with regard to the four realms that we have outlined earlier; secondly it is inclusive in that it serves to simultaneously deal with the development of self, organisation, community and society. Furthermore, in both of the above inclusive respects, it encompasses the rich cultural diversity that we represent within an altogether shared humanity. It is also for this reason that the perspectives shared in this book come from all corners of the world.

Thereby, Integral Development is an attempt to create a space where a reconfigured, and now inclusive human choir of cultures can develop in dynamic harmony, with each participant on an equal, though different, level. For it is in the space between two or more perspectives that the new is born. Renewal can never be brought about by the imposition of one perspective alone.

TAPPING INTO THE CRADLE OF HUMANKIND

Africa is the cradle of humankind. It therefore seems almost 'natural' to turn first to Africa to begin the exploration of human nature. Applying ancient African wisdom to oneself is beneficial not only for Africans, but to any human being. In a way, listening to Africa's wisdom is like listening to our collective human ancestors, as we all came, one early day of human evolution, out of Africa. We are not of course implying, here, that all of Africa is exactly the same. The continent contains enormous natural as well as cultural diversity. Yet, for us there are underlying, historically laden essences that all Africans, just like all Europeans, share in common.

So what do we hear when we carefully listen to Africa in relation to human development? Though only orally transmitted for most of its historical existence, the wealth of African traditional wisdom remains so vast, that at this point we are only able to provide selective excerpts which may entice the reader into his or her own deeper investigation. With the help of the African American healer, psychologist and scholar Clyde Ford and his fascinating work *The Hero with an African Face*, we shall introduce two cultural perspectives on the human development from Africa: one from the Kongo in Central Africa, one from the Yoruba people in West Africa.

THE KONGO COSMOLOGY AND THE HUMAN JOURNEY

In Kongo civilisation, life and the journey of human existence was understood in circular form. The most important symbol of this understanding was the Yowa Cross, a circular ideogram including a cross-like shape, usually traced on the ground.

From Ford we learn that 'with solar disks at the end of each cross arm and arrows suggesting a counter clockwise direction of motion, the cruciform represents the four stations of the sun's movement through the sky'.[1]

BaKongo interpreter Fu-Kiau Bunseki states 'The cross was known to the BaKongo before the arrival of the Europeans, and corresponds to the understanding in their minds of their relationship to their world'.[2] For the BaKongos the human life cycle was closely aligned with the cycle of the earth – and could be pictured by three movements, that correspond with the daily rhythm of the sun: emergence (sun rise), fulfilment (ascendency) and dissolution (sun set). The fourth movement was invisible, alluding to the sun's disappearance during the night, its dwelling in 'the other world', and its eventual rebirth on the following day. The human being rises in the morning, becomes active, then we go to rest in the evening and enter into the fourth phase of sleep, after which we rise again to a new day. For Bunseki, the sun's circle is the first geometric form given to humankind; reflecting on our own human rhythm – as per every day, as per our whole life – in this sun-like circular form, enables us to reconnect and align with the larger nature to which we belong. All of this is depicted in the Kongo cosmogram, as illustrated in Figure 7.1.[3]

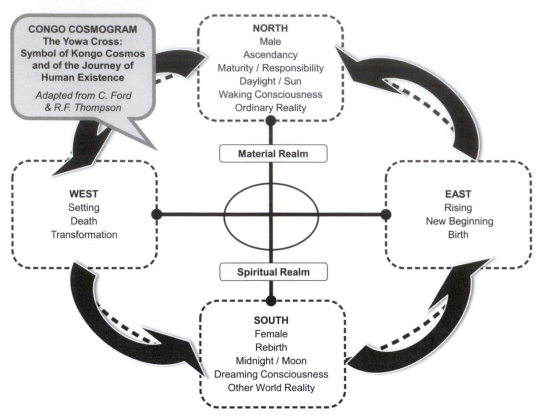

Figure 7.1   Congo cosmogram

From Ford we learn that the 'central ellipse represents the mythic waters of Kalunga separating two worlds that are mirror images of each other: the ordinary world (Ntoto) and the "land of the death" (Mputo)'[4] Bunseki explains that 'between these two parts, the land of the dead and the living, the water is both a passage and a great barrier'[5] We are reminded of an age-old mythic truth that tells us that a deep understanding of life includes death, and is not opposed to it. Again and again, we need to cross the 'Kalunga-Line' (the horizontal line in the Yowa Cross). Like the moon that is disappearing at the end of one cycle, to be then mysteriously reborn to begin a new one, so life as a whole is a process of continuous death and renewal.

This ancient truth is echoed in Goethe's famous verse: 'As long as thou hast not got/This dying or becoming/Thou art but a gloomy guest/Upon the dark Earth'. It is in this very spirit that Ford interprets the Yowa Cross as an emblem of the quest that each individual is called to embark upon, passing, like the sun, through the stages of departure (the hero goes on a quest), fulfilment (the hero resolves his or her task) and return (the hero returns to his people with the newly acquired insight or treasure). We revisit this mythic journey portrayed by Clyde Ford through the work of Joseph Campbell (⇨11), as it provides deep clues into a comprehension of ourselves, and of the 'development tasks' we are called to fulfil in our own lives.

Ford explains that the Yowa Cross – similar to Mandalas in Hinduism and Buddhism – is also a meditation tool, helping the adept to connect deeper to his or her nature and calling, as well as of the nature of life in general. Often, the initiate has to stand in the middle of the cross – often called the 'God-Point', the origin and source of all consciousness – to engage in meditation. If the adept had learned the lesson, it signified, so Bunseki, that he or she 'knew the nature of the world, [and] that he [or she] had mastered the meaning of life and death'.[6] The centre of the cross, however, holds also the task for the initiate, as in this one point lies the potential of all that this person can become. In Ford's words: 'This is the aspect of creation, so imperfectly rendered by any symbol, that is suggested by the dot in the middle of the ellipse in the Kongo cosmogram: the person within the fertilised egg; the oak tree within the acorn; the universe within a dimensionless point; the potential prior to its manifestation'.[7]

For the BaKongo, the cosmogram is a dynamic, sacred circle, whose evocation held healing power, as it reconnected the individual and the community to an eternal, wholesome truth, 'symbolising the movement of the sun, the movement of life from birth to rebirth, and the movement of human consciousness'.[8] With this in mind, we shall now move to the Yoruba people of West Africa, whose interpretation of their principle divinities resonates strongly with the Kongo cosmogram, and provides further insight into our human nature.

YORUBA COSMOLOGY: UNDERSTANDING THE GODS – UNDERSTANDING YOURSELF

For Ford, one of the differences between Africa and the West is that deities are seen as personifications of characteristics that are to be found in nature as much as within ourselves. He argues:

> These two different ways of regarding divinity give rise to two different ways of interpreting mythology, for where deities are considered to be facts, tales of those deities are understood historically, and where deities are viewed as personifications of source energies in nature and within ourselves, tales of those deities are understood symbolically. As facts, deities are worshipped and believed in primarily as entities outside one's self – 'up there' or 'down there', in a heaven or hell beyond human existence. But as symbols representing the source energies of life, deities are experiences as part of one's self: from birth to death, from hunger to anger, from love to pain, the forces that motivate us are themselves the gods and goddesses within us.[9]

For us, this insight is of enormous importance, as it provides another clue of how traditional Africa has seen the individual human being as well as the development tasks he or she is facing, including the driving inner forces and motivations of a person. It was the Swiss psychoanalyst C.G. Jung who confirmed this insight in the twentieth century by making a strong case for understanding god(s) and deities as archetypal manifestations of the human psyche. This matches with the ancient perspectives that have, according to Ford, prevailed in indigenous Africa.

Ford goes on to introduce the Yoruba culture from West Africa (Nigeria and Benin) as one of the strongest examples of an archetypal interpretation of divinity. Yoruba deities are called 'orishas'. They are significant not only because of their 'central standing in Yoruba culture but also because the orishas have survived in the Americas, forming the vibrant core of such Afro-Carribean and Afro-South American spiritual practices as Santeria, Macumba, Capoeira, and Candomblé, into which Christianity has been folded'.[10]

For the Yoruba, in understanding ourselves, we are called to understand the gods in ourselves. By connecting to these archetypal phenomena deep within ourselves, we are tapping into our own divine nature. The Nigerian Nobel Laureate and Yoruba Wole Soyinka calls these inner divine aspects 'essence-ideals',[11] a term that Ford sees closely related to Jung's notion of the 'archetype':

> Jung thought that such archetypes are so fundamental to the human species that they were first formed in the very earliest stages of human development, millions of years ago, and like the basic structures of our bodies, they have undergone little significant change in the intervening aeons. So universal are these templates of the psyche that Jung suggested they exist not within the unconsciousness of each individual but in the shared, collective unconsciousness of humanity, rather like the common atmosphere in which we all live.[12]

If we agree with Jung's theory on the archetypes, we acknowledge our shared humanity, our profound interconnectedness through the collective unconsciousness, as well as that Africa – our common origin – is still alive in all of us.

The Yoruba pantheon of deities is impressive. There is no 'shortcoming' of gods – numbers range between 200 and many thousands – given that the orishas themselves owe their existence – according to the creation myths of the Yoruba – to the shattering of the original, single godhead called Orisa-nla (meaning 'Great Orisha') into many pieces.[13] Ford then introduces the four principle deities or orishas of the Yoruba pantheon and presents them in a fascinating fourfold and holistic fashion, demonstrating, as did the Kongo Cosmology, an almost striking resonance with our generic integral approach of human development. Ford bases this representation on the work of Leo Frobenius, the great German archaeologist and ethnologist, of whom Senegal's founding president and poet Leopold Senghor once said that his work contributed to give Africa back its dignity and identity. Frobenius had understood that one of the central Yoruba myths that circles around the fourfold hat of the Orisha Eshu provides a summation of the Yoruba cosmology (see Figure 7.2), introducing the four orishas Obatala (South), Eshu (East), Ogun (North) and Shango (West) as the four principles archetypes.[14]

Ford explains that this:

> integrated system is based on the counter clockwise motion of the sun through the four cardinal directions. Each compass direction is associated with a principle Orisha, element, psychological aspect, colour, object from the earth, time of the year, and day of the week ... At the heart of this system is a cross uniting a horizontal axis known as the 'Chief Way' with a vertical axis, the 'Secondary Way'; these are the principal paths by which this mystery system is apprehended.[15]

For the Yoruba, the development task of each person is to bring forth in one's own life the archetypal qualities represented by the two orishas of the principal way, or, alternatively, of the secondary way. These are the two routes of accessing the sacred wisdom, whose acquisition is seen as the core human development purpose. The key to personal development is hence to be embedded in a comprehensive mythic order 'that at once reclaims and rejoins the mysteries of the cosmos, the earth, and the social order with the mysteries of a divine self'.[16]

Both the Kongo and the Yoruba cosmology illustrate how closely Africans see the human journey as interrelated with the circle of the sun, and of all life on earth. Everything, from an African understanding, is interrelated. That brings us to Ubuntu.

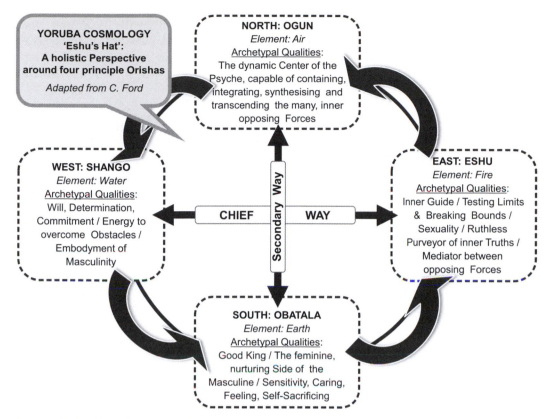

Figure 7.2   Yoruba cosmology

UBUNTU: I AM BECAUSE YOU ARE!

Not many philosophies capture the principle of interconnectedness and a shared humanity better than the Pan-African ethical and humanist system Ubuntu. Simply soak in the response that Ubuntu gives to the question 'Who am I?' It answers: 'I am because you are!' Or, in the words of Liberian peace activist Leymah Gbowee who was responsible for leading a woman's peace movement that was instrumental in ending the Liberian Civil War in 2003: 'I am what I am because of what we all are'.

The South African Archbishop and Peace Nobel Laureate Desmond Tutu provides further insights:

> *Africans have a thing called Ubuntu; it is about the essence of being human, it is part of the gift that Africa is going to give to the world. It embraces hospitality, caring about others, being willing to go that extra mile for the sake of another. We believe that a person is a person through other persons; that my humanity is caught up and bound up in yours. When I dehumanise you, I inexorably dehumanise myself. The solitary human being is a contradiction in terms, and therefore you seek to work for the common good because your humanity comes into its own in community, in belonging.*[17]

In conclusion, these opening lessons from Africa set the scene for all of the four realms of Integral Development. In particular, it enables us to see the role of this Southern realm in contributing to the restoration of life in nature and community with its ultimate goal to promote 'healthy and participatory co-existence'. Before we now move on to consider indigenous people from all over the world, we give a final word on Africa, Ubuntu and interconnectedness to our friend and colleague Barbara Nussbaum, a South African authority on Ubuntu:

> *Ubuntu is the capacity in African culture to express compassion, reciprocity, dignity, harmony, and humanity in the interests of building and maintaining community. Ubuntu calls on us to believe and feel that: Your pain is my pain; my wealth is your wealth; your salvation is my salvation. In essence, Ubuntu ... addresses our interconnectedness, our common humanity, and the responsibility to each other that flows from our connection.*[18]

Needless to say, many African communities and societies are bereft of Ubuntu. For us this is because such a natural 'Southern' realm, starting out on the level of the individual unit and family unity, has hardly been considered in development. In other words, exploitation from within and/or without has all too often inhibited such evolution, from the development of self and community to that of a whole society. We now turn from a particular African perspective to the indigenous worldview, in more general terms.

7.3   The Indigenous Fourfold Way: Personal Development from the Fourth World

INSPIRED DEVELOPMENT: TURNING TO THE FOURTH WORLD

For the renowned US American cultural anthropologist Angeles Arrien, development should not seek primary inspiration in the First World, but in the so-called Fourth World.[19] The Fourth World was described by Sushwap Chief George Manuel of the World Council of Indigenous People and former leader in the North American Indian movement as the 'name given to indigenous peoples descended from a country's aboriginal population and who today are completely or partly deprived of the right to their own territory and riches'.[20]

To distinguish the four worlds from each other, Arrien maintains that while those in the First, Second and Third Worlds believe that land belongs to the people, the Fourth World believes that people belong to the land. In order to 'heal and restore Mother Earth', bridges between these four worlds have to be built. In that process it is important that people of the first three worlds understand and accept the Fourth World. Indeed, she claims, there is not only much to learn from the peoples of the Fourth World, but it is also in the interface of all worlds, that our shared planet can heal.[21]

What is it that needs to be learned from the Fourth World? Julian Burger states in his *Gaia Atlas for First Peoples*:

> *Indigenous peoples are one of the world's most persistent voices of conscience, alerting humankind to the dangers of environmental destruction. And as the world searches for alternative strategies to deal with global problems, it is turning more and more to indigenous peoples. Much of their respect for nature, their methods of resource management, social organisation, values and culture are finding echoes in the writings of scientists, philosophers, politicians, and thinkers.*[22]

Arrien adds that 'no matter what world we live in now, we are all people of the earth, connected to one another by our mutual humanity. When we listen to land-based peoples, we are listening to our oldest selves'.[23] Arrien herself has listened to those peoples all her life, and what she found is that many of the shamanic traditions of indigenous peoples worldwide draw on the power of four archetypes in order to live in harmony and balance with outer nature as well as with our own inner nature. She called it the Fourfold Way.

THE FOURFOLD WAY: THE HEALER, THE VISIONARY, THE WARRIOR AND THE TEACHER

The four almost universal archetypal images that Arrien surfaced are those of the healer, the visionary, the warrior and the teacher. She argues that these archetypes are rooted in the deepest mythological layer of humanity and are hence accessible to all of us. Reconnecting and engaging with these archetypes is not only necessary for the individual journey, but it has profound implications for the world as a whole. Arrien emphasises that 'when we learn to live these archetypes within ourselves, we will begin to heal ourselves and our fragmented world'.[24]

Though the traditional roles within community and society have dramatically changed, the relevance of the four archetypes remains:

- The archetype of the healer is expressed through the care we give to the physical well-being of others and ourselves, as well as to nature and the earth as the whole.
- The archetype of the visionary is reflected by our capacity to imagine, to be creative and to realise our dreams, as well as to support the realisation of the dreams of others.
- The archetype of the teacher mirrors our individual striving for knowledge and wisdom.
- The archetype of the warrior is articulated through personal leadership skills, applied to family and work.

All of these aspects are important. For individual well-being all of them need to be addressed within ourselves. Arrien explains: 'In many shamanic traditions, optimum health is considered to be the equal expression of these archetypes. Indigenous peoples consider it vitally important to be balanced in all four areas: leading, healing, visioning, and teaching'.[25] She invites us to critically reflect on the importance of all four aspects within our psyche and to embark on a journey of self-discovery and healing that has served as a valid roadmap for tens of thousands of years for diverse civilisations. If you don't know where to start, begin with the following question:

> If you think of yourself as a warrior or leader, for example, do you feel fully competent in this area, or would learning the skills of the visionary help you express your vision of what might be possible? Would learning the skills of the healer help you work with people out of love rather than out of competition? Would learning the skills of the teacher open you to new dimensions you have not considered?[26]

In the following Table 7.1 we introduce the core qualities of each of the four archetypes.

Table 7.1   The fourfold way: The four archetypes and their qualities

Healer

- Pays attention to what has heart and meaning
- Recognises the power of love as the most potent healing force
- Extends the arms of love: acknowledgement, acceptance, recognition, validation, gratitude

Visionary

- Tells the truth without blame or judgement
- Knows and communicates his/her creative purpose and life dream
- Acts from authentic self
- Freedom from patterns of denial and indulgence
- Honours the four ways of seeing: intuition, perception, insight, vision

Warrior

- Shows up
- Chooses to be present
- Aligns words and action
- Shows honour and respect for all things
- Employs judicious communication
- Sets limits and boundaries
- Acts responsible and disciplined
- Demonstrates right use of power
- Understands three universal powers (presence, communication, position)

Teacher

- Displays wisdom: clarity, objectivity, discernment
- Open to outcome, not attached to outcome
- Flexibility
- Teaches trust
- Understands the need for detachment

THE ARCHETYPES AND THEIR SHADOWS: CLUES FOR INDIVIDUAL DEVELOPMENT WORK

Each of us is regularly faced with inner imbalances, which, according to the fourfold way, are caused by an overemphasis of one or more qualities and/or a neglect of certain qualities. Due to such overemphasis or neglect these qualities play out within us in a distorted way, and hence disturb our sense of inner balance. The same applies to organisations and whole societies. To explain those imbalances more concretely, Arrien employs Jung's approach of the shadow to which we shall later return (⇨11). The shadow refers to those inner aspects that are repressed and hence unnoticed by the individual consciousness.

The work of personal development is to make the shadow conscious. In fact, each imbalance, if noticed, understood, as well as acted upon, serves to promote the rhythm of Integral Development. In the Table 7.2 we provide a first intimation of the shadow aspects of each archetype. It may serve as a template for self-reflection in order to identify development shortfalls.

Table 7.2 The fourfold way: The shadows of the four archetypes

Healer

- Non-attendance to personal health and well-being
- Neediness and withdrawal
- Martyr syndrome
- Life-negating patterns
- Addictions: to intensity; to perfection; to the need to know; to being fixated on what's not working rather than what is working

Visionary

- Self-abandonment and self-denial in order to receive love or acceptance, to keep peace, to maintain balance, to stay in state of harmony
- Supporting the false-self system rather than staying in authenticity
- Projection
- Fixed perspectives/blind spots

Warrior

- Rebellion: over-identification with being independent and self-sufficient/underlying fear of being limited, restricted or restrained
- Authority issues: projection of our own authority on others/unwillingness to claim personal responsibility
- Invisibility patterns: avoidance of reclaiming personal power/underlying fear of exposure and accountability

Teacher

• Righteous positionality	• Confusion
• Judgement	• Doubt
• Control	• Inflated inner critic
• Ignorance	

INTEGRATION OF THE ARCHETYPES: THE MEDICINE WHEEL

Making the shadow aspects conscious and striving for a harmonious balance between the qualities of the four archetypes within us is a lifelong task.

For Fourth World People an ever-deeper understanding of our inner and outer nature is crucial for mastering this task. They believed that both, inner and outer nature, resonate profoundly. That is reflected in the fact that each of the four archetypes corresponds to one of the four seasons (spring, summer, autumn, winter), four elements (earth, fire, air, water) and four directions (south, east, north, west), altogether echoing our integral realms. Furthermore, each archetype is 'equipped' with certain supporting creatures, healing salves, instruments and helpful meditations. Each represents a way of living. And each accesses and evokes a particular human resource: from power to vision, from wisdom to love. For indigenous people, all four archetypes require attention, though each of us has a different set of gifts and strengths. However, it is for each of us, to seek dynamic balance between all of our inner aspects, and for each of the four paths there are healing processes to vitalise the particular resource of the path. The full wealth of the fourfold way is depicted in a medicine wheel (Figure 7.3), in which each of the

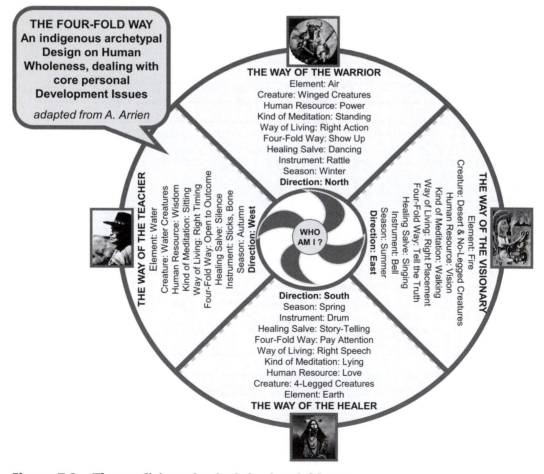

Figure 7.3   The medicine wheel of the fourfold way

four interconnected archetypes occupies an equal space. Note that America's First Nation People regarded the terms 'medicine' and 'power' as interchangeable.

Arrien explains, that cross-culturally there have been many different perspectives offered by indigenous peoples of each continent regarding the directions and seasons – if you like variations on the integral theme – and that the illustration shown here reflects the most common interpretation. In its circular form, the medicine wheel mirrors a human and natural cosmos in equilibrium. Its elements, however, are forever changing and highly interdependent which requires us to participate in the 'dance of creation', seeking to evolve (or develop) in harmony with creation and with our fellow human beings. That is the key developmental rhythm we receive from indigenous people. For us this age-old development wisdom is a powerful scene-setter for a renewed orientation to development. It starts out not only with aligning human and ecological development by seeing the human being as an integral part of nature, but also by highlighting the individual responsibility for personal and communal development, in association with others.

RELEVANCE OF FOURTH-WORLD DEVELOPMENT WISDOM FOR OUR DAY AND AGE

In recent decades we have noticed a gradual rediscovery of such indigenous wisdom, though it is often either romanticised or pushed to the margins, being seen as relevant only for a negligible part of the world's population. However, there are more and more voices that proclaim that it is exactly those marginalised people that hold a key to the future of sustainable development. Renowned American activist and writer Jerry Mander, for example, demands that 'we need to rethink our relationship with nature and with native peoples'. For him, that includes 'relearning history' and 'grappling with the forces that caused this history to occur'. Passionately, he argues that:

> there is no denying that all of this amounts to considerable adjustment, but it's not as if there were much choice. Truly, such change is inevitable if sanity and sustainability are to prevail. To call this adjustment 'going back' is to conceive of it in fearful, negative terms, when the changes are actually desirable and good. In fact, it is not really going back; it is merely getting back on track, as it were, after a short unhappy diversion into fantasy. It is going forward to a renewed relationship with timeless values and principles that have been kept alive for Western society by the very people we have tried to destroy.

Mander defies the critique of being a romantic as he goes on:

> As for whether it is 'romantic' to make such a case, I can only say that the charge is putting the case backwards. What is romantic is to believe that technological evolution will ever live up to its own advertising, or that technology itself can liberate us from the problems it has created. So far, the only people who, as a group, are clear-minded on this point are the native peoples, simply because they have kept alive their roots in an older, alternative, nature-based philosophy that has proven effective for tens of thousands of years, and that has nurtured dimensions of knowledge and perception that have become opaque to us. It is the native societies, not our own, that hold the key to future survival.[27]

The striking relevance of the indigenous fourfold way for an integral understanding of the realms of human existence and its rhythmical evolution is mirrored in C.G. Jung's work on psychological types introduced in the twentieth century.

7.4 Psychological Types: An Exploration into Human Nature

A PRELUDE TO THE UNDERSTANDING OF HUMAN NATURE: A LONG HISTORY OF NATURAL CLASSIFICATION

Throughout human history we find order giving systems that sought to conceive of the functioning of the human being as an integrated (or disintegrated) composition of natural elements. In Greek, Medieval, and Renaissance thought, the traditional four elements form the basis for a theory of medicine and later psychological typology known as the four humours. While in Western thinking the idea of elements as substances took pride of place, Chinese philosophy, to provide another example, conceived of the five elements (earth, metal, wood, water, fire) as dynamic states of change. These five elements were themselves linked to natural phenomena such as the seasons of the year, different types of weather, directions (south, east, north, west), organs, tastes and shapes.

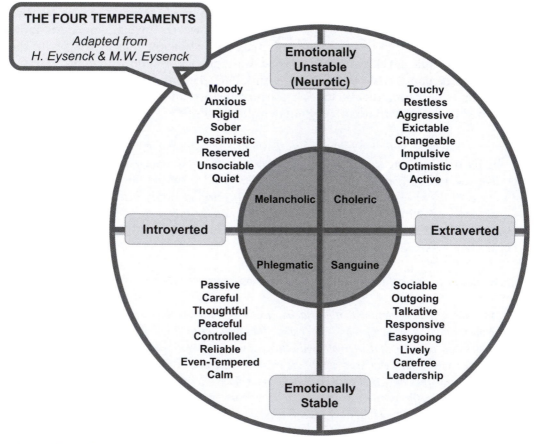

Figure 7.4   The four temperaments

All of these early typologies were clearly guided by nature and natural elements and were oriented towards health and healing. In Western classical tradition, it was in particular the Greek philosophers Plato (in his *Republic*), Hippocrates and Aristotle, as well as the Roman physician Galen, who built on the concept of the four humours in articulating their approach to health, disease and the functioning of the body. The four humours or temperaments – sanguine, melancholic, choleric and phlegmatic – were linked to the four bodily substances of blood, yellow bile, black bile and phlegm, which themselves pointed to major bodily organs – liver, spleen, gall bladder and brain/lungs – and to the core elements – air, fire, water and earth. During European Renaissance these concepts experienced a major revival. Later, in the nineteenth and early twentieth century, it was the anthroposophist Rudolf Steiner who developed these concepts further. In the twentieth century it was the work of Hans Eysenck,[28] whose work introduced the four temperaments to a global audience. Eysenck took the extrovert-introvert polarity, developed by Jung, and a stable-unstable gradient, to come up with four quadrants that can be associated with the classic four temperaments. Each quadrant (see Figure 7.4 on the page opposite) is divided by keywords, creating a 360° gradation.

With our integral realms we have generally taken on from where all of the above have left off. And so did Jung. His approach to psychological types builds on a long history that was profoundly informed by nature, including human nature. The work of the Swiss psychoanalyst has been a particular source of inspiration for us and has been of seminal influence in the development of our integral perspective.

WHO AM I? A SELF-REGULATING SYSTEM, OPERATING ON THE NATURAL PRINCIPLE OF DYNAMIC OPPOSITION

C.G. Jung's oeuvre as a whole is one of the most outstanding intellectual achievements of the twentieth century (especially in the context of the Western/Northern world). Almost single-handedly, he established Analytical Psychology as a new field within psychology. His work provides multiple entry points for self-discovery and a deeper understanding of the human nature. We shall hence return or refer to Jung at various occasions throughout this book. At this initial stage we are particularly interested in getting a sense for the basic nature and scope of his 'psychological types', following the question 'Who am I?'

For Jung – who rejected any separation between mind and body, physical and psychological nature – all the essential functions of the physical body and of the human psyche operate in accordance with the principle of dynamic opposition. In other words, they are arranged in opposing systems, which in health are kept in balance through a process of positive and negative feedback. Thus, hunger is balanced by satiation, sleep by wakefulness, and vice versa. Jung was convinced that the human psyche, like the body, was a self-regulating system. We strive to perpetually maintain a balance between opposing propensities, while, at the same time, seeking our own individuation. A dynamic polarity exists then between surface personality and deep self, between masculine and feminine consciousness, between extraverted and introverted attitudes, between modernity and tradition. Thus the greatest and most important problems of life and work are all fundamentally insoluble. They must be, because they express the necessary polarity inherent in every self-regulating system. They can never be 'solved', but rather need to be transcended.

JUNG'S THEORIES OF PSYCHOLOGICAL TYPES

Through his observations of his patients as well as of people in his personal and professional environment, Jung gradually developed his theory of types. For many, Jung's notion of the psychological types was not only the most evolved concept but also the most important. For Jung, understanding our type is the alpha and omega of the individuation process. 'Without that insight one stands little chance of any true self-realisation or development as an individual'.[29]

More precisely, Jung distinguished between attitude-types and function-types. In distinguishing the various types Jung describes that he started out with:

> two basic types [that] I have termed introverted and extroverted. This will be followed by a description of those more special types whose peculiarities are due to the fact that the individual adapts and orients himself chiefly by means of his most differentiated function. The former I would call attitude-types … the latter I would call function-types.[30]

According to Jung, distinguishing between these psychological types is crucial, for it is one's psychological type that determines and limits a person's judgement:

> Just as the lion strikes down his enemy or his prey with his fore-paw, in which his strength resides, and not with the tail like the crocodile, so our habitual reactions are normally characterised by the application of our most trustworthy and efficient function; it is an expression of our strength. However, this does not prevent our reacting occasionally in a way that reveals our specific weakness. The predominance of function leads us to construct or to seek out certain situations while we avoid others, and therefore to have experiences that are peculiar to us and different from those of other people.[31]

WHAT TYPE AM I?

After wrestling for many years to find suitable differentiations and definitions of the core psychological functions of human beings, Jung concluded that there are four functions inherent to all of us, in the same way (see above) – going back to the indigenous world and to ancient times – as there are four elements. Sensation and intuition, as the pair of opposite functions regulating our direct experience, and thinking and feeling as the pair of opposite functions regulating how we organise this experience internally. For Jung:

> these four function types correspond to the obvious means by which consciousness obtains its orientation to experience. Sensation (i.e., sense perception) tells you that something exists; thinking tells you what it is; feeling tells you whether it is agreeable or not; and intuition tells you whence it comes and where it is going.[32]

Jung often referred to the functions as compass points for the personality that guide us within a situation. Lenore Thomson, a US American analytical psychologist, explains:

> For example, people who are well developed in sensation or intuition prefer direct experience. They live in the present, and they are alert to situations that require an immediate response. They may resist situations that require them to organise their experience systematically or

to follow a plan. People who are well developed in thinking or feeling prefer to organise their experiences and plan for them. Once they've established a plan, they can be irritated by the unpredictability of the direct experience.[33]

In addition to the four functional types it is important to note the relevance of what Jung called our attitudes-types: introversion and extraversion. 'We experience each of our functions from two distinct perspectives – one that involves the person we are inside (the introverted view) and one that involves our relationship to others (the extraverted view)'.[34]

The Myers-Briggs Type Indicator is perhaps the most renowned translation of Jung's work on psychological types into practice. Applied to an almost infinite range of fields – and well known also in the context of organisation development and team building – it has been developed from Jung's theories on basic attitudes (introvert versus extravert) and the functional types (feeling, thinking, intuiting, sensing). Myers-Briggs came up with a personality test and a corresponding matrix of 16 types, distinguishing people according to their style of perception and judgement. These 16 types are the result of the total possible options of combining Jung's basic attitudes and functional types.[35] The impressive work that has been done in and around the Myers-Briggs Type Indicator and the vast literature that has been produced in this field, allows everyone to engage with it in depth and to explore further its value on our journey to wholeness. Some further clues are provided here.

THE FOUR FUNCTIONAL TYPES, THE ATTITUDES-TYPES AND OUR STRUGGLE TOWARDS WHOLENESS

If we arrange Jung's four types in a circle (see Figure 7.5 on the next page) we get an image that resonates profoundly with our own integral realms. The circle was used by Jung to represent the whole person. The circle represents the totality of a context, an individual or a group, a whole society or even the world at large'. In a way, Jung's types – extrapolated from self to organisation and society – can be seen as a constant underlying structure of the realms underlying Integral Development.[36] The circular representation allows also for arranging the functional types in a way that the polar opposite types face each other.

It is exactly in these opposites that we find a key to resolving our personal development struggles. For example, a person whose thinking function is strongly developed is likely to have a relatively weak articulation of his feeling type. Thus, a strong thinking type is likely to approach a particular development context with sophisticated theories and statistics, while he may not be able to distinguish the important from the unimportant aspects, which intimates a common lack of an internal value hierarchy in thinking types. On the contrary, the feeling type is likely to have an instant 'feel' for the situation and the crucial issues to focus on, while the analytic representation of the results of the development work may lack clarity and logic.[37] The task for the individual remains: to be aware of both, the strong and the weak types, and to gradually evolve the weaker functions, to arrive at a more complete and balanced perception of himself, others and the world. The same applies for an organisation, community or whole society, as we shall later see.

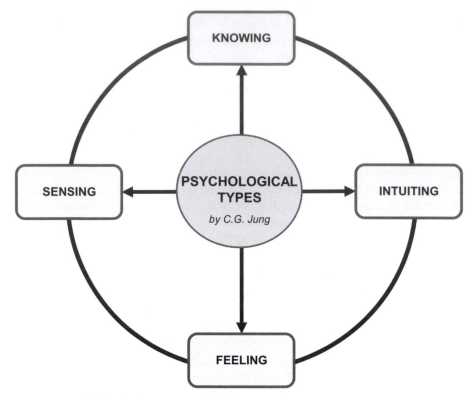

Figure 7.5   Psychological types

You will notice throughout the book that quite a number of researchers have built either directly on Jung's typology, such as David Kolb with his famous learning cycle (⇨15), or have come up with similar distinctions translated to their particular field. In fact, Kolb's learning 'cycle', serves to translate Jung's psychological types into a learning 'rhythm', analogous to our own integral developmental rhythm. Such emergence of resonating rhythms across fields, space and time may well be an indicator that we are tapping into a deeper psychological field common to the human psyche in general. Jung called such deeply anchored, shared structural images within our collective human psyche 'archetypes'. Our circular model with its four vectors is almost an archetypal image, like a mandala (the Indian and Tibetan Buddhist circular paintings derived from the Sanskrit word *mandala* which means 'circle'). It is a symbol of wholeness.

Jung used the drawing of mandalas as a pedagogical tool, for himself as well as for his patients. The resulting images allowed him and others to reflect on their state of inner wholeness. That points to the notion that the major personal development struggle that an individual faces in life, is the struggle towards wholeness, or, in Jung's terms: to find a meaningful balance between the polar opposite attitudes-types as well as between the opposing functional types.

THE IMPORTANCE OF THE TYPES FOR THE INTEGRAL DEVELOPER

It is because of our habitual reactions, of our seeking and avoiding of certain experiences that we as Integral Developers are required to have a sense for our psychological type, and our 'typical' ways of reacting that come with it. Engaged in decisions that are likely to affect the lives of many, we need not only to understand our own type but also to learn how to overcome the limitations that come with it, to arrive, after all, at a sound and integral judgement. Moreover – for us, though not explicitly for Jung – the culture and society (or societies) to which we belong, exercise a major influence on our individuation journey.

The work of the Swiss Jungian analyst and professor of economic planning Theodor Abt confirms the strong influence of the psychological disposition of the development agent on the outcome of the development project. With regards to the attitudes-types, he explains, most development projects favour from the outset development agents with an extraverted personality: because of the strong focus on outer objects and practical realities in development projects and due to the requirement that the development agent interacts easily with people on the ground. Furthermore, the extraverted personality is in general favoured in the Western world with its strong emphasis on – to name just a few characteristics – pragmatism, communication skills and entrepreneurship. However, as Abt experienced in his own development projects in rural Switzerland, each type, the extraverted and the introverted, has much to learn from the other. A purposeful collaboration between development workers representing both attitudes-types can help each to become more conscious of hitherto unknown aspects of one's personality. This process, says Abt, would also lead to a more balanced outcome of the development work they are engaged in.[38] Equally important, as we explained earlier, is a balance with regards to the function-types. Abt laments that due to an overemphasis on the thinking function and on extraversion in development work, much of it has become rather uniform, disregarding the particularity of a context, its specific nature, its communal and social fabric, its cultural and spiritual characteristics.

In engaging with Jung's psychological types we need to start our Integral Development journey with understanding our own individual nature and realm/type. We also receive initial clues with regards to our personal development needs and capacities. The work of American developmental psychologist Daniel Levinson, to whom we now turn, provides further insights into the inner development work that we face on an individual level and that subsequently affects our outer way of working. Levinson, a disciple of Jung, serves as a bridge between integral realms (psychological types) and rhythms (individuation process).

7.5 The Seasons of Human Life: A Circular Development Perspective

THE CYCLE OF LIFE AND THE RESPONSIBILITY OF THE INTEGRAL DEVELOPER

Daniel Levinson sees human life going through different stages within a life cycle. His acclaimed *Seasons of a Man's Life*[39] is a classic of adult development studies written in the late 1970s, and has also informed our previous work on *Transformation Management*.[40] Later, he complemented his original work with *Seasons of a Woman's Life*,[41] co-written with his wife Judy. These life seasons can be regarded as a modern translation of a traditional understanding of life phases that had been cultivated and practised in almost all indigenous societies.

Like nature, we undergo a seasonal rhythm. Like all life in nature, human life moves in a cycle. In traditional societies, each stage of a person's life cycle brings a new function and altered responsibilities to the community. Initiation rites or rites of passage helped the individual to make the transition from one state to another and to get acquainted with his or her new role within the community. Mastering these transition stages were the main development tasks of the individual.

Modern society lacks any such explicit support as we transit from one phase to another. One of the many reasons for this situation is that modern society has become so fragmented and heterogeneous that generalised rites of passage that are designed for overtly homogeneous societies won't provide the necessary meaning any more. Furthermore, we are living in an age of transition without a clear picture as yet to where our collective journey is going. Today, individuals are required to master the transitions connected to one's life phases through a much more individualised, self-reflective, and self-responsible process. This is in particular true for the Integral Developer.

THE CYCLE OF OUR INDIVIDUAL LIFE: FROM TEENS TO MATURITY

Levinson tells us that the components of our life are not a random set of items, like pebbles washed up at the shore. Rather, like threads in a tapestry, they are woven into an encompassing design. Like nature, we – and as we shall later see, organisations and societies – move rhythmically through different seasons. Recurring themes in various sectors of our life and work help to unify the overall patterns of the tapestry. Individual's lives differ widely in the nature and patterning of these themes.

A core finding of Levinson is that our life structure consists of a series of alternating stable and changing periods. We can refer to these as structure building periods and transitional structure-changing periods. Together they make up transformation.

The primary task of every stable period is to build a life structure. We must make certain key choices, form a structure around them, and pursue values and goals within that structure. A transitional period terminates the existing life structure, and creates the possibility for a new one. The primary tasks of every transitional period are to question and reappraise the existing structure, to explore various possibilities for change in self and society, and to move towards commitment to the crucial choices that form the basis for a new life structure in the ensuing stable period. We now introduce the four life stages that Levinson distinguished in greater detail, and that underlie our developmental rhythm.

FIRST FORMATIVE LIFE STAGE: CHILDHOOD AND YOUTH

Forming a Dream: Levinson identifies four 'exploratory tasks' that engage us in the course of a 'healthy' childhood and youth. Sadly enough, should the early stage of our lives be socially and psychologically 'unhealthy' we will carry such an unfulfilled load into the future. For some that may provide an extra spur to development, for others an extra burden. The first task is that of 'forming a dream'. The vicissitudes and fate of the dream have fundamental qualities for development. In its primordial form, the dream is a vague sense of self-in-world. It is associated with a sense of identity, the 'I am' feeling, the experience that 'I exist', that self and society are ultimately properly matched. At the start, it is poorly articulated and only tenuously connected to reality, although it may contain concrete images, such as winning the Nobel Prize or setting up an enterprise.

It may take a dramatic form as in the great artist or an outstanding political leader. It may take the forms of the excellent craftsman, the husband-father in a certain kind of family, the high-performing manager, or the greatly respected member of a community. However, the full articulation and prospective realisation of the dream is dependent on a mentor relationship.

Forming Mentor Relationships: A mentor may act as a teacher to advance the youth in honing skills and intellectual development. Serving as a sponsor, he or she may use his or her influence to facilitate young person's entry and advancement into organisation and society. Such a mentor may be a host and guide, welcoming the initiate to a new occupational and social world and acquainting the novice with its values, customs, resources and cast of characters. Through his or her own virtues, achievements and way of living, the mentor may be an exemplar that the young person can admire and seek to emulate. The mentor has another function though, one that has great relevance also at a societal level, and this is developmentally the most crucial one: to support and facilitate the realisation of a dream. He or she fosters development by believing in the other, by sharing in the other's dream and giving it his or her blessing. The third task in this first season is finding an occupation.

Forming an Occupation: Young people who make a strong occupational commitment in the early twenties, without sufficient exploration of external options and inner preferences, often come to regret it later. However, those who don't make a commitment until the thirties, or who never make one, may feel deprived of the satisfaction of engaging in enduring work that is suitable for the self and valuable for society. Now we come to the fourth youthful endeavour.

Forming Love Relationships: One of our first developmental tasks as a young person is to form the capability of having adult, peer relationships with a 'loved one'. Our formative development, according to Levinson, prepares us partially, but never sufficiently to undertake this work of love and reconciliation. In the light of the formative difficulties we experience, it is small wonder that relating to the other should be a lifelong task. Interestingly enough, at a societal level, the so-called developed world receives increasingly the call from the so-called developing world to love and respect them. It is not enough, for example, to offer aid or debt forgiveness, but justice in trade involves resolving the need for reconciliation for the injustices of the past, those of economic as well as social nature. We now turn to the second life stage: reformative adulthood.

SECOND REFORMATIVE LIFE STAGE: ADULTHOOD

Reformative Orientation: Unlike the conventional wisdom on life stages, from psychotherapists like Jung and Levinson, who come from Europe and America, and who claim that the major 'reformation' starts at midlife, we claim that, for those of us coming from societies in transition it is different. Levinson does give us a prospective bridge across this developed-developing society divide, though, in terms of what he describes as an 'early adult transition'. For us, such a reformative stage, and particularly for those of us based in societies in transition, can extend from young adulthood to early midlife, which is from the late teens to the early/mid forties. Furthermore, the term transition society, to our mind, is not any more only applicable for those states that transit from a so-called developing to a developed society. Increasingly, the so-called developed world is acutely aware of its own need for fundamental transformation. It is in this sense that we propagate a very broad understanding of the term transition society and welcome reformative development impulses already at this second life stage.

Early Adult Transition: For Levinson, the first task for the young adult is to move out of the pre-adult world, to question the nature of the world and our place in it, to modify or terminate relationships with important persons. The second task is to make a preliminary step into the adult world, to explore its possibilities; to imagine oneself as a participant in it; to consolidate an initial adult identity; to make and test some preliminary choices for adult living.

In a society in transition, such an individual developmental agenda is set within the context of a similar process going on in the society as a whole. The great danger that such transitional societies, and the managers and organisations within them, face, is that they are led prematurely to conform to external norms suggested or often thrust upon them by development agents and agencies, rather than evolving their own norms through a process of thorough reformation. We have experienced this danger, again and again, in our own work in southern Africa and the Middle East.

First Adult Structure: Levinson argues that as a young person we have two primary yet antithetical tasks. First, we need to explore the possibilities for adult living, to keep our options open, to avoid strong commitments and maximise our alternatives. This task is reflected in a sense of adventure and wonderment. The second task is to create a stable life structure, to become more responsible and 'make something of one's life', and thereby to be involved in institution building in some shape or form. If the first task predominates, life has an extremely transient, rootless quality. If the second predominates, there is a danger of committing oneself prematurely to a structure.

Age 30 Transition: According to Levinson, in the late twenties the provisional quality of the twenties begins to end and life becomes more serious, more for real. A voice from within the self says 'if I am to change my life – if there are things in it I want to modify or exclude, or things missing I want to add, I must now make a start, for soon it will be too late'. In most cases then, the life structure of the late twenties is incomplete or fragmented. The 'Age 30 Transition' therefore provides an opportunity to work on the flaws in the life structure formed during the previous period, and to create the basis for a more satisfactory one. For some the transition proceeds smoothly. For most it takes a more stressful form.

Settling Down to a Point: As a young adult, the 'settling down' phase is our main vehicle for realising youthful ambitions and goals. In this period a person has two major tasks. First we need to establish a niche in the world, to anchor ourselves more firmly in an institution, and to develop competence in a chosen field. We thereby seek to become a valued member of a valued world. Second we have to work to 'make it'. Whereas the first task contributes to the stability and order of a defined structure, the second involves a progression within that structure. However, at this reformative stage, there will still be a lack of overall resolution.

THE THIRD NORMATIVE LIFE STAGE: MIDLIFE

Tasks of Renewal: To the extent that an individual has consciously engaged with reformation, it will create a firmer basis for life and work in the ensuing phase. To the extent that adult reformation fails, there will be inner contradictions that wait to be addressed.

Midlife Transition: Developmentally, this is the period when the creative tension between self, organisation and society comes to a head. The midlife transition – for the individual self as much as for enterprise and society – is a time of severe crisis. The butterfly is struggling to emerge from the chrysalis. We question nearly every aspect of our life and feel that we cannot go on as before. The neglected parts of our self urgently seek expression. Internal voices or competencies that have been muted for years now clamour to be heard. 'I cannot live with myself any more'. Oftentimes, a successful business entrepreneur or executive, like Microsoft's Bill Gates or financier-philanthropist George Soros, will create a foundation to serve such a hitherto neglected purpose or part of the world that calls their attention.

Balancing and Integrating: The rapidly lengthening life span in modern society has stimulated widespread concern with the era of late adulthood. We are beginning to seek ways of improving the quality of life for the elderly, and of managing the economic burdens involved. Much less attention has been given to a problem of equal or greater significance, specifically the rapidly growing percentage of the population in middle adulthood. Unless the quality of life in this generation can be improved, Levinson asserts, the middle age will be under strain and society will continue to be short of creative leadership. While occupational roles have become more specialised we need more people who can contribute as leaders, managers, mentors, sources of traditional wisdom as well as vision and imagination. This represents a return to the relationship orientation at the formative stage of development, but at a whole new level. Yet, at this stage, our newly formed self-concept is inclusive but still divisive. In a few cases this division yields to the call of radical actualisation. Levinson calls this 'Legacy Stage'.

FOURTH TRANSFORMATIVE LIFE STAGE: MATURITY

Imagery of the legacy tends to flourish during the midlife transition, as part of the work of the young/old polarity. Our legacy is what we pass on to future generations. People differ enormously in their views about what constitutes a legacy, but, for whole societies, their cultures are manifestations of this. Although the real value of our legacy is impossible to measure, in our mind it defines to a large degree the ultimate value of our lives – and our claims to immortality – thereby ultimately realising, as an individual, organisation and society, what we intended, or indeed were destined, to develop.

LIFE'S SEASONS: A HELPFUL TOOL FOR SELF EXAMINATION FOR THE INTEGRAL DEVELOPER

Levinson's seasons are a helpful tool for the Integral Developer to examine where he or she stands in life. What are the personal development tasks that I am facing according to my life stage? And how are these tasks potentially projected to an outer development context? How can the larger development context I am embedded in help me in my own evolution, as, whatever I do and wherever I am, I am not developing in isolation, but always in interaction with others. In that sense, it is totally legitimate that the chosen context also feeds my own development needs. The utterly important task for the Integral Developer, however, remains: to be conscious of one's own developmental needs and tasks, and being equally conscious and empathetic about the developmental needs and tasks of others.

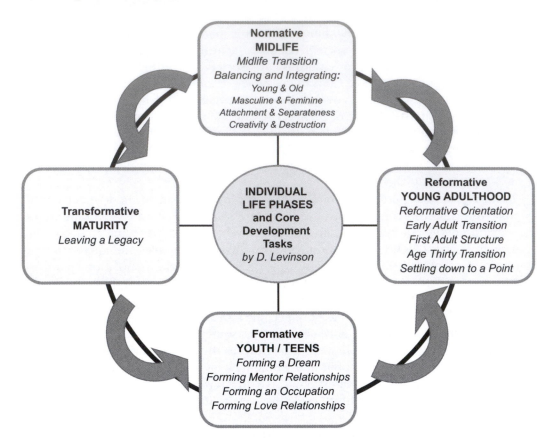

Figure 7.6   Individual life phases and core development tasks

When we discovered Levinson's distinction in four core life phases, we were struck by the closeness to our own work, though Levinson focuses purely on the individual level. Each phase builds on the then following phase, and in each the (self-)developer is faced with core development tasks. Figure 7.6 sums up the four phases and the key development tasks.

7.6   Integration

We are now ready to move to the next organisational level. Yet, at one and the same time, we have already anticipated this move. For the formative grounding in self prepares the way for a reformative emergence, through an organisation, and ultimately community and society, that befits our very self, and that potentially co-evolve with us. Inevitably, such an institution, and such a community, involves in some shape or form, a fusion between our particular local, indigenous grounds and more global perspectives.

Indeed, where the world at large has done most of us a major disservice, is to impose a particular form of organisation, and indeed a particular form of 'development' upon all of us. The prevailing form of both is the 'Western' model of a private enterprise – conveyed to millions of students through the Anglo-Saxon-derived MBA (Masters of Business Administration) and thereby onto the world at large – and of economic development, running alongside. That means, if you yourself come, for example from Belgium or Benin, Singapore or Senegal, conventional organisational designs, and approaches to community and economic development, may well not befit your natural and community-based origins: a deplorable state of affairs that we seek to address through Integral Development.

Before we move on, however, we invite you to engage – through reflection and prospective action – with the guiding questions and theory presented in this chapter, as well as with the major development challenges derived thereof for yourself.

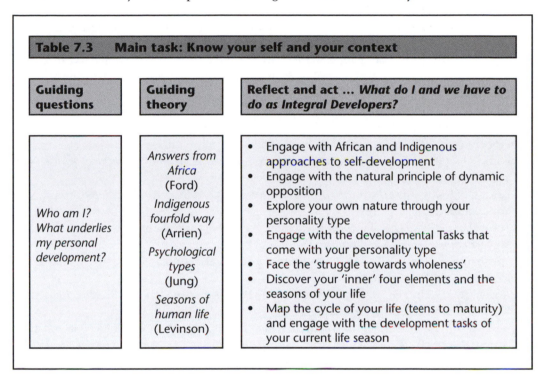

Table 7.3	Main task: Know your self and your context	
Guiding questions	**Guiding theory**	**Reflect and act ... What do I and we have to do as Integral Developers?**
Who am I? What underlies my personal development?	Answers from Africa (Ford) Indigenous fourfold way (Arrien) Psychological types (Jung) Seasons of human life (Levinson)	• Engage with African and Indigenous approaches to self-development • Engage with the natural principle of dynamic opposition • Explore your own nature through your personality type • Engage with the developmental Tasks that come with your personality type • Face the 'struggle towards wholeness' • Discover your 'inner' four elements and the seasons of your life • Map the cycle of your life (teens to maturity) and engage with the development tasks of your current life season

We now turn from self to organisation within this 'Southern' integral realm.

References

1 Ford, C. (2000). *The Hero with an African Face: Mythic Wisdom of Traditional Africa*. New York: Bantam Books, p. 194.

2 MacGaffey, W. (1993). *Modern Kongo Prophets*. Bloomington, IN: Indiana University Press, p. 128.

3 Ford, C. (2000). *The Hero with an African Face: Mythic Wisdom of Traditional Africa*. New York: Bantam Books, p. 195, and Thompson, R.F. (1983). *Flash of the Spirit*. New York: Random House.

4 Ford, C. (2000). *The Hero with an African Face: Mythic Wisdom of Traditional Africa*. New York: Bantam Books, p. 195.

5 MacGaffey, W. (1993). *Modern Kongo Prophets*. Bloomington, IN: Indiana University Press, p. 127.

6 Thompson, R.F. (1983). *Flash of the Spirit*. New York: Random House, p. 109.

7   Ford, C. (2000). *The Hero with an African Face: Mythic Wisdom of Traditional Africa*. New York: Bantam Books, p. 197.

8   Ford, C. (2000). *The Hero with an African Face: Mythic Wisdom of Traditional Africa*. New York: Bantam Books, p. 198.

9   Ford, C. (2000). *The Hero with an African Face: Mythic Wisdom of Traditional Africa*. New York: Bantam Books, p. 144.

10 Ford, C. (2000). *The Hero with an African Face: Mythic Wisdom of Traditional Africa*. New York: Bantam Books, p. 145.

11 Soyinka, W. (1992). *Myth, Literature and the African World*. Cambridge: Cambridge University Press, pp. 1–2.

12 Ford, C. (2000). *The Hero with an African Face: Mythic Wisdom of Traditional Africa*. New York: Bantam Books, p. 146. Referring to: Jung, C.G., Archetypes of the Unconscious, in: De Laszlo, V.S. (ed.), (1959). *The Basic Writings of C.G. Jung*. New York: Random House.

13 Soyinka, W. (1992). *Myth, Literature and the African World*. Cambridge: Cambridge University Press, p. 152.

14 Frobenius, L. (1968). *Voice of Africa*. New York: Benjamin Blom, pp. 252–64.

15 Ford, C. (2000). *The Hero with an African Face: Mythic Wisdom of Traditional Africa*. New York: Bantam Books, p. 169.

16 Ford, C. (2000). *The Hero with an African Face: Mythic Wisdom of Traditional Africa*. New York: Bantam Books, p. 169.

17 Tutu, D. (1999). *No Future without Forgiveness: A Personal Overview of South Africa's Truth and Reconciliation Commission*. London: Doubleday.

18 Nussbaum, B. (2004). Ubuntu: Reflections of a South African on Our Common Humanity. In: *Reflections*, Vol. 4, Issue 4.

19 Arrien, A. (1993). *The Four-Fold Way: Walking the Paths of the Warrior, Teacher, Healer and Visionary*. San Francisco, CA: Harper, p. 4.

20 Manuel, G. (1974). *The Fourth World: An Indian Reality*. Toronto, ON: Collier Macmillan.

21 Arrien, A. (1993). *The Four-Fold Way: Walking the Paths of the Warrior, Teacher, Healer and Visionary*. San Francisco, CA: Harper, p. 4.

22 Burger, J. (1990). *The Gaia Atlas of First Peoples: A Future for the Indigenous World*. Garden City, NY: Anchor Books.

23 Arrien, A. (1993). *The Four-Fold Way: Walking the Paths of the Warrior, Teacher, Healer and Visionary*. San Francisco, CA: Harper, p. 6.

24 Arrien, A. (1993). *The Four-Fold Way: Walking the Paths of the Warrior, Teacher, Healer and Visionary*. San Francisco, CA: Harper, p. 7.

25 Arrien, A. (1993). *The Four-Fold Way: Walking the Paths of the Warrior, Teacher, Healer and Visionary*. San Francisco, CA: Harper, p. 9.

26 Arrien, A. (1993). *The Four-Fold Way: Walking the Paths of the Warrior, Teacher, Healer and Visionary*. San Francisco, CA: Harper, p. 9.

27 Mander, J. (1991). *In the Absence of the Sacred: The Failure of Technology and the Survival of the Indian Nation*. San Francisco, CA: Sierra Club Books, pp. 383f.

28 Eysenck, H.J. and Eysenck M.W. (1958). *Personality and Individual Differences*. New York: Plenum

29 Maidenbaum, A. (1998). In: Thomson, L. (ed.), *Personality Type: An Owner's Manual*. Boston, MA: Shambhala, p. ix.

30 Jung, C.G. (2009). *Psychological Types*. London: Routledge, p. 330.

31 Jung, C.G. (1933). *Modern Man in Search of a Soul*. San Diego, CA: Harcourt, p. 88.

32 Jung, C.G. et al. (1968). *Man and His Symbols*. New York: Laurel, p. 49.

33 Thomson, L. (1998). *Personality Type: An Owner's Manual*. Boston, MA: Shambhala, p. 7.

34 Thomson, L. (1998). *Personality Type: An Owner's Manual*. Boston, MA: Shambhala, pp. 7f.

35 Briggs-Myers, I. and Myers, P.B. (1995). *Gifts Differing: Understanding Personality Types*. Mountain-View, CA: Davies-Black.

36 Comment: Jung's work – in particular his approach to quaternity – has already inspired profoundly our previous integral work, in particular also our recent book: Lessem, R., Schieffer, A., Tong, J. and Rima, S. (2013). *Integral Dynamics: Nature, Culture, Science and Enterprise*. Farnham: Gower

37 Abt, T. (1978). *Entwicklungsplanung ohne Seele? Sozio-ökonomische und psychologische Aspekte der Entwicklungsplanung im Berggebiet*. Bern: Lang, pp. 111ff.

38 Abt, T. (1978). *Entwicklungsplanung ohne Seele? Sozio-ökonomische und psychologische Aspekte der Entwicklungsplanung im Berggebiet*. Bern: Lang, pp. 111ff.

39 Levinson, D.J. et al. (1979). *The Seasons of a Man's Life*. New York: Knopf.

40 Lessem, R. and Schieffer, A. (2009). *Transformation Management: Towards the Integral Enterprise*. Farnham: Gower.

41 Levinson, D.J. and Levinson, J.D. (1996). *The Seasons of Woman's Life*. New York: Knopf.

8 *The Ecosystemic Organisation: A Southern Organisational Perspective*

Guiding Questions: Who are we? Where do we come from and where are we going to as a group and as an organisation?

8.1 Orientation

You now expand your radius within this 'Southern' integral realm. From the first level of the individual, that is the grounding of the self, you move to the second level, that is our emergence as a group and organisation. Such institutional emergence needs to reflect our prior self. In most cases – sad to say in the world at large and most particularly in the 'Global South' today – this is not the case. Most development efforts leading to institutionalisation (thereby read modernisation), ignore the first level of 'self', unable or unwilling to build institutions that emerge out of local, individual and communal development impulses.

In our case here, we are determined to purposefully interconnect individual, group and organisational development. Thereby we seek to avoid falling victim to the predominant, largely Anglo-Saxon approach to institutionalisation. That does not mean that you need to have all the organisational answers yourself, but you need to be able to formulate who you are institutionally, and which institutional form befits you.

At this level we purposefully draw upon organisation development theory. Characteristically, the three levels from self to society remain disconnected. But we claim there is a great deal that the three levels can learn from each other. And indeed, we do need all three levels, so that the development impulse that we seek to nurture can be fully actualised. The organisation development field has a lot to offer in that respect, and the enormous pressure for change and transformation particularly in the private sector organisations, has produced a vast amount of research in this arena.

On this organisational level, we looked in particular for organisation development literature that served to restore our connection with nature and community. It is indeed fascinating to witness, how some of the more recent research in this field serves to re-ground the organisation in organic metaphors inspired by nature and life, as opposed to earlier mechanistic, machine-inspired ones. The organisation as a living organism is thus embedding and embedded in smaller and larger living organisms. This is the interconnected picture that is increasingly being painted. This new understanding of an organisation can be regarded as a fundamental paradigm shift. In a way, quite a number of path-breaking organisations, which are fully rooted in a nature-inspired organisational paradigm – like Interface in USA (⇨22) and Broad in China[1] – anticipate the mind-shift that society as a whole might experience.

Moreover, you do not act in isolation. In our development efforts we are either already part of an organisation that is our major operational vehicle, or we emerge from our 'Southern' individual grounding to become a group or organisation through which we engage with a particular development context. We thus address the following development questions:

* Who are we as a group and organisation?
* How have we emerged from our formative individual grounding?
* What then is our reformative natural and communal organisational role?
* What are our aspirations and gifts that nurture and serve the development process?
* What do we know about group and organisational life? How do organisations in a 'Southern' natural and community context live and renew themselves?
* How do we relate to and what do we do to restore nature and community, both within our own context and in the world without?
* What requires 'restoration' in our group and organisation and in the larger context we are part of?
* What are therefore our collective developmental issues and capacities?
* How do these issues and capacities relate to the development needs of the community and society of which we are part?

To be able to go further, we first seek guidance from one of the key thinkers on organisational development of the twentieth century, the Dutchman Bernard Lievegoed and his work on organisational life cycles. That will also help us to reflect on the differences and similarities between individual and organisational approaches to such cycles. Thereafter, we follow the American management consultant James Moore, who takes Lievegoed's original work forward, but gives it a much more natural and community-based edge. He thereby integrates the collaborative principle that is found in nature into organisational thinking, in addition to the hitherto sole 'Western' focus on competition as the guiding mechanism for a private enterprise.

8.2　Life Cycles in Organisations: Towards Association

THE ORGANISATIONAL LIFE CYCLE: FROM PIONEERING TO IMPLEMENTATION

Bernard Lievegoed was one of the major path breakers in organisational development. His book *The Developing Organisation*,[2] published in 1969, provides invaluable insights in how the phases in the development of a human being informed the development of organisations. Though his main focus was on business enterprises, he also showed great interest in community development, and the generic phases have relevance beyond the economic arena. It is also for this reason that we have built on Lievegoed's approach also in our work on the Integral Enterprise.[3]

Lievegoed described three phases typical in the development of organisations. His colleague Fritz Glasl has added a fourth phase, thereby enabling us to liken that approach to that of Levinson, and indeed to our own model. The first phase is the formative pioneer phase, common to such entrepreneurial ventures across the globe.

FIRST FORMATIVE PHASE OF PIONEERING

'In its pure form, a pioneer enterprise is an enterprise that is still being run by its founder. It comes into being as a result of a creative act by a human being'.[4] For Lievegoed, the characteristics of so-called pioneer enterprises are:

- Leadership is autocratic.
- Communication is direct.
- The style of organisation is person-oriented.
- The working style is improvisational.
- The work force or community: 'one big family'.
- The pioneer's market or environment: known customers, clients or members.

The characteristics are equally familiar to the start-up phases of almost any organisation, including, for example, NGOs focusing on any aspect of communal and societal development. Lievegoed illustrates vividly what may happen when a pioneer organisation becomes 'over-ripe' and has reached the threshold of a new development. Such a stage is reached when the original strength of the pioneer organisation, its closeness, has become its weakness. Often, at this moment, the founding pioneer and his/her leadership and management style are increasingly questioned by the staff and demands are made to (a) respond in a different way to external challenges (new technologies, altered economic situation, etc.) and (b) to organise the operations in a more systematic, differentiated way.

SECOND PHASE OF REFORMATIVE DIFFERENTIATION

For Lievegoed, the 'historical answer to the problems of the over-ripe pioneer enterprise came in the form of scientific management',[5] or, in other words, of classical management. When private sector organisations, in the second half of the nineteenth century were for the first time confronted with the challenge of industrial production on a large scale, large-scale enterprises emerged and called for a reorientation and reorganisation of management. It was primarily two people who laid the foundation for such a new kind of scientific management: the engineers Frederick Taylor (1856 to 1915) from the USA and Henry Fayol (1841 to 1925) in France:

Scientific management is based on a logical ordering of functions, tasks, things and processes. It assumes that the productivity of an organisation increases the more the people concerned succeed in behaving according to the formal organisational plan. The norms for human behaviour in the work situation comply first and foremost with the demands made by the technical process.[6]

The core principles of the phase of differentiation were:

- Principle of mechanisation.
- Principle of standardisation.
- Principle of specialisation.
- Principle of coordination.

The differentiation of the second phase is an essential prerequisite for a group, community or organisation if it is to function on a long-term basis on a larger scale and with greater complexity. That having been said, such reformative differentiation is much more commonplace in the 'North' and 'West' than elsewhere. By and large reformative institutional emergence conventionally falls short in the 'Global South', in part because neither management consultants nor schools of public or private enterprise have taken the time and trouble to re-conceive nature and community-based enterprise in such differentiated terms. Indeed not only business schools and consultancies, but also professional associations, be they scientifically, engineering or management based, are all modelled on the 'West'. Most academic disciplines, such as physics or chemistry, and most organisational knowledge domains, such as finance or marketing, were all developed as differentiated fields in Europe and America. By and large no authentically 'Southern' (or 'Eastern') reformulation of these has taken place, building on the prior grounds of nature and community.

That said, increasing differentiation and systemisation of an organisation can lead to rigidity, coordination problems, vertical communication problems, decrease of motivation and thereby reduced individual productivity and many more such problems. All of the large-scale development institutions – from World Bank to IMF, from ILO to WHO – went through this phase, and most, critics argue, got stuck in it and turned in bureaucratic over-standardised, over-specialised institutional dinosaurs. For Lievegoed 'in order to escape from the dilemma of the over-ripe second phase ... the time seems to have arrived for a complete revision of the model'.[7] At this stage the organisation enters the phase of (in our terms) normative integration, if it continues to develop – but most in fact do not.

THIRD NORMATIVE PHASE OF INTEGRATION WITH SOCIETY

In this third phase, argues Lievegoed, it is crucial, that the institution develops a social subsystem, and integrates it with the already existing economic and technical subsystems. Such integration, we would add, needs to include the organisational embeddedness within the particular community or society in which it is lodged. For Lievegoed this is a gradual process, but a necessary one. It is characterised by the following assumptions:

- Interlinked, smaller, relatively independent units are set up.
- Self-planning, self-organisation and self-control ensue.
- The system rests on the conviction that every person can and wants to develop.
- Personal fulfilment can be achieved in the work situation.
- Organisation and society are intimately interlinked.

It is noteworthy that the above characteristics blend in well with those of a fully functioning learning community, within a research and educational environment, as well as in a conventional, public or private enterprise. The Austrian management consultant, Fritz Glasl, a close collaborator of Lievegoed, has taken Lievegoed's three-phase model of organisational development on to a fourth stage, reflecting the challenges of our times. This phase is called the associative phase.

FOURTH PHASE OF TRANSFORMATIVE ASSOCIATION

Glasl claims that organisations have arrived indeed at a new threshold, which requires another evolutionary step. He argues that:

it is not only important to structure and manage one's own organisation well, but we have to recognise that our own organisation can only be successful if it sees itself as:

- *a whole interdependent network of relationships between different organisations and stakeholders.*
- *this does not mean that 'my' organisation becomes subordinate and disappears, but that it is important how this entity related to others in an ongoing network of cooperative relationships.*
- *these are the 'shared destiny relationships' because an enterprise has to enter into a relationship with a variety of organisations in its environment; a relationship which is characterised by an attitude of responsibility, or a certain permanence, and which is based on continuous development.*[8]

Over the course of this book, you will notice that this kind of associative organisation resonates strongly with the new educational-developmental institutions ('Uni-Versities') that we propose as the culmination of each realm. Figure 8.1, on the next page, sums up the four phases of the organisational life cycle.

It is easy to see the resonance between our own Integral Development rhythm with Lievegoed and Glasl's four phases. However, neither Glasl nor Lievegoed take into account the particular cultural and societal context, with whom an organisation is developmentally becoming associated.

In the 'Global South', especially, where large-scale organisations invariably become dysfunctionally bureaucratic, and remain that way, nobody has taken the time and trouble to develop a new form of natural and community 'integration' and 'association', of the kind to which Lievegoed and Glasl allude, one that is attuned to a particular 'Southern' people and circumstances. A well-known practical example, that illustrates this case, is that of the closely inter-networked family based enterprises of Middle Italy, especially in the 1970s and 1980s, which were highly successful for two decades, in fields ranging from textiles to machine tools, before they began to be overtaken by large-scale, Anglo-Saxon style multinationals.

That having been said, Glasl's additional fourth phase of association builds a perfect bridge to James Moore's ecosystemic approach to organisational development. We can clearly see the connection between Lievegoed's and Glasl's more socially centred approach and Moore's ecological orientation.

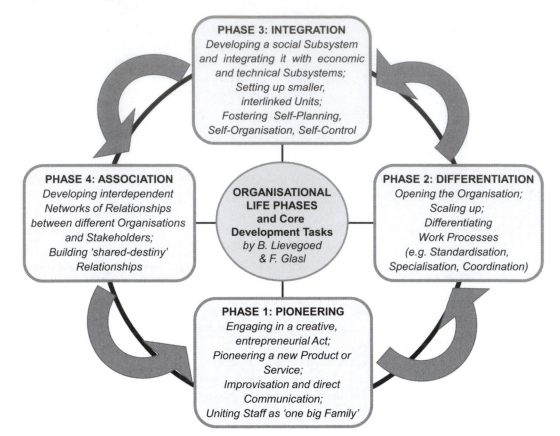

Figure 8.1   Organisational life phases and core development tasks

8.3   Organisational Evolution via an Ecosystemic Shift: Beyond Competition

BUSINESS ECOSYSTEMS

James Moore is a respected American business consultant, drawing ostensibly upon conventional Darwinian evolutionary biology. Yet his orientation towards *The Death of Competition: Leadership and Strategy in the Age of Business Ecosystems* is startling. For Moore, the presumption that there are distinct, immutable businesses within which players scramble for supremacy is a tired idea whose time is past. The new business paradigm requires thinking in whole systems:

> *With nature and not machines as their inspiration, today's innovators are showing how to create a different future by learning to see the larger systems of which they are a part and to foster collaboration across every possible boundary. These core capabilities – seeing systems, collaborating across boundaries, and creative problem solving, form the underpinnings for the shift in thinking we now require.*[9]

Starting with understanding the big picture rather than specific products and services, business evolution becomes a more important concept than simply competition or cooperation. Moore argues that an enterprise would have to undergo a mind-shift from one of competing to co-evolving with the institutions and individuals to which it relates.

As leaders then evolve into what Moore terms 'gardeners' so they develop what he calls an eco-community supported by a foundation of interacting organisations and individuals. This emerging community – which would equally be reflected in a 'Communiversity' (⇨10) – produces goods and services (which could include educational programmes and processes) of value to customers, learners or researchers, who are themselves members of the ecosystem; member organisms also include suppliers, lead contractors, and even competitors.

Over time, they co-evolve their capabilities and roles, and tend to align themselves with the directions set by one or more of the companies. The function of an ecosystem leader, which for example INTEL plays in the world of semiconductors, is valued by the community. For it enables members to move toward shared visions so as to align their investments, and to find mutually supportive roles. Organisations compete to unite disparate contributors to create powerful total solutions, and then to establish thriving business ecosystems dedicated to providing these solutions to customers and communities. These solutions depend not only on the core product or service, but on a variety of complementary offers that enhance the experience of customer or community. Ultimately, as Moore affirms, returns from the core enterprise are also invested in leadership and support for the social and economic ecosystem itself, for 'alliance community development' activities.

The major factor today limiting the spread of realised innovation, for Moore, is not a lack of good ideas, technology or capital. It is rather the inability to command cooperation across broad, diverse communities of players or learners who must become intimate parts of a far-reaching process of co-evolution. In the classical paradigm of industry-based competition, products and even product leadership have become comparatively easy to dislodge. Newcomers simply clone the required technologies or programmes, make the requisite investments in technologies and people, and have a go at it. By contrast, the environment-shaping leader of an organisational ecosystem like a Microsoft or a Benneton, set the stage for a co-evolving system, which becomes difficult to dislodge.

For a leading evolutionary strategist:

- Finds ways to better embed contributions into the products and processes of adjacent institutions, as well as to shape architectural standards and customer and community preference.
- Ties together stronghold sub-ecosystems and/or uses them to create new positions in adjacent territories.
- Finds some aspect of value creation where the niche is becoming important and no player has made a strong stand.

How then, in such an evolutionary context, do organisations evolve over time? Moore takes a similarly developmental perspective to Lievegoed and Glasl. While the Lievegoed's approach was lodged in what he terms 'social ecology', Moore roots his orientation more in 'natural ecology'. He came up with the following four developmental stages, illustrating the corporate world's increasing affinity with nature-based metaphors.

FOUR DEVELOPMENT STAGES: FROM PIONEERING TO RENEWAL

First Stage = Pioneering: According to Moore, business, social and even eco-entrepreneurs firstly struggle to form embryonic ecosystems that, while hardly mature, are at least complete enough to fulfil the needs of initial customers and communities. Doing something of dramatic value, compared to what is already available, is the *sine qua non* of the early days of a business or social ecosystem.

The pioneering goals then are primarily to do with learning, that is learning what value proposition works and discovering how to provide it, through a combination of:

- intense customer/community interaction to find out how they think and to get clues of how they want to use the product;
- finding sponsor/patron customers/communities committed to helping the core offer evolve fruitfully, as early adopters perceiving the dramatic potential of the innovation at an early stage.

Second Phase = Expansion: At a second stage of an emerging enterprise ecosystem, the successful formula is more broadly applied and made more reliable and replicable. Additional waves of customers and other stakeholders are recruited. The overall focus is upon identifying and rounding up the most desirable potential allies available, that is, the best customers, strongest suppliers and most important channels of distribution.

Moore continuously draws comparisons to nature. Ecological communities mature in at least two ways: first they expand in biomass, grasslands get denser, trees grow taller, and populations of animals multiply. Second they mature through increased genetic diversity, adding species, elaborating synergistic relationships, becoming ever more artful in turning resources into community life. The diversity of members in an enterprise ecosystem makes it more robust and resilient, providing variety to its offerings, and a host of creative ideas to help spawn further evolution. Expansion, hence, requires a compelling vision of value, and the ability to scale up the ecosystem to provide this.

Third Phase = Authority: To stay successful, a lead institution must maintain and fortify its ability to shape the future direction and investments of the ecosystem's key customers and suppliers, thereby maintaining the authority and the uniqueness of its contribution to the community, while also encouraging community-wide innovation and co-evolution.

INTEL's systems business, for example, and its relationship to the microprocessor business had traditionally been seen in industry, not in ecosystem, terms. The INTEL products group in the early 1990s saw the potential to drive new ideas and innovation into the business system in a new way. INTEL used to design circuits. Now, according to Moore, they worry more about the nature of industrial democracy and the design of the interactions among companies, organisations and individuals who shape markets. INTEL's architecture labs are now promoting an open framework for investment, a framework that invites others to bring their innovation to the personal computer platform. The framework is particularly valuable in making a place for smaller, highly creative companies; to help coordinate the investments of others, rather than make these themselves. In Moore's terms, as 'chip heads willing to learn', managers starting out with a semiconductor industry orientation became ambassadors to a larger, more diverse community of companies. Over time, INTEL got Wall Street to recognise that the company is not simply a capital-intensive producer of a commodity but an important member of the fabric of information industries.

Moore argues that regardless of whether stage three enterprises lead or follow, the opportunity environments in which they operate are populated by centres of intense co-evolution. Such organisations do not necessarily need to be the shapers of the business ecosystem they join. This is especially the case if they trust and respect its leadership, but they must find a valued contribution to make. Most of all, they need to make a contribution enduringly critical to the ecosystem, and embed it in the fabric of the community. This brings us to the ultimate stage of either renewal or death.

Fourth Phase = Renewal or Death: For Moore, longevity or sustainable development comes from finding ways to inject new ideas into the existing ecosystem, thereby establishing a system of symbiotic relationships of lasting value relative to what else is available. Few institutions around the world have reached such an ultimate stage of development.

In most stage four ecosystems, individuals are competent and dedicated in their specific contributions. It is the ecosystem as a whole, which is under-performing, and not the individual species. Leadership and strategy in the age of business or communal ecosystems must therefore bring several elements together for organisational reform and corporate renewal to have a chance to:

- survey the opportunity landscape and understand the current power players and their interests and assets;
- develop valid information about the performance of the whole enterprise ecosystem, and what it means for this ecosystem to succeed. How can this be measured? What factors are required for success? How might these factors be influenced to improve performance?
- organise things to affect the aspects of the enterprise ecosystem that require transformation, taking responsibility for the most important co-evolving factors and actors.

We now turn to the economic system as a whole.

FROM BUSINESS ECOSYSTEMS TO AN ECOSYSTEMIC ECONOMY: FROM EGO-AWARENESS TO ECO-AWARENESS

Moore's organisational approach to business – or, analogous, for social or educational – ecosystems is mirrored in the latest thinking on rebuilding the economic system as a whole. We shall come back to this issue at a later stage (⇨21), but it is worthwhile now intimating with one example the degree to which visionary thinking on reinventing economics as a whole seeks guidance in nature's principles. The German management thinker Otto Scharmer, based at Boston's MIT, sees seven so-called 'acupuncture points' that we need to deal with systemically, in order to make the shift from what he calls 'Capitalism 2.0' – beyond a free market, laissez faire capitalism towards *a* more regulated European-style stakeholder capitalism with a focus on redistribution) – to 'Capitalism 3.0', 'an (as-yet unrealised) intentional, inclusive, ecosystem economy that upgrades the capacity for collaboration and innovation throughout all sectors of society (focus on ecosystem innovation)'.[10]

The first two of Scharmer's acupuncture points relate directly to natural principles:

- *Ecosystemic Coordination Mechanisms:* Upgrade the economic operating system from one driven by competition and special interest group led legislation ('ego-system awareness') to one that operates from shared seeing and common will (driven by an intentional 'ecosystem awareness').
- *Nature:* Design all production and consumption cycles completely earth-to-earth (without the need for landfills and in co-evolution with the natural ecosystem).

8.4 Integration

As far as Lievegoed's and Moore's reformative work is concerned, we can conclude, that both their developmental approaches emerge out of a prior grounding in natural cycles, rooted initially in the 'self'. In Figure 8.2 we illustrate, for example, how Moore's developmental stages for an organisation can be aligned with those of Levinson' life seasons for the individual self (⇨7). Pioneering, expansion, authority, and renewal or death, in Moore's case, correspond with formative youth, reformative adulthood, normative midlife and transformative maturity, in Levinson's case.

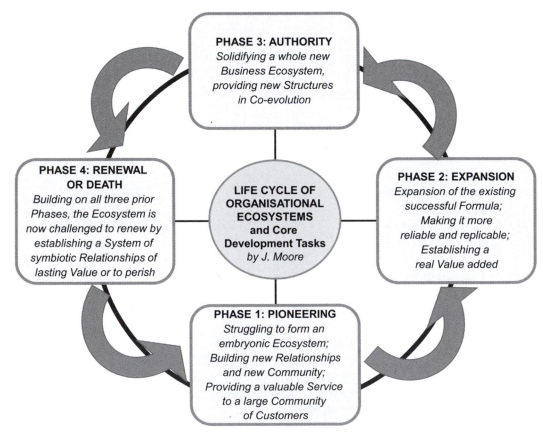

Figure 8.2   Life cycle of organisational ecosystems

Such a cyclical rhythm, lodged within physical and human nature, is deeply resonant with archetypal fourfold realms and rhythms lodged in antiquity and in indigenous worldviews. All too often, though, such an integral orientation does not emerge from an individual to an organisational level. Then, this 'Southern' orientation does not make its way from the individual toward society. That said, with Moore's work on business ecosystems, and in particular with Scharmer's call for an ecosystemic society, we are reminded again of the interconnectedness between the organisational and the societal level, to which we now turn.

Before we move on we invite you to engage – through reflection and prospective action – with the guiding questions and theory presented in this chapter, as well as with the major development challenges derived thereof for yourself and your organisation or community. If you are not yet associated with a particular organisation or community (or initiative, network or movement), you may want to envision founding one, together with others. If your primary association is with a university – be it as member of its faculty or as participant in an educational or research programme – you may want to consider using this as your core transformational, organisational context.

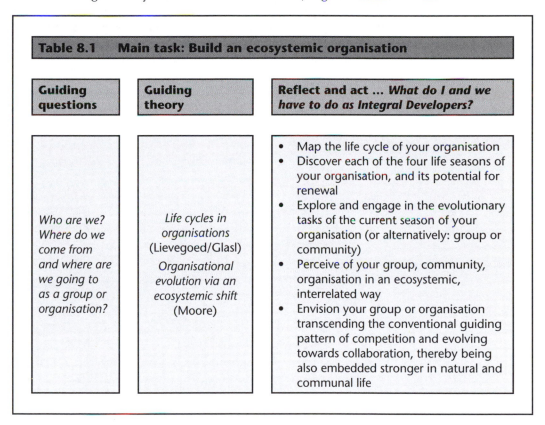

Table 8.1	Main task: Build an ecosystemic organisation	
Guiding questions	**Guiding theory**	**Reflect and act ... *What do I and we have to do as Integral Developers?***
Who are we? Where do we come from and where are we going to as a group or organisation?	*Life cycles in organisations* (Lievegoed/Glasl) *Organisational evolution via an ecosystemic shift* (Moore)	• Map the life cycle of your organisation • Discover each of the four life seasons of your organisation, and its potential for renewal • Explore and engage in the evolutionary tasks of the current season of your organisation (or alternatively: group or community) • Perceive of your group, community, organisation in an ecosystemic, interrelated way • Envision your group or organisation transcending the conventional guiding pattern of competition and evolving towards collaboration, thereby being also embedded stronger in natural and communal life

We now turn from individual, group and organisation onto society at large.

References

1   Schieffer, A., Ying, X. and Lessem, R. (October 2006). Rooted in China – Reaching out to the World. Part 1 and Part 2. In: *Transformation*, Vol. 20, Issues 16/17. World Business Academy.
2   Lievegoed, B. (1969). *The Developing Organisation*. London: Tavistock Publications.
3   Lessem, R. and Schieffer, A. (2009). *Transformation Management: Towards the Integral Enterprise*. Farnham: Gower.
4   Lievegoed, B. (1991). *Managing the Developing Organisation*. Oxford: Basil Blackwell.
5   Lievegoed, B. (1991). *Managing the Developing Organisation*. Oxford: Basil Blackwell.
6   Lievegoed, B. (1991). *Managing the Developing Organisation*. Oxford: Basil Blackwell.
7   Lievegoed, B. (1991). *Managing the Developing Organisation*. Oxford: Basil Blackwell.
8   Glasl, F. (1997). *The Enterprise of the Future: Moral Intuition in Leadership and Organisation Development*. Stroud: Hawthorne Press.
9   Moore, J. (1997). *The Death of Competition: Leadership and Strategy in the Age of Business Ecosystems*. New York: Wiley.
10 Scharmer, O. (2009). Seven Acupuncture Points for Shifting Capitalism to Create a Regenerative Ecosystem Economy. Paper presented at the Roundtable on Transforming Capitalism to Create a Regenerative Economy, Boston, MA, September 2009.

9 *Embeddedness in Society: A Southern Societal Perspective*

Guiding Question: How do we develop as a community or society based on our own development needs, aspirations and capacities?

9.1 Orientation

We now enter the field that 'normal' development thinking deals with exclusively: spanning community and society – disconnected from individual, group and organisation. As a result, most of such thinking has taken place in a rather distant, intellectualised manner and much of the subsequent work has thereby proven to be out of touch with the actually experienced life worlds and cultural contexts of the people it seeks to benefit. The reason for this is that such a societal approach has not emerged out of prior individual and organisational contexts. As a result, it is plucked out of societal mid-air.

Among development thinkers there is only a relatively small group of primarily anthropologists that have not only delved into the depth of such development contexts, but also managed to understand local conditions and to see development with the eyes of those 'to be developed'. They foster thereby a bottom-up perspective that this book as a whole also promotes, and that the 'Communiversity' to which we will allude in the next chapter builds upon. In their work they often critically comment on the disastrous effects that much of the prevailing top-down approach to development has caused within local communities, despite their often genuine intentions to contribute to the betterment of social conditions. However, even in their community orientation, they do not start out from the developmental perspective of the individual, as well as the small group, and they completely bypass the development of the organisation. Their development 'norming' is thereby bereft of prior individual 'forming', and institutional 're-forming'.

Having worked through the levels of self and other, group and organisation, you are now ready to engage with community and society. By now it has become evident, that you and your immediate context are not outside society, but an integral part of it. Thereby, every engagement in development on a communal or societal level is always also to be reflected on a personal and organisational level. Development takes place 'in here' as well as 'out there'. The development agent is co-evolving with the development context. We thus part company from top-down development – through a new understanding of life, through a better understanding of ourselves and others.

The natural starting point for working with society is the immediate community of the Integral Developer. Starting there, rather than with society as a whole, helps us to bring things back to human scale, back into a sphere were interaction is possible and tangible. Geoff Mulgan, founder of the British think tank Demos, has a similar reason why he prefers community as a starting point:

> *Community is deliberately a different word from society. It may refer to neighbourhoods or workplaces, but to be meaningful it must imply membership in a human-scale collective: a scale at which it is possible to encounter people face to face ... and to nurture human-scale structures within which people can feel at home. Social science is ill at ease with such ideas. Strangely there is very little theory about the importance of scale and form in economics and sociology.*[1]

In today's academic as well as common language, terms like 'the system', 'society', 'the region', 'the world' come very quickly to our lips. We tend to throw quite readily the whole world into one basket and discuss its problems in a general manner. Mulgan reminds us that we often overlook not only social realities that many communities are facing, but that we also detach ourselves from what makes communities 'tick'. He invites us to take a fresh look at the notion of community.

> *The first is the simple recognition of people's social nature, and one might add, of the sociability, sense of fairness, sympathy and duty that evolutionary psychologists now see as hardwired into our genetic make-up. Two hundred years of history have done much to nurture institutions for freedom and equality, but very little for the fraternity and solidarity that hold societies together. Yet, this softer value – a social capital that enables people to work together, to trust each other, to commit to common causes – has proved absolutely critical to societal success, whether in narrow economic terms of in terms of well-being.*[2]

Focusing in this realm on restoring natural and community life, we clearly promote a developmental attitude that simply recognises the natural and social realities on the ground and subsequently contributes to reactivating the restorative potential that can be found in each physical nature and human community, as well as in each individual and organisation of which such is constituted.

It is in that guise that you are faced now with the following developmental questions:

- How do we develop as a community and wider society based on our own development needs, aspirations and capacities?
- What do we know about the life of communities and societies and their ways to renew themselves?
- How well do we know the communal and societal context we seek to develop?
- What are the true developmental issues faced by the specific local community and national society, or even wider region, with which we intend to work?
- How do these relate to the major development issues that the world is facing at large, and to the development capacities and issues of myself, my group and my organisation?

In exploring these questions, we seek guidance from some of the most renowned development thinkers of our time, who focus in particular on the perspective of local communities, through which we seek to link individual, community, organisation and society. We learn from them about the importance of land, territory and place within development contexts, and notice that there remain a significant number of people on Earth, whose understanding of nature is a profoundly existential and spiritual one. For them, land, nature, and development are not separate issues, but they belong together, as much as they, the people, belong to their land. Yet, this basic premise of the deep relationship between people and their land has been almost entirely ignored and absent from development theory and practice since its emergence in the 1950s. We have no desire to present such issues in a purely romantic fashion, but we argue that there is a lot to learn from cultures that see themselves as guardians and safe keepers of the Earth rather than its owners.

9.2 Development as a Whole Life Project: Rooted in the Grounds of a Society

For anthropologist Arturo Escobar, a renowned Colombian American voice in the development arena, development thinking fostered a way of conceiving of social life as a technical problem, as a matter of rational decision and management to be entrusted to development professionals whose specialised, usually 'economic' knowledge allegedly qualified them for the task. Escobar argues that instead of seeing development as an emergent process rooted in the grounds of each society's history, cultural tradition, human psyche, and existing indigenous institutions, these development professionals sought to devise mechanisms and procedures to make society fit a pre-existing imported model that embodied the structures and functions of modernity.

Development assumed a teleology that proposed that the original 'natives' will sooner or later be reformed from without, rather than developmentally from within. In other words, the indigenous self and organisation are either bypassed, or else accommodated in their traditionally static form, rather than enabled to re-form, thereby combining tradition with modernity. At the same time, it reproduced endlessly the separation between reformers and those to be reformed by keeping alive the image of the 'underdeveloped' Third World as different and inferior, as having limited humanity in relation to the accomplished, 'developed' First World, and as needing to be modernised.

The pioneers of Anglo-Saxon-based development economics, according to Escobar, conceived of development as something to be achieved by the more or less straightforward applications of savings, investment and productivity increases. It precluded thereby a view of development as a project that could be conceived of not only in economic terms but as a whole living and learning project, intimately connected with education. Material aspects would be not the goal and limit but a space of possibilities for broader individual and collective endeavours to emerge.

Succinctly stated, universal economic models – whether neoclassical or Marxist – continuously reproduce and rediscover their own assumptions. Escobar argues that in the process they deny the capacity of people – like yourselves, individually and communally – to model your own behaviour, through self-reflection and self-criticism.

Escobar contrasts such a universal approach with what might be termed the 'peasant model'. Rooted in the peasant model is the notion that the Earth 'gives', based on its 'strength'. Humans must 'help' the land to give its products through work. There is a relation of give and take between humans and the Earth, modelled in terms of reciprocity. Peasants, villagers, or indeed those working in the informal urban sector are aware, however, that they are being increasingly pushed into the market. They interpret this fact as a diminishing margin for manoeuvring.

There are then two levels that must be considered in rethinking development from this nature and community perspective. The first refers to the need to make explicit the existence of a plurality of models of the community-and-economy. This requires the development agent to place him- or herself in the space of local 'grounds'. But this by itself will not make it. A second concern must be added. One – including those of you involved in communal learning programmes and processes – must have a theory about the forces that drive this inscription. What needs to be studied are the mechanisms by which local cultural knowledge and economic resources, including land and natural resources are appropriated by larger forces, such as unequal exchange between centre and periphery, rural and urban areas, upper and lower classes and dominant and dominated ethnic groups.

Escobar's claim that development needs to be seen as a whole life project, rather than merely focusing on its economic aspects, is strongly supported by the Hungarian intellectual Karl Polanyi, who was one of the first voices, who warned of the negative consequences of an economy that dominates society, rather than being embedded in it.

9.3   Embeddedness in Society: Embedding Livelihood and Economics in Society

Karl Polanyi was one of the great development economists in the first half of the twentieth century.[3] Albeit that his work has been largely ignored by the economic establishment, it has been recognised in development thinking, as Björn Hettne stresses in his book *Thinking about Development*.[4] The reason why Polanyi's work has been bypassed by economists was that his approach was substantively anthropological, working upwards from the local community.

For Polanyi, in referring to human activities, the term 'economic' is a compound of two meanings that have independent roots. Polanyi calls them substantive and formal. The substantive meaning of economics (*oikos* – ancient Greek for household, house or family) derives from man's dependence for his living on nature and his fellows. It refers to the interchange with his natural and social environment, insofar as this results in supplying him with the means of material want-satisfaction. The anthropologist, the sociologist and the historian then, each in his study of the place occupied by the economy in human society, is therefore faced, Polanyi emphasises, with a great variety of institutions other than markets, in which man's livelihood is embedded. The formal meaning of economics, Polanyi laments, is derived from abstract mathematical formulae, devoid of any natural, community-oriented, psychological or spiritual connotations.

Concentrating on numerically derived demand and supply curves, mediated by price-based equilibria is the formal economic approach par excellence. Here, economic activities are determined by choices induced by an insufficiency of means. The conceptual tools by which this is performed make up the discipline of economic analysis. The use of this formal meaning denotes the economy as a sequence of acts of economising, that is of choices induced by scarcity situations. The laws of the one, formal economy are those abstract 'scientific' laws of the mind; the laws of the other, the substantive one, are part of concrete physical and human nature. These two meanings could not be further apart.

The substantive economy, in sum, is embedded and enmeshed in institutions, economic and non-economic. The inclusion of the non-economic institutions is vital for Polanyi. For religion or government may be as important for the structure and functioning of the economy as monetary institutions, or the availability of tools and machines themselves that lighten the toil of labour. This substantive economy is the one with which we are concerned with at this point, though it is substantively not one the international development community is now taking into account.

How disastrous the Western market economy was in the eyes of Polanyi, is reflected in Hettne's contemplation on Polanyi's work: 'The rise of the market society was above all a cultural catastrophe ... Polanyi's ideal view on modernity – freedom in a complex society – contained the spirit of a social order in which the economy was embedded in the social structure and subordinated to wider social concerns'.[5]

In conclusion, Polanyi argued not only for a perspective on development that put the economy in the midst rather than on top, of society. The economy is to be embedded in society and seen in its interdependent relationship with society and a wide range of supporting and contributing institutions from all sectors of society. In that sense, Polanyi already anticipates the ecosystemic perspectives, earlier introduced by Moore and Scharmer, although he does so with less ecological emphasis, and indeed ignores individual psychology. Polanyi can be regarded as much a social scientist as a philosopher with enormous foresight. Already in the 1940s, he had indicated in his famous *The Great Transformation*,[6] the deficiency of conventional economic development models and the need to ground any approach to economic development firmly in the particular societal hand. Stephen Gudeman, to whom we now turn, does exactly that.

9.4   Unleashing Community Potential: On the Immersion in Local Value Domains

THERE IS NO ONE TRUE MODEL OF ECONOMY

Stephen Gudeman, a graduate of both Cambridge University's School of Anthropology in the UK and also Harvard Business School in the US, is today Professor Emeritus in the Department of Anthropology at the University of Minnesota. For Gudeman, there is no one 'true' model of economy, but only multiple meaningful formulations within particular cultures, each with their own value domains, in which we need to reflectively immerse ourselves as researchers.[7] Thereby we uncover the origins of a particular community. As a representative of modern economic anthropology, a school of thought that uses anthropology in trying to understand economy in human terms, he calls on us to understand 'local models'.

COMMUNITY AND MARKET

For Gudeman, economy consists of two realms, which he calls community and market. Both facets make up economy, for humans are motivated by social fulfilment, curiosity and the pleasure of mastery, as well as by instrumental purpose, competition and the accumulation of gains. In one guise (community), economy is local and specific, constituted through social relationships and contextually defined values. In the other guise (market), it is impersonal, even global, and abstracted from social context.

LOCAL VALUE DOMAINS: NATURE AND COMMUNITY AS FOUNDATIONS

In addition to community and market as the two constituting realms for economic practices and relationships, Gudeman distinguishes four value domains: base, relationships, trade and accumulation.

The first value domain is the base or foundation. It consists of a community of shared interests, which include lasting resources, such as land and water, produced things and ideational constructs such as knowledge, technology, laws, practices, skills and customs. The base comprises of cultural agreements and beliefs that provide a structure for all other domains.

The second domain, relationships, consists of valued communal connections maintained as ends in themselves. Through these relationships the base is created, allotted and apportioned to people in community.

The third and fourth domains consist of trade and accumulation. Accumulated value includes resources, relationships, goods, money and capital, all of which may become components of other domains. Amassed value is held, invested, consumed and displayed. Such an overall perspective of a social and economic base and its accompanying value domains, has, for us, distinct 'Southern' connotations, not surprisingly, given Gudeman's anthropological background.

For example, in areas of Panama, Columbia, and Guatemala, where Gudeman has conducted extensive fieldwork, the base consists of material things, human character, work, and divinity. The concept of 'force' or 'strength' (*la fuerza*) unites the several parts of the base, provides the mooring for a household, and offers a rationale for caring for it. According to Gudeman, strength has divine and mundane referents; overall, it is life energy. For him, people must continually secure such vital energy from their surroundings. The often-heard expression 'meeting the needs of the house' refers to the necessity of gathering and preserving the needs of the base. In a market, people exchange goods, buying and selling at the best price available until they cannot better any further their personal holdings. Exchanges in community are different. Gudeman critiques that much of development work emphasises only the latter two of the four value domains – trade and material accumulation – while it is crucial to engage initially with the first two value domains: base and relationships. Interesting enough, an inquiry into aid effectiveness commissioned in 2005 by the UK All Party Parliamentary Group (APPG) for Debt, Aid and Trade and involving researchers from the Institute of Development Studies confirmed that effective aid requires as much investing in relationships as in managing money.[8] While this critique only partly reaches in the second community value domain of relationships, it nevertheless points in the same direction as Gudeman.

UNLEASHING COMMUNITY POTENTIAL

For Gudeman, development is not primarily about capital accumulation, but rather about innovation in the relationships of you, your immediate learning community, your external community, organisations and society. Community in this wider sense offers, according to Gudeman, a reservoir of possibilities, and the key to development is to unleash the innovative potential that lies in it. One important dimension for such unleashing lies in what Arturo Escobar calls the 'vitality of place'.

9.5   Reactivating Vitality of Place: Place Making and Localisation Strategies

REVERSING LOCAL-GLOBAL IMBALANCE: REFOCUSING ON THE VITALITY OF A PLACE

If anything has characterised social science debates since 1990, states Arturo Escobar in his work on *Territories of Difference*,[9] it is the concern with globalisation. These debates, he says, have been characterised by a perfect imbalance as the global dimension is all about space, capital and the capacity to transform, while the local dimension is restricted to geographical location, labour as a resource, and backward tradition.

For Escobar, it is time to reverse this imbalance by focusing anew on the continued 'vitality of place' in the creation of culture, nature and economy. Place continues to be important in the lives of most people, if by place we mean the engagement with and experience of a particular location with some measure of groundedness (however unstable), boundaries (however permeable) and connections to everyday life. The reversion of asymmetry between the global and local happens, for Escobar, through localisation.

From the perspective of local communities and social movements, Escobar sees two kinds of indigenous strategies of localisation: first, place-based strategies that rely on the attachment to territory and culture; and second, network strategies that enable social movements to enact a politics of scale from below.

How does this apply, for example, to the Columbian Pacific region, in which Escobar has undertaken many years of ethnographic research alongside his passionate engagement in political activism for social change?

EXAMPLE: LOCALISATION STRATEGIES AND PLACE MAKING IN THE COLOMBIAN PACIFIC IN THE 1990S

Most regions of the Colombian Pacific had an open frontier until about 1950. After the 1950s, with increasing decolonisation, technological changes in mining, fishing and timber extraction – for example the use of high-power pumps for mining, gasoline-powered saws for timber, and large nylon nets for fishing – great land concessions were granted to foreign companies. With the arrival of the big oil palm companies in the 1980s, large-scale technology development and market forces, more than ecological dynamics or local cultural practices, began to shape the territorial transformation of the entire Tumaco region in Colombia.

From the 1950s on, peasant struggles all over Latin America were carried out over land ownership. Since 1985, communities with the help of Catholic groups inspired by liberation theology began to delimit their territory and develop strategies for resource use. There thus appeared a growing number of local organisations, grouped under the name ACIA – Integral Peasant Association of the Atrato River – intended to secure a measure of self-governance. By 1987, ACIA had negotiated with government the demarcation of 60,000 hectares that, though still not fully secured under legal title, were put under a special management plan based on cultural practices of the communities. Not until 10 years later did ACIA, by then representing 120 organisations, receive legal title.

Members of ACIA describe their shared ambition as follows: 'We are an association of men and women that fights for the well-being of our communities and for the future of our children, defending our right for territory, protecting the natural environment, and formulating a development model emerging from our own vision and culture as black people'.[10]

Calling for a new approach to ethno-development, the ACIA process fostered the pioneering development of a series of concepts and technologies that had illustrious careers throughout the 1990s. The idea that the 'territory' was fundamental to the physical and cultural survival of the communities, and the argument that these communities have unique ways of using the diverse spaces constituted by forest, river, mangrove, hills and oceans, were the two most important social innovations:

> *Chants and dances became an integral part of political meetings, the elders narrated the story of the peopling of the river, the original places of settlement were marked on maps, somebody taught the history of slaves and masters, other about food and fiestas of the past, and yet others told of the history of encounters between Indians and Blacks. Hundreds of people took to their boats, stopping in each town and enlivening the trip at each stop with music and dances. The voyage was a geographical recognition of a territory they now learned to be their own. It was thus that a region became manifest through a lived-in process.[11]*

In an Ecological Zoning Project in the 1990s, conducted by government, interdisciplinary teams of natural and social scientists worked together with local communities in the elaboration of the communities' mental maps, subsequently contrasting them with the maps afforded by modern cartography. But the most critical achievement of a social movement that came together in Perico Negro, a predominantly black region, when blacks and indigenous peoples came together, was the discussion of the 'cosmovision' and conception of the territory of the various movement organisations: Embera, Wounaan, Zenu, Tule.

They emphasised the integration of people and nature, traditional practices, and the resulting conservation of the environment. A declaration of principles followed on the defence of resources and traditional knowledge through strategies regarding unity, territory, identity, autonomy and self-sufficiency. If the territory embodied the life project of the community, the region-territory articulated the political project of the social movement.

The territory, then, was considered a challenge to developing local economies and forms of governability. The strengthening and transformation of traditional production systems and local economies, the need to press on with the collective titling process, and working towards territorial governability were all-important. Besides being influenced by larger debates and interactions with academics, other activists, state experts, and NGOs, the conclusions reached were based on an analysis of the situation of the local population and intensive interaction with communities and their leaders.

Within such communities, while men demarcated the territory in mobilisation of production, women were seen as consolidating it through socialisation processes and the construction of identities through a panoply of food practices, production and healing. When these practices were disrupted, for example by the introduction of food markets, the links to territory started to weaken. Hence the crucial nature of the gender dimension.

To sum up, for Escobar, the concept of territory and vitality of place, produced by a number of movements in the 1990s, articulated a place-based framework linking history, culture, environment, social and economic life. It showed the development of a spatial consciousness among movement activists and, to some extent, within the involved communities themselves. The conception resonates with academic frameworks in which nature and culture are seen as interconnected in overlapping webs, and communities are seen as multiply located – place-based and networked across places. In our example of the Colombian Pacific, the region, so Escobar, may be seen as a complex matrix of processes in which people, territories, species and so forth are held in relation within a socioeconomic context.

This example links back to Escobar's earlier argument for development as a whole life – living and learning – project. It also makes a strong case to re-evaluate our relationship with nature within development contexts. While the case of the black and indigenous population in the a region in Colombia might be a remote one for an Integral Developer engaged in, say, Switzerland, the catastrophic impact of the so-called 'Western way of life' on nature, is one we cannot ignore in any development context. The life-giving and sustaining role of nature for our individual and communal life, as well as for humankind as a whole, is the main reason, why we place nature and community at the beginning of the development journey. Indeed, probing even deeper into the matter, we learn that nature can even be seen as a central agent in reconfiguring development.

9.6 Alignment with Nature as Central Development Agent: Recognising Nature's Role in Reconfiguring Development from a Local Perspective

LEARNING FROM THE MODEL OF COMMUNITY DEVELOPMENT IN THE COLOMBIAN PACIFIC

The Colombian model of community development, for Arturo Escobar, leads to another nature related lesson in development.[12] Throughout history, many place-based peasant and indigenous communities have internalised cultural and ecological conditions in the social relations and productive systems of their societies. Theoretically, one can say that in these cases the environment may be seen as a productive system based on the stability and productivity of the ecosystem and the cultural styles of the groups that live in it. These observations point at an alternative theory of production and subjectivity that entails a triple articulation and vitalisation of ecological-economic, cultural-spiritual and sociotechnical processes.

Because of their focus on locality and difference, the political ideologies of social movements question universalised modernity and standardised development, in favour of the phenomenology of place and time. By privileging such localised knowledges, these political ideologies articulate uniquely questions of diversity, difference and interculturality – with nature as central agent. Sustainability, thereby, may become a de-colonial project.

LEARNING FROM THE WORLD'S OLDEST PEOPLE – THEIR STORY EMBODIES SUSTAINABILITY

Let us look at a further example for nature's central role for human development, going much further back into history. The aboriginal societies in Australia – referring to themselves as 'the world's oldest people' – sustained themselves for about 60,000 years, before they were overtaken by the 'white man'. From the Scandinavian Knowledge Management expert Karl-Erik Sveiby and the Australian Aboriginal Elder Tex Skuthorpe, we learn that for the aborigines – in this particular case the Nhunggabarra – it was what they called the 'story' that embodied sustainability.[13]

What was crucial for the Nhunggabarra story was how and where it was linked to the land, the people and the law. At the same time each story had a high level of stability and continuity over thousands of years, containing hidden levels of meaning.

Simplified, the story would have been one of the first a child heard. Its first level is the text itself and it explained natural features and animal behaviours. The natural environment then reinforces the learning on a daily basis. Typically, this first level is also exciting and entertaining. The second level of meaning concerns the relationships between the people in the community. It does not come explicitly from the story; the implicit meaning had to be extracted as part of the education. Many of those inferences arise out of the recognition that the imposition of a single view on another person is an abuse of power. There are an infinite number of truths and what is true for one person is not true for another. The third level concerns the relationship between one's own community and the wider environment – that is the Earth and other aboriginal communities. Again, the third level is never told explicitly. The learner had to pull out the meaning himself, and needed to have some knowledge of the law. Many, but not all stories, have a fourth level. The fourth level included practice, ceremonies and experiences, which give access to special esoteric knowledge hidden in the story. In that overall context, the development of self, institution, community and society, for the Nhunggabarra, were congruent. Think of all four of these levels in relation to your own learning community.

Sustainability then, in this aboriginal case, was strongly linked to the specific characteristics of their land and people as well as to the value base of the particular society. Hence the need, to tap into what Escobar called the 'vitality of a place' and what Gudeman called 'local value domains'. In disciplinary terms, it would likely be anthropology and literature that would be most applicable to further our understanding of Nhunggabarra 'sustainability' and 'development', rather than biology or ecology.

Understanding nature and community, as we can see, is a most multifaceted theme in itself. Delving thoroughly into one's own human nature, and consequently into that of one's group and organisation, followed by the larger community and society, provides the necessary foundation within the Integral Development process.

9.7   Integration

We have now journeyed within our gradually opening southern realm of nature and community from individual-formative grounding to organisational-reformative emergence to normative societal navigation. One of the reasons for the Nhunggabarra aboriginal peoples being able to sustain their community and society for some 60,000 years is that self, organisation, community and society were resonant with one another. In other words, normative navigation was in tune with community structures and organisational patterns that themselves were supporting and had emerged out of the life worlds of individuals and groups altogether grounded in nature: the land and their story embedded within it.

Thereby, Nhunggabarra society may not have evolved rapidly, at least to any marked degree, but it remained in a stable, sustainable state, one in which (wo)man and nature, one aboriginal group and another, lived in relative harmony with one another.

The approach to economic and societal development, that economic anthropologists like Stephen Gudeman, Arturo Escobar and Karl Polanyi have adopted, has also aligned the vitality of place, so to speak, with economy and society. For them, grounding in physical, if not also human nature, precedes the emergence of 'embedded institutions', from which new community-based forms of economic behaviour are derived. Unfortunately though, the likes of Gudeman, Escobar and Polanyi are rather the exception than the norm in economic and development circles. Indeed, the theoretical field of economic development has been dominated by formal economists and sociologists, at the expense of cultural anthropologists and depth psychologists.

Therefore, in the 'Global South', where closeness to nature is the norm, and the formation of the self is closely interwoven with both nature and community, orthodox 'North-Western' development economics and the accompanying institutional forms have been antithetical to such 'Southern' worlds. It is time for development economists and modernising sociologists to shift perspective and to evolve organisational forms that befit local nature and communities.

Before we move on to the fourth level or round, serving to fully actualise individual, communal, organisational and societal development from this 'Southern' perspective, we pause to engage – through reflection and action – with the guiding question and theory presented in this chapter. This includes the major development challenges derived thereof for you and your community, your organisation, as well as for society at large. At this stage, it is of primary importance to identify, how you and your organisation or community can reach out into society at large, thereby becoming a veritable agent for societal development. For this to happen, you are challenged to articulate and conceptualise your own learnings and findings with regards to development, based on your experiences in Round 1 (the formative grounding of your own self within your context) and in Round 2 (the reformative response of your group and organisation). Hence, this normative Round 3 is very much about coming up with new development norms, so it can inform – large-scale – the learning and development of your society at large.

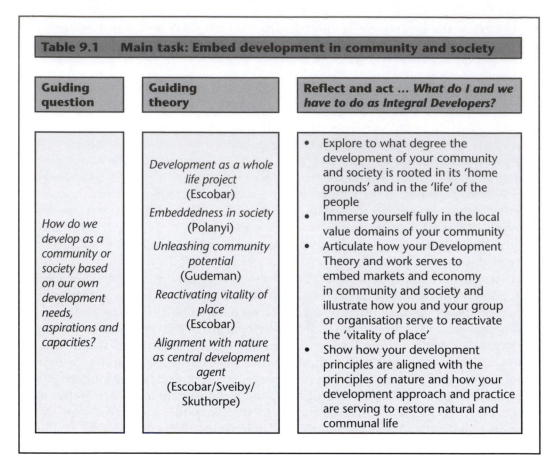

Table 9.1   Main task: Embed development in community and society

Guiding question	Guiding theory	Reflect and act … *What do I and we have to do as Integral Developers?*
How do we develop as a community or society based on our own development needs, aspirations and capacities?	*Development as a whole life project* (Escobar) *Embeddedness in society* (Polanyi) *Unleashing community potential* (Gudeman) *Reactivating vitality of place* (Escobar) *Alignment with nature as central development agent* (Escobar/Sveiby/Skuthorpe)	• Explore to what degree the development of your community and society is rooted in its 'home grounds' and in the 'life' of the people • Immerse yourself fully in the local value domains of your community • Articulate how your Development Theory and work serves to embed markets and economy in community and society and illustrate how you and your group or organisation serve to reactivate the 'vitality of place' • Show how your development principles are aligned with the principles of nature and how your development approach and practice are serving to restore natural and communal life

We are now ready to move from individual grounding, organisational emergence and societal navigation, to a practical, developmental effect. This effect will be illustrated in this 'Southern' case by Chinyika in Zimbabwe and the US-based institute and network First Peoples Worldwide. Both cases gave birth to what we call a 'Communiversity' – which is the educational-developmental vehicle that allows for the full realisation of this 'Southern' realm.

References

1   Mulgan, G. (2005). A Sense of Community. *Resurgence*, No. 172, pp. 18f.
2   Mulgan, G. (2005). A Sense of Community. *Resurgence*, No. 172, pp. 18f.
3   Polanyi, K. (1991). *Primitive, Archaic and Modern Economics*. Boston, MA: Beacon.
4   Hettne, B. (2009). *Thinking about Development: Development Matters*. London: Zed.
5   Hettne, B. (2009). *Thinking about Development: Development Matters*. London: Zed, p. 7.
6   Polanyi, K. (2001). *The Great Transformation: The Political and Economic Origins of Our Time*. Boston, MA: Beacon.
7   Gudeman, S. (2001). *The Anthropology of Economy: Community, Market and Culture*. Oxford: Blackwell.

8   Hopper, R. and Birch, J. (2005). *A Report of the All Party Parliamentary Group on Debt, Aid and Trade: A Parliamentary Inquiry into Aid Effectiveness*. Available at: www.ids.ac.uk/files/dmfile/AEIXX.pdf / Accessed 11 October 2013.

9   Escobar, A. (2008). *Territories of Difference: Place, Movements, Life, Redes*. Durham, NC: Duke University Press.

10 CHOCO website. Available at: www.choco.org / Accessed: 15 May 2012. Translation by the authors.

11 Escobar, A. (2008). *Territories of Difference: Place, Movements, Life, Redes*. Durham, NC: Duke University Press.

12 Escobar, A. (2008). *Territories of Difference: Place, Movements, Life, Redes*. Durham, NC: Duke University Press.

13 Sveiby, K. and Skuthorpe, T. (2004). *Treading Lightly: The Hidden Wisdom of the World's Oldest People*. London: Allen & Unwin.

10 *Southern Integration via a Communiversity: The Cases of Chinyika and First Peoples Worldwide*

Guiding Question: How can we sustainably actualise the Southern realm of Integral Development, rooted in nature and community?

10.1   Orientation

In this final chapter of the 'Southern' realm, we come to its fourth round of actualisation. Here we shall illustrate through practical cases, not only how the first three rounds of individual, organisational and societal development can be meaningfully integrated in theory and practice, but also how they can altogether be further actualised through an educational institution. We thereby seek to explore how such a new educational-developmental space can stimulate widespread innovation in and beyond the particular society in which the original development impulse was lodged.

In this 'Southern' realm with its core theme of 'Restoring Life in Nature and Community', the actualising educational institution – or Uni-Versity – is a 'Communiversity'. Being an enabling space for 'healthy and participatory coexistence' as

Table 10.1 Towards a Communiversity	
The Southern reality and realm of relationship	**Transformative educational institution (Uni-Versity)**
Core perspectives: nature and community Theme: Restoring life in nature and community Core value: Healthy and participatory coexistence	*Communiversity* Main focus: Community-based learning and development Key terms: Context, community, care

the core 'Southern' value, such a university type focuses on community-based learning and development. Key defining terms of a Communiversity are 'context', 'community' and 'care'. Deeply rooted in one or more local communities, it is a true motor for the self-development of communities.

We shall now intimate in a series of short case stories how the Southern realm as a whole can be actualised. We pave the way first with a case in Zimbabwe, in which we ourselves are intimately involved.

10.2   Integrated Southern Practice: Chinyika in Zimbabwe and First Peoples Worldwide in the USA

THE CASE OF CHINYIKA AND COMMUNITY-BASED TRANSFORMATIVE EDUCATION-AND-RESEARCH PROGRAMMES IN ZIMBABWE

Introduction

The fascinating case of Paul Chidara Muchineripi, Steven Kada and the Chinyika Community in rural Zimbabwe, and the transformative community economic development initiative that grew out of it, is perhaps the most prominent showcase that emerged directly out of our own development work through Trans4m. As we have already written extensively about Chinyika, in particular in *Integral Community*,[1] we shall provide in this book only a snapshot, serving to illustrate the outstanding case of Integral Development it embodies.

Round 1, 2, 3, 4 – The first loop: The remarkable transformation of Chidara Muchineripi and Steve Kada into catalysts for community self-development

It was in 2005, that Paul (nicknamed Chidara) Muchineripi and Steven Kada, both based in Harare, Zimbabwe, enrolled in the master's programme on Social and Economic Transformation, run by Trans4m, our Center for Integral Development, in Johannesburg, in conjunction with South Africa's CIDA (stands from Community and Individual Development Association) City Campus, and UK's Buckingham University. While Buckingham University acted as the academic accreditation entity and CIDA City Campus as the academic host of the programme, it was Trans4m that designed and executed the programme. This partnership served to link a new form of transformational educational programme (Trans4m), with a reputed but conventional UK university (Buckingham) and a context that invited transformation (CIDA/South Africa). For Trans4m, as the core architect of this partnership, it was an important step on our way to 'push' education out of the confined, often sterile atmosphere of typically 'ivory tower' universities right into the centre of southern African society (participants came from South Africa, Zimbabwe and Lesotho), and to enable participants to become effective agents of transformation within their particular contexts and communities.

Before such transformation could take place, participants themselves had to transcend their own conventional understanding of education. Chidara and Steve, then both in their late fifties and friends since their early twenties, found themselves on our programme with the primary intention of adding a master's title to their academic credentials. Chidara, who ran an independent management training company called BTD (short for Business Training and Development) and Steve, at that time Head of Human Resources of Cairns Food, Zimbabwe's then largest food processing company, shared an interest in management and organisational development. The nature of our programme requested, however, from every participant, that he or she related the content of the transformational master's programme to a burning issue in their own work or community context and to activate for its resolution the particular problem-solving capacity of that context.

The starting point, for each participant was the transformation of the self within its particular context. In that process both Steve and Chidara made personal discoveries that would change their lives and that of their organisation (Cairns Food) and community (Chinyika) forever.

Steve was prompted to come to the realisation that rather than research organisational development in general, he needed to address the fact, that the supposedly 'African' company he served had never uncovered its 'organisational soul'. Cairns Food, at that time, was imitating Western management styles and techniques, as opposed to developing an organisational framework that would build authentically on the 'African-ness' of its shareholders, employees and customers. In particular, employees felt alienated from the organisation and demonstrated a severe lack of intrinsic motivation. Catalysed through three projects that were embedded in the master's programme – focusing progressively on individual, organisational and societal transformation – Steve underwent profound personal development discovering his own 'African humanity'. He was thereby guided by a childhood question of his mother to him that pushed him to continuous self-reflection: *Uri Munhu Here?* – Are You Human? Steve then spearheaded the transformation of Cairns Food that ultimately led to Cairns Food's new engagement with African communities in rural Zimbabwe. The initial point in case was the Chinyika Community in Masvingo Province, about 250 km south of Harare.

The choice was made for Chidara's home community Chinyika, as he, in a parallel and interactive process of self-reflection, rediscovered not only his own African heritage, but also the need to contribute to resolving the severe food crisis with which his own local community Chinyika as well as Zimbabwe as a whole was then confronted. As a local chief in Chinyika and next in line for the paramount chieftainship of the larger region, Chidara took it on himself to lead the local transformation process. In his master's level research, Chidara was focusing on understanding how his ancestors had dealt with severe food crises in times of draught and gradually tapped into those rare sources of wisdom within the community that were still alive. Subsequently he started experimenting successfully with finger millet (Rapoko) as a traditional, highly nutritious and draught-resistant crop that the local communities had used in the past, but that got replaced by irrigation intensive maize cultivation during colonial times. With the help of the local village committee, run primarily by women, Chidara gradually engaged the entire Chinyika Community in a process of re-establishing traditional planting methods. This undertaking was supported through modern-day agronomic methods that were brought to the community by Steve's organisation Cairns Food.

In working together, Steve and Chidara forged a community-private–public partnership that served to bring food security initially to over 5,000 villagers,[2] and, slowly, through processes of dissemination into surrounding villages, to over 100,000 villagers. Over time, the communities not only achieved food security, but managed to generate a surplus of grains that were sold to Cairns Food and to the wider market. Cairns itself was thereby able to satisfy a number of parallel organisational interests: firstly, it could make a tangible contribution to an increasing number of rural communities which had a positive impact on the motivation of its workforce as a whole; secondly, it gained an opportunity to co-evolve with these communities, transcending at least in part, the typical one-sided learning flow from the private to the community sector; thirdly, it was able to create new nutritious products, that were developed from traditional grains and thereby enter into new food markets.

The then agricultural minister Gumbo got personally interested in the case of Chinyika, and what was learnt from Chinyika subsequently influenced agronomic policies of the country.

Through Steve and Chidara's master's programme projects, one notices the full-fledged engagement with the Southern realm of Integral Development. All four rounds were touched: self, organisation and society, altogether interconnected through a transformational educational programme.[3] However, we also became aware that such a programme would have to be further institutionalised within the local context, were it to bear fruits on a sustainable basis.

Luckily, Steve and Chidara, were highly motivated to take the transformation journey to higher levels. Inspired by the impact they themselves had through a single master's programme and by the capacity for development that had been unleashed and significantly realised, Chidara and Steve began to dream of transformational village learning centres that could in time give birth to a new university for community economic development in Zimbabwe. Here is how they took this challenge on. In the process, we can see how, a Communiversity-to-be was gradually taking shape, actualised through individual and communal learning – both inside and outside an academic institution.

Round 1, 2, 3, 4 – The second loop: Transforming BTD into a research and development institute with a focus on community economic development

Steve and Chidara's ambition, spurred on by Trans4m, was to move beyond the mere cases of the Chinyika Communities and Cairns Food, beyond food security for a particular region alone.

They intended to develop a new theory and practice that could enable Chinyika and other communities to move from food security to economic self-sufficiency, and that could demonstrate how Zimbabwe, as an entire society, could come up with its own 'research-and-education-vehicles' to enact a sustainable economy. For that purpose they enrolled in 2008 in Trans4m's international PhD programme on Integral Development, a programme that was accredited by the South African higher learning institute Da Vinci. In Figure 10.1 we illustrate one of the key concepts on Integral Community Economic Development that Kada and Muchineripi co-evolved with Trans4m.

The concept describes how our fourfold model starts in the South. Through the activation of community voices the participation of a large group of community members is encouraged. The objective of this first stage is not only to tap into the collective wisdom of the community but also to develop a sense of shared identity and community self-assertion. What follows in the emergent stage is an active engagement with relevant

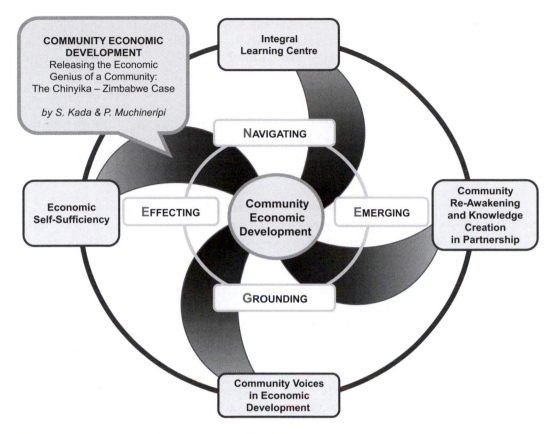

Figure 10.1 Community economic development

partners – from private enterprise and public sector institutions, to other communities and civic organisations. The objective of this second stage is to initiate a process of knowledge creation, whereby local wisdom is juxtaposed with other local, national and global knowledge sources. This emergent stage leads to a gradual 'community awakening', giving rise to new insights and ideas. Such insights and ideas need then to be further evolved in the third, navigational stage that is dedicated to the systemisation of knowledge and to the evolution of practical know how. Such know how is then, in the fourth, effecting stage, to be applied to foster economic self-sufficiency for the entire community. In their respective doctoral research and innovation Chidara and Steve have evolved this approach in great detail.[4]

About two years into the programme, Chidara began, with Steve's help, to evolve his hitherto conventional Management Consultancy BTD into an ecosystemic hub for communal and societal development. What followed was an agreement with Da Vinci Institute in South Africa and with Trans4m in Geneva to host, via BTD, master's and doctoral programmes in Integral Development directly in Zimbabwe. Both Chidara and Steve saw this transformation of BTD and the hosting of the programme not only as an organic evolution of their own research-and-education journey but also as a crucial further step towards a new kind of university – a Communiversity – in Zimbabwe, one that could spearhead the renaissance of the entire society. Establishing a programme, however, that actively engages with the remaking of a society was a most delicate endeavour in the difficult, if not dangerous, political environment that Zimbabwe was and still is facing. Despite that, the programme was established in 2011 and by 2012 over 40 participants had inscribed for both the master's and PhD programme.

Through these programmes, participants are again led through a self (in community)–organisation–society trajectory. In this case we have formed, from the very beginning, research communities around shared topics. Building on the success of the cooperation between Steve and Chidara, pairs and groups of researchers are encouraged to set up communities of shared research and practice. By now, only about one year into the programme, we see already three thematic groups emerging:

- Education/research and innovation/knowledge creation.
- Enterprise development, urban and rural.
- Economic transformation of Zimbabwe as a whole.

Together, we reckon that this programme has the potential to influence the recreation of society, bottom-up through specific individuals and their local communities, and can serve as a role model for Integral Development. At the time of concluding this book (autumn 2012), Steve and Chidara have handed in their final PhD theses. They thereby laid an initial knowledge and practice foundation for a new community economic development reality in Zimbabwe. The existing group of master's and doctoral students, albeit in some cases more than others – for some the priority remains securing a reputable individual degree – is determined to further develop this foundation, and to conclude in its own way the journey through the Southern integral realm. We are hopeful that in time, this foundation provides the solid ground for a Zimbabwean Communiversity – a university that develops entire communities, urban and rural, and gradually the country as a whole.

The challenges, however, on the way to such a Communiversity are manifold and need to be creatively resolved by ourselves in the years to come. What are the core issues? Firstly, the starting position for participants is still all too often the achievement of a personal degree (master's or PhD), rather than the collective uplifting of their communities and society. That is understandable, given the highly individualised nature of today's education systems throughout the world. Intense catalysation and contextualisation is required to connect individuals to their community grounds, and develop, in the process, a research to innovation trajectory, that is geared to contributing to burning issues in those communities.

Secondly, current day educational and research programmes (such as master's and PhD) are by and large designed – in terms of enrolment, assignments, thesis formats and evaluation – for individual participants. What Trans4m with its partners is attempting, is to match these individualised formats with a communal process and vision. That, inevitably, leads to conflicts between the individual pursuit of status and recognition, and the group pursuit of a shared vision. In time, further harmonisation is required to enable truly community-lodged research and education. Such an evolution would then allow and encourage participants to work together in order to adequately deal with the complexity of the burning issues they are seeking to address; furthermore, it would not only positively acknowledge the generation of new theory, but would facilitate its implementation in the respective local communities. The final outcome would have to be an authentic improvement, as a combination of locally resonant and relevant theory and practice.

Finally, acknowledgement for the final innovation would then be given to the participants as well as to the participating communities. Why? Because such a community-based approach – see for example Figure 10.1 – requires that research is not done on or about such communities, but together with them, with a view to coming up with an integral innovation. Indeed, in our case, the community would not only have to be acknowledged for it (perhaps with some kind of yet to be invented community degree), but it would also itself evaluate the merits of the research and innovation. Altogether, these are crucial ingredients for the Communiversity that Chidara and Steve – via BTD and together with Trans4m and many others – intend to build in Zimbabwe. In fact it is with this end in mind that Muchineripi has recently renamed BTD as 'BTD Integral Institute for Research and Development in Africa'. In Table 10.2 we summarise this Zimbabwean case.

Table 10.2 Chinyika in Zimbabwe: Seedbed for societal transformation	
Integral development	**A 'Southern' case for Integral Development (summary)**
Round 1: **Self-Development** *Formative* *Grounding*	*Self-discovery of Muchineripi and Kada: 'I am an African'* • Both deeply steeped in African traditions: Africa as primary identity, with Christianity and modern business world as secondary identities • Both strongly emotionally affected by the disastrous socioeconomic-cultural situation many of Zimbabwe's communities are facing • Jointly enrolled in Trans4m's South African master's programme for Socioeconomic Transformation to rediscover themselves and to address, jointly, burning Issues in their communities in Zimbabwe
Round 2: **Organisational Development** *Reformative* *Emergence*	*Building an ecosystemic partnership around Chinyika* • Muchineripi and Kada consequently supported Chidara's home community Chinyika to reconnect to its communal and cultural Capacities to renew itself • Jointly set up an ecosystemic partnership between Chinyika (community), Kada's company Cairns Food (private) and government (public): this partnership achieved local food security (for up to 100,000 Villagers) • Established, together with the local village council, run by Chinyika women, the Chinyika Learning Center, with a long-term vision to create a Rural University

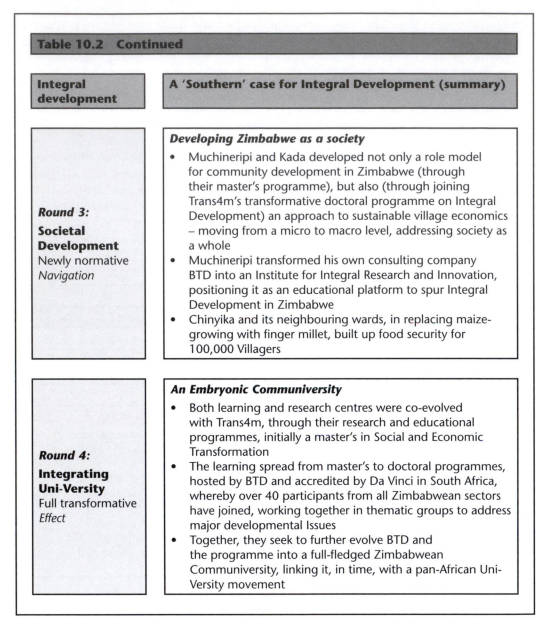

Integral development	A 'Southern' case for Integral Development (summary)
Round 3: **Societal Development** Newly normative *Navigation*	**Developing Zimbabwe as a society** • Muchineripi and Kada developed not only a role model for community development in Zimbabwe (through their master's programme), but also (through joining Trans4m's transformative doctoral programme on Integral Development) an approach to sustainable village economics – moving from a micro to macro level, addressing society as a whole • Muchineripi transformed his own consulting company BTD into an Institute for Integral Research and Innovation, positioning it as an educational platform to spur Integral Development in Zimbabwe • Chinyika and its neighbouring wards, in replacing maize-growing with finger millet, built up food security for 100,000 Villagers
Round 4: **Integrating Uni-Versity** Full transformative *Effect*	**An Embryonic Communiversity** • Both learning and research centres were co-evolved with Trans4m, through their research and educational programmes, initially a master's in Social and Economic Transformation • The learning spread from master's to doctoral programmes, hosted by BTD and accredited by Da Vinci in South Africa, whereby over 40 participants from all Zimbabwean sectors have joined, working together in thematic groups to address major developmental Issues • Together, they seek to further evolve BTD and the programme into a full-fledged Zimbabwean Communiversity, linking it, in time, with a pan-African Uni-Versity movement

We now move from Chinyika as an Indigenous African case to a First Nations people's perspective, rooted originally in Indigenous America.

THE CASE OF FIRST NATIONS DEVELOPMENT INSTITUTE AND FIRST PEOPLES WORLDWIDE: AN INDIGENOUS HOLISTIC DEVELOPMENT APPROACH

Introduction

Rebecca Adamson is a Cherokee activist from the USA, who became the founder of the First Nations Development Institute (1980) and subsequently of First Peoples Worldwide

(1997). In her work, Adamson discovered and helped to resurface a traditional, integrated approach to development, deeply 'embedded' in the culture of Indigenous people. This underlying process, however, unfolded out of her own life story, within and across all four rounds.

Round 1 – Self: Rebecca Adamson – It started with a dream

Adamson started her remarkable developmental journey as an unemployed single mother and cancer survivor who decided, in 1979, to become a spokesperson and activist for the rights of the so-called First Nation people in the United States of America. Having witnessed herself over an extended period the social and economic marginalisation of the Indigenous people of America – in her own Cherokee tribe as well as with other tribes and ethnicities – Adamson's dream was to build 'an organisation that would forever rid Native Americans of their dependence on the federal government'.[5]

Rebecca Adamson was born in 1949 of a Swedish father and a part-Cherokee mother. A quiet student, she was recognised early for her acute powers of observation. Several trips to her Cherokee relatives in North Carolina 'not only acquainted her with the traditional beliefs of her grandfather, but also left her a keen judge of human character'.[6] From an early age, Adamson engaged in the journey of knowing herself and others. She observed the lack of opportunity of First Nation peoples and started, after short stints of studying philosophy, law and economics, to engage in Native American movements. In 1972, she became director of the Coalition of Indian Controlled Schools Boards, fighting for Native American control of their own schools. Adamson recognised the significance of education for authentic development from early on in her activist career. The Coalition she worked for responded to the fact that 'generations of Indian children had been taken from their families and sent to Indian boarding schools, where they were not allowed to speak their own language or follow their tribes' cultural and spiritual teachings'.[7]

Round 2 – Organisation: From early experiments with tribal economic development to the set-up of First Nations Development Institute

In the following years, Adamson experimented with different ideas to promote tribal economic development, until she set up, with financial support from the Ford Foundation, the First Nations Development Institute. A later collaborator of Adamson, Sherry Salway Black, an Oglala Sioux, described the institution as 'a national Native American economic development organisation working with tribes and Native people to change the economic environment of reservations to one that builds on local resources, recognises Native knowledge and culture, and supports development from within'.[8] Adamson crafted the institute as an antidote to conventional development approaches. 'Instead of Euro-American values of individualism, equal opportunity, private property and accumulation she emphasised kinship, communal usage, sharing, cultural identity and spirituality'. Nature and community, culture and context became the core building blocks of the institute. 'Four principles provided the foundation for First Nations: Community is essential for survival; Nature is a source of knowledge, a model to emulate, and a mentor; Subsistence emphasises the interplay of spiritual beliefs with hunting and fishing; Culturally, subsistence derives its meaning from the context of the group'.[9]

Of particular importance for First Nations was the control of Indigenous people over their assets. The institute takes a comprehensive view of assets. 'First Nations' asset topography includes financial holdings, natural resources, cultural property, human capital, and social, political, institutional and legal assets'.[10] Assets are regarded as the major prerequisite of wealth, and the core source of income, jobs and other benefits. Adamson and her colleagues argue, that this is particularly relevant for Native communities, as opposed to other low-income communities. For them, 'Native American tribes and individuals technically own many assets, including land, but often do not control these assets and thus do not reap the benefits'.[11] However, the ability of the tribes to build self-sustaining communities, and to restore their 'vitality of place' is, for Adamson, determined by the control of local assets. In the case of First Nation people, the communal nature and scope of asset control is to be emphasised. Adamson points out that 'although most economic systems comprise a comprehensive collection of laws, institutions, and social activities that govern the accumulation, distribution, and management of individual assets, many Native economic models consider these mechanisms as part of the local asset pool and crucial to the community's sustainability'.[12]

Over time, First Nations Development Institute grew to provide more than USD 3 million in annual aid to support Native American self-sufficiency. The institute deployed a variety of programmes, such as the Eagle Staff Fund (making grants to various Native American projects), and the Oweesta Program, dealing with Micro-Finance. Gradually, the impact of First Nations on society grew. In a conversation in spring 2012, Adamson shared with us that the institute can look back on the following major achievements: the first reservation-based microenterprise loan fund in the United States; the first tribal investment model; a national movement for reservation land reform; and legislation that established new standards of accountability regarding federal trust responsibility for Native Americans. With these achievements on the table, First Nations began to articulate an alternative approach to development, one that is authentically rooted in First Nations culture.

Round 3 – Society: Towards large-scale societal impact – an alternative, Indigenous approach to development and the foundation of First Peoples Worldwide

From the early beginnings of First Nations, it was Adamson's vision to create an alternative approach to development. Gradually the institute came up with a development model that was deeply steeped in the natural and communal context as well as building on the historical-cultural traditions of the Native Americans. As Figure 10.2 on the page opposite illustrates, this 'development ecology' has four primary vectors – kinship, spirituality, assets and personal efficacy. Altogether, they show a remarkable resonance with our approach to Integral Development, and similarly remind us of the work of Angeles Arrien on the Indigenous fourfold way (⇨7).

The four main elements of the model can be described as follows:[13]

- *South = Kinship:* This element relates to the networks among community members and families. The kinship network connects the individual to the family and the tribe.
- *East = Spirituality:* This element refers to the underlying value systems of the community, and the sense of well-being among community members. Spirituality gives people a sense of vision, a sense of who they are and meaning within the community and the larger universe.
- *North = Control of Assets:* This element refers to the ability to control assets in order to create wealth.
- *West = Personal Efficacy:* This element refers to a sense of confidence in one's own abilities.

The interactions between the four primary sectors produce a variety of subtle development outcomes,[14] as is intimated in Figure 10.2. It is noteworthy that Adamson and her colleagues have developed an entire inventory of indicators to evaluate, measure and map each component of the model. Furthermore, in the centre of this model is the individual or a group of individuals, who, through engaging with the second project layer gradually contribute – 'inside-out' – to the development of the entire tribe and subsequently to the nation as a whole. It reflects thereby also the deep conviction of Adamson and First

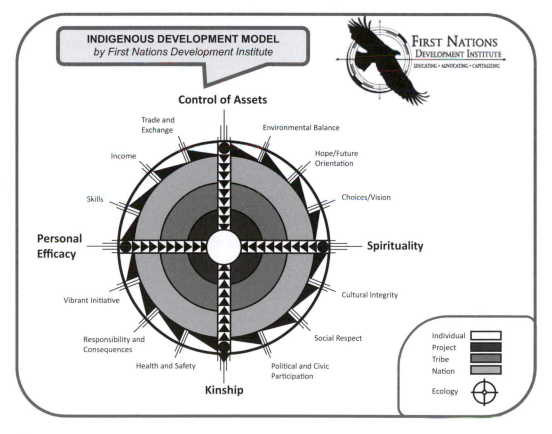

Figure 10.2 First Nation's holistic Development ecology

Nations Development Institute that 'development comes from within. It cannot be done to people, or for people, but must ultimately come from people'.[15]

Over time, Adamson and the First Nations Development Institute spread their wings beyond the United States. Increasingly, requests for assistance came from abroad, primarily from Indigenous people from Africa, Australia, Latin America and Russia. That led Rebecca Adamson, together with her daughter Neva, to the foundation of First Peoples Worldwide in 1997, an initiative that seeks to develop and implement solutions for Indigenous communities' issues all over the world. That includes the facilitation of the use of traditional Indigenous knowledge in solving today's challenges, from climate change to food security, to medicine, governance and sustainable development. Thereby, the organisation does not single-mindedly promote Indigenous solutions, but sees them in combination and co-evolution with contemporary practices. Such collaboration, however, does have to start, so the institute, on a local level from which it can gradually spread to a larger scale.

The development philosophy of First Peoples Worldwide clearly mirrors Adamson's approach, acquired over a lifetime of working with Indigenous people:

> *Everything we do is geared toward helping our communities achieve control over their own assets, including land, cultural rights and intellectual property. We recognise that our communities have their own unique needs, worldviews and problem-solving strategies, and must be allowed to determine their own definitions of success. We believe that a sea change in which communities are empowered on the local level will make a drastic improvement to the success of development efforts worldwide.*[16]

What remains central in the organisation's work is its holistic and multifaceted approach to development. For First Peoples Worldwide, the 'Indigenous approach to problem-solving considers the effect each part of a system has on the whole, whether it is economic, environmental, or social. Everything is connected, related, and interdependent. All of our work at First Peoples is grounded in this understanding of wholeness and balance'.[17]

First Peoples Worldwide consults extensively with policy councils, governments, funders, and economics development institutions on behalf of Indigenous Peoples. Furthermore, First Peoples Worldwide bridges Indigenous Peoples into broader partnerships, as they reach out to network and share common experiences and best practices. Today, both institutions – First Nations Development Institute and First Peoples Worldwide – coexist, with the former focusing on the national US American level, and the latter on the world at large. Jointly they have built up a vast experience and knowledge base that increasingly is translated in developmental, educational programmes.

Round 4 – Integrated practice: Educational actualisation – The Keepers of the Earth Program

First Peoples Worldwide is continuously evolving its rich experience, research and learnings into educational capacity building programmes. Particularly noteworthy is the example of the Keepers of the Earth Program to build the capacities of Indigenous people for managing protected areas on their own homelands. This programme seeks to support Indigenous people in their growing attempts to restore the relationship between the sustained protection of natural resources and their own sustainable productivity. Purposefully, it is building on the century old ability of Indigenous people to protect their natural environment.

The main case that First Peoples Worldwide is making through its Keepers of the Earth programme is the following:

> Indigenous Peoples inhabit more than 80 percent of the earth's protected areas; their territories span most of the last remaining, biodiversity-rich, conservation priority areas of the new century; and they maintain traditional land claims on 18 to 20 percent of the earth's land surface. This convergence of significant, biodiversity-rich areas on Indigenous territories presents an enormous opportunity to expand conservation beyond any current strategies, and on a scale to save the planet. If only half of Indigenous territories became Indigenous Conservation Areas, it could place an additional 12 percent of the world's land surface under protected status. These protected areas, combined with the over 12 percent of the earth's land surface already under conventional protected status, would double the world's land surface under conservation protection – almost one quarter of the globe would be protected from environmental degradation, and much of it would still be available for sustainable productive use.[18]

The case presents not only an enormous potential to revive traditional communities, but it holds one important key for the survival of humanity as a whole. Promoting an alternative approach to development – grown out of Indigenous tradition and contextualised for the requirements of today's world – the ultimate goal of the Keepers of the Earth Program is to support Indigenous people:

> to establish and manage Indigenous Stewardship Areas on their own homelands. Immeasurable human costs, in addition to hundreds of millions of dollars in administrative costs, could be saved by empowering Indigenous Peoples to practice biodiversity conservation and sustainable land use on their homelands, rather than evicting them in favour of outside management. In the process, Indigenous Peoples will restore the relationship between sustained protection of natural resources, and their sustainable productivity – a contribution of incalculable value to conservation and the global environment.[19]

Adamson affirms that there is still a long way to go. Reviewing her lifelong engagement she now sees spirituality and education as the two major keys to 'unlock a sustainable future'. Indeed, First Peoples Worldwide nowadays often uses an evolved version of Figure 10.2, placing 'spirituality' in the very centre of the development model – with 'values systems' becoming the fourth vector. Hence, for Adamson and her team, the development of educational programmes that incorporate and revitalise the ancient spirituality and wisdom sources of Indigenous people to capacitate them to 're-take' their role as Keepers of the Earth is much more than fighting for the rights of a social minority: rather, meaningful bridges between these age-old wisdom sources and modern ways of living are of vital importance for the survival of our species and planet. For Adamson, if Indigenous people and their knowledge die, humankind as a whole loses its foundation for a sustainable future.

The unfolding journey of Adamson, First Nations Development Institute and First Peoples Wordwide is summarised in the following Table 10.3.

Table 10.3   First Nations and First Peoples Worldwide

Integral Development	A 'Southern' case for Integral Development (summary)
Round 1: **Self-Development** Formative *Grounding*	***The self-discovery of Rebecca Adamson*** • Recognised early her acute powers of observation • Observed during childhood and youth the lack of opportunity of First Nation Peoples • Several trips to her Cherokee relatives acquainted her with the traditional beliefs of her grandfather and left her a keen judge of human character • Acknowledged the significance of education for authentic development from early on in her activist career and started out as director of the Coalition of Indian Controlled Schools Boards
Round 2: **Organisational Development** Reformative *Emergence*	***Setting up First Nations as a learning ecosystem*** • First Nations as a national Native American development organisation working with tribes and Native People to change the economic environment of reservations to one that builds on local resources, recognises native knowledge and culture, and supports Development from within • Four principles provided the foundation for First Nations: community is essential for survival; nature is a source of knowledge, a model to emulate, and a mentor; subsistence emphasises the interplay of spiritual beliefs with hunting and fishing; culturally, subsistence derives its meaning from the group's context
Round 3: **Societal Development** Newly normative *Navigation*	***Developing First Peoples Worldwide*** • An integrated, culturally sensitive, inside-out development model ('Learning and Development Ecology') was evolved that was deeply steeped in the natural and communal context as well as building on the historical-cultural traditions of the Native Americans – a major contribution to development theory and practice. its four core pillars are kinship, spirituality, assets and personal efficacy • From First Nations to First Peoples Worldwide: Foundation of First Peoples Worldwide in 1997 to develop and implement solutions for Indigenous communities' issues all over the world

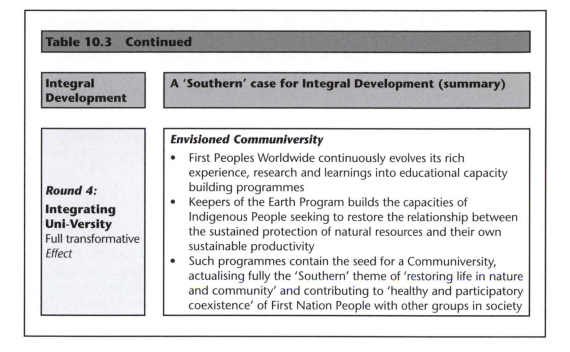

Table 10.3 Continued	
Integral Development	**A 'Southern' case for Integral Development (summary)**
Round 4: Integrating Uni-Versity Full transformative *Effect*	**Envisioned Communiversity** • First Peoples Worldwide continuously evolves its rich experience, research and learnings into educational capacity building programmes • Keepers of the Earth Program builds the capacities of Indigenous People seeking to restore the relationship between the sustained protection of natural resources and their own sustainable productivity • Such programmes contain the seed for a Communiversity, actualising fully the 'Southern' theme of 'restoring life in nature and community' and contributing to 'healthy and participatory coexistence' of First Nation People with other groups in society

Backed by these three case stories for integrated 'Southern' practice, we are now ready to provide a first conceptual overview of the nature and scope of the Communiversity – as a novel form of a context-and-community-based university.

10.3   Actualising the Communiversity: Motor of Community-Based Learning and Development

In this 'Southern' realm, the translation of the four-round-trajectory results in the establishment of what we call a 'Communiversity'. In all the cases introduced in this chapter, the natural evolutionary path points towards such a new type of educational entity. A Communiversity is a deeply contextualised research-and-education platform with a primary focus on communal learning and development, both within the institution and outside it. This platform serves to catalyse intensive processes of communal learning, through which communities reclaim their full problem-solving potential. The 'vitality of a particular place', in Escobar's terms (⇨9), becomes restored.

A university with a 'communiversity-character' can then take forward, on a larger scale – though always locally contextualised – the impressive restoration work with regards to nature and community that we have seen in the cases presented. Through a similar process, such a new type of university can also serve to complement, if not reform the existing educational system of a society.

The term 'Communiversity' has gradually emerged in recent years. We came across it a number of times, for example in the case of Stroud Common Wealth in UK's Gloucestershire, with which we are closely related. Stroud Common Wealth is a fascinating initiative, started by Martin Large and others, with the purpose of building community wealth for social, cultural and economic renewal.[20] The initiative is driven by the quest for a community to make a tangible difference to its affairs and take responsibility for its own present and future needs. Accordingly, in the case of Stroud Common Wealth their (still young) Communiversity pursues the objective 'to build a community of practice for sustainable livelihoods and a local living economy'.[21]

Other examples that show clearly elements of Communiversities are the Barefoot College in Rajastan in India, founded by Sanjit Bunker Roy,[22] the Universidad de la Tierra in Oaxaca in Mexico, founded by the renowned development economist Gustavo Esteva[23] and the Earth University (Bija Vidyapeeth) in North India's Dehradun, founded by the eco-feminist and social activist Vandana Shiva in partnership with the UK-based Schumacher College.[24] Most notable is also the Kliptown Youth Program in South Africa's formerly black township Soweto, providing academic support for over 400 children. Such academic support includes school fees, tutoring programmes, tertiary education programmes and employment networking. Furthermore, in almost integral fashion, the programme offers access to technology and to a library, organises cultural, artistic and sports activities, as well as a 'roots and shoots' environmental programme, inspired by the work of British primatologist and anthropologist Jane Goodall. Kliptown Youth Program was founded in 2007, not by a single individual but by a small group of passionate young people, all of them hailing from Kliptown's squatter camps themselves. Among the founders is 'community crusader' Thulani Madondo who was selected a 'CNN Hero' in 2012.[25] The mission of this fascinating community-education based programme is 'to eradicate the poverty of mind, body and soul and to fight against the disadvantages imposed on the children of Kliptown, by providing educational support and after school activities. It seeks to develop young and dynamic individuals who are willing to contribute effectively for the betterment of their community'.[26]

Another remarkable case is the Ecuadorian intercultural university Amawtay Wasi (Universidad Intercultural de las Nacionalidades y Pueblos Indígenas). An educational project of the Indigenous movement, officially founded in 2004, it declared as its core objective the creation of an 'integral university that works to overcome the divide between practice and theory'.[27] Its strong relationship to nature, its focus on community, and its focus on 'healthy and participatory coexistence' are reflected in the purpose behind Amawtay Wasi:

> *Our purpose is to contribute to the formation of human talents that will prioritise an harmonious relationship between the Pachamama (Mother Nature) and the Runa (Human Being), based upon the principle of Sumak Kawsanamanta Yachay, which means 'Learning Wisdom and the Good Way to Live'. Our university is part of the living web that we weave in the intercultural cosmos.*[28]

The university philosophy is based on the four natural elements: air, fire, water and earth – projected in a fourfold design with life as an integrating force in their shared centre. These four elements have been translated into the official university structure that maintains the Indigenous fourfold design (see Figure 10.3).

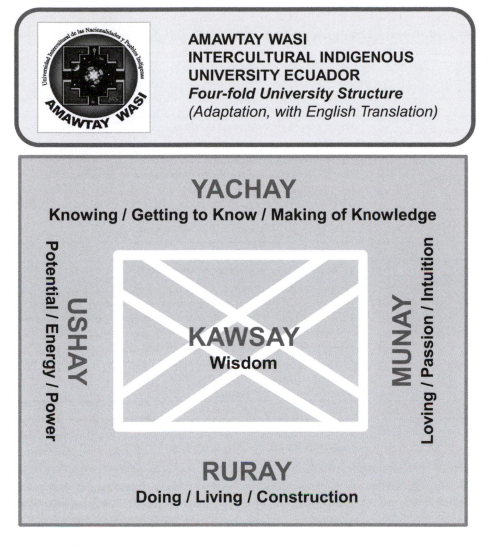

Figure 10.3 The fourfold university structure of Amawtay Wasi, Ecuador

All cases presented in this chapter have started out by setting up research and/or educational programmes and processes. The major challenge that comes with a more formal institutionalisation as a Communiversity is not to lose the transformative power of the original journey (Rounds 1, 2, 3) and of the initial programmes and processes (early stage of Round 4). The official higher educational standards often oblige new institutions to adopting conventional curricula and educational processes that are not geared towards effective community, as well as individual and organisational, development.

Based on the theory and practice introduced in this 'Southern' realm, we summarise in the following Table 10.4 core steps, highlighting how we can work towards the establishment of Communiversities.

Table 10.4 Integral Development rhythm of the 'Southern' realm	
Core theme: Restoring life in nature and community **Core value: Healthy and participatory coexistence**	
Round 1: **Self Development** Formative *Grounding*	**Know your self and your context** You engage in a process of deepening self knowledge (in relation to your particular communal context), dealing with respective insights from nature and from your own and other traditions and cultures. You develop a sense for 'whom am I' in Relation to others, for your personal life cycle and for related Development tasks. In the same process, you also seek to understand your contribution to a larger organisational and communal context.
Round 2: **Organisational Development** Reformative *Emergence*	**Build an ecosystemic organisation** Having deeply connected with your individual self, and being in touch with the cyclical, interconnected nature of life, you now bridge personal Development tasks with those of a group or entire organisation. In that process, you now altogether understand organisational life cycles and engage reformatively in building ecosystemic organisations that allow for continuous evolution. Doing so, you contribute to the reformation of the conventional, more static and isolated notion of an organisation.
Round 3: **Societal Development** Newly normative *Navigation*	**Embed development in community and society** The organisation, seeing itself as an integrated part within a larger societal ecosystem, now seeks, through its design and actions, to contribute to the development of the communities and society it is part of. Livelihood and economics thereby become increasingly embedded in society, and the organisation contributes to unleashing community potential and to reactivating the 'vitality' of its natural and societal environment. In the process, the organisation formulates new developmental norms and becomes a role model for sustainable organisational theory and practice.
Round 4: **Integrating University** Full transformative *Effect*	**Fully actualise the 'Southern' realm through a Communiversity** These new developmental norms and practice are translated into research and educational programmes, serving to codify and then effect large-scale, community-based Integral Development. Programmes and processes are institutionalised in this 'Southern' context through a 'Communiversity'. Such a university is grounded in a particular context, and seeks to build research and learning communities that are able to unleash their own potential and are directed at addressing their community's developmental issues, drawing on Indigenous knowledge and capacities, on an ongoing level. Courses for individual students are a by-product rather than its reason for being: restoring life in nature and community.

10.4 Integration: Integral Development as Healthy and Participatory Coexistence

INTEGRATING THE 'SOUTHERN' ROUND 4

We have learned in this final round about the need to evolve a potent 'developmental vehicle' out of the first three rounds, that facilitates the interconnection of the development journeys experienced for self, organisation and society. In this 'Southern' case we called such a transformational entity a 'Communiversity'. Use the following summarising Table 10.5 to reflect back on this fourth and final round of the 'Southern' realm and record your own thoughts and prospective actions in order to bring about such individual and communal, organisational and societal development, through a Communiversity.

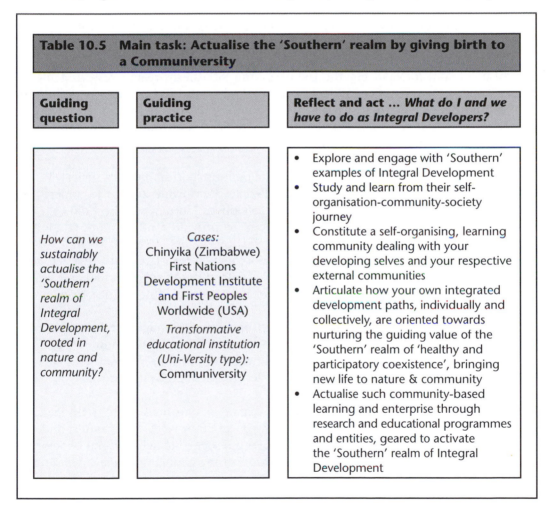

Table 10.5 Main task: Actualise the 'Southern' realm by giving birth to a Communiversity		
Guiding question	**Guiding practice**	**Reflect and act ... *What do I and we have to do as Integral Developers?***
How can we sustainably actualise the 'Southern' realm of Integral Development, rooted in nature and community?	*Cases:* Chinyika (Zimbabwe) First Nations Development Institute and First Peoples Worldwide (USA) *Transformative educational institution (Uni-Versity type):* Communiversity	• Explore and engage with 'Southern' examples of Integral Development • Study and learn from their self-organisation-community-society journey • Constitute a self-organising, learning community dealing with your developing selves and your respective external communities • Articulate how your own integrated development paths, individually and collectively, are oriented towards nurturing the guiding value of the 'Southern' realm of 'healthy and participatory coexistence', bringing new life to nature & community • Actualise such community-based learning and enterprise through research and educational programmes and entities, geared to activate the 'Southern' realm of Integral Development

INTEGRATING THE FULL 'SOUTHERN' REALM

We are now ready to conclude this 'Southern' nature-and-community-based perspective on Integral Development.

Over the course of the past four chapters you have worked yourself progressively through the four rounds of self (Round 1), organisation (Round 2), society (Round 3), and, finally, through integrated educational-and-developmental practice (Round 4). At the fourth round, you were presented with the case stories of Chinyika in Zimbabwe and First Peoples Worldwide in the USA that serve to illustrate the organic and authentic interweaving and integration of the first three rounds.

Both cases are representations of a Communiversity, the culmination of the 'Southern' realm. Such a Communiversity stands for a new type of community-based research and learning platform that allows for the development of communities and facilitates the effective resolution of community development issues. We regard it as the main objective of this 'Southern' part of the Integral Developer's (or Developers') journey to give rise to such Communiversities. They allow for maximising the potential for communities to engage in their own development.

As we shall see in the chapters to come, the Communiversity is not the only institutional solution offering 'education with a difference' that Integral Development proposes. However, it represents the most relevant institution for local community development and for realising the theme of the 'Southern' realm: restoring life in nature and community. According to our integral rhythm that starts with 'nature and community', we 'naturally' propose the Communiversity as the first institutional solution, as communities, first and foremost, require such natural and communal well-being or vitality to effectively engage in addressing their own developmental issues.

We have illustrated how such vitality can be built up 'bottom-up' in a society. While the phenomenal cases of Chinyika and First Peoples Worldwide help us to understand and get motivated to undertake the Integral Developer's journey, we also hold that the learnings derived out of such cases can be used to provide a much more conducive development environment for other transformation agents. If the core innovators' journeys get decoded (as we attempt in this book), then translated into research-and-education processes (as for example in Chinyika or First Peoples Worldwide) and finally institutionalised within Communiversities, we have a reasonable chance to generate widespread sustainable development.

In the concluding Figure 10.4 we take you once more through the journey of the 'Southern' realm: we indicate the main developmental tasks of each round; we provide an overview of the core thinkers and practitioners that illustrate the nature of each of the four rounds; and we summarise the core developmental challenges that you, your organisation and your community face.

Ultimately, the journey through this 'Southern' integral realm is not to be understood in linear fashion. However, the composite view on the four integrated rounds, and the large variety of relevant thinkers and practitioners is designed to help Integral Developers to build, step by step, a developmental foundation strong enough to make a meaningful contribution to restoring life in nature and community.

We shall now enter the 'Eastern' integral realm of culture and spirituality.

Your Development Calling & Challenge	MAIN TASK	GUIDING THEORY / GUIDING PRACTICE	LEARNING AND DEVELOPMENT PROCESSES FOR INTEGRAL DEVELOPMENT – AGENT & AGENCY
G — Round 1: **Self Development** — *Formative Grounding*	KNOW YOUR SELF AND YOUR CONTEXT	**Answers from Africa** (Ford) **Indigenous Four-Fold Way** (Arrien) **Psychological Types** (Jung) **Seasons of Human Life** (Levinson)	• Engage with African and indigenous Approaches to Self Development • Engage with the natural Principle of Dynamic Opposition • Explore your own Nature through your Personality Type • Engage with the developmental Tasks that come with your Type • Face the *'Struggle towards Wholeness'* • Discover your *'inner'* Four Elements and the Seasons of your Life • Map the Cycle of your Life (Teens to Maturity) and engage with the Development Tasks of your current Life Season
E — Round 2: **Organisational Development** — *Reformative Emergence*	BUILD AN ECO-SYSTEMIC ORGANISATION	**Life Cycles in Organisations** (Lievegoed / Glasl) **Organisational Evolution via an Ecosystemic Shift** (Moore)	• Map the Life Cycle of your Organisation (or Group or Community) • Discover each of the four Life Seasons of your Organisation, and its potential for Renewal • Explore and engage in the evolutionary Tasks of the current Season • Perceive of your Organisation in an ecosystemic, interrelated Way • Envision your Organisation transcending the conventional guiding Pattern of Competition and evolving towards Collaboration, thereby being also embedded stronger in natural & communal Life
N — Round 3: **Societal Development** — *Normative Navigation*	EMBED DEVELOPMENT IN COMMUNITY AND SOCIETY	**Development as a Whole Life Project** (Escobar) **Embeddedness in Society** (Polanyi) **Unleashing Community Potential** (Gudemann) **Reactivating Vitality of Place** (Escobar) **Alignment with Nature as Central Development Agent** (Escobar / Sveiby / Skuthorpe)	• Explore to what Degree the Development of your Community & Society is rooted in its *'Home Grounds'* and in the *'Life'* of the People • Immerse yourself fully in the local value Domains of your Community • Articulate how your Development Theory and Work serves to embed Markets and Economy in Community and Society and illustrate how you and your Group or Organisation serve to reactivate the *'Vitality of Place'* • Show how your Development Principles are aligned with the Principles of Nature and how your Development Approach and Practice is serving to restore natural and communal Life
E — Round 4: **Integrating Uni-Versity** — *Transformative Effect*	GIVE BIRTH TO A COMMUNIVERSITY	**Cases:** Chinyika (Zimbabwe) First Nations Development Institute and First Peoples Worldwide (USA) **COMMUNIVERSITY**	• Explore & engage with *'southern'* Examples of Integral Development • Study and learn from their self-organisation-community-society Journey • Constitute a self-organising Learning Community, dealing with your internal developing Self and your respective external Communities • Articulate how your own integrated Development Paths. Individually and collectively, are oriented towards nurturing the guiding Value of the *'southern'* Realm of *'healthy and participatory Co-Existence'*, bringing new Life to Nature & Community? • Actualise such Community based learning through educational and Research Programs and Entities, geared to activate the *'southern'* Realm. • Build on a relevant local and global Movements

Figure 10.4 Releasing the gene-ius of the 'Southern' realm

References

1   Lessem, R., Muchineripi, P. and Kada, S. (2012). *Integral Community: Political Economy to Social Commons*. Farnham: Gower-Ashgate.

2   Muchineripi, P. (2008). *Feeding Five Thousand: The Case of Indigenous Crops in Zimbabwe*. London: Africa Research Institute.

3   Muchineripi, P. and Kada, S. (2009). Together We Grow. A Transformative Approach to Food Security in Africa. In: *Forum CSR International*, January 2009.

4   Muchineripi, P. (2012). Thesis on Social and Economic Transformation: A Case Study for Chinyika Communities in Gutu, Zimbbwe. PhD thesis, Modderfontein. Kada, S. (2012). *Social and Economic Transformation of Rural Communities in Africa: The Case of Chinyika Community in Zimbabwe*. Modderfontein: Da Vinci.

5   Stoesz, D., Guzzetta, C. and Lusk, M. (1999). *International Development*. Boston, MA: Allan and Bacon, p. 184.

6   Stoesz, D., Guzzetta, C. and Lusk, M. (1999). *International Development*. Boston, MA: Allan and Bacon, p. 187.

7   Ridley, K. (1997). Indian Giver. *HOPE Magazine*. May/June 1997, p. 35.

8   Black, S.S. (1994). *Redefining Success in Community Development: A New Approach for Determining and Measuring the Impact of Development*. Richard Schramm Paper on Community Development. Medford, MA: The Lincoln Filene Center at Tufts University.

9   Stoesz, D., Guzzetta, C. and Lusk, M. (1999). *International Development*. Boston, MA: Allan and Bacon, p. 188.

10 Adamson, R., Salway Black, S. and Dewees, S. (2003). *Asset Building in Native Communities*. Fredericksburg, VA: First Nations Development Institute, p. 4.

11 Adamson, R., Salway Black, S. and Dewees, S. (2003). *Asset Building in Native Communities*. Fredericksburg, VA: First Nations Development Institute, p. 5.

12 Adamson, R., Salway Black, S. and Dewees, S. (2003). *Asset Building in Native Communities*. Fredericksburg, VA: First Nations Development Institute, p. 10.

13 Adamson, R., Salway Black, S. and Dewees, S. (2003). *Asset Building in Native Communities*. Fredericksburg, VA: First Nations Development Institute, p. 16.

14 Black, S.S. (1996). Indigenous Economics. In: *Yes! A Journal of Positive Futures*. Spring/Summer 1996.

15 First Peoples Worldwide and First Nations Development Institute (30 June 2006). *Okiciyab 'To Help Each Other' Promoting Best Practices in Indigenous Community Development*. Report submitted to the United States Agency for International Development.

16 First Peoples Worldwide website. Available at: www.firstpeoplesworldwide.org / Accessed: 1 October 2012.

17 First Peoples Worldwide website. Available at: www.firstpeoplesworldwide.org / Accessed: 1 October 2012.

18 First Peoples Worldwide website. Available at: www.firstpeoplesworldwide.org / Accessed: 29 August 2012. Includes changes based on interview with Neva Morrison (1 October 2012).

19 First Peoples Worldwide website. Available at: www.firstpeoplesworldwide.org / Accessed: 29 August 2012.

20 Large, M. (2010). *Common Wealth: For a Free, Equal, Mutual and Sustainable Society*. Stroud: Hawthorn Press.

21 Stroud Commonwealth website. Available at: www.stroudcommonwealth.org.uk / Accessed: 6 September 2012.

22 Kristen Nehemiy, H. (2011). *Bunker Roy. Barefoot College, Tilonia, Indian NGOs*. London: Dign Press.

23 Prakash, M. and Esteva, G. (1998). *Escaping Education: Living as Learning at the Grassroots*. New York: Peter Lang Publishing.

24 Navdanya website. Available at: www.navdanya.org/earth-university / Accessed: 12 September 2012.

25 CNN website. Available at: http://www.cnn.com/SPECIALS/cnn.heroes/2012.heroes/thulani.madondo.html / Accessed: 20 November 2012.

26 Kliptown Youth Program website. Available at: www.kliptownyouthprogram.org.za / Accessed: 22 November 2012.

27 Amawtay Wasi website. Available at: www.amawtaywasi.edu.ec / Accessed: 17 September 2012.

28 Amawtay Wasi website. Available at: www.amawtaywasi.edu.ec / Accessed: 17 September 2012.

PART IV

The Eastern Realm of Integral Development: Regenerating Meaning via Culture and Spirituality

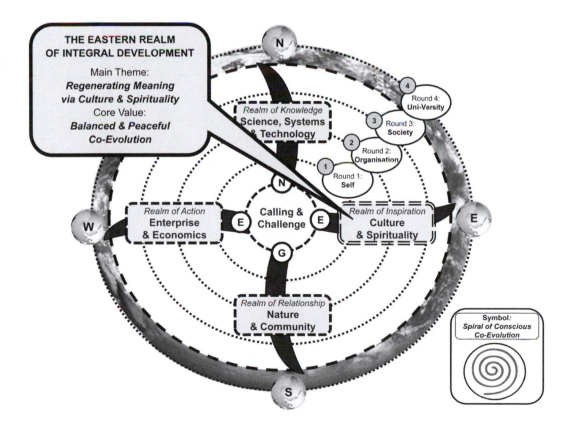

THE EASTERN REALM
OF INTEGRAL DEVELOPMENT

Main Theme:
*Regenerating Meaning
via Culture & Spirituality*
Core Value:
*Balanced & Peaceful
Co-Evolution*

Realm of Knowledge
**Science, Systems
& Technology**

4 Round 4:
Uni-Versity
3 Round 3:
Society
2 Round 2:
Organisation
1 Round 1:
Self

N

Realm of Action
**Enterprise
& Economics**

E Calling &
Challenge E

Realm of Inspiration
**Culture
& Spirituality**

G

Realm of Relationship
**Nature
& Community**

Symbol:
*Spiral of Conscious
Co-Evolution*

N

W

E

S

11 *The Journey of the Self: An Eastern Individual Perspective*

Guiding Questions: How am I evolving? What creative sources within and around me can provide insights into my development?

11.1   Orientation

We now turn from the 'Southern' realm of relationship comprised of nature and community to the 'Eastern' realm of inspiration comprised of culture and spirituality. We thereby also turn from a pre-emphasis on context and community to a focus on consciousness. Starting out by raising individual consciousness on this first level, we end up with societal awakening, drawing on Sarvodaya in Sri Lanka as well as on Om Creations and Aravind in India, on the concluding level (or round). For us, the conventional 'Eastern' orientation towards the development of the 'self', set apart from the wider organisation, community and society, severely limits its developmental reach. The practical cases we cite will have healed this divide, at least to a considerable degree.

As this 'Eastern' reality perspective seeks to contribute to the generation of new meaning in a development context, we first need to have a clear understanding of what gives meaning to our lives, and how we regenerate meaning at times of disorientation. In other words: as we seek to engage in co-evolutionary development with others, we need to have a sense of direction for ourselves. Such a developmental direction will then inform the development of a particular organisation, community and/or society. On this first level of individual, formative grounding in culture and spirituality, we pursue the following questions:

- How am I evolving at this point of time?
- What is my calling?
- What gives me meaning?
- What regenerates me?
- What is the myth or guiding image I live by and that also informs my own development work? To what degree is this image informed by my own cultural background? How does it connect with other cultural predispositions?
- What creative sources within and around me can provide insights in my development?
- What sources of wisdom can I tap into, alone and with others?

- How can I align my own evolution with those of others, and also with my organisation or community, to contribute to a larger societal, if not even cosmic context?

Facing our own difficulties in finding adequate answers to these questions will also help us to develop our empathy for others who are struggling like us to find their own answers. These questions are particular challenging when we feel weak and have lost our sense of direction. This is a situation in which many people in so-called developing countries live, due to their recent history, which destroyed the ancient foundations of their cultures and spiritualities through conquest, colonisation, religious conversion, dispossession, forced labour and displacement. Despite the formal end of colonisation, the destabilisation continues today through economic globalisation that is inimical to the autonomous cultural and spiritual renewal of these countries. It is also for that reason, that we started our Integral Development journey with 'restoring life' – a necessary first step to vitalise ourselves for the development journey.

As difficult as the answers to these questions are, we find many sources of guidance on our way, as countless individuals before us have undertaken the same process of self-questioning and achieved higher levels of consciousness. The spiritual and religious literature of the world provides rich nourishment. And yet, it is not easy to find our way through it. We have selected four eminent thinkers that can help us on our way. We start out with the 'Eastward'-oriented American mythologist, whose book *The Hero with a Thousand Faces*[1] tells the timeless wisdom embedded in the world's cultures of how to embark on the heroic journey of uncovering your innermost treasures. It also serves as a bridge with the 'Southern' individual realm of nature and community, where we first introduced the journey of the African hero, through Clyde Ford (⇨7).

Campbell's scholarly yet highly accessible work has inspired an entire generation of students, researchers and artists across disciplines. The work of the Swiss psychoanalyst C.G. Jung complements Campbell's, as Jung has translated the mythological truths with which Campbell deals into a whole new school of psychological thinking. We shall draw in particular on his work on the 'shadow', which constitutes for Jung the seat of human creativity.

We shall then turn to the South Africa-based Iraqi Sufi Master Shaykh Fadhlalla Haeri and his work *The Journey of the Self*[2] and conclude with insights from the fascinating life, work and global impact of Swami Vivekananda, drawing on the great wisdom sources of India. Both Haeri and Vivekananda are powerful voices in their own right of linking individual and societal development.

There are many more fascinating thinkers that we could have introduced in this section. Spiritual masters from all over the world come to our mind. We have chosen to start with Campbell and Jung, as both of them have not only drawn on incredible knowledge and wisdom from a wide range of global sources, but also have been picked up by others, building bridges between the development of the self and that of organisation or society. With Haeri, we purposefully introduce a voice that at times is underrepresented in the self-development literature: the 'Eastern' wisdom of the Muslim world. Altogether, we feel, that with Campbell, Jung, Haeri and Vivekananda we shall be sufficiently initiated into the world of self-development from the 'Eastern' cultural and spiritual perspective, in order to then move on to the level of group and organisation.

11.2   The Hero's Journey: The Need for Myth and Images for Personal Development

QUO VADIS? WHERE ARE YOU GOING?

For the great and late American mythologist Joseph Campbell the key question for anyone to answer is: where am I going? What direction is my life taking? For Campbell, the answer to this question lies in mythology. All through the history of humankind, collective myths have given entire civilisations direction and orientation. The mythologies of the Australian Aborigines, or of our African ancestors, have functioned relatively stably for tens of thousands of years. That worked, so says Campbell, as long as the context in which people lived was not overly disruptive. In a relatively slow changing outer world, ancient myths can provide for a long time relevant interpretations of the world to help people to deal with it.

THE POWER OF MYTH

For Campbell, the function of myths is to:

> first, awaken us to the fascinating mystery of life. The second function is to interpret the mystery in order to give meaning to life. The third function is that of sustaining the moral order by shaping the individual to the requirements of his geographically or historically conditioned group. The fourth function is the most vital one of fostering the unfolding of the individual, in accord with himself, his culture and the universe, as well as that awesome ultimate mystery, which is both beyond and within himself and all things.[3]

In other words, myths are often seen as sacred narratives. They provide culturally specific explanations of how the world has come to be and they function as role models and ethical codes for how to live an honourable life, how to behave, communicate and interact in this lifetime, and how to die in dignity. The stories of, for example, Odysseus, Heracles, King Arthur and his knights – in particular of Perceval, the Knight of the Holy Grail – are all powerful myths that inform how mortals can live heroic, exemplary lives. The life stories of Buddha, Krishna, Moses, Jesus and Mohammed, the founding fathers of religious traditions, continue to inform the making and evolution of civilisations. The almost magnetic resonance these myths and stories evoked for long in millions of people was only possible because their content mirrored an inner truth that the recipient could experience inwardly. Listening to these stories filled humans with a sense of awe and wonder in the face of creation and the creator, and more importantly, inspired humans to emulate their prophets and heroes in their own lives. Each prophet or hero offers a template, a role model for our own lives, an inspiration to rise above the mundane profanity of our existence to fulfil a higher purpose.

   This is captured, almost lyrically, by the cultural philosopher and poet Jean Gebser:

> Myth is the closing of the mouth and eyes; since it is a silent inner gaze (and inner listening), it is essentially a gazing at the psyche, which can be seen and represented as well as heard and

made audible. Myth is the representing and making audible; it is the articulation, the report …
about that which has been seen and heard inwardly.[4]

THE DECLINING POWER OF COLLECTIVE MYTHS

Today, we are living in a time of transition. Our era is characterised by such rapid change, that many myths do not carry any more their initial powers to interpret the world and the cosmos around us, nor do they give guidance in orienting us in our social lives. On many levels, myths have become meaningless – unless we are able to understand their symbolic meaning, re-interpret and subsequently reactivate the myths within ourselves and hence see them in the light of our current day and age. However, the faster a society changes and the more it is fragmented into pockets of subcultures, the more it is the role of the individual to become the maker of his or her own myth. Campbell argues that:

> with respect to the development of each individual's psychology, we have such varied sources
> from which we've come and such varied opportunities in our lives that there is no single
> mythology that can do it for us. My belief is that within the field of a secular society, which is
> a sort of neutral frame that allows individuals to develop their own lives.[5]

Campbell's crucial indication for the present age is this: '… each of us has an individual myth that's driving us, which we may or may not know'.[6] It is our responsibility to uncover that myth so that we can live it, and indeed live up to it, consciously. The present dichotomised age requires each individual to live the life of a hero, shaping her or his own unique hero's journey, writing his or her own myth in line with the challenges of his or her specific cultural and spiritual context, and in accord with our times. Understandably, says Campbell, for we do need myths, which are guiding images that provide us with an inner compass to navigate our complex world. While for former times we could say – not having collective myth equals collective lack of direction, Campbell declares for our time: not having a personal myth equals individual disorientation!

Although formally the vast majority of the world's population, particularly in the so-called developing countries, follows a religion, for many people the power of the original myth, which lies at the heart of each religion, is largely lost. In our rationalistic age, the time of awe and wonder is gone. It is also for that reason, that we find a growing percentage of human beings embarking on a spiritual search, seeking new or renewed meaning in their lives. For humans can't live without meaning and purpose.

The search for meaning as the central motivation in the lives of human beings was affirmed by the work of the renowned psychologist Victor Frankl – the founder of logo-therapy (*logos* signifies 'meaning'). In his classic book *Man's Search for Meaning*,[7] one of the most influential books in psychotherapy, Frankl testifies how it was this belief in the intrinsic meaning of life even amidst profound suffering and oppression that helped him to survive the concentration camps of the Nazis, and how this traumatising personal experience – which is so strongly emphasised also by Campbell – helped him to further evolve his theory and practice as a logo-therapist.

So where are you going? Quo vadis?

THE HERO WITH A THOUSAND FACES: THE DEPARTURE – THE JOURNEY – THE RETURN

In perhaps his most popular book, *The Hero with a Thousand Faces*,[8] Campbell compared the world's mythologies and came to an astounding result: The basic pattern that he identified in all great myths anywhere in the world is basically the same. In almost all cases, the hero goes on a quest, leaving his or her familiar environment, faces dangerous adventures and nearly insurmountable challenges, often is even confronted with death – and sometimes dies and is miraculously resurrected – and returns with enormous riches (usually in the form of knowledge and wisdom) to his society, which he subsequently serves, be it as a warrior, king, religious leader or sage.

Laurens Van der Post echoes this finding of the common pattern underlying all myths. Van der Post himself lived a most adventurous life, and was one of the first outsiders with whom the Bushmen of the South African Kalahari shared their own creation myths.[9] Van der Post describes that the deepest of all the patterns in the human spirit is that of departure and return, and the journey implicit in between. The life of man is the journey, a voyage such as that of Odysseus, the wanderings of the Israelites from bondage in Egypt in search of the Promised Land, the walkabouts of the aborigines in Australia, and of the stone-age people in the vast lands of southern Africa. The same pattern underlies the Tao of China, and the one and only way of Confucius, and the New Testament parable of the prodigal son.[10]

The question then is how to find out what his or her development adventure is about, and how to gain the cultural and spiritual insights and orientation to guide his or her development and life journey. In other words, on what do we focus with regards to our own inner development, and to which target do we direct our outer development energies, thereby concretely contributing to a specific development context. The answer that Campbell gives us is simple, yet challenging: 'Follow your Bliss!' Campbell stops, however, at the individual level or round, whereas we argue, that such individual development would need to be further 'rounded out' – organisationally, communally and societally.

FOLLOW YOUR BLISS!

Campbell's own life journey is a good example of someone following his personal bliss. Campbell inspired the inner development process of thousands of his students, and millions of his readers.[11] The American director and entrepreneur George Lucas is one of those cases. His space opera *Star Wars* and his movie series of the archaeologist-adventurer *Indiana Jones* were both strongly influenced by Campbell's work. For Campbell, in turn, *Star Wars* represents a fascinating showcase of reactivating and transporting the ancient hero-myth into our day and age.

In Campbell's terms, we are called to find out what truly gives us happiness. Campbell explains bliss as follows:

> *Your bliss can guide you to that transcendent mystery, because bliss is the welling up of the energy of the transcendent wisdom within you. So when the bliss cuts off, you know that you've*

cut off the welling up; try to find it again. And that will be your Hermes guide, the dog that can follow the invisible trail for you. And that's the way it is. One works out one's myth that way.[12]

Campbell leaves us with an enormous personal challenge, claiming that one's life is wasted if one's bliss is not found. He asserts, however, that if we find what gives us bliss, we can release enormous energy and creativity within ourselves, which then naturally serves the development of ourselves and society. If we were to translate his advice to our own quest, it would mean finding our bliss in bringing about Integral Development within the development contexts with which we engage. Jung's work provides further clues for that challenging task.

11.3 The Pathway to Individuation: Owning the Shadow to Uncover the Seat of Creativity

OWNING THE DEVELOPMENT SHADOW

Having pursued Joseph Campbell's mythology laden journey, we feel, it is important to return once more to the Swiss psychologist C.G. Jung, whose theory of psychological types (as a tool to make sense of our own nature) we introduced earlier (⇨7).

As we learned from Campbell, the journey that heroes in the world's myths undertake is in large part a symbol for the inner journey that each of us is invited to undertake. For Campbell and for Jung, the monsters, dragons, dark knights or evil spirits that the heroes have to fight represent nothing else than the unknown, often suppressed, parts of our psyche. They represent those inner aspects that we don't dare to face: our anxieties, our powerlessness, our perceived insufficiencies. Instead of accepting these aspects as part of ourselves, we tend to suppress and disown them, and in a next step project them onto others. Jung called this amalgam of undesired and feared facets of our psyche the 'shadow', a psychological concept that has gained such popularity that the term has become almost part of everyday knowledge. However, while we intellectually may have integrated this knowledge, it still requires tremendous personal strength to truly face these shadow parts within us.

This process is inevitably painful, as we deal here with no less than overcoming a limited and limiting, illusionary self-perception that, over time, has become not only dear, but existential to us. Looking at ourselves in a more 'complete' light, requires us to recognise that the harm or 'evil' we accuse others of is all too often a projection of our own shadow. It demands the courage to acknowledge this and accept and integrate this. This can be a shattering experience for the solid ego image we have built of ourselves as 'respectable, good and socially accepted individuals'. Yet, Jung believes that when we reintegrate our shadows it releases enormous energy that was so long repressed. This is the creative potential we referred to earlier that is suppressed with our shadows. The task of letting go, of overcoming our old sense of self is a crucial stepping stone towards acknowledging and embracing a much larger, but also much more complex understanding of ourselves. The task, according to Jung, is akin to a death experience. It is for that very reason that most people never face their shadow. Yet, as we shall examine further below, without this death experience of the small, reduced perception of our self, we cannot awaken to our much larger self.

For Jung, the core problem that arises if we do not face our individual shadows – we would argue that the same applies to organisations and whole societies – is that it leads inevitably to a projection of the repressed, perceived insufficiencies within ourselves to the outer world. That is what Rahnema meant (⇨5) when he said of development workers that 'instead of claiming to be able to change the world and to save 'humanity', we rather need to save ourselves from our own compelling need for comforting illusions'.[13] In grounding our cultural and spiritual self-development, we are hence called to avoid such projections to our best abilities, as they are bound to severely distort our development efforts and to cause irritation and conflict among the people we work with.

THE REWARD OF THE JOURNEY: UNCOVERING THE SEAT OF CREATIVITY

But the task of facing our shadow side is not an altogether negative one. Quite the contrary. Jung asserts us that there is indeed much to gain if we dare to journey. For him, the answer to our core personal development needs lies clearly in our shadow. Facing our suppressed, inner shadow side, then involves learning to integrate what we hitherto rejected, a process that can be applied to whole communities, thereby transforming the negative, initially frightening material into positive, creative life energy.

For Campbell, the shadow that the hero needs to face in the form of, say, a dragon is none other than his or her own ego. It is 'beyond' that perceived superior side of us that we seek to display as we feel it is impressive enough to present to the world, of course according to the standards the world has set for our day and age. Behind that ego-mask we equally carefully hide those aspects within us that we perceive as inferior. We often hide them so well, that we ourselves believe in their absence. The hero's mission is to slay the ego-dragon, in order to arrive at his or her true sense of self. In the myth the 'true self' is often symbolised by a treasure (representing our inner gold) or by a maiden (representing our personal purity, fertility and creativity) that are guarded by the dragon.

Jung would agree with this interpretation of myths by Campbell, as he himself saw the shadow as the source of personal creativity. How then do we lift to consciousness what is hitherto in 'shadowland'. For Jung, the answer to this question is to be found in our dreams. They are the most potent 'access providers' to the individual shadow.

WORKING WITH DREAMS: A KEY TO CONSCIOUS PERSONAL DEVELOPMENT

Jung, who had analysed over 80,000 dreams in his lifetime, discovered 'not only that all dreams are relevant in varying degrees to the life of the dreamer, but that they are part of one great web of psychological factors'. He also found that, on the whole, they seem to follow an arrangement or pattern. This pattern Jung called 'the process of individuation', a process of psychic growth that a person undergoes.[14] Individuation is the term he coined to describe the process of the gradual integration of the unconscious, feared shadow-aspects of the psyche into consciousness. Jung called the 'inventor, organiser, and source of dream images' the inner centre or self, 'and described it as the totality of the whole psyche, in order to distinguish it from the 'ego', which constitutes only a part of the total psyche'. For Marie Louise von Franz, one of Jung's closest collaborators, the 'Self can be defined as an inner guiding factor that is different from the conscious personality and that can be grasped only through the investigation of one's own dreams. These show it to be the regulating center that brings about a constant extension and maturing of the personality'.[15] Von Franz underlines the crucial task to carefully seek to understand one's dreams, as she affirms, that the degree to which the self of a person develops 'depends to whether or not the ego is willing to listen to the message of the self'.[16]

Von Franz explains further that in all ages, cultures have been aware of the existence of such a centre. The Greeks called it 'daimon', while the Romans referred to it as a man's inner 'genius' that is inborn in each individual.

As illustrated in earlier chapters (⇨5, 6), we use the concept of 'releasing genius' in the Integral Development paradigm as well. This intimates another interesting – though initially unconscious – resonance between Jung's and the integral approach proposed here.

Both, Jung and von Franz observed in their work that those people who gave active attention to their dreams and their deeper meaning, and allowed themselves to be guided by them in their conscious life, would gradually develop not only a richer dream life, but also live a more balanced life. Going back to the self-regulation theory of Jung that we briefly introduced earlier (⇨7), in those cases the content of the unconscious that had been made conscious through dream work, could function as a balancing, or regulating force to the conscious life of a person. In other words: if we regard our dreams as a source of inner wisdom, they can not only help to become conscious of hitherto unseen, or even suppressed aspects of psyche, but they can also provide guidance in our inner, personal development work, as well as in working with concrete outer development contexts. Later, when we move to the community and society level, we shall illustrate the potential relevance of dreams for societal development work with the example of Swiss economic planner Theodor Abt (⇨13).

OUTLOOK ON THE PATHWAY TO INDIVIDUATION

While Western psychological traditions deal intensively with the inner confrontation and reconciliation with one's own shadow, as a crucial stepping stone to individuation, Eastern spiritual traditions put an overall stronger emphasis on the realisation of 'emptiness', a 'still mind', and an uncompromising focus on the higher self within us. Both pathways point to the same destination. Both we regard as complementary.

Having then paid particular attention to Campbell and to Jung, based respectively in America and in Northern Europe, we now turn to the internationally renowned, Iraqi Sufi Master Shaykh Fadhlalla Haeri and his work on the *Journey of the Self*,[17] which stresses the importance of the development of the self for culture and civilisation.

11.4   The Evolution of the Self: Towards Integration and Unity

THE ONE SELF

For Haeri, currently resident in South Africa, our life's journey has a clear direction: towards integration and unity, towards the 'one self'. For him, our 'purpose in this life is to discover and know the basic nature of the self and the spiritual foundation which underlies it. We will only attain contentment when our potential as a spiritual being is fulfilled'.[18]

While for the Muslim Haeri the Qur'an is the primary source of spiritual inspiration, in his work and teachings he demonstrates a remarkable ability to translate the central message of the Qur'an in a language of universal relevance. Simultaneously appreciative and critical of his own faith as well as how it is interpreted and practised throughout the world, Shaykh Fadhlalla has become a transformational voice within and without the Muslim world.

For Robert Frager from the Institute for Transpersonal Psychology at California, Haeri's work is a 'spiritual psychology', containing an alternative model of human nature.[19] In translating the wisdom of the Qur'an for a contemporary audience of seekers of self-knowledge, Shaykh Fadhlalla clearly transcends his own spiritual origins and links them to the spiritual and philosophical foundations of other belief systems. In this respect it is revealing to learn from his autobiography *Son of Karbala*[20] that his own 'spiritual initiation' has, among others, been catalysed by personal encounters with two of the great wisdom teachers of India of the twentieth century: Chinmayananda, the Hindu sage and foremost exponent of the Vedanta, and Jiddu Krishnamurti, the world-famed spiritual philosopher. Indeed, Haeri's readiness to transcend his own faith and openness to reach out to other belief systems while remaining deeply connected to his own cultural and spiritual origins makes Haeri's work particularly resonant and relevant for this 'Eastern' realm of Integral Development. In our own focusing on the regeneration of meaning, Haeri's own journey illustrates how cultural and spiritual renewal can be powerfully facilitated by the creative interaction between one's original source (here: Haeri's Islamic belief) and other sources (here: 'Eastern' spirituality). We regard such creative, dialogical interaction, within and without ourselves, as crucial for individual and collective renewal.

In our conversations with Haeri in his Academy for Self Knowledge (ASK) near Johannesburg, he emphasised that, according to the Qur'an, human beings were created from one self. Each individual self has a higher and lower nature. We function on a spectrum that at one end resembles the lowest of animalistic impulses and thoughtless responses, and at the other end, a sublime, patient, considerate and independent yet loving and compassionate nature. Whether we reflect our higher or our lower self, there remains within us an unchanging, steady state of the one self. As one matures one realises that the outer, material satisfactions have no end, and that the physical world offers little stability, whereas knowledge and wisdom are unending and provide a reliable, stable base.

THE DRIVE FOR KNOWLEDGE: STRIVING FOR INNER AND OUTER KNOWLEDGE

At all times, we match new information and facts with past experiences, in order to add new dimensions to the ever-expanding network of perceptions and knowledge that we are building. Our drive to expand this network increases with the expansion of our knowledge and understanding. It is a never-ending process. Each new level, stratum or dimension of knowledge opens up new vistas for further search and assimilation, and the whole process is absorbing because of the connective, integrating and unifying characteristic of its very nature. Ignorance has the opposite effect. It is sterile, disruptive and limiting. Since this is contrary to man's nature, he is repulsed by its oppressiveness and darkness, and attracted to knowledge and light because it is connective, expansive and unifying, both for the individual and for his or her society.

Haeri argues that according to prophetic traditions there are two types of knowledge available to humankind.[21] One type is based on facts and information, is related to existential realities and deals with causality. It is factual and objective. The second type is more complex and permanent in nature. This type of knowledge relates to higher or inner awareness, psychologically or culturally, and to fundamental reality. This knowledge has its root within the human heart, and access to it is available only as a result of the quest for and unfolding of our inner essence. The inner knowledge, for Haeri, belongs to a subtle, multidimensional network that is stimulated by external facts and information. So the greater the development of our innate knowledge, the more will we be able to appropriately absorb, coordinate, relate and utilise the factual knowledge and external information which comes to us. Both kinds of knowledge are essential and complementary for human and societal evolution – the outer knowledge reflecting upon the network of inner knowledge to bring about a state of stability, reliability and harmony.

In his work *The Journey of the Self*, Haeri illustrates that 'life is a journey of unfolding discovery towards self-knowledge, and that knowledge begins with physical and material consciousness at birth and evolves into emotional, mental and intellectual consciousness, then culminates at maturity with higher spiritual consciousness, or pure awareness'.[22] Haeri asserts, however, that the Qur'an gives the individual self the freedom to choose to follow the path of wholesomeness. Of course, he adds, the 'wise person actually has no choice but to accept the path of unity'.[23] How then does the journey of the self unfold?

ORIENTATION TO THE JOURNEY OF THE SELF: FIVE INTERCONNECTED PHASES

The journey of the self, for Haeri, consists of five distinct yet connected phases, which complete the cycle of the journey of the integrated individual. Each phase is dependent upon, and a product of, the previous phase. Each phase unfolds into the next one. Haeri argues that the journey is based on a pattern that charts a parallel progression of the outer (biological) and inner (conscious) development of the human being. There will inevitably be overlapping between phases. Earlier phases – to varying degrees of intensity – will remain active throughout one's life, even as one progresses in one's journey.

PHASE 1 – ABSOLUTE UNITIVE REALITY

The Qur'an challenges us with the insight that there existed an absolute unified state before the act of creation. 'Was there not a period of time that came upon man when he could not be mentioned'.[24] In the beginning, the eternal void was an infinite, boundless ocean without waves or movement. It was from this original void that creational waves surfaced. So from the unmanifest emerged the physically manifest. From the world of the unseen came the command 'Be'. At that point, from the realm of the unseen emerges the spark of creation, seen and bounded. From the formless void of the cosmos came the first shattering explosion of the big bang. Analogically, for Haeri, it is in the dark void of the human womb, that the emergence of the light of consciousness occurs. Indeed, for him, there is not only coherence between the inner (psychological, spiritual) and outer (biological) development of an individual, but also between the microcosm of a person and the macrocosm of society. It is on that level, that all our journeys are interconnected.

PHASE 2 – INNER DEPENDENCE

Haeri argues that the first phase of absolute reality is followed by a second phase of inner dependence. It begins with the inner dependence of the foetus upon its own primal laws. Within the first few weeks of its life it is virtually formed and the remaining months of its life in the mother's womb are a process of gradual completion and development. During this phase of inner dependence the identity and individualisation of the foetus begin to occur. The physical self is developed; it grows and nourishes itself in an ecology of limited mobility, wrapped in itself, unfolding by itself.

PHASE 3 – OUTER DEPENDENCE

In this third phase, so Haeri, the self begins to mature and the individual gradually grows and strengthens on a physical level. The self that is predominant in the life of the newborn possesses three powers – those of feeding, growth and expulsion. These systems develop in complexity and are refined as the child matures. As it develops the child acquires two additional powers – of movement and that of comprehension. Ultimately, this phase takes the individual to full maturity – physically, mentally, intellectually – and also towards awakening of higher consciousness.[25]

PHASE 4 – INTERDEPENDENCE

The phase of interdependence is the main creational nursery of the self. As we mature we attain maximum coordination, integration and connection. Generally, as the self develops and evolves, there is a trend or movement from the outer towards the inner, from the sensory towards the meaning, from the terrestrial towards the celestial. A balanced and stable situation comes about when the opposites counteract each other. Haeri advises that 'the one who seeks a state of healthy equilibrium places himself in the middle of the spectrum of opposites'.[26]

PHASE 5 – INNER RELIANCE: RECOGNISING A HIGHER, ALL-PERVADING REALITY

As we emerge from the experiences of interdependence, we begin to rely more and more on the store of experiences and inner awareness. The creational nursery of the world of interdependence has served its purpose as a laboratory in which we have tested and have been tested in situations of interaction and interrelationships. For Haeri, all of these have aided in spurring on and refining the development of the rational self. We are now beginning to approach the state of inner reliance. As a result, our inner practices of self-development increase, reflected in virtuous outer behaviour. At this stage we are able to see more clearly the stages of the journey through which we have evolved.

It is also at this point, claims Haeri, that one knows that the entity called the self, that is the 'I' or 'me', is none other than a passing shadow and is dependent on a higher and all-pervading reality. The truly realised being has become the pivotal interlink, master of outer knowledge and possessor of inner awareness. For Haeri, our love and communion with nature are reminders of the vast ecosystem that rules over all systems. It is a reflection that is reminiscent of that which is already within us – that primordial ocean of perfected unity that is self-regulated and everlasting. The Qur'an and the prophetic traditions recommend the contemplation of nature in all its multitudinous harmony, in order to see the divine attributes of beauty and perfection, both on the horizon and within oneself. At this final stage, the individual reconnects to the original unity, which has become accessible through a process of ongoing purification and self-perfection. We are simultaneously aware of our origin and our destination. In this phase we have returned to 'unity' – transcending our original duality in which we were caught in between an earthly and physical self and a 'heavenly', unseen and intangible soul, which for Haeri is 'the seat of consciousness and the source of life'.[27]

RENEWING SELF – RENEWING SOCIETY

Haeri stressed that everything in life has two facets, including the human being: the personal and the social (collective). The journey of the self focuses on the microcosm of the human being, although – and that is critically for our integral perspective on human development – the stages of development are echoed in the macrocosm of society and the universe. For Haeri, there is indeed not only resonance between the inner and outer development of the individual, but also between the microcosm of a person and the macrocosm of society. 'Thus the human being is a microcosm resonating with the macrocosm, and reflects the unifying field and one reality or truth that holds the universal realities'.[28]

Haeri further links the development of the human self with the establishment and maintenance of culture and civilisation. The building of a noble character and the acquisition of virtue are an integral part of the development and growth of individuals and societies. Just as a family is composed of individual beings, a society comprises an amalgamation of family units and its strengths and weaknesses are a direct result of the quality and coherence of its values and goals. 'A review of the lifespan and success of various societies, cultures and nations shows that the more vigorously practised are the higher values in a society, the stronger, healthier and more durable that society will be'.[29]

TOWARDS HARMONY: ALIGNMENT WITH NATURE'S ETERNAL LAWS

Haeri encourages us to follow the inner call urging us to enter the path of self-perfection. This call, so Haeri, comes almost naturally to us:

> Humanity has a natural tendency to seek and understand ways that will lead to a lasting and harmonious state. The ultimate harmony comes about by the discovery of and adherence to the unchanging laws of nature, and by moulding our own individual direction and orientation to fit within those laws. Only then can conflict disappear, and our desires and wishes move in harmony with the original and ultimate power of creation.[30]

For Shaykh Fadhlalla, this human tendency towards consciousness and harmony is engrained in us, as creation itself ultimately seeks to be understood, to be made conscious. He emphasised that it was revealed to the Prophet Muhammad 'that the essence of all creation is the greatest hidden treasure, and that it loved to be known; so it created, in order that it might be known'.[31]

For Haeri, we can arrive at a stage of harmony and real fulfilment when there is:

unison between heart and head or soul and self. To achieve this unison or harmony the challenge for all spiritual seekers is the constant need to act appropriately at every moment, aiming for excellence in intention and action. To do the right thing in the right way, at the right time and place, is the foundation of quality living. Freedom from confusing choices and habitual mistakes will gradually increase with heightened self awareness and continual reference to higher wisdom.[32]

In our conversations in South Africa, Shaykh Fadhlalla shared that he has been discovering that a person's self-soul connectivity and the degree to which self-soul is in unison, indicates the likelihood that the person is in the best possible state of psychological well-being that he or she can be. He added that psychiatric medication can reduce damage from psychological illness but it cannot heal: only the self-soul connectivity can heal. In all that, he asserts we have an inner guide, that helps us to understand whether we are on the right path: 'Any activity that leads us towards realising our inner potential and essential nature we will find to be nourishing, enriching and conducive to fulfilment; and any other activity will be palliative, detractive to growth, and even destructive'.[33] Staying committed to this path leads, so Haeri, to the glorious essence of the human being, culminating in enlightenment: 'Enlightenment is the outcome of an evolution from basic personal need for survival and growth to pure consciousness. It is a metamorphosis from the dark cocoon of delusion to the ever-present garden of light and delight'.[34]

Aligned with the work of Haeri, who himself was profoundly influenced by Hindu philosophy, we now turn from the Middle East to the Far East, to India's Swami Vivekananda. Like Haeri, Vivekananda emphasised the interconnectedness of individual and societal development.

11.5   Inner Liberation and Freedom: On Becoming the Truth

INTRODUCTION

This 'Eastern' chapter on individual development would not be complete without a voice from India, perhaps the world civilisation that has dedicated most time and effort to the spiritual development of the individual self. Selecting one out of India's countless saints and sages for this chapter was a difficult task. We ultimately decided to introduce Vivekananda (1863 to 1902), because he, like hardly any other recent cultural and spiritual representative of India, built bridges between India's past and future, between individual development and societal development, between faith and reason, between spirituality and science, between East and West. Furthermore, he was, at one and the same time, a self-realised Yogi and a force for societal renaissance. Almost single-handedly, he brought the wealth of India's spiritual heritage to the consciousness of the world, during the memorable speeches that he gave at the World Parliament of Religions in Chicago in 1893, and numerous subsequent speeches in the US and in the UK. He articulated the cultural-spiritual contribution that India as a whole could and would have to make to the world, in order to balance the one-sided economic-technological orientation of a 'West', that he also understood and appreciated for its own achievements. In that respect, even hundred years after his death, his thinking is of utmost relevance for our day and age, and a most valuable contribution to Integral Development.

LIBERATING THE SELF

Swami Vivekananda, born as Narendra Nath Datta, grew up as an agnostic with a thorough belief in science. He questioned vehemently those who proclaimed the existence of god. It was only when he met Sri Ramakrishna, a Hindu Saint hailed by many as India's greatest mystic of the nineteenth century that he turned to religion and spirituality. Becoming a disciple of Ramakrishna transformed him completely, and led him, in his own words, to self-realisation.

Vivekananda passionately rejected rituals and priesthood. He encouraged his own followers to free themselves from outer authority and to explore life's innermost truths by pursuing relentlessly the ultimate questions of existence and by rigorously analysing one's mind.

Fiercely critical of religious dogma and of most religious institutions and structures, he maintained that religion, well understood, is a matter between the individual and god alone. For him 'religion is a question of fact, not of talk. We have to understand it and realise what is understood. That is religion. No amount of talk will make religion. So the question of whether there is a God or not can never be proved by argument, for the arguments are as much on one side as on the other. But if there is a God, he is in our hearts'.[35] He went on, sharing that 'it is the heart that takes one to the highest plane, which intellect can never reach. It goes beyond intellect and reaches what is called inspiration. The intellect can never become inspired ... Man will have to go beyond intellect in the end.[36]

In that regard, Vivekananda pointed early to a solution to overcome the massive conflicts and cruelties arising over millennia till today out of so-called religious belief. Self-righteous, argumentative belief is, for Vivekananda, always related to dogma and institutions, but never to profound personal religious experience. In his challenging of formalised religion he can be regarded as an early pioneer of today's increasingly individual search for a spirituality beyond institutionally formalised religious systems. In that respect he was also a predecessor of Jiddu Krishnamurti, one of the greatest spiritual philosophers from India of the twentieth century who also advocated an individual search for the truth as a means to achieving inner freedom.[37]

For Vivekananda, religion is not about 'believing'. One either has experienced and hence realised inner truth, or one hasn't. He proclaimed:

> This is one great idea to learn and to hold on to, this idea of realisation. This turmoil and fight and difference in religions will cease only when we understand that religion is not in books and temples. It is in actual perception: Only the man who has actually perceived God and the soul has religion. There is no difference between the highest ecclesiastical giant, who can talk by the volume, and the lowest, most ignorant materialist ... Mere intellectual assent does not make us religious.[38]

For Vivekananda, for those who indeed have perceived the truth within themselves, this experience is of an utmost liberating quality and profoundly transformative as then, in his words, 'you will know the truth because you have become the truth'.[39]

The great Indian philosopher-poet and Nobel Laureate Rabindranath Tagore affirmed Vivekananda's liberating impact, declaring that his teachings 'showed the path of infinite freedom from man's tiny egocentric self beyond the limits of all selfishness' and his work 'marked the awakening of man in his fullness'.[40]

For Vivekananda, individual development is not disconnected from societal development but intimately linked to it:

> The individual's life is in the life of the whole, the individual's happiness is in the happiness of the whole; apart from the whole, the individual's existence is inconceivable – this is an eternal truth and is the bedrock on which the universe is built. To move slowly towards the infinite whole, bearing a constant feeling of intense sympathy and sameness with it, being happy with its happiness and being distressed in its affliction, is the individual's sole duty.[41]

In that respect, and as we have come to learn from such a wholesome 'Eastern' viewpoint, the individual and the societal dimension of development are closely interconnected, while the organisational dimension goes missing.

AWAKENED SELF – REALISED SOCIETY

Vivekananda relentlessly connected the awakening of the individual with the evolution of society. Famously, he proclaimed: 'The world will change if we change'.[42] Furthermore, he continuously emphasised the particular contribution that his homeland India had made to the world's history and would need to make to the world's future. The contribution of a particular society, said Vivekananda, can only meaningfully occur through a thorough understanding of its own path. 'Out of the past is built the future',[43] he declared. In the case of India, he argued, she would have to return to the original meaning of her greatest wisdom sources, the wisdom of the Vedas and the Upanishads. For him, as for us, economic and political renewal would have to be preceded by spiritual renewal.

The devastatingly impoverished socioeconomic state of colonial India, which Vivekananda witnessed around the turn of the twentieth century, was for him a symptom of India's unrealised spiritual potential as a civilisation. 'The degeneration of India came not because the laws and customs of the ancients were bad, but because they were not allowed to be carried to their legitimate conclusion'.[44]

He clearly put the immaterial dimension before the material dimension. This is the same process as suggested by Integral Development, whereby the more immaterial and implicit 'South' and 'East' precedes the more material and explicit 'North' and 'West'. While ultimately all 'Worlds' need to interact freely and simultaneously with each other, we maintain that times of restoration and regeneration of a human system require its 'Southern' re-grounding to enable its revitalised 'Eastern' re-emergence. From there, it can then proceed to new 'Northern' navigation, developing new knowledge, which can then be effected and actualised in 'Western' fashion.

The necessary re-grounding of society, for Vivekananda, would have to be facilitated through authentic education.

AUTHENTIC EDUCATION AS THE NECESSARY BRIDGE BETWEEN FAITH AND REASON, BETWEEN SPIRITUALITY AND SCIENCE

In all his works, Vivekananda put primary emphasis on education. He maintained that 'through education comes faith in one's own self, and through faith in one's own self the inherent Brahman is waking up ...'.[45]

Reading Vivekananda's works it becomes quickly evident, that his understanding of education begins with the spiritual evolution of individuals, and thereby differs strongly with a knowledge and skills driven educational approach:

> *Education is not [about] filling the mind with a lot of facts. Perfecting the instrument and getting complete mastery of my own mind is the ideal education … To me the very essence of education is concentration of mind, not the collecting of facts. If I had to do my education again, and had any voice in the matter, I would not study facts at all. I would develop the power of concentration and detachment, and then with a perfect instrument I could collect facts at will.*[46]

For Vivekananda, education is about getting in touch with the inner truth of life. That involves a process of 'unveiling' and 'discovering' – a process that removes the cover off one's own soul that, for him, is a 'mine of infinite knowledge'.[47]

Vivekananda argued that education would need to be restructured in a way that it leads to self-knowledge by connecting people to the wisdom treasures of their own civilisation.[48] He argued for educational systems that are authentic to a particular society and that mirrored its cultural essence, rather than imitating other cultures. He heavily critiqued India's university system of his time – as we have critiqued the universities of our time, with their lack of developmental sensitivity – describing such education as 'almost wholly one of defects. Why, it is nothing but a perfect machine for turning out clerks'.[49] For him, without authentic knowledge creation and without increased self-knowledge – of individuals, and of the society as a whole – there was no chance for real development that brings about the best in a particular culture. Ironically the formal education system in India, including its universities and business schools to this day, has not taken heed of Vivekananda's or indeed Gandhi's wise insights. For A.P.J. Abdul Kalam, India's recent president and leading nuclear atomic scientist, the country's current education system emphasises 'acquiring skills as compared to research. The common trend today is to follow what is laid out rather than to innovate'.[50] Advocating that 'we cannot continue to deliver a 20th Century, scientific-management, factory-model education',[51] Kalam calls for a 'scientific mindset guided by conscience, and by action that take the complex values of our social and moral worlds into accounts'.[52] Indicating how he envisions such a transformation to happen, the culminating chapter of his recent work *You are Born to Blossom* is entitled 'Education as a Spiritual Journey'.

Vivekananda's belief in home-grown knowledge creation is reflected in the following episode: On a ship, he once met Jamshedji Tata, the founder of Tata Group, today India's largest business conglomerate. Tata was on his way to Japan to import industrial products. Vivekananda critically observed that, according to him, economic enterprise was not enough for the upliftment of India, and he advised Tata to also fund a research institute. Tata followed his advice and set up the by-now world-renowned Indian Institute of Research, located in Bangalore.[53]

The transculturally oriented Vivekananda hoped that 'India would set an example of how science and religion could meet, science taking care of man's physical needs and religion of his moral and spiritual needs'.[54]

His own life, though short, reflected his dedication to reconnect India with its own wisdom sources. He left for posterity his four classics *Jnana-Yoga*, *Bhakti-Yoga*, *Karma-Yoga*, and *Raja-Yoga*, all of which are regarded as outstanding treatises on Hindu philosophy. His complete writings, including his speeches and letters, are compiled in eight volumes.

OUTLOOK

Vivekananda's influence on both India and the West cannot be underestimated. India acknowledges the importance of Vivekananda's life, work and teaching for her own spiritual renewal, by celebrating his birthday every year as National Youth Day. The Swami's national and international impact is well captured in this short paragraph issued by the Ramakrishna-Vivekananda Center of New York:

> In his own motherland Vivekananda is regarded as the patriot saint of modern India and an inspirer of her dormant national consciousness. To the Hindus he preached the ideal of a strength-giving and man-making religion ... Many political leaders of India have publicly acknowledged their indebtedness to Swami Vivekananda. The Swami's mission was both national and international. A lover of mankind, he strove to promote peace and human brotherhood on the spiritual foundation of the Vedantic Oneness of existence. A mystic of the highest order, Vivekananda had a direct and intuitive experience of Reality.[55]

Within the context of Integral Development, Vivekananda represents a voice for individual inner liberation and development beyond formalised religion, coupled with a dedication to the development of one's society. Both, for Vivekananda, have to be understood as an inseparable unity.

We are now ready to conclude.

11.6 Integration

With a view to Integral Development, we see one core problem in this first individual 'Eastern' level of grounding the self in culture and spirituality. All too often it is assumed that journeying oneself in such progressively consciousness-raising guise, automatically leads to societal development. Such an assumption invariably leaves out of account the organisational dimension in between, as well as the particular community. In other words, such individuation or self-realisation is rightfully seen as a necessary precondition for societal development, but it is wrongly assumed that such self-development is sufficient. What usually remains unrecognised, amidst self and society, is the organisational evolution in between. Furthermore, many of those leading lights focusing on the individual journey tend toward universalism, whereas we, in each individual, organisational and societal case, focus in addition on the particularity of any given development context.

In turning then in the following organisational chapter to such seminal thinkers and practitioners as David Bohm (Dialogue), Harrison Owen (Organisational Transformation), and Ryuzaburo Kaku (Organisational Co-evolution), we move again from formative individual grounding (Round 1) to reformative organisational emergence (Round 2). In this 'Eastern' realm of culture and spirituality, the focus will no longer be on the organisation as an ecosystem, but rather on its co-evolution. To that extent the journey of the organisation, so to speak, takes on from where the journey of the self has left off.

Before we move on, however, we invite you to engage – through reflection and prospective action – with the guiding questions and theory presented in this chapter, as well as with the major development challenges derived thereof for yourself.

Table 11.1 Main task: Embark on the journey of the self		
Guiding questions	**Guiding theory**	**Reflect and act … What do I and we have to do as Integral Developers?**
How am I evolving? What creative sources within and around me can provide insights into my development?	The hero's journey (Campbell) The pathway to individuation (Jung) The evolution of the self (Haeri) Inner liberation and freedom (Vivekananda)	• Awaken to the fascinating mystery of life • Interpret the mystery in order to give meaning to life • Unfold, in accordance with yourself, your culture, and the universe • Own the development shadow – uncover the seat of creativity • Engage in conscious personal development (e.g. through your dreams) • Strive simultaneously for inner and outer knowledge • Evolve from inner-outer dependence to interdependence to inner reliance • Explore, free from outer authority, life's innermost truths by pursuing relentlessly the ultimate questions of existence and by rigorously analysing your mind

We now turn from self to organisation within this 'Eastern' integral realm, recognising that this is seldom an easy transition to make.

References

1   Campbell, J. (1969). *The Hero with a Thousand Faces*. Princeton, NJ: Princeton University Press.
2   Haeri, F. (1989). *The Journey of the Self: A Sufi Guide to Personality*. Shaftesbury, Dorset: Element Books.
3   Campbell, J. (1969). *The Hero with a Thousand Faces*. Princeton, NJ: Princeton University Press.
4   Gebser, J. (2003). *Ursprung und Gegenwart*. Quern-Neukirchen: Novalis, p. 77. Translated by Georg Feuerstein.
5   Campbell, J. (2004). *Pathways to Bliss: Mythology and Personal Transformation*. Novato, CA: New World Library, p. 86.
6   Campbell, J. (2004). *Pathways to Bliss: Mythology and Personal Transformation*. Novato, CA: New World Library, p. 87.

7   Frankl, V.E. (2006). *Man's Search for Meaning*. Boston, MA: Beacon.
8   Campbell, J. (1969). *The Hero with a Thousand Faces*. Princeton, NJ: Princeton University Press.
9   Van der Post, L. (2004). *The Lost World of the Kalahari*. London: Vintage.
10 Van der Post, L. (1955). *The Dark Eye of Africa*. Cape Town: Lowery Press.
11 Comment: A highly popular PBS TV Series, broadcasting interviews with Joseph Campbell by Bill Moyers, gave a fascinating account on Campbell's thinking in 1988. The series was later accompanied by an excellent book: Campbell, J. (with Bill Moyers) (1988). *The Power of Myth*. New York: Anchor.
12 Campbell, J. (2004). *Pathways to Bliss: Mythology and Personal Transformation*. Novato, CA: New World Library, p. xxiv.
13 Rahnema, M. (1997). Towards Post-Development: Searching for Signposts, a New Language and New Paradigms. In: Rahnema, M. and Bawtree, V. (eds), *The Post-Development Reader*. London: Zed, p. 392.
14 Von Franz, M.-L. (1968). The Process of Individuation. In: Jung, C.G. et al. *Man and His Symbols*. New York: Laurel, p. 159.
15 Von Franz, M.-L. (1968). The Process of Individuation. In: Jung, C.G. et al. (eds), *Man and His Symbols*. New York: Laurel, p. 163.
16 Von Franz, M.-L. (1968). The Process of Individuation. In: Jung, C.G. et al. (eds), *Man and His Symbols*. New York: Laurel, p. 163.
17 Haeri, F. (1989). *The Journey of the Self: A Sufi Guide to Personality*. Shaftesbury, Dorset: Element Books.
18 Haeri, F. (1989). *The Journey of the Self: A Sufi Guide to Personality*. Shaftesbury, Dorset: Element Books, p. 3.
19 Frager, R. (1989). Foreword to: Haeri, F. *The Journey of the Self: A Sufi Guide to Personality*. Shaftesbury, Dorset: Element Books, p. x.
20 Haeri, F. (2006). *Son of Karbala*. Brooklyn, NY: O Books.
21 Haeri, F. (1989). *The Journey of the Self: A Sufi Guide to Personality*. Shaftesbury, Dorset: Element Books, p. 23.
22 Haeri, F. (1989). *The Journey of the Self: A Sufi Guide to Personality*. Shaftesbury, Dorset: Element Books, p. 4.
23 Haeri, F. (1989). *The Journey of the Self: A Sufi Guide to Personality*. Shaftesbury, Dorset: Element Books, p. 11.
24 Qur'an: 76:1.
25 Haeri, F. (1989). *The Journey of the Self: A Sufi Guide to Personality*. Shaftesbury, Dorset: Element Books, p. 4.
26 Haeri, F. (1989). *The Journey of the Self: A Sufi Guide to Personality*. Shaftesbury, Dorset: Element Books, pp. 60ff.
27 Haeri, F. (2008). *Witnessing Perfection*. Brooklyn, NY: O Books, p. 51.
28 Haeri, F. (2009). *101 Helpful Illusions*. Brooklyn, NY: O Books, p. 3.
29 Haeri, F. (1989). *The Journey of the Self: A Sufi Guide to Personality*. Shaftesbury, Dorset: Element Books, p. 23.
30 Haeri, F. (2008). *Witnessing Perfection*. Brooklyn, NY: O Books, p. xii.
31 Haeri, F. (1989). *The Journey of the Self: A Sufi Guide to Personality*. Shaftesbury, Dorset: Element Books, p. 3.
32 Haeri, F. (2008). *Witnessing Perfection*. Brooklyn, NY: O Books, p. xiii.

33 Haeri, F. (1989). *The Journey of the Self: A Sufi Guide to Personality*. Shaftesbury, Dorset: Element Books, p. 4.

34 Haeri, F. (2009). *101 Helpful Illusions*. Brooklyn, NY: O Books, p. 7.

35 Vivekananda, S. (2009). *Vedanta: Voice of Freedom*. Kolkata: Advaita Ashrama, p. 85.

36 Vivekananda, S. (2009). *Vedanta: Voice of Freedom*. Kolkata: Advaita Ashrama, pp. 236f.

37 Krishnamurti, J. (1996). *Total Freedom: The Essential Krishnamurti*. New York: HarperOne.

38 Vivekananda, S. (2009). *Vedanta: Voice of Freedom*. Kolkata: Advaita Ashrama, p. 86.

39 Vivekananda, S. (2009). *Vedanta: Voice of Freedom*. Kolkata: Advaita Ashrama, p. 87.

40 Tagore, R. (2008). Some Great Men on Swamiji. In: Vivekananda, S. (2008). *My India, the India Eternal*. Kolkata: Ramakrishna Mission Institute of Culture, p. 196.

41 Vivekananda, S. (2008). *My India, the India Eternal*. Kolkata: Ramakrishna Mission Institute of Culture, p. 29.

42 Vivekananda, S. (2009). *Vedanta: Voice of Freedom*. Kolkata: Advaita Ashrama, p. 97.

43 Vivekananda, S. (2008). *My India, the India Eternal*. Kolkata: Ramakrishna Mission Institute of Culture, p. 31.

44 Vivekananda, S. (2008). *My India, the India Eternal*. Kolkata: Ramakrishna Mission Institute of Culture, pp. 32f.

45 Vivekananda, S. (2008). *My India, the India Eternal*. Kolkata: Ramakrishna Mission Institute of Culture, p. 37.

46 Vivekananda, S. (2008). *My India, the India Eternal*. Kolkata: Ramakrishna Mission Institute of Culture, pp. 55f.

47 Vivekananda, S. (2008). *My India, the India Eternal*. Kolkata: Ramakrishna Mission Institute of Culture, p. 54.

48 Vivekananda, S. (2008). *My India, the India Eternal*. Kolkata: Ramakrishna Mission Institute of Culture, p. 60.

49 Vivekananda, S. (2008). *My India, the India Eternal*. Kolkata: Ramakrishna Mission Institute of Culture, p. 61.

50 Kalam, A.P.J. and Tiwari, A.K. (2008). *You are Born to Blossom: Take My Journey Beyond*. New Delhi: Ocean Paperbacks, pp. 10f.

51 Kalam, A.P.J. and Tiwari, A.K. (2008). *You are Born to Blossom: Take My Journey Beyond*. New Delhi: Ocean Paperbacks, p. 152.

52 Kalam, A.P.J. and Tiwari, A.K. (2008). *You are Born to Blossom: Take My Journey Beyond*. New Delhi: Ocean Paperbacks, pp. 153f.

53 Lokeswaranda, S. (2008). The Message of Swami Vivekananda. In: Vivekananda (2008). *My India, the India Eternal*. Kolkata: Ramakrishna Mission Institute of Culture, p. 11.

54 Lokeswaranda, S. (2008). The Message of Swami Vivekananda. In: Vivekananda (2008). *My India, the India Eternal*. Kolkata: Ramakrishna Mission Institute of Culture, p. 11.

55 Ramakrishna-Vivekananda Center of New York website. Available at: www.ramakrishna.org / Accessed: 25 November 2012.

CHAPTER 12 *Organisational Co-Evolution: An Eastern Organisational Perspective*

Guiding Questions: How do institutions evolve? What creative sources underlie the development of organisations, further to that of ourselves?

12.1 Orientation

In the previous chapter, we have pursued the journey of the self in 'Eastern' guise, whereby organisation, community and society were at best subject of implicit concern. For us as Integral Developers, development does not stop on the individual level. We move on, in this next step, to the organisational level.

Hence: Quo Vadis? Where are you going is an equally important question on the organisational level. For long the answer to this question had been institutionally relegated to top management, and disconnected from the journey of the individual self. All too often, organisational development had more to do with competitive strategy than with providing meaning to the members of the organisation as well as to those that the organisation is supposed to serve. An organisation, though, that focuses for direction solely on top-down strategy, and does not purposefully engage with the creative potential and source for renewal that its organisational culture holds, is likely to underperform in terms of organisational development. Such an organisation has not understood the potential of co-evolution, which begins, first and foremost, within the organisation and through its people.

As Integral Development moves through the 'Eastern' realm from the formative individual to the reformative group and organisational level, we need to explore the following questions in order to help us engage with and further release our own co-evolutionary potential. These are the questions that need to be asked:

- How do groups and organisations evolve and develop?
- What creative sources within and around us can provide momentum for organisational development?

- What gives us meaning, what regenerates us? What wisdom sources can we tap into, alone and with others?
- What role does culture play in organisational development?
- How does an organisation co-evolve and co-arise with others, thereby contributing to the co-evolution of organisations and society at large?

Interestingly enough, for reasons already given, these are not questions that geographical Easterners (Japan being the one exception, as we shall see), in the Middle, Near of Far East address. We argue that it is also for that reason that Business Schools in China, India or Egypt are the same as those in the USA.

We start our explorations on this organisational level by learning from the American physicist David Bohm about the power of dialogue to create shared meaning. The US management thinker Harrison Owen takes the developmental story on from there, illustrating how we can activate the meaning giving layers in an organisation by purposefully engaging with the transformational capacity of the organisational culture. Our focus on organisational development culminates in the fascinating, authentically 'Eastern' example of Japan's Canon that illustrates how an entire organisation has built its corporate culture on the principle of co-evolution by activating internally a major cultural philosophy of its society called Kyosei, a term that means co-evolution.

12.2 Deep Dialogue: The Creation of Shared Meaning

CO-GENERATION OF MEANING IN A GROUP

We start then by considering the nature and scope of the human group, before turning to the organisation at large. Not often has the work of a physicist contributed so much to our understanding of the processes by which we generate meaning. That of the late quantum physicist David Bohm, who worked in his younger years alongside Albert Einstein, certainly did. It is a strange fact that it was a natural scientist who helped re-sensitising the world for deep dialogue.

Bohm, often seen as one of the most provocative and creative thinkers of our time, argued that in most cases it is not true dialogue that is taking place when people communicate with each other. He distinguished carefully between the terms 'discussion' and 'dialogue'. Discussions take place when people merely justify, hold, and defend their positions through a hurtling of preconceived opinions and well-constructed arguments. Such conversations don't go beyond a certain depth, and they can't lead to the generation of profound insights out of which new meaning can arise.

THE NATURE OF DIALOGUE: CO-CONSTRUCTED BY ALL

Bohm declared that true dialogue requires all participants to suspend their preconceived positions, to fully listen to the other, and – during the time of listening – to not think about one's own response. Afterwards, one is called not to speak immediately, but to carefully listen to what emerges from the inside. Participants in a dialogue thus enter jointly a 'space of unknowing'. In this space something new can arise, co-constructed by all. Such dialogue requires an enormous honesty, as participants are asked to reflect on and share the underlying assumptions of their beliefs and to thereby explore potential blind spots in their thinking. Such dialogue demands courage, strength, discipline, and the longing for learning. It is a difficult undertaking; enriching, but often painful. However, it opens us, it connects us as equal participants and it allows for the generation of new meaning, shared by all. It is only then that dialogue can live up to its essence, as the word (derived from logos = meaning, and dia = through) originally signifies 'flow of meaning'.

For Bohm, the capacity for activating 'flows of new meaning' is a crucial skill for our human survival. We are in need of dialogue to discover the world anew, to challenge and let go of unjustified beliefs, and to coexist peacefully with a multitude of viewpoints, instead of imposing a single one. Bohm maintained, however, that our enormous difficulties to simply allow different viewpoints to coexist, stands in the way of most true dialogue. The dilemma, Bohm argued, that people can't share anymore any meaning, if each holds on to his or her particular 'truth'.

He lamented in that respect the scientific fundamentalism of our time, where science has become the new religion, thereby cutting humanity off a much richer perception of reality, or even multiple realities. Here Bohm echoes Gebser (⇨4, 13), both of whom claim that humanity is caught in an over-rationalistic 'either or' thinking and thereby stuck in its own evolution. At times, Bohm's language with its focus on emergence and evolution has an almost 'Eastern' ring to it. And indeed, the resonance with evolved Eastern spirituality is strong, as, for example, the famous dialogues between Jiddu Krishnamurti, one of the most eminent spiritual teachers of the past century, and David Bohm, illustrate.[1]

Bohm derived his thinking however from his own experiences with quantum physics, according to which the web of reality is continuously co-created through the interaction of all particles. Analogous, participants in a true dialogue participate in the creation of a pool of shared meaning, which itself is constantly evolving.

TOWARDS COLLECTIVE INTELLIGENCE

David Bohm regarded thought primarily as a collective phenomenon, made possible only through culture and communication. 'Human conversations arise out of and influence an ocean of cultural and transpersonal meanings in which we live our lives, and this process he called dialogue'.[2] Bohm maintained that such collective learning increases our collective intelligence.

The field of collective intelligence is a fascinating, though still relatively young one that enjoyed growing prominence in the past few decades. In particular the increased acceptance of a 'noosphere' – the sphere of human thought – gave rise to the field. Among the earliest protagonists of a noosphere were the Ukranian mineralogist and geochemist Vladimir Vernadsky, the French philosopher and Jesuit priest Pierre Teilhard de Chardin and the French sociologist Émile Durkheim. In the original theory of Vernadsky, the noosphere is seen as the third sphere in the Earth's evolution, after the geosphere (unanimated matter) the biosphere (biological life). Phenomena of collectively intelligence, including the noosphere are increasingly researched worldwide, for example by the MIT Institute for Collective Intelligence and the Princeton Global Consciousness Project, the latter funded by the Institute for Noetic Science. For Teilhard de Chardin, the noosphere emerges through and is constituted by the interaction of human minds, and grows in awareness through human beings engaging in ever more complex social networks and interactions.[3] For him, the noosphere develops towards ever-greater unification and integration, until its culmination, a final state that he coined Omega Point. The implications of such thinking are breathtaking.

There are more and more indications that there is indeed some kind of field of collective intelligence. From C.G. Jung's Collective Unconsciousness, to Rupert Sheldrake's Theory of Morphic Resonance,[4] from James Lovelock's Gaia Theory[5] to Lynne McTaggart's synthesising research on The Field,[6] from Richard Tarnas and John Heron's Participatory Theory[7] to the Indian Sage Sri Nisargadata who states in his classic book *I am That*[8] that each of us is the source of all knowledge. There is an increasing body of emergent theory as well as an age-old body of spiritual wisdom that all points to the invisible interconnectedness of life ... and to the potential of collective intelligence we can activate.

The most crucial requirement, however, for tapping into the field of collective intelligence, is that we step out of our over-individualised sense of self. And the key ingredients for that are trust and love. When we trust and love, we go beyond our narrow borders, we reach out, connect on a deep level, and step into a shared, collective space. That's why we make our first experiences with what is 'beyond our self' almost always in a state of love. To this truth points also the famous neurobiologist Humberto Maturana, when he claims that at the core of human life is the 'biology of love'.

Bohm was convinced that deep dialogue had an enormous potential to foster collective intelligence. For him:

> dialogue holds out the possibility of direct insight into the collective movement of thought, rather than its expression in any particular individual. Bohm suggests that the potential for collective intelligence inherent in such groups could lead to a new and creative art form, one which may involve significant numbers of people and beneficially affect the trajectory of our current civilisation.[9]

THE RELEVANCE OF (BOHMIAN) DIALOGUE FOR DEVELOPMENT

There is no shortage of people referring to 'dialogue'. Dialogue is applied to all kinds of fields, from conflict resolution to organisational development, from marriage counselling to teambuilding. The term is frequently used – as stakeholder, civic, cross-sector, intergovernmental dialogue, and so on. For example, when the Global Compact Initiative was established by the UN under the stewardship of the then Secretary-General Kofi Annan, to foster collaboration among corporations to elevate social, labour and environmental standards around the world, 'policy dialogue' was introduced as a key aspect.

And yet, despite all of that, dialogue remains probably one of the most overused, misused and abused terms. In reality, our time is still averse to deep dialogue. Only gradually do we awake to the fact that 'dialogue as usual' won't do any longer. This gradual awakening is illustrated by the enormous resonance with Bohm's thinking that is increasingly emerging. One exceptional 'fruit' of this awakening process is the World Cafe, an increasingly popular dialogue tool, applied to a multitude of contexts all over the world. The originators of the World Cafe as a social technology, Juanita Brown and David Isaacs, close friends of ours, have developed a global network and resource centre for people applying the Cafe to diverse contexts. They regard the World Cafe as a living network around conversations that matter and that have the power to shape our future.[10]

From our perspective, Bohmian dialogue offers an enormous potential for development work, in that it enables developers to truly tune into a particular development context. For Irene Mutalima, a colleague who has long been the Executive Director of ECLOF, the microfinance arm of the World Council of Churches, the lack of such true dialogue is at the heart of much of the failure of today's development work. She is now back in her homeland Zambia, where she seeks to engage in a different kind of development that truly, in her words, 'listens to the voices of the people'. For us, the capacity for dialogue in the spirit of David Bohm, that includes such deep listening, is an essential ingredient in the Integral Development toolbox.

In his foreword to Bohm's popular book *On Dialogue*,[11] Peter Senge, one of the leading management thinkers of our time, concluded his appreciation of Bohm's work and person as follows:

> It is easy to dismiss Bohm as a romantic idealist ... But my experiences over the past fifteen years with both the possibilities and challenges of dialogue leads me to see him quite differently. I would call David Bohm an extreme realist. He knew that no society has ever faced the sort of global predicament we face and that we are not likely to muddle through without radical changes of our ways of being – together.[12]

Senge himself strongly recommends the Bohmian dialogue in his influential management classic *The Fifth Discipline*,[13] and was involved in an MIT research project on dialogue inspired by David Bohm. One of the results of this research projects is the highly acclaimed book on *Dialogue and the Art of Thinking Together*,[14] authored by William Isaacs.

One could summarise Bohm's notion of *dialogue as people truly listening to people truly speaking*. That is how American management thinkers John Adams and Harrison Owen once described Bohmian dialogue. It is to Harrison Owen and his artistic work on organisational transformation that we now turn, incorporating also his orientation to 'corporate culture', Owen being one of the first management thinkers to authentically enter into that field.

12.3 Myth, Ritual and Storytelling: Activating Collective Meaning and the Developmental Role of Organisational Culture

THE ART OF COLLECTIVE STORYTELLING

While 'corporate culture' was first promoted in the management literature as a field worthy of study and application by the famed Tom Peters and Robert Waterman duo through their work *In Search of Excellence*,[15] their treatment of such 'culture' tended towards trivialisation: the way we do things around here. It was Harrison Owen who picked it up seriously. Owen considers that one of the greatest art forms, as well as means of organisational transformation, is 'collective storytelling'. 'For it is such stories that transform energy into spirit and back again'.[16] The organisational starting point, for Owen – as it was for Joseph Campbell on the individual level (⇨11) – is 'mythos', that is the language of spirit. Like Campbell, Harrison Owen, though a 'Westerner' by geographical location, worldview-wise is a mix of 'Southern' and 'Eastern', not least because his background is in anthropology and theology rather than in business and economics.

THE NATURE AND SCOPE OF MYTHOS

Mythos in an organisational context, for Owen, is the collective term for organisational myth and ritual. These two elements make up the fundamental building blocks of corporate culture. They represent what capital and labour represent for the business enterprise. Myths then are the stories of a group's – or community's or society's – culture that describe its beginning, continuance and ultimate destination.

To know the myth, according to Owen, is to know the institution in a way that balance sheets can never tell. Ritual, moreover, is the dramatic re-enactment of the myth, whereby the members of the organisation or community really experience being there, and participating in the original event.

A myth may be defined as a likely (but not necessarily true) story, arising from the life experience of a community, through which it comes to experience its past, present and future potential. It is gripping, it creates a world, and to some extent transforms it. It not only reflects life, but becomes life. The true function of myth and ritual is to bring the individual, or group, into a self-validating relationship with the spirit of the enterprise, community or society. Such mythos continues to grow over time, as succeeding generations add their imagination – their spirit – to the original act of creation and its continual re-creation.

THE LIFE CYCLE OF MYTHOS

Myth and ritual, for Owen, go through a life cycle. In the early days, stories are acted out by a key protagonist, be it a Prophet Mohammed (Islam), a Nelson Mandela (South Africa), or a Ryuzaburo Kaku (Japan's Canon). They are part of everyday reality rather than carriers of meaning. It is only later, once the stories have become increasingly familiar to an ever-growing number of people, that their presence begins to offer comfort as well as excitement. Eventually it becomes important that the stories are told, or interpreted, in the right way, if they are to continue to be meaningful. In their more flexible form, for Owen, they provide also an outlet for creativity and innovation.

Mythos then completes its life cycle with renewal, whereby an individual, organisation or community is infused with new meaning and purpose. This new spirit is generated during a period of what Owen calls 'open space', whereby a new storyline is being crafted out of the old. In fact, rigid and formal tradition is quite deadly to the spirit. Myth and ritual need to change at different points of the life cycle, if organisational transformation is to take place. At first, it only tacitly embodies transformation. Secondly, it serves as a record of such. The intent embodied in mythos at the second point is not to just talk about what transpired but to create the conditions whereby that prior journey may be re-experienced and renewed. The third phase of mythos, in its life cycle then, is to become an agent of transformation. Just as everybody becomes accustomed to a tale, it changes and exposes some new area of meaning. This ongoing shifting continually creates new spaces and invites the group spirit in, to consider new forms of expression. Owen then turns to 'liturgy'.

MYTH AND RITUAL TO LITURGY

Liturgy is formed of the two Greek words – *laos*, meaning people, and *êrgos*, meaning work. In fact, it is the sum of what people do as an expression of their innermost being. When myth and ritual are deeply and continuously integrated into the life of an organisation or community that, according to Owen, is liturgy. Liturgy at its best, then, is the conscious production and orchestration of myth and ritual, so that spirit is focused and directed in a particular, intended way.

While the raw material of liturgy is myth and ritual, the processes for 'liturgy making', according to Owen, are form and structure. Form is the way we do things, structure is the delineated field of operation in which they are done. To be effective, in liturgical terms, the form and structure should accord with the image and channel of the spirit of the organisation or community.

At some point of the life of an organisation, the special sense of space and time, in which the spirit is lodged, needs to be given formal expression. Initially sparse, it ultimately becomes a kind of rulebook. How then is organisational transformation taking place?

FACILITATING TRANSFORMATION – THE ULTIMATE FORM OF TWENTY-FIRST CENTURY ART

Ultimately Owen's concern, in relation to corporate culture and organisational transformation, is how you facilitate the kind of development, or indeed transformation, that draws on all of the above, and takes the story collectively forward. He distinguishes four steps in a process of facilitating organisational transformation:

Step 1 = Conducting a Historical Scan: The process starts with a 'historical scan' of an organisation, community or even a whole society, to uncover how it got started, where and under what conditions, who were and are now the key parties concerned, and what currently is the overall structure and key affiliations of the entity with which you are individually or institutionally concerned.

Step 2 = Uncovering the Leader's Vision: In interviewing the president or prime minister, the Dalai Lama or archbishop, the vice chancellor or chief executive, or a community leader, the key question is where the organisation, community or society is going, and where it should be going. This is set against the backdrop of facts and figures about the social and economic 'state of the nation' or state of the enterprise or community.

Step 3 = Unravelling the Culture: In the 'corporate' sense in which Owen is addressing culture, the three main questions to be asked of a dozen or so key and representative people in the organisation or community are – who are you and how did you get here; what is this place; what should it be? The real concern, then, is less the factual responses but the stories that are told, and the key words that continually crop up. The actual number of major myths (stories pregnant with meaning) are, from Owen's experience, unlikely to be more than a dozen or so. The findings then are presented to a focal leadership group. Thirdly, some 100 or so representative people are interviewed to broaden the base.

Step 4 = Collective Storytelling: The ultimate, and most important, objective is to create a new and composite story out of the existing elements contained within the myths and rituals uncovered. In collectively constructing a new tale, with the focal group concerned, the objective is to create a new storyline woven out of the old, where a place must be found for the heroes and rebels of the past as a connecting point for the future. Weaving such a new tale lies at the heart of development, or transformation, in this cultural context. In constructing it, it is necessary to link back to the organisational or communal potential, created through its depths, vision and language. Whatever this new tale might be, it must not jettison what came before.

The facilitating individual or group may start with an opening storyline, distilled from the prior research, but, most importantly, the overall future story should be co-constructed, leaving sufficient open space to allow members to participate in its enactment. The story must become their story, 'our story'. Constructing such a story, for Owen, may be the ultimate form of twenty-first century art. The story, once told, will be subsequently lost if it is not somehow embedded in the organisation, as such mythos is linked up with liturgy (structure and form), as it were. The structure of the enterprise or community, its physical fabric, as well as the cycle of organisational activities, all need to reinforce it. Celebrations, at regular intervals, and suitable 'rites of passage', serve to build on a newfound story.

For Owen, such a newfound story generates meaning and reenergises the organisation. It prepares it for further evolution, or better, for co-evolution. This brings us to the renowned electronics group, Canon in Japan. Canon has a compelling story to tell about co-evolution. In fact, it is one of the very few cases we have experienced of a genuinely 'Eastern' enterprise, which has come up with a fully fledged theory of management and organisation, building on its own societal and organisational ethos.

12.4 Releasing the Spirit of Organisational Co-Evolution: The Philosophy of Kyosei

WORKING TOGETHER FOR THE COMMON GOOD

In a way, Kyosei can be seen as the corporate myth that Canon lives by. As a cultural force, Kyosei – a Japanese term signifying coexistence or co-evolution – has a long-standing Buddhist heritage. From about 1500 to 1640 Japanese traders were among the most successful in the world. Merchants travelled to China, Thailand, Indonesia and the Philippines. As people came together to exchange goods, however, cultural differences led to conflict. So a successful merchant teamed up with a Confucian scholar and developed a set of guidelines known as *shishu kiyuka*. The guidelines said that trade must be carried out not only for one's own benefit, but also for the benefit of others. For Canon's late chairman Ryuzaburo Kaku, this policy sowed the seeds of Kyosei today. Canon and Kaku have fascinated us already for many years, and we extensively introduced this case within *Transformation Management*.[17]

Kaku, a former shipyard worker, was company chairman at Canon, in Japan, during the 1970s and 1980s, and thereafter life president, until his death in 2001. Initial foundations for the corporate philosophy that Kaku was to develop had already been laid at Canon, as one of its original founders was a Buddhist, establishing Buddhist principles within the organisation (Canon's company name is derived from Kannon, the name of the Buddhist goddess of mercy.) Kaku then developed what he came to describe as *kyosei*, addressing that it was Canon's moral duty, as Kaku saw it, to respond to global problems like Third World poverty, the deterioration of the environment and endless trade battles. But to his view, only few companies had realised that their very survival depended on their response. Global corporations relied on educated workers, consumers with money to spend, a healthy natural environment, and peaceful coexistence between nations and ethnic groups. For that reason, Kaku maintained that global companies had no future if the Earth had none. How then were such companies to promote peace and prosperity, while at the same time enhancing their profitability?

The answer lay for Canon in a 'spirit of co-operation' and co-evolution, where individuals and organisations work together for the common good:

> *A company practising Kyosei establishes harmonious relations with its customers, suppliers and competitors, as well as with the government with which it deals, and the natural environment. When practised by a group of corporations, Kyosei can become a powerful force for social, political and economic transformation.*[18]

Kaku identified five states of Kyosei, starting from economic survival and culminating in the alleviation of global imbalances.

THE FIVE STATES OF KYOSEI: FROM ECONOMIC SURVIVAL TO RECTIFYING GLOBAL IMBALANCES

For Kaku, Kyosei begins with laying a sound business foundation, and ends in political dialogue for global change. The strength of each layer depends on each level before it. The same was the case for Aurobindo, in relation to self and society, and indeed for Maslow in his hierarchy of needs. Kaku starts from the immediately and locally practical, and works his way towards the more far-reaching and global 'life-world'.

> *Stage 1 – Economic Survival:* Companies at the survival stage work to secure a predictable stream of profits and to establish strong market positions in their industries. They contribute to society by producing needed goods, purchasing locally produced raw materials, and employing workers to realise business goals. However, they tend to exploit workers. For Kaku, making a profit is only the beginning of a company's obligations. As a company matures, it needs to understand that it plays a larger role in a global context. Two years before Kaku became president, in 1975, Canon was

losing money. He had to set aggressive targets for each division, reorganise around the main product lines, and invest heavily in manufacturing, marketing and R&D. Later, it became market leader in copiers and desktop printers, and, by the 1990s, net profits had grown, over 10 years, 20 per cent per year.

Stage 2 – Cooperating with Labour: A company enters a second stage when management and workers begin to cooperate with each other. The two sides are in the same boat, sharing the same fate. Canon started cooperating with its employees well before other companies. It had no distinctions between factory and office workers: we are all 'sha-in', members of the company. Because employees tend to spend their entire lives with the company it invests heavily in them.

Stage 3 – Cooperating outside the Company: At this stage, customers are treated respectfully and reciprocally, suppliers are provided with technical support in return for high quality materials. Competitors are invited to form partnerships for mutual gain, while the company links up with community to solve local problems. At this point, the focus is still more local than global. Aside from getting close to its customers and suppliers, Canon, for Kaku, contributes its technological know-how to the general public and communities.

Stage 4 – Global Activism: By cooperating with foreign companies, large corporations can reduce trade frictions by building local plant; they can set up R&D facilities in foreign countries to upgrade their local know-how; and they can improve the living standards of people by paying and training them well. And by developing and using technology that reduces pollution, companies can help preserve the global environment. So, for Kaku, Canon addresses trade imbalances by situating production facilities in countries where Japan has the greatest trade surpluses; it creates employment in poor countries by building manufacturing plants there. Further, to protect the environment, Canon has a major recycling initiative in over 20 countries for photocopiers and laser copiers. And the company is involved in developing bioremediation products, which break down microbes in chemical pollutants, which will enable Canon in the future to generate profits and help the planet.

Stage 5 – The Government as a Kyosei Partner: When a company has established a worldwide network of Kyosei partners it is ready to move onto the final stage. Fifth stage companies, for Kaku, are very rare. They urge governments to rectify global imbalances. Substantiated by Canon's ever-increasing investment in R&D, it is committed to neither support military activities nor harm the environment. It encourages cooperation, worldwide, not duplicating work of others.

KYOSEI IN PERSPECTIVE

Nowadays, Kaku goes on, 400 years after Kyosei was first conceived, multibillion-dollar corporations control vast resources around the globe, employ millions of people, and create and own considerable wealth. They literally hold the future of the planet in their hands. Although governments and civil society need to play their part, they do not possess the same degree of wealth and power. So Kaku's point is this:

> *if corporations run their businesses with the sole aim of gaining more market share, and earning more profits, they may well lead the world towards economic, social and environmental ruin. But if they work together, in a spirit of Kyosei, they can bring food to the poor, peace to war-torn areas, and renewal to the natural world. It is our obligation, as business leaders, to join together to build a foundation for world peace and prosperity.*[19]

Interestingly enough, it was left to a business leader to come up with such a far-reaching, developmental perspective, steeped in his 'Eastern' Buddhist heritage. At the same time, regrettably, there is no major body of theory established in Japan, based on Kyosei, at least to our knowledge. That serves to reinforce the way in which the 'North-West', that is Western Europe and America, dominates in the theory of management and organisation development. As we have seen, Kyosei is a philosophy that has individual, organisational and societal, if not also global implications. It totally redefines the organisation's role and position in society. As its fifth stage requires the organisation to even address global imbalances, Kaku has set an early tone for the enterprise as a development agent. It is also for these reasons, that the example of Canon and Kyosei leads us, almost naturally, into the third level of societal development.

12.5   Integration

We have learned through the work of Bohm in America and Europe, Owen in America, and Kaku in Japan, that spiritually infused consciousness-raising can be applied just as well to the evolution of organisations as to the individual. However, many 'Eastern' philosophies have restricted themselves to the latter.

Canon's Kaku is one of few exceptions, but then he was a business practitioner as well as a philosopher. We reckon that it may well require a marriage between an 'Eastern' sensitivity towards culture and spirituality, and a 'Northern' orientation toward management and organisation to bring about the emergent approach to organisational co-evolution that follows from the individual journey of the self.

We now turn from such individual grounding and organisational emergence in this 'Eastern' realm, to the third level of society based navigation. This leads us also onto approaches to cultural development that have hitherto been seldom recognised.

Before we move on, we invite you again to engage – through reflection and action – with the guiding questions and theory presented in this chapter, as well as with the major development challenges derived thereof. If you are not yet associated with a particular organisation or community (or initiative, network or movement), you may want to envision founding one, together with others. If your primary association is one with a university – be it as member of its faculty or as participant in an educational or research programme – you may want to consider using this as your core transformational context.

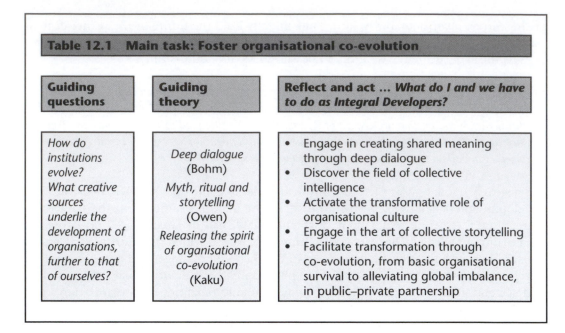

Table 12.1 Main task: Foster organisational co-evolution

Guiding questions	Guiding theory	Reflect and act ... *What do I and we have to do as Integral Developers?*
How do institutions evolve? What creative sources underlie the development of organisations, further to that of ourselves?	*Deep dialogue (Bohm)* *Myth, ritual and storytelling (Owen)* *Releasing the spirit of organisational co-evolution (Kaku)*	• Engage in creating shared meaning through deep dialogue • Discover the field of collective intelligence • Activate the transformative role of organisational culture • Engage in the art of collective storytelling • Facilitate transformation through co-evolution, from basic organisational survival to alleviating global imbalance, in public–private partnership

We now turn to the third 'Eastern' level of societal development.

References

1 Krishnamurti, J. and Bohm, D. (1985). *The Ending of Time*. San Francisco, CA: Harper Collins.

2 The Co-Intelligence Institute website. Available at: www.co-intelligence.org / Accessed: 27 January 2012.

3 Teilhard de Chardin, P. (2005). *Das Herz der Materie. Kernstück einer genialen Weltsicht.* Ostfildern: Patmos.

4 Sheldrake, R. (2009). *Morphic Resonance: The Nature of Formative Causation*. South Paris, ME: Park Street Press.

5 Lovelock, J. (2000). *Gaia: A New Lock at Life on Earth*. Oxford: Oxford Paperbacks.

6 McTaggart, L. (2008). *The Field Updated Ed: The Quest for the Secret Force in the Universe*. New York: Harper Perennial.

7 Tarnas, R. (2007). *Cosmos and Psyche: The Quest for a New World View*. New York: Plume.

8 Nisargadatta, M. (2003). *I am That*. Bombay: Chetana.

9 Nichol, L. (1994) Foreword. In: Bohm, D. (1994). *Thought as a System*. London: Routledge, p. xiv.

10 Brown, J. and Isaacs, D. (2005). *The World Cafe: Shaping Our Futures through Conversations that Matter*. San Francisco, CA: Berrett-Koehler.

11 Bohm, D. (2004). *On Dialogue*. London: Routledge.

12 Senge, P. (2004). In: Bohm, D. *On Dialogue*. London: Routledge, p. xiv.

13 Senge, P. (2004). *The Fifth Discipline: The Art and Practice of the Learning Organisation*. New York: Broadway Business.

14 Isaacs, W. (1999). *Dialogue and the Art of Thinking Together: A Pioneering Approach to Communicating in Business and in Life*. New York: Currency.

15 Waterman, R. and Peters, T. (2004). *In Search of Excellence: Lessons from America's Best Run Companies*. 2nd Edition. New York: Profile Books.

16 Owen, H. (1987). *Spirit, Transformation and Development in Organisations*. Potomac, MD: Abbott.

17 Lessem, R. and Schieffer, A. (2009). *Transformation Management: Towards the Integral Enterprise*. Farnham: Gower.

18 Kaku, R. (1997). The Path of Kyosei. In: *Harvard Business Review*, July–August.

19 Kaku, R. (1997). The Path of Kyosei. In: *Harvard Business Review*, July–August.

13 *Evolutionary Stages in Society: An Eastern Societal Perspective*

Guiding Question: How does our community and society co-evolve creatively and harmoniously with others?

13.1   Orientation

Further to the formative journey of the self (⇨11), and reformative organisational co-evolution (⇨12), we now turn to evolutionary stages on this third societal level of the 'Eastern' realm. Until now, developmental approaches on this level that are rooted in culture and spirituality have been almost completely missing from the 'development' literature.

To our surprise, however, we discovered an unexpected 'forerunner'. Until recently, we were unaware that by using the term 'integral development', we are also building on Pope Paul VI. But so it is. Gregory Baum, who teaches religious studies at McGill University in Montreal, states that, for him, Pope Paul VI took seriously the religious arguments he formulated against development. He repudiated the generally accepted and materialistic idea of development current at the time (1960s) and suggested instead what he called 'integral' development, alluding to a development that improves people's material conditions in the context of the fuller realisation of humanity in social, cultural, political and religious terms. For the late pope, economic development had to go hand in hand with the intensification of social solidarity, political freedom and responsibility, access to education, cultural continuity, and the search for greater religious depth.[1]

If we look at other major religious systems, we find similar 'integral' statements. The Muslim faith with its major emphasis on balance and justice, Buddhism and Hinduism with their rejection of material accumulation beyond the fulfilment of basic needs, First Nation people with their resource-conscious way of living in harmony with a sacred Mother Nature are further examples. All of them provide powerful proof how development (before the so-called development era, commencing after World War II) was strongly informed by the culture and spirituality of a people. Indeed, the secular approach to development that followed is regarded by many people in so-called developing countries with distrust. Baum, for example, asserts that:

First Nations peoples, whether they are Christians or practice their traditional cosmic religion, regard with great suspicion the secular approach to life taken for granted in business, government, economics, and other social sciences. As all these endeavours systematically exclude the spiritual dimension of life, native peoples often regard them as a form of brainwashing designed to undermine their cultural identity.[2]

As Integral Developers we purposefully tap into the realm of a society's culture and spirituality. Indeed, analogous to the individual level (or 'round', as we call it), it is here where we seek a community's or society's 'seat of creativity'. The regularly proclaimed, generalised 'self help' approach often falls short in truly helping a particular society to connect with its own co-evolutionary potential, guided by its own cultural values and beliefs. By 'self help' is often meant that the to-be-developed-people learn to help themselves on their path to become like the developed-people.

To take us out of that conventional cul-de-sac and re-enter the path of co-evolution, now in societal terms, we explore together the following questions:

- How does our community and society co-evolve creatively and harmoniously with others?
- How does a community's or society's culture inform its developmental path and provide useful responses to its core developmental issues?
- How does the interaction between various cultures create fields for creative co-evolution?
- How can our own creative potential, rooted in our own cultural identity, ultimately also contribute to the evolution of the world at large?
- How can societal evolution build on the organisational co-evolution and the journey of the self that come before it?

We begin with the African social philosopher Laurens Van der Post who takes us back to our shared origin, to the collective story of humankind. The German-born philosopher Jean Gebser takes this original story on, charting out the evolutionary stages of human consciousness. He emphasises the need to be in touch with our 'ever-present origin' in order to master the steps of human evolution that lie ahead of us. The Indian sage Sri Aurobindo will then provide us with an evolutionary concept of societal development that interconnects individual and society. The Swiss expert on rural development and Jungian analyst Theodor Abt subsequently shares how communities and society can 'progress without loss of soul'.

We then move on to consider a few, renowned exponents of the international development scene who resonate with this cultural if not also spiritual orientation. These range from the Argentinean semiotician Walter Mignolo to the Hispanic American Gloria Anzaldua who introduces us to the notion of 'transculturation', a concept on which the Portuguese sociologist Boaventura de Sousa Santos builds in his promotion for 'translation between cultures'. We end this societal, developmental round with the Indian social philosopher Paulin Garg and his perspective on the 'culture of transience', whereby he emphasises the need for a society to reconnect to its own cultural identity in order to find the strength to walk its own unique development path in today's world. This all paves the way for the 'Eastern' Developmental University, towards which we will ultimately turn (⇨14) to actualise self and organisational, communal and societal development with a cultural and spiritual pre-emphasis.

We begin our 'Eastern' societal journey with the South African writer, adventurer and storyteller Laurens Van der Post.

13.2   Reconnecting with Our Collective Story: Looking Back to Our Origins to Move Forward

THE STORY IS TIMELESS

Van der Post provides us with fundamental insights into the stories of our unfolding lives. Van der Post was born in South Africa in 1906, to an Afrikaans family living out in the 'bush veld'. His independent expedition to the Kalahari Desert in search of the Bushman was the subject of a famous documentary film.

Van der Post complained that people always laughed at Bushmen stories and said they had no meaning. They had no meaning, he argued, because we onlookers had lost the key and the code. We had lost the meaning of the stories. So he started in 1952 to decode them. This was after he had returned to Africa, war shattered, at a time when he was beginning his life again:

> *My story was moving into a new phase, and I had to begin it again. And it almost seems to me as if in this there's a parable for all of us, mankind. All of us who are discouraged, who sit back and say what's the point of trying, well this is heresy to me, because the story is timeless. Life is timeless. If we play our role in it we redeem it from time.*[3]

Long before he went to school, Van der Post had received a kind of 'African' schooling. First of all he received through his nursemaid Klara the stories and legends of her bushman people. Then, on the family farm, he imbibed the myths and legends of the Bantu and Khoikhoi people as he was playing amongst them. Also there were the Cape Coloured and Malay people who told him stories about Malaya. All of this provided his real teaching before Laurens was given the *Iliad* by his father, alongside the Bible. So his real education came from stories, myths and legends.

EVERYTHING IN LIFE IS A STORY

The word 'myth' in common usage, Van der Post argues, is the label applied to what the rationalist in command of the day dismisses as illusion, non-existent, apocryphal, or some other means of denying the existence of any invisible and non-conceptual forms of reality. It is perhaps understandable that the literal-minded scientist does not see the obvious significance of myth. But he cannot, Van der Post maintains, ignore their proven therapeutic importance. None of us can fail to realise that ultimately, known or unknown, we have derived meaning from what we have experienced in the story in ourselves and throughout its evolution from myth, legend, dream and fairy-tale into its most sophisticated present day form.

For Van der Post, everything in life is a story. The story of mankind, then, is history, and without history we have no meaning. Both are part of the same indivisible process.

Stories provide us with our sense of wonder. They provide us with the sense of living mystery in life. They help us to heighten our sensitivities, our awareness.

The story, moreover, presents the options and possibilities of life that might have been and still can be lived. C.G. Jung – Van der Post's great mentor about whom he even wrote a biography[4] – said that in every disturbance of personality one could discern the elements of an interrupted personal story. And the person could only be cured or healed by the psychiatrist getting hold of the story. That story was the personality's, or indeed society's, most precious possession.

THE DIFFICULTY OF WESTERN MAN TO RETURN TO THE BEGINNING OF HUMANITY'S STORY

Africa is the cradle of humankind. From there our collective story unfolded. For Van der Post, modern man has cut himself off so dramatically from his origins that he can't do other than looking down on them.

Van der Post argues, that it is modern man's excessive rationalism and fanatic adherence to outer physical reality – our 'North-Western' reality viewpoint – together with his overvaluation of the demonstrable objective world around him, which is the cause of much of his undoing. There are, all manner of invisible and imponderable values which modern man has neglected in his or her own life and therefore ignored in the lives of those in his power, or those with whom he or she is thrown into contact, and those factors sooner or later combine in rebellion against him.

LINEAR STORIES – MISUNDERSTOOD TIME

Our stories unfold in time. Van der Post goes on to critique the Western understanding of time. He argues that for most, time is only a 'when', a linear current measured by ticking of clocks over which it flows like water over a wheel, a measure completely at human's disposal over which dates are made and business appointments kept. People are so caught up in this linear movement that one never stops to consider that time may also have a content and a nature, a specific meaning of its own which makes it not merely a 'when' but also a 'what' and perhaps, more importantly still, also a 'how' and a 'way' to eternity.

> I suggest therefore that incorporated somewhere in the inner patterns of misunderstood time there exists a blueprint from the master architect of life itself, a chart of the ultimate design of being which ceaselessly communicates to us our own unique share in time's fashioning. Or, if you like a more modern comparison, I believe there exists a kind of radar which, if we are properly tuned in, can bring us to our appropriate landing ground through the thickest fogs and darknesses of existence. The moment we neglect to fly by this radar, then increasingly panicky unrest invades our aboriginal hearts and minds and infests our behaviour, institutions and societies like a new black plague.[5]

ENTERING THE ORIGINAL STORY – FACING THE SHADOW

For Van der Post, indigenous societies and in particular Africa give the most dramatic example of life developing from an invisible point in time where history has as yet no size and magnitude but only position, right on into our own age.

The bushman makes gods of all the animals that surround him; the Khoikhoi kneel to an insect, the praying mantis; the Bantu listens to the spirits of his ancestors in the roar of the lion and in the noise of his cattle stirring.

Then suddenly European man arrived on the scene. A long period of pure reason that began with the Reformation and had been stimulated by the French Revolution was deeply at work in the European spirit, setting him at variance with his instincts:

> *European man walked into Africa by and large totally incapable of understanding Africa, let alone of appreciating the raw material of mind and spirit with which this granary of fate, this ancient treasure house of the lost original way of life, was so richly filled. He had, it is true, an insatiable appetite for the riches in the rocks, diamonds and gold … but not for the precious metal ringing true in the deep toned laughter of the indigenous people around him.[6]*

For Van der Post, most Western people have swung to an extreme wherein the natural 'Southerner' within us not only has had very little honour but wherein also his rich and instinctive promptings have been thrown summarily out of the courts of our reason.

By evoking the universal story of humanity, Van der Post takes us deep into our own psyche. With reference to C.G. Jung's concept of the shadow, he argues:

> *Now in a deep sense every man has two profound sides to his being, a child of darkness who is equal and complementary to the more obvious child of light. Whether we know it or not we all have within us a natural and instinctive man, a dark brother, to whom we are irrevocably joined as to our shadow. Now the white man of Africa sees reflected in the natural dark man around him that dark aspect of himself that he has rejected. The black man is therefore condemned to play that part which the increasingly exacting projection of the white man expects of him. He is therefore prevented from being himself and from living out his own unique being.[7]*

For Van der Post, the whole problem of modern culture expresses the need for some transcendent factor or purpose wherein neither white nor black, neither natural nor thinking man, will have to be sacrificed to one another. Instead both will be joined and made complete in one transcending purpose. After all, the two opposites of electricity need no longer be expressed through the bright and dangerous medium of lightning but can now be transformed and resolved together into a source of creative energy.

LOCAL MICROCOSM – GLOBAL MACROCOSM

Van der Post maintains that the unrest in the 'Global South' is plainly an extension of modern man's own individual inner unrest. Modern man with his grievous and crippling realisation of having lost the sense of his own beginnings, with this agonising feeling of great and growing estrangement from nature, finds that life holds up Africa like a magic mirror miraculously preserved before his darkening eyes. In this great glass of time the innermost reflections of this ancient, timeless spirit stare out at him, and he can, could he but realise it, rediscover therein his despised and rejected natural self.

That's why Van der Post urges us to revisit the collective story of humanity and thereby also revisit the origins of our story:

I believe the greatest of all mirrors of our age is Africa. We ... bewildered 20th (and 21st) century man, stare into it as if hypnotised, but we do not see and recognise in it the reflection of our own hidden selves. Nevertheless the interest of the world is compelled by events in Africa because, unconsciously, the world apprehends that Africa may the secret of its own lost and hidden being. Without this miraculously preserved Africa, without this land and its allegiance to the original meaning and charter of life, this timely reflection may not be possible.[8]

We need a sense of wonder, for it is part of our wholeness and keeps us humble. One of the more harmful by-products of the excessively one-sided scientific concentration of the past centuries, Van der Post maintains, has been the tendency to eliminate the sense of the mystery of life in men and to depreciate any feelings which lie outside the range of our conscious awareness. The process too was made easier as European civilisation became more and more a metropolitan culture and man's conquests in the physical world increased the distance between man and nature. So man's natural contacts with the great mysteries became more remote. Africans so far have not lost contact with that great mystery, and its influence on their make-up is immense. For the African can still experience the full blast of the ancient spirit of man, taking us along, thereafter, the 'mythological journey', helping us to experience our stories, individually and collectively. Indeed it was Van der Post's unique ability, as a writer, a philosopher and an adventurer, who entered, through his travels, into the very heart and soul of Europe and Asia, as well as Africa, that positions him in our 'Eastern' cultural and spiritual developmental light. For him, in the final analysis, 'every culture is a unique idiom of beauty'.

This 'primordial original experience' is the starting point of the work of the European philosopher Jean Gebser who urges humanity to become conscious of its ever-present origin, as it seeks to evolve to a new civilisational level.

13.3 Co-Evolving towards the Integral Society: In Touch with the Ever-Present Origin

EVOLUTIONARY STAGES IN SOCIETY: FROM MAGICAL TO INTEGRAL

Jean Gebser was a Professor of the Study of Comparative Civilisations at the University of Salzburg in the middle of the last century. What was becoming increasingly evident for Gebser, was that the individual was being driven into isolation while the collective was degenerating into mere aggregation. These two conditions, isolation and aggregation, were, for him, clear indications that individualism and collectivism were becoming deficient and a new form was required.

However, before we can describe the new, Gebser maintains, we must know the old, or, as per the title of Gebser's book, we must know our *Ever-Present Origin*.[9] Looking back on human endeavour, Gebser distinguishes three structures of societal consciousness – magical, mythical and mental – and a fourth one to come – integral, altogether preceded by an original archaic structure. According to him, a true process of development always occurs in quanta, which is in leaps, or in mutations.

STAGE 0: ORIGIN OR ARCHAIC STRUCTURE

Taken together, micro- and macrocosmic harmony is nothing less than the perfect identity of man and the universe, in their original form.

STAGE 1: MAGICAL STRUCTURE

The man of magic has been released from his identity with the whole. The more man became conscious of himself the more he began to be an individual. Man now stands up to nature. He tries to exercise her, to guide her, striving to be independent of her; then he begins to be conscious of his own will. Here is man the maker, fighter and indeed entrepreneur.

STAGE 2: THE MYTHICAL STRUCTURE

While the magic structure leads to a liberating struggle against nature through a disengaged awareness of the external world, the mythical structure, in turn, leads to the emergent awareness of the internal world of the soul. To look into the mirror of the soul is to become conscious; to apprehend the soul, through myth, is to become conscious of self. Everyone who is intent on surviving – with worth and dignity – must sooner or later pass through the agonies of emergent consciousness. For Gebser, as reflected by the German-Canadian Indologist Georg Feuerstein, the mythic consciousness 'led humanity to an awareness of its internal environment ... imagination (imago = picture) or inner experiencing is distinctive of the mythic consciousness. The mythic consciousness is "introvertive"'.[10] It is this introvertive capacity, out of which myth and meaning are born, which – so argues Gebser, as well as Campbell and later Ken Wilber – got lost when human consciousness evolved to the mental structure.

STAGE 3: THE MENTAL STRUCTURE

Events of 500 BC in Greece had to be repeated, according to Gebser, around AD 1250 by European man. Then, however, his basis was considerably broadened because of three major achievements: the Greek theory of knowledge, the Hebrew doctrine of salvation and Roman legal and political theory. From the standpoint of the perspectival European world this mental structure is 'rational', from the root *ratio* meaning to calculate, to think, to understand. Indeed the name for the Indian lawgiver Manu, the Cretan King Minos and the Egyptian King Menes are all most likely derived from the root 'man', the 'measurer'.

STAGE 4: THE INTEGRAL STRUCTURE

By integration Gebser means a fully completed and realised wholeness – the re-establishment of the inviolate and pristine state of origin by incorporating the wealth of all subsequent achievement. The concretion of everything that has unfolded in time and coalesced in a spatial array is the integral attempt to reconstitute the 'magnitude' of man from his constituent parts, so that he can consciously integrate himself with the whole.

OUTLOOK ON THE EVER-PRESENT ORIGIN

While Levinson (⇨7), Lievegoed (⇨8), and Gebser, all adopt somewhat different, transformational orientations, they all build upon an original 'vitality' in the living systems and its progressive unfolding. Indeed, it is this very 'vitality' of Africa to which Van der Post has continually alluded.

Our task in this societal round, therefore, is to promote a new, integral structure without forfeiting the efficient forms of the previous ones. The new societal consciousness has nothing to do with might, rule and overpowering. It cannot be striven for, only elicited or awakened. What is needed therefore is care, a great deal of patience, and the laying aside of many preconceived opinions. There is a need for a certain detachment toward oneself and the world in order to prepare from the leap into the new mutation, a theme now picked up by India's Sri Aurobindo.

13.4   The Co-Evolution of Self and Society: Interconnecting Individual and Societal Development

SRI AUROBINDO: SAGE, PHILOSOPHER, ACTIVIST

Sri Aurobindo was an Indian 'sage' and also a political activist who was a very influential figure in the early part of the twentieth century. Aurobindo's life and work present a strong inspiration to a developmental perspective rooted in culture and spirituality.

THE BACKDROP OF AUROVILLE: ESTABLISHING THE 'UNITY OF MANKIND'

Auroville, a whole city located near South India's Pondicherry, has been created and named after him to establish the 'unity of mankind'. Auroville can be seen as a 'development project', strongly rooted in Aurobindo's spiritual philosophy, and oriented, simultaneously, towards individual and societal development. Some of its key philosophical constituents are:

• Auroville belongs to nobody in particular. Auroville belongs to humanity as a whole. But to live in Auroville, one must be the willing servitor of the Divine Consciousness.
• Auroville will be the place of an unending education, of constant progress, and a youth that never ages.
• Auroville wants to be the bridge between the past and the future. Taking advantage of all discoveries from without and from within, Auroville will boldly spring towards future realisations.
• Auroville will be a site of material and spiritual researches for a living embodiment of an actual Human Unity.

In his reflections (on) *The Human Cycle*,[11] Aurobindo combines his own thinking with that of German nineteenth-century social philosopher Karl Lamprecht as articulated in Weintraub's *Visions of Culture*.[12] Aurobindo, building on Lamprecht, distinguishes four stages of development, altogether interconnecting individual and societal development.

STAGE 1: SYMBOLISM – ORIGINAL – PRIMAL

For Aurobindo, symbolism and a widespread imaginative or intuitive religious feeling, has a natural kinship with primal formations. When man begins to be predominantly intellectual, sceptical or rational he is already preparing for the individualist society and the age of symbols and conventions lose their lustre. If we look at the beginnings of Indian society, in the far off Vedic age, not only the actual religious worship but also the social institutions of the time were penetrated through and through with the symbolic spirit. So too, in times of old, the poet was a seer, a revealer of hidden truths. The image was used because it could hint luminously in the mind what the precise intellectual word, apt only for logical or practical thought, could not hope to manifest. Rigidly 'backward' communities, on the other hand, have already passed out of the symbolic into the conventional stage on a curve of degeneration rather than growth. Symbolic forms then become fixed.

STAGE 2: SYMBOLIC – TYPAL – CONVENTIONAL

The first symbolic stage of evolution is predominantly religious and spiritual, with other elements – economic, psychological, ethical – subordinated to it. The second typal stage that follows creates the social forms that remain impressed on the human mind, even when the stage itself is past.

The tendency of the conventional age of society is to fix, to arrange firmly, to formalise, to erect a system of grades and hierarchies, to bind education to a traditional and unchangeable form, to subject thought to infallible authorities. In this conventional period there is much that is helpful to human progress, but they are the age when the Truth we strive to arrive at is not realised, not accomplished. The form prevails and spirit recedes.

Aurobindo goes on, describing that then there arrives a period when the gulf between convention and truth becomes intolerable and the men of intellectual power arise, strike at the walls of the prison-house and seek by individual reason, moral sense or emotional desire the Truth that society has lost or buried. For him, it is then that the individualistic age of religion and thought and society is created; the Age of Protestantism, of Reason, of Revolt and of Freedom. But still a necessary passage to the subjective period of humanity is required, whereby man has to circle back to the recovery of his deeper self and toward a new upward line or revolving cycle of civilisation.

STAGE 3: CONVENTIONAL TO INDIVIDUAL REVOLT

According to Aurobindo, an individualistic age of human society comes as a result of the corruption and failure of the conventional, as a revolt against the reign of the petrified type. The individualism of the new age is an attempt to get back from conventionalism to some solid bedrock of real and tangible Truth. And it is necessarily individualistic, because the old moral standards have become bankrupt and can no longer give any inner help. For Aurobindo, it is therefore the individual who has to become a discoverer, a pioneer. When he has found or thinks he has found a law of the world, he will strive to rebase it on a firm foundation and remould in a more vital form a religion, institution or societal ethos.

It is in Europe, for Aurobindo who wrote early in the twentieth century, that the age of individualism had exercised its full sway. Yet the truths that Europe found covered only the first, more obvious physical and outward facts of life. Aurobindo argues that Europe's rationalistic civilisation had swept so triumphantly over the world, because it found no deeper and more powerful truth to confront it; for all the rest of humanity was still in the inactivity of the dark hours of the conventional age. The individualistic age of Europe, then, was in its twentieth-century culmination a triumphal progress of physical science. Through such progress, the individual finds a religion being imposed upon him, based on the letter of an ancient book, the infallible dictum of the pope, the tradition of the Church. Thereby the individual must ask, does all of such convention agree with the facts of the world, with his experience of reality? And if it does not, the individual flings off the yoke, declares the truth as he sees it, striking inevitably at the rots of the religious, social or political order.

Eventually, the evolution of Europe, for example, was determined less by the Reformation than by the Renaissance. It flowered by the vigorous return of the ancient Greco-Roman mentality, giving back to Europe on the one hand the free curiosity of the Greek mind, its eager search for first principles and rational laws, and on the other hand the Romans' practicality and robust utility. It was from these sources that the individualistic age of Western society sought order and control.

In the modern era, however, there are forces in operation, which seem likely to frustrate or modify development before it reaches its consummation. Aurobindo maintains that in the first place, rationalistic-physical science has overpassed itself and must before long be overtaken by a mounting flood of psychological and psychic knowledge which cannot fail to compel quite a new view of human being and to open a new vista before mankind. At the same time, the Age of Reason is visibly drawing to an end; novel ideas are sweeping over the world and are being accepted with a significant rapidity, ideas subversive of any economic rationality.

Secondly, Aurobindo argues, the West in its conquest of the world has awakened a slumbering East. Some believe, indeed, that Asia will reproduce Europe's Age of Reason with all its materialism and secularist individualism while Europe will be pushing forward into new forms and ideas. However, if the East follows its own bent and evolves a novel social tendency and culture that is bound to have an enormous effect on the direction of the world's civilisation.

It now seems that social development and well-being is not merely a flourishing of an upper class, or the mass. In addition there is the deeper truth that individualism has discovered, the individual not being merely a social unit, not merely a member of the human pack. He is something in himself, a soul, a being who has to fulfil his own individual truth and law, his own part in the truth and law of collective existence.

STAGE 4 – COMING OF THE SUBJECTIVE AGE

The whole tendency of development of an individualistic age of mankind goes back to the one dominant need of rediscovering the substantial truths of life, thought and action. For these have been overlaid by the falsehood of conventional standards no longer alive to the truth of ideas from which their conventions started.

The need of a developing humanity is not always to return to old ideas. Its need is to progress to a larger fulfilment in which, if the old is taken up, it must be transformed and exceeded. For the underlying truth of things is constant and eternal, but its mental figures, its life forms, its physical embodiments call constantly for growth and change.

Throughout the East, the subjective Asiatic mind is being driven to adapt itself to the need for changed values of life and thought. What it did not do from within, has come on it as a necessity from without and this externality has carried with it immense advantages as well as great dangers. A revolutionary reconstruction of religion, philosophy, science, art and society is the ultimate outcome.

It proceeds at first by the light of the individual mind and reason, by its demand on life and experience of life; but it must go from the individual to the universal. Of the universe we are a part; in all but our deepest layer we are the subject; a small cell in the tremendous organic mass: our substance is drawn from its substance and by the law of life the law of our life is governed.

In Europe and in modern times this has taken the form of physical science, by the laws of the physical universe and the economic and sociological conditions of human life. Yet our economic state and social institutions are themselves governed by our psychological demand on the possibilities, circumstances, and tendencies created by the relation between the mind and soul of humanity in its life and body. Therefore we must go deeper and discover the subjective secret of ourselves and our surroundings.

This we may attempt to do for a time through the power of critical and analytical reason, but not for long. For in our study of ourselves we cannot but come face to face with the soul in ourselves and the soul in the world and find it to be an entry so profound and complex, so full of hidden secrets that intellectual reason proves to be a fumbling seeker; it is analytical only of superficialities. More and more we need to live within our souls and act out of such rather than floundering on the surfaces. In this process the rationalistic ideal begins to subject itself to intuitional knowledge and a deeper self-awareness; the utilitarian standard gives way to the aspiration toward self-consciousness and self-realisation.

The art, music and literature of the world, always a sure index of the vital tendencies of the age, have also undergone a profoundly deepened subjectivism, with the great objective art and literature of the past no longer commanding the mind of our age. Often, however, such subjective art describes the malady of life rather than its health and power.

At the same time, in the practical dealing with life there are progressive tendencies that take their inspiration from profounder subjectivism. Take the example of new ideas about education that focus on bringing out a child's intellectual and moral capacities. Such subjectivism is a return to the lost knowledge of the ancients. First deepening man's inner experience, restoring self-knowledge to our race, it must end by revolutionising our social and collective powers of self-expression. Yet, the nascent subjectivism preparative of the new age has shown itself not so much in the relations of individuals or in tendencies of social development, which are still largely rationalistic and materialistic, but in the new collective self-consciousness of man: the discovery of the nation-soul.

THE DISCOVERY OF THE NATION-SOUL

The primal law and purpose of a society, for Aurobindo, is to seek its own self-fulfilment; it strives rightly to find itself, to become aware within itself of the law and power of its own being and to fulfil it as perfectly as possible, to realise all its potentialities, to live its own self-revealing life. The nation or society, like the individual, has a body, an organic life, a moral and aesthetic temperament, a developing mind and soul for the sake of which it exists. There is only this difference between individual and society, that the group-soul is much more complex.

At first, for this very reason, it seems more crude, primitive and artificial in the forms it takes; for it has a more difficult task before it, needs a longer time to find itself, it is more fluid and less easily organic. When it does succeed in getting out of the stage of vaguely conscious self-formation, its first definite self-consciousness is more objective than subjective. And so far as it is subjective, it is loosely and vaguely so. Yet potentially, in its inner self, there lies a great corporate soul with all the dangers and possibilities that go with it.

The objective view of society has reigned throughout the historical period of humanity in the West. Rulers, people and thinkers alike have understood by their national existence a political status, the extent of their borders, their economic well-being and expansion, their laws, institutions and the working of these. For this reason political and economic motives have everywhere predominated on the surface and history has been a record of their operations and influence.

Scientific history has been conceived, as if it must be a record and appreciation of the motives of political action, of the play of economic forces and developments and the course of institutional evolution. It is when this subconscious power of the group-soul comes to the surface that societies begin to embrace their subjective selves; they set about getting, however vaguely or imperfectly, at their souls.

Religion, argues Aurobindo, ought to be subjective as its very reason for existence – where it is not merely an ethical creed with supernatural authority – but seeks to realise the individual and communal soul. Yet religious history has been almost entirely – except in the time of its founders and their immediate successors – an insistence on objective things, that is on rites, ceremonies, authority, dogmas and forms of belief. It is only recently that men have begun to seriously consider what Buddhism, Christianity, Catholicism and Islam really mean, in their essence.

It is necessary, Aurobindo concludes, that if the subjective age of humanity is to produce its best fruits, societies need to become conscious not only of each other's souls, but also learn to respect, to help and to profit each other, not only economically and intellectually, but subjectively and spiritually.

OUTLOOK ON THE CO-EVOLUTION OF SELF AND SOCIETY

As unusual as some of Aurobindo's thinking comes across in our modern day and age, he challenges us as Integral Developers, to rediscover the substantial truths of life, thought and action. These truths, for him, are eternal and the development task, for each of us, is to move beyond old and used-up forms of living and thinking, and to progress towards larger fulfilment of this truth.

We discover an enormous proximity between the philosophical thought of Gebser and Aurobindo. Aurobindo himself has also influenced profoundly a number of today's leading integral thinkers, in particular the US philosopher Ken Wilber (⇨19). As Aurobindo stresses the necessity of seeing individual and societal evolution as an inseparable whole, so does the Swiss development thinker Theodor Abt, to whom we now turn.

13.5   Societal Development without Loss of Soul: Healing Divides by Co-Evolving Polarities

PROGRESS WITHOUT LOSS OF SOUL

Swiss German agronomist, economic planner and Jungian analyst Theodor Abt, based at the ETH Swiss Federal Institute of Technology in Zurich, has developed a holistic approach to development. He coined his approach *Progress without Loss of Soul*.[13] His work, based on his experiences as project director of a comprehensive economic development plan for two Swiss mountain areas, is strongly inspired by the oeuvre of C.G. Jung and Jung's closest collaborator Marie Louise von Franz. In his analysis, Abt draws simultaneously on empirical research as well as on deep psychological insights.

UNIFICATION OF OPPOSITES

Abt illustrates in his research the importance of atonement in today's development work between the polar opposites of tradition and modernity, of organically grown well-tried ways of life and the paths of progress, between wisdom and knowledge, between presentiments and hard facts.[14] His work takes us away from an 'either or' towards a 'both and'. Abt's approach to the unification of opposites does not mean to statically take diverse aspects of a development problem into consideration and to subsequently label it 'holistic'. Rather, the integration work has to take place, first and foremost, within the individual person. It requires an active reconciliation of one's unconscious suppressed psychic elements with its conscious parts. It requires, as we learned earlier, the facing of the shadow, now on an individual and collective level. Abt goes on to illustrate how with the help of dreams we can actively engage with the process of making the unconscious conscious, in relation to our development work.

WORKING WITH DREAMS IN DEVELOPMENT

To our knowledge, Abt is a rare example of one of those few development experts who have dared to explicitly use, quote and communicate the interpretation of their dreams that occurred to them during development projects. He shares the example of his assignment to present a development concept for Uri, one of the mountain cantons in central Switzerland. After his intense analysis of all relevant factors and dealing with the enormous complexity of the assignment for many months, he retreated for a couple of weeks into a mountain house to progress with the report. He got frustrated that no coherent concept was arising. Then he had a dream, in which he finds himself holding the development report of Uri in his hands. In the middle of the open page was a vertical line. To the right of the line was a piece of bacon fat, to the left a flower. We shall only present here the gist of the subsequent interpretation. Abt interpreted the bacon fat as a symbol for wealth (as it was indeed, traditionally, in the mountain areas), biological needs, in short for material well-being. The flower symbolised meaning, love and imagination, and time for relaxation. It represented human needs on the level of soul and spirit: in short, it stood for life quality. Abt organised his report along these two complementary images. The report was extremely well received and the images subsequently served as guiding symbols for the development of the region.[15]

Abt's work provides important clues how we, in pursuing Integral Development, can actively learn from his dreams to access an inner resource of knowledge that has hitherto been unconscious. According to Jung's theory of dream analysis, dreams reflect, at least to some degree, our conscious life and can provide support to correct or direct our conscious actions. In order to understand one's dreams, one need, as we have seen, to be able to decipher the symbolic language of dreams.[16, 17]

Laurens Van der Post, with whom we started this chapter, supported Abt's stance as he writes in his foreword to *Progress without Loss of Soul*:

In our centuries of the pursuit of reason and the indulgences of a hubris of a tyrannical rationalism, we have lost touch with [the] dreaming element which still, night and day, seeks to redirect us to a destination where beginning and origin are one and whole ... Human beings, I believe, can endure anything except a state of meaninglessness, and ultimately what Abt is concerned about is bringing back meaning, and the sense of totality it confirms on all life on earth, back to progress and make it what it should not have ceased to be: a part, an instrument also, of man's dreaming self.[18]

NO GENERALISED SOLUTIONS TO DEVELOPMENT

Abt purposefully did not prescribe any generalised solutions for development. He rebuked a subsequent critique to his work with the following remark:

Has it not been the general solutions and approaches themselves that have rendered impossible specifically appropriate, unique, and hence organically natural solutions, to social problems? Doubtless the answer to this is 'yes'.[19]

Accordingly, he calls for unique local solutions that find their originality, strength and sustainability in the personal dealing with the unconscious emotional reality, solutions that are grown within and out of the concerned population. Hence, the responsibility for development is not so much with some distant politicians or development planners that are out of touch with the local reality. Rather, it lies with those Integral Developers that deal 'hands-on' and 'hearts-on' with the particular local development issues, and that are willing and able to unearth those suppressed unconscious material, that points to the inner source of hitherto inhibited development. By unearthing this material, prior divides can be healed and the constructive energy needed for the actual development process can flow. The task ahead for us, on the one hand, may be daunting. But on the other hand, rather than getting lost in or unjustifiably reducing the enormous complexity that any development context contains, Abt illustrates that following his approach to development we can actually activate guidance from within to provide orientation. Indeed, he concludes his work by stating that the development of the whole person can well serve as a guiding image for societal development.

THE WHOLE PERSON AS GUIDING IMAGE FOR SOCIETAL DEVELOPMENT

Looking at oneself from a whole person perspective requires the healing of inner divides, and the unification of the opposite poles of our psyche. It invites us, however, also to discover the evolutionary stages of humankind. Here Abt strongly echoes Gebser's notion of the 'ever-present origin', on which Ken Wilber much later built his transpersonal view on human evolution titled *Up from Eden*.[20]

What Abt adds to Gebser's and Wilber's perspective is a much stronger rooting in Jung's work on archetypes, which are psychological structures that all humans share and that provide us with powerful images of self-discovery and discovery of our own evolution.

> *According to what is known today, the human being is not simply a rational creature ... but rather a highly complex and ultimately inscrutable psychological phenomenon, for the psyche does consist of far more than just consciousness. Consciousness is simply a small part of the total psychic reality, namely the youngest result of developmental history extending over eons. The individual stages in this psychic development are found in the genotype of every human being, namely in the archetypal modes of imaging common to all people. On the one hand these archetypal modes are shaped by the experience of our ancestors. On the other hand, we can find all the prehuman development steps in the unconscious structure of our psyche, much as the animal, autonomic, and elemental stages of development can be demonstrated in our body.*[21]

As much as our human evolutionary stages reflect a development journey towards higher consciousness, such a consciousness has to integrate our natural, biological origins and needs as well as our mystic, knowledge-seeking and spiritual needs. For Abt, the quintessence of his work is:

> *to make visible an image of humanity consisting not only of basic biological but also of fundamental spiritual structures that must be given scrupulous attention. Making the whole human being the center of the future guiding image is the need of our age, both for our personal way of life and for our political actions, if the gulf between human and environment as well as between people themselves is not to grow even wider.*[22]

Van der Post, Gebser, Aurobindo and Abt have all helped us strengthen our link between individual and societal development. Altogether, they provide a significant foundation for Integral Development with an 'Eastern' orientation to culture and spirituality. We turn now to a group of development thinkers with a stronger emphasis on a purely societal perspective, that has less of an integral connection with the individual and organisational level, but nevertheless offers us some seminal insights into stages of societal evolution, which will serve to inform the full actualisation of this 'Eastern' realm.

13.6   Transculturation: The Creation of New Civilisational Consciousness

NEW EMERGENT HORIZONS

From a cultural perspective, it is the interconnection between local and global, indigenous and universal worldviews, and between tradition and modernity, where the foundations for rich interpretation, insights and innovation lie. This is the space where new consciousness can emerge. While we engaged with such new consciousness from a psychological and spiritual perspective through Van der Post, Gebser and Abt, we now turn to more cultural and sociological perspectives with the help of a group of development economists, anthropologists and sociologists: these are the South Americans Mignolo, Anzaldua, Ortiz, De Sousa Santos and Escobar, the Iranian Rahnema and India's Garg.

FROM DECALTURATION AND ACULTURATION TO TRANSCULTURATION

This cultural – or better intercultural – theme is picked up by Walter Mignolo, an Argentinian-born semiotician (study of signs and symbols) now based at Duke University in North Carolina, who has joint professorial appointments in cultural anthropology and romance studies. In his *The Idea of Latin America*,[23] Mignolo focuses on *'interculturalidad'*, whereby he cites his Hispanic American colleague, social activist and poet, the late Gloria Anzaldua, and the importance of the *mestiza* – a term used for the mixed breed of indigenous South Americans and people of European heritage – for transcultural renewal:

> *the future will belong to the mestiza. Because the future depends on the breaking down of paradigms, it depends on the straddling of two or more cultures. By creating new mythos – that is a change in the way we perceive reality, the way we see ourselves, and the way we behave – mestiza creates a new consciousness.*[24]

Interculturalidad, Mignolo goes on to say, does not mean merely speaking the same logic in two different languages, but putting into collaborative conversation two different logics for the good of all. Whereas 'multicultural' means that the hegemonic control remains, interculturalidad means, instead, that two different cosmologies – Western and Indigenous – are at work.

Cuban philosopher and polymath Fernando Ortiz argues in similar guise: For him, while 'acculturation' points towards cultural changes in one direction, 'transculturation' means to call attention to the complex and multidirectional processes in cultural transformation. Ortiz is:

> *of the opinion that the word transculturation better expresses the different phases of transition from one culture to another because this does not consist merely in acquiring another culture, which is what the English world acculturation implies, or the process of uprooting from a previous culture, that is deculturation. In addition it carries the idea of the creation of a new cultural phenomenon, which could be called neoculturation. In the end, the result of a union of cultures is similar to that of the reproductive process between individuals; the offspring always has something of both parents but is always different from each of them.*[25]

BORDER THINKING: BEYOND ADAPTATION AND REACTION

By introducing the theme of 'travelling', Mignolo takes the transcultural story on. Theories that travel in economics and development tend to travel from North to South, for Mignolo, if not also from West to East, for us. The language in which they travel, he says, are colonial ones. When this happens, there are several possibilities. One is to adapt or to react, and to thereby propose civilisation, modernisation, development (adapt) or to propose resistance, to close the doors and defend against it (react). A third approach is to think critically, at the intersection of the dwelling place and the new travellers, that is to think from the border, implying a new epistemology, neither adopting the modern not defending tradition. This alternative involves a double critique, of the foreign travellers and the local homeowners, thereby creating a space for new thinking to take place.

Mignolo argues, that such a new way of 'border thinking', in which dichotomies can be replaced by the complementarity of apparently contradictory terms, could open up the doors to another tongue, another thinking, another logic superseding the long history of the modern-colonial world. For this to happen we need to engage with the work of so-called 'translation'.

13.7   Translation: The Crucial Work of Translation between Cultures for Co-Evolution

TRANSLATION BETWEEN ONE WORLD AND ANOTHER

Rahnema argues that on our way to build a new development paradigm we need to:

> overcome the hegemony of one universal language, which, like the global village, tends to destroy the real languages used by millions of people everywhere to express themselves and their worlds ... Unfortunately, most local and culturally construed terms that define the perception of different communities in those things close to their hearts – such as poverty, conviviality, abundance, freedom, deference, the good the virtuous – have all been reduced to 'amoebas' or 'plastic' words, called upon to mean the same thing the world over. So long as these words colonise people's languages, it will be difficult ... to talk seriously about such problems.[26]

It is for that very reason, that the Portuguese sociologist Boaventura de Sousa Santos, an active protagonist in the World Social Forum, stresses the importance of translation between one world and another, as an alternative to adopting one general (alien) theory.[27] Translation is the procedure that allows for mutual intelligibility among the experiences of different worlds, both available and possible, without jeopardising their identity and autonomy, without reducing them to homogeneous entities. Such translation of knowledges consists of interpretation work between two or more cultures.

De Sousa Santos introduces the following example for what he means by translation: he proposes a comparative exploration of concerns for human dignity between the Western concept of human rights, the Islamic concept of *umma* (community) and the Hindu concept of *dharma* (cosmic harmony).

Thereby a space is opened for dialogue, mutual knowledge and understanding and for identification of commonalities from which practical combinations for action can emerge. Seen from the perspective of *dharma*, for example, human rights are incomplete in that they fail to establish the link between the part (individual) and the whole (cosmic reality), or even more strongly that they focus on what is merely derivative rights, rather than on the primordial imperative, the duty of individuals to find their place in the order of the entire society and of the entire cosmos. On the other hand, so de Sousa Santos, seen from the perspective of human rights, *dharma* is also incomplete, owing to its strong bias in favour of the social and religious status quo, totally neglecting the value of conflict as a way towards a richer harmony. Moreover, dharma is unconcerned with the principles of democratic order, with individual freedom and autonomy.

The same work of translation can be attempted between the concept of human rights and that of *umma* in Islamic culture. Seen from the latter perspective, the incompleteness of individual human rights lies in the fact that on their basis alone it is impossible to ground the collective linkages, duties and solidarities without which no society can survive, and much less flourish. Conversely from the perspective of human rights, *umma* overemphasises duties to the detriment of rights, and for that reason condones inequalities.[28]

In sum, the work of translation in the intercultural contact zone among movements and organisations expounding different conceptions of human dignity allows us to identify the fundamental weaknesses of Western culture. For these consist in dichotimising too strictly between individual and society, thus becoming vulnerable to possessive individualism, narcissism and alienation. On the other hand, the fundamental weakness of Hindu and Islamic culture lies in the fact that they both fail to recognise that human suffering has an irreducible individual dimension, which can only be addressed in a society not hierarchically organised.

The work of translation among knowledges starts from the idea that all cultures are incomplete and can therefore be enriched by dialogue and confrontation with other cultures. For de Sousa Santos, the World Social Forum has granted this idea a new centrality and a higher urgency. Once the exchange of experiences has begun, the idea and feeling of want and incompleteness create motivation for the work of translation among social groups. In order to bear fruit, translation must be the coming together of converging motivations with their origins in different cultures.

What, more concretely, is involved?

CREATING INTELLIGIBILITY IN A WORLD ENRICHED BY MULTIPLICITY AND DIVERSITY

The work of translation aims to create intelligibility, coherence and association in a world that sees itself enriched by multiplicity and diversity. Translation is a work of dialogue and politics. It has an emotional dimension as well, because it presupposes both a nonconformist attitude vis-à-vis the limits of one's knowledge and practice, and the readiness to be surprised and learn from the other's knowledge and practice.

What need to be facilitated, however, are what de Sousa Santos calls 'cosmopolitan contact zones'. For him, the World Social Forum is a key example for a facilitator of such a contact zone among NGO movements, their leaders and activists. The workings of the contact zone generate a new kind of citizenship, a cosmopolitan attitude of reflection and self-reflection, reaching beyond familiar territories. The partners in the contact zone must be deeply embedded in the practices and knowledges they represent, having both a profound and a critical understanding. This critical understanding grounds the want, the feeling of incompleteness and the motivation to discover in other practices the answers that are not found in the limits of a given knowledge or practice.[29]

TRANSLATION AS A WORK OF EPISTEMOLOGICAL AND DEMOCRATIC IMAGINATION

For de Sousa Santos, the work of translation is the procedure we are left with to give coherence and generate coalitions among the enormous diversity of struggles against neo-liberal globalisation. Such can only arise when there is no general theory of progressive social transformation to be brought about by a privileged culture. When social transformation has no automatic meaning and neither history nor society nor culture can be centrally planned, the movements have to create, through translation, partial collective meanings that enable them to join together in courses of action that they consider most adequate to bring about the kind of social transformation they deem most desirable. It is a work of epistemological and democratic imagination, aiming to construct new and plural conceptions of social emancipation upon the ruins of the automatic social emancipation of the modernist project.

The objective of the translation work is to nurture among progressive social movements and organisations the will to create together knowledges and practices strong enough to provide credible alternatives to neo-liberal globalisation.

The possibility of better prospects, for de Sousa Santos, lies therefore not in a distant future, but rather in the reinvention of the present. To affirm the credibility and sustainability of this possibility is for him the most profound contribution of the World Social Forum to counter-hegemonic struggles. The work of translation permits the creation of meanings and directions that are precarious but concrete, short-range but radical in their objectives, radical but shared. The aim of translation between knowledges is to create cognitive justice from the standpoint of the epistemological imagination.[30]

With his proposal of establishing a university movement, de Sousa Santos has illustrated his concern to building new educational spaces in which the practice of translation can be actualised in large scale.

13.8   A Culture of Transience: A Key to Activate the Regenerative Cultural Potential

The Indian social philosopher Paulin Garg promotes a culture of transcience as a way for a country to connect and build on its own cultural identity while simultaneously engaging with modernity. As cited by Mignolo, Garg claims:

> Western theory which has been the only theory available for universalisation is definitely culture specific and grounded in the Judeo-Christian and Greco-Roman assumptions of man. These may have been internalised by educated groups of people but not by the masses; and any way they have not been introjected. Hence they have not yet become enlivened and energised by the psychic energy held in the cultural identity of India.[31]

Garg presents three possible options: two of them are pernicious, one carries some hope. The first one, which produced economic growth and a resurgence of Indian nationalism, was established in 1830 by the renowned Bengali social reformer Ram Mohan Roy. But it also opened up the doors for corruption and disengagement, violence and problems of law and order, and a whole set of unethical practices. The second option is to continue operating on the ethos of the West and believe that technology will take care of all of the problems, which is pretty much what is happening in India today. The third option, for Garg, is the culture of transience and its dynamics:

The identification of the basic assumption and processes of our own ethos can become the best anchor to formulate a new cultural identity relevant for the times as well as to evolve forms and processes which aim for dynamic and creative transactions between individual and our social systems. This option also involves going backward and forward. The past is forever present in our introjected ethos. It is a heritage and source of dynamicity, but it is also a pathology and source of immobility and degeneration. The past ethos can be regenerative if we can decode the processes and use them to unleash energy held in cultural identity. As an Indian, I believe that this third option is the only one for us to survive as a self-respecting society.[32]

We are now ready to assimilate the rich and diverse feast of ingredients that constitute this 'Eastern' societal development chapter.

13.9   Integration

Paulin Garg, Boaventura De Sousa Santos and Walter Mignolo, in focusing on transculturation, revisit David Bohm's orientation towards dialogue, though in their case with more of a sociopolitical as well as cultural orientation. Prior to that, Jean Gebser and Laurens Van der Post, and also Sri Aurobindo, 'follow' the organisational course set by Harrison Owen and Ryuzaburo Kaku, in promoting stages of societal evolution. Theodor Abt adds to that the necessity to heal the divides between opposite polarities in development for a holistic approach to development to be actualised.

The overall 'Eastern' developmental tone is somewhat different from the 'Southern' orientation toward nature and community, whereby the conscious evolution of individual and societal consciousness is much more prominent than in the 'Southern' orientation. When we later turn to the 'Northern' realm of science, systems and technology, the overall tone will again change fundamentally.

In the following chapter, which serves as transformative culmination of this 'Eastern' developmental path, we turn towards a Developmental University, serving to actualise the first three rounds of self, organisation and society. It embodies, at least to some degree, a new kind of educational and developmental institution, which can effect the journey of the self, the co-evolution of organisations, and the furthering of communal and societal consciousness altogether.

Before we move on to this fourth round we pause to engage – through reflection and prospective action – with the guiding question and theory presented in this chapter. This includes the major development challenges derived thereof. At this stage it is of primary importance to identify, how you and your organisation or community can reach out into society at large, thereby becoming a veritable agent for societal development. For this to happen, you are challenged to articulate and conceptualise your own learnings and findings with regards to development, based on your experiences in Round 1 (the formative grounding of your own self) and in Round 2 (the reformative emergence of your organisation and community). Hence, this normative Round 3 is very much about coming up with new development norms, so it can inform – large-scale – the development of your society at large.

Table 13.1	Main task: Catalyse evolutionary stages in society	
Guiding question	**Guiding theory**	**Reflect and act ... What do I and we have to do as Integral Developers?**
How does our community and society co-evolve creatively and harmoniously with others?	*Reconnecting with our collective story* (Van der Post) *Co-evolving towards the Integral Society* (Gebser) *Co-evolution of self and society* (Aurobindo) *Development without loss of soul* (Abt) *Transculturation* (Mignolo/Anzaldua) *Translation* (De Sousa Santos) *A culture of transience* (Garg)	• Enter the story of your society. Rediscover origins to move forward • Tune into your society's evolutionary story: from magical to integral • Show how the development of your self and your society are linked • Explore the soul of your community and society and its path to fulfilment • Reconfigure the notion of societal progress in your societal context • Articulate how your society can evolve without losing its soul • Explore how its consciousness can expand through transculturation • Elaborate how your community and society can evolve by translating in between inner and outer multiplicity and diversity • Seek ways to activate the regenerative potential of your society's culture – by purposefully building on its current state of transience

We are now ready to move from individual grounding, organisational emergence and societal navigation, to practical effect. This effect will be illustrated, in this 'Eastern' case, by Sarvodaya in Sri Lanka, as well as by the two Indian institutions Om Creations and Aravind, culminating in an envisaged 'Developmental University'.

References

1   Baum, G. (2000). Solidarity with the Poor. In: Harper, S.M.P (ed.), *The Lab, the Temple and the Market: Reflections at the Intersections of Science, Religion and Development*. Ottawa. ON: International Development Research Center, p. 66.

2   Baum, G. (2000). Solidarity with the Poor. In: Harper, S.M.P (ed.), *The Lab, the Temple and the Market: Reflections at the Intersections of Science, Religion and Development*. Ottawa, ON: International Development Research Center, p. 63.

3   Van der Post, L. (1955). *The Dark Eye of Africa*. Cape Town: Lowery Press.

4   Van der Post, L. (1976). *Jung and the Story of Our Time*. London: Vintage.

5   Van der Post, L. (1955). *The Dark Eye of Africa*. Cape Town: Lowery Press.

6   Van der Post, L. (1955). *The Dark Eye of Africa*. Cape Town: Lowery Press.

7   Van der Post, L. (1955). *The Dark Eye of Africa*. Cape Town: Lowery Press.

8   Van der Post, L. (1955). *The Dark Eye of Africa*. Cape Town: Lowery Press.

9   Gebser, J. (1985). *The Ever-Present Origin*. Athens, OH: Ohio University Press.

10   Feuerstein, G. (1992). *Wholeness or Transcendence: Ancient Lessons for the Emerging Civilisation*. New York: Larson Publications, p. 27.

11   Aurobindo, S. (1950). *The Human Cycle: The Psychology of Social Development*. Twin Lakes, WI: Lotus Press.

12   Weintraub, K. (1966). *Visions of Culture*. London: University of Chicago Press.

13   Abt, T. (1988). *Progress without Loss of Soul: Toward a Wholistic Approach to Modernisation Planning*. Wilmette, IL: Chiron.

14   Abt, T. (2007). *Wissen und Ahnung: Landentwicklung mit Seelengewinn*. Niederaltaich: Landvolkshochschule St. Gunther.

15   Abt, T. (1986). *Planung ohne Schatten? Vom Umgang mit komplexen Problem*. Speech given at the International Congress for Analytical Psychology in Berlin.

16   Jung, C.G. et al. (1964). *Man and His Symbols*. New York: Dell.

17   Jung, C.G. (2001). *Traum und Traumdeutung*. Munich: DTV.

18   Van der Post, L. (1988). Foreword to: Abt, T. *Progress without Loss of Soul: Toward a Wholistic Approach to Modernisation Planning*. Wilmette, IL: Chiron.

19   Abt, T. (1988). *Progress without Loss of Soul: Towards a Wholistic Approach to Modernisation Planning*. Wilmette, IL: Chiron, p. xix.

20   Wilber, K. (1996). *Up from Eden: A Transpersonal View of Human Evolution*. Wheaton, IL: Quest Books.

21   Abt, T. (1988). *Progress without Loss of Soul: Towards a Wholistic Approach to Modernisation Planning*. Wilmette, IL: Chiron, p. 353.

22   Abt, T. (1988). *Progress without Loss of Soul: Towards a Wholistic Approach to Modernisation Planning*. Wilmette, IL: Chiron, p. 365.

23   Mignolo, W.D. (2005). *The Idea of Latin America*. Malden, MA: Blackwell.

24   Anzaldua, G. (2006). *Borderlands/La Frontera: The New Mestiza*. San Francisco, CA: Aunt Lute Books.

25   Font, M. (2004). *Cuban Counterpoints: The Legacy of Fernando Ortiz*. Lanham, MD: Lexington Books.

26   Rahnema, M. (1997). Towards Post-Development: Searching for Signposts, a New Language and New Paradigms. In: Rahnema, M. and Bawtree, V. (eds), *The Post-Development Reader*. London: Zed, p. 400.

27   De Sousa Santos, B. (2006). *The Rise and Fall of the Global Left: The World Social Forum and Beyond*. London: Zed Books.

28   De Sousa Santos, B. (2006). *The Rise and Fall of the Global Left: The World Social Forum and Beyond*. London: Zed Books.

29   De Sousa Santos, B. (2006). *The Rise and Fall of the Global Left: The World Social Forum and Beyond*. London: Zed Books.

30   De Sousa Santos, B. (2006). *The Rise and Fall of the Global Left: The World Social Forum and Beyond*. London: Zed Books.

31   Mignolo, W.D. (2000). *Local Histories/Global Designs: Coloniality, Subaltern Knowledges and Border Thinking*. Princeton, NJ: Princeton University Press, pp. 322ff.

32   Mignolo, W.D. (2000). *Local Histories/Global Designs: Coloniality, Subaltern Knowledges and Border Thinking*. Princeton, NJ: Princeton University Press, pp. 322ff.

14 *Eastern Integration via a Developmental University: The Cases of Sarvodaya, Om Creations and Aravind*

Guiding Question: How can we sustainably actualise the Eastern realm of Integral Development, rooted in culture and spirituality?

14.1 Orientation

In this final chapter of the 'Eastern' realm, we come to its fourth round of integrated and institutionalised practice. As in the final 'Southern' chapter (⇨10), we illustrate through practical cases, how the first three rounds of individual, organisational and societal development can be actualised through what we term a '*Developmental University*'.

In this 'Eastern' realm, such an educational institution needs to serve the realm's core theme of 'Regenerating Meaning via Culture and Spirituality'. Being an enabling space for the core 'Eastern' value of 'balanced and peaceful co-evolution', a Developmental University focuses on societal learning and consciousness-raising. Key tasks of it are 'catalysation', 'consciousness' and 'conscientisation'. The latter term had been coined by the Brazilian Paulo Freire, one of the twentieth century's greatest educators, for whom 'conscientisation' was the development of a critical awareness of one's own reality through reflection and action.[1] Deeply embedded in a societal fabric, a Developmental University is a catalytic force for societal development around a particular issue, or even a whole group of issues. Invariably, there is a strong psychological and spiritual motive behind a Developmental University. To enable it to fully actualise, it requires elements of a Communiversity (⇨10), ensuring it is directly serving one or more communities – and from there reaching out into society at large.

As in the 'Southern' case of a '*Communiversity*', we are again stepping consciously in relatively unchartered waters. Why? The '*Developmental University*' that we introduce in this chapter has not yet been fully conceived of. It is, however, clearly emergent, as our cases show.

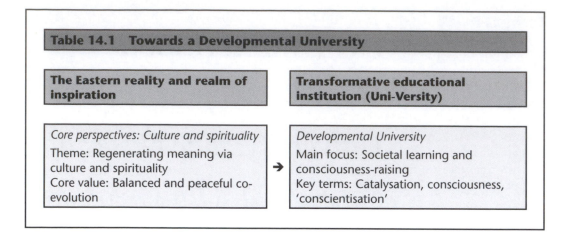

Table 14.1   Towards a Developmental University

The Eastern reality and realm of inspiration	Transformative educational institution (Uni-Versity)
Core perspectives: Culture and spirituality Theme: Regenerating meaning via culture and spirituality Core value: Balanced and peaceful co-evolution	*Developmental University* Main focus: Societal learning and consciousness-raising Key terms: Catalysation, consciousness, 'conscientisation'

We could see already glimpses of a Developmental University in the thoughts of Julius Nyerere, the founding president of the liberated Tanzania. Nyerere viewed development as the process of advancing from a lower, less satisfying, less peaceful stage to struggle to higher, more satisfying and emancipating conditions. Development represents not only material achievement, but also cultural freedom, and the psychological upliftment of people. It is a process, not an integral end. To this effect, Nyerere asserts that education (both formal and informal) is a productivity factor and an indicator of development: No education = no development, and no further national progress.[2]

Why have both the 'Communiversity' and the 'Developmental University' not yet been fully expressed? Because, as per the introductory chapters to this book (⇨1, 2, 3), the 'Southern' and 'Eastern' realms have both been dramatically neglected within development theory and practice. Hence, the full articulation of these two realms has not yet taken place. It was only in recent decades, with an increased affirmation of local communities on the one hand and of diverse cultural perspectives on the other hand, that we can observe such new forms of community- and culture-bound development. Such new development forms have laid the foundations for the 'Southern' Communiversity and the 'Eastern' Developmental University.

What makes this 'Eastern' case particularly complex is that the cultural and spiritual realm of development is perhaps the most neglected and undervalued one. This is for the following two reasons: firstly, the enormous dominance of the 'Western' cultural perspective has paved the way for a solely universalistic understanding of the world (e.g. 'global village') with little to no attention given to local cultural perspectives; secondly, phenomena like 'culture' and 'spirituality' require a very refined combination of sensitivity, receptivity and empathy from any would-be Integral Developer, as well as our having the courage to deal with inner, subjective and unquantifiable aspects of such development.

Furthermore, whenever developmental cases have emerged with an obvious and strong cultural and spiritual dimension, they are generally considered as singular phenomena having minimal implications for development at large. Also – in conventional development terms – they were merely looked at from a community or societal perspective. Due to the hitherto lack of an integral perspective, such cases have not been understood from a multi-level or 'fully rounded' (self/organisation/ society/Uni-Versity) perspective, nor have they been looked at through a four-realm-lens.

Because of all that, no deeper understanding of such cases has been attained, and – with the individual (Round 1) and organisational (Round 2) perspectives missing – those individual and organisational development agents that were eager to engage in culturally and spiritually infused forms of development, were left without a requisite frame of societal orientation.

The final inhibiting factor is that the university world has equally been dominated by one prevailing 'North-Western' design, with an overall focus on individual education and research, largely devoid of a particular context and culture. If that were not enough, higher education has by now become a highly competitive 'business', making it extremely difficult to enter this 'market' with new, innovative, culturally sensitive programmes.

In fact, if new, more sustainable forms of development are to have a chance, we need to create collective learning and innovation spaces, where individuals and their organisations and communities can work towards new societal realities. For this to happen, we require new types of universities that can act as transformational institutions for societal – as well as individual and organisational – development.

As we shall learn later (⇨18), there was a time when universities did indeed at least somewhat play such a development role within societies, and we see the time ripe for reconnecting universities to this particular role, albeit now in a newly integral way.

The following case stories of Sarvodaya in Sri Lanka, Om Creations in India, and – in brief – Aravind in India, illustrate not only the transformative impact on society of each one of them, but also the additional potential they could release as fully evolved Developmental Universities.

14.2   Integrated Eastern Practice: Sarvodaya in Sri Lanka and Om Creations in India

THE CASE OF SARVODAYA IN SRI LANKA: THE AWAKENING OF ALL

Introduction

Starting with the Sarvodaya *Shramadana* Movement (in short: Sarvodaya) in Sri Lanka we come to one of the most fascinating development initiatives in the world. Having celebrated its fiftieth birthday in 2008, Sarvodaya has stood the test of time and in the process has offered us unique insights into a development theory and practice that deeply roots itself in the particular cultural and spiritual context of Sri Lanka, while also maintaining, from the outset, a universal outlook. We were fortunate to recently become significantly involved with Sarvodaya, thereby co-evolving our respective integrated approaches. At the same time, we have been cooperating in promoting the emergence of a potential Developmental University – spearheaded by the founder's son and current General Secretary of the movement. Dr Vinya Ariyaratne. As you will see in the course of the subsequent case story, such a Developmental University is almost a natural evolutionary step for Sarvodaya, emerging out of its prior history. Indeed, such an emergent university is seeking to make explicit, what is – to a considerable degree – already developmentally implicit in Sarvodaya's way of thinking and acting. Sarvodaya's story begins in the mind of its founder A.T. Ariyaratne, often dubbed the 'Gandhi of Sri Lanka'.

Round 1 – Self: A.T. Ariyaratne – A Buddhist-Ghandian social philosopher-revolutionary-activist

Born in 1931 into the little village of Unawatuna in Sri Lanka's Galle district, Ahangamage Tudor (A.T.) Ariyaratne, called Ari by most of his friends, was attracted from an early age to the country's predominant religion: Buddhism. Ariyaratne, who was later to become a teacher of a whole nation, attended, after finishing his high school education, a teacher's college. In line with his Buddhist orientation, he thereafter acted, until 1972, as a teacher at Nalanda, a renowned Buddhist college in Colombo. With Buddhism having been the country's formal religion, or belief system for over 2,000 years, Sri Lanka is one of the world's oldest Buddhist nations. Central Buddhist concepts such as non-violence, impermanence, no-self and the Four Noble Truths, were as much a guiding force in the life of Ariyaratne, as they would later become in the Sarvodaya Movement. For him, living a Buddhist non-violent life means to be 'grounded in a systematic "attitude adjustment" in which negative, reactive states such as hatred, greed, and delusion are transformed into positive social orientations through meditative self-training'.[3] To our mind, Ariyaratne's profound, developmental orientation to life has laid the early 'Eastern' Sarvodayan grounds for a Developmental University to emerge more explicitly at a later stage.

Already in his youth, Ariyaratne developed a highly meditative, reflective way of being – an attitude that was to result in countless books and papers that he wrote in order to shape his thinking and that of his 'learning organisation'. The acclaimed Sri Lankan social scientist Nandasena Ratnapala edited the collected works of Ariyaratne.

What led Ariyaratne to adopt Sarvodaya as the lead-theme and name for his organisation? The concept of Sarvodaya, borrowed from Gandhi, seemed to best capture the social vision he developed for Sri Lanka. For him, Sarvodaya aims at the complete opening up or awakening of all – as individuals, as families, as rural and urban groups, as nations and as a global society of human beings. With 'sarva', meaning all and 'udaya' meaning awakening – both Sanskrit words also used in Sri Lanka's Sinhala language – the name embodies the objective and spirit of the later movement. Inspired by Mahatma Gandhi's translation of John Ruskin's famous economics essay *Unto This Last*,[4] entitled by Gandhi as *Sarvodaya*, Ariyaratne sees such an awakening in its fullest sense with inner and outer aspects: spiritual, moral, cultural as inner ones and social, economic and political aspects as outer ones. What could be a better basis for a holistically oriented Developmental University than this?

Gandhi's thinking on Indian independence was another crucial influence for Ariyaratne. For Gandhi, in the first part of the twentieth century, Indian independence was much more than a political issue. So-called 'constructive work' such as homespun cloth, village industries, and local self-reliance (*khadi*) was at the heart of genuine independence, not just political democracy. In that way he encouraged Indian farmers to grow what they needed themselves. The same was true for essential village industries. Only when an equal share had been given 'unto the last' person, in Ruskin's terms, was a non-violent social order (*ahimsa*) possible. For Gandhi, only such a society could attain truth (*satya*) and self-realisation (*swaraj*) could grow. For him, political independence was only one small step towards such-realisation. A day before he was assassinated, Ghandi wrote that 'India has still to attain social, moral and economic independence in terms of its seven hundred thousand villages …'.

Indeed these thousands of villages were to contain, within them, the seeds of development within the person, and enterprise, the community and the whole nation.

For Ariyaratne, Sri Lanka – that had gained its political independence from British colonial rule in 1948 (one year after India) – was equally far from attaining social, moral and economic independence. For him, as for Gandhi, the starting point for true independence, and hence for authentic development, was to be found in the Sri Lankan villages – concretely it had to begin with the awakening of the individual villager. That's how Sarvodaya as a movement came into being, and that is from where Sarvodaya as a would-be Developmental University traces its foundations.

Round 2 – Organisation: The Sarvodaya Shramadana movement as a new organisational approach to culture and spiritually based holistic development

In our overall developmental-educational context, it is noteworthy that Sarvodaya has its origins as an offshoot of an educational institute: Colombo's Buddhist college Nalanda. Already at the time of its inception in 1958, Sarvodaya expressed a distinct, socially revolutionary development philosophy. Though culturally clearly rooted in Sri Lankan Buddhism, it had a particular 'universal philosophical openness'. For example, in addition to the teachings of the Buddha as its strongest influence,[5] a philosophy of non-violence imported from India, in particular that of Mahatma Gandhi and his close disciples Vinoba Bhave and Sri Jayaprakash Narayan, were the other major influences. Indeed, Ariyaratne has always displayed a remarkable ability to integrate philosophies and practices from other cultures and civilisations with his own indigenous sources. Even his approach to Buddhism, as George Bond observed, has an almost 'ecumenical' touch to it, with Ariyaratne believing in a spiritual unity underlying all religions.[6] He hence interprets Sarvodaya as a 'synthetic ideology' that tries to embrace all forms of creative altruism and evolutionary humanism. Its main concern is to keep things going, not to make them grow.

But Sarvodaya did not only employ Buddhism as a guiding philosophy, it also used – or better: regenerated – the nation's existing 'Buddhist infrastructure'. At different stages of Sarvodaya's evolution, large number of monks served the movement, many of them on what they considered a full time basis. Indeed, without this contribution Sarvodaya could never have penetrated into the country the way they have done. In as much as the monks serve as extension agents for Sarvodaya so Sarvodaya serves to revitalise their order and their sense of vocation, restoring the wider social responsibilities they carried in pre-colonial days. In this respect, Sarvodaya has become an agent of cultural and spiritual, as well as communal and societal renewal within Sri Lanka, if not also on behalf of the wider world.

For US environmental activist and Buddhist scholar Joanna Macy, Sarvodaya's integration of religion into its approach to development can be viewed as generating an Asian Buddhist form of 'social gospel' parallel to 'liberation theology' in the West. As has occurred in relation to the teachings of Jesus, the Buddha's teaching on social equality, economic sharing, and political participation are being brought to the fore as a challenge – to inspire not just the enlightenment of individuals but the transformation of society itself.[7]

In line with such individual and societal transformation, it is therefore Sarvodaya's mission, in Ariyaratne's words, 'to generate a non-violent revolution towards the creation of a Sarvodaya Social Order which will ensure the total awakening of human personalities, human families, village communities, urban communities, national community and the world community'.[8] We can clearly see how the seeds of a Developmental University were sewn, into Sarvodaya, from an early stage of its evolution.

The initial core principles of the movement, that still hold today – and that would equally be relevant for the Developmental University to follow – were:

- to mould the youth in conformity with the local culture, bearing in mind the vast changes taking place in the country;
- to provide the rural population with an understanding of the social revolution taking place, and making them contributors in accordance with their culture and responsibility;
- to create in every person a condition of national solidarity without distinction of community, caste, language and religion, making them share in common in a national re-awakening through truth, non-violence and self-sacrifice, achieving thereby fundamental human rights and social justice;
- to join together in a spirit of brotherhood, with people living in other countries with the aims of world peace, human brotherhood, cooperation and development.

In the years before the official foundation of Sarvodaya, Ariyaratne had already experimented with these principles together with some of his colleagues and his students. In a first step, he had taken his privileged 16–17-year-old high school students to a village in Kanatoluwa, as an attempt to give an urban elite insights into some of their fellow low-caste countrymen in rural areas. Ariyaratne inspired and helped to organise a two-week work-camp in a remote and destitute outcast village. The main goal of the work-camp was to 'understand and experience the true state of affairs that prevailed in the rural poor urban areas ... and to develop a love for their people and utilise the education they received to find ways of building a more just and happier life for them'.[9]

What follows is legendary. A hard core of volunteers – more than 300,000 between 1958 and 1966,[10] with Ariyaratne as the 'convenor' – started to organise *Shramadana* camps in downtrodden rural areas over weekends and on school holidays. The objective always was 'to teach the rural poor how to liberate themselves by working together on projects that would benefit the community'.[11] *Shrama* means energy and *dana* means sharing. The volunteers pledged themselves to economic and spiritual regeneration, according to Buddhist values and principles.

The *Shramadana* camp had two major objectives: experiencing traditional social living based on the principles of sharing, pleasant language, constructive activity and equality; and sharing labour to complete a physical task that satisfies a long felt community need. Furthermore, the camps always also had a strong educational component that was actualised during the family gatherings that accompanied the process. For example:

- A mass education programme was set in place where the history of the village, their habitual customs and beliefs, their problems and aspirations were readily discussed.
- Relevant questions from great religious teachers and other great men and women were read and explained.

- Song and dance items were intermixed with serious discussions regarding community, national and international problems.
- Family get-togethers were held daily; here one could see the rare sight of a university professor seated on a mat with an illiterate villager.

Reflecting on the significance of the *Shramadana* process, Macy concluded: 'I came to believe that Shramadana's distinctive contribution to grassroots development lies in the way it combines physical work with town meetings'.[12]

In 1967, Ariyaratne decided to test the validity of the approach by initiating the Hundred Villages Development Scheme in some of the most impoverished of Sri Lanka's 23,000 villages. 'Under this plan, Sarvodaya selected one hundred villages across the countries and organised *shramdana* and *gramadaya* (village awakening or village development in each). This campaign served as a laboratory for refining the village-development techniques that Sarvodaya would employ in thousands of villages in the next few years'.[13] The scheme was successful. What began with one village has expanded to about 15,000 (of a total of 38,000) Sri Lankan villages in 2012 that are directly or indirectly involved, making up a huge proportion of Sri Lanka's population. Sarvodaya estimates that a total of 11 million Sri Lankan's have directly benefited by at least one of the movement's programmes. Such an extensive engagement with about one-third of the entire population of Sri Lanka, required the building up of a potent organisation. As in 2012, the total workforce of Sarvodaya counts almost 1,800 staff.

Sarvodaya's vision of a 'village society' gets often criticised as utopian or naïve. However, Bond argues that:

> viewed from a socially engaged Buddhist perspective, Sarvodaya's use of the vision reflects a good understanding of what is needed to build a society around humanistic and spiritual values. Sarvodaya does not seek a return to the past ... it seeks to orient society to values such as spirituality, equality, simplicity, and conservation. Sarvodaya envisions a network of village democracies where people are free to live in a way that fulfils their human potential and awakens them spiritually to pursue the Dharmic path.[14]

Sarvodaya's articulation of how it seeks to develop an entire society – bottom-up and in an integrated fashion – is perhaps its greatest contribution to the field of human development – and for the Developmental University to come. Moving to Round 3, we are now ready to delve deeper into this unique developmental combination of education, research, catalysation and social activism.

Round 3 – Society: Articulating and demonstrating a new approach to development, for Sri Lanka and the world

Overview
Ariyaratne's aspiration was nothing other than to:

> redefine development based on our 'Eastern' values. We wanted to go to the people and learn from them while working with them. We wanted to discover the types of techniques and methodologies of development that were most suitable to the rural situation. We wanted to

study and experiment on the most suitable institutional arrangements for our village people. Above all we wanted to generate a people's force from the bottom-up, which would bring to focus that tradition and modernity could be given a new dimension. We drew on Gandhi, but our greatest source of ideological strength was drawn from Buddha's teachings. We also wanted to give a new meaning and purpose to education.[15]

Such a bottom-up, experience-based co-evolutionary way of revisiting development gradually led to Sarvodaya's distinct approach. Against the advice of the economic planners, Ariyaratne set out to build a 'righteous' as opposed to 'industrial' society. What then is that?

In Buddhist terms, the 'revolution of rising expectations' associated with an industrial society, involves people suffering and extinguishing their insight into the true nature of things: impermanent (*anicca*), harmful (*dukkha*), and devoid of any essence (*anatta*). In other words, through conventional development, as per modernisation, a traditionally unindustrialised region is integrated into a modern industrial one. From then on the economic relationships in such a region would depend not so much on timely rains and mutual cooperation among farmers but, as is indeed ever more so today, on the ups and downs of the stock exchange in commercial centres which the average farmer will never have the chance to see.

In that context, Sri Lanka's Sarvodaya does not ask what has to be done to overcome the growth crisis and the distributive problems of a national economy. Instead it begins, for Ariyaratne, with a Buddhist definition of man and an insight into the causes of his suffering. According to Buddhist doctrine, the illusion of permanence, craving for existence, and violent competition to realise one's identity through material acquisition, are the real causes of underdevelopment. Such a 'Buddhist definition of man' led to the formulation of 10 basic needs that provide guidance for all of Sarvodaya's development work.

Table 14.2 Awakening through meeting the 10 basic needs

The focus of Sarvodaya development work (Source: Sarvodaya)

1.	A clean and beautiful environment
2.	Clean drinking water
3.	Adequate supply of clothing
4.	Adequate and balanced nutrition
5.	Simple housing
6.	Basic health care
7.	Basic communications facilities
8.	A minimal supply of energy
9.	Holistic education
10.	Satisfaction of spiritual and cultural needs

Development activities related to the 10 basic needs range from capacity building in the community, early childhood development, community health, relief and rehabilitation, village development, infrastructure projects, environment and biodiversity, communication projects, development of integrated education, applied research and projects in relation to peace and conflict resolution.

Sarvodaya workers believe that they have a universal message: the history of mankind need not founder on the insanities of private capitalism or the hypocrisies of totalitarian Communism, since Sarvodaya offers a third alternative. What then is the process that Sarvodaya developed to realise such an alternative to development? Like concentric circles, Sarvodaya understands development as an inside-out process, gradually evolving through the following six so-called 'levels of awakening': individual, family, village, urban, nation, and world. This can be seen as a further elaboration of our own distinction between self, organisation, society, Uni-Versity. We shall now introduce four of the six levels of awakening in more detail, which serve to underpin, unlike purely individual education, a Developmental University, which is individually and collectively oriented.

Self-awakening ('paurushodaya'): Sarvodaya as building of a new person

It is the chief premise of the Sarvodaya Movement that the notion of development can only be meaningful in terms of human fulfilment. While this fulfilment involves the production and consumption of goods, it entails a great deal more – such as the unfolding of potential for wisdom and compassion. Though present conditions neither reflect nor encourage this potential, it is real and can be awakened. In the concept of Dharma – specific to Hinduism and Buddhism – this awakening to one's true nature is the ultimate goal of existence. Since *udaya* means awakening, and *sarva* means all, entire or total, the movement's name is given a dual meaning. In addition to the awakening of everybody, it denotes the awakening of the total human personality. As Joanna Macy observed:

> The transformation of personality – the 'building of a new person' – is presented as the chief aim of the Movement. Ariyaratne consistently stresses this, declaring that 'the chief objective of Sarvodaya is personality awakening' – that is, 'with the effort of the individual as well as with help from others, to improve oneself to the highest level of well-being.[16]

For us, as is now becoming evident, this is the authentic starting point of a Developmental University.

Implicit in this goal is the belief that a root problem of poverty is a sense of powerlessness. While most modern planners would view the goal of spiritual awakening as idealistic and irrelevant, the Sarvodaya Movement sees any development programme as unrealistic which does not recognise and alleviate the psychological impotence gripping the rural poor. Sarvodaya believes that by tapping the innermost beliefs and values, one can awaken people to their *swashkati* (personal power) and *janashkati* (collective or people's power).

Rahnema stressed exactly this point, stating:

> When one studies some of the significant grassroots movements of recent times (for example, the Swadhyaya in India, the Sarvodaya in Sri Lanka), which seem to have followed the Gandhian path, it is apparent that a dimension has emerged out of the people's art of resistance (both

at a group and individual levels) that requires a much more attentive reading. I call this the dimension of the inner world ....[17]

Toward the end of his *Post-Development Reader*, Rahnema declares the end of conventional development and offers, however, a number of 'signposts' towards a new development future. For him, Sarvodaya provides one of such signposts, in particular through its emphasis on the need to begin development processes with individuals attending to their own self-development to bring about 'right action' on a personal level: 'This way of being has firm roots in the traditions of resistance by the weak. In these traditions, 'right action' involving others starts always as a personal work on oneself'.[18]

Sarvodaya sees individual awakening taking place, not in monastic solitude, but in social, economic and political interaction. While many capitalists and Marxists take spiritual goals to be private quests, Sarvodaya's process of awakening pulls one headlong into the 'real' world and into the Movement's multifaceted programmes for health, food, education and productive enterprise. These programmes are undertaken because people's basic material needs must be met if they are to develop their potential. In other words: one cannot listen to the Dharma on an empty stomach!

Furthermore, in working together to meet their needs, people gain wisdom about the interdependence of life. This is important to Buddhists, for whom the interconnectedness and relativity of all phenomena is clearly evident. Indeed, 'dependent co-arising' is central to their doctrine. Because reality is seen systemically, each and every act is deemed to have an effect on everything else. A Sarvodaya worker learns to understand intellectually and to experience spiritually the interrelationship that exists between different manifestations of the living world. One's personal awakening (*purushodaya*) is integral to the awakening of one's family (*kutumbodaya*), one's village (*gramodaya*), one's city (*nagarodaya*) and all play an integral role in the awakening of one's country (*deshodaya*) and the world (*vishvodaya*). That leads us to the next layer of village awakening.

Gram Swaraj: Local awakening and economic emancipation
Gram swaraj signifies the liberation of the village through the creation of grassroots economic and social programmes, alongside a raising of consciousness. Each *Sarvodaya* 'Village' goes through the following five levels of awakening, towards village self-governance:

- *Stage 1:* Inquiry from the village and organisation of an introductory *Shramadana* camp for the village, during which problems are analysed together and needs identified.
- *Stage 2:* Establishment of various groups (children's, youngsters, mothers' and farmers' groups), construction of a child development centre, and training of staff.
- *Stage 3:* Programme for meeting the basic needs and setting up institutions (including the founding of the Sarvodaya Shramadana Society, which is responsible for the village's development initiatives).
- *Stage 4:* Measures to produce income and employment; establishment of complete self-reliance and self-financing.
- *Stage 5:* Support for other village communities, which includes sharing of some financial profits.

For Katherine Marshall – a long-term former World Bank scholar and Senior Fellow at the Berkeley Center for Religion, Peace and World Affairs – who has researched Sarvodaya extensively, this approach 'clearly echoes the Gandhian model of sustainability'.[19]

To achieve maximum coverage of the country, the process is designed in such a way that several villages are always grouped around a pioneering village that has already reached the fifth stage.

To provide some examples of what village economic rebuilding activities comprise of: today there are 670 Sarvodaya village financial centres, run by the villagers themselves, and 3,000 villages with finance programmes supported by SEEDS (Sarvodaya Economic Enterprise Development Services), Sarvodaya's financial arm, altogether providing for economic empowerment and self-reliance. Moreover, Sarvodaya is in the process of setting up its own Development Bank, serving half a million people with loans and savings. It also facilitates the establishment of regional telecentres to service 'decentralised people-centred development' through the use of modern information and communications technology (ICT).

Thereby, Sarvodaya gradually developed a *'dharmic* citizenry', so to speak, aiming to generate a cultural-spiritual revolution to build up a *dharmic* civil society. In other words, because people at the grass roots are trapped between oppressive state and market forces, Sarvodaya seeks to liberate the grass roots from both.

Sarvodaya's leaders have long argued that the colonial powers destroyed the traditional horizontal axis of village power in order to build up a vertical axis of governmental hierarchy, a pattern that postcolonial governments have continued. From Sarvodaya's perspective, the recent waves of globalisation and modernisation have further reinforced the hierarchical structures by imposing a layer of economic and consumerist oppression on top of the subjugation of people by the government hierarchy. Sarvodaya has been intent, over five decades, on showing the people of Sri Lanka how to rebuild a *dharmic* civil society, in order to progress toward enlightenment. We now turn to societal awakening.

Deshodaya: National awakening and political liberation

Simultaneously, Sarvodaya has been involved at a national level in facilitating a process of political liberation, a community-based participatory democracy, beginning from the grassroots that parallels and builds upon the economic liberation that has begun with the village finance programmes and banks. Power is thus transferred from the elites to the lowest possible level, leading to village self-determination.

Sarvodaya established a Deshodaya organisation in 2001 to build up a consensual political culture, devoid of political parties, and to enact a 'new constitution' to establish such a system. Over the past two years (at our time of writing in the latter part of 2012), Sarvodaya has even increased its *deshodaya*-driven efforts significantly. The movement believe that full-fledged *deshodaya* will result when a critical mass of villages reach the stage of *gram swaraj* and the people move to take charge of their own political destiny. Moreover, as Ariyaratne shared with us in a conversation in 2011, when the present economic system collapses, the way will be paved for *deshodaya*.

Given the critical state that Sri Lanka's political system is presently in, with a central government adverse to full-fledged political participation across all ethnic groups, Sarvodaya regards it as one of its major current foci to develop through its *deshodaya* activities a more mature democracy, stabilised through checks and balances and supported by responsible citizenship of a maximum number of Sri Lankans. The movement's intense efforts are led by Ariyaratne himself, now over 80 years old, together with his son Vinya Ariyaratne. We finally turn from societal to global awakening.

Vishodaya: World awakening

Perhaps the most significant theme that Sarvodaya seeks to contribute to the global dialogue is that of development based on spirituality and spiritual consciousness. Although Sarvodaya has aimed for a balanced development that integrates social, economic, political and spiritual elements, the key to its integrated system is spirituality. In essence, Sarvodaya is a spiritual movement that seeks social justice and development, culminating in a social revolution. Sarvodaya evokes Gandhian and Buddhist values to orient society towards spirituality, equality, simplicity and conservation. These are the alternatives they propose to the violent paradigm of global materialism and consumerism that threatened to undermine cultural values and bring social and environmental chaos to the world.

Emphasising the importance of the spiritual aspect, Ariyaratne continuously directs the attention to the implicit, rather than the explicit qualities and outcome of Sarvodaya's work:

> *My story is not so much in what Sarvodaya, as an organisation, does to start, nurture, and support businesses. It is the overall philosophy that says we need to create and nurture what I would call a psychosocial and spiritual 'infrastructure' as a basis for economic development and business strategies. I have always said – and Sarvodaya's philosophy and practice have demonstrated – that if we focus on earning money and 'doing business' before establishing the values orientation, which encompasses kindness, compassionate action, altruistic joy, and equanimity, we will find that people get into conflict over money. To be frank, that sharing that makes the difference is the giving, not the 'I want my share'. Does this approach set us up to resent wealth? No, it should not, because if we are sufficiently detached from material and transitory things we don't overly concern ourselves with getting, keeping and protecting what we have.*[20]

Integrated levels and dimensions of awakening

Cultivating a critical mass of spiritual consciousness as its core dimension over the course of 50 years, Sarvodaya has always sought to develop six dimensions of awakening in parallel: spiritual, moral, cultural, social, economic and political. In addition, the six awakening levels from self to world and the six dimensions of awakening are complemented, in interdependent form, by three core programme areas: social, economic and technological empowerment. Awakening levels, dimensions of awakening and programme areas, altogether, form the core ingredients of Sarvodaya's integrated development architecture (see Figure 14.1).

It is this integrated model that also provides the foundation for Round 4, to which we now turn.

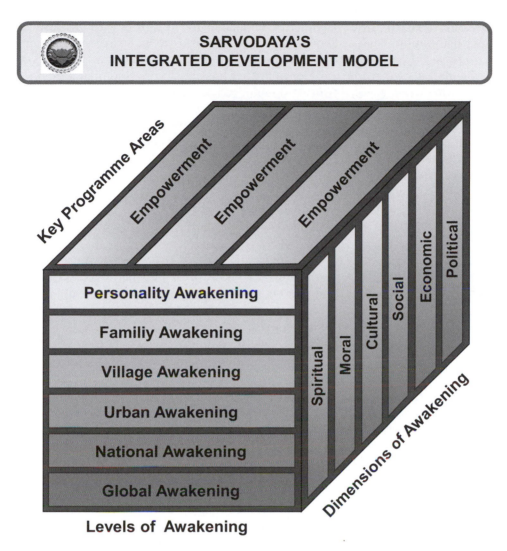

SARVODAYA'S INTEGRATED DEVELOPMENT MODEL

Key Programme Areas

Empowerment

Empowerment

Empowerment

Personality Awakening

Familiy Awakening

Village Awakening

Urban Awakening

National Awakening

Global Awakening

Levels of Awakening

Spiritual

Moral

Cultural

Social

Economic

Political

Dimensions of Awakening

Figure 14.1 Sarvodaya's approach to Integrated Development

Round 4 – Towards the Sarvodaya Developmental University

Sarvodaya entering a new phase in its own evolution
Sarvodaya is currently undergoing a transition phase. In the first five decades of its existence, Sarvodaya was primarily focused on development work according to the needs of Sri Lanka's villages. Nowadays, however, Sarvodaya has shifted to empower communities to express, autonomously, their particular needs towards government. The core reasons for this shift in perspective are the following: firstly, many of the most urgent development needs of the rural communities had by now been catered for; secondly, in its attempt to tighten its grip on the country, the national government has increasingly taken control

over the supply part of the development agenda, refusing to partner with established civil society organisations such as Sarvodaya; thirdly – and to some degree arising from the first two reasons – Sarvodaya sees its future role strongly oriented towards education and societal consciousness rising, in order to further leverage its developmental orientation, locally if not also on a global scale. It thereby, as an organisation, intends to follow the same developmental pattern it promotes within society. How?

Sarvodaya, in its early days, had been primarily driven by the vision of its founder. Thereafter such vision and drive also came from his own family and an ever-growing community of co-workers. For decades the core focus of the Sarvodaya Community's work was on the community level, promoting village self-governance. With an outreach in over 15,000 villages, Sarvodaya, 50 years since its inception, is now not only concerned with moving from a community-village level to a national level (*deshodaya*), but also to transform itself into a sound and lasting foundation for a 'self-sustaining people's movement'.

Responding innovatively to these inner and outer challenges, Sarvodaya is undergoing intensive organisational changes. While Sarvodaya in the past had been very much in the centre of the developmental movement it spearheaded, thereby being a 'centre-centric movement', it sees itself now becoming a catalytic force within a network, hence advancing towards a 'network-centric movement'.

As a network-centric movement, Sarvodaya's main interdependent tasks for the next decades would be:

- *Stimulating Political Awakening (deshodaya):* Supporting villages in moving from self-governance to becoming active agents of responsible democratic self-determination and political participation on a national level; this task would need to be underpinned by
- *Promoting Macro-Developmental Alternatives:* Shaping and providing alternatives on a macro level, politically and economically, suitable to Sri Lanka's societal and cultural context, leading to a sustainable society; to respond adequately to tasks of such magnitude, Sarvodaya needs to gradually set up a
- *Co-Evolving a Developmental University:* Such a university would build on the profound Sarvodayan developmental impulse that has come before, to now design and implement innovative educational-developmental processes and programmes, that can drive, support and stimulate the agenda of national (and global) awakening, as well as the development of economic and political macro alternatives.

When we met with Dr A.T. Ariyaratne and his son Dr Vinya Ariyaratne for the first time in 2009, we immediately began to explore how Sarvodaya's approach could be translated into an 'education with a difference'. Given the strong philosophical, conceptual and practical overlapping of Sarvodaya's integrated approach to development and Trans4m's own integral orientation – to enterprise and economics on the one hand, research and development on the other – we saw each other almost instantaneously as natural partners. From that moment onwards we began to interact closely with Vinya Ariyaratne, who had already done significant groundwork through the establishment of the Sarvodaya Institute for Higher Learning at Bandaragama. For him, education – as can be seen from the basic needs Table 14.2 earlier – has always been a core pillar of the Sarvodaya ideology and he sees it as a 'process of awareness and consciousness that moves individuals and communities to understand the dynamics of social development, and participate in the process of improving their own well being'.[21] It was in this spirit that a Sarvodaya Development University was to be institutionally and programmatically conceived.

The vision for a Sarvodaya Developmental University as a major catalyst for the holistic development of communities, society and the world

From the very outset it was clear, that the envisioned university would need to authentically build on the foundations that Sarvodaya had laid in the past decades. It would hence have to be a higher learning institution that would directly serve the – spiritual, moral, economic, political and ecological – development needs of Sri Lanka's communities, thereby building on existing cultural and community-based capacities and knowledge which Sarvodaya had hitherto tapped and further 'awakened'.

In addition, it would naturally build on and make use of Sarvodaya's existing extensive village network and infrastructure, thereby being fully embedded within Sri Lankan society. That would enable the university to authentically contribute to societal awakening at large. Besides its strong rural and societal rooting, however, the Sarvodaya Developmental University would seek to connect and cross-pollinate with other community-based development initiatives all over the world – thereby also reflecting the universal philosophy of Sarvodaya.

Therefore, the Sarvodaya Developmental University is to be seen not only as a local initiative, but also as a cornerstone in a transculturally based global movement for integrated development of self, community and society that purposefully activates – rather than just acknowledges – the world's rich cultural diversity, thereby supporting the balanced and peaceful co-evolution of all cultures.

At the core of the Sarvodaya Developmental University would be its integrated approach to development – combining an inner directed (consciousness-raising) and outer directed (political and economic) approach to development. Transformational research and education processes would need to be designed (a) for groups and communities instead of merely for individuals, and (b) to generate relevant local knowledge that, applied, leads to tangible contributions to communities' most burning issues and desires.

Finally, the Sarvodaya Developmental University would – in the double sense of its name – also be a vital source for the renewal of Sarvodaya itself, and hence be seen as the main catalyst for Sarvodaya's transformation towards a 'self-sustaining people's movement'.

In the process of designing the Sarvodaya Developmental University – evolved and evoked out of its journey so far – it became ever more clear, that such a university, at least to some significant degree, already existed – albeit only implicitly. A close look at Sarvodaya, its processes, structures, institutions and networks, reveals, that it could already be called a 'Development University' – indeed, it is, and has always been, a learning institution for an entire nation. What is missing, though, is to make this implicit design explicit, articulate its underlying processes and frame it in developmental curricula, research and educational programmes and, ultimately, in an institution, designed to leverage its existing knowledge and achievements.

In other words: from the early days of Sarvodaya, its approach was essentially learning-by-doing, harnessing the knowledge and skills available within the community. Sarvodaya is now of the view that its future educational services need to be developed at greater depth and over a wider range, that is beyond 'on-the-job learning' to cope with immediate problems. People should experiment and learn to solve their own problems but they need to be assisted through transformative research and educational processes. Thereby, the Sarvodaya Developmental University seeks to build up a knowledge foundation that serves as an alternative paradigm for socioeconomic development paradigm for Sri Lankan villages and can simultaneously contribute to the socioeconomic renewal of the country as a whole.

Towards the realisation of the Sarvodaya Developmental University: From implicit existence to explicit articulation

Reviewing Sarvodaya's existing structure and network, one notices that Sarvodaya's primary education and knowledge basis is embedded in about 3,000 villages: All of them have registered Sarvodaya Shramadana Societies fostering village self-governance programmes. They are the core knowledge carriers and community linkage points for future university. In addition, Sarvodaya has built up a vast network of community-based learning institutions all over the country, through which it reaches out to about one-third of the Sri Lankan population. Among them are:

*   main campus – the Development Education Institute Bandaragama;
*   further development education institutes, e.g. in Avissawella, Anuradhapura, Tanamalvila, Kegalla, Palletalawinna, Saturukondan, Trincomalee;
*   multipurpose community centres, e.g. in Kalutara (Lagoswatte), Balapitiya, Ambalangoda;
*   various education farms, e.g. Padaviya Farm, Wellawaya Farm, Saliyapura Farm.

While each entity works largely independently they could become part of a loosely knit interdependent network of educational units associated with the university. Across these units, one finds many areas of expertise, which will be further developed and expanded within the university as a whole. Among them are: environment; agriculture; child development; women empowerment and gender; appropriate technology; community health; disaster mitigation and risk reduction; art and culture; information and communication technology; enterprise development and economic empowerment; peace and good governance; as well as spiritual development. These would need to be further evolved with the formal academic disciplines in each area, by maintaining the transdisciplinary perspective required to address complex problems in communities and society. To further consolidate knowledge and optimise resources, units with particular areas of expertise will be grouped in clusters, such as an agriculture and an environmental cluster. Such clusters would need to be woven into Sarvodaya's overall integrated development model (see Figure 14.1 earlier). This structure enables the Sarvodaya Developmental University to operate in a very decentralised and yet integrated way, and to develop and direct expertise according to particular local needs.

Outlook

While design, concretisation and preparation of the Sarvodaya Developmental University is well on the way, the actual set up may still take a number of years. Not only is Sarvodaya facing an extremely complex and inhibiting political environment together with severe constraints of financial funding, its evolved focus on 'national awakening' (*deshodaya*) is also of gigantic scale. However, the determination to ultimately give rise to a Sarvodaya Developmental University is clearly apparent. Though the final name of this university may be quite different, there is no doubt of its orientation towards the development of entire communities and of society as a whole along a set of evolutionary stages: from self to nation, and ultimately to the world at large. The concluding Table 14.3 sums up the four-round trajectory of Sarvodaya.

Table 14.3 Sarvodaya in Sri Lanka: Catalysing societal development	
Integral Development	**An 'Eastern' case for Integral Development (summary)**
Round 1: **Self-Development** Formative *Grounding*	*Awakening A.T. Ariyaratne* • Deeply steeped in Buddhism, Sri Lanka's main religion: highly self-reflective personality, able to link original spiritual thought and action • Belief that awakening starts with the self and the courage to develop one's inner power • Began his career as a teacher at Buddhist college • Strongly influenced by Gandhi's emphasis on village self-governance as a means to develop a whole society • Personally grounded in systematic attitude adjustment in which negative states such as hatred, greed, and delusion are transformed into positive social orientations through meditative self-training
Round 2: **Organisational Development** Reformative *Emergence*	*Awakened Sarvodaya Shramadana movement* • Emerged out of an educational-development project (Ariyaratne with his students) • Based on a 'synthetic ideology': a fusion of Buddhism, Gandhian thinking and universal sources • Oriented as a non-violent revolution towards the creation of a Sarvodaya social order which will ensure the total awakening of human personalities, human families, village communities, urban communities, national community and the world community • Rooted in Shramadana (= sharing of energy) processes: participatory development activities co-evolving villagers and urban development agents • Designed as a co-learning organisation – the initiative sharing its knowledge continuously, based on real-life experiences

Table 14.3 Continued	
Integral Development	**An 'Eastern' case for Integral Development (summary)**
Round 3: **Societal Development** Newly normative *Navigation*	*Awakening of All: Awakening the Nation* • Focus on developing a 'righteous' rather than an 'industrial' society • Reaches through self-governance programmes to over 15,000 Villages • Impact on all spheres of life: agriculture, education, disaster management, ethnic reconciliation, etc. • Developed and articulated a new Integrated Development approach, integrating rounds (self to world) and dimensions (economic to spiritual) of development through key programmes • Engaged in training and educational programmes, plus research projects
Round 4: **Integrating Uni-Versity** Full transformative *Effect*	*Emergent Sarvodaya Developmental University* • Instigating individual and community-based research and educational programmes at undergraduate and postgraduate levels geared towards Integral Development as a means to develop a whole society • Involving processes for total awakening of human personalities, families, village communities, urban communities, national community and the world • Spanning spiritual, moral, cultural, political, economic, ecological disciplines • Oriented toward political, economic and technological empowerment in Sri Lanka, in the broader context of Asia and the world as a whole

We now turn from the hugely illustrative case of Sarvodaya to its Indian counterpart Om Creations. Albeit more recent in origin, and not quite as expansive in nature and scope, it is a case full of developmental (Uni-Versity) potential.

THE CASE OF OM CREATIONS AND THE EVOLUTION TOWARDS AN 'INCLUSIVE INDIA'

Introduction

With Om Creations we are introducing a second case story that is focused on one particular developmental issue in holistic fashion: the meaningful integration of mentally disabled – which the organisation terms 'specially abled' – women into Indian society. Om Creations provides a nurturing learning and productive environment, in which such women can not only strengthen their sense of self-worth, but also demonstrate to society their ability to positively contribute to it. The case shows, how the integrated, spiritual and evolutionary outlook to life of Om Creation's founder Dr Radhike Khanna has led to the development of an integrated organisation, that itself became a catalyst for societal evolution in India. Finally, the following story intimates how such a self-organisational-societal journey is incrementally providing the ingredients for what we coin a Developmental University.

Round 1 – Self: Following her bliss – The heroine's journey of Rhadike Khanna

When one meets Dr Radhike Khanna for the first time, one quickly notices the fruitful (and, for us, integral) balance between a warm and open heart, a reflective, intuitive and spiritual approach to life, a sharp and vibrant mind, and a will and ability to 'make things happen'. Having been a 'free spirit' with a tendency to independent thinking already in her childhood, Khanna, born in 1963 into an affluent family from Amritsar, decided – initially against the will of her family – to turn down the conventional role of a married woman that was reserved for most of her female peers in the conservative India of the 1980s. By choosing 'the road less travelled',[22] Khanna embarked, in the terms of the renowned mythologist Joseph Campbell on 'The Hero's – or indeed Heroine's – Journey' (⇨11). Consciously engaging with the difficulties of living as an independent woman in India, and fighting the cause of one of the least privileged groups in society, Khanna had to win many inner and outer battles. For Campbell, the hero's (in this case, heroine's) journey ends with her return to society, where she uses the insights she gained during her journey for the betterment of society.

Hence Khanna's was not a decision for personal freedom alone; it became a decision to engage in the liberation of women in general, and in particular on behalf of those who were considered as the most 'unwanted', who were the most 'hidden' from their communities. The mentally disabled women Khanna was to dedicate her life's work to, were, and still often are, condemned to a life outside the Indian society, with no rights, no freedom, no voice. As a catalyst for societal consciousness, Khanna and her organisation have brought this fundamental injustice to the consciousness of Indian society. Through Om Creation's example, society is confronted with the following questions: How do we (dis-)value and how are we dealing with our disabled members? How do we deal with disabled women in particular? And what is the value that such people can bring to everyone's life, if they are allowed to bring their own inner richness to society and to thereby make a valuable contribution?

Radhike Khanna has been giving such disabled women a voice. Perhaps that was one of the instinctive reasons why she chose the name 'Om Creations' for her organisation, with *Om* being the original sound of creation, the primary voice of an awakened consciousness. Indeed, for Joseph Campbell, Om is a truly integral, multifaceted sound, capturing the entire creational cycle that underlies all life. For him, OM, composed out of the three vowels A – U or O – M signifies the rising of a new sound (A), the full maturation of the sound (U or O), and the decline and its ultimate disappearance (M). But Campbell insists that there is a fourth element, that of silence that lies between the ending of one sound, and the beginning of a new.[23] For the new (A) to rise, one needs to be able to listen deeply into the silence underlying all sound. Such an understanding of OM reminds us of the cosmologies, that we encountered, for example, in Central Africa (⇨7), that depicted the human life cycle as mirrored in the cycle of the sun with its four phases: sunrise in the morning, the full ascendance of the sun by midday, and the setting of the sun in the evening, followed by its disappearance in the night.

As we shall soon see in Round 2, Radhike Khanna was able to translate her own integral personality, and the 'integral sound' of her organisation's name into an integral enterprise design.

Before Khanna, however, was to set up Om Creations, she knew that she had to learn everything possible on how effective help to mentally disabled women could be provided. She underwent as a result an intensive course of studies, culminating with her PhD in Special Education.

Round 2 – Organisation: Om Creations as an integral enterprise

Om Creations was founded in 1991 as a trust for developmentally challenged, 'specially abled' women. The organisation is 'run on the conviction that with professional training and support, women born with Down syndrome and other mental disabilities can imbibe professional skills and become productive contributors to society',[24] which includes, Radhike Khanna emphasises, the simple act of paying taxes. Through her vision she sees mentally challenged women and men – within and through a supportive environment – earning a sustainable livelihood and becoming responsible citizens.

Khanna founded Om Creations when she was 28 years old, just hours before she was to be engaged. While the engagement never led to a marriage, Om Creations flourished as her 'vocational marriage partner'. Perhaps it was destined to happen, as the name *Radhike* is derived from an old Sanskrit term meaning 'successful' and 'prosperous'.

Located in Mumbai's Mahalaxmi area, and strongly supported by Tata Group, one of India's most eminent corporations, Om Creations employs today around 70 specially abled women. They produce 'unique items in three departments – Om Foods, Om Visual Arts & Crafts and Om Flowers – all of which are sold in the Om Creations shop as well as other retail outlets through exhibitions, website and private orders'.[25]

The women entrusted to Om Creations earn between 2,000 and 6,000 Indian Rupees a month. Besides enabling them to become economically self-sufficient, Om Creations also looks after the physical and mental well-being of all its women. In addition to Om Creations, Khanna had also founded another charitable trust for mentally challenged boys, called *Shradda*.

From an early stage, Om Creations understood itself as an educational-developmental institution, which is underpinned by its close partnership with the S.P. Jain Sadhana School, also located in Mumbai. Khanna has known the Sadhana School from her early university days. Studying textile design at Mumbai's Sophia Polytechnic, Khanna almost coincidentally started to work part-time for Sadhana. The Sadhana School is a nationally and internationally acknowledged 'resource centre for training persons with special needs, as well as updating teachers in effective methodologies'.[26] The school praises itself for being the only centre in the world offering five-year polytechnic courses to the mentally challenged young adult and guaranteeing employment. The school's vision is not only to help the mentally challenged, 'specially abled' individual to learn to adjust to the world but more 'to become a useful member of the human community, independent and self-sufficient, with a contribution to make to society'.[27] It is about helping them to realise their full potential. This is Sadhana School's main objective. As its second objective it aims 'to be a support system for the families of the mentally challenged students'. The third objective is to encourage special educators 'in planning innovative programmes, which are flexible in nature so as to cater to the needs of each child and allow individual creativity to spring forth'.[28] In order to stick to its innovative educational-developmental programme, the school does not accept government grants, as this would oblige it to follow a set schedule.[29]

Om Creations employs almost exclusively graduates from Sadhana School, and all graduates of Sadhana are absorbed by either Om Creations or Shradda. Over time, the Om Creations and Sadhana co-developed the Sadhana Suyojan educational programme to build capacities, designed to evolve each child's level of learning, starting from its particular level of disability. Through studying latest brain research, Radhike Khanna came to the realisation that the brain can grow at any age. With this conviction, each beneficiary is given intense personal attention to help her developing her full potential. What does that mean?

Khanna and her staff are always looking simultaneously at the inner and outer potential of each woman as well as of the organisation as a whole. Such a dialectic perspective is, for Khanna, deeply steeped in Hindu philosophy that regards the creative interplay of the immaterial and material, the spiritual and physical as the core feature of life. This dialectic is also mirrored in the name of the organisation, with *Om* representing the immaterial, spiritual world and 'Creations' the material, physical world. Furthermore, Khanna believes in the Hindu principle, that it is the spiritual domain, expressed through energy, that is underlying and permeating all material aspects of life, be they economic, environmental or social. In a way, the spiritual (*Om*) is the deeper reality, out of which all matter (Creations) arises, and to which it returns.

While choosing a core term of Hindu religion as the lead element of the organisation's name, Khanna, however, does not confine her spiritual orientation to Hinduism alone. Rather, she readily acknowledges her belief in universal unity underlying all religions, indeed all creation. It is this particular openness for learning from people from all walks of life and from all cultures, that Khanna seeks to cultivate within Om Creations, thereby allowing, in her terms, 'creative energy' to flow freely through the organisation. Infact, Khanna shared with us, that she sees one of her main tasks to resolve 'energy blockages' within the organisation. Thereby she is guided by her intuition that, to her, is one of her greatest personal strengths. In resolving energy blockages, Khanna sees her contribution in bringing about the 'new order' that she feels is required in our day and age. In her own words: 'I know that a new order can be created as we individually break down our psychological barriers and gain inner freedom. I have been putting a lot of energy into building the capacity of my teams, so that their personal growth coincides with the growth of the organisation'.[30]

Recently, Rishab Khanna – a young development economist, organisational developer and nephew of Radhike – has researched the organisational model underlying Om Creations. He chose to employ Trans4m's approach to an Integral Enterprise[31] for his analysis of the transformational functioning of the organisation. The Integral Enterprise, that is later described in some detail (⇨20), looks at the five core functions of an enterprise in an integrated manner, and in the process evolves each function, so it, firstly, dynamically integrates the three rounds of self, organisation and society and, secondly, fosters transfunctional interaction. Thereby, it stimulates the ongoing evolution of an organisation towards ever-growing dynamic balance between all of its functions. In that process, the core functions of the enterprise are transformed as follows:

* marketing into community building;
* human resources into conscious evolution;
* operations into knowledge creation;
* finance into sustainable development;
* corporate strategy into strategic renewal (as the central, integrating function).

In his own analysis, Rishab Khanna built on the original concept, and adapted it creatively to the specific context of Om Creations. In Figure 14.2 we illustrate, in summary, the outcome of Khanna's research.

The role of the transformative leader within an Integral Enterprise is to support the continuous, constructive interaction between all of its functions. Such an interaction always has a balancing and a dynamic aspect at the same time. For Radhike Khanna as the leading force behind Om Creations, the image of the Integral Enterprise reflects her in the centre (see Figure 14.2) – not on top as in conventional leadership frameworks – enabling the free flow of creative energy throughout the organisation.

Altogether, Om Creations has come a long remarkable way, and one can expect even more development in future. In a recent (2012) workshop attended by all employees, staff and beneficiaries expressed their future vision and dream for the organisation with

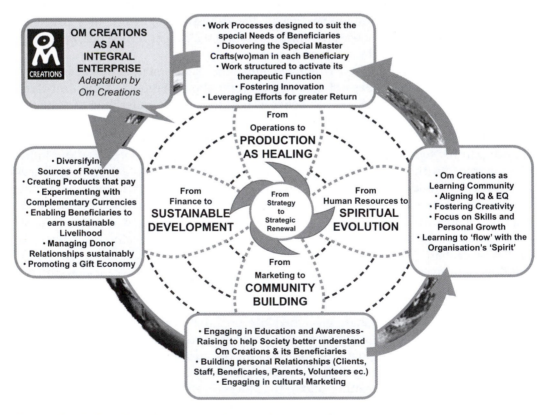

Figure 14.2 Om Creations as an Integral Enterprise

the following terms: 'Quality, joy, global, capacity building, child-centric, increase in production, happiness with young adults, team work, care for young adults, create an Om Creations Centre'.[32]

For Radhike Khanna, her major concern is now shifting towards ensuring Om Creations' long-term sustainability so that the women in its care continue to have a sustainable livelihood. Furthermore, she would like to enable Om Creation's beneficiaries to be looked after once they can't work any longer at Om Creations due to health or ageing. Khanna is now considering seriously the construction of residential premises for disabled women – and also one for men – on a piece of land recently entrusted to Om Creation by the parents of one of their women.

Certainly, such premises would add to Om Creations' overall sustainability. But Khanna is equally concerned with the society at large, and how Om Creation's work can sustainably catalyse the transformation of public awareness in India with regard to women and men with disabilities, in particular mental disabilities.

Round 3 – Society: Om Creation as an evolutionary catalyst for awareness creation and organisational innovation in India and beyond

Though being still a relatively small organisation, Om Creations has undergone remarkable achievements.

Society, a leading popular magazine in India recently proclaimed: 'From being an NGO that aimed at empowering mentally challenged and disabled women, Om Creations has grown to be the only brand for mental retardation and for children with cognitive delays'.[33]

On a societal level, we see two distinct achievements that were catalysed by Om Creation: the first has to do with awareness creation of both the plight and potential of hitherto marginalised, mentally disabled women, the second has to do with innovating and articulating an approach towards a, what we would call, spiritually driven and integrated 'education-development-activist-organisation'. We now elaborate on both achievements in more detail.

Firstly, Om Creations has been a path breaker for integrating mentally disabled women and men into specially designed work processes, thereby enabling such women and men to live a life in dignity and earn (or at least significantly contributing to earning) a sustainable livelihood for themselves. Doing so, Om Creations demonstrates the unique qualities that people with mental disabilities have, and showcases their capacity to productively contribute to society. The impact: not only a major cause of injustice is addressed, but also society as a whole becomes enriched. In this regard, Om Creations can be regarded as a major evolutionary catalyst.

Secondly, Om Creations has articulated – in practice, and subsequently also in theory – a new organisational model. As Figure 14.2 has illustrated, it has not only creatively evolved and integrated the major functions of an organisation, it has also built into the organisation a strong educational-developmental character. The latter is expressed through the close cooperation with the Sadhana School, and through the focus on continuous education of the entrusted women and men. While from the outside an organisation with an activist focus, from the inside it is clearly a 'healing institution'. It contributes not only to healing wounded individuals psyches through bringing new confidence and dignity into the lives of mentally disabled women and men, it also contributes to healing a psychic split in society. Indeed Indian society, for a long period, did not want to see and engage with any kind of disability. Through Om Creations, a space is created in which society can witness and learn the mutual enrichment (and peaceful co-evolution) of physically and mentally able and disabled people. Finally, Om Creations contributes to healing the divide between the spiritual and the material, in that it enables both qualities to co-evolve.

How can these achievements be fully actualised in the fourth and final round of Integral Development?

Round 4 – Towards the next evolutionary step – a developmental venture

Until recently, Om Creations has been doing its groundbreaking work almost intuitively naturally. Yes, there was a great deal of systematic management and financial ingenuity behind it. And yes, in more recent years Om Creations and its founder have increasingly been acknowledged for their outstanding achievements, for example with the Sadguru Gnanananda National Award (2002), India's National Award (2005), the Woman of the Year Award (2008) and the NCPEDP-Shell Helen Keller Award (2008).

However, until recently the underlying uniqueness of the organisation had not been sufficiently articulated in a way that it could, firstly, inform and inspire other organisations, secondly, be used as a case story in educational and research contexts and thirdly, and in our context most significantly, that it could be further evolved into a veritable Developmental University. What do we mean by such a university?

Based on what we have learnt from this case, we consider Om Creations as more than 'just' a developmental enterprise. Much more, it holds the potential of becoming a Developmental University, with a particular focus on mentally disabled women and men. Its strong focus on education and development, its close-knit, almost symbiotic cooperation with the Sadhana School, its organisational model that simultaneously fosters individual and societal transformation constitute crucial ingredients for such a Developmental University.

Khanna laments that training and educational institutions for mentally disabled young adults are woefully short in India. In a recent television interview on BBC World News India she argued that India needs to create more infrastructure for social inclusion.[34] Furthermore, she criticises the way in which the enormous mainstreaming of administration and education processes in India over the past few years, makes it ever more difficult to integrate children with special needs into the education system. From her experience, children with special needs can't excel in heavily standardised systems. Rather, they require specially trained teachers. The awareness for such requirements, however, is not yet developed in India. Khanna goes on to state, that much of the population in India still entertains false assumptions about mentally challenged people, their capacities and their potential to be educated. That often includes the parents and other close family members of such children.

The recent research on Om Creations undertaken by Rishab Khanna was an important start with a view to laying a more systematic foundation for leveraging the knowledge basis and practical experience of the organisation in the future. As a next step, he seeks to convince Indian universities to integrate the Om Creations case into their curricula.

Together with Trans4m, Om Creations, through Radhike and Rishab Khanna, have explored opportunities to evolve the integral organisational model further in order to make the next evolutionary step – research and education-wise – towards a Developmental University for mentally disabled young adults more explicit. We also began, jointly, to envision concrete steps how to make such a new form of university a reality. Indeed, it would be the first university for the 'specially abled'. Naturally, the actualisation of such a vision requires careful consideration and enormous ingenuity. But it has the potential to leverage Om Creations' existing achievements dramatically – thereby responding to the huge task, that, according to Radhike Khanna, India still has to face in order to fully integrate her mentally disabled citizens as worthy and respected members into society.

In the concluding Table 14.4 we sum up the journey-to-date of Radhike Khanna and Om Creations towards the further evolution of India into an inclusive society.

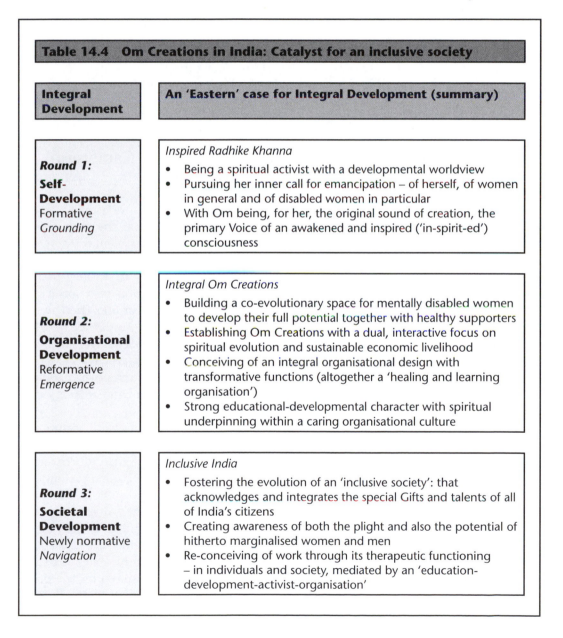

Table 14.4 Om Creations in India: Catalyst for an inclusive society

Integral Development	An 'Eastern' case for Integral Development (summary)
Round 1: **Self-Development** Formative *Grounding*	*Inspired Radhike Khanna* • Being a spiritual activist with a developmental worldview • Pursuing her inner call for emancipation – of herself, of women in general and of disabled women in particular • With Om being, for her, the original sound of creation, the primary Voice of an awakened and inspired ('in-spirit-ed') consciousness
Round 2: **Organisational Development** Reformative *Emergence*	*Integral Om Creations* • Building a co-evolutionary space for mentally disabled women to develop their full potential together with healthy supporters • Establishing Om Creations with a dual, interactive focus on spiritual evolution and sustainable economic livelihood • Conceiving of an integral organisational design with transformative functions (altogether a 'healing and learning organisation') • Strong educational-developmental character with spiritual underpinning within a caring organisational culture
Round 3: **Societal Development** Newly normative *Navigation*	*Inclusive India* • Fostering the evolution of an 'inclusive society': that acknowledges and integrates the special Gifts and talents of all of India's citizens • Creating awareness of both the plight and also the potential of hitherto marginalised women and men • Re-conceiving of work through its therapeutic functioning – in individuals and society, mediated by an 'education-development-activist-organisation'

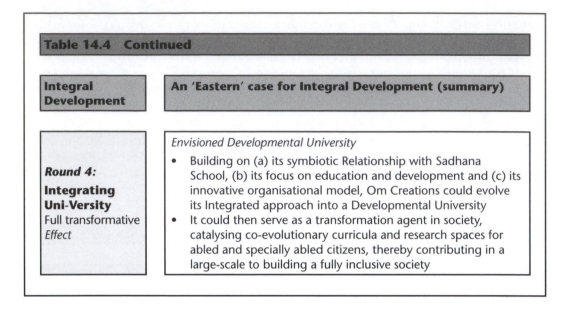

Table 14.4 Continued	
Integral Development	**An 'Eastern' case for Integral Development (summary)**
Round 4: **Integrating Uni-Versity** Full transformative *Effect*	*Envisioned Developmental University* • Building on (a) its symbiotic Relationship with Sadhana School, (b) its focus on education and development and (c) its innovative organisational model, Om Creations could evolve its Integrated approach into a Developmental University • It could then serve as a transformation agent in society, catalysing co-evolutionary curricula and research spaces for abled and specially abled citizens, thereby contributing in a large-scale to building a fully inclusive society

14.3   Actualising the Developmental University: Catalysing Societal Learning and Consciousness-Raising

In this 'Eastern' realm, the Integral Development journey builds up towards what we call a Developmental University. In the two cases introduced in this chapter, the evolutionary path points towards such a new type of educational entity. A Developmental University shows, as does the Communiversity, a strong rooting in context and community, but has, as its main focus, societal learning and consciousness-raising. To achieve that, it purposefully builds on and activates the cultural-spiritual foundation of a society. In the process it renews this societal foundation and generates new meaning. Thereby, the Developmental University also helps the society to evolve, or – in Aurobindo's (⇨13), Gebser's (⇨13) or Beck's (⇨4) terms – to advance to a new evolutionary stage. Further, a Developmental University addresses particular imbalances (e.g. in Sarvodaya's case, for example, the urban-rural divide in Sri Lanka or that between wealth and poverty), and it fosters co-evolution of hitherto imbalanced aspects of society (e.g. in Om Creations' case a healthy co-evolution between abled and disabled citizens).

The Developmental University is transformatively oriented toward scaling up the already impressive cultural-spiritual renewal work that we have seen in the cases presented. Furthermore, as in the Communiversity case, the Developmental University can serve to complement, if not altogether reform the existing educational system of a society.

We have come across other cases of emergent Developmental Universities. The FUNDAEC University Center for Rural Well-Being in Colombia, founded by the Iranian physicist and development activist Farzam Arbab[35] and few of his university colleagues, is one of such examples. It contains strong aspects of both, a Communiversity as well as a Developmental University. Its strong spiritual foundation was inspired by the Bahai Movement. FUNDAEC 'dedicated itself to the creation of the University for Integral Development ... which was defined as a social space in which the inhabitants of a given region learn to choose and walk the paths of their own communities' development'.[36] For Gustavo Correa, one of the co-founders of FUNDAEC, the basic idea behind the initiative is 'spiritual transformation'. SAT (System for Tutorial Learning), FUNDAEC's major educational programme, won the Best Practice Award by the Club of Budapest in 2002 for its achievements in providing high school education and training to more than 50,000 people living in rural areas in Latin America and was coined by German physicist and eco-philosopher Ernst Ulrich von Weizsäcker as 'the best educatory project of the time'.[37]

At this concluding stage, we would like to give a glimpse of just one further case, Aravind Eye Care System, as it showcases in highly condensed form all rounds of the 'Eastern' realm, with each round organically unfolding out of the previous one. Furthermore, this case is powerfully informed by one of the seminal thinkers that we introduced in the previous chapter: the Indian sage Sri Aurobindo (⇨13). His teachings inspired the foundation of the eye care hospital Aravind in South India, dubbed 'the World's greatest business case for compassion'.[38] It was founded in Madurai in 1976 by the late Dr Govindappa Venkataswamy (called Dr V. by his colleagues and patients), an eye doctor and disciple of Aurobindo. Aravind's vision is directly informed by the spiritual teachings of Aurobindo. In fact, Dr V. made Aurobindo's emphasis on 'being of service for society' and on the 'co-evolution of self and society' the foundation of his organisation and called it even after the sage, Aravind being another name for Aurobindo. Aravind's reason for being is to fight 'unnecessary blindness' in India. By addressing a major health problem in India, Aravind not only provides eyesight for hundreds of thousands, but it literally 'gives life'. The life expectancy of blind people is – due to their unemployability – dramatically less than that of people with normal eyesight. Underlying Aravind is a unique 'high volume high quality business model', that allows for everyone who needs eye care to receive treatment from Aravind. That model kept the organisation remarkably resilient in financial terms. The core logic is that everyone who is financially able pays for his or her own surgery plus for two more surgeries, covering those who can contribute nothing or little.

Thereby an Aravind that is committed to 'providing compassionate and high quality eye care for all'[39] can provide surgery to those 70 per cent of its patients that could otherwise not afford treatment. Over time, Aravind grew into the largest cataract facility in the world. Its eye surgeons undertake about 2,000 surgeries each per year, compared to the national average of about 220 per ophthalmologist. Community outreach is the backbone of Aravind. The organisation sends experts with so-called mobile village units into local communities to examine villagers with eye problems. Patients are then brought with Aravind's buses to one of its numerous eye-clinics all over the country. The organisational model of Aravind has been replicated all over the world, and a case on Aravind is by now mandatory reading for every MBA student at Harvard Business School.[40]

For Dr V. the key reason for Aravind's success remains its spiritual orientation that turned the organisation in servicing the evolution of society as a whole. 'Holding a vision for each person's highest potential, whether employee, patient or partner, shaped Aravind's model in important ways'.[41] For DrV., each and every day began and ended at the hospital with a visit to the meditation room for, what he called 'a silent talk with God'. He stated:

When I go to meditation room at the hospital every morning, I ask God that I be a better tool, a receptacle for the divine force. We can all serve humanity in our normal professional lives by being more generous and less selfish in what we do. You don't have to be a 'religious' person to serve God. You serve God by serving humanity.[42]

In summary, like Sarvodaya and Om Creations, Aravind embodies multiple characteristics: to begin with, Aravind is a spiritual-activist organisation that provides eye treatments for millions 'serving everyone from penniless farmers to the president';[43] further, it has addressed a major health problem in India that came along with immense poverty, marginalisation and exclusion, and has hence contributed to the raising of societal consciousness; and it has done all that through a spiritually inspired, evolved business model.

Finally – and so important for our approach to development – Aravind shows clearly features of an emergent Developmental University. According to Dr V., the direct dealing with local communities and the intense experience that doctors and nurses gain through treating very large numbers of patients has turned Aravind into a veritable educational institution. In time, Aravind had also undertaken its own research, and came up with a number of technological innovations, all catered to deliver low cost eye surgery to anybody. All the knowledge acquired, however, has never been kept hidden. Quite the contrary, Aravind shared its knowledge widely, even with competitors. For Aravind 'giving away secrets of its success is part of the organisational DNA'.[44] The organisation sees itself as an 'open source model' – ready to develop, educate, share, and hence co-evolve with anyone who is aligned with the greater vision of restoring eyesight and/or of serving humanity.

Based on the theory and practice introduced in this 'Eastern' realm, we summarise in the following Table 14.5 core steps, highlighting how we can work towards the establishment of a Developmental University to fully actualise this realm.

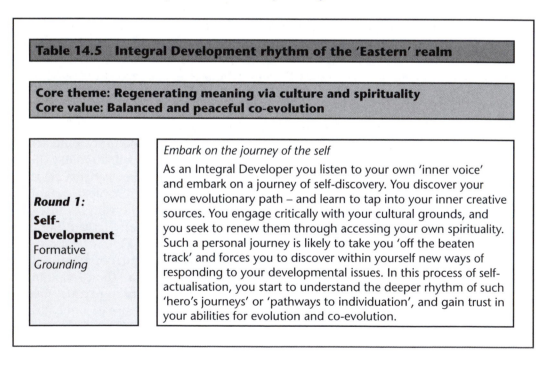

Table 14.5   Integral Development rhythm of the 'Eastern' realm

Core theme: Regenerating meaning via culture and spirituality
Core value: Balanced and peaceful co-evolution

Round 1: **Self- Development** *Formative Grounding*	*Embark on the journey of the self* As an Integral Developer you listen to your own 'inner voice' and embark on a journey of self-discovery. You discover your own evolutionary path – and learn to tap into your inner creative sources. You engage critically with your cultural grounds, and you seek to renew them through accessing your own spirituality. Such a personal journey is likely to take you 'off the beaten track' and forces you to discover within yourself new ways of responding to your developmental issues. In this process of self-actualisation, you start to understand the deeper rhythm of such 'hero's journeys' or 'pathways to individuation', and gain trust in your abilities for evolution and co-evolution.

Table 14.5   Continued

Core theme: Regenerating meaning via culture and spirituality
Core value: Balanced and peaceful co-evolution

Round 2: **Organisational Development** Reformative *Emergence*	*Foster organisational co-evolution* Through your 'inner journey', you now bridge – through deeply dialogical interactions – personal development tasks with those of a group or entire organisation. The insights of your personal journey are translated into a spiritual foundation for the organisation. In that process, the creative, inner sources of the organisation are activated (e.g. through myth, storytelling, alignment of organisational culture with individual and societal aims) and the organisation's 'spirit of co-evolution' is gradually released.
Round 3: **Societal Development** Newly normative *Navigation*	*Catalyse evolutionary stages in society* The organisation, seeing itself as an agent of evolution, now contributes – in theory and action – to the further evolution of society as a whole – culturally and spiritually, technologically and economically. It is able to share through its own example new ways of cultural and spiritual being in society, helping society to progress 'without loss of soul'. The organisation fosters not only the co-evolution of self and society, but it also builds ever-larger co-evolutionary partnership-networks. Finally, it is engaging in research and development geared towards societal evolution.
Round 4: **Integrating Uni-Versity** Full transformative *Effect*	*Fully actualise the 'Eastern' realm through a Developmental University* Now, these new developmental norms and practice are translated into research and educational programmes, straddling relevant disciplines, serving to codify and then effect large-scale societal transformation. These programmes and processes are then institutionalised, in this 'Eastern' context through a 'Developmental University'. Such a university has a primary focus on healing divides in society to enable co-evolution, societal learning and consciousness-raising. courses for individual students are a by-product rather than its reason for being: renewing the cultural-spiritual basis of society through integral innovation, serving also to further evolve the developmental enterprise with which it is aligned.

14.4   Integration: Integral Development as Balanced and Peaceful Co-Evolution

INTEGRATING THE 'EASTERN' ROUND 4

We have learned in this Uni-Versity round about the need to evolve a potent 'developmental vehicle' out of the first three rounds, that facilitates the interconnection of the development journeys experienced for self, organisation and society. In this 'Eastern' case we called such a transformational entity a 'Developmental University'. We invite you to use the following summarising Table 14.6 to reflect back on this fourth and final round of the 'Eastern' realm. Record your own thoughts and prospective actions in order to bring about such a Developmental University.

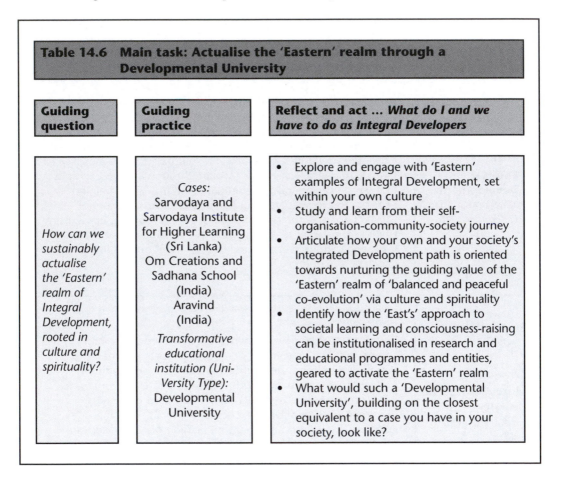

Table 14.6	Main task: Actualise the 'Eastern' realm through a Developmental University	
Guiding question	**Guiding practice**	**Reflect and act ... *What do I and we have to do as Integral Developers***
How can we sustainably actualise the 'Eastern' realm of Integral Development, rooted in culture and spirituality?	*Cases:* Sarvodaya and Sarvodaya Institute for Higher Learning (Sri Lanka) Om Creations and Sadhana School (India) Aravind (India) *Transformative educational institution (Uni-Versity Type):* Developmental University	• Explore and engage with 'Eastern' examples of Integral Development, set within your own culture • Study and learn from their self-organisation-community-society journey • Articulate how your own and your society's Integrated Development path is oriented towards nurturing the guiding value of the 'Eastern' realm of 'balanced and peaceful co-evolution' via culture and spirituality • Identify how the 'East's' approach to societal learning and consciousness-raising can be institutionalised in research and educational programmes and entities, geared to activate the 'Eastern' realm • What would such a 'Developmental University', building on the closest equivalent to a case you have in your society, look like?

INTEGRATING THE FULL 'EASTERN' REALM

We are now ready to conclude this 'Eastern' culture-and-spirituality-driven perspective on Integral Development.

Over the course of the past four chapters you have worked yourself progressively through the four rounds of self (Round 1), organisation (Round 2), society (Round 3), and, finally, through integrated educational-and-developmental practice (Round 4). In this final round, you were presented with the case stories of Sarvodaya in Sri Lanka and Om Creations in India – as well as, in brief, with Aravind in India – that altogether serve to illustrate the organic and authentic interweaving and integration of the first three rounds.

All of these cases are representations, at least to a significant degree, of a Developmental University, the culmination of the 'Eastern' realm. The Developmental University's particular focus is on societal learning and consciousness-raising. It stands for a new type of university that purposefully builds on and activates the cultural-spiritual foundation of a society, building upon a prior, developmental enterprise or initiative. In the process, it helps the society to advance to a new evolutionary stage. Further, a Developmental University addresses particular imbalances and it fosters co-evolution between hitherto imbalanced aspects of society. We regard it as the main objective of this 'Eastern' part of the Integral Developer's (or Developers') journey to give rise to such Developmental Universities.

The Developmental University is our approach to an 'education with a difference' that helps to fully actualise this 'Eastern' realm of Integral Development. It represents the most relevant institution for societal learning and collective consciousness-raising, and for realising the theme of the 'Eastern' realm: regenerating meaning via culture and spirituality.

We introduced the 'Eastern' Developmental University *after* the 'Southern' Communiversity, as we see a vital need to first restore life in nature and community (the 'Southern' theme of the Communiversity), before societal learning and broadly based consciousness-raising can effectively take place. Sarvodaya's evolution from village self-governance to societal awakening illustrates this argument to a large extent, though it is still to formalise its Developmental University. Yet, such processes don't happen in linear fashion. As we progress further through this book, we will see, that each realm, initially, has to pursue its own authentic actualisation. Ultimately, however, each realm would need to interact with all other realms, to gradually enable the integration of all realms. While each realm's actualising Uni-Versity type illustrates already some kind of integral inclination (notice for example, Chinyika's and Sarvodaya's integrated development approaches), we shall finally reach out to create a prospective university that integrates all realms, thereby being fully integral. That is the integral university, towards which we progressively work and that we shall sketch out in the concluding chapter (⇨25).

The 'Eastern' realm holds vital keys to the realisation of a fully integral university. Not only is this realm the most ignored and neglected in most development work, it is also the one that has the greatest demands with regards to personal evolution. Embarking on the inner journey, getting in touch with one's inner voice and power, and evolving out of it new perspectives on personal, organisational, communal and societal development may well be the single most decisive factor for the enormous task ahead. The individual journeys of Dr A.T. Ariyaratne of Sarvodaya, Dr Radhike Khanna of Om Creations and Dr Govindappa Venkataswamy of Aravind, the developmental scope of their respective organisations, and the extent of each of their societal reach certainly provide us with a sense of the magnitude of this task.

In the concluding Figure 14.3 we take you once more through the journey of the 'Eastern' realm: we indicate the main developmental tasks of each round; we provide

Your Development Calling & Challenge

	MAIN TASK	GUIDING THEORY / GUIDING PRACTICE	LEARNING AND DEVELOPMENT PROCESSES FOR INTEGRAL DEVELOPMENT – AGENT & AGENCY
G — Round 1: **Self Development** *Formative Grounding*	EMBARK ON THE JOURNEY OF THE SELF	The Hero's Journey (Campbell) The Pathway to Individuation (Jung) The Evolution of the Self (Haeri) Inner Liberation and Freedom (Vivekananda)	• Awaken to the fascinating Mystery of Life • Interpret the Mystery in Order to give Meaning to Life • Unfold, in accordance with yourself, your Culture, and the Universe • Own the Development Shadow – Uncover the Seat of Creativity • Engage in conscious personal Development (e.g. through your Dreams) • Strive simultaneously for inner and outer Knowledge • Evolve from inner-outer Dependence to Interdependence to inner Reliance
E — Round 2: **Organisational Development** *Reformative Emergence*	FOSTER ORGANISATIONAL CO-EVOLUTION	Deep Dialogue (Bohm) Myth, Ritual and Storytelling (Owen) Releasing the Spirit of Organisational Co-evolution (Kaku)	• Engage in creating shared Meaning through deep Dialogue • Discover the Field of Collective Intelligence • Activate the transformative Role of organisational Culture • Engage in the Art of collective Storytelling • Facilitate Transformation through Co-evolution, from basic organisational Survival to alleviating global Imbalance, in public-private Partnership
N — Round 3: **Societal Development** *Normative Navigation*	CATALYSE EVOLUTIONARY STAGES IN SOCIETY	Reconnecting with our Collective Story (van der Post) Co-Evolving towards the Integral Society (Gebser) Co-Evolution of Self & Society (Aurobindo) Development without Loss of Soul (Abt) Transculturation (Mignolo / Anzaldua) Translation (de Sousa Santos) A Culture of Transience (Garg)	• Enter the Story of your Society – Rediscover Origins to move forward • Tune into its evolutionary Story: From magical to integral • Show how the Development of your Self and your Society are linked • Explore the Soul of your Community / Society and its Path to Fulfilment • Reconfigure the Notion of societal Progress in your societal Context • Articulate how your Society can evolve without losing its Soul • Explore how its Consciousness can expand through Transculturation • Elaborate how your Community and Society can evolve by translating in between inner and outer Multiplicity and Diversity • Seek Ways to activate the regenerative Potential of your Society's Culture – by purposefully building on its current State of Transience
E — Round 4: **Integrating Uni-Versity** *Transformative Effect*	ENABLE THE EMERGENCE OF A DEVELOPMENTAL UNIVERSITY	**Cases:** Sarvodaya & Sarvodaya Institute for Higher Learning (Sri Lanka) Om Creations & Sadhana School (India) Aravind (India) **DEVELOPMENTAL UNIVERSITY**	• Explore & engage with 'eastern' Examples of Integral Development, set within your own Culture • Study and learn from their self-organisation-community-society Journey • Articulate how your Development Paths, individually and collectively, are oriented towards nurturing the guiding Value of the 'eastern' Realm of 'balanced & peaceful Co-Evolution' • Identify specifically how the 'East's' Approach to societal Learning and Consciousness Raising can be institutionalised in Research & educational Programs and Entities, geared to activate the 'eastern' Realm • What would such a 'Developmental University' in your Case look like?

Figure 14.3 Releasing the gene-ius of the 'Eastern' realm

an overview of the core thinkers and practitioners that illustrate the nature of each of the four rounds; and we summarise the core developmental challenges that you, your organisation and your community face.

As in all of the four realms, the journey through this 'Eastern' integral realm is not to be understood in linear fashion. However, the composite engagement with the four interconnected rounds and the large variety of relevant thinkers and practitioners is designed to help Integral Developers to build, step by step, a developmental foundation strong enough to make a meaningful contribution to regenerating meaning via culture and spirituality.

We shall now enter the 'Northern' integral realm of science, systems and technology.

References

1   Freire, P. (2000). *Pedagogy of the Oppressed*. London: Continuum.
2   Nyerere, J.K. (1974). *Man and Development*. Dar es Salaam: Oxford University Press, p. 125.
3   Queen, C.S. (1998). The Peace Wheel: Nonviolent Activism in the Buddhist Tradition. In: Smith-Christopher, D.L. *Subverting Hatred*. Maryknoll, NY: Orbis, p. 31.
4   Ruskin, J. (2006). *Unto This Last*. New York: Cosimo.
5   *Sarvodaya Shramadana: Growth of a People's Movement*. Sarvodaya booklet, p. 11.
6   Bond, G.D. (2004). *Buddhism at Work: Community Development, Social Empowerment and the Sarvodaya Movement*. Bloomfield, CT: Kumarian, p. 13.
7   Macy, J. (1983). *Dharma and Development: Religion as a Resource in the Sarvodaya Self-Help Movement*. West Hartfold, CT: Kumarian.
8   Ariyaratne, A.T. (1999). *Buddhist Economics in Practice*. Salisbury, UK: Sarvodaya Support Group, p. 2.
9   Ariyaratne, A.T. (1999). *Buddhist Economics in Practice*. Salisbury, UK: Sarvodaya Support Group.
10 Ariyaratne, A.T. (1970). The Sarvodaya *Shramadana* Movement: Hundred Village Development Scheme. In: *Collected Works* (ed. N. Ratnapala), vol. 1. Moratuwa, Sri Lanka: Sarvodaya Press, p. 58.
11 Bond, G.D. (2004). *Buddhism at Work: Community Development, Social Empowerment and the Sarvodaya Movement*. Bloomfield, CT: Kumarian, p. 18.
12 Macy, J. (1983). *Dharma and Development: Religion as a Resource in the Sarvodaya Self-Help Movement*. West Hartfold, CT: Kumarian, p. 58.
13 Bond, G.D. (2004). *Buddhism at Work: Community Development, Social Empowerment and the Sarvodaya Movement*. Bloomfield, CT: Kumarian, p. 21.
14 Bond, G.D. (2004). *Buddhism at Work: Community Development, Social Empowerment and the Sarvodaya Movement*. Bloomfield, CT: Kumarian, p. 49.
15 Ariyaratne, A.T. (1999). *Buddhist Economics in Practice*. Salisbury, UK: Sarvodaya Support Group.
16 Macy, J. (1983). *Dharma and Development: Religion as a Resource in the Sarvodaya Self-Help Movement*. West Hartfold, CT: Kumarian, p. 32.
17 Rahnema, M. (1997). Towards Post-Development: Searching for Signposts, a New Language and New Paradigms. In: Rahnema, M. and Bawtree, V. (eds), *The Post-Development Reader*. London: Zed, p. 401.

18 Marshall, K. and Van Saanen, M. (2011). *Development and Faith: Where Mind, Heart and Soul Work Together*. Washington, DC: World Bank, p. 120.

19 Rahnema, M. (1997). Towards Post-Development: Searching for Signposts, a New Language and New Paradigms. In: Rahnema, M. and Bawtree, V. (eds), *The Post-Development Reader*. London: Zed, p. 401.

20 Field, L. (2007). *Business and the Buddha: Doing Well by Doing Good*. Boston, MA: Wisdom Publications, p. 78.

21 Ariyaratne, V. (2011). Internal presentation. Unpublished document.

22 Note: 'The road less travelled' is a metaphor the US psychiatrist Scott Peck used for those who follow their own inner path. Peck, S. (2008). *The Road Less Travelled: A New Psychology of Love, Traditional Values and Spiritual Growth*. London: Rider.

23 Campbell, J. (with Bill Moyers) (1988). *The Power of Myth*. New York: Anchor, p. 286.

24 Khanna, R. (2012). *Surging Beyond the Bottom Line: Insights into a Successful, Integral Enterprise*. Bombay: Om Creations Trust, p. 6.

25 Khanna, R. (2012). *Surging Beyond the Bottom Line: Insights into a Successful, Integral Enterprise*. Bombay: Om Creations Trust, p. 6.

26 Sadhana School website. Available at: www.spjsadhana.org / Accessed: 10 September 2012.

27 Sadhana School website. Available at: www.spjsadhana.org / Accessed: 10 September 2012.

28 Mathias, L. and Jain, R. (2008). Mind over Matter. In: *Marwar*, May–June 2008, p. 93.

29 Mathias, L. and Jain, R. (2008). Mind over Matter. In: *Marwar*, May–June 2008, p. 94.

30 Gopalakrishnan, G. and Bakshi, A. (2010). *See Beyond: SPJ Sadhana School Empowering Persons with Special Needs*. Mumbai: Silverpoint Press, p. 46.

31 Lessem, R. and Schieffer, A. (2009). *Transformation Management: Towards the Integral Enterprise*. Farnham: Gower.

32 Khanna, R. (2012). *Surging Beyond the Bottom Line: Insights into a Successful, Integral Enterprise*. Bombay: Om Creations Trust, p. 21.

33 Salokhe, U. (2012). A Woman of Substance. In: *Society*, July 2012, p. 126.

34 BBC World News India, broadcast 9 September 2012.

35 Harper, S. (ed.) (2000). *The Lab, the Temple and the Market: Reflections at the Intersection of Science, Religion and Development*. Ottawa, ON: IDRC.

36 FUNDAEC website. Available at: www.fundaec.org / Accessed: 16 September 2012.

37 *Baha'i inspired education system for the poor of the world honored by the Club of Budapest*. Bahai World News Service, 22 December 2002. Available at: http://news.bahai.org/story/185 / Accessed: 16 September 2012.

38 Metha, P.K. and Shenoy, S. (2011). *Infinite Vision: How Aravind Became the World's Greatest Business Case for Compassion*. San Francisco, CA: Berrett-Koehler.

39 Aravind website. Available at: www.aravind.org / Accessed: 15 September 2012.

40 Kasturi Rangan, V. (1993). *Aravind Eye Hospital, Madurai, India: In Service for Sight*. HBS Premier Case Collection. Boston, MA: Harvard Business School.

41 Metha, P.K. and Shenoy, S. (2011). *Infinite Vision: How Aravind Became the World's Greatest Business Case for Compassion*. San Francisco, CA: Berrett-Koehler, p. 138.

42 Aravind website. Available at: www.aravind.org / Accessed: 15 September 2012.

43 Metha, P.K. and Shenoy, S. (2011). *Infinite Vision: How Aravind Became the World's Greatest Business Case for Compassion*. San Francisco, CA: Berrett-Koehler, Backcover.

44 Metha, P.K. and Shenoy, S. (2011). *Infinite Vision: How Aravind Became the World's Greatest Business Case for Compassion*. San Francisco, CA: Berrett-Koehler, pp. 180ff.

PART **V**

The Northern Realm of Integral Development: Reframing Knowledge via Science, Systems and Technology

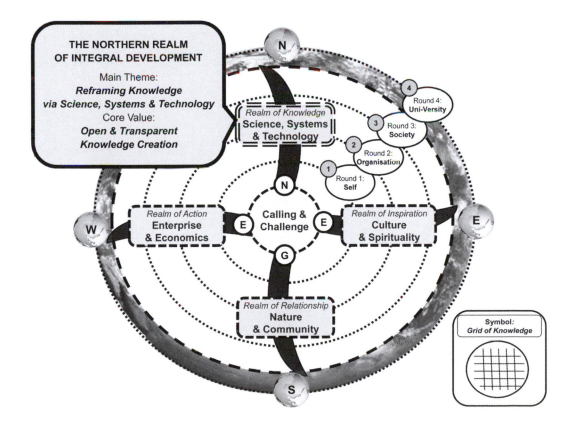

CHAPTER # 15 *Transdisciplinary Learning and Research: A Northern Individual Perspective*

Guiding Questions: How do I learn and research? How do I address my development needs with relevant new knowledge, generated by myself, together with others?

15.1   Orientation

Having reviewed 'Southern' and 'Eastern' developmental realms, we now enter into the first of the two conventionally acknowledged development worlds, that of the 'North', to be followed by that of the 'West'.

The theme of the 'Northern' integral realm is 'reframing knowledge via science, systems and technology'. Again, we start out with the first level of self-development: here we revisit 'research and learning' as our formative means of grounding. On the second level of organisational development, we pursue 'organisational knowledge creation', reformatively emerging out of the prior individual development impulse. What follows on the third level of community and societal development, is the pursuit of a 'knowledge and network society'. This then becomes our 'Northern' navigation. Finally, in this realm of science, systems and technology, we turn to both Mondragon in the Spanish Basque country and to our own prospective African University as our core 'Uni-Versity' cases. Both cases are linked to a reframed 'Research University', as our educational-developmental means of fully actualising the 'Northern' development story.

Why is this fundamental reframing of the established '*North*' necessary? As Integral Developers, we seek to contribute to the creation of new knowledge in a development context. This means that we need to build on the communal and developmental orientations that have come before. In other words, 'Southern' relationship and experience and 'Eastern' inspiration and imagination come before 'Northern' conceptualisation and knowledge creation. We then need a clear understanding how experiences and images are translated into research and learning processes, and how such research and learning are translated into relevant new knowledge that addresses the burning development issues at hand. Thereafter, as we turn to the '*West*', we will need to have in mind how such new knowledge can be applied to practice. Given the unfortunate fact, that little of our education and research seems to address and resolve the major social issues we are facing, we are called upon to look at learning and knowledge creation anew. The Integral Developer is thus invited – now from a 'Northern' perspective – to explore at this individual level the following questions:

- How do I learn and know?
- What do I need to know based on deep reflection on my self and my society, the burning development issues I face, and the natural, communal, spiritual and cultural facets of the development contexts of which I am part?
- How do I address these development needs with relevant new knowledge, generated by myself, together with others?
- What learning models, knowledge creation concepts, forms of research and education, and learning tools can inform me and my context?
- How do I envisage building up my learning and research from an individual to organisational and societal perspective, to begin with in theory and later in practice?

To explore these questions we are initially guided by the American MIT-based educational theorist David Kolb who is particularly recognised for his work on experiential learning. Kolb's learning model has been widely picked up and applied to all kinds of fields and has proven its theoretical strength and practical applicability. With Kolb's help we explore our individual learning styles and learn how our learning styles can evolve during our lifetime. From Kolb's focus on learning, we then move to a model that we ourselves have developed and applied in educational and research programmes: Integral Research. Through the Integral Research model we gain firstly an understanding of how social science research can actually be reinvented in order to truly lead to social innovation. Secondly, the approach invites us to probe into different research paths, that are (a) suitable to our personal/institutional research disposition, (b) adequate to address a particular developmental issue and (c) that lead the researcher all the way from knowledge creation to implementation, from theory to action.

Thus, we see Integral Research as an important addition to our Integral Development toolbox. While Integral Research focuses primarily on social science research and social innovation, we shall look for further inspiration with regards to learning and knowledge creation to the natural sciences. Here, in particular in the fields of biology, neurobiology, quantum physics, systems thinking and cybernetics, we find an enormous wealth of new knowledge that increasingly revolutionises our very understanding of social systems and their functioning – which includes the way how social systems learn, create knowledge, develop and adapt. For this we turn to the Austrian American physicist Fritjof Capra, who has demonstrated already various times his outstanding ability to synthesise and communicate these findings to a wide public. With Kolb, our own work and Capra, we will have made a considerable contribution to a deepened understanding of learning and knowledge creation not only on a personal level, but we will have already received significant pointers how this understanding can also inform us on an organisational, communal and societal level.

15.2   The Learning Cycle: Learning is Development

WHAT DO YOU KNOW ABOUT HOW YOU LEARN?

It may be strange to revisit here what should have been clear to us all along: the way in which we learn. Understanding how we learn, we consider a necessary, scientific precondition for individual as well as organisational and societal development. And yet, though we are schooled from an early age, we often have relatively little knowledge about learning in general and about our personal learning style in particular. It is somehow bizarre that in our formal education, from pre-school to school to university, we not only discover little about how we learn individually, but also how this relates to collective learning. Of course, we may study such individual learning processes in a programme of pedagogy, but even this will be restricted to individual, as opposed to organisational or community based learning.

While our objective in this book is not to fully fill that gap, we nevertheless feel it is important to have at least a reasonable sense of how we learn, individually and collectively, as such an understanding is amongst the most needed qualities of the development agent. This is in particular true in our case, as we are seeking to continuously create new knowledge from the ground up, relevant to a particular context, and at least to a significant degree evolved out of the learnings we generate in a specific development context. Such a primarily inside-out approach is totally different from the typical outside-in approach to economic development, in which preconceived knowledge is merely applied to a context, usually with unsustainable results, as we have argued earlier (⇨3).

THE (INTEGRAL) LEARNING CYCLE OF DAVID KOLB

One of the most helpful introductions into learning in our specific context comes from the American educationist David Kolb, world renowned for the development of his experiential learning theory (ELT), together with his colleague Ron Fry.[1] Like Jung in the case of psychological types (⇨7), Kolb argues that it is our preferred learning style that determines how and what we learn, and also what we rather not learn or even avoid learning.

Kolb acknowledges that his work was strongly inspired by C.G. Jung, but also by the Swiss developmental psychologist and philosopher Jean Piaget and the American psychologist Carl Rogers, one of the founders of humanistic psychology. Furthermore, the experimental orientation of Kolb's approach to learning was heavily influenced by the fathers of Action Research, John Dewey and Kurt Lewin.

Kolb's model works on two levels, as he explains in *Experiential Learning*.[2] The first level is represented by the learning cycle that includes four learning stages that, ideally, progressively build on each other. Table 15.1, on the following page, introduces each of them – and illustrates also the corresponding steps in Jung's typology and in our own transformational process – the GENE-ius – that underlies the Integral Development approach:

Kolb argued that his learning stages are to be seen in circular or even spiralling form. The learner is supposed to engage with the full circle of experiencing, reflecting, thinking and acting. Concrete experiences lead to observations and reflections. These reflections are then assimilated and translated into abstract concepts, which then inform a person's

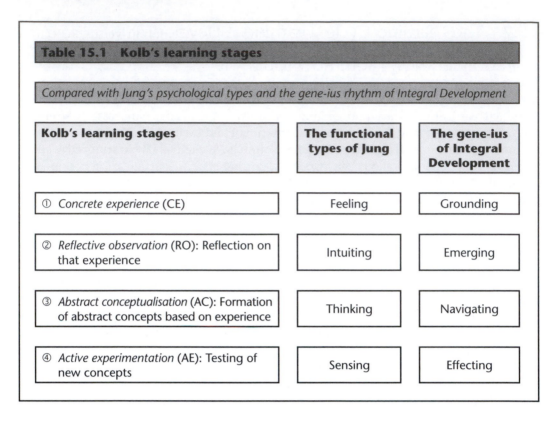

Table 15.1   Kolb's learning stages

Compared with Jung's psychological types and the gene-ius rhythm of Integral Development

Kolb's learning stages	The functional types of Jung	The gene-ius of Integral Development
① Concrete experience (CE)	Feeling	Grounding
② Reflective observation (RO): Reflection on that experience	Intuiting	Emerging
③ Abstract conceptualisation (AC): Formation of abstract concepts based on experience	Thinking	Navigating
④ Active experimentation (AE): Testing of new concepts	Sensing	Effecting

action, where the person actively tests and experiments. This fourth and final step, in turn, enables the creation of new experiences, which makes the cycle start all over and turns it into a spiral.[3]

LEARNING STYLES

The second level of Kolb's model includes a four-type definition of learning styles, each representing the combination of two preferred styles, for which Kolb uses the terms:

- Diverging (CE/RO).
- Assimilating (AC/RO).
- Converging (AC/AE).
- Accommodating (CE/AE).

Whatever influences the choice of style, the learning style preference itself is the product of two pairs of variables, or two separate 'choices' that we make. Again, we are reminded of the polar-opposite nature of the two sets of functional psychological types, distinguished by Jung. Like in Jung's analytical psychology, Kolb presented these two choices with lines of axis, each with 'conflicting' modes at either end:

- Perception Continuum Axis: Concrete Experience CE (feeling) versus Abstract Conceptualisation AC (thinking) – this axis illustrates our emotional response, how we think or feel about a task.

- Processing Continuum Axis: Active Experimentation AE (doing) versus Reflective Observation RO (watching) – this axis illustrates how we approach a task.

A typical way to visualise Kolb's two continua is that the east–west axis depicts the processing continuum, and the north–south axis depicts the perception continuum. In Figure 15.1 we illustrate the four different learning stages, as well as the four learning styles. The learning stages, building on each other, are represented in circular form. Note, that each learning style represents a combination of two lines of axis (continuums). Each style links what Kolb calls the 'dialectically related modes' of 'grasping experience' (doing or watching), and 'transforming experience' (feeling or thinking).

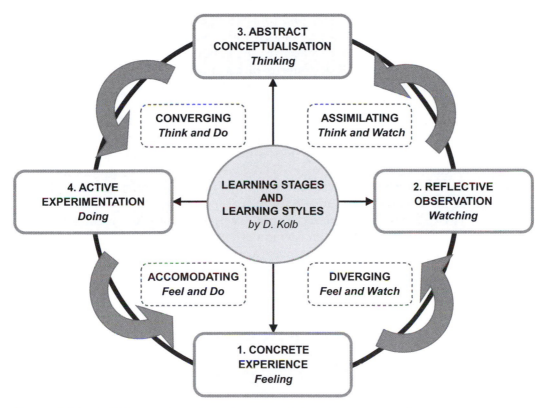

Figure 15.1 Kolb's four learning stages and four learning styles

TOWARDS INTEGRATION: THE THREE DEVELOPMENT PHASES OF A LEARNER

According to Kolb, different people naturally prefer a certain learning style. Various factors influence this preference. One important factor, says Kolb, is the development stage of a learner. In his experiential learning theory model (ELT), Kolb defined three phases of a person's development. He suggests – and that is important for our purpose here – that our tendency to reconcile and successfully integrate the four different learning styles improves as we mature through our development phases.

The development phases that Kolb identified are the following three, whereby we notice a certain resonance with Levinson's life phases (⇨7):

- *Phase 1 = Acquisition:* Birth to adolescence – development of basic abilities and cognitive structures.
- *Phase 2 = Specialisation:* Schooling, early work and personal experiences of adulthood – the development of a particular specialised learning style shaped by social, educational and organisational socialisation.
- *Phase 3 = Integration:* Mid-career through to later life – expression of non-dominant learning style in work and personal life.

LEARNING EQUALS DEVELOPMENT

Kolb argues that learning equals development. The subtitle to his influential book *Experiential Learning* anticipates already this conclusion: *Experience as the Source of Learning and Development.*[4] Starting the learning process with concrete experience, and allowing it to pass through a second phase of reflective observation, we recognise Kolb's approach as a truly integral one. The holistic character of his approach is further emphasised by the potential of a gradual integration of learning styles over the course of our lives. This is an important call for us as Integral Developers to gradually deepen and broaden our learning experiences. Thereby we also strengthen significantly our capacity to create relevant new knowledge – that includes all four realms – for the development issue and context we are dealing with. What we notice though, that much of the work that has been done on learning and learning styles – and here Kolb's approach is no exception – is primarily focusing on the individual. That is mirrored in conventional university designs that emphasise individual education and research.

As much as we have to gain greater clarity on stages, styles and development phases of learning we also desperately need a broader understanding of the methods of knowledge creation that are used. For this exploration we now turn to what we coined Integral Research, which was originally developed for individuals pursuing their research in the social sciences. We will recognise the conceptual resonance between Kolb's four learning styles and stages on the one hand, and Integral Research's four research realms and rhythms on the other. Indeed, at the root of both approaches lie the four psychological types of Jung (⇨7) that themselves can be traced back to profound archetypal structures in human psyche.

15.3   Research for Development: Integral Research to Enable Individual and Societal Transformation

OUR FRUSTRATION WITH SOCIAL SCIENCE RESEARCH

It has been our long-standing passion to conceive of learning and research in a transformational way. Learning, for Kolb as for ourselves, should not primarily be geared toward recipients gaining factual knowledge, but should rather be liberating and transformational, for the individual and, by extension, for their societies. Equally research should not merely lead to yet another all too often irrelevant publication on the library shelf, but should indeed go all the way from theory to action, with the final objective being that of leading to transformation on the ground. In other words, social science research and innovation should generate relevant knowledge to address issues that truly matter in particular social and economic contexts.

Unfortunately, most of social science research that is produced today does not function that way. It is all too exclusively 'Northern', rather than the 'North' and 'West' building on the 'South' and 'East'. The fact that much of it does not lead to social innovation is an important reason for the multitude of severe social problems we are facing today – from an increasing lack of communal cohesion, to inefficient means of conflict resolution, from inappropriate education systems to dysfunctional economic and financial systems. The list is endless. Designing integrally oriented master's and doctoral programmes ourselves – always drawing on participants' burning social issues within their contexts – we started to explore in more depth the underlying reasons for the predicament of today's social science research. During this exploration we received three wake-up-calls, that we then responded to with the development of *Integral Research*[5] – as a contribution to heal this predicament, so to say.

TOWARDS A NEW INTEGRAL RESEARCH PARADIGM: THREE WAKE-UP CALLS

The more we wandered through the all too often desert-like landscapes of social science research, the more we saw emergent pictures of the promised land. It was the following three insights that gave us clues for the renewal of the existing research paradigm:

First Wake-Up Call = Social science research can lead to social innovation: We noticed increasingly that the majority of social researchers are totally oblivious to the rich and diverse portfolio of research methods. Instead, most social science research employs 'Western' (read: American) case studies and survey methods, the latter characteristically using questionnaires and interviews. That's it. These represent, however, only a limited number of research methods, reflecting in particular a pragmatic-experimental and rational-theorising approach to knowledge generation. What we saw as left out were all those more humanistically descriptive and interpretively narrative oriented research methods that could accommodate cultural regions where the predominant way of thinking is different to the Western way. Employing exclusively 'Western' methods almost invariably leads to a stifling lack of originality in research. In Europe and America, we noticed the difficulty students often have to methodologically reach out to other parts of the world and their worldviews; this is a core reason of the reasons for a continuous reinforcement of a one-sided way of knowledge generation.[6] We concluded that a new approach to social science research would have to expose the researcher to culturally appropriate and relevant ways of doing research.

Second Wake-Up Call = We need to overcome our blurred perspective on research method and research methodology: We noticed that much of the literature on social science research confuses research method with research methodology. This phenomenon we witness over and over again also among researchers. While the term 'research method' points towards research techniques (like, e.g., experiment, survey, grounded theory), the term 'research methodology' points towards profound philosophical perspectives (like, e.g. Empiricism, Feminism, Phenomenology, Hermeneutics, Postmodernism, Critical Rationalism). In other words, research methodology is all about challenging, evolving and even revolutionising our view of the world and of our understanding of knowledge and its creation.

Each research methodology then represents an entirely different worldview, and seeing the diversity of these methodologies – or indeed paradigms or philosophies – helps us as researchers to position our own worldview while at the same time not neglecting all other perspectives. Research methodologies, however, are rarely seen in this revolutionary light, and furthermore, they are not purposefully connected with research method, thereby interlinking the more philosophical worldview with a concrete technique to enact the research. We also became aware that whereas Europeans have conceived of most research methodologies, most research methods come from the USA. In a nutshell, philosophy comes from Europe, while pragmatic translation of research comes from the US. The rest of the world has been left out, which leads, again, to a perpetuation of American/European perspectives, and inhibits other perspectives from participating. This is a matter of enormous importance, as the research methodologies and methods that are employed have become a powerful, but almost hidden, vehicle for the cementation of basically a combined European/American worldview. As we explained earlier, any domination is ultimately to the detriment of the dominator as well. A lack of diversity always kills the resilience of a social system and its capacity to adapt.[7] A new Integral Research paradigm would have to not only integrate research method and research methodology in a new way, it would also have to allow the integral researcher to choose more freely from combinations of research methods and methodologies that the whole world has to offer.

Third Wake-Up Call = Research Needs Integration: The third agonising fact that we encountered in social science research is the rift between theory and action. In other words, not only does much of social science research never see the light of active day, but there is also a strong division between highly theoretically oriented social researchers, who are familiar with the depth of research methodologies but are often out of touch with concrete realities on the ground, and those social science researchers who work in more applied ways, but are out of touch with the philosophical roots of their research field. While the former fall short by not having any impact on the ground, the latter fail in contributing to a more radical revision of the underlying philosophy and worldview, which is so important for our time today.

INTEGRAL RESEARCH: A NEWLY EMERGENT RESEARCH PARADIGM

Having received the three wake-up calls and having started to understand the inherent dilemmas in social science research in more depth, we gradually began to develop our approach to *Integral Research and Innovation*. Addressing all of those dilemmas, Integral Research allows the researcher to choose between four (or a combination of two or more) research paths that jointly fulfil the following criteria:

- Integral Research paths reflect different modes of thinking and being (if not from all over the world, at least from all over Europe as well as America).
- Integral Research paths are culturally rooted and relevant to the specific context to which they are applied.
- Integral Research paths interconnect research method and methodology, action and research, thereby stretching over the full trajectory: leading from a burning social issue to transformative action on the ground.

In addition, what became a real discovery for us is that research method would now serve as a starting point and not at an end point of research. We see it as an access point to the research issue and context. That ensures that the research is from the very beginning practically and experientially rooted in a burning social issue on the ground.

WORKING WITH INTEGRAL RESEARCH

Let us have a look at Figure 15.2 through which we provide a summary overview of the Integral Research realms ('Southern', 'Eastern', 'Northern' and 'Western' paths) and rhythms (four trajectories with Levels 1, 2, 3, 4) that we distinguish within each research path:[8]

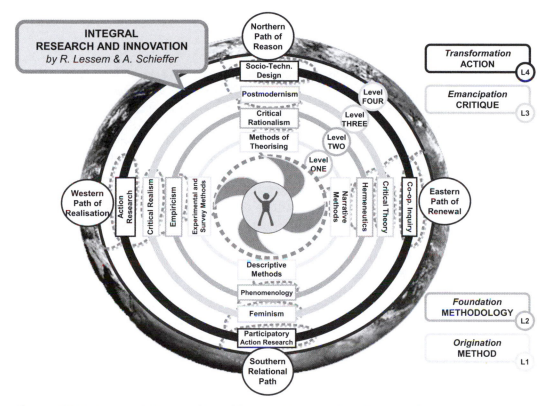

Figure 15.2 Integral Research and innovation model: An overview

According to Integral Research the researcher begins in the centre of the model by reflecting on his or her own personality, his or her burning research issue and desire, specific research context, cultural background, and personal research style. S/he then chooses a research path or even a combination of two or more paths.

Then the research is firstly grounded in a research method (Figure 15.2/Level 1) where the researcher gets really in touch with his or her issue, desire and context. Thereafter the integral researcher gradually builds up a theoretical foundation by applying Level 2 of the research path. On Level 2 he or she lays the foundation for new theory, primarily by working through one of the classical research methodologies, such as Phenomenology, Hermeneutics, Critical Rationalism and Empiricism. This, however, is only a foundation, which then on Level 3 is to be radically challenged, by surfacing the shortcomings of the existing theory base. On this level the researcher works with one of the so-called emancipatory methodologies – such as Feminism, Critical Theory, Postmodernism, or Critical Realism. The radical critique is not merely an intellectual exercise, but is then to be tested in practice through the application of Action Research on Level 4. On Level 4 we distinguish four different types of Action Research methodologies: Participatory Action Research, Cooperative Inquiry, Socio-Technical Design and the Western original form for Action Research.

In conclusion, we start with an active engagement with the context (through applying research method on Level 1) and we end – having built a strong theory basis and developed a radical critique to its shortcomings – with Action Research (Level 4) that leads to transformative results on the ground within the given research context.

APPLICATION OF INTEGRAL RESEARCH

By now quite a number of our masters and doctoral students have applied Integral Research in theory and practice. Bethel University in St Paul in the USA has even made Integral Research a requirement for many of their doctoral classes. Among the most encouraging results was the research of our Zimbabwean master's (and now doctoral) students whose masters research led effectively to a sustainable project that delivered food security for over 100,000 people in rural Zimbabwe (⇨10). Their research was firmly lodged within communal grounds and within Zimbabwe's cultural and societal context. An excellent piece of Integral Research is also embodied in the doctoral work of Sam Rima.[9] His research led him to the development of a theory on Spiritual Capital, and to the subsequent founding of a Movement for the Advancement of Spiritual Capital called MASC. A compelling example from the Middle East is that of Maqbouleh Hammoudeh, who developed through Integral Research a theory on Islamic management[10] that she is now putting into practice in collaboration with her clients through her consulting work in Jordan and the Middle East. Finally, we, through our Trans4m Center for Integral Development in Geneva, have teamed up with Da Vinci Institute in South Africa (⇨18) to apply such an integral approach to research and innovation at undergraduate, masters and doctoral levels.

As Integral Research focuses primarily on the Social Sciences and the Humanities as well as the integration of the two fields, we shall now turn in complementary fashion to the natural sciences, seeking inspiration from a few enlightened natural scientists that have helped to revolutionise our understanding of how social systems learn and generate knowledge. You may notice that while our approach to integral research and innovation has a slight 'North-Western' bias (though in an inclusive, integral way), the work of Capra and his natural science colleagues is more 'North-Eastern' in orientation.

15.4   To Live is to Know: Self-Making as a Key to Human Knowledge Generation

TURNING POINT

With the Austrian-born American physicist Fritjof Capra we turn to a scientist who has achieved almost cult status. Already his first book *The Tao of Physics*[11] became widely recognised. Capra reveals the remarkable similarities between Eastern and Western (primarily Greek) mystical traditions and the findings of twentieth-century physics. However, it was in particular his book *The Turning Point*[12] that articulated in the early 1980s the need for a fundamental paradigm shift across all disciplines. Turning Point also expressed eloquently the flaws of the existing mechanistic Newtonian/Cartesian paradigm. Capra became an influential voice for a whole new movement propagating new ways of thinking, of knowledge creation and of living sustainably on the planet. One of his later works, *The Hidden Connections*,[13] extends the framework of systems theory and complexity theory to social organisms, from international corporations to local communities. It also helps us to realise the importance of 'autopoiesis', when it comes to our understanding of living, learning, knowing and knowledge creation.

AUTOPOEISIS: THE SCIENCE OF SELF-MAKING – AN INVITATION TO THE 'DANCE OF LIFE'

Coming to 'self-making', we turn to the life sciences, in particular chemistry, biology, and ecology. As ecosystems are understood in terms of food webs (networks of organisms) so organisms are viewed by Capra as networks of cells, organs and organ systems, and cells as networks of molecules. Wherever we see life, we see networks. This is the key to the systemic definition of life: living networks continually create, or recreate, themselves by transforming or replacing their components. In this way they undergo continual structural changes while preserving their web-like patterns of organisation.[14]

This dynamic of self-generation was identified as a key characteristic of life by Chilean and French biologists, respectively, Humberto Maturana and Francisco Varela,[15] who gave it the name 'autopoiesis', literally 'self-making'. A theory designed to explain the nature of living systems – such as cells or entire human beings – autopoiesis points to the ability of a living system to recreate itself by itself through dialectical interaction between its structure, mechanism and functioning. According to autopoiesis, any living system is operationally closed, which means that it recreates itself out of itself. In the case of human beings it means that we also create meaning out of ourselves.

Our structure, mechanism and function also define how we interact and consequently conceive of the world. As interaction between living systems is dynamic and continuously changing, so is our self-constructed picture of reality. Thus, reality is a fluid, ever changing process. This process is oriented towards bringing about some kind of stability, harmony and balance between our internal structure, mechanism and function and what we perceive the world to be. It is important to see that we share this ambition for harmony and balance with every living system. As each human being does continuously engage in this process based on his or her particular constitution as well as on the given time and place, so each one of us holds a different part of a larger ever-unfolding truth.

Varela argues that once we fathom the profundity of this insight, we can't but develop humility and respect for the other and his view of the world. Knowing that we continuously create the world through interaction, this perspective also invites us to engage joyfully and playfully in dancing together, thereby making full use of the infinite possibilities that the great dance of life offers us. However, as each living system seeks for balance and harmony, Varela suggests that we use this new perspective on reality and its co-creation, to jointly bring about a world of balance and harmony – for the sake of each and every one of us, for a world worth living – and dancing – in.[16]

EMERGENCE OF ORDER

Most people tend to believe that biological form is determined by a genetic blueprint, and that all the information about cellular processes is passed onto the next generation through DNA when a cell divides and its DNA replicates. This is not at all, Capra asserts, what happens. When a cell reproduces, it passes on not only its genes, but also its membranes, enzymes, organelles, – in short, the whole cellular network.

Detailed studies of the flow of matter and energy through complex systems have resulted in the theory of dissipative structures by Ilya Prigogine and his collaborators. A dissipative structure is an open system that maintains itself, in a state far from equilibrium, yet is nevertheless stable: the same overall structure is maintained in spite of an ongoing flow and change of components. Prigogine chose the term 'dissipative structures' to emphasise the close interplay between structure on the one hand and flow and change (or dissipation) on the other. The dynamics of these dissipative structures specifically include the spontaneous emergence of new forms of order. This spontaneous emergence of order at critical points of instability is one of the most important concepts of the new understanding of life.[17]

It is technically known as self-organisation, analogous to self-making, and is often referred to simply as 'emergence'. It has been recognised as the dynamic origin of development, learning and evolution. In other words, creativity for Capra, the generation of new forms, is a key property of all living systems. Whereas traditionally the study of complexity has been study of complex structures, the focus is now shifting from structures to the processes of their emergence.

TO LIVE IS TO KNOW

As it keeps interacting with its environment a living organism will undergo a series of structural changes, and over time it will form its own individual coupling pathway. Living structure then is always a record of prior development. So is cognition, which is not a representation of an independently existing world, but rather a continual bringing forth of a world through a structure of living. For Maturana and Varela 'to live is to know'. Learning and development are the two sides of the same coin. In the languages of ancient times, both soul and spirit are identified with the metaphor of the breath of life – Sanskrit *atman*, Greek *psyche* and Roman *anima* – all mean both breath and soul. The relationship between mind and brain, then, is that of process and structure.

Primary consciousness arises when cognitive processes are accompanied by basic perceptual, sensory and emotional experience, and is experienced by most mammals. Secondary consciousness, sometimes called 'higher order consciousness', involves self-awareness, which Capra terms 'reflective consciousness'. This involves an ability to hold mental images such as values, beliefs, goals and strategies. This evolutionary stage is central to his work – the extending of the new understanding of life to the social domain.

THE BREATH OF LIFE

This new understanding of life is a systematic understanding, which means that it is based not only on the analysis of molecular structures, but also on the analysis of patterns of relationships among these structures and of the specific processes underlying their formation. As we have seen, the defining characteristic of a living system is not the presence of certain macromolecules, but the process of a self-generating network of metabolic processes.

Similarly, the original meaning of spirit in many ancient philosophical and religious traditions, in the West as well as in the East, is that of the breath of life. Our spiritual moments are those when we feel most intensely alive. Buddhists, according to Capra, refer to this as mental alertness or 'mindfulness'. Spiritual experience, moreover, is an experience of aliveness of mind and body as a unity. This experience of unity, for Capra, transcends not only the separation of body and mind but also the separation of self and world. The central awareness in these spiritual moments is a profound sense of oneness with all, a sense of belonging to the universe as a whole.

The sense of oneness with the natural world is fully borne out by the new scientific conception of life. As we understand how the roots of life reach deep into physics and chemistry, how the unfolding of complexity began long before the formation of the first living cells, and how life has evolved for billions of years by using again and again the same basic patterns and processes, we realise how tightly we are connected with the entire fabric of life. We belong to the universe, we are at home in it, and this experience of belonging can make our lives profoundly meaningful.

FORM TO MEANING

A full understanding of any biological phenomenon, for Capra, must incorporate three perspectives. Take for example the metabolism of a cell. It consists firstly of a network 'form', secondly of chemical reactions or 'processes', which involve the production of the cell's components or, thirdly, 'matter'. Similarly, the phenomenon of emergence (process) is characteristic of dissipative structures (matter), which involve multiple feedback loops (form). When we try to extend the new understanding of life to the social domain, we immediately come up against a bewildering multitude of phenomena – rules of behaviour, values, intentions, goals, strategies, designs, power relations – that play no role in most of the non-human world but are essential to social life. However, these diverse characteristics of social reality all share a basic common feature, which provides a natural link to the systems view of life. Such a systemic understanding is extended into the social domain, for Capra, by adding the perspective of meaning.

The metabolic network of a cell, for example, generates material structures. Some of them become structural components of the network, forming parts of the cell membrane or of other cellular structures. Others are exchanged between the network's modes as carriers of energy or information, or as catalysts of metabolic processes. Social networks too generate material structures – buildings, roads, technologies – that become structural components of the network; and they also produce material goods and artefacts that are exchanged between the network modes. However, the production of material in social networks is quite different from that in biological and ecological networks. The structures are created for a purpose, according to some design, and they embody some meaning. Such meaning is essential to human beings. We continually need to make sense of our outer and inner worlds, find meaning in our environment and in our relationships with other humans, and act according to that meaning. This includes in particular our need to act with a purpose or goal in mind. This brings us onto culture.

THE DYNAMICS OF CULTURE

On the one hand, the network continually generates mental images, thoughts and meaning; on the other hand, it continually coordinates the behaviours of its members. From the complex dynamics and interdependence of these processes emerges the integrated system of values, beliefs and rules of conduct that we associate with the phenomenon of culture. In our time the different meanings of 'culture' that are associated with the active cultivation of the mind coexist with the anthropological use as a distinctive way of life of a people or social group. In addition, the original biological meaning of culture as cultivation continues to be used, as in agriculture.

We discover that culture arises from a complex, highly nonlinear dynamic. It is created by a social network involving multiple feedback loops through which values, beliefs and rules of conduct are continually communicated, modified and sustained. It emerges from a network of communications among individuals; and as it emerges, it produces constraints on their actions. The social network also produces a shared body of knowledge – including information, ideas, skills – that shapes the culture's distinctive way of life. This social network is engaged in communication with a cultural boundary that its members continually recreate and negotiate. The situation is not unlike that of the metabolic network of cell, which continually produces and recreates a boundary – the cell membrane – that confines it and gives it identity.

We are now ready to conclude.

15.5   Integration

We have now come to the end of our individual perspective on reframing knowledge, whereby our integral approach to research, and Kolb's integral orientation towards learning, predominate. Alongside both approaches, we introduced the concept of 'self-organisation', drawn from recent developments in the natural sciences, which complements the integral approach.

What is distinctive about these 'ways of knowing' is not only the fact that they explicitly draw on different worldviews, but also that such individual learning and research can be aligned with organisational, and ultimately societal approaches to knowledge creation. Before we move on to illustrate this, we invite you again to engage – through reflection and prospective action – with the guiding questions and theory presented in this chapter, as well as with the major development activities derived thereof for yourself.

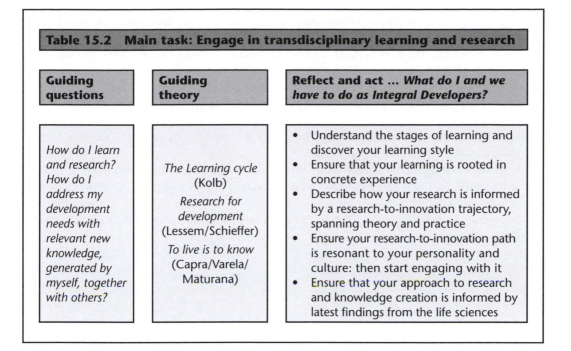

Table 15.2 Main task: Engage in transdisciplinary learning and research

Guiding questions	Guiding theory	Reflect and act ... *What do I and we have to do as Integral Developers?*
How do I learn and research? How do I address my development needs with relevant new knowledge, generated by myself, together with others?	*The Learning cycle* (Kolb) *Research for development* (Lessem/Schieffer) *To live is to know* (Capra/Varela/Maturana)	• Understand the stages of learning and discover your learning style • Ensure that your learning is rooted in concrete experience • Describe how your research is informed by a research-to-innovation trajectory, spanning theory and practice • Ensure your research-to-innovation path is resonant to your personality and culture: then start engaging with it • Ensure that your approach to research and knowledge creation is informed by latest findings from the life sciences

We now turn from self to organisation within this 'Northern' integral realm.

References

1   Kolb, D.A. and Fry, R. (1975). Toward an Applied Theory of Experiential Learning. In: C. Cooper (ed.), *Theories of Group Process*. London: John Wiley.

2   Kolb, D. (1983). *Experiential Learning: Experience as the Source of Learning and Development*. New York: Financial Times/Prentice Hall.

3   Business Balls website. Available at: www.businessballs.com/kolblearningstyles.htm / Accessed: 18 May 2012.

4   Kolb, D. (1983). *Experiential Learning: Experience as the Source of Learning and Development*. New York: Financial Times / Prentice Hall.

5   Lessem, R. and Schieffer, A. (2010). *Integral Research and Innovation: Transforming Enterprise and Society*. Farnham: Gower.

6   Lessem, R. and Schieffer, A. (2010). *Integral Research and Innovation: Transforming Enterprise and Society*. Farnham: Gower, pp. 12f.

7   Lessem, R. and Schieffer, A. (2010). *Integral Research and Innovation: Transforming Enterprise and Society*. Farnham: Gower, pp. 13f.

8   Lessem, R. and Schieffer, A. (2010). *Integral Research and Innovation: Transforming Enterprise and Society*. Farnham: Gower, p. 57.

9   Rima, S.D. (2013). *Spiritual Capital: A Moral Core for Social and Economic Justice*. Farnham: Gower.

10 Hammoudeh, M. (2012). *Islamic Values and Management Practice: Quality and Transformation in the Arab World*. Farnham: Gower.

11   Capra, F. (1975). *The Tao of Physics: An Exploration of the Parallels between Modern Physics and Eastern Mysticism*. Berkeley, CA: Shambhala.

12   Capra, F. (1982). *The Turning Point: Science, Society and the Rising Culture*. New York: Bantam.

13   Capra, F. (2002). *The Hidden Connections: A Science for Sustainable Living*. San Francisco, CA: Harper Collins.

14   Capra, F. (2002). *The Hidden Connections: A Science for Sustainable Living*. San Francisco, CA: Harper Collins.

15   Maturana, H. and Varela, F. (1992). *The Tree of Knowledge: The Biological Roots of Human Understanding*. Boston, MA: Shambhala.

16   Reichle, F. (2005). *Monte Grande: Francisco Varela*. Documentary. Switzerland: Franz Reichle & t&c Film. Last two paragraphs informed by various interviews with Francisco Varela in this documentary movie.

17   Prigogine, I. and Stengers, I. (1993). *Order out of Chaos: Man's New Dialogue with Nature*. London: Flamingo.

16 *Organisational Knowledge Creation: A Northern Organisational Perspective*

Guiding Questions: How do organisations learn? How do they become knowledge-creating entities able to generate concepts and theories to adequately respond to the development issues they face?

16.1   Orientation

We now turn from individual learning and research to organisational knowledge creation. Over the course of the last two decades there has been much talk of the 'Knowledge Society' if not also of the 'Knowledge Economy' and indeed of 'Knowledge Management'. Unfortunately, over that period, such talk has been dominated by the onset of information technology, and the link between individual learning and research on the one hand, and organisational as well as societal learning and knowledge creation on the other hand, has not been coherently forged. To that extent individual education, organisational knowledge creation and societal development have not been integrated. It is our intention, in this 'Northern' orientation to Integral Development to do just that, now turning from formative individual research and learning as our grounding, to reformative organisational knowledge creation as an emergent form of reframing science, systems and technology.

Organisations play a most important role in societal knowledge creation. At a time where the shelf life of much of our operational knowledge is continuously decreasing, it is actually organisations, in particular private enterprises, that have looked for new ways to improve their ability to learn and to create new knowledge. Thus, the value of products is increasingly defined through so-called immaterial knowledge components, as opposed to material and physical components. It is for that reason that the late management guru Peter Drucker heralded almost half a century ago the rise of the knowledge worker, and our era as the one of the knowledge society.[1] Interestingly enough, it was private enterprises, at least in some notable cases, which have paved the organisational way to such knowledge creation, and not universities. Hence, for our reframed Research

University, to which we come at the end of this 'Northern' realm, we shall draw on significant insights from such organisational knowledge creation.

In short, there is much to learn from prior research on how organisations learn and create knowledge. For us, this is the key question on this second reformative level in the 'Northern' realm. As we now engage as a whole group or organisation with development, the following questions need to be reviewed:

*   How do we learn and create knowledge as a group or organisation?
*   How do we become a knowledge-creating entity able to generate concepts and theories to adequately respond to the development issues we face?
*   How does organisational knowledge creation build on individual research and learning and lead onto the modernisation of society as a whole?

Much has been said about knowledge management within organisations, but much less about knowledge creation that can be related to prior learning processes. We have chosen two outstanding contributions to the field, both of which do relate knowledge creation to individual and organisational learning, though not, as we do, to academically based research. We start out with the Japanese management thinkers Ikujiro Nonaka and Hirotaka Takeuchi, and their globally acclaimed work on The Knowledge-Creating Company. Both authors argue in particular from a sociological perspective and offer the design of the 'hypertext organisation' as a new organisational model. South African-born management thinker Ralph Stacey, in turn, argues from a perspective of complexity sciences and social psychology. In his work we shall find strong resonance with the concepts of autopoiesis and systems thinking that were introduced earlier (⇨15) by Fritjof Capra. In the combination of these two perspectives we will find highly valuable clues to advance in our own efforts with regards to organisational knowledge creation.

16.2   The Knowledge-Creating Enterprise: Geared Up for Innovation

KNOWLEDGE CREATION: UNCOVERING THE SECRET UNDERLYING INNOVATION

The Japanese organisational sociologists Ikujiro Nonaka and Hirotaka Takeuchi – both Professors Emeritus from Tokyo's eminent Hitotsubashi University – are among the best-known scientists in the area of organisational knowledge management. Their acclaimed work *The Knowledge-Creating Company*,[2] published in the mid 1990s, drew the world's eyes on the 'secret' underlying the innovation strength of Japanese companies at that time. With their well-grounded research, Nonaka and Takeuchi turned the conventional wisdom that Japan's success lay primarily in its capacity to imitate, on its head. They illustrated with case studies like Honda, Matsushita and Canon that Japanese companies were indeed highly innovative by themselves. What was the key?

SURFACING TACIT KNOWLEDGE: ACTIVATING THE SECI SPIRAL

For Nonaka and Takeuchi, the key for such innovation strength was the ability to turn tacit or implicit knowledge into explicit knowledge and thereby create new products, services and also organisational processes. More precisely, they discovered and subsequently mapped an iterative process that they coined the 'SECI spiral' (Figure 16.1). This spiral interconnects four stages of Socialisation, Externalisation, Combination and Internalisation, hence the acronym SECI. The linkages between these four stages take place in a way that tacit knowledge that is hidden in shared experiences and mental models (stage 1: socialisation) is made conscious through externalisation (stage 2). At this second stage knowledge is articulated, which is often facilitated through dialogue. At the third stage such externalised knowledge is turned into systemic knowledge. At this level also new knowledge is created through the combination of existing patterns, processes and technologies with new ideas. At the fourth and last stage of internalisation, the newly systemised and invented knowledge then becomes operationalised and integrated into individual and organisational practice.

The SECI model of organisational learning and knowledge creation is depicted as an integrated process, as is demonstrated by Figure 16.1.

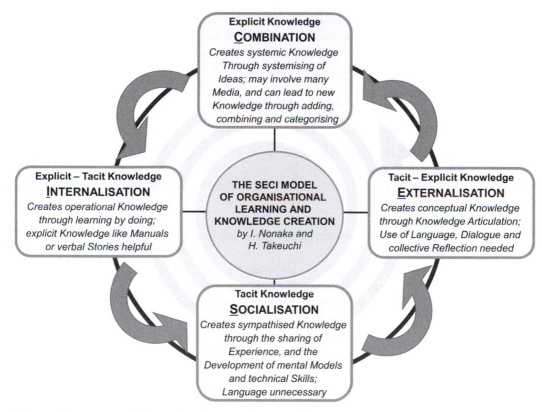

Figure 16.1 The SECI model of organisational learning and knowledge creation

For Nonaka and Takeuchi, a key to innovation lies in the purposeful activation of the SECI spiral – indeed analogous to our GENE rhythm (Grounding = Socialisation, Emergence = Externalisation, Navigation = Combination, Effect = Internalisation) – thereby turning knowledge into continuous innovation. To give the spiral the necessary focus, the definition of the main knowledge domain of the enterprise is an important preliminary step.

DEFINING A KNOWLEDGE DOMAIN

Through defining its main knowledge domain, the enterprise generates a mental map of the world in which it lives. Such a map then provides a general direction regarding what kind of knowledge the enterprise seeks to create. Most organisations think here only about products and services. However, such products and services have clear boundaries. In contrast, boundaries for knowledge are more fluid, serving to expand the organisation's economic, technological and social scope.

Nonaka and Takeuchi offer Matsushita – the Japanese multinational manufacturer of consumer electronics, now called Panasonic Corporation – as an example that declared itself in 1990 a 'possibility-searching company' and subsequently came up with a knowledge-based vision. Here is an excerpt of that vision, illustrating the relatively open boundaries that Matsushita chose:

- *We are in the 'human innovation business', a business that creates new lifestyles based on creativity, comfort and joy in addition to efficiency and convenience.*
- *We produce 'humanware technology', technology based on human studies such as artificial intelligence, fuzzy logic, neuro-computers and networking technology, all necessary for the 'human innovation business'.*[3]

Once the knowledge domain is defined, the organisation is called to provide enabling conditions for knowledge creation to take place.

ENABLING CONDITIONS FOR THE KNOWLEDGE-CREATING COMPANY

Nonaka and Takeuchi identify three enabling conditions that a knowledge-creating enterprise needs to supply:

- *Knowledge Capability*: The organisational capability to acquire, create, accumulate and exploit knowledge.
- *Autonomous Projects*: Autonomous individuals and groups, that set their task boundaries by themselves to pursue the ultimate intention of the organisation.
- *Crisis and Ideal*: A sense of crisis as well as a lofty ideal that together increase the creative tension within the organisation.

Ultimately, we arrive at a new design of the organisation, that Nonaka and Takeuchi call the 'hypertext organisation'.

THE HYPERTEXT ORGANISATION: DEVELOPING, CHANNELLING AND DISTRIBUTING KNOWLEDGE

The term 'hypertext organisation' is inspired by the multiple layers that serve to develop, channel and distribute knowledge through the organisation. The three layers that are distinguished are the project layer, the business system and the knowledge basis. In Figure 16.2, Nonaka and Takeuchi illustrate the three layers as well as the relationships between them, providing a first overview of the overall functioning of the hypertext organisation.

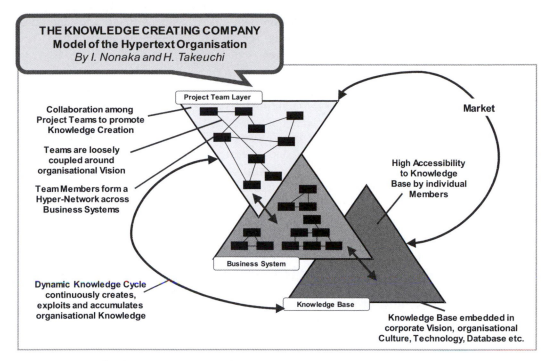

Figure 16.2 The hypertext organisation

Let us have a closer look at the three layers of the hypertext organisation:

- *Project Layer:* Multiple project teams engage in knowledge-creating activities such as new product and systems development. In all such cases the team members are brought together from a number of different units across the business system, and are assigned exclusively to a project team until the project is completed.
- *Business System:* Alongside the project layer – but occupying a lower order of knowledge creation significance – is the conventional business system. While the project layer is engaged with developing new knowledge through self-organising groups, the business system is primarily concerned with categorising, ordering, distributing and commercialising or operationalising such knowledge. With regards to the SECI spiral, we can say that the project layer is relatively more engaged in the socialising, externalising and in the innovative aspects of the combination stages, while the official business system is primarily occupied with combination and internalisation. Underlying both project layer and business system is the knowledge base of the enterprise.
- *Knowledge Base:* This third layer does not exist as an actual organisational entity, but is embedded in corporate vision, organisational culture and technology.

As indicated, a knowledge-creating organisation – be it a private enterprise, a public institution, a civic NGO, or a university – must have the ability to acquire, accumulate, exploit and create knowledge, continuously and dynamically. Also, the organisation must both be able to recategorise and recontextualise this knowledge strategically for use by others in the organisation or by future generations. For Nonaka and Takeuchi, a hierarchy is the most efficient structure for the acquisition, accumulation and exploitation of knowledge, while a task force is the most effective for the creation of new knowledge.

COMPLEMENTARITY OF DESIGNED AND EMERGENT STRUCTURES

The layered structure of the hypertext organisation provides much inspiration for any institution that aspires to be a knowledge-creating organisation, whether based in commerce, community or academics. The complementarity of a structured hierarchy and an autonomous task force corresponds with the findings of the Austrian-American ecologist Fritjof Capra (⇨13). Capra illustrates in his *Hidden Connections*[4] the emergence of novelty in human organisations. Human organisations always contain both designed and emergent structures. The designed structures are the formal structures of the organisation described by its official documents. The emergent structures – whether in companies, communities or universities – are created by its informal networks and communities of practice. The two types of structures are very different, and every organisation needs both. Designed structures provide the rules and routines that are necessary for the effective functioning of the organisation. They enable an organisation to optimise its processes and to deliver its products, services and solutions effectively to its customers or the people it serves. Emergent structures, however, provide novelty, creativity and flexibility. They are adaptive, capable of changing and evolving.

A final remark on Nonaka and Takeuchi: though the primary focus of their work is the corporate world, it is intriguing to see how they have dissolved the notion of 'labour' or even 'human resources', and replaced these terms with knowledge creators. We often noticed that such a transformation from labour to knowledge is widely absent from most of the Western literature on knowledge management, which is much more strongly rooted in technology. We are aware, how much this research into the corporate world resonates with the overall orientation of this chapter whereby the northern realm positions 'open and transparent knowledge creation' as one of the main principles of Integral Development.

While Nonaka and Takeuchi look at organisations primarily from a sociological perspective, we now move to the much more interdisciplinary systems perspective of Ralph Stacey. This approach, like that of Fritjof Capra, casts significant light on the 'emergent' role that organisational complexity plays in developmental thinking from a 'Northern' scientific perspective. Interestingly enough, while Stacey is a social scientist, Capra is a natural scientist. Yet both come to similar conclusions.

16.3   The Complex Organisation: Dealing with Uncertainty

THE PROBLEMATIC SCIENCES OF CERTAINTY

Ralph Stacey, based at the University of Hertfordshire in Britain, was originally an academic economist and corporate planner, before he discovered the complexity sciences and social psychology. It is this multifaceted background that enabled him to develop his transdisciplinary perspective on organisational complexity and to describe ways through which organisations learn and adapt creatively in an ever more uncertain environment. Moreover, like Nonaka and Takeuchi, he is greatly concerned with the interaction between organisational hierarchy (bureaucratic system) and network (project layer).

Stacey's research has been partly rooted in his frustration that the application of a scientific perspective to management and organisational theory brought with it an illusionary sense of certainty. For him, to understand organisations we need to grasp 'organisational reality'. 'At the heart of understanding organisational reality is causality. Causality addresses how and why organisations move into the future, becoming what they become. Management's view of causality, whether explicit or implicit, leads to particular approaches to leadership, management, and, of course, strategy'.[5] So what is wrong, for Stacey, with the prevailing understanding of organisation?

REVIEWING CAUSALITY: THE SCIENCES OF CERTAINTY CAN'T BE APPLIED TO MANAGEMENT

Stacey argues that early rationalist moves in Europe and America to link organisations, management and systems to science, brought with it both 'efficient causality' expressed in scientific management (e.g. Taylorism) and 'formative causality' expressed in systems models of organisations.[6]

For example, much of today's corporate planning is still based on the belief that through plans the future is rendered largely predictable. Most managers assume that there can't be any coherent pattern in the development of the organisation without such plans. In keeping with the classical 'scientific' tradition, the 'scientist' manager is hence required to understand the organisation in reductionist terms –as a mechanism driven by 'efficient causality' and by 'formative causality' (developing in predefined stages).

Stacey makes the point that in identifying management with such a rationally based science we have imported three very important concepts from science into management that we now take so much for granted we hardly notice them. However, all of these three concepts are not only profoundly limited and limiting, but also dangerous as they are erroneous and misleading.

- *The Autonomous Individual:* First, there is the notion of the autonomous, rational individual: individuals are seen as split off from each other and the natural world. This goes hand in hand with an atomistic view of society and the objectification and control of nature.
- *The Objective Observer:* The second 'import' is that of the objective observer who identifies and isolates causality in nature, and then tests hypotheses based on these identifications.
- *A Mechanistic, Formative and Rational Causality:* The third import from science to management is the following understanding of causality:

  - a mechanistic, efficient cause producing a stable environment over time and change that is predictable;

- formative cause producing movement to an already given, supposedly mature state;
- rational cause producing autonomously chosen goals and strategies.

Stacey adopts a radically different, much more developmental approach, drawing on both contemporary complexity sciences and psychodynamic psychology. It is important to note that there is not yet a single science of complexity but rather a number of different strands comprising what might be called the complexity sciences. Those writing about complexity in organisations usually draw on concepts to be found in one or more of these strands, namely chaos theory, dissipative structure theory, and the theory of complex adaptive systems.

Stacey builds up his argument for a new organisational perspective with the help of the work of Nobel Prize-winning chemist and leading figure in the complexity sciences, Ilya Prigogine.

COMPLEXITY AND THE SCIENCES OF UNCERTAINTY: TOWARDS TRANSFORMATIVE CAUSALITY

At the beginning of his book *The End of Certainty*,[7] Prigogine posed what he saw as a central question: is the future given, or is it under perpetual construction? His answer is clear: he sees the future for every level of the universe under perpetual construction, whereby development can only be understood in nonlinear, non-equilibrium terms, where instabilities, or fluctuations, are the norm.

For Prigogine, nature is about the creation of unpredictable novelty. According to him, evolution encounters bifurcation points where micro details of interaction determine the evolutionary paths. Prigogine sees evolution and development at all levels in terms of instabilities, with humans and their creativity as part of it. For him, as for Ralph Stacey and Fritjof Capra, human creativity is essentially the same process as nature's creativity. This is the basis for his call for a 'new dialogue with nature' that moves away from domination and control. These features – unknowable futures emerging in here-and-now disorderly interactions – present a paradoxical form of 'transformative causality'.

Central to Prigogine's approach is the distinction between individual entities and ensembles. He points to how classical physics takes the trajectories of individual entities as the fundamental unit of analysis. He criticises this conventional perspective and argues, as illustrated in Table 16.1 opposite, that individual trajectories cannot be specified for complex systems. Rather, interaction between particles produces resonance, which makes it impossible to identify individual trajectories. Since individual trajectories cannot be identified, Prigogine takes the ensemble as fundamental and argues that changes in whole ensembles, like populations, emerge over long periods through amplification of slight variations in individual entities.

Transferring Prigogine's thinking to the organisational level, Stacey argues that any kind of organisation is a dynamic interplay of stability and change, of continuity and novelty, of decay and generation, of the sameness of identity and the difference of changes in that identity. The fundamental question about organisation then follows:

Table 16.1 Transformative causality	
Movement towards a future that is:	perpetually constructed by the movement itself as continuity and transformation, known and unknown
Process of movement in order to:	express continuity and transformation individually and collectively, in local interaction, forming and being formed by population-wide patterns
Nature of variation: freedom/constraint	diverse micro-interaction and escalation of small changes; freedom and constraint arises

what are the sources of both stability and change, of decay and generation, of identity and difference?[8]

MOVING TOWARDS AN UNKNOWABLE FUTURE

In this movement of identity, there is both the possibility of sameness or continuity, and the potential for spontaneous transformation at the same time. This movement is paradoxical in that it is simultaneously both: the repetition and the transformation of identity. Stacey calls, as Prigogine does, such a movement towards an unknowable future 'transformative teleology' (teleology meaning a process that is oriented towards a final cause).

It is worth to distinguish such transformative from other types of teleology. Stacey and his colleagues Douglas Griffin and Patricia Shaw differentiate four kinds:[9]

- *Natural Law Teleology:* In which movement is regular and predictable, and the parts add up to a whole;
- *Rationalist Teleology:* In which movement is towards a goal autonomously chosen by humans as an expression of universal principles;
- *Formative Teleology:* In which movement is to a final form, a pre-given state already contained within the formative process that produces it;
- *Transformative Teleology:* In which movement is toward an unknown form that is in the process of being shaped, to a form that is itself evolving.

These distinctions are so important for our understanding of 'organisation' that we take a closer look at them through the following Table 16.2. Here a fifth perspective – of a more random adaptive teleology – is added:[10]

Following the thread of a formative teleology, Stacey sees a number of limitations of conventional management science as well as of systems thinking that are predominant in today's management thinking.

Table 16.2 Comparison of frameworks

Adapted from Stacey, Griffin and Shaw

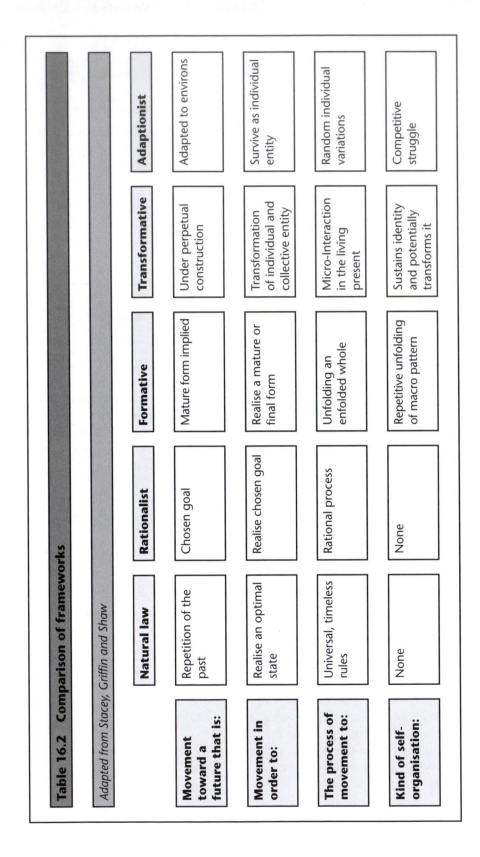

	Natural law	Rationalist	Formative	Transformative	Adaptionist
Movement toward a future that is:	Repetition of the past	Chosen goal	Mature form implied	Under perpetual construction	Adapted to environs
Movement in order to:	Realise an optimal state	Realise chosen goal	Realise a mature or final form	Transformation of individual and collective entity	Survive as individual entity
The process of movement to:	Universal, timeless rules	Rational process	Unfolding an enfolded whole	Micro-Interaction in the living present	Random individual variations
Kind of self-organisation:	None	None	Repetitive unfolding of macro pattern	Sustains identity and potentially transforms it	Competitive struggle

LIMITATIONS OF MANAGEMENT SCIENCE AND SYSTEMS THINKING: HOW TO DEAL WITH HUMAN PARTICIPATION AND FREEDOM?

For Stacey, both management science and systems thinking provide powerful ways of thinking about and designing means of securing organisational stability and continuity. However, they both encounter difficulties when it comes to explaining the role of ordinary human freedom and participation, as well as the closely related possibility of transformative change. Furthermore, organisational change of a fundamental kind also cannot be adequately understood from either mechanistic or systems perspectives. That's why he proposes a new perspective – transformative teleology.

He asks, though, why managers are not normally engaged in such transformation? Till today, a combined rationalist and formative teleology prevails in organisational life, causing stressful daily experience for people working within it. The argument that he and his colleagues give, is that most managers are caught in ways of thinking that do not pay adequate attention to their own participation in what is happening. Instead, they focus on the 'systems' that attempt to control ordinary, everyday freedom in order to preserve stability or secure regular, global intended change. The very practical problem with thinking about organisations in either mechanistic or systemic ways is that no sooner has the mechanism or the system been identified or designed – than real organisational life, which is rather different from the design, moves on.[11] In a time of overwhelming velocity of change, sooner or later we are forced to look at organisations differently.

In order to evolve our organisational understanding towards a transformative teleology we are required to challenge the dominant management thinking. It requires us to face and actively deal with:[12]

- severe limitations on predictability in the evolution of complex organisational processes;
- the centrality of self-organising interaction as transformative cause of emergent new directions in the development of an organisation;
- the limits to individual choice;
- the fact that stability emerges in relationships;
- the importance of diversity and difference as complex systems evolve only when there is micro diversity, or fluctuations;
- the limits to planning as creative development cannot be designed and complex systems emerge spontaneously and unpredictably;
- the potentiality of success as we face the paradox that evolution is creative as well as destructive;
- the centrality of the expression of identity because the movement of stability and change arises in the human need to express identity, both individually and collectively. Competitive survival and profit, both conventionally considered to be priorities, become subordinate to identity.

Such a fundamental change of perspective leads us to a new understanding of the organisation.

A NEW ORGANISATIONAL UNDERSTANDING: TOWARDS COMPLEX RESPONSIVE PROCESSES

For Stacey and his colleagues, an organisation is not just a tool of joint action. Rather it *is* joint action. In other words, the organisation is a pattern of cooperative interaction that is continually recreated and potentially transformed simultaneously. The organisation then is not a system or a tool, but rather systems are some of the communication tools employed by people in organising joint action.

Stacey, Griffin and Shaw call these interactive patterns 'complex responsive processes'. These processes are characterised by the paradox of the known-unknown and in this paradox emerges the aims people formulate and the choices they make. What is being expressed is individual and collective identity at the same time.

The perspective of complex responsive processes accords priority to the individual and the social simultaneously, forming and being informed by each other. The individual is the singular aspect and the social is the plural aspect of the same phenomenon. Stacey confirms and further evolves his thinking on complex responsive processes in later research, seeing the individual and the social emerge in communicative interaction.[13]

In conclusion, some of the principal insights to be gained from the complexity sciences for such a new view on the organisation are:

- Relationships seem to have the intrinsic capacity for self-organisation, producing emergent patterns of coherence in themselves.
- Such abstract relationships are capable of emergent novelty only when the relationships are between diverse entities in the presence of fluctuations.
- Such emergent change is predictable and unpredictable, stable and unstable at the same time.

INSPIRED BY COMPLEXITY SCIENCES: IMPLICATIONS FOR DEVELOPMENT

Stacey's shift of perspective towards complex responsive systems serves to establish a bridge for us to move from the organisational to the societal level. Indeed we have already left behind the conventional organisational viewpoint where organisations are seen within rather narrowly defined institutional borders. Though systems sciences had already taken us out of that restrictive box decades ago, it is with the help of complexity theories that we are gradually developing a totally new lens on human interaction in organisational environments in general. Such new viewpoints have profound implications for any development organisation and process. We are challenged to review our beliefs on how organisations work. We are invited to think in parallel about stability and change, continuity and transformation, individual and collective standpoints.

As we progress to the community and societal level, we will notice that this perspective was for long absent in societal development practice. Yet, the ability to navigate complexity is even more in demand when we come to societal or even global perspectives. However, even there, we are still deeply steeped in the conventional 'either/or' mode of thinking. The shift to 'both/and' – embracing the polarities of stability and change, tradition and modernity, local and global, competition and collaboration, etc. – is only just beginning. The integral perspective invites us to go even 'beyond the both/and'. The circular fourfold of Integral Development transcends polarised thinking towards an interactive engaging with a complex diversity – with a pull towards continuous and dynamic reintegration and rebalancing of diversity.

16.4   Integration

In this chapter, we have reviewed the second organisational level of Integral Development from a 'Northern' perspective, with a particular emphasis on complex social systems and organisational knowledge creation. In purposefully linking the prior chapter on individual learning and research with this chapter on organisational knowledge creation, we have bridged the divide not only between self and enterprise but also between academe and industry. In moving from the formative grounding of self in learning and research, to the reformative emergence of an organisation through knowledge creation and complex responsive processes, we have also paved the way for renewing the normative focus on societal development to which we now turn for our 'Northern' navigation.

Before we move on we invite you again to engage – through reflection and prospective action – with the guiding questions and theory presented in this chapter, as well as with the major development challenges derived thereof. If you are not yet associated with a particular organisation or community (or initiative, network or movement), you may want to envision founding one, together with others. If your primary association is one with a university – be it as member of its faculty or as participant in an educational or research programme – you may want to consider using this as your core transformational context.

Table 16.3 Main task: Bring about organisational knowledge creation		
Guiding questions	**Guiding theory**	**Reflect and act ... *What do I and we have to do as Integral Developers?***
How do organisations learn? How do they become knowledge-creating entities able to generate concepts and theories to adequately respond to the development issues they face?	*The Knowledge-creating enterprise* (Nonaka/Takeuchi) *The complex organisation* (Stacey)	• Understand how you can tap into the tacit knowledge of your organisation and how to activate the spiral of organisational learning and innovation • Provide the enabling conditions for knowledge creation and innovation • Map your organisation as a hypertext organisation and articulate the subsequent development tasks • Explore to what degree your organisation is designed to overcome a mechanistic and rational paradigm and to deal with uncertainty • Explore how your organisation can give simultaneous priority to individual and collective identity via 'complex responsive processes'

We now turn to the third round of societal development, 'Northern' style.

References

1   Drucker, P. (1990). *The New Realities: In Government and Politics/In Economics and Business/ In Society and World View*. New York: Harper Collins.
2   Nonaka, I. and Takeuchi, H. (1995). *The Knowledge-Creating Company: How Japanese Companies Create the Dynamics of Innovation*. Oxford: Oxford University Press.
3   Nonaka, I. and Takeuchi, H. (1995). *The Knowledge-Creating Company: How Japanese Companies Create the Dynamics of Innovation*. Oxford: Oxford University Press, p. 115.
4   Capra, F. (2002). *The Hidden Connections: A Science for Sustainable Living*. San Francisco, CA: Harper Collins.
5   Create Advantage website. Available at: www.createadvantage.com/glossary/causality / Accessed: 3 February 2012.
6   Stacey, R. (2010). *Complex Organisational Reality: Uncertainty and the Need to Rethink Management after the Collapse of Investment Capitalism*. London: Routledge.
7   Prigogine, I. (1997). *The End of Certainty: Time, Chaos and the New Laws of Nature*. New York: Free Press.
8   Stacey, R., Griffin, D. and Shaw, P. (2000). *Complexity and Management: Fad or Radical Challenge to Systems Thinking*. London: Routledge.
9   Stacey, R., Griffin, D. and Shaw, P. (2000). *Complexity and Management: Fad or Radical Challenge to Systems Thinking*. London: Routledge·
10 Stacey, R., Griffin, D. and Shaw, P. (2000). *Complexity and Management: Fad or Radical Challenge to Systems Thinking*. London: Routledge.
11 Stacey, R., Griffin, D. and Shaw, P. (2000). *Complexity and Management: Fad or Radical Challenge to Systems Thinking*. London: Routledge.
12 Stacey, R., Griffin, D. and Shaw, P. (2000). *Complexity and Management: Fad or Radical Challenge to Systems Thinking*. London: Routledge.
13 Stacey, R., (2001). *Complex Responsive Processes in Organisations: Learning and Knowledge Creation*. London: Routledge.

17 The Knowledge and Network Society: A Northern Societal Perspective

Guiding Question: How do we become a knowledge-creating community and society, able to assist the necessary transformation of our scientific, technological and political systems?

17.1 Orientation

Having spanned the grounds of individual learning and research and those of organisational learning and knowledge creation in 'Northern' developmental guise, we now enter more conventional, though difficult, societal development terrain. For it is here, in the 'Northern' realm of science, technology and systems, that some of the most popular development theories have been generated. For decades, it was social science, in particular sociological thought, that has heavily influenced development discourses. Many of these sociological contributions to development theory, so our earlier argument goes, were highly abstract, predominantly universalist and as such disconnected from real life development contexts.

Two bodies of theory that we see in particular in this critical light are modernisation theory and dependency theory. We have dealt with both of them in some detail in the beginning of the book, when we critically reviewed the history of development (⇨2).

Another critique that we made with regards to these sociological studies was that the majority of them had been generated to the exclusion of individual and organisational development, which we have now duly considered in the previous two chapters. In other words, much of societal modernisation theories have been disconnected from individual research, learning and development (⇨15) as well as from organisational learning and knowledge creation (⇨16).

That said, our major critique of the 'Northern' and 'Western' domination in economic and developmental thought and practice, is their overall, paradigmatic disconnect from the 'Southern' and 'Eastern' realms of Integral Development. It is the overemphasis on science, systems and technology, as well as on enterprise and economics as the sole panacea – to the exclusion of nature, community, culture and spirituality – which we believe is responsible for much of the predicament with regards to development. For us, it is this imbalance that causes much of the world's social and economic problems.

Having reconnected to the 'Southern' and 'Eastern' realms in the previous parts of this book, and having now developed – on an individual and organisational level – a new, more integral approach to learning and research (Round 1) as well as organisational knowledge creation (Round 2), we are now (Round 3) faced with the challenge of coming up with a transformed approach to societal knowledge creation. As we seek to reconstruct this 'Northern' sociological, developmental realm we need to reflect on the following questions:

- How do we learn and create knowledge as a community and society?
- How do we become a knowledge-creating community and society able to generate new theories and technologies to respond adequately to the development issues we face?
- How do we ensure that these theories and technologies relate to our natural and communal development needs and are informed by our own culture and spirituality?
- What technologies are appropriate for our development?
- How can individual research and learning, organisational knowledge creation and societal learning interconnect?
- How can we sustainably modernise?

On this societal level we shall start out with World Systems Analysis – a highly influential theory conceived of by US sociologist Immanuel Wallerstein. While still characterised by a degree of abstraction that is conventionally associated with sociology, World Systems Analysis offers a societal development perspective that synthesises and transcend its two predecessors: modernisation theory and dependency theory. It is particular helpful, as it provides explanation for the extraordinary 'world systemic' changes that humanity is currently facing.

Furthermore, with the help of the Colombian anthropologist Arturo Escobar, we seek to understand how the theories on self-making, self-organisation and emergence, to which we were exposed on an individual and organisational level, can be translated into local development contexts, thereby providing a new way of looking at the development of community and society. Escobar will also provide us with some clues as to how social movements are important, yet often undervalued, spaces of knowledge production. One could say, we are thereby revisiting the 'Northern' realm from the local ground up. Finally, we shall move from the local to the global perspective, and reflect on the notion of the Knowledge Society, now in an integral manner. We hereby are guided by the eminent Spanish sociologist Manuel Castells.

We begin with World Systems Analysis.

17.2   World Systems Analysis: A New Perspective on Human Development Indicating a Global Transition towards a Post-Capitalist World System

THE HISTORICAL CONTEXT OF THE WORLD SYSTEM PERSPECTIVE

When the United States became a superpower after World War II, American social scientists were called upon to study the problems of Third World development. This started the modernisation school, which dominated the field of economic development in the 1950s. However, the failure of modernisation programmes in Latin America in the 1960s led to the emergence of a neo-Marxist dependency school. This coexistence of contrasting approaches in the field of development by the 1970s made for a time of intellectual fertility. By the mid 1970s, the ideological battle between the two, modernisation and dependency, began to gradually subside, and a group of radical researchers led by American sociologist Immanuel Wallerstein found that many new activities in the capitalist world economy could not be explained within the confines of the modernisation or dependency perspectives.[1]

First, East Asia began to experience a remarkable rate of economic growth and it became harder and harder to explain such in terms of 'dynamic dependency', especially when the East Asian industrial states began to challenge the economic superiority of the United States. Second, there was a crisis among the socialist states, notable the failure of the Chinese Cultural Revolution, and, third, there was an emerging crisis in US capitalism, with the combination of 'stagflation' in the 1970s.

THE THEORETICAL HERITAGE OF WORLD SYSTEMS ANALYSIS

Wallerstein started out as a specialist on Africa, when he incorporated many concepts from the dependency school – such as unequal exchange, core-periphery exploitation, and the imbalanced world market – into his World Systems theory. However, at a later stage he moved beyond the *dependentistas*, as he became strongly influenced by Fernand Braudel and the Annales School.

The Annales School arose as a protest against the overspecialisation of social science disciplines within conventional academic boundaries. First, its key proponent Fernand Braudel sought to develop 'total' or 'global' history.[2] Instead of subordinating history to other disciplines, he saw it as all-embracing. Second, Braudel argued for the synthesis of history and social science through an emphasis on the 'longue durée' (the long term). In this way history would move away from the uniqueness of events (eventism) and the social sciences would gain a historical perspective. For Braudel, it is only through a study of the long term that the totality, the deepest layers of social life, the 'subterranean history' and the continuing structures of historical reality are revealed. Thirdly, Braudel was instrumental in shifting the centre of concern in historical discourse towards problem-oriented history.

THE WORLD SYSTEMS METHODOLOGY AND ITS CRITIQUE

For Wallerstein, today based at Yale University, the world system perspective is not a theory but a protest. In particular he feels uncomfortable with the following five assumptions of traditional social scientific inquiry that have informed research approaches over the past 150 years.

One: Division of social sciences in distinct disciplines – beyond existing social science disciplines

In traditional scientific inquiry the social sciences are constituted of a number of distinct disciplines. All these divisions are derived intellectually from the dominant liberal ideology of the nineteenth century, which argued that state (politics) and market (economics) were analytically separate domains,[3] that sociology was supposed to explain the irrational phenomena that economics and political science could not account for, and that anthropology specialised in the study of primitive people beyond our civilised worlds. However, as the real world evolved, so these divisions increasingly blurred. From a World Systems perspective the various disciplines are interdependent and single.

Two: Towards the historical social scientist – combining particular and universal modes of analysis

In traditional social science inquiry, history is the study of and the explanation of the particular event as it happened in the past. Social science is the statement of the universal rules whereby human social behaviour is explained. This is the famous distinction between ideographic (particular) and nomothetic (universal) modes of analysis. For Wallerstein, there is a need to combine the two in scholarship. World Systems Analysis therefore combines trans-historical generalisations and particularistic narrations. This implies that at every instant we look for both the cyclical rhythms of the system and for the patterns of internal transformation that will eventually bring about the demise of the system. There is neither historian nor social scientist but only a historical social scientist.[4]

Three: Towards a new unit of analysis – state-society versus historical system

Wallerstein argues that the basic unit of analysis should be the historical system rather than the state-society. Such an entity is historical and systemic simultaneously. He maintains that in human history there have been three known forms of historical systems: mini-systems, world empires and world economies. In the pre-agricultural era there were a multiplicity of mini-systems that were small in space and brief in time. The basic logic was one of reciprocity and exchange. In the period between 8000 BC and AD 1500 the world empires were dominant in the historical system. The basic logic was extraction of tribute. Around AD 1500 the capitalist world economies were born. The underlying logic was accumulated surplus distributed unequally in favour of those able to achieve monopolies in the market networks. These expanded all over the globe so that, by the late nineteenth century, for the first time ever, there existed only one historical system on the globe.

Four: Towards a new definition of capitalism

For Wallerstein, the anomalies in the pure definition of capitalism – competition between free producers using free labour with free commodities ('free' meaning available for purchase and sale in the market) – supersede the norm, and therefore should open up new research questions.

Five: The questionable nature of progress

World System Analysis wants to remove the idea of 'modern' progress from the status of a trajectory and open it up as an analytical variable. It is not at all certain, for Wallerstein, that there has been a linear trend – upward, downward or straightforward. Furthermore, Wallerstein concludes, we are now living in the long moment of transition wherein the contradictions of the capitalist world economy have made it impossible to continue to adjust its machinery. Thus we are living in a period of real historical choice, and World System Analysis is a call for the construction of a historical social science that feels comfortable with the uncertainties of transition, that contributes to the transformation of the world by illuminating the choices without appealing to the crutch of a belief in the inevitable triumph of the good.

We would reckon our own integral approach to be part of such a transitional social science. Integral Development combines also, as suggested by the World Systems theory, ideographic and nomothetic frames of analysis, though our starting point is the ideographic mode, moving from the particular local narrative towards a global perspective. This for us occurs not in form of a linear trajectory, but rather in continuous dynamic interaction of both the local and global perspectives.

Wallerstein's new approach to look at the world's development as within world systems brings us to his critique of the dependency school.

FROM A BI-MODAL TO TRI-MODAL SYSTEM: CORE, SEMI-PERIPHERY AND PERIPHERY

Wallerstein has criticised the construction of a bi-modal, core-periphery system of the *dependentistas* as overly simplistic. Instead he proposes a tri-modal system: core, semi-periphery, periphery. If the semi-peripheral countries were not there, the capitalist system would rapidly face a crisis. According to Wallerstein, success in moving from periphery to semi-periphery depends on whether the country can adopt one of the following development strategies: seizing the chance, promotion by invitation, or self-reliance.

First, in 'seizing the chance', one solution is 'import-substitution', involving aggressive state action. However, all too often in such a case, technological dependence then replaces manufacturing dependence. The second strategy of 'development by invitation' involves 'inviting in' the multinationals, as has been the case, for example, in Singapore and now in China. The third strategy involves 'development through self-reliance', as had been the case for Tanzania in the Nyerere days.[5]

However, being successful in the transition from a peripheric to a semi-peripheric country is almost certainly not a long-lived solution, as World Systems Analysis sees the existing global economic system undergoing a fundamental transformation.

THE CAPITALIST WORLD ECONOMY IN TRANSFORMATION

According to Wallerstein, a capitalist world economy began to form in the European continent in the sixteenth century, possessing a set of integrated production processes that he called 'commodity chains'. The total surpluses extracted from these were always concentrated to a disproportionate degree on some zones rather than others. Indeed, the gap between rich and poor has widened enormously over the past four centuries.

Yet the absolute expansion of the world economy, for Wallerstein, has probably been as great since 1945, in terms of value produced and accumulated wealth, as had been the case in the entire period between 1500 and 1945.

At the same time, the strength of anti-systemic or anti-establishment movements has also increased enormously, although recently these – whether socialist, social democratic or post-colonial – have come under question. On the one hand, anti-systemic movements have sought greater internal equality, which demands fundamental social transformation. On the other hand, they have historically desired rapid economic growth that means catching up with core states. The World Social Forum today has become an exception to this contradictory expectation, focusing on equality, while having abandoned the postulate of growth, engrained in today's mainstream capitalistic thinking.

Movements and organisations such as the World Social Forum are important catalysts for the transformation capitalism is currently exposed to. Wallerstein leaves it open what kind of new system is ultimately emerging, stating that all depends on the interplay of a growing number of actors in a field of enormous possibility and complexity.

OUTLOOK ON WORLD SYSTEMS ANALYSIS

In sum, the World Systems school is different from the dependency school in that it treats the whole world as its unit of analysis, adopts a historical methodology that perceives reality as a state of flux, develops a tri-modal theoretical structure, abandons the deterministic progress-driven view on the direction of development, and has a broader overall focus.

While we agree with the overall critique of World Systems Analysis and regard it as an important evolution in breaking out of narrow disciplinary thinking and the dualistic approach adopted by modernisation and dependency schools, we see a need for stronger emphasis on local particularities within the global perspective. Furthermore, World Systems Analysis is primarily driven by historians and sociologists, which holds the danger of the inclusion of the wide range of other perspectives, as promoted by Integral Development. Overall, however, World Systems Analysis provides a key stepping-stone towards reimaging 'the world as we know it', to toy with the title of one of Wallerstein's books: *The End of the World as We Know It: Social Sciences for the 21st Century*.

Wallerstein's own conclusion that the shape of the new post-capitalist system that is ultimately emerging out of the current transition the world is currently undergoing depends on the interplay of a growing number of actors on a local and global level. That resonates strongly with the new way of thinking that natural scientist like Capra, Maturana, Varela, Prigogine and others promoted earlier (⇨15, 16) – based on complexity theories, self-organisation, autopoiesis and other recently emergent theories from the natural sciences. It is as if we come increasingly to a point where the perspectives on knowledge creation, reality perception and reality construction within the natural and social sciences begin to converge. Wallerstein thereby invites us also, as Varela has done earlier in this chapter, to actively engage in the transformation process of our time, as any single contribution can stimulate a decisive shift of the entire system. Wallerstein encourages us to seize our chance. However, he also reminds us that the transition to any new world system will be highly turbulent as:

the modern-world system, as a historical system, has entered into a terminal crisis and is unlikely to exist in fifty years. However, since its outcome is uncertain, we do not know whether the resulting system will be better or worse than the one we are living in, but we do know that the period of transition will be a time of terrible troubles, since the stakes of the transition are so high, the outcome so uncertain, and the ability of small inputs to affect the outcome so great.[6]

The Colombian American anthropologist Arturo Escobar – whom we met already in the 'Southern' and 'Eastern' integral realms – has indeed picked up these signs and translated them into an evolved development theory and practice. With Escobar we begin to explore how the 'Northern' realm can be reconceived, taking on from where other scientists like Capra (self-organisation) and Stacey (complex responsive organisational processes) have left off.

17.3   Self-Making, Self-Organisation, Emergence: New Bottom-Up Ways for Development and Knowledge Creation through Local Social Movements

BOTTOM-UP DEVELOPMENT: CHANGING THE WHOLE FROM THE INTERACTIONS OF THE PARTS

Concepts like 'autopoiesis', 'self-making' and 'self-organisation', drawn from biology and complexity theory, constitute still relatively new forms of thinking about life and organisation, including networks and social movements. They altogether have a profound impact on our new understanding of development.

For Escobar, this thinking emphasises bottom-up processes where agents working at a local scale give rise to sophistication and complexity at another level.[7] Emergence happens through the actions of multiple agents acting dynamically and following local rules rather than top-down commands.

The consequences are far-reaching. Conventional approaches to economics or development assume two levels (micro, macro) or a nested series of levels (the proverbial Russian doll). The alternative approach is to show, from the ground up, how, at each scale, the properties of the whole emerge from the interaction between the parts. Such a macro-micro interaction is clearly apparent in the Sarvodaya case (⇨14), depicted in the simultaneous processes of individual, family, community and national development.

These interdependent frameworks provide an alternative to established state-centric, capitalocentric and globalocentric thinking in development, with their emphasis on larger forces, hierarchies, determination and unchanging structures. For Escobar, these newer perspectives contrast the old, as they see entities as made up of always unfolding intermeshed sites.

LIVING IN AN EMERGENT WORLD: CONSEQUENCES OF SELF-ORGANISATION AND ENACTION FOR DEVELOPMENT

'Self-organisation' and 'enaction' were two concepts that influenced Escobar strongly in his approach to development. While the notion of 'self-organisation' has its roots in the systems thinking and cybernetics movement of the 1950s and 1960s – spearheaded by Norbert Wiener, Gregory Bateson and Heinz von Förster – the term enaction was coined by Humberto Maturana and Francisco Varela:

- *Self-Organisation:* The key idea in self-organisation was that cognition takes place not in terms of a system of rules and symbols, but on the basis of vast numbers of interconnected elements which, operating locally, create local-global modes of cooperation that emerge spontaneously, depending on conditions. This transition from simple local rules to global coherence is at the heart of what in the days of cybernetics was called self-organisation, and has been more recently talked about in terms of nonlinear dynamics, emergence and complex adaptive systems.
- *Enaction:* The world is seen not as something predefined and representable, but is always emerging from one's actions. One can never stand fully detached from the world because one is inevitably thrown into it.[8]

Consequently, Escobar argues that social researchers and developers today need to move away from ways of thinking based on rigid laws, ideologies, macropolitics, genetic determination, towards tracings, indetermination, movements, multiplicities, micropolitics and assemblages. If the dominant institutions of modernity have tended to operate on the basis of the first set of concepts, it would make sense now, in the trans-modern age, to build an approach to development building on the second set, being mindful that both exist.

For Escobar this perspective has profound implications on our understanding of knowledge creation and shifts local social movements to the centre of attention.

SOCIAL MOVEMENTS AS IMPORTANT SPACES OF KNOWLEDGE PRODUCTION

Escobar sees social movements as important spaces of knowledge production about the world. Furthermore, it in such spaces that the value of activist knowledge for the creation of new theory is recognised. Escobar hence promotes that communities and individuals are seen as the core knowledge producers – as opposed to, for example, the state, international development institutions or universities. Such local knowledge creation then can give gradually rise to larger knowledge systems.

According to Escobar, through such multiplication of the landscape of knowledge production, the dominance of academy (universities, research centres) as the knowledge space par excellence can be broken. The knowledge landscape then becomes flatter, in the sense of being populated by many. With a shift towards local knowledge creation, Escobar foresees also a change in the objects of studies. Naturally, now chosen on a local level, these objects will have greater relevance for the local contexts for which knowledge is to be created. Also, the core development questions asked have a much more inside-out direction, focusing on inner issues first before outer issues are regarded, than the previous outside-in direction, where the development question asked was defined by external developers.

Escobar takes the root paradigm of development out of former liberal or Marxist boxes into a new post-structural perspective. In this perspective, the core criteria for change is not progress but representation – allowing a multitude of local communities to participate in the discourse on development (see Table 17.1 opposite).

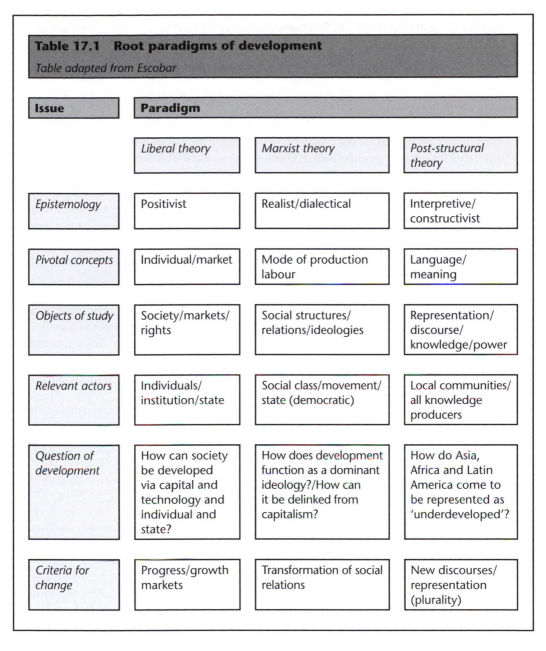

Table 17.1 Root paradigms of development

Table adapted from Escobar

Issue	Paradigm		
	Liberal theory	*Marxist theory*	*Post-structural theory*
Epistemology	Positivist	Realist/dialectical	Interpretive/ constructivist
Pivotal concepts	Individual/market	Mode of production labour	Language/ meaning
Objects of study	Society/markets/ rights	Social structures/ relations/ideologies	Representation/ discourse/ knowledge/power
Relevant actors	Individuals/ institution/state	Social class/movement/ state (democratic)	Local communities/ all knowledge producers
Question of development	How can society be developed via capital and technology and individual and state?	How does development function as a dominant ideology?/How can it be delinked from capitalism?	How do Asia, Africa and Latin America come to be represented as 'underdeveloped'?
Criteria for change	Progress/growth markets	Transformation of social relations	New discourses/ representation (plurality)

TOWARDS A POST-STRUCTURAL DEVELOPMENT PARADIGM

There is indeed a lot of resonance between our integral approach and Escobar's post-structural orientation to development, though we arguably put a much stronger emphasis on culture and spirituality. Altogether, we begin to see emergent facets within the development world of the post-capitalist society that Wallerstein postulates.

What we regard together with Escobar as crucial, is that a post-structural paradigm is not merely about multiplicity of discourses – for us 'Northern' and 'Southern', 'Eastern' and 'Western' – but that the co-evolutionary and meaning-generating potential that lies in the space between these discourses, is purposefully considered. As we have seen in our 'Eastern' organisational chapter (⇨12), this quality is rather evoked through dialogue than through discourse. It is evoked through listening to each other in carefully orchestrated processes of transculturation (⇨13) and translation (⇨13), and through respectfully co-engaging with the particular developmental paths that individuals, communities and societies chose.

As Integral Developers, we clearly resonate with Escobar's bottom-up approach. For us this not only means that we engage in an individual transformation process before we work towards organisational, communal and societal level, it also means that we have worked ourselves first through the 'Southern' realm of healthy coexistence and the 'Eastern' one of peaceful co-evolution. Restored life, the Southern theme, and regenerated meaning, the Eastern theme, are crucial inner prerequisites for our Northern engagement for open and transparent knowledge creation. We need the restored strength of the South and the emergent clarity of the East to engage in knowledge creation. For in this realm we need to face the dominant discourses of the field, which weigh heavily over it.

It is indisputable that the international power structure, for example the power of the so-called 'Washington Consensus' together with the financial markets, weighs in against the alternative knowledge systems that different communities possess, but are unable to make manifest on a global stage. That capacity to emerge is both constrained internally, by inhibited capacities to interweave one field of discourse with another, as it is also constrained, externally, by dominant power structures, including language and meaning-making systems.

Overall, we regard both the current dominance of the neo-liberal economic system, and the prior dominance of Marxism as monocultural systems that inhibited the emergence of something new. The co-evolutionary principle that we developed in the Eastern realm has never been applied in the confrontational relationship between both systems. In both cases, their approach to modernisation has been severely constraining of development rather than serving to promote it. Both have served to bypass local grounds, rather than accommodate them.

Hence, in the entire modern period, the so-called Global South has been continually on the back foot, continually having to defend, adapt or react. Even for the intellectuals, predominantly from South America in the development field, they have had to react to what has come before. The Portuguese sociologist Boaventura de Sousa Santos argues that the World Social Forum came as a dynamic reaction to the World Economic Forum. That is a good argument to a point, but it tends to lose out on the particular qualities that particular cultures have, in and of themselves, beyond being a dialectical reaction to the other.

Perhaps with the multiplicity of discourses (and dialogues) that Escobar (and we as Integral Developers) promote, we can gradually move towards, bottom-up, a post-structural development paradigm. In that process, we need to be fully aware of the enormously powerful dynamics that the world as a whole is facing with regards to information and communications technology (ICT) and whole new patterns of interactions, collaboration and social networking. With that we come to a final perspective in this societal 'Northern' chapter, the knowledge and network society.

17.4   The Network Society: The Challenge to Reconcile Technological Overdevelopment and Social Underdevelopment

THE RISE OF THE NETWORK SOCIETY

The world-renowned Spanish sociologist Manuel Castells is among the foremost scholars in the fields of network and information society, and of communications research. His Information Age Trilogy has become one of the most influential texts in this field. For Castells, the technological revolution of the last quarter of the twentieth century, centred around information, has transformed the way we think, we produce, we consume. A dynamic, global economy has been constituted around the planet, linking up valuable people and activities from all over the world, while switching off from networks of power and wealth, people and territories, dubbed as irrelevant from the perspective of dominant interests.[9]

NEW EMERGENT SOCIAL STRUCTURES

For Castells, partly based at the University of California, a new world is taking shape. It originates in the historical coincidence, around the late 1960s and mid 1970s, of three independent processes: the information technology revolution; the economic crisis of both capitalism and statism, and their subsequent restructuring; and the blooming of cultural social movements, such as libertarianism, human rights, feminism and environmentalism. The interaction between these processes, and the reactions they triggered, brought into being a new dominant social structure, the network society; a new economy, the informational, global economy; and a new culture, the culture of real virtuality. The logic embedded in this economy and society and culture underlies all institutions in an interdependent world. Particularly important is the role of ICT in allowing the development of networking as a dynamic, self-expanding form of organisation of humanity. This prevailing networking logic transforms all domains of social and economic life.

THE RISE OF INFORMATIONAL CAPITALISM

Castells argues that the new capitalism we witness today is characterised by the globalisation of core economic activities, organisational flexibility, and greater power for management in relation to labour, leading to the retrenchment of the welfare state, the cornerstone of the social contract in the industrial era. New information technologies played a vital role in facilitating the emergence of such a revitalised capitalism, by providing the tools for networking, and coordinating the individualisation of work. The emergence of a powerful, competitive Asia Pacific broadened the scale and scope of the global economy. Networks of capital, labour and information linked up, while switching off from those networks those people and territories deprived of value and interest for the dynamics of global capital. What followed was the social and economic exclusion of segments of societies, and of entire countries. Castells refers to such excluded segments and countries as 'the Fourth World'. He affirms that as social inclusion grows, we shall witness increasingly expressions of social resistance to informationalisation and globalisation. Such social resistance is mainly built around primary identities. That includes different forms of fundamentalism, creating defensive communities in the name of God, locality, ethnicity and family.

INCREASING POLARISATION: PARALLEL DEVELOPMENT AND UNDER-DEVELOPMENT

For Castells, the ascent of global informational capitalism is characterised by simultaneous economic development and underdevelopment, social inclusion and exclusion. There is a polarisation in the distribution of wealth at the global level, differential evolution of intra-country income inequality, and substantial poverty and misery in the world at large and in most, but not all developed and developing countries.

Castells discloses that the rise of informational capitalism in the past 30 years coincided with the collapse of Africa's economies, the disintegration of many of its states, and the breakdown of most of its societies. Africa, with the exception of South Africa, was for a long time excluded from the information technology revolution, and much of Africa still is. Furthermore, technological dependency and technological underdevelopment, in a period of accelerated technological change in the rest of the world, makes it literally impossible for Africa to compete internationally. For Castells, the disinformation of Africa at the dawn of the Information Age may be the most lasting wound inflicted on this continent by new patterns of dependency.[10]

THE RISE OF SOCIAL MOVEMENTS

Societies, however, are not just the result of technological and economic transformation, nor can social change be limited to institutional crises and adaptations. At the same time that these changes began to take place in the 1960s, powerful social movements exploded almost simultaneously around the industrialised world, first in the US and France, then in Italy, Germany, Spain, Japan, Brazil, Czechoslovakia, with echoes and reactions in many other countries. They were essentially cultural movements. Their ambitions encompassed a multidimensional reaction to arbitrary authority, a revolt against injustice, and a search for personal experimentation. From these movements sprang the source of environmentalism, feminism, the defence of human rights, of sexual equality, of ethnic equality and grassroots democracy.

HOPE FOR LIBERATION: THE NECESSARY SHIFT FROM RESISTANCE TO PROJECT IDENTITY

For Castells, societies today are constituted of the interaction between the 'net' and the 'self'', the network society and the power of identity. The net, for him, will increasingly lead to the replacement of vertical hierarchies as the major form social organisation, while the self refers to the sum of activities that individuals use to reaffirm social identity and meaning. Yet, the self serves to fragment rather than reconstitute society. People's experience remains confined to simple, segregated locales, while global elites retrench within immaterial palaces made up of communication networks and information flows. With no Winter Palace to be seized, so Castells, outbursts of revolt may implode, transformed into everyday senseless violence. Thus, he foresees that a long march is required from communes built around resistance identity to the heights of new project identities, sprouting from the values nurtured in these communes. The concept of sustainable development and the universal mobilisation in defence of human rights represent that. For this transition from resistance to project identity, a new politics will need to emerge. This will be a cultural politics that connects to values and experiences that spring from people's life experience.

Castells affirms that such new local cultural politics – connected to values and rooted in people's life experience – are the basis for liberation. According to him, it is for people to free themselves from uncritical adherence to theoretical or ideological schemes, to construct their practice on the basis of their experience, while using whatever information or analysis is available to them. Such social, economic and political action is essential for the betterment of society, which needs change and hope.

Castells evokes here – as a 'Northener' with a good feel for the other worlds' realities – something very close to our Integral Development approach. To sum it up in our words: a rooting in people's life experience and in local communes (South), an evolution linked to values and local culture (East), a critical use of suitable information and knowledge (North), to ultimately arrive at new economic and political projects (West) – and in the overall process progressing from a resistance identity to a project identity, thereby actively participating in the remaking of society. We have creatively adapted the development rhythm proposed by Castells into an integral perspective (Figure 17.1).

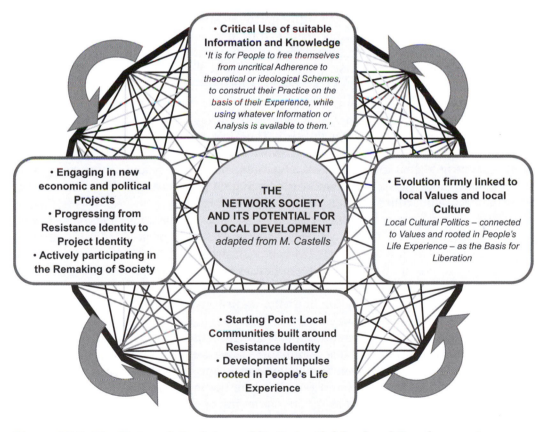

Figure 17.1 The Network Society and its Potential for local Development

Furthermore, Castells argues that such development processes would necessarily start on local grounds, and it is there where they do have a chance to succeed. As for him, the era of globalisation of the economy is also the era of the localisation of the polity. What local and regional governments lack in power and resources they make up in flexibility and networking. They are the only match to the dynamism of global networks of wealth and information. It is on this level, where Escobar's more local perspective and Castells' more global perspective meet. Further, there seems to be growing insights also from the international development community into the need to avoid the polarisation and exclusion Castells refers to, as well as to support local communities to find meaningful ways to integrate ICT into existing structures.

ICT4D: INFORMATION AND COMMUNICATIONS TECHNOLOGY FOR DEVELOPMENT

Ban Ki-moon, the current UN Secretary-General recently confirmed that:

> *information and communications technologies have a central role to play in the quest for development, dignity and peace. The international consensus on this point is clear. We saw it at the 2000 Millennium Summit and at the 2005 World Summit. And we saw it in the two phases of the World Summit on the Information Society.*[11]

The translation of this consensus into practice, for the time being, still remains relatively weak. Many ICT4D projects suffered from a poor cost-benefit ratio, of cultural insensitivity, environmental unfriendliness and in parts even resulted in widening the digital divide. Anriette Esterhuysen, an advocate for ICT4D and human rights in South Africa, pointed out that some ICT4D projects often give more emphasis to how ICT can help its beneficiaries economically rather than helping them create a society where social justice and equal rights prevail.[12] The renowned development expert Jan Nederveen Pieterse even warns in a chapter entitled 'The Unbearable Lightness of ICT4D' that ICT4D often comes with the fragrance of 'cyber utopianism', and is frequently packaged with marketing 'digital capitalism'. He advocates, that ICT4D 'should move away from development aid, NGOs and externally funded digital projects and focus on the central question of disembedding technology from capital'.[13]

A 2010 research report from the Governance and Social Development Resource Centre confirmed that very few ICT4D activities have proved sustainable. The report stressed the need to shift from a technology-led approach, where the emphasis is on technical innovation towards an approach that emphasises innovative use of already established technology (mobiles, radio, television).[14] The report's author Hannah Beardon agues that ICTs cannot create communication capacity, and should not start from scratch. They should be built into existing structures to enhance what works, or to increase equal participation in existing communication channels. This means enhancing resources provided by other projects, such as community radio, television stations or telecentres, and recognising less formal communication arenas and structures. Beardon concludes that E-government, E-learnings and E-health were the few areas that were found to be possible of great success, as well as the strengthening of social networks and boosting of security (particularly of women).

The model of an information society that every society seeks to build should depend on the values that people and governments put forward. Castells warns, however, that we will have to articulate sustainable values for the transformation of society and the economy, otherwise the contradictions of the social transformation will trigger social explosions and violent opposition from a diversity of quarters.[15] That brings us to the probably most profound developmental challenge to an emergent network society.

OVERCOMING SOCIAL UNDER-DEVELOPMENT

Castells laments that there is an extraordinary gap between our technological overdevelopment and our social underdevelopment. Our economy, society and culture are built on interests that, by and large, limit collective creativity, confiscate the harvest of information technology, and deviate our energy into self-destructive confrontation. The overcoming of humankind's social underdevelopment, for Castells, is likely to be the decisive factor in the world's social and economic evolution. Building a network economy requires foremost, in this emergent stage, the development of a learning economy that is addressing this very challenge.

But Castells also shows the potential that the newly emergent structures offer:

> *If people are informed, active and communicate; if business assumes its social responsibility; if the media become the messengers rather than the message; if political actors react against cynicism and restore democracy; if culture is reconstructed from experience; if humankind feels the solidarity of the species throughout the globe; if we assert intergenerational solidarity by living in harmony with nature; if we depart for the exploration of the inner self, having made peace among ourselves; if all this is made possible by our informed, conscious, shared decision, while there is still time, maybe then, we may, at last, be able to live and let live, love and be loved.[16]*

OUTLOOK: BEYOND DEFENCE IDENTITY – TOWARDS PROJECT IDENTITY

With the help of Manuel Castells we gained insight in the potential as well as threats that come with the emergent network society. The major challenge we need to address is to close, or at least dramatically narrow, the gap between technological overdevelopment and social underdevelopment. The network society, so Castells, is likely to increase social injustice and exclusion. From leading protagonists of the international development arena, we learned that the hopes that are put into ICT to close the digital divide and to link hitherto excluded communities and societies to the global economy, thus lifting them out of material poverty, are still overwhelmingly unsustainable. Castells and others, however, come to the conclusion, that such exclusion needs to be dealt with primarily on a local level, progressing from a 'defence identity' to a 'project identity'. We illustrated that Castells' work shows tangible traces of an integral logic, as he emphasises the potential that the network society also offers on local levels, if linked to communities, local values and culture and with a critical perspective on informationalism. Given the enormous dynamics of an ICT driven network society, we become aware of the extraordinary challenge – but also potential – we are facing as Integral Developers.

17.5   Integration

In this chapter we dealt with the challenge of bringing about a new societal perspective on 'organisational and societal knowledge creation', thereby building on the foundation that was provided through individual learning and research (⇨15) and organisational knowledge creation (⇨16). We engaged with new ways of thinking that could help us to go beyond approaches to societal modernisation coming out of a narrow sociological or technological modernisation perspective but rather repositions societal learning in the light of today's civilisational transition.

With World Systems Analysis, Immanuel Wallerstein provided us with a useful societal perspective on development. This approach takes development not only out of the national modernisation box, but also transcends the bi-modal, core-periphery standpoint of the dependency school. Instead, World Systems Analysis places development in the context of the dramatic shift of one (current) world system towards a (yet unknown) new world system that brings with it the end of capitalist economics.

This perspective created a platform for Arturo Escobar to follow with the translation of 'self-making', 'self-organisation' and 'emergence' (altogether still relatively new concepts from biology and complexity theory) into new sociological concepts for societal knowledge creation – bottom-up through local social movements. He thereby promotes a new, post-structural development paradigm.

With Manuel Castells' interpretation of the emergence of a global network society, we added a 'global society' perspective on knowledge creation – with its primary challenge of balancing today's technological overdevelopment with social underdevelopment. Escobar's work may be seen as one partial response to this challenge.

With these three pre-eminent thinkers, we provided insights into the highly transitive world of societal learning and knowledge creation, caught in the midst of paradigmatic shifts. What became apparent in the past three chapters of this 'Northern' realm of science, systems and technology is that a link between research and learning, at the level of self, organisation, and now society is only tenuously apparent.

To promote this link between individual learning and research, organisational knowledge creation and societal transformation in a much more effective way, we now turn to Mondragon in Spain as well as to a prospective new African University – both aligned with the concept of a reframed 'Research University', as well as to a telecoms giant at the heart of Europe.

Before we move on, we shall, once again, conclude this chapter with an invitation to engage with the guiding question and theory presented in this chapter. This includes the major development challenges derived thereof. At this stage it is of primary importance to identify, how you and your organisation or community can reach out into society at large, thereby becoming a veritable agent for societal development.

For this to happen, you and your organisation or community are challenged to articulate and conceptualise your own learnings and findings with regards to development, based on your experiences in Round 1 (the formative grounding of your own self) and in Round 2 (the reformative response of your organisation or community). Hence, this normative Round 3 is very much about coming up with new development norms that can inform wide ranging knowledge creation as well as learning and development in your society at large.

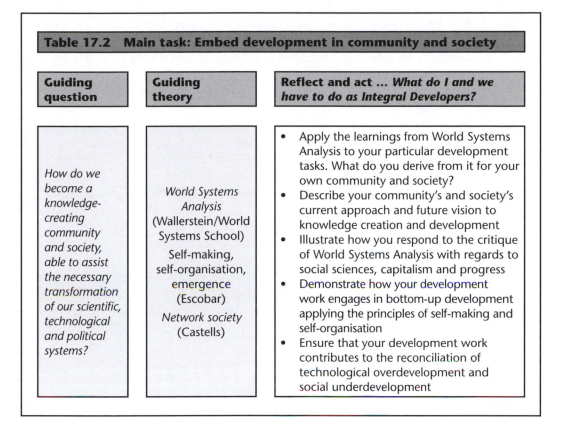

Table 17.2   Main task: Embed development in community and society

Guiding question	Guiding theory	Reflect and act ... *What do I and we have to do as Integral Developers?*
How do we become a knowledge-creating community and society, able to assist the necessary transformation of our scientific, technological and political systems?	*World Systems Analysis* (Wallerstein/World Systems School) Self-making, self-organisation, emergence (Escobar) *Network society* (Castells)	• Apply the learnings from World Systems Analysis to your particular development tasks. What do you derive from it for your own community and society? • Describe your community's and society's current approach and future vision to knowledge creation and development • Illustrate how you respond to the critique of World Systems Analysis with regards to social sciences, capitalism and progress • Demonstrate how your development work engages in bottom-up development applying the principles of self-making and self-organisation • Ensure that your development work contributes to the reconciliation of technological overdevelopment and social underdevelopment

We now turn, finally, in this 'Northern' realm, to a renewed Research University.

References

1   Wallerstein, I. (2004). *World Systems Analysis: An Introduction*. Durham, NC: Duke University Press.
2   Braudel, F. and Mayne, R. (1995). *A History of Civilisations*. Harmondsworth: Penguin Books.
3   Wallerstein, I. (ed.) (1996). *Open Social Sciences*. Palo Alto, CA: Stanford University Press.
4   Wallerstein, I. (1999). *Social Science for the 21st Century: The End of the World as We Know It*. Minneapolis, MN: University of Minnesota.
5   Nurnberger, K. (1999). *Prosperity, Poverty, and Pollution*. London: Zed
6   Wallerstein, I. (1999). *The End of the World as We Know It: Social Science for the 21st Century*. Minneapolis, MN: University of Minnesota.
7   Escobar, A. (2008). *Territories of Difference: Place, Movements, Life, Redes*. Durham, NC: Duke University Press.
8   Maturana, H. and Varela, F. (1998). *The Tree of Knowledge: The Biological Roots of Human Understanding*. Boston, MA: Shambhala.
9   Castells, M. (1996). *The Rise of the Network Society*. Oxford: Blackwell.
10   Castells, M. (2003). *The Power of Identity*. Oxford: Blackwell.

11 Ban, K.-M. (2011). Quoted from Asia-Pacific Development Information Programme. Available at: www.apdip.net/ Accessed: 14 June 2012.
12 ICT4D website. Available at: http://ict4d.at/2009/07/09/coop-20-interview-anriette-esterhuysen / Accessed: 16 June 2012.
13 Nederveen Pieterse, J. (2010). *Development Theory: Deconstructions/Reconstructions*. Los Angeles, CA: Sage, p. 166.
14 Beardon, H, (2008). *ICT for Development: Empowerment or Exploitation*. A GSDRC document. Available at: www.gsdrc.org.
15 Castells, C. and Himanenen, P. (2002): *The Information Society and the Welfare State: The Finnish Model*. Oxford: Oxford University Press.
16 Castells, M. (1996). *The Rise of the Network Society*. Oxford: Blackwell.

18 Northern Integration via a Renewed Research University: The Cases of Mondragon and a Future University for Africa

Guiding Question: How can we sustainably actualise the Northern realm of Integral Development, rooted in science, systems and technology?

18.1   Orientation

THE REINVENTION OF THE RESEARCH UNIVERSITY

In this final chapter of the 'Northern' realm, we come to its culminating 'Uni-Versity round'. As in the final 'Southern' (⇨10) and 'Eastern' (⇨14) chapters before, we illustrate through practical cases, not only how the first three rounds of individual, organisational and societal development can be meaningfully integrated in theory and practice, but also how they can altogether be further actualised through an educational institution.

In this 'Northern' realm, with its core theme of 'Reframing Knowledge via Science and Technology', the actualising educational institution is a reframed 'Research University'.

Being an enabling space for 'open and transparent knowledge creation' as the core 'Northern' value, such a university type focuses on education and research with a view to technological *and* social innovation. Key defining terms of a reframed Research University are 'content', 'conceptualisation' and 'complexity'. The latter term alludes to its ability to adequately respond and deal with complexity – for example, through a transdisciplinary orientation rather than the still prevailing disciplinary compartmentalisation of most existing universities. What is of further significance for the reframed Research University is that the content and concepts it generates are relevant for addressing burning issues of our time. This, so our argument, requires that it builds on the 'Southern' communal grounds and 'Eastern' cultural-societal context that have come before. It is hence crucial that this university type has elements of a Communiversity (⇨10), ensuring its serving particular communities, and of a Developmental University (⇨14), enabling it to relate to the particular consciousness of the societal context it is embedded in.

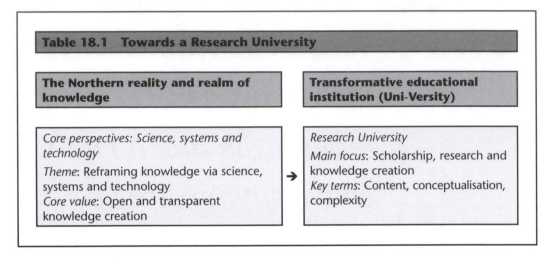

Table 18.1 Towards a Research University	
The Northern reality and realm of knowledge	**Transformative educational institution (Uni-Versity)**
Core perspectives: Science, systems and technology *Theme*: Reframing knowledge via science, systems and technology *Core value*: Open and transparent knowledge creation	*Research University* *Main focus*: Scholarship, research and knowledge creation *Key terms*: Content, conceptualisation, complexity

Why have we chosen the Research University as the actualising institution in this realm, and in what respect do we see the need for its reinvention?

A Research University, in its best sense, focuses on education, research and knowledge creation, altogether relevant for society. We argue that today, many universities that had originally been conceived as Research Universities, fail to bring about social and technological innovation that is required to respond adequately to a society's most burning issues. Indeed, most of such universities have over time degenerated into mere educational entities. They focus mainly on delivering standardised (usually in 'North-Western' guise) productised courses. In the process, they have lost their innovative power. In those cases where there is still significant knowledge creation taking place, it is often primarily focused on technological innovation, rather than, simultaneously, on social innovation. As a result we experience a severe lack of social innovation.

Furthermore, many students leave universities with an education that is not contextualised within their particular society, hence inhibiting the potential contribution that they might make to their respective employers as well as to their society at large. In our integral terms, we see such limited Research Universities being insufficiently in touch with context and community (our 'Southern' realm) as well as with consciousness and catalysation (our 'Eastern' realm). In other words, education and research are often not sufficiently in tune with the needs and capacities of the communities and organisational-societal contexts for which they intend to cater, nor do they act as catalytic forces for evolving the consciousness of society, responding to society's most urgent evolutionary requirements.

Linking the argument back to the institutional solutions that we introduced for the 'Southern' and 'Eastern' realms, we argue, that most Research Universities have not integrated enough elements of a 'Southern Communiversiy' nor of an 'Eastern Developmental University', leaving them isolated from society in the proverbial 'ivory tower'. The reinvention of such 'inhibited' Research Universities is necessary because of the vital role of education, knowledge creation and innovation (technological *and* social) for society.

The cases of reinvention that we are introducing in this chapter illustrate how such reframed Research Universities can indeed grow through a process of self-organisational-societal-development (Rounds 1, 2, 3). As such, they gradually build up an integrated approach to learning and research on an individual level (Round 1); then evolve such individual approaches towards a learning and knowledge producing organisation (Round 2); moving on to enabling knowledge creating communities and society. On such a 3-level foundation we can then envision the establishment of relevant, reframed Research Universities (Round 4).

The two cases we present differ significantly in scale. In the first and major case, Mondragon Corporation and Mondragon University in Spain, we retrospectively illustrate the full four-level process. In the second case, we share the emergent case of CISER in Nigeria, a Centre for Integral Social and Economic Research, that regards itself as a seedbed for a Nigerian, if not African Research University. Later in this chapter (⇨18.3) we additionally provide a short glimpse of an interesting development with the German corporation Deutsche Telekom Group, driven by innovative social science research. Before we introduce our cases, though, we feel the need to give a backdrop of the history of the original Research University, illustrating, at what point in time it lost its course.

LOOKING BACK TO MOVE FORWARD: THE STORY OF THE RESEARCH UNIVERSITY SO FAR

Birth of the Research University in Germany – Towards Wissenschaft and Bildung

The Research University, which originated in Germany in the nineteenth century, has been characteristically associated with the natural sciences and material technologies. However, it was initially established with a much broader scientific base, including also the humanities, in mind.

These Research Universities, according to the English historian Peter Watson in his work on *The German Genius: The Second Scientific Revolution*,[1] showed a couple of unique characteristics that intimate its potential role in establishing a learning and knowledge creating society:

- *Increased Access to Education:* Early eighteenth-century Germany had far more universities – about 50 – as compared with Oxford and Cambridge in England. It was therefore far easier for the gifted sons of poorer families to obtain higher education.
- *Combining Natural Sciences, Social Sciences and Humanities:* At Göttingen, for instance, in addition to the traditional subjects of logic, metaphysics and ethics, the philosophical faculty offered law of nature, physics, politics, natural history, mathematics, history and geography, art and modern languages. On top of these, dancing, riding and fencing, drawing and music, conversation in foreign languages, were on offer.
- *Redefining Research – The Drive towards 'Wissenschaft':* Göttingen also developed and refined the seminar, which led on to the modern concept of research, and the organisation of the university into departments divided between education and research. In the research seminar, criticism was welcome, knowledge was regarded as mutable, and the aim was to cultivate taste, judgement and reason. Thereby, the fostering of research put a premium on originality, which reached its climax in the

Romantic period, when research was considered an art form. In the early nineteenth century, *Wissenschaft* (the German term for science, or, more precisely, knowledge creation), evolved further, incorporating science, learning, knowledge, scholarship, also implying a research-based element, and the idea that knowledge is a dynamic process, discoverable for oneself, rather than something handed down. It was out of such an evolution that the PhD emerged.

Education turned from something that was outer directed to something more inner-directed, expressed in the concept of *Bildung*, referring to the inner shaping and development of the person, a process of fulfilment through education and knowledge, representing progress and refinement in knowledge and moral terms, a combination of wisdom and self-realisation. Unlike in Britain or Russia, in Germany the intelligentsia was drawn from all social classes: also because university education was needed for a government position.

Bildung and the inborn drive for perfection

Wilhelm von Humboldt played a major part in the emergence of the German university. For him, nature consisted of specific individual centres of energy and activity, each centre revealing its own character in the activity it displayed. Activity – sheer movement – was key here. In classical (Newtonian) physics, motion was always the result of some outside source. However, many thinkers were dissatisfied with the application of Newton's science as an explanation for living systems. They preferred what they called 'the living order of nature': it was here where nothing stood still, and where 'self-generated motion' meant that every living part of nature was constantly in movement. Unlike mechanical concepts of force (magnetism, electricity, gravitation), these internal powers were thought to operate directionally toward self-realisation.

Bildung, for someone like Humboldt, was partly a biological force, partly a spiritual necessity. *Bildung* was an interior force whereby an individual could work on himself, or herself, to improve his or her self-consciousness, to move closer to perfection. The concept of genius – individuals whose creations offered glimpses of divine wisdom, glimpses of perfection – meant that self-cultivation offered the cultivated individual the prospect of achieving an approximation of divine wisdom right here on earth. Such an approach to self-realisation is of course in stark difference to the more 'Eastern' approach where 'alignment to a larger, divine force' or to nature takes pride in place of 'working on yourself'.

The advent of the Research University in Germany

The culmination of Humboldt's reforms was his design of the University of Berlin, founded in 1810. Consolidating the trend begun at Göttingen, Humboldt promoted Berlin's philosophical faculty, ultimately subordinating the natural sciences to the humanities, over and above the more practical law, medicine and theology, and fearing that the natural sciences would otherwise slide into 'mindless empiricism'.

For Humboldt, the development of social morality within an individual was an all-important progression which depended on that individual's self-transformative progress from a natural state of ignorance to 'self-willed citizenship': a belief that spiritual emancipation through education in the humanities was the true path to inner freedom and willing citizenship. According to Humboldt, such true inner freedom involved three things: a non-utilitarian orientation, inwardness and scholarliness.

The development of modern scholarship, the concept of *Bildung*, and the innovation of the research-based university was seen at the beginning of the nineteenth century in Germany as a form of moral progress.

Education was not simply the acquisition of knowledge but looked upon as a process of character development during the course of which a person would learn to form critical judgements, make an original creative contribution, and learn about his or her place in society. Education as *Bildung* involved a process of 'becoming'.

When the Research University was exported from Germany to America in the latter part of the nineteenth century, it initially saw its role primarily as a creative contributor to societal development – a role that most US universities, by now, have abandoned and replaced with 'upgrading of individuals'.

The rise of the Research University in the USA

In his brilliant work *From Higher Aims to Hired Hands*,[2] Rakesh Khurana, Professor of Management at Harvard Business School, uses the case of business education in the USA to illustrate how the original idea of the Research University, after taking successful roots in the USA, gradually degraded. Khurana's insights are particularly helpful, given the all-pervasive impact that the enterprise approach – promoted by the MBA, the flagship of Anglo-Saxon business education – has all over the world, not only on business, but also on the field of development.

Khurana describes the role that the American Research University initially played for the evolution of the entire American society, as well as for shaping the individual character of its graduates. Many of the early universities in the US were faith-based, and saw their role clearly in ethical formation of individuals as well as societal betterment overall.

By the era early on in the twentieth century, science was widely viewed not only as a means of solving concrete problems, but also as an intrinsically moral and even quasi-religious activity. The scientist's dedicated search for truth was seen to resemble the religious believer's pursuit of spiritual truth. At the same time, the drive for social progress through science offered an outlet for a distinctly Protestant moral fervour. Thus, American society's embrace of scientific authority represented as much a cognitive and ideational revolution as it did a revolution in problem-solving methods.

As much as the pioneering scientists of early modern Europe conceptualised a basis for knowledge that promised delivery from murderous conflicts inspired by religious dogmatism, Americans from the late nineteenth century onwards sought a cognitive and normative framework within which to resolve the often intense social conflicts caused by the disruption of traditional communities and mores by such forces as industrialisation, urbanisation and the rise of the large corporation. Because science itself was concerned primarily with discovering the true constitution of the natural and social worlds, its most passionate advocates believed that it represented a prescription for society's ills.

Then, Khurana affirms, as science came under the wings of the universities and consequently was recast as public service rather than idle indulgence for the elite, both social scientists and natural scientists enjoyed a new kind of social stature and prestige.

Together, scientific associations offered an overarching vision that combined social welfare and science to convey the conviction that the process of scientific inquiry could alter the world, making it more responsive to human purpose. Part of such a moral appeal derived from the organisational structure of science, conducted in a communal setting, where individuals bound together through intense socialisation, shared values and common norms.

Thus, Khurana argues, the goals of science were viewed as collective and rooted in the disinterested pursuit of truths about nature, using knowledge to advance collective goods having to do with human social progress and equality. What followed is that science, with its emphasis on truth, service and community, stood in stark contrast to an increasingly bureaucratic and materialistic culture that arguably dominated. Indeed, scientists tended to produce not tangible products but rather ideas taking the form of principles and norms. Science became the pervading faith, the laboratory was the temple, and scientific method was the path to salvation, envisioned as a new era of social order and harmony. Yet, as Khurana intimates, science had started to lose touch with the social realities and cultural contexts it was facing by becoming ever more abstract and remote.

During this entire period, the American Research University was emerging. In many ways, so Khurana, its rise and development represented the most significant institutional challenge of the time. This was the case not only because the American Research University was, and remains, one of the most vital, dynamic, and influential institutions in the modern world, but also because it enabled both science and the professions to come into its own as institutions. In proclaiming its mission of creating and disseminating knowledge for the public good, the Research University drew on the cognitive and normative legitimacy of its new commitment to scientific method. By strengthening its links with the professions, it affirmed its dedication to useful knowledge and to service.

In the early nineteenth century, new states' colleges and universities began expanding access to higher education, giving it a more practical cast. In the ensuing decades, the growing belief that universities in a democratic society needed to provide practical benefits for the public, an American hybrid university emerged, dedicated to serving society with the provision of opportunities for individual cultivation and economic advancement.

In the progressive heartland of the US the 'Wisconsin Idea'[3] took hold: the University of Wisconsin's School of Economics, Political Science and History was founded with the objective of turning the university into an efficient practical servant of the state, offering its know-how in practical sciences to support the state, while providing widening education through satellite campuses.

The universities received increasing attention because they performed a dual function: they infused knowledge into the young who would apply it in their professions and whose lives would be illuminated by its possession, and they contributed to the improvement of the stock of knowledge, penetrating further into the nature of reality. The knowledge that was appreciated was secular knowledge that continued the mission of sacred knowledge, complemented it, led to it, or replaced it; systematically acquired knowledge as seen to be a step toward redemption. This kind of knowledge held out the promise of the transfiguration of life by improving man's control over resources; offering the prospect of the better understanding of society, leading to its improvement. According to Khurana, at a time of faltering theological conviction, the university scholar or scientist assumed the role of an earnest seeker after fundamental truth. The scholar, like the priest or minister, lived a life oriented toward ultimate things. We now turn, specifically with Khurana, to management, an area with which both of us authors have been intimately concerned.

The emergence of management as science and profession

Gradually, management appeared on the university scene and attempted to establish itself as a discipline on its own. In alignment, management as a profession began to articulate its role in society more clearly: just as natural science was enabling man to gain previously unimaginable control over the physical world and thus to dramatically improve the material conditions of human existence, and social science was creating knowledge for a more balanced ordering of psychic and social life, so management in turn would harness the tremendous forces of technology, markets and corporations to advance both material prosperity and social harmony.

As management became gradually accepted as an independent scientific discipline, the leading business schools of the USA – from Pennsylvania's Wharton School to Dartmouth and Harvard – positioned management as a force for good in society. According to Khurana, they intended to form a new kind of manager, instilled with the sense of social obligation, who would run corporations in ways consistent with the broader interests of the country.

When Leon Marshall became Dean of Wharton Business School at the advent of the Great Depression in 1933, he called upon the business schools to shift their gaze so as to serve the needs of the nation: 'The world demands that we step up the quality of our understanding of the complex and changing phenomena with which we deal so that the basis for a more stable and better planned society may be present'.[4]

By the time one of the authors, Ronnie Lessem, became a student at Harvard Business School in the mid 1960s, little evidence of the sense of overall moral purpose and social scientific intent that had been imbued within the early business schools was left. The original intent behind the American university business school, as an offshoot of a Research University that explicitly served societal, as well as organisational and individual learning and research ends, was nowhere to be seen. This is in particular dramatic in a time like ours, where new sustainable social designs of sustainable micro- and macroeconomics, as well as a renewed management education and practice that is actualising such new designs, are desperately needed.

Rise and fall of Research Universities: From 'societal development' to 'upgrading of individuals'

When we compare Humboldt's approach to education that was at the very root of the Research University to the conventional approach to research and education that we encounter in most universities today, we don't find much of the original educational vision left: not only has natural sciences clearly taken pride of place over social sciences – not to speak of the humanities, that are almost living a shadow existence in most universities – also the focus on the inner moral evolution of the human being has almost been lost completely. Rather, instead of fostering original creative contributions of their students, most universities have become extremely impoverished, focusing primarily on 'producing degree holders'.

To the extent that research is taking place at all – many universities have already been reduced to mere 'degree factories' – it is often not leading to innovation. This is in particular true for the social sciences, where research is suffering of the following interrelated predicaments: not being embedded in social realities; not responding to natural and community needs; culturally insensitive; undertaken individually rather than in research teams; career advancement of the social scientist as the primary motive; lack of accountability of social scientists towards society.

Given this desolate state of affairs in the social sciences, natural sciences today account for most of society's innovation power. Indeed, most people understand by now the term 'innovation', or indeed knowledge creation, in relation to 'technological innovation' alone. That has led to a disastrous lack of relevant social designs (be it in politics, economics, environment etc.) that balance and frame technological innovations. That in turn has made many of today's technological innovations unrelated to context: meaning they either not respond to actual needs in communities and society, or are even harmful to natural and social environment.

The challenge ahead: Reinventing the Research University

What did the overall demise of the Research University mean for us personally? The extent to which universities at large – including our own Alma Maters, the University of St Gallen and Harvard Business School – had departed from the original Research University purpose, motivated us to create alternative educational and research designs and curricula. Through our Trans4m Center for Integral Development, we have developed new approaches to integral research, enterprise and economics, altogether geared toward societal, as well as organisational and individual, betterment. Some of these approaches we have introduced in this book, embedded in the overall paradigmatic approach of Integral Development.

In some cases, our work has led to the establishment of integral research centres on the ground, such as CISER (Centre for Integral Social and Economic Research) in Nigeria and, more recently, CISER in Zimbabwe. Both centres are a direct result of our PhD programme on Integral Development. In both cases, the centres can be seen as an institutionalisation of a research-to-innovation journey (framed and catalysed through the PhD programme) geared to address burning socioeconomic issues in the contexts of the participants. Both are stepping stones towards an envisioned, new University for Africa. CISER Nigeria we shall introduce as a 'case in progress' in this chapter.

We begin, however, with the case story of Mondragon in Spain, which allows us to retrace the evolutionary journey that led to the establishment of an authentic Research University – one that is geared to societal transformation, and that is located geographically in the northern hemisphere.

18.2   Integrated Northern Practice: Mondragon Corporation in Spain and a Prospective New African University

THE CASE OF MONDRAGON CORPORATION AND MONDRAGON UNIVERSITY: SOCIAL AND TECHNOLOGICAL INNOVATION FOR THE BASQUE COUNTRY, SPAIN AND THE WORLD

Introduction

The Mondragon Corporation, headquartered in the city of Mondragon in Spain's Basque country, has grown since its official foundation in 1956 into the largest worker cooperative in the world. With a revenue of about €15 billion (2010) and a workers' force of almost 84,000 (2010), Mondragon Corporation is the leading business enterprise in the Basque country, and among the seven largest corporations in Spain. Today, it consists of over 250 enterprises and is committed, according to its current president José María Aldecoa, 'to the creation of greater social wealth through customer satisfaction, job creation, technological and business development, continuous improvement, the promotion of education and respect for the environment'.[5] Mondragon Corporation – whose logo carries the slogan 'Humanity at Work' – is focusing simultaneously on four areas: industry, retail, finance and knowledge.

Mondragon was founded against all odds in a post-World War II environment, where not only Spain as a whole sought to recover from its own civil war, but in which also the Basque country was economically and politically shunned by the Franco regime for its support of the republican forces during the war.

The story begins with the arrival of a young Catholic priest, Don José María Arizmendiarrieta – called, in short, Arizmendi – in the economically and socially depressed city of Mondragon (in Basque: Arrasate) in 1941. This period became later known as 'the hunger period'.[6] The story of Arizmendi and Mondragon Corporation, as well as its collective impact on the Basque country and on Spain, including its international repercussions as one of the most innovative cooperative organisational models of our time, is a fascinating tale. For it involves local economic development, underpinned by a fervent moral and social vision, as well as with a strong drive for education and technological excellence. At the root of Mondragon is Arizmendi's philosophical and practical reinterpretation of work as simultaneously being a catalyst for self-realisation and societal betterment, a combination of 'auto-realisation de la persona' and 'servicio a la communidad'.[7]

Round 1 – Self-development: Work as self-realisation and societal betterment with education as the key

Arizmendi, born in 1925, was only 26 years old, when he arrived in Mondragon. At the time, he was already engaged in deeply critical thinking vis-à-vis the nature and scope of capitalism. His personal search for economic alternatives was then primarily influenced by Christian social philosophers, such as the French Catholic intellectuals Jacques Maritain and Emmanuel Mounier.

Arizmendi embraced Mounier's philosophy of 'Personalism', advocating that economic renewal needed to be moral or else it would not exist. Following the message of the so-called worker priests, Arizmendi believed that 'work should be seen as a means of achieving personal growth and development and contributing to the overall well-being of society. The aim was to encourage workers to see themselves as agents for the transformation of industry, and ultimately society as a whole'. In his sermons, he stressed that 'work should not be seen as a punishment but as a means for self-realisation'.[8] Thus an educational – personal growth and development – mission was built into the prospective Mondragon Cooperatives from the outset.

Gradually, Arizmendi developed his own vision of 'cooperativism', which he saw as an alternative to egoistic capitalism and depersonalising socialism. His key concern was to create an economic system that surpassed capitalism without losing its dynamism, and that would serve to shift the focus from individual self-interest to what he called 'supreme human values' – such as cooperation, solidarity and mutual support. For Arizmendi:

> We want cooperatives, which constitute a new social potential and, thus, are built by those who are not impelled by a myopic and limited egotism or by a simple gregarious instinct. Cooperativism seeks to create a new state of conscience, of culture in a word, through the humanisation of power, through democracy in affairs, and through solidarity, which impedes the formation of privileged classes. Here and now it assigns a functional value to property. That is, property is valued in so far as it serves as an efficient resource for building responsibility and efficiency in any vision of community life in a decentralised form.[9]

Arizmendi himself seemed to have embodied the cooperative philosophy also in his personal life. He was known for never accepting any rewards or personal privileges, and got around on foot or bicycle. In his own continuous search for new ideas, Arizmendi did not restrict himself to Christian thinkers at all, but would increasingly explore more secular philosophers, including Karl Marx, Herbert Marcuse and Paulo Freire. Indeed, Arizmendi, though a Catholic priest, always remained highly critical of religion in general and of his church. Also, in contrast to many of his priest colleagues, his focus was not on individual salvation but on societal renewal.[10]

For Arizmendi – whose widespread interests extended from economics and sociology to philosophy and pedagogy – the key to a different kind of socioeconomic development was education which he coined 'el primer fundamento'[11] (the primary foundation) of transformation. Soon after his arrival in Mondragon, Arizmendi opened a school to teach craft and industrial skill to boys of age 14 to 16. He was convinced that in order to democratise power knowledge had to be socialised. Years later, he reflected: 'It therefore involved, in the early days, a process of mobilisation, consciousness-raising and training, of theory and practice, of self-management and self-government of young people. It was these youth who later would become protagonists of the cooperative experience'.[12]

In 1943 Arizmendi set up a Technical College, the Escuela Politecnica, a democratically administered educational body that was open to everyone and which ultimately became the seedbed out of which the first cooperative grew. Arizmendi was relentless in educating young people, combining teachings about a form of humanism based on solidarity and participation with technical knowledge and skills. 'In 1955, he selected five of these young people who were working at the Unión Cerrajera company (Usatorre, Larrañaga, Gorroñogoitia, Ormaechea and Ortubay) to set up Talleres Ulgor (an acrostic for their surnames), known today as Fagor Electrodomésticos, the pioneering company of the experience and industrial embryo of the corporation'.[13] From then on an intensive co-creative process started between Arizmendi and the Mondragon cooperativists – with Arizmendi as an integrated part of an ever-growing group of workers rather than a top-down operating leader.

What did Arizmendi mean by 'the cooperative experience'? He defined it as:

> *An economic effort that translates itself into an educational action ... an educational effort that employs economic action as a vehicle for transformation. One is not born a cooperator, because to be a cooperator requires a social maturity, a training in social living. For one to be an authentic cooperator it is necessary to have learnt to tame one's individualistic instincts, through education and the practice of virtue.*[14]

Don José María's interest in philosophy and education, moreover, never disconnected him from reality. On the contrary, he was concerned with theory only to the extent that it helped him link words to action and beliefs to practice. And it was out of this unique combination that the foundation for this unusual and till today highly successful organisational experience grew.

Round 2 – Ongoing organisational learning: Growing the cooperative experience in a complex societal environment

Though Arizmendi never got directly involved in the business operations, he remained the guiding philosophical, moral and often also strategic force behind Mondragon Corporation until his death in 1976, ensuring that the cooperative model was well institutionalised and reflected in the cooperation's philosophy, core values and management model. Thereby, the spirit of personal mastery was carried forward.

This spirit is well captured in the statement of one of Mondragon's founders, Alfonso Gorroñogoitia, made with regards to the continuous drive towards personal mastery and competence:

> *What surprises other entrepreneurs is the poetic-philosophical vein that we have as entrepreneurs. This humanistic inclination that surprises people we owe to Don José María, because we could never dissociate our entrepreneurial attitudes from a philosophy, a concept, an ideology, after the contact we had with him. We could not be pure technocrats, who know perfectly the process of chemistry or physics or semiconductors and nothing more. We see the development of our firms as a struggle, a duty.*[15]

In the period from the 1950s to 1970s Mondragon Corporation enjoyed dynamic growth. Not only did a variety of further industrial cooperatives emerge, but it was also in this period that the financial arm of Mondragon, the Caja Laboral, was founded (1959) as well as the corporation's social welfare arm Lagun Aro (1966), and Eroski (1969), by now Spain's third largest retailer. In 1972 followed the foundation of Ikerlan, an applied industrial research cooperative – again Don José was accredited with giving it its general orientation.[16]

The enormous growth, together with a rapidly changing outer environment, catalysed a gradual restructuring of the organisation, preparing it for new development steps. In 1985 Mondragon Cooperative Group was created, the predecessor of the existing Mondragon Cooperation. Over time, the organisation got divided into four core areas: industry, finance, retail and knowledge.[17] Though to a variable extent in each case, the cooperative model is clearly to be found in all four areas.

- *Industry:* The industrial division – that focuses on consumer goods, capital goods, industrial components, construction and services to companies – operates widely internationally, with about 60 per cent of its sales coming from outside of Spain – either through exports or via the approximately 75 subsidiaries located in 17 countries.
- *Finance:* In the financial division, Caja Laboral is the lead organisation, providing not only finance to Mondragon's member organisations and others, but it also, through its business consulting arm, provides assistance in setting up new, as well as managing and restructuring existing businesses. In that sense, Caja Laboral is almost a development bank. In an independent consulting report, published in 2009, Caja Laboral has been elected as the No. 1 in terms of excellence in the quality of service among 105 Spanish financial institutions.[18] Part of the financial division is also the insurance company, Seguros Lagun Aro. The voluntary social welfare fund Lagun Aro had in 2012 funds of more than €4 billion under management. With the returns from this fund long-term retirement schemes, widowhood and benefits for disabled workers are covered; all of them are complementary to those offered by the national social security systems.
- *Retail:* In the retail division, the main player is Eroski with over 2,600 subsidiaries all over Spain and in Southern France, and with a total turnover of about €8.3 billion (2010). At Eroski, both, worker-owners and consumer-members, are involved in Eroski's decision-making processes.
- *Knowledge:* The Knowledge Division of Mondragon – of particular significance for us here in 'Northern' knowledge production terms – comprised Mondragon University (that itself includes the original Escuela Politecnica) as well as a large variety of research and innovation centres (with a workforce totalling about 750 people (2011) – is supposed to support the development of existing cooperatives as well as stimulate the formation of new ones.

'La persona es el origen y el objetivo de la cooperativa'.[19] At the philosophical core of Mondragon Corporation is its management model, driven by the sovereignty of labour, as opposed to the conventional sovereignty of capital. This principle of 'work over capital' is expressed in the fact, that each worker – from the president to the cleaner, from the research expert to the university professor – has one vote in the annual General Assembly to approve the strategic goal of the corporation. Sophisticated participation models ensure that each employee's voice is heard and recognised in the decision-making processes.

The corporate culture is defined by 10 basic cooperative principles. They have been approved by the 'Co-operative Congress', Mondragon's highest executive body, comprising over 600 delegates from all member cooperatives. The 10 principles are open admission, democratic organisation, sovereignty of labour, instrumental and subordinate nature of capital, participatory management, payment solidarity, inter-cooperation, social transformation; universality and education.[20]

During our visit to Mondragon in April 2012, we encountered a compelling example of the principle of 'payment solidarity'. Faculty and staff of Mondragon University were in the midst of discussions to lower their salaries – voluntarily.

Despite the overall successful development of the university, the move was one of solidarity with the economic difficulties that many of the partner enterprises of the university were facing at that time. Anticipating that it might threaten the university's own financial sustainability in the mid-to-long term, the staff took the initiative to adjust its own salary structure.

The corporate principles are reflected in the four core values that Mondragon aspires to follow:[21]

- *Cooperation:* Everyone is acting as owner and protagonist.
- *Participation:* The work force is committed to shared management.
- *Social Responsibility:* A dedication to distribute wealth based on solidarity.
- *Innovation:* An organisational determination to promote constant renewal.

For Mondragon Corporation, the generation of profits is a limiting condition, but not the primary driving force, which remains social and economic development. The organisation is committed to maintain existing, and create further, employment. As many of the existing cooperatives have faced or are facing a difficult economic environment, this commitment requires that workers retrenched in one cooperative need either to be offered a job in another cooperative, or they are to be supported with substantial payments.

But a tough economic environment is not the only challenge that Mondragon Cooperation is faced with today. Perhaps the most critical challenge, as we see it, is the continuous revitalisation of a unique organisational development process. As a major determinant of Mondragon's success we regard the following creative dynamic between three core factors:

1. Moral-philosophical inspiration.
2. A strong inclination to education, knowledge creation and personal mastery.
3. A strong drive towards entrepreneurship that is committed to a unique cooperative philosophy and management model and to serve simultaneously the needs of its workers and of society at large.

The question today – so Unai Elorza from Mondragon University in a conversation in April 2012 – is how to keep this dynamic alive and to make it relevant to the challenging times to come. Yes, Mondragon Cooperation is still – and rightfully so – an internationally admired organisational model – but with Arizmendi gone and with changing needs of workers, society and the planet, Mondragon is faced to fully live up to its fourth core value – 'innovation' – ensuring that it equally brings about social as well as technological innovation. It is only then that Mondragon can continue to build on the enormous contribution it has made over time to society – a contribution that we shall now revisit.

Round 3 – Mondragon in society: Living, co-evolving and teaching cooperative principles within Basque country, Spain and the world

Reviewing Mondragon's origin, one can say that it clearly arose from the cultural roots of Basque country. Arizmendi, who grew up in Markina-Xemein, a village not far from the city of Mondragon, was known for his particular interest in Basque language and culture. During the Civil War, he even acted for a while as a journalist for a Basque newspaper. Understanding the cooperative experience of Mondragon, its unique spirit and corporate culture is impossible without acknowledging its link to the cooperative, democratic and egalitarian principles deeply rooted in Basque culture. Indeed, Foote Whyte and King Whyte affirm, that the Basque country has been fertile ground for cooperatives well before the Civil War.[22] This link is reflected in the organisation's mission up to today: 'Mondragon Corporation is a business-based socioeconomic initiative with deep roots in the Basque Country, created for and by people and inspired by the Basic Principles of our Co-operative Experience'.[23]

Mondragon's socioeconomic impact on the Basque country is indisputable. This goes for its entrepreneurial contribution as much as for its technological innovativeness, and also for Mondragon's influence in shaping policies and programmes in the Basque Government.[24] We argue, however, that its full cultural significance is still to be discovered. For most interpreters fail to articulate Mondragon's strong anchoring in a supportive Basque cultural and spiritual soil as well as in community-based cooperative and democratic principles, thereby running the risk of reducing the 'cooperative experience' to a mere social and economic phenomenon. That may in turn lead to the assumption that the Mondragon model can be transplanted to other parts of the world, without engaging in the threefold dialectic described earlier that functioned as the creative engine of Mondragon and without anchoring it in a particular cultural and social context.

If that process, however, can be articulated and recognised as a crucial ingredient for bringing about the social innovation, that the Mondragon model represents, then it can serve as a basis not only for the ongoing renewal of Mondragon Corporation, but it can help evolve other such organisations in Spain and in the wider world. Indeed, we would suggest this as a major focus of the Mondragon University. In recent years, the 'authentic export' of the Mondragon Model has gradually been recognised as one of the cooperative's most important challenges. For now, Mondragon's organisations in Spain are fully embracing the cooperative approach; its subsidiaries in other parts of the world, however, are still in the process of evolving towards participatory models that are locally relevant and culturally resonant to the particular context in which they are lodged.

Mondragon's recognised relevance all over the world is mirrored in a large number of national and international engagements to promote the cooperative model. Mondragon was founder member of the European Association for Cooperative Groups (ECG) and works closely with the International Cooperative Alliance. It is also closely associated with Social Economy Europe, an EU-level representative institution, representing enterprises and social actors that are set up in order to meet citizens' needs. In October 2009 the United Steelworkers (USW), North America's largest industrial union, announced an agreement for collaboration with Mondragon to establish Mondragon Cooperatives in the manufacturing sector in the USA and Canada. At the signing ceremony, Josu Ugarte, president of Mondragon International commented on the significance of this agreement: 'What we are announcing today represents a historic first – combining the world's largest industrial worker cooperative with one of the world's most progressive and forward-thinking manufacturing unions to work together so that our combined know-how and complimentary visions can transform manufacturing practices in North America'. USW president Leo Gerard added:

> We are excited about working with Mondragon because of our shared values, that work should empower workers and sustain families and communities ... We see Mondragon's cooperative model with 'one worker, one vote' ownership as a means to re-empower workers and make business accountable to Main Street instead of Wall Street.[25]

Indeed, we recognise the transformational potential of the Mondragon model. In *Integral Economics*, an earlier book of ours, we have showcased Mondragon as an innovative organisational approach that can serve as a role model for a new kind of economy, concretely: a social, knowledge-based economy. Critically in such a process would be a deeper understanding of the self-organisation-society journey initiated by Arizmendi, as well as, from the reframed Research University perspective adopted here, the ongoing knowledge creating process involved, from a communal and cultural, as well as a technological and economic point of view.

The Mondragon story is a powerful case for sociotechnical-economic development of an entire region, which, through its strong rooting in the local culture has not only survived for almost 60 years but also emerged as the world's largest workers' cooperative. In Figure 18.1 we illustrate the integral orientation of Mondragon, capturing core

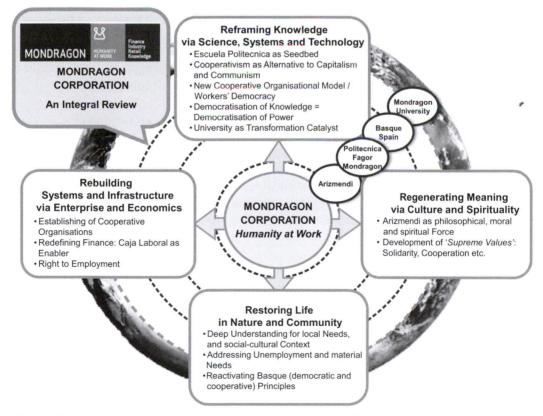

Figure 18.1 Mondragon cooperation: An integral review

'ingredients' of each of the four integral realms. As you can see, Mondragon in practice, like Castells in theory (⇨17), has a primarily 'Northern' orientation, though with a strong link to the communal 'South' and developmental 'East'. It also contains a clear element of 'Western' action orientation. All of these elements serve to inform the reframed Research University.

The challenge ahead for Mondragon may well lie in reactivating the interactive dynamic between all realms, by:

- revisiting citizens' changed needs for the future, thereby restoring life in nature and community;
- reviewing and renewing the value base of the organisation, through engaging (as did Arizmendi) anew with culture, spirituality and philosophy;
- engaging in knowledge creation, in particular through its university and research centres, in a way, that the cooperative model originated in Mondragon is continuously evolved and reframed;
- contributing to bringing about new systems and infrastructure relevant for the twenty-first century, and capable to addressing some of the major social and financial dysfunctionalities in today's macroeconomic framework.

To address these challenges, the Knowledge Division – spearheaded by Mondragon University – will have to play a major role. Indeed, as the following Round 4 indicates, Mondragon University has clearly the potential to act as a major catalyst for the renewal of Mondragon Corporation, as well as for the further evolution of viable – participation-based – micro- and macroeconomic frameworks for the future.

Round 4 – Fully actualising Mondragon: The role of Mondragon University

Mondragon University was officially inaugurated in 1997, and has been evolved out of the Escuela Politecnica that was founded by Arizmendi himself and has functioned as the original seedbed for Mondragon Corporation.

The Polytechnic School itself is by now fully integrated in the university, alongside two other faculties: Business Studies as well Humanities and Education. Altogether, these three faculties – the technology oriented Polytechnic School, management oriented Business Studies and culture and learning oriented Humanities and Education – mirror the three core pillars of Mondragon Corporation. More recently, in 2011, a fourth faculty on Culinary Science has been added.

The founding impulse and declared vision of Mondragon University, located close to the Headquarters of Mondragon Corporation, is clearly rooted in Mondragon's orientation to societal change and its unique participatory approach. As its social vocation, the university affirms its commitment to 'social transformation, which is specified in our participatory model'.[26]

The unique humanistic philosophy of Mondragon and Arizmendi, articulated in the commitment to renew human beings, communities and society, remains tangible at Mondragon University. Equally present is the strong cultural rooting in Basque culture, expressed, for example, through its trilingual (Basque, Spanish, English) educational model. For Mondragon University 'is deeply rooted in the Basque Country and is committed to the Basque language and culture, whilst, at the same time, being open to the changes demanded by the 21st century society. Our educational model is based on values such as innovation, humanism, solidarity and cooperation'.[27]

The cooperative spirit of Mondragon is also reflected in the legal constitution of the university, which is established as a non-profit cooperative. That 'makes it easier for students to economically access our University and for them to finance their own studies. The idea is to enable everyone who wants to take part in our educational model to do so, regardless of their economic situation'.[28]

Being part of the cooperative family of Mondragon and embedded in the Knowledge Division of Mondragon Corporation, the university itself directly serves the educational and research needs of Mondragon cooperative enterprises.

One may see Mondragon's over 250 (2011) cooperatives with their about 83,000 (2011) workers as the core community Mondragon University is lodged in and catering for. Many of its education and research programmes and activities are directly aligned with the requirements of those 'enterprise-communities'. The university thereby acts as an authentic bridge between theory and practice, between community and research, as well as between individual learning, organisational knowledge creation, and social needs. Mondragon University describes its 'embedded approach' as follows: 'Our teaching model involves a system of relationships which, with the educational system as the central theme, aims to involve the companies and institutions in the area, in order to guarantee social accessibility, the combination of work and study, the development of research and the provision of continuing education'.[29]

Building on the original legacy of the Polytechnic School, Mondragon University puts a strong emphasis on research and innovation for which it gained national and international recognition. According to the Basque Foundation for Science:

> The R+D activity in Mondragon Unibertsitatea is not only limited to generating new know-how; it also pursues applicability in the target area or field, in training in the courses that it imparts, and in the services of innovation that it renders the organisations that ask for them. This activity is conducted through research teams bringing researchers together under a defined and shared strategy and a plan for carrying out the investigation and transferring it to society.[30]

While the Polytechnic School, however, in its early days gave birth to a combination of social and technological innovation, recent focus has been more strongly on technological innovation. In conversations with young researchers from Mondragon University, we noticed a perceived lack of social innovation coming out of the university. There is, however, an increased self-critical awareness of this situation, and a clear intention to make the university also a facilitator of social innovation through knowledge creation – within the Mondragon Group of cooperatives and outside it.

Altogether, we identified Mondragon University as a renewed version of a Research University for its explicit integration of 'Southern', 'Eastern', 'Northern' and 'Western' aspects – with the 'Northern' dimension, in this case, understandably in the lead. In a nutshell, the university's integrated orientation can be expressed as follows:

- *Community/Context:* Mondragon University is clearly embedded in society and catering to the needs of closely connected 'workers' communities', with the university

Table 18.2 Mondragon Corporation and Mondragon University	
Integral Development	**A 'Northern' case for Integral Development (summary)**
Round 1: **Self-Development** Formative *Grounding*	*Arizmendi: Education is the key* • Arizmendi was a learner-philosopher-researcher-teacher with a profound philosophical foundation and a constant drive to individual and societal betterment • He saw work, anew, as a means to self-realisation (personal mastery) and societal betterment – with education as the key • Early on in his life and work engaged in critical thinking vis-à-vis the nature of capitalism • Gradually, through intense studies, he developed his own vision of 'cooperativism', which he saw as an alternative to egoistic capitalism and depersonalising socialism • Arizmendi was relentless in educating young people, combining teachings about a form of humanism based on solidarity and participation with technical knowledge and skills
Round 2: **Organisational Development** Reformative *Emergence*	*Mondragon: A cooperatively learning organisation* • Start: Set-up of a polytechnic school as seedbed for first cooperative • The cooperative experience was defined as an economic effort that translates itself into an educational action … an educational effort that employs economic action as a vehicle for transformation • Mondragon's corporate culture is defined by 10 basic cooperative principles, among them democratic organisation; sovereignty of labour; subordinate nature of capital; participatory management; inter-cooperation; social transformation; universality and education • Three core success factors: a moral-philosophical inspiration; a clear commitment to education, knowledge creation and personal mastery; a strong drive towards entrepreneurship that is committed to cooperative philosophy and management model and to serve simultaneously the needs of its workers and of society at large

Table 18.2 Continued	
Integral Development	**A 'Northern' case for Integral Development (summary)**
Round 3: **Societal Development** Newly normative *Navigation*	*Mondragon: Catalyst for societal learning and development* • Mondragon sees itself as a business-based socioeconomic initiative with deep roots in Basque country, created for and by people • Mondragon as an innovative organisational approach that can serve as a role model for a new kind of economy, concretely: a social, knowledge-based economy • Mondragon's recognised its relevance all over the world which is reflected in a large number of national and international engagements to promote the cooperative model (e.g. as founder member of the European Association for Cooperative Groups (ECG))
Round 4: **Integrating Uni-Versity** Fully transformative *Effect*	*Mondragon University: A Reframed Research University* • Mondragon University was evolved out of polytechnic school that was founded by Arizmendi and gave rise to first cooperative • The university, itself a non-profit cooperative, is strongly committed to Basque society and culture, and clearly rooted in Mondragon's orientation to societal change and its unique participatory approach • Its education and research caters primarily to the needs of the Mondragon Cooperative (as its larger community). Altogether, through its knowledge-creating activities, it integrates context, consciousness, content and contribution • Challenge ahead: university, together with mondragon corporation, is to bring about new systems and infrastructure relevant for the twenty-first century, and capable to addressing some of the major social and financial dysfunctionalities in today's macroeconomic framework

fostering community-based learning and development (though with a particular focus on socioeconomic-technological development).

• *Consciousness/Catalysation:* With a primary focus on societal transformation (building on Arizmendi and Mondragon Corporation), Mondragon University clearly catalyses societal learning and consciousness-raising, promoting new forms of participatory working and workplace democracy.

- *Content/Conceptualisation:* With educational programmes that are closely aligned with the learning needs of its network of enterprises, Mondragon University ensures that content is not 'out of context' and 'relevant for community'. Equally, through its dedicated research activities and its high-level research network, the university has positioned itself as a knowledge creator, instigating (primarily) technological innovation, applicable and useful for the communities it is serving.
- *Contribution/Capacity:* With an educational model that is reflecting Mondragon's core values (humanism, solidarity, innovation, corporation, etc.) and a strong orientation towards building relevant capacities (e.g. through intense periods of practical work as part of the studies), the university is able to link its philosophical foundation and educational orientation with relevant practice, altogether resulting to meaningful contribution to organisations and society.

We have summarised the Mondragon case story in Table 18.2 on the previous two pages. It illustrates the strong focus on (social and technological) learning and knowledge creation throughout all four rounds.

THE CASE OF A PROSPECTIVE NEW AFRICAN UNIVERSITY: CISER IN NIGERIA (AND BEYOND)

Introduction

We now turn from Europe to Africa, illustrating how a 'Northern' perspective is applicable in both cases. With the story of a prospective, new University in Africa and CISER Centre for Integral Social and Economic Research in Nigeria we introduce a 'case in progress' that serves to illustrate the need for locally relevant research centres and their potential to renew society. Before we reveal its (not yet fully realised) four levels, two important preludes to CISER are necessary.

Prelude 1: New education and research programmes geared to stimulate local research and the institutionalisation of research centres

Building upon such illustrious case stories like that of Mondragon Cooperative University as well as many others, we have designed, through our Geneva based institute, transformative educational and research programmes that can be seen as seedbeds for innovative, locally rooted research centres that strengthen the ability of a society to generate its own knowledge catering for its own burning issues and evolutionary tasks.

Based on our research conducted over the past decades, we have come up with master's and doctoral programmes that are geared to Integral Development, thereby addressing burning socioeconomic issues in the societal and cultural contexts of our participants. These programmes incorporate our integral knowledge basis rooted in the Integral Worlds approach (⇨4), spanning economics and enterprise, community and development, and thereby offer participants catalytic support to generate and practically actualise new knowledge relevant to the particular burning issue they address. In a nutshell, these programmes enable their journey all the way from fundamental research to transformative action.

It has been not always easy for us to find a university that would act as accrediting partner for our programmes. The core problems we faced were threefold. Firstly, our programmes promoted a local-global approach, rejecting a universalist (one-size-fits-all) attitude to education and research. They were less standardised, as they aimed at integrating relevant local knowledge from the contexts of the participants. That made our programmes, however, more difficult to 'market' in a standardised way. Secondly, with our programme's focus on addressing burning issues, students were emancipated to critically deal with their unique gifts and particular contexts. Part of that context was, of course, also their educational-research context, and that included the programme as well as the accrediting institution. We always sought to change our participants' role from students (conventional perspective) to co-evolvers (renewed perspective). Emancipated, they became, however, less easy to deal with from a conventional institutional perspective, and more difficult to fit into existing educational and research standards. Thirdly, we always saw ourselves becoming co-creators, at least in prospect, of a new developmental-educational space (Uni-Versity) on the ground, rather than merely running postgraduate degree programmes. Hence, we had to look hard for a compatible partner university. One university that we found being resonant with and supportive of our work, as well as open for co-evolution, was the South African Da Vinci Institute. Their story began with Nelson Mandela.

Prelude 2: From Nelson Mandela to Robben Island University to Da Vinci Institute with a focus on knowledge production

Nelson Mandela, the Robben Island University and the Long Walk to Freedom
In 1994 Nelson Mandela was installed as the new president of a new South Africa. In a famous speech at the time, he said:

> *I am not truly free if I am taking away someone else's freedom, just as I am surely not free when freedom is taken away from me. The oppressed and the oppressor alike are robbed of humanity. When I walked out of prison that was my mission, to liberate the oppressed and the oppressor both. Some say that has been achieved, but that is not the case. The true test of our devotion to freedom is just beginning. I have walked that long road to freedom. I have tried not to falter; I have made mishaps along the way. But I have discovered the secret that after climbing a great hill, one only finds that there are many more hills to climb. I have taken a moment here to rest, to steal a view of the glorious vistas that surround me, to look back on the distance I have come. But I can rest only for a moment, for with freedom comes responsibilities, and I dare not linger, for my long walk is not yet ended.*[31]

Mandela, in his 27 years of imprisonment in South Africa's Robben Island, has undergone a remarkable personal transformation, that led him to believe that both, the oppressor and the oppressed, needed to be liberated and that not violence, but the liberation of the minds – through education – was the key to such freedom. Mandela, himself, together with his imprisoned comrades, has experimented with a new kind of university – the so-called Robben Island University – that helped him and his imprisoned comrades not only to individually transform, but also to develop a vision for a new South Africa. We quote Mandela at length from his fascinating autobiographical account *The Long Walk to Freedom*:

In the struggle, Robben Island was known as 'the university'. This was not only because of what we learned from books, or because prisoners studied English, Afrikaans, art, geography and mathematics, or because so many of our men earned multiple degrees. Robben Island was known as the university because of what we learned from each other. We became our own faculty, with our own professors, our own curriculum, our own courses. We made a distinction between academic studies, which were official, and political studies, which were not. Our university grew up partly out of necessity.

As young men came to the island, we realised that they knew very little about the history of the ANC. Walter Sisulu, perhaps the greatest living historian of the ANC, began to tell them about the organisation in its early days. Gradually this informal history grew into a full course of study, which became known as Syllabus A, involving two years of lectures on the ANC and the liberation struggle. Syllabus A also included a course taught by Kathy on 'A History of the Indian Struggle'. Another comrade added a history of the Coloured people. Mac Maharaj, who had studied in the German Democratic Republic, added a course on Marxism. The style of teaching was Socratic in nature; ideas and theories were elucidated through the course leaders asking and answering questions.

As the courses became known in the general section of the prison, we began to get inquiries from our men on the other side. This started what became a kind of correspondence course with the prisoners from the general section. The teachers would smuggle lectures over to them and they would respond with questions and comments. This was beneficial for us as well. These men had little formal education, but great knowledge of the hardships of the world. Their concerns tended to be practical rather than philosophical.

For a number of years I taught a course in political economy. In it I attempted to trace the evolution of economic man from the earliest times to the present, sketching out the path from ancient communal societies to feudalism to capitalism and socialism. I am by no means a scholar and not much of a teacher, and I would generally prefer to ask questions than to lecture.[32]

From Robben Island University to Da Vinci Institute

We have been inspired by Nelson Mandela's story and by the *'Robben Island University'* ever since. There is a follow up to Robben Island University of which few people are aware. Soon after the new South Africa was born, President Nelson Mandela took a trip to Europe and America, with a group of educators including Roy Marcus, who was to become the founder of the Da Vinci Institute in South Africa. Together, they looked for the kind of university establishment that would befit the new South African society. Roy, a prominent South African academic and engineer, was known to Mandela because Gilbert Marcus, who had been Mandela's human rights lawyer, was Roy's brother.

The university that caught Marcus' and Mandela's eye, was the Warwick School of Manufacturing based in the UK. The reason that it attracted them was because it had recently established itself as a so-called 'Mode 2' university. A Mode 2 university is rooted in the practical world, and therefore resonated with both: the political activist Mandela and the engineer Marcus.

Inspired by Warwick School and Mode 2, Marcus intended to establish an offshoot of this British university in South Africa – an attempt that was, however, barred by the new Higher Educational Authorities in South Africa. After many trials and tribulations, Marcus – who was later to be joined by Bennie Anderson – established their own Mode 2 University in 1992: the Da Vinci Institute in Modderfontein near Johannesburg. Before we share how the story continues, now including ourselves, we shall elaborate on the crucial difference between a Mode 2 and a Mode 1 University.

From Mode 1 to Mode 2 Universities

In 1994, shortly after Mandela's and Marcus' visit to Europe and America in search for institutions models for education and research that could inform South Africa, an illustrious group of natural and social scientists came together to research on 'The New Production of Knowledge: The Dynamics of Science and Research in Contemporary Societies':[33] Michael Gibbons, Director of SPRU at Sussex University, Helga Nowotny, then Professor of Sociology at the Institute for Theory and Social Studies of Science at the University of Vienna, Camille Limoges, recently retired as Quebecan Minister of Research, Science and Technology, Simon Schwartzman, Professor of Political Science at the Universidade de Sao Paulo in Brazil, Peter Scott as Professor of Education at the University of Leeds, and Martin Trow, Professor (Emeritus), Graduate School of Public Policy, at the University of California, Berkeley.

For them, so-called 'Mode 2' knowledge production was different in nearly every respect from what they termed 'Mode 1' universities. For the latter was a form of knowledge production – a complex of ideas, methods, values and norms – that perpetrated a Newtonian model of classical, analytic 'scientific method' to more and more fields of enquiry. For many, Mode 1 was identical with what was conventionally meant by rational-pragmatic science. Here, problems are set and solved in a context governed by largely academic interests in a specific, self-contained, scientific discipline.

By contrast, Mode 2 knowledge is carried out in an applied context. Comparing the two modes, Gibbons and his colleagues draw the following conclusion:

- Mode 1 is generally uni-disciplinary while Mode 2 is transdisciplinary.
- Mode 1 is characterised by homogeneity while Mode 2 is heterogeneous.
- Organisationally, Mode 1 is hierarchical and tends to preserve its form, while Mode 2 is heterarchical and transient.
- Mode 2 involves the close interaction of many actors, not just academics.

The emergence of 'Mode 2', for Gibbons and his colleagues, was a profound development. It called fundamentally into question the adequacy of familiar knowledge producing institutions, whether universities, government research establishments, or corporate laboratories. In Mode 2, knowledge production is manifest as a group phenomenon, with the individual's contribution seemingly subsumed in a socially distributed process that accommodates many interests.

According to Gibbons, the transformation of knowledge production in the Mode 2 sense is one of the central processes characterising the societies of the technologically advanced industrial world. Knowledge production is less and less a self-contained activity. Increasingly, it is a distributed process. At its base lies the expansion of numbers of sites that form the sources for a continual combination and recombination of knowledge resources; the multiplication of the nerve centres of knowledge. The management of a distributed knowledge production process needs to be open-ended, and break away from classical planning perspectives. That management style can be summarised in two notions – increasing permeability of boundaries and brokering. Furthermore, the social accountability of such a (Mode 2) management style tends also be significantly higher than that of Mode 1.

To that extent, the self-contained Mode 1 university – which is still the by far predominant university type in today's world – is anathema to Michael Gibbons and his co-researchers. Knowledge production rather had to be understood as a socially distributed process.

The Da Vinci–Trans4m partnership

Such a Mode 2 university seemed infinitely more resonant for our research-to-innovation geared programmes, than the conventional Mode 1 type. We regarded it, hence, as good fortune when one of us got to meet up with Da Vinci's CEO Bennie Anderson, and an initial connection was made.

Da Vinci – working in close cooperation with South African business, in particular technology-driven enterprises – has developed an expertise to address so-called 'work-based challenges' rather than mere academic challenges. Its programmes, therefore, focus primarily on organisational development. Trans4m's programmes – focusing interconnectively on individual, organisational and societal development – can be seen as a perfect complement to the Da Vinci offering. It is for that reason that Da Vinci and Trans4m decided to cooperate. Da Vinci is now not only accrediting our Zimbabwean master's and doctoral programme, but also our international PhD programme, all of them geared to bring about Integral Innovation. It is here, where the story of Basheer Oshodi and CISER in Nigeria begins.

Round 1 – Self: The integral learning and research journey as formative grounding of Basheer Oshodi from Nigeria

Born in 1974 into a noble Muslim Yoruba family in Lagos, Basheer Oshodi grew up in a chaotic, highly paradoxical society. Reflecting on his youth, Oshodi remembers:

> I watched as the Nigerian economy swung between periods of austerity into the Structural Adjustment Programme (SAP) and then into persistent poverty. I experienced several military take-overs, political killings, worker strikes, infrastructure decay, loss of primary health and educational standards, consistent loss of the value of the Naira, conversions of factories, industries and warehouses turning into churches, and today's new dawn of democracy.[34]

To deal with this situation, Oshodi became soon an avid learner, and became particularly interested in understanding how his country could get out of its state of paralysis and instead successfully develop economically. He looked for answers at universities, studied Estate Management at the University of Lagos, followed by a master's in Management in 2001 at the same university. Unsatisfied, he was looking for alternative economic models, and in the process undertook a postgraduate course on Islamic Finance in London at the Institute of Islamic Banking and Insurance, and subsequently enrolled at London Metropolitan University for a master's in Research, Business and Management.

Though inspired by his learning journey, he still felt ill-equipped with the economic knowledge he accumulated and decided to pursue a PhD, in order to develop an economic approach, resonant to the cultural and societal context of Nigeria and Africa. It was then, in 2008, that Oshodi joined our PhD programme, accredited by UK's Buckingham University. Soon, however, we jointly noticed that Buckingham University could not accommodate Oshodi's broad vision for an alternative economic-developmental approach for Nigeria. Embedding his research in the complex and volatile environment of Nigerian economy and society, the transdisciplinary perspective of our programme, and in particular Oshodi's articulation of it, increasingly clashed with the conventional research standards of Buckingham University. Given our new partnership with Da Vinci in South Africa, Oshodi transferred to our Trans4m–Da Vinci PhD programme. He experienced DaVinci as a much more supportive educational and research environment. Also, Oshodi saw the Da Vinci content module – that formed part of our PhD programme – with a particular focus on the interrelationship of Technology, Innovation, People and System (in short: TIPS) as an enrichment to the programme.

At the time of joining our programme, Oshodi was a manager with Stanbic Bank IBTC in Lagos, a member of Standard Bank Group, headquartered in South Africa, one of Africa's largest banking institutions. Oshodi headed the department on Islamic Finance, Risk & Compliance, and he used his PhD programme to revisit Islamic Finance, and to develop new financial instruments – aligned with Islamic belief and equally with indigenous Nigerian knowledge systems – fitting in the particular cultural context of Nigeria. These new instruments were not only envisioned to restore moral trust in the banking system overall, but also to increase financial inclusion of Nigeria's poorer population. In that process, Oshodi not only significantly influenced the thinking of Stanbic IBTC Group with regards to the potential of new financial instruments to make a significant contribution to society, he also became strongly involved in a research group comprised of the country's foremost specialist on regulatory reforms for Islamic Finance, altogether concerned with further developing the Nigerian economy and society through financial innovations. By the time of concluding his PhD research,[35] Oshodi was ready to institutionalise his research und network by founding – together with close colleagues and with us at Trans4m – CISER, a Centre for Integral Social and Economic Research.

Round 2 – Organisation: The set-up of CISER as a reformative research centre

The date for the foundation of the centre coincided with the PhD viva presentation of Oshodi in May 2012 for which we went to Lagos. At the same time, four Nigerian colleagues of Oshodi joined not only our PhD programme, but also became founding members of CISER. CISER regards itself as an integral research-to-innovation initiative. As one of their core objectives the founding members see the addressing of 'the challenges of poverty alleviation through the promotion of sustainable livelihoods and enterprises, also underpinned by environmental conservation, peaceful co-evolution and open society'.[36] To achieve this goal, the centre enables 'collaboration between local researchers and policy makers – in the ecological and anthropological, cultural and philosophical, scientific and technological, as well as economic and political fields – with regards to the formulation of policies that resonates with local culture and are relevant for the economic growth of Africa'.[37]

The emphasis on knowledge creation evolved out of Oshodi's personal experience of having undergone a PhD programme that catalysed transformation – through new theory but also through evolved organisational practice at Stanbic IBTC Bank. It was further encouraged by one of Africa's leading contemporary thinkers, philosopher-statesman and Benin's former Minister of Education and Culture, Paulin Hountondji, who emphasises the need for Africa – and indeed for the entire so-called developing world – to create its own knowledge:

> *What is needed in Africa today is not just to apply traditional knowledge in agriculture or medicine, while continuing to import from the West technologies that are poorly understood and mastered by the local users. What is needed, instead, is to help the people and their elite to capitalise and master the existing knowledge, whether indigenous or not, and develop new knowledge in a continual process of uninterrupted creativity, while applying the findings in a systematic and responsible way to improve their own quality of life. Instead, we have been serving as learned informants for a theory-building activity located overseas and entirely controlled by the people there. Africa needs to invent ways in which knowledge can be better shared by the North and South in all its phases, be it the phase of production, accumulation and capitalisation, or of application. It needs to develop an ambitious strategy of knowledge appropriation that will allow Africans to freely and critically take up anything that can be useful for us in the intellectual heritage now available in the world.[38]*

Oshodi and his colleagues understood that the actualisation of Hountondji's claim required functional African universities or research centres that produce original ideas through research, and promote individual education through providing a developmental, learning environment. CISER was founded in this spirit. CISER's intention to draw in a wide network of national and international transformation agents is to make the centre a catalytic entity for knowledge creation processes that can purposefully inform the renewal of Nigeria: from the individual to the organisational level, onto the societal and Uni-Versity level.

Round 3 – Society: The aspiration to evolve CISER into a forceful catalyst for societal innovation

CISER started from the very beginning with a dual focus on local communities and a continental, African perspective. That vision was born not just out of the need for a pan-African renewal, but also out of the felt requirement to make Africa's voice heard in the world – in a way, that it contributed to the development of humanity whereby local cultural particularities are valued. 'The big picture for CISER is … to contribute to the well being of humanity within an ethno-religious and socio-political diverse global environment'.[39] On the local community level, the founding members of CISER, all of them dedicated to undertake research that leads to innovation, make already significant progress. Here are examples of the existing activities as represented by the founding members. All of these examples are catalysed through the Trans4m–Da Vinci PhD programme or (as a post-doc programme) evolved out of it:

- Basheer Oshodi (Post-PhD): Oshodi focuses, at Group Head of Non-Interest Banking of Nigeria's Sterling Bank, on the development of new, culturally rooted and morally based financial products that foster financial inclusion in Nigeria especially for the poor.

- Ade Adegbenjo (PhD): Adegbenjo, a former Member of the National Assembly and Senior Lecturer at the University of Lagos, focuses on funding for the real estate sector – agriculture, manufacturing and infrastructure.
- Folusho Titiloye (PhD): Titiloye, a Learning and Development Consultant with Stanbic IBTC Bank, Lagos, focuses on improving the learning styles and knowledge creating orientations in academic institutions.
- Akeem Oyewale (PhD): Oyewale, Head of Global Markets Sales of Stanbic IBTC Bank, Lagos, focuses on entrepreneurial development amongst Nigerian youth.
- John Adewale Akingbade (PhD): Akingbade, Group Head, Direct Sales Force and Bancassurance of Sterling Bank, Lagos, is working on community currencies for Nigeria (especially Lagos).
- Anselm Adodo (PhD): Reverend Father Adodo, Director of Pax Herbals, Ewu (Edo-State), focuses on surfacing and expanding the holistic business and community development model underlying Pax Herbals, thereby bringing about community health and well-being. Adodo, through Pax Herbals, puts particular emphasis on revitalising African indigenous knowledge systems for current times.[40]

For all members of CISER, their individual and collective research-to-innovation projects are stepping stones towards their larger vision to become a force for societal innovation, in Nigeria, Africa and the world. They are aware that the current institutional form of CISER will have to either evolve into a full-fledged Research University itself, or, alternatively, CISER will have to facilitate the set-up of such. Conversations about that have already begun.

Round 4 – Towards a University for Africa

Debbie Tarr, a Namibian born, former South African based Private Banker, and now Group CEO of a number of companies active in physical security, engineering, construction, agriculture and electronics, has joined our international PhD programme, together with four of the founders of CISER Nigeria. Tarr's key vision is the establishment of a new University for Africa, thereby further co-evolving the vision of Nelson Mandela through the Da Vinci Institute that has so far primarily been focusing on industry. Such a university is meant to be profoundly rooted in African culture, activate African indigenous knowledge systems, engage in knowledge creation relevant for Africa, offering education formats and educational content that is resonant with African culture, and thereby, altogether, becoming a catalyst for an African Renaissance. While this giant vision is to be evolved further by Tarr and many others in the future, her close link with CISER Nigeria and the bottom-up knowledge creation that is already taking place within CISER makes this vision more concrete. Indeed, CISER Nigeria is now aligning itself with the ultimate goal of co-creating a University for Africa – focusing simultaneously on education, research and knowledge creation.

While the third and fourth rounds are not yet actualised, the goal and path towards the goal has become clearer. For the evolution of CISER as well as for the realisation of a University for Africa, Trans4m is seen as a major co-evolutionary partner.

At the time of concluding this book, the foundation of another CISER, this time in Zimbabwe, has taken place. This new research and innovation centre is born and bred within our Zimbabwean PhD programme. CISER Zimbabwe was spearheaded by a group of five out of our 40 doctoral and masters participants (2013) that initially formed around shared research issues – in particular rural and urban economic development and new forms of African entrepreneurship. As they began to work closer, a collective vision to institutionalise their group research within a formal research centre arose. This centre is designed to enable them to address more effectively the burning issues of their country, but also to serve others as a platform for individual, communal and societal transformation.

Similar to CISER Nigeria, the core aspiration of CISER Zimbabwe is 'to provide a centre for integral research and development that uses innovative eco-systems grounded in local knowledge systems and practices that are internationally relevant for the improvement and economic wellbeing of the local people, particularly the previously marginalised members of our society'.[41] The centre sees itself as a 'socio-economic revolutionary initiative' determined to unlock – through research, innovation, education and capacity building – the potential of Zimbabwean communities.

With Trans4m in a mediating role, CISER Nigeria and CISER Zimbabwe have started to work together. In addition, Debbie Tarr is in the process of setting up a shared platform for all these impulses that she calls PISERI (Platform for Integral Social and Economic Research and Innovation). Altogether, PISERI and the two CISERs see themselves as building blocks towards a new type of a university in (and for) Africa – incorporating elements of Research University, Communiversity and Developmental University – that is grounded in Africa and contributes to the continent's integral development. We shall now sum up this case in Table 18.3.

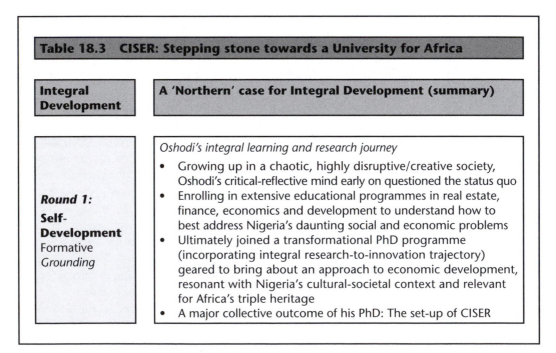

Table 18.3   CISER: Stepping stone towards a University for Africa

Integral Development	A 'Northern' case for Integral Development (summary)
Round 1: **Self-Development** Formative Grounding	*Oshodi's integral learning and research journey* • Growing up in a chaotic, highly disruptive/creative society, Oshodi's critical-reflective mind early on questioned the status quo • Enrolling in extensive educational programmes in real estate, finance, economics and development to understand how to best address Nigeria's daunting social and economic problems • Ultimately joined a transformational PhD programme (incorporating integral research-to-innovation trajectory) geared to bring about an approach to economic development, resonant with Nigeria's cultural-societal context and relevant for Africa's triple heritage • A major collective outcome of his PhD: The set-up of CISER

Table 18.3 Continued	
Integral Development	**A 'Northern' case for Integral Development (summary)**
Round 2: **Organisational Development** Reformative *Emergence*	*CISER Nigeria: Reformative research and innovation centre* • Founded by Oshodi and a group of Nigerian doctoral researchers as an 'integral research and innovation initiative' • Seeks to address poverty alleviation through promotion of sustainable livelihoods and enterprises, underpinned by environmental conservation, peaceful co-evolution and open society • To achieve this goal, the centre enables collaboration between local researchers and policy makers with regards to policies that resonate with local culture and are relevant for the economic growth of Africa • Intention to draw in a wide network of national, regional African and international transformation agents to make the centre a catalytic entity for knowledge production processes
Round 3: **Societal Development** Newly normative *Navigation*	*CISER: Building a catalyst for societal renewal* • CISER, as a Centre for Integral Social and Economic Development, started from the very beginning with a dual focus on local communities and continental Africa. • That vision was born not just out of the need for a pan-African renewal, but also out of the felt requirement to make Africa's voice heard in the world – in a way, that it contributed to the development of humanity whereby local cultural particularities are valued • The big picture for CISER is to contribute to the well-being of humanity within an ethno-religious and sociopolitical diverse world
Round 4: **Integrating Uni-Versity** Full transformative *Effect*	*Towards a University for Africa:* • Education, research and innovation for Africa • CISER sees itself as a stepping stone towards a new University for Africa, one that is focusing on community development, societal learning, and organisational knowledge creation, for the continent • In that respect, CISER Nigeria has begun to cooperate with similar initiatives in Africa (such as CISER Zimbabwe and PISERI in South Africa) and to align itself, together with these Initiatives, to a shared vision of a new University for Africa

Equipped with the two cases of Mondragon in Spain and CISER in Nigeria, we are now ready to formulate some generic conclusions concerning the nature and scope of a reframed Research University.

18.3   Actualising the Research University: Driving Societal Innovation

In this 'Northern' realm, the translation of the four-level-trajectory results in the establishment of a reframed Research University. In the two cases introduced in this chapter, the natural evolutionary path points towards such a fundamental reinvention of an educational entity. A reframed Research University is focused on scholarship, education, research and knowledge creation aiming, simultaneously, for social and technological innovation. Natural sciences are neither dominating, nor are they subordinated to the social sciences. And humanities are restored to their rightful place alongside social and natural sciences.

A reframed Research University reconnects to the original vision of Humboldt, ensuring that:

- Education:

  - Education is understood as 'inner-directed', and as a process of constant personal (trans-)formation.
  - It is focusing not primarily on the conveying of content but on character development, perceiving the individual as being in a continuous process of becoming.
  - Ultimately education is to be geared towards 'self-willed citizenship'.
  - Education was closely related to *Bildung*, a German term that refers to the inner shaping and development of the person, a process of fulfilment through education and knowledge, representing progress and refinement in knowledge and moral terms, a combination of wisdom and self-realisation.

- Knowledge:

  - Knowledge is equally not regarded as static, but as continuously and dynamically unfolding.
  - It is something to be cultivated for oneself, not something to be handed on from outside.

- Research:

  - Research is seen as an 'art form' fostering the originality of the researcher (and hence his/her potential to innovate).

Such reframed 'Northern' Research Universities are not to be seen as an isolated innovation in the education and research field. Rather, with their particular orientation towards content, conceptualisation and complexity, they are to be understood as complementary forces to, for example, the 'Southern' Communiversity with its orientation towards community, context and care, and the 'Eastern' Developmental University with its orientation towards consciousness, conscientisation and catalysation.

We have not come across many such reframed Research Universities. There are impressive examples of universities that are icons of technological innovation. But the dual focus on social and economic innovation, authentically articulated in respective education and research processes, are rare, and only recently emerging.

As illustrated in this chapter, such reinvention requires grounding in individual learning and research processes (Round 1) that subsequently get translated in new, reformed knowledge-creating organisational designs (Round 2). What would then be required is to embed, in such a new organisational form, a research and innovation centre that can act as catalyst for the social and technological innovativeness of this organisation on an ongoing basis. This innovativeness then needs to transcend the organisational boundaries and radiate into society at large.

The case of Reza Moussavian may serve as a further intimation for how such a process can practically work within a modern technology-driven business enterprise. Moussavian has been active as a strategy consultant and managing partner of Detecon International in their regional office in Abu Dhabi. Detecon, headquartered in Bonn, Germany, is an international ICT (Information and Communication Technology) consulting company that is part of Deutsche Telekom Group. In 2007, Moussavian joined our PhD programme on Social and Economic Transformation and focused – as his personally perceived burning issue – on the development of an integral enterprise design, that would enable an enterprise to balance community, cultural-spiritual, technological and economic-financial requirements.[42] His research was to be complemented by his colleague and then Detecon consultant Tanja Misiak, who joined our PhD programme about two years after Moussavian. In order to enable Detecon to engage in processes of social innovation, Moussavian championed, with the help of Misiak and others, the institutionalisation of a Centre of Excellence for Integral Business within Detecon, whose objective is to develop and implement social innovation solutions for Detecon's corporate customers. For this, he secured not only the support of Detecon's then CEO, but also lots of voluntary engagement of a group of young consultants from within Detecon who saw themselves as internal and external change agents.

In tandem with this Centre of Excellence, we developed a model for Integral Innovation, which was a creative adaptation – for corporate purposes – of Trans4m's approach to Integral Research and Innovation (⇨15). The intention was that this centre – based on its underlying approach to Integral Innovation – would help Detecon not only to renew from within but to also make the organisation a role model for contributing – through knowledge creation and innovation – to societal betterment. The vision was to further link up Detecon's approach to social and technological innovation with its parent company Deutsche Telekom.

Therefore, Moussavian was assigned to lead a newly designed unit called 'Group Transformational Change' to facilitate the 'continual impetus for Deutsche Telekom's transformation processes' and that aims to respond to 'changes happening in our society, culture and the world of technology'.[43] In addition to current and future employees, the new group unit regards as its stakeholders: society as a whole, the scientific community, research and education, and institutional partners. Altogether, we find here all the required ingredients for a transformative research and innovation centre, potentially acting a seedbed for an integrated Research University. The new function started operations in January 2013 and is envisioned to drive Deutsche Telekom's transformation towards aligned social and technological innovation.

Based on the theory and practice introduced in this 'Northern' realm, we summarise in Table 18.4 below core steps, highlighting how we can work towards the establishment of renewed forms of a Research University.

Table 18.4   Integral Development rhythm of the 'Northern' realm

Core theme: Reframing knowledge via science, systems and technology
Core value: Open and transparent knowledge creation

Round 1: **Self-Development** Formative *Grounding*	*Engage in integral learning and research* As an Integral Developer you seek to understand different approaches to learning and research and discover your unique learning/research style, factoring in latest findings from the life sciences. Throughout you ensure that your approach is rooted in concrete experience. Curious to explore different ways to research and innovation – and in the process choosing the one most authentic and culturally resonant to him/her – you then set out on a research-to-innovation path, dedicated to come up with new knowledge, relevant for your burning issue and building on your particular capacities
Round 2: **Organisational Development** Reformative *Emergence*	*Bring about organisational knowledge creation* Being yourself on a knowledge creation path, you – now individually and institutionally – seek to uncover the dynamics behind organisational knowledge production, eager to align both. In that process you aspire to provide an organisational environment that is conducive for research and innovation. You also explore how the organisation can embrace an evolutionary perspective – considering knowledge as dynamic and ever-changing – and gradually learn how to deal with complexity and uncertainty, be it in technological, social, political, economic or cultural terms

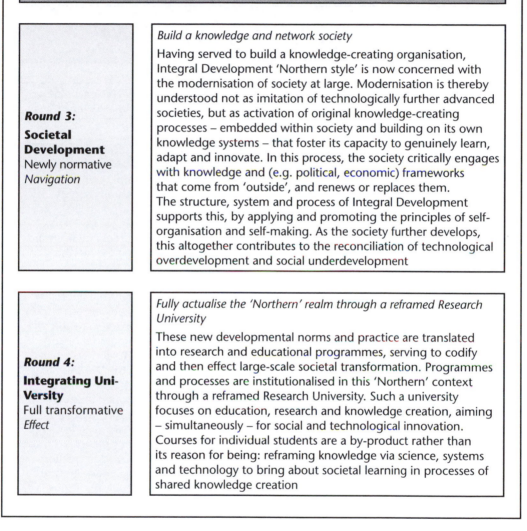

Table 18.4 Continued

Core theme: Reframing knowledge via science, systems and technology
Core value: Open and transparent knowledge creation

Round 3: **Societal** **Development** Newly normative *Navigation*	*Build a knowledge and network society* Having served to build a knowledge-creating organisation, Integral Development 'Northern style' is now concerned with the modernisation of society at large. Modernisation is thereby understood not as imitation of technologically further advanced societies, but as activation of original knowledge-creating processes – embedded within society and building on its own knowledge systems – that foster its capacity to genuinely learn, adapt and innovate. In this process, the society critically engages with knowledge and (e.g. political, economic) frameworks that come from 'outside', and renews or replaces them. The structure, system and process of Integral Development supports this, by applying and promoting the principles of self-organisation and self-making. As the society further develops, this altogether contributes to the reconciliation of technological overdevelopment and social underdevelopment
Round 4: **Integrating Uni-** **Versity** Full transformative *Effect*	*Fully actualise the 'Northern' realm through a reframed Research University* These new developmental norms and practice are translated into research and educational programmes, serving to codify and then effect large-scale societal transformation. Programmes and processes are institutionalised in this 'Northern' context through a reframed Research University. Such a university focuses on education, research and knowledge creation, aiming – simultaneously – for social and technological innovation. Courses for individual students are a by-product rather than its reason for being: reframing knowledge via science, systems and technology to bring about societal learning in processes of shared knowledge creation

18.4   Integration: Integral Development as Open and Transparent Knowledge Creation

INTEGRATING THE 'NORTHERN' ROUND 4

We have learned in this final round about the need to evolve a potent 'developmental vehicle' out of the first three rounds, that facilitates the interconnection of the development journeys experienced for self, organisation and society. In this 'Northern' case we called such a transformational entity a reframed 'Research University'. Use the following summarising Table 18.5 to reflect back on this fourth and final round of the 'Northern' realm and reality and record your own thoughts and prospective actions in order to bring about such a reframed Research University.

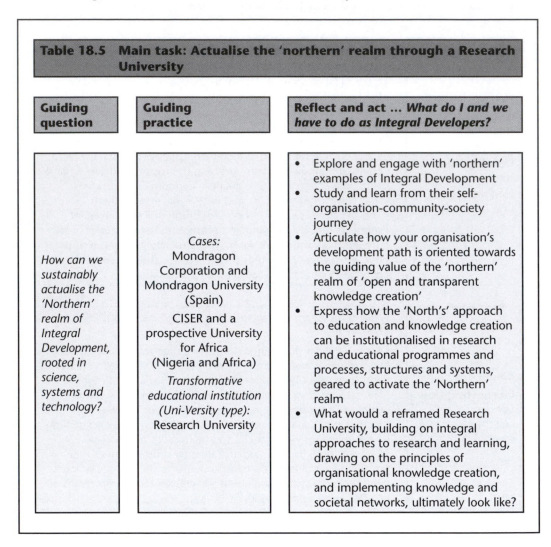

Table 18.5   Main task: Actualise the 'northern' realm through a Research University

Guiding question	Guiding practice	Reflect and act ... *What do I and we have to do as Integral Developers?*
How can we sustainably actualise the 'Northern' realm of Integral Development, rooted in science, systems and technology?	*Cases:* Mondragon Corporation and Mondragon University (Spain) CISER and a prospective University for Africa (Nigeria and Africa) *Transformative educational institution (Uni-Versity type):* Research University	• Explore and engage with 'northern' examples of Integral Development • Study and learn from their self-organisation-community-society journey • Articulate how your organisation's development path is oriented towards the guiding value of the 'northern' realm of 'open and transparent knowledge creation' • Express how the 'North's' approach to education and knowledge creation can be institutionalised in research and educational programmes and processes, structures and systems, geared to activate the 'Northern' realm • What would a reframed Research University, building on integral approaches to research and learning, drawing on the principles of organisational knowledge creation, and implementing knowledge and societal networks, ultimately look like?

INTEGRATING THE FULL 'NORTHERN' REALM

We are now ready to conclude this 'Northern' realm of a science-systems-technology-driven perspective on Integral Development.

Over the course of the past four chapters you have worked yourself progressively through the four levels of self (Round 1), organisation (Round 2), society (Round 3), and, finally, through to a reframed Research University (Round 4). At the fourth level, you were presented with the case stories of Mondragon Corporation in Spain and a prospectively new University for Africa that serve to illustrate the organic and authentic integration of the first three rounds. These cases are representations, at least to some significant degree, of a reframed Research University, the culmination of this 'Northern' realm. Such a Research University needs to build authentically on what has come communally ('Southern') and culturally developmentally ('Eastern') before.

With our claim for the reinvention of the Research University, we underline the challenge that we pose to most of today's universities – including knowledge-creating enterprises that see themselves aligned with such Research Universities. With their often-unilateral emphasis on education alone, such education lacks the mechanisms of cooperative knowledge creation. Moreover, we witnessed in many cases that instead of the pursuit of integral research and learning, arid research and teaching protocols are followed. What then happens is a by now common phenomenon – education not only degenerates to a mere product to be delivered to individuals (primarily feeding individual aspirations in terms of personal career advancement), but it also becomes increasingly irrelevant for societal betterment. It is for this reason that the reframed Research University is required to align individual research and learning, with organisational knowledge creation, and subsequent societal modernisation.

Given the difficulties that we are aware of (and personally experienced many times) in transforming existing universities, we suggest a bottom-up approach that begins on the level of individual learning and research. The example of Arizmendi in Mondragon who started (Round 1) with the foundation of a Polytechnic School, in which he offered formative education to a group of young men, linking technological knowledge and social philosophy, which then (Round 2) gave birth to a reformative organisation (Mondragon Corporation) that institutionalised a newly developed cooperative model, which in the process (Round 3) provided the nation and the world with a whole new cooperative working model, that then led (Round 4) to the establishment of a full-fledged Research University that actualised and leveraged the three-level evolutionary trajectory that has come before, remains a powerful showcase for such a newly framed Research University.

Integrating the learnings from such illustrious cases, we have ourselves designed transformative educational and research programmes that can be seen as seedbeds for innovative, locally rooted research centres that strengthen the ability of a society to generate its own knowledge catering for its particular burning issues and evolutionary tasks. In this respect, the set-up of the research and innovation centre CISER in Nigeria, founded by Basheer Oshodi and his colleagues and born out of the transformational PhD that Oshodi himself undertook, serves as another useful example to illustrate how research can be activated for the betterment of society.

In the concluding figure, Figure 18.2 on the next page, we take you once more through the full journey of the 'Northern' realm: we indicate the main developmental tasks of each round; we provide an overview of the core thinkers and practitioners that illustrate the nature of each of the four rounds; and we summarise the core developmental challenges that you, your organisation and your community face in each round.

As with all four transcultural reality viewpoints and transdisciplinary realms, the journey through this 'Northern' integral realm is not to be understood in a linear fashion. However, the composite view on the four integrated rounds, and the large variety of relevant thinkers and practitioners, is designed to help you to build, step by step, a

Your Development Calling & Challenge	MAIN TASK	GUIDING THEORY / GUIDING PRACTICE	LEARNING AND DEVELOPMENT PROCESSES FOR INTEGRAL DEVELOPMENT – AGENT & AGENCY
G — Round 1: Self Development / *Formative Grounding*	ENGAGE IN TRANS-DISCIPLINARY LEARNING AND RESEARCH	The Learning Cycle (Kolb); Research for Development (Lessem / Schieffer); To Live is to Know (Capra / Varela / Maturana)	• Understand the Stages of Learning and discover your Learning Style • Ensure that your Learning is rooted in concrete Experience • Describe how your Research is informed by a Research-to-Innovation Trajectory, spanning Theory and Practice • Ensure your Research-to-Innovation Path is resonant to your Personality and Culture: then Start engaging with it • Ensure that your approach to Research and Knowledge Creation is informed by latest Findings from the Life Sciences
E — Round 2: Organisational Development / *Reformative Emergence*	BRING ABOUT ORGANISATIONAL KNOWLEDGE CREATION	The Knowledge Creating Enterprise (Nonaka / Takeuchi); The Complex Organisation (Stacey)	• Understand how you can tap into the tacit Knowledge of your Organisation and how to activate the Spiral of organisational Learning and Innovation • Provide the enabling Conditions for Knowledge Creation and Innovation • Map your Organisation as a Hypertext Organisation and articulate the subsequent Development Tasks • Explore to what Degree your Organisation is designed to overcome a mechanistic and rational Paradigm and to deal with Uncertainty • Explore how your Organisation can give simultaneous Priority to individual and collective Identity via 'Complex Responsive Processes'
N — Round 3: Societal Development / *Normative Navigation*	BUILD A KNOWLEDGE- AND NETWORK-SOCIETY	World Systems Analysis (Wallerstein / World Systems School); Self-Making, Self-Organisation, Emergence (Escobar); Knowledge- and Network Society (Castells)	• Apply the Learnings from World Systems Analysis to your particular Development Tasks. What do you derive from it for your own Community and Society? • Describe your Community's and Society's current Approach and future Vision to Knowledge Creation and Development • Illustrate how you respond to the Critique of World Systems Analysis with regards to Social Sciences, Capitalism and Progress • Demonstrate how your Development Work engages in Bottom-Up Development applying the Principles of Self-Making and Self-Organisation • Ensure that your Development Work contributes to the Reconciliation of technological Over-Development and Social Underdevelopment
E — Round 4: Integrating Uni-Versity / *Transformative Effect*	REINVENT THE RESEARCH UNIVERSITY	**Cases:** Mondragon Corporation and Mondragon University (Spain); CISER and a prospective University for Africa (Nigeria & Africa); RESEARCH UNIVERSITY	• Explore & engage with 'northern' Examples of Integral Development • Study and learn from their self-organisation-community-society Journey • Show how your Development Paths, individually and collectively, are oriented towards the guiding Value of the 'northern' Realm of 'open & transparent Knowledge Creation'? • Envision how the 'North's' renewed Approach to Education & Knowledge Production can be institutionalised in Research & educational Programs, Processes & Systems, geared to activate the 'northern' Realm. • What would a reframed Research University (Research Center) in your Case look like (e.g. as a knowledge creating, cooperative Enterprise)?

Your Development Calling & Challenge

Figure 18.2 Releasing the gene-ius of the 'Northern' realm

learning and research foundation strong enough to make a meaningful contribution to reframe knowledge via science, systems and technology in a way that knowledge caters for the integral development of individuals, organisations, communities and society.

We shall now enter the 'Western' integral realm of action.

References

1   Watson, P. (2010). *The German Genius: Europe's Third Renaissance, The Second Scientific Revolution and the 21st Century*. New York: Harper.

2   Khurana, R. (2007). *From Higher Aims to Hired Hands: The Social Transformation of the American Business Schools and the Unfulfilled Promise of Management as a Profession*. Princeton, NJ: Princeton University Press.

3   Stark, J. (1996). The Wisconsin Idea: The University's Service to the State. *Wisconsin Blue Book: 1995–1996*. Madison, WI: Wisconsin Legislative Reference Bureau.

4   Khurana, R. (2007). *From Higher Aims to Hired Hands: The Social Transformation of the American Business Schools and the Unfulfilled Promise of Management as a Profession*. Princeton, NJ: Princeton University Press.

5   Aldecoa, J.M. (2009). *Corporate Profile*. Mondragon: Mondragon Corporation, p. 4.

6   Foote Whyte, W. and King Whyte, K. (1991). *Making Mondragon: The Growth and Dynamics of the Worker Cooperative Complex*. Ithaca, NY: Cornell University Press, p. 26.

7   Altuna, L. (2008). *La Experienca Cooperativa de Mondragon. Una Síntesis General*. Eskoriatza: Lanki-Huhezi, pp. 51f.

8   Foote Whyte, W. and King Whyte, K. (1991). *Making Mondragon: The Growth and Dynamics of the Worker Cooperative Complex*. Ithaca, NY: Cornell University Press, p. 29.

9   Foote Whyte, W. and King Whyte, K. (1991). *Making Mondragon: The Growth and Dynamics of the Worker Cooperative Complex*. Ithaca, NY: Cornell University Press, pp. 253f.

10 Foote Whyte, W. and King Whyte, K. (1991). *Making Mondragon: The Growth and Dynamics of the Worker Cooperative Complex*. Ithaca, NY: Cornell University Press, pp. 246ff.

11 Altuna, L. (2008). *La Experienca Cooperativa de Mondragon. Una Síntesis General*. Eskoriatza: Lanki-Huhezi, p. 45.

12 Foote Whyte, W. and King Whyte, K. (1991). *Making Mondragon: The Growth and Dynamics of the Worker Cooperative Complex*. Ithaca, NY: Cornell University Press.

13 Foote Whyte, W. and King Whyte, K. (1991). *Making Mondragon: The Growth and Dynamics of the Worker Cooperative Complex*. Ithaca, NY: Cornell University Press, p. 33.

14 Foote Whyte, W. and King Whyte, K. (1991). *Making Mondragon: The Growth and Dynamics of the Worker Cooperative Complex*. Ithaca, NY: Cornell University Press.

15 Foote Whyte, W. and King Whyte, K. (1991). *Making Mondragon: The Growth and Dynamics of the Worker Cooperative Complex*. Ithaca, NY: Cornell University Press.

16 Foote Whyte, W. and King Whyte, K. (1991). *Making Mondragon: The Growth and Dynamics of the Worker Cooperative Complex*. Ithaca, NY: Cornell University Press, p. 64.

17 Altuna, L. (2008). *La Experienca Cooperativa de Mondragon. Una Síntesis General*. Eskoriatza: Lanki-Huhezi, p. 210.

18 Caja Laboral website. Available at: https://www.cajalaboral.com/clweb/en/quienes_somos. aspx / Accessed: 2 May 2012.

19 Altuna, L. (2008). *La Experienca Cooperativa de Mondragon. Una Síntesis General*. Eskoriatza: Lanki-Huhezi, p. 232.

20 Mondragon Corporation website. Available at: http://www.mondragon-corporation.com/ ENG/Cooperativism/Co-operative-Experience/Co-operative-Culture.aspx / Accessed: 3 May 2012.

21 Mondragon Corporation website. Available at: http://www.mondragon-corporation.com/ ENG/Cooperativism/Co-operative-Experience/Co-operative-Culture.aspx / Accessed: 3 May 2012.

22 Foote Whyte, W. and King Whyte, K. (1991). *Making Mondragon: The Growth and Dynamics of the Worker Cooperative Complex*. Ithaca, NY: Cornell University Press, pp. 20f.

23 Mondragon Corporation website. Available at: http://www.mondragon-corporation.com/ ENG/Co-operativism/Co-operative-Experience/Co-operative-Culture.aspx / Accessed: 18 May 2012.

24 Foote Whyte, W. and King Whyte, K. (1991). *Making Mondragon: The Growth and Dynamics of the Worker Cooperative Complex*. Ithaca, NY: Cornell University Press. p. 196.

25 United Steelworkers website. Available at: http://www.usw.org/media_center/releases_ adviseries?id=0234 / Accessed: 18 May 2012.

26 Mondragon University website. Available at: www.mondragon.edu / Accessed: 18 September 2012.

27 Mondragon University website. Available at: www.mondragon.edu / Accessed: 18 September 2012.

28 Mondragon University website. Available at: www.mondragon.edu / Accessed: 18 September 2012.

29 Mondragon University website. Available at: www.mondragon.edu / Accessed: 18 September 2012.

30 Basque Foundation for Science website. Available at: www.ikerbasque.net / Accessed: 20 September 2012.

31 Mandela, N. (1994). *The Long Walk to Freedom*. New York: Abacus.

32 Mandela, N. (1994). *The Long Walk to Freedom*. New York: Abacus.

33 Gibbons, M., Limoges, C., Nowotny, H., Schwartzman, S., Scott, P. and Trow, M. (1994). *The New Production of Knowledge: The Dynamics of Science and Research in Contemporary Societies*. London: Sage.

34 Oshodi, B. (2013). *An Integral Approach to Development Economics: Islamic Finance in an African Context*. Farnham: Gower, p. 13.

35 Oshodi, B. (2013). *An Integral Approach to Development Economics: Islamic Finance in an African Context*. Farnham: Gower.

36 Oshodi, B. et al. (2012). *CISER Nigeria*. Draft concept paper – unpublished (September 2012).

37 Oshodi, B. et al. (2012). *CISER Nigeria*. Draft concept paper – unpublished (September 2012).

38 Hountondji, P. (2002). *The Struggle for Meaning*. Buckingham: Open University Press.

39 Oshodi, B. et al. (2012). *CISER Nigeria*. Draft concept paper – unpublished (September 2012).

40 Adodo, A. (2013). *Nature Power: Natural Medicine in Tropical Africa*. Bloomington: AuthorHouse.

41 Rushesha, T.S. & Mhaka, W. .(2012). *CISER Zimbabwe*. Draft concept paper – unpublished (September 2012).

42 Moussavian, R. (forthcoming). *Crafting an Integral Enterprise: Towards a Sustainable Telecommunications Sector*. Farnham: Gower.

43 Deutsche Telekom website. Available at: www.cr-report.telekom.com / Accessed: 19 September 2012.

PART VI

The Western Realm of Integral Development: Rebuilding Infrastructure and Institutions via Enterprise and Economics

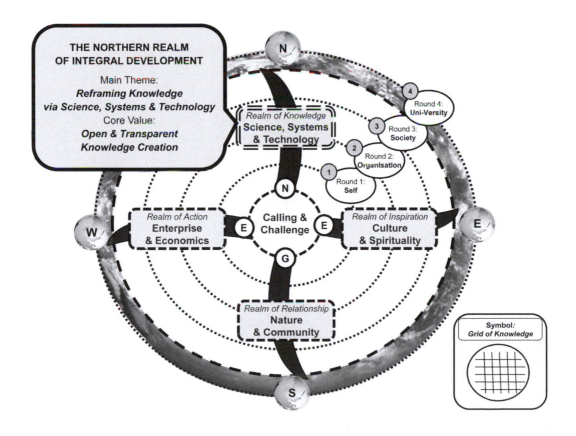

THE NORTHERN REALM OF INTEGRAL DEVELOPMENT

Main Theme:
Reframing Knowledge via Science, Systems & Technology
Core Value:
Open & Transparent Knowledge Creation

Realm of Knowledge
Science, Systems & Technology

Round 4:
Uni-Versity
Round 3:
Society
Round 2:
Organisation
Round 1:
Self

Realm of Action
Enterprise & Economics

Calling & Challenge

Realm of Inspiration
Culture & Spirituality

Realm of Relationship
Nature & Community

N · E · G

W · E · S

Symbol:
Grid of Knowledge

19 The Full Life: A Western Individual Perspective

Guiding Questions: What can I do? How do I meaningfully contribute to sustainable livelihood, for myself and others?

19.1 Orientation

We have now spanned the communal and relational 'South', the culture-laden and inspirational 'East' and the research and knowledge oriented 'North', all of which we need to consider before embarking 'West'. In other words: when we ultimately come onto the University of Life (⇨22), we will need to take account of the Communiversity, the Developmental University and the reframed Research University. However, in this first level of the 'Western' realm of enterprise and economics, we focus, fair and square, on you as an individual, in the fullest possible light.

Starting with individual development, we immediately stumble over the question of what 'infrastructure and institutions' to propose at this juncture? We need to take both terms out of their usual – organisational and societal – context, and translate them into their individual equivalent. Infrastructure then points towards the physical 'equipment' (our body and mind), the philosophical underpinning, and our intentions and our beliefs. This personal infrastructure then enables and informs our personal and behaviourally oriented institutionalisation of an actual life practice.

The focus of this chapter is on 'doing' – an 'enriched doing', however, that integrates 'Southern being', 'Eastern becoming' and 'Northern knowing'. The questions that we as Integral Developers need to explore on this first individual level are:

• What can I do?
• What can I do based on the learnings from all other realms of the Integral Development approach?
• How do I meaningfully contribute to sustainable livelihood, for myself and others?

We start this Round 1 with a brief introduction into a development topography, an instrument that is designed to link any practical development action to the deeper layers of reality, thereby enabling us to design deep-rooted, sustainable action. Afterwards, we are guided by one of the most influential social philosophers of the USA, Ken Wilber, and his renowned integral approach. Based on his enormously rich body of integral theory that he originated in the past decades, he has recently developed – together with a group of colleagues – an Integral Life Practice. Seeking to integrate physical, emotional, spiritual and mental dimensions of the individual in a most practical and coherent manner, his approach helps us to practically reground our lives and thus to build a foundation for sustainable livelihoods.

19.2   Co-Creating Full Realities: Activating the Development Topography, Bottom-Up

THE IMPORTANCE OF 'DIGGING DEEP'

In our own work on integral enterprise and economics, research and development, we continuously observed how most of the practical work in these fields is unilaterally focused on surface phenomena. Thereby, the 'generative mechanisms' of reality, so to speak, remain overlooked. This leads to a rather incomplete understanding of how the phenomena at hand have been brought about. The notion of 'generative depths' comes from the Indian-English social philosopher Roy Bhaskar. He originated a theory called 'critical realism' which critiques empiricism and any form of pure positivism as being too 'superficial' as a research methodology. His core argument is that a mere empirical understanding of reality does not account for the generative depths or layers under the surface of reality. These layers, however, so his point, constitute the very foundation for observable and measurable phenomena.[1] Ignoring this foundation leads to a false perception of reality.

The topography that we developed[2] seeks to build such generative depths into the ongoing awareness of the Integral Developer. It also serves to illustrate that any of the outer activities that we engage in are profoundly influenced by a number of invisible layers that are beneath the surface. If those layers are not recognised and activated in the development process, any outer change is bound to be short-lived and hence unsustainable.

THE DEVELOPMENT TOPOGRAPHY

Our development topography distinguishes between four layers – images, ideologies, institutions and inclinations – that we playfully dubbed 'the four Is'. In Table 19.1, opposite, we sketch out the characteristics of each layer. We also illustrate how the four layers are related – roughly – to our four integral realms.

As Integral Developers we see immediately the relevance of the development topography for all our three layers of self, organisation and society. We positioned it, though, in Round 1 of this realm, to ensure that we purposefully ground ourselves in this topography, and then carry it forward to the following rounds. Let us now explore how to activate the development topography.

INTERCONNECTED AND DYNAMICALLY INTERACTIVE: UNDERSTANDING THE DEVELOPMENT TOPOGRAPHY

For thoroughgoing development to occur, all four levels need to become dynamically interconnected. We begin with the images at the deepest level of our self. They form the source of creativity and imagination.

Topography	Developmental layers	Expressions	Integral realms
Table 19.1 Development topography			
Topsoil	*Inclinations*	Visible attitudes and behaviours/ outer practice	West
Subsoil	*Institutions*	The institutional frameworks that organise and direct our attitudes and behaviours, as well as the scientific disciplines underlying them	West North
Bedrock	*Ideologies*	The philosophies and worldviews that inform our way of thinking/ This layer includes ontology and epistemology, defining what counts as valid knowledge and how new knowledge is to be created	North East
Core	*Images*	The deep-rooted images, beliefs and archetypal structures that inform, often unconsciously, our lives and that are directly related to our physical, psychological and spiritual existence ('human infrastructure')/These root images provide in turn the foundation for philosophies and worldviews, as well as for institutional and conceptual frameworks	East South

Images – Touching the core

The deepest source of development are archetypal images drawn from the ancient stories (such as creation myths), the humanities, from the cultural depths of religion and spirituality, inclusive of language in its original context. They inform our imagination.

Ideologies – The bedrock on which we stand

At the bedrock level, we are dealing with philosophies and ideologies that lie well below the everyday surface. All too often, such a bedrock is globally imported from elsewhere

– as was the case for both Russia and China in relation to Communism – without being aligned with the local cultural and societal core. This always serves to distort whatever processes of renewal take place, unless such dis-integration is consciously addressed. Often, outer ideological imprints fall upon stony ground if they are not embedded or creatively assimilated in the individual, organisational and societal consciousness.

Institutions – Built up from our collective intelligence

Institutional and conceptual frameworks are the object of concern on this next layer. It includes legal systems, political and economic structures, and predominating forms of public, private or civic enterprise. Here we are called to carefully distinguish whether we deal with a Spanish cooperative, a Zimbabwean family enterprise, an American corporation or a Japanese *kereitsu* (a Japanese-style business group). Included in this subsoil layer of depersonalised systems are also management models that we study at Business Schools and that inform the design of much of our institutions. We notice that here American models inevitably predominate. Whereas it is individuals who characteristically get things going, with their personal and formative and idiosyncratic inclinations, institutions keep things going over the long haul, with their standardising rules and procedures. The power of the system is something that everyone who deals with institutional change recognises quickly.

Inclinations – The visible surface

We finally come to the practice of our individual inclinations, including attitudes and behaviours. Engaging with diverse development contexts, here we learn and discover how to exchange business cards in Japan, whether or not to shake hands with Arab women, how formal or informal we should be with the French, what your attitude is to time in Harare or Hamburg. Many of our everyday conversations and dealings with different people and cultures tend to be conducted in these sort of almost instinctive 'topsoil' terms, and are thus focused on individual traits and identities.

What is crucial is that we tap into and stay connected to all layers. In many individuals and societies – in particular in the so-called developing world – we will discover ruptures in between the four layers. We will notice, that often ideologies (bedrock) are imported, and not sufficiently home-grown or assimilated on the level of the core. Equally, in particular in the business world, we see a lack of connectedness with the institutional design of a private enterprise in Anglo-Saxon style (institutional layer), with the guiding cultural philosophy (bedrock) within many societies. And so on. The development topography can help us to surface these ruptures, make them conscious and subsequently engage in healing the divide. Figure 19.1, on the opposite page, sums up the development topography.

IMPLICATIONS FOR INTEGRAL DEVELOPERS

For us as Integral Developers – and for the institutions, communities and societies we engage with – the development topography has specific implications on each of its four layers:

- *Inclinations:* The activation of individual inclinations, that enables us to adeptly engage in development processes across cultures, requires both behavioural change through exposure to diverse regions and countries (including language training) and attitudinal change through appropriate simulations and role plays (backed up by suitable instrumentation and measurement).
- *Institutions:* The perception of institutional frameworks and organisational models, on the one hand, is enhanced by appropriate case material, both live and documented – in book and case form. Their conception, on the other hand, is enhanced by didactively based teaching, provided by seasoned Integral Development practitioners

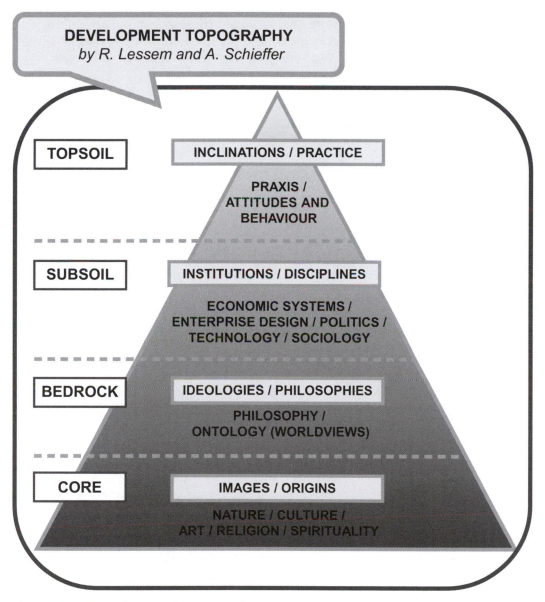

Figure 19.1 Development topography

and thinkers from diverse cultural backgrounds, together with seminal, related books that have been written in the particular society we are dealing with.

- *Ideologies:* The development of philosophical ideas about culture, economy and society requires an exposure to all walks of life in a particular developmental context, as well as the assimilation of its seminal philosophical and ontological ideas through lectures and readings. Linking the levels of topsoil, subsoil and bedrock, the regeneration of a community or society requires a combination of attitudinal change, model rebuilding, and philosophical exploration.
- *Images:* The activation and transformation of root images within a particular developmental context requires both an affinity with the indigenous art and culture, as well as locally relevant spirituality, mediated through appropriate interpreters, and an ability to use archetypal images, in order to create new forms of livelihood, organisations and systems that are properly built upon such relevant local foundations.

It is with this development topography in mind that we move on towards an Integral Life Practice, originated by America's Ken Wilber.

19.3   The Integral Life: Linking Integral Theory and Integral Life Practice

INTEGRAL THEORY – AN ALMOST IMPOSSIBLE ENDEAVOUR

Ken Wilber, America's renowned contemporary psychologist and integral philosopher, has almost single-handedly undertaken the attempt to develop a transdisciplinary and transcultural integral theory, that maps coherently humanity's individual and collective development stages, states, levels and types.[3] Wilber's approach has inspired countless thinkers and practitioners around the world. His ability to weave together threads across disciplines and time are remarkable. Though widely admired, his work is often criticised, especially by conventional academia, for being overly simplistic. While in some areas this critique may well be right, the sheer depth and breadth of his work is mind-boggling, and he is to be applauded for the significant and highly relevant attempt of bring together a highly fragmented 'knowledge world' with which we are faced in a new way.

One could say that Wilber has undergone a similar journey to the one we have, though his focus is much more strongly on the individual than on institutional and societal levels. Also, his work is primarily anchored in the theoretical sphere – and on that level much richer – while our work is seeking to combine theory and practice on a continuous base. Our focus on practice has also given our work a more transformational and developmental orientation. Nevertheless, Wilber's work has at all times been a profound inspiration for us, and this book would not be complete without incorporating his fascinating integral approach. As an introduction to Wilber, we provide a brief overview of his four quadrants, before we progress to a recent work of his, in which he translates the integral theory into an Integral Life Practice.

KEN WILBER'S FOUR QUADRANTS

According to Wilber, the four quadrants in their different manifestations represent the four compass points of the known cosmos. All of them are needed to accurately navigate through personal, organisational and societal worlds. Concretely, these quadrants are represented as:[4]

- *Upper Left 'Me' Quadrant (individual-interior):* This so-called 'intentional' quadrant focuses on the individual consciousness (and its different states, stages, levels and types). 'Intentional' refers to the individual's possibility to respond socio-psychologically to those stimuli that fall within its interior space. The 'me' quadrant is the 'subjective' quadrant.
- *Lower Left 'We' Quadrant (collective-interior):* This 'cultural' quadrant focuses on collective consciousness (and its different states, stages, levels and types). 'Cultural' refers to all of the interior meanings that we share with similar communities like, for example, a shared worldview, value systems and stories. The 'we' quadrant is the 'inter-subjective' quadrant.
- *Upper Right 'It' Quadrant (individual-exterior):* This 'behavioural' quadrant focuses on individual behaviour and physical individual expressions – like skills and performance – (and its different states, stages, levels and types). 'Behavioural' refers to our individual physical expressions like skills and performance, but also to our physical formation that materially corresponds with our ability for different levels of consciousness. The 'it' quadrant is the 'objective' quadrant.
- *Lower Right 'Its' Quadrant (collective-exterior):* This 'social' quadrant focuses on socio-technical forms and systems (and their different states, stages, levels and types). 'Social' refers to all of the exterior, material, institutional forms of the community, from its sociotechnical base to its written codes. The 'its' quadrant is the inter-objective quadrant.

In Figure 19.2, on the next page, we provide an overview of the four quadrants. Altogether, they represent the interior and exterior of the individual and the collective. All four quadrants show growth, development or evolution not as rigid rungs of a ladder, but as flowing waves of unfolding. Wilber urges that our future development efforts need to take all quadrants into account. If not, he states, we will go limping into the future; we will be ordinary local driftwood on the shore of this extraordinary global stream.

Though Wilber uses different levels of abstraction and categorisation, we clearly notice the resonance between our two integral approaches. His two interior quadrants correspond very much with our 'Southern' and 'Eastern' integral realms, while his two exterior quadrants mirror, to some extent, our 'Northern' and 'Western' ones. Furthermore, as we differentiate in each realm between the levels of self, organisation and society, Wilber has built this differentiation in between his four quadrants (Figure 19.2).

Over the past decades, Wilber has developed these four quadrants into a sophisticated body of theory thereby building on a wealth of thinkers of a large variety of disciplines. For all of the quadrants Wilber distinguishes, among others, between:

- stages or levels of development;
- lines of development;
- types of development; and
- states of consciousness.

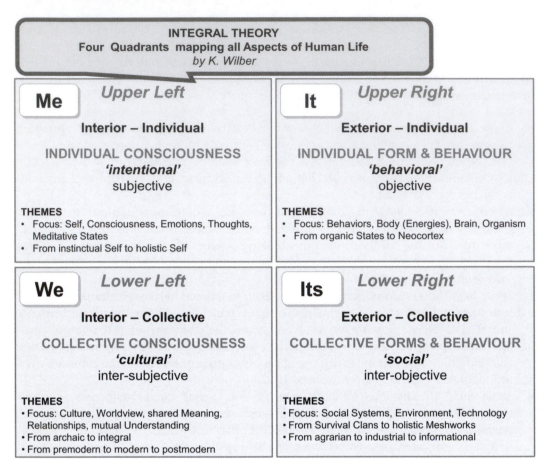

INTEGRAL THEORY
Four Quadrants mapping all Aspects of Human Life
by K. Wilber

Me *Upper Left* **Interior – Individual** INDIVIDUAL CONSCIOUSNESS *'intentional'* subjective THEMES • Focus: Self, Consciousness, Emotions, Thoughts, Meditative States • From instinctual Self to holistic Self	**It** *Upper Right* **Exterior – Individual** INDIVIDUAL FORM & BEHAVIOUR *'behavioral'* objective THEMES • Focus: Behaviors, Body (Energies), Brain, Organism • From organic States to Neocortex
We *Lower Left* **Interior – Collective** COLLECTIVE CONSCIOUSNESS *'cultural'* inter-subjective THEMES • Focus: Culture, Worldview, shared Meaning, Relationships, mutual Understanding • From archaic to integral • From premodern to modern to postmodern	**Its** *Lower Right* **Exterior – Collective** COLLECTIVE FORMS & BEHAVIOUR *'social'* inter-objective THEMES • Focus: Social Systems, Environment, Technology • From Survival Clans to holistic Meshworks • From agrarian to industrial to informational

Figure 19.2 The four quadrants of Ken Wilber's Integral approach

In order to tease out a bit more of Wilber's conceptual genius, we shall shed some brief light on these four differentiations.

STAGES OR LEVELS OF DEVELOPMENT: EGOCENTRIC, ETHNOCENTRIC, WORLD-CENTRIC

Where states of consciousness are temporary, stages of consciousness are permanent. Stages represent the actual milestones of growth and development. Once we are at a stage it is an enduring acquisition. In the Indian *chakra* system, for example, there are seven major stages or levels of consciousness. Jean Gebser, as we have seen earlier (⇨13), used five: archaic, magical, mythical, rational and integral. Each stage represents a level of consciousness or complexity. Wilber's integral model works with eight to ten stages in each quadrant.

An example: if we look at individual, moral development, we find that an infant at birth has not yet been socialised into the culture's ethics and conventions. That is the so-called pre-conventional stage. It is also-called egocentric in that the infant remains self-absorbed. But as the young child begins to learn the culture's rules and norms it grows into the conventional stage of morals. This stage is also-called ethnocentric, in that it centres on the child's particular group, tribe, clan or nation, and it therefore tends to exclude those not in one's group. But at the next post-conventional stage of moral development, the individual's identity expands once again. This time it includes a care and concern for all peoples. This stage is called world-centric. With the help of Howard Gardner's work, Wilber then comes to what he calls 'lines' of development.

LINES OF DEVELOPMENT: ACKNOWLEDGING MULTIPLE INTELLIGENCES

With lines of development, Wilber acknowledges different forms of intelligence with which humans can operate. The renowned American educationalist Howard Gardner distinguishes between seven different human intelligences – interpersonal, intrapersonal, verbal, mathematical, visual, musical and kinaesthetic.[5] Each intelligence can grow through the three stages identified. Emotional development, at the first and egocentric stage for example, focuses on 'me', especially the emotion of hunger, survival and protection. As we continue to grow from 'me' to 'us' to the second and ethnocentric stage, we begin to develop commitments and attachments to loved ones, from friends and family to tribe and nation. If we grow into the third and world-centric stage we will develop further our capacity for care and compassion to include all sentient beings. Wilber not only refers to Gardner's multiple intelligences. Building on them he also uses different articulations to express the nature of development lines, such as cognition, needs, self-identity, values, emotions, aesthetics, morals, kinaesthetic, interpersonal relating and spirituality.[6] These lines can develop within a quadrant relatively independent from each other.

TYPES OF DEVELOPMENT: MASCULINE OR FEMININE

Wilber then turns from stage and line to 'type'. Here he distinguishes male and female logic that can operate on every quadrant. Let's turn to some examples that Wilber provides: male logic tends to be based on terms of autonomy, justice, and rights whereas women's logic tends to be based on terms of relationship, care and responsibility. Men tend toward individualism, women towards relationships. However, there are healthy and unhealthy versions of each type. If the healthy masculine principle tends towards autonomy, strength, independence and freedom, when this type becomes pathological all of these positive virtues are under fire. There is not just autonomy but alienation; not just strength but domination; not just independence, but fear of relationship and commitment; not just drive towards freedom, but also a drive to destroy. If the healthy feminine principle tends towards flowing, relationship, care and compassion, the unhealthy feminine flounders in each of these. Instead of healthy relationships the person becomes lost in one; instead of a healthy self in communion with others, the person is dominated; instead of being in a flow state the person is in a panic state. In each quadrant we need to recognise that this male–female dialectic is at play.

STATES OF CONSCIOUSNESS: GROSS, SUBTLE, CAUSAL

Wilber argues that states of consciousness do not float in the air, dangling and disembodied. On the contrary, every mind has its body. For every state of consciousness there is an energetic component. Wilber distinguishes three levels of consciousness experience: there is a coarse or gross experience, subtle or refined experience, and very subtle or causal experience. These are what philosophers would call phenomenological realities, or realities that present themselves in immediate awareness. These three consciousness experiences relate to three states of consciousness. In a waking state we are aware of our gross physical and material body. In a dream state, it is our subtle body, light and energetic, emotional and fluid, with flowing images. Wilber explains further that as we ultimately pass from dream state to the third, formless state, there is only emptiness as thoughts and feelings drop away, a formless state beyond the individual ego. Out of this causal body great possibilities can arise.

Wilber argues that the greater the consciousness, the more complex the system housing it. For example, in living organisms, the reptilian brain stem is accompanied by a rudimentary interior consciousness of basic drives such as food and hunger, physiological sensations and sensorimotor based actions centred on 'me'. By the time we get to the more complex mammalian limbic system, basic sensations have evolved to include quite sophisticated feelings and desires that we experience in the subtle body, which can expand from 'me' to 'us'. As evolution proceeds to even more complex physical structures, the neocortex, consciousness expands to a world-centric awareness of 'all of us'. Wilber argues, that we are now collectively moving towards a more world-centric awareness.

THE INTEGRAL MAP – FOSTERING WORLD-CENTRIC AWARENESS AND ENABLING GLOBAL PERSPECTIVES

Wilber makes the point that during the last 30 years we have witnessed a historical first: all of the world's cultures are now available to us.[7] He explains that in the past, if one was born, say a Chinese, one was likely to have spent the entire life in one culture, often in one province, sometimes in one house, living and loving and dying in one small plot of land. But today, not only are people geographically mobile, but we can study, and have studied, virtually every known culture on the planet. All cultures are exposed to each other. Wilber asserts that by using his integral approach as a map or operating system, we are able to dramatically accelerate cross-disciplinary and transdisciplinary knowledge, thus creating the world's first integral learning community.

We have now ended our brief tour of Wilber's main framework and illustrated its potential to catalyse a fundamentally new perspective on human systems and the world at large. At this first 'Western' level we are now interested in how we can build such an integral perspective into our own lives, as a fundament for sustainable livelihood.

FROM THEORY TO PRACTICE: TOWARDS AN INTEGRAL LIFE PRACTICE

Wilber, together with his colleagues Terry Patten, Adam Leonard and Marco Morelli has recently translated the integral theory into an *Integral Life Practice: A 21st-Century*

Blueprint for Physical Health, Emotional Balance, Mental Clarity, Spiritual Awakening. In this work they are dealing simultaneously with all four quadrants. 'Since our life arises in and as all four quadrants, we can engage it with more balance and intelligence by accounting for these four primordial perspectives'.[8] However, their intention is not to break life into four or more pieces. Rather, they have grounded Integral Life Practice 'in awakening to life's wholeness and singleness, its "Integral-ness"'.[9]

The authors remind us that human beings, in almost all cultures, have engaged for thousands of years in practices to transform and balance their lives. In an attempt to do justice to the enormous variety of practices, 'Integral Life Practice is a way of organising the many practices handed down through the centuries – along with those developed at the cutting edge of psychology, consciousness studies, and other leading fields – using a framework for life in the 21st century'.[10] Wilber and his colleagues regard Integral Life Practice as a synthesis of 'the best of the best' that tradition and modern science has to offer.

WHY ENGAGE IN INTEGRAL LIFE PRACTICE AS AN INTEGRAL DEVELOPER

Integral Life Practice is written for a large audience and is aiming to serve many different reasons for engagement. We present some of these reasons here, that may in particular resonate with us as Integral Developers: to embrace and work with crisis, pain, or suffering; to live with integrity and excellence; to become a better person – on all levels, on all areas; to live according to our highest ideals; to become more fully alive and creative; to make our highest possible contribution; to participate in the evolution of consciousness; to love and care for ourselves and others more fully.

THE INTEGRAL LIFE PRACTICE MATRIX

With Integral Life Practice, Wilber and his colleagues have excelled with regards to two important achievements. First of all, they have come with a comprehensive and applicable matrix that enables everyone to get on the journey or to evolve one's current practice. Secondly, they continuously interlink the practices they introduce with the four quadrants.

Evaluating their Integral Life Practice matrix, we find it grounded in four core modules that focus on body, mind, spirit and shadow. We regard it as an invaluable asset of the matrix, that the shadow dimension is prominently included. In earlier chapters we have already introduced the relevance of the shadow extensively (⇨11), but we emphasise together with Wilber the importance of integrating shadow work into one's life practice. In addition to the four core modules, Wilber and his colleagues regard the following additional practice modules as relevant: ethics, work, relationships, creativity and soul. For each of the modules they are offering a variety of concrete exercises, complemented by rich advice how and when to use these exercises and how to compose a meaningful menu for oneself, selected from the proposed variety and by adding additional own practices. Tables 19.2 and 19.3 present the Integral Life Practice matrix.[11] Together, these modules – adapted to personal choice – provide a solid fundament on an individual level to bring about sustainable livelihood.

Table 19.2   Integral Life Practice matrix (1)

Four core modules (sample practices)

Body	Mind	Spirit	Shadow
3-body workout FIT (strength-training) Aerobic exercise Balanced diet and conscious eating Yoga Martial arts Sports and dance	Reading and study Discussion and debate Writing and journaling Looking at your meaning making Pursuing a degree	Meditation Prayer The 3 faces of spirit integral inquiry Spiritual community worship, song and chant Compassionate exchange	3–2–1 Process (Face it/talk to it/be it) Dream work Journaling Psychotherapy Family and couples therapy Transmuting Emotions Art, music and dance therapy

Table 19.3   Integral Life Practice matrix (2)

Five additional modules (sample practices)

Ethics

- Moral inquiry
- Professional ethics
- Integral ethics
- Philanthropy
- Volunteer work
- Heartfelt service
- Social activism

Work

- Right livelihood
- Time management
- Integral communication
- Personal productivity systems
- Professional development
- Financial intelligence

Relationships

- Conscious commitment
- Integral parenting
- Weekly check-ins
- Being vulnerable
- Intimacy workshops

Creativity

- Integral Artistry
- Dance and drama
- Practicing, playing and writing music
- Cooking and interior decorating
- Creative writing
- Creative community

Soul

- Solitude
- Psychology
- Nature communion
- Resonance with art, music and literature
- Discovering and living
- Your purpose
- Depth
- Vision quest Journeys

LINKING INTEGRAL LIFE PRACTICE WITH THE FOUR QUADRANTS

Wilber and his colleagues invite us to adopt each practice in a four-quadrant manner. That enables us to continuously connect the inner and the outer perspective, as well as the individual and collective viewpoint. In other words, we evaluate on a regular basis what we feel or think ('me' quadrant), what the perspectives of others are ('we' quadrant), what possible interconnections with larger systems exist ('its' quadrant) and what possible actions we can take on each issue ('it' quadrant). Figure 19.3 illustrates this ongoing evaluation process.[12]

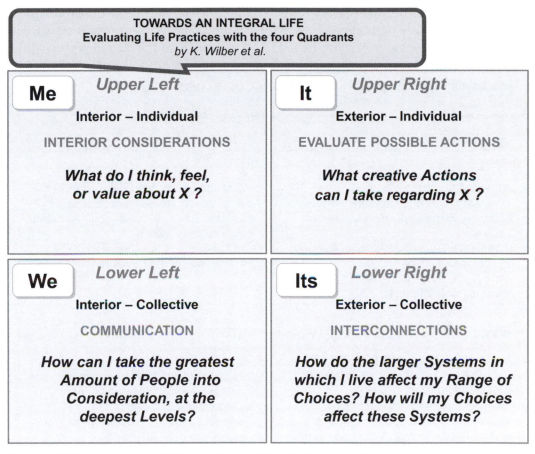

Figure 19.3 Evaluating life practices with the four quadrants

MUTUALLY ENRICHING INTEGRAL APPROACHES

We regard Wilber's and his colleagues' work as an invaluable complement to and strong affirmation of our own integral approach. For us, Wilber is the key thinker within a newly emergent field of integral thinking. If there are missing components in Wilber's approach, it is firstly the lack of a dynamic principle built into the quadrants, and secondly, the lack of reference to one world or another, in cultural and communal terms. In other words, whether I am an Indian or an African, an American or Japanese, Wilber's approach is seemingly universally relevant. The quadrants are an organising mechanism for a profoundly inclusive map, yet, it remains problematic how to navigate and effect in that map in a particular context.

With Integral Life Practice a convincing step towards actualising the integral theory into our lives has been made. However, to some degree we are left with a rich matrix and rich advice for its implementation, but without an inner transformational process to activate it. It is for that reason, that we feel that both our approaches are deeply complementary. We further illustrate this through Figure 19.4, in which we aspired to link the four quadrants with our own integral perspective.

In both cases that we presented in this Round 1 – the development topography and Wilber's integral theory and practice – we have already well transcended the individual level. Indeed, we see both approaches as profoundly relevant for organisational and societal development as well. With this in mind, we move on to conclude this chapter.

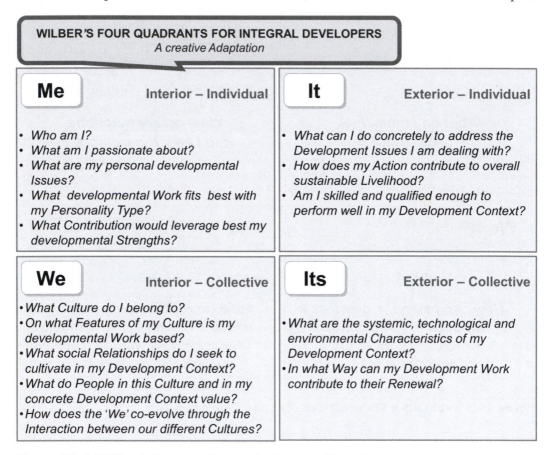

WILBER'S FOUR QUADRANTS FOR INTEGRAL DEVELOPERS
A creative Adaptation

Me — Interior – Individual

- Who am I?
- What am I passionate about?
- What are my personal developmental Issues?
- What developmental Work fits best with my Personality Type?
- What Contribution would leverage best my developmental Strengths?

It — Exterior – Individual

- What can I do concretely to address the Development Issues I am dealing with?
- How does my Action contribute to overall sustainable Livelihood?
- Am I skilled and qualified enough to perform well in my Development Context?

We — Interior – Collective

- What Culture do I belong to?
- On what Features of my Culture is my developmental Work based?
- What social Relationships do I seek to cultivate in my Development Context?
- What do People in this Culture and in my concrete Development Context value?
- How does the 'We' co-evolve through the Interaction between our different Cultures?

Its — Exterior – Collective

- What are the systemic, technological and environmental Characteristics of my Development Context?
- In what Way can my Development Work contribute to their Renewal?

Figure 19.4 Wilber's four quadrants for Integral Developers

19.4 Integration

We have now, finally on our Integral Development journey, entered the 'Western' world of action. The renewal of development practice begins not on an institutional or societal level, but with us, as Integral Developers. It begins with our own 'life practice', albeit in relation to our immediate context and community.

The development topography with which we opened this chapter, helps us link our 'surface action' (inclinations) with underlying images, ideologies (philosophies) and institutional designs. The topography enables us to remain conscious of the deeper foundations on which we root our action.

The subsequent approach of Ken Wilber and his colleagues on Integral Life Practice is another potent 'tool' (note the 'Western' ring of the term 'tool') to analyse, in practical terms, our lives, and to seek alignment between its various, complex facets. Through such alignment we can then keep focus on our overriding goal as Integral Developers in this 'Western' realm: contributing to equitable and sustainable livelihoods.

In conclusion, we invite you to engage – through reflection and prospective action – with the guiding questions and theory presented in this chapter, as well as with the major development challenges derived thereof for yourself.

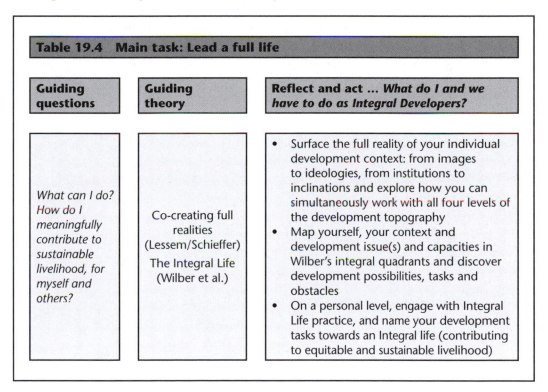

Table 19.4	Main task: Lead a full life	
Guiding questions	**Guiding theory**	**Reflect and act ... *What do I and we have to do as Integral Developers?***
What can I do? How do I meaningfully contribute to sustainable livelihood, for myself and others?	Co-creating full realities (Lessem/Schieffer) The Integral Life (Wilber et al.)	• Surface the full reality of your individual development context: from images to ideologies, from institutions to inclinations and explore how you can simultaneously work with all four levels of the development topography • Map yourself, your context and development issue(s) and capacities in Wilber's integral quadrants and discover development possibilities, tasks and obstacles • On a personal level, engage with Integral Life practice, and name your development tasks towards an Integral life (contributing to equitable and sustainable livelihood)

We now turn from self to organisation within this 'Western' integral realm.

References

1   Bhaskar, R. (2000). *Meta-Reality: Creativity, Love and Freedom*. London: Sage.
2   Lessem, R. et al. (2013). *Integral Dynamics: Nature, Culture, Science and Enterprise*. Farnham: Gower

3   Wilber, K. (2000). *A Theory of Everything: An Integral Vision for Business, Politics, Science and Spirituality*. Boston, MA: Shambhala.

4   Wilber, K. (2000). *Marriage of Sense and Soul: Integrating Science and Religion*. New York: Broadway Books.

5   Gardner, H. (2006). *Multiple Intelligences: New Horizons in Theory and Practice*. New York: Basic Books.

6   Wilber, K. et al. (2008). *Integral Life Practice: A 21st-Century Blueprint for Physical Health, Emotional Balance, Mental Clarity, Spiritual Awakening*. Boston, MA: Integral Books, pp. 81f.

7   Wilber, K. (2008). *Integral Spirituality: A Startling New Role for Religion in the Modern and Postmodern World*. Boston, MA: Shambhala.

8   Wilber, K. et al. (2008). *Integral Life Practice: A 21st-Century Blueprint for Physical Health, Emotional Balance, Mental Clarity, Spiritual Awakening*. Boston, MA: Integral Books, p 29.

9   Wilber, K. et al. (2008). *Integral Life Practice: A 21st-Century Blueprint for Physical Health, Emotional Balance, Mental Clarity, Spiritual Awakening*. Boston, MA: Integral Books, p 29.

10   Wilber, K. et al. (2008). *Integral Life Practice: A 21st-Century Blueprint for Physical Health, Emotional Balance, Mental Clarity, Spiritual Awakening*. Boston, MA: Integral Books, p. 1.

11   Wilber, K. et al. (2008). *Integral Life Practice: A 21st-Century Blueprint for Physical Health, Emotional Balance, Mental Clarity, Spiritual Awakening*. Boston, MA: Integral Books, p. 20.

12   Wilber, K. et al. (2008). *Integral Life Practice: A 21st-Century Blueprint for Physical Health, Emotional Balance, Mental Clarity, Spiritual Awakening*. Boston, MA: Integral Books, p. 112.

20 *Enterprise as a Force for Good: A Western Organisational Perspective*

Guiding Questions: What can we do? What kind of organisation do we build that meaningfully contributes to the sustainable development of community and society?

20.1   Orientation

Now that we have mapped out the Integral Development of the individual from a 'Western' perspective, we set out to identify what kind of evolved organisational designs 'fit the integral bill'. At this 'Western' stage of our journey, we want to get 'real', in that our organisational ways of operating practically in society need to mirror our progressive findings from the 'Southern', 'Eastern' and 'Northern' realms. We seek to find out how an organisation can actually function in totally different ways, in order to become an authentic vehicle for the Integral Development of the community and society of which it is part. What kind of experiments have already been made that can inform our understanding of a new organisational design? What kind of theory has been developed?

Filled with experiences, insights and new knowledge, gained and developed in the previous three realms, where we asked progressively the questions of 'Who are we?' ('South'), 'How are we co-evolving?' ('East') and 'What do we need to know?' ('North'), it is now time to deal concretely with 'What can we do?' As Integral Developers we are called to explore the following questions:

- What can we do?
- What can we do based on what we have learnt from the other realms of Integral Development?
- What kind of organisation do we build accordingly?
- How do we meaningfully contribute as an organisation to the sustainable development of community and society, in which we are embedded?

As a first step we shall find out – with the guidance of the UN Global Compact, of Nobel Laureate Muhammad Yunus and others – what types of new enterprises are emerging that effectively deal with development issues, thereby transcending the conventional notion of a private enterprise. We will come to the conclusion that what we find at this stage, is highly promising, but overall still 'a fertile chaos'. As we observe promising new organisational types 'up and running' in practice, we also notice their shortcomings. What has not yet taken place is a fundamental transformation of the very functioning of the enterprise. As long as that that does not happen, we continue to address societal problems with defunct organisational designs. It is for that reason that we shall introduce, as a second step, the concept of an Integral Enterprise – a concept that has been carefully developed over the past 10 years, and is starting to see the light of organisational practice.

20.2   The Renewal of Enterprise: Reorientation of Private Enterprise, Social Business and Other Emergent Enterprise Forms

EXPANSION OF THE TRADITIONAL NOTION OF PRIVATE ENTERPRISE

The role of business in society over the past two decades has come a long way from promoting general philanthropy, corporate social responsibility and corporate social investment. We have seen a gradual expansion of the traditional notion of private enterprise, whereby an increasing number of organisations are putting more and more emphasis on societal engagement. Corporations are reaching out towards culture, education, environment and other fields. Cross-sector partnerships are encouraged, and the term public–private–civic partnership is by now part of business vocabulary. Increasingly, business is reaching out to society at large, acknowledging that such engagement is vital in order to ensure its own survival and growth.

A prominent case in point is the International Business Leaders Forum (IBLF), initially established in 1990 in the UK by the Prince of Wales to promote responsible business practices in developing and transition economies. Working closely with more than 100 large multinational corporations, IBLF is exploring new approaches to developing the role of 'business in society', in trans-sectoral partnership with public, civic and multilateral enterprises.[1] IBLF argues that business needs to move to 'the heart of sustainable development', to the benefit of both itself and also the communities within which it operates. The growing gap between the rich and the poor, the advent of climate change, peak oil, food crises, massive corruption and international terrorism are just few of the complex issues that make business leaders realise that something more than CSR (corporate social responsibility) is required.

A well-known representative of such new thinking is Unilever's former Group CEO Patrick Cescau who is praised for putting sustainable development and corporate social responsibility firmly onto Unilever's agenda. For him, as for us, CSR does not go far enough. Cescau claimed that social innovation together with sustainable development need to become core drivers of business growth.[2]

PRIVATE ENTERPRISES FOR DEVELOPMENT: SUPPORTING THE MILLENNIUM DEVELOPMENT GOALS

This combined new focus on conventional business growth and profit on the one hand and the promotion of societal development on the other is increasingly promoted in business circles. The UN Global Compact Initiative, launched in 2000 under the stewardship of the then UN Secretary-General Kofi Annan, is one of the most prominent signs for an emergent shift of mind. While from the outset Global Compact is a global initiative focusing on the private sector, it describes itself as 'global and local, public and private, voluntary yet accountable'. Participants subscribe to an established policy framework for the development, implementation and disclosure of environmental, social and governance policies and practices. One of the tasks of Global Impact is to make best practices available to its members to enhance practical solutions and strategies to common challenges.

Global Compact sees business as the key agent for globalisation. As the world largest corporate citizen initiative it pursues two primary goals: firstly, it seeks to institutionalise 10 distinct business principles within mainstream business practice and secondly, it aims to catalyse action of the corporate sector supporting the Millennium Development Goals (MDGs). The 10 principles are internationally agreed targets covering Human Rights, labour standards, environment and anti-corruption. According to the website of the UN Global Compact, by now over 4,000 organisations have become members, among them trade unions, NGOs, and over 3,100 businesses.[3]

Another reflection of a new thinking in the corporate world are the World Business and Development Awards, organised in partnership by the International Business Leaders Forum (IBLF), the International Chamber of Commerce (ICC), the United Nations Development Programme (UNDP) Agency, the UN Global Compact and others. These annual awards, initiated in 2002, honour selected organisations that have developed innovative business models that deliver both commercial success and helping improve social, economic and environmental conditions. According to ILBF, the awards are designed to demonstrate how companies can – through their core business activities – help achieve the MDGs. Clare Melford, IBLF's former CEO claims: 'When businesses apply the full force of their core business activities to development challenges and measure their success both by profit and social outcomes, there is no limit to what can be achieved'.[4]

A prominent example for such a business is Richard Branson's Virgin Group, a part of which (Virgin Money) we have been working with for many years. The Virgin Group has set up an entire non-profit organisational entity called Virgin Unite that describes itself as follows:

> We unite people to tackle tough social and environmental problems with an entrepreneurial approach. Our aim is to help revolutionise the way businesses and the social sector work together – driving business as a force for good. This is based on the belief that this is the only way we can address the scale and urgency of the challenges facing the world today. Virgin Unite also works on behalf of vulnerable young people across the globe.[5]

It also oversees the by now famous initiative of Richard Branson, Peter Gabriel, Nelson Mandela and Graça Machel to set up *The Elders*,[6] a group of outstanding global leaders who 'use their experience and wisdom to work on behalf of humanity'.[7]

While then the private sector is looking for new and more meaningful ways of societal engagement, the civic sector has developed its own approach: the 'social enterprise'.

ENTREPRENEURSHIP IN THE CIVIC SECTOR: THE RISE OF SOCIAL AND SOCIETAL ENTERPRISE

Social Enterprises are often defined as organisations that apply business strategies to pursue developmental or philanthropic goals in society. Usually, social enterprises are set up as non-profit organisations, but not in all cases. However, whether they are aiming for profit or not, what is an important distinguishing factor is that the primary goal of the organisation is a social one. According to Charles Leadbetter of the British Think Tank Demos, today non-profit social enterprises are the fastest growing category of enterprises in the USA. In policy-making and in discussions on how to balance the role of government, business and civil society, social and civic entrepreneurs get central attention.[8] 'Social entrepreneurship' is engaging in many different initiatives, in the health sector, in the environment, amongst NGOs, in the informal sector in the third world, and in other cultural and social domains. Such new initiatives are often viewed as a form of R&D in the welfare system, innovating new solutions to intractable social problems. Concluding, social enterprises help communities to build up social capital.

Another newly emergent enterprise type, transcending the social enterprise, is the 'societal enterprise'. In recent years, this model, particular discussed and practised in Sweden[9] and South Africa, points towards new field of entrepreneurship emphasising societal utility.[10] According to Tony Bradley, Director of the SEED Centre of the Business School of Liverpool's Hope University, a key to societal entrepreneurship is 'the range of stakeholder and social capital networks that have been developed to deliver a regional change in capacity-building for social entrepreneurs'.[11] For him, this kind of 'entrepreneurship-based community development' is already happening all over the world. Mondragon in Spain (⇨18) and Grameen in Bangladesh are two prominent examples to which he points. That, however, also demonstrates how blur the line between such new enterprise types still is, as we turn now to the case of the social business.

ENTREPRENEURSHIP BETWEEN THE PRIVATE AND THE CIVIC SECTOR: EMERGING SOCIAL BUSINESS

Nobel Laureate Muhammad Yunus, by way of his own example through the Grameen enterprises in Bangladesh, has promoted the 'social' business as a new 'hybrid' between conventional private and social enterprise. For him, both concepts fall short. The private entrepreneur, for Yunus, is deemed to be dedicated to one mission only – the maximisation of profit. Yet the reality is very different. People are not one-dimensional. They are multidimensional. They have the potential to self-actualise, to realise heightened levels of consciousness. Mainstream free-market theory, for Yunus, suffers from a 'conceptualisation failure', a failure to capture the essence of what it is to be human. For him, it actually ignores higher levels of 'world-centric' consciousness.[12]

Yunus goes on and argues that in the conventional theory of business we have created a one-dimensional human being to play the role of business entrepreneur, the so-called economic entrepreneur. We have insulated him or her from the rest of life, the religious, emotional, political and social that characterise the social entrepreneur. However, that puts also the latter into a box. This is where Yunus' concept of 'social business' comes in. Entrepreneurs establish a social business not to achieve limited personal gain but to pursue social goals. A social business respects the multifaceted motivations of the entrepreneur, including his or her business orientation, which, of course, includes the generation of profits to secure the economic sustainability of the business. Hence, such an enterprise is simultaneously social *and* economic.[13]

For Yunus, the singular focus on profit of Western-style capitalism is also one of the root causes of poverty. Thus, he sees social business as a way to build a new kind of capitalism. He argues, that social businesses have to operate within the same capitalist system as conventional businesses. Like profit-maximising companies, they must find ways to sell their products that will cover their costs and generate enough money to fund their expansion. They must respond effectively to market challenges, price their products so that the target audience can afford them, and, when possible, take advantage of opportunities to generate additional income through sales at higher prices to affluent people. However, a social business has one advantage. It is less exposed to the downside risks experienced when markets fluctuate, because the future of the business is not tied to its stock price. Above all, social business represents, for Yunus, a new way for human being to express their entrepreneurial spirit.[14]

By now the concept of the Social Business has become very popular. A number of organisations have been established to research and promote the further dissemination of the social business concept – such as the Yunus Center in Bangladesh, Social Business Earth, the Grameen Creative Lab in Germany and the Yunus Social Business Center at the University of Florence.

We now turn from the social business to the environmentally oriented eco-enterprise.

THE RE-EMERGING ECO-ENTERPRISE

There is a fundamentally new enterprise form increasingly visible, which so far has been subsumed under the social enterprise: the eco-enterprise. With eco-enterprise we mean enterprises, which have a strong environmental orientation, and are deeply rooted in nature and nature's principles. For Catherine Campbell, a South African social psychologist currently based at the London School of Economics:

> growing ourselves and our communities in harmony with the land is seldom recognised as an entrepreneurial activity. Although a majority of the world's population lives on the land, only a tiny fraction of people in the industrialised world do, and most theories of entrepreneurship emanate from the latter. We have discredited our enterprising physical selves and commoditised the business of living. In fact, we exist today because our foremothers foraged and gathered and, later, accomplished the transition to gardening and agriculture.[15]

According to Campbell, modern notions of entrepreneurial behaviour are in many ways idealisations of the mythical hunter. But our species did not survive by hunting alone. Close study of a subsistence relationship with 'Mother Earth' reveals the quintessential entrepreneurial responsibility for our individual and collective process of self-creation and self-nurturing. Unlike industrial production or knowledge work, work that occurs with and for the land is axiomatically concerned with space and place. Such 'grounded' entrepreneurial activity becomes a mutually beneficial interaction between and among individuals, and between people and nature, as they collectively create meaning for themselves and their community. Indeed, Catherine Campbell is calling for a transformation in our understanding of enterprise, one that is grounded in nature rather than in economics.

'Bioregionalism', for example, is a result of such eco-entrepreneurial efforts. Bioregions – or ecoregions – dramatically reframe the entrepreneurial process, shifting the emphasis from a human to an ecosystemic orientation, whereby we become more rooted in place and space.[16] Modern-day permaculture – a concept that has been pioneered in the 1970s by David Holmgren and Bill Mollison – is another influential entrepreneurial attempt to move towards more localised energy-efficient and productive living arrangements.[17] Permaculture claims, that this is not a choice, but an inevitable direction for humanity. According to Rob Hopkins, one of the key proponents of permaculture, rebuilding local agriculture and food production, localising energy production, rethinking healthcare, rediscovering local building, in the context of zero energy building, rethinking how we manage waste – all of these activities build resilience and offer the potential of an extraordinary renaissance of humanity – and of enterprise in a whole new guise.[18]

Finally, we shall take a look at a newly emergent form of enterprise in the public sector.

EMERGING PUBLIC ENTERPRISE IN A REDEFINED PUBLIC SPACE

Recently upcoming discourses from Scandinavian academics Daniel Hjorth and Bjorne Bjerke make the case for the emergence of a public form of entrepreneurship via a redefinition of 'public space'. Starting from a conviction that entrepreneurship belongs primarily to society rather than to the economy, and that we need to understand life rather than simply business to fully appreciate the entrepreneurial processes, Hjorth and Bjerke suggest locating entrepreneurship in the public domain.[19] According to them, it would be appropriate to conceive of today's society as consisting of three sectors:

- one common sector (the traditional public sector financed by taxes);
- one business sector driven by market forces;
- a newly called public sector, where community goals are achieved by engaging in social processes, including 'public businesses'.

Hjorth and Bjerke use the concept 'public' to think their way back from 'social and society'. They do this as a reaction against how managerial economic rationality has come to define and refer to the 'social' in a derogatory manner while being called upon to provide expert knowledge in the recent urge for 'reinventing government'. Such a perspective on public enterprise can be contrasted with the neo-liberal attempt to limit citizenship to the role of consumer choices in a market. Hjorth and Bjerke claim that a different view of citizenship is developed, that involves a creative 'making use' of the public space between state institutions and civic society. In this new discourse on social entrepreneurship the public citizen is reviewed as an enterprising self. Public entrepreneurs, for Hjorth and Bjerke, serve to create new forms of 'sociality' in the face of withering state institutions.

RENEWING ENTERPRISE IN SOCIETY: A STATE OF FERTILE CHAOS

In introducing the changing face of enterprise in today's society we have focused on three core trends. We have firstly described the ongoing expansion of business' engagement in society – increasingly in partnership with international and local development actors – and its reaching out to society's other sectors while exploring new concepts of doing so. Secondly, we have reviewed how social enterprises have established themselves as a counterbalance to the shortcomings of the private and public sectors. Thirdly, we have indicated that there are now a variety of emerging entrepreneurial forces, such as the 'social business' (positioning itself simultaneously in the business and in the social world), the eco-enterprise, as well as attempts to a redefinition of public enterprise. Figure 20.1 illustrates such core trends.

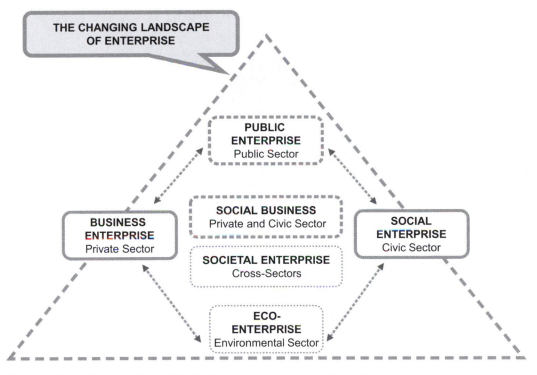

Figure 20.1 Types of established and emergent enterprises

Note: Established types = full line/Emerging types = dotted line.

Further building upon these trends is the emerging notion of cross-sector partnerships, most commonly termed public–private-civic partnerships. There are also significant efforts to consolidate upon such partnerships from an educational perspective. This is, for example, illustrated by the 'Partnering Initiative',[20] an educational joint venture of the International Business Leaders Forum and Cambridge (UK) University.

We regard these developments as 'fertile chaos'. They serve to acknowledge a need for transformation. They also acknowledge a need for new forms of trans-sectoral entrepreneurship and transformed enterprises, including new ways of partnering between different types of enterprise.

For us as Integral Developers, organisational designs like those of a social enterprise, societal enterprise, social business, eco-enterprise and public enterprise offer valuable steps along the way to something more fundamentally new. In particular the social business is a big step towards a more holistic approach to organisational sustainability. Yet, we still see an urgent requirement to challenge not only the outer orientation of enterprise, which is well on its way, but to review the inner functioning, which has often been uncritically transferred into new types of enterprises. Thereby the risks of perpetuating – at least in part – the negative 'side effects' of conventional business are carried forward. It is for this reason that we now turn to the concept of the Integral Enterprise.

20.3   The Integral Enterprise: Transforming the Enterprise into a Core Development Agent in Society

THE SEARCH FOR A NEW UNDERSTANDING OF THE ENTERPRISE EMBEDDED IN, CO-EVOLVING WITH AND SERVING SOCIETY

In our own work with organisational development and transformation we have long been struggling with the question of how organisations can be designed more sustainably, and in the process become more embedded in society. Thereby, the organisation would not only be responding much more directly to the real needs of society, it would also help to evolve society and to co-evolve with it. In other words, it would strengthen at one and the same time its own sustainable organisational functioning as well as the sustainable functioning of society. Such a perception would take the organisation out of its narrow and rather artificial institutional borders, and would place it as a living, interacting and continuously adapting entity within its equally living, interacting and ever changing societal environment.

The penny started to drop when we noticed the applicability of the integral model and its three levels of self, organisation and society to the enterprise. We then engaged in intensive research, examining organisational theory and advanced sustainable practice from all over the world. We gradually came up with a new organisational design, that enabled us to represent the organisation in an integral manner and to illustrate through advanced organisational practice that indeed a number of highly sustainable enterprises operate in an integral manner. We called such organisations Integral Enterprises. The process of consciously evolving an organisation into an Integral Enterprise we called Transformation Management, to indicate that the organisational functioning would have to undergo a fundamental transformation process. As we have described this approach at length in *Transformation Management: Towards the Integral Enterprise*,[21] we focus at this stage on a short introduction to the core concept, as we feel that it can strongly contribute to a transformed understanding of an organisation as an agent for the development of society.

HURDLES ON THE WAY TOWARDS AN INTEGRAL ENTERPRISE

According to the inner logic of our integral approach, whereby the four vectors and the centre represent the core functions of any social organism, so can the major functions

Figure 20.2 The conventional enterprise functions within an integral framework

of an enterprise be depicted in an integral manner. This is illustrated by Figure 20.2. The integral representation takes the organisation visually out of the conventional hierarchical or matrix format. We begin to envision the organisation more as a living organism, with the coordinating force (CEO, managing director, president), not on top of the organisation but in its very centre. Organised around this centre are the four core functions of the enterprise: Sales and Marketing; Human Resource Management and Organisational Development; Operations Management and IT; Financial Management and Accounting.

However, what is crucial is that the functions operate in an integral and thereby transformational manner. In many of the private sector enterprises we worked with we noticed, among others, four major interconnected shortcomings that inhibit continuous transformation processes that are necessary for fast and purposeful inner development.

• *Disconnected Functions:* The functions of the organisation are disconnected from each other, or at least do not sufficiently build on each other. What is required is that the organisational functions would need to build on each other and mutually reinforce each other – similar as in Integral Development.

- *North-Western Dominance:* An overemphasis is given to the 'Northern' and 'Western' functions of the enterprise: operations and finance. As in conventional development theory and practice (⇨2, 3), we witness a privileging of the technological and financial dimension over the human and ecological dimension. In many private sector organisations we even come across a singular dominance of the financial function over the other functions. An example: if one follows organisational founding stories, we often find that at the origins of organisations like, for example, Unilever, Bodyshop, Grundig or Avon, was a profound societal vision – an urge to respond to a societal predicament. Such organisations were deeply grounded in the societies they originated from. Many enterprises, however, lose this initial grounding in the course of their evolution and focus on ever more efficient operational processes ('Northern' function) and on cash flow and return on investment ('Western' function). Thereby the enterprise is in danger of becoming static, as the functions stop playing an equal role – interaction and continuous evolution of each of the organisational functions and thus of the organisation as a whole are inhibited. We find similar disturbing patterns in many development organisations. Though mandated to 'serve the poor', we see a majority of such organisations spending most of their time and resources on fundraising and project evaluation ('West') as well as gathering and preparing relevant statistics ('North'). Thereby they lose touch with the communities they are supposed to serve ('South') and fail to understand and activate the cultural and spiritual context of their activity field ('East').
- *Limited Functional Definition:* The understanding of the organisational functions is often very narrow. In such cases the functions do not reach out and connect to individual functioning (our Round 1) and societal functioning (our Round 3). An example: the 'Southern' sales and marketing function of an enterprise is often primarily focusing on the communication and distribution of products and services providing for individual wants, rather than being in touch with the nature and community of a society, and responding consequently – through products and services – to the developmental needs in society. Another example: in such organisations, the individual becomes a mere 'human resource' (what a disrespecting term for the working human being), and consequently feels alienated from the organisation – a situation which many organisations face today.
- *Overall Closedness of the Organisation:* All of the above shortcomings result in an internal and external closedness of the organisation, which leads to a limited flow – from within and without – of new perspectives. That diminishes the innovation potential of the organisation. An example: If we consider only the ideas and practices already introduced in Round 2 of Integral Development, we find enormous transdisciplinary stimulation for the organisation. Many organisations, however, don't deal proactively with such new insights provided by other disciplines.

The Integral Enterprise seeks to overcome these shortcomings. Not only are the three levels of self, organisation and society interconnected, but, furthermore, the organisational functions are also interconnected among each other. In that process, each of the original function transforms and broadens its scope. This is intimated in Table 20.1.

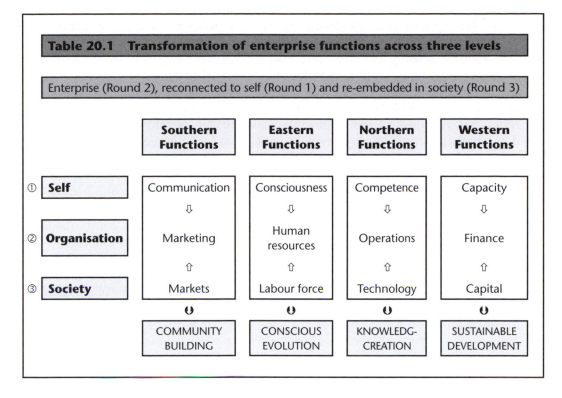

Table 20.1 Transformation of enterprise functions across three levels

Enterprise (Round 2), reconnected to self (Round 1) and re-embedded in society (Round 3)

	Southern Functions	Eastern Functions	Northern Functions	Western Functions
① **Self**	Communication ⇩	Consciousness ⇩	Competence ⇩	Capacity ⇩
② **Organisation**	Marketing	Human resources	Operations	Finance
③ **Society**	⇧ Markets	⇧ Labour force	⇧ Technology	⇧ Capital
	☊ COMMUNITY BUILDING	☊ CONSCIOUS EVOLUTION	☊ KNOWLEDG-CREATION	☊ SUSTAINABLE DEVELOPMENT

FUNCTIONAL TRANSFORMATION: BUILDING THE INTEGRAL ENTERPRISE

The transformational process that each individual function has to undergo is complex. In our work we demonstrate what such transformation processes could look like. We are building on latest organisational theory and advanced practice that precedes such functional evolution – and which is well on its way, although as yet only in pockets. For example, the evolution of the function of marketing towards 'relationship management', 'social marketing' and 'eco-marketing', is a clear sign of a reorientation and broadening of the marketing function towards nature and community and to community building. Equally, concepts like 'knowledge management', 'intellectual capital', the 'networked operation' and the 'virtual organisation' signal a fundamental change of the 'Northern' function. Furthermore, new enterprise forms, such as social enterprise and the social business, illustrate a strong orientation towards community building and sustainable development.

So what we find are promising 'pockets' and 'cases', but not yet a fundamental redesign of the enterprise. What has not happened as yet is a redefinition and subsequently reintegration of the core organisational functions. Also, the business curricula have not all been changed towards a more integral organisational theory and practice – though what we find are lots of 'add ons', such as 'corporate social responsibility', 'business ethics' and 'social business'.

With our theory on Integral Enterprise as well as in our own educational practice, we seek to promote such a transformational renewal of the enterprise functions. True to our 'South-East-North-West' rhythm we seek to transform the very functions of the enterprise in the following way:

- *South:* We reground the enterprise and its products and services in nature and community, as well as in societal developmental needs, thereby promoting 'Community Building'.
- *East:* We relink the enterprise's evolution to its own cultural and spiritual foundations and to those of its surrounding society thereby tapping into its creative resources and initiating a process of 'Conscious Evolution'.
- *North:* We rebuild and design organisational structures and processes based on developmental needs and co-evolutionary processes, thereby transforming the northern function from technocratic operations to 'Knowledge Creation'.
- *West:* We redefine the role of finance within the organisation as a supportive one to all other functions, and redesign it in a way that it supports the overall 'sustainable development' of the organisation and society.
- *Centre:* The role of the centre is an inspiring, coordinating and overall transformational one. Strategy ceases to be implemented top-down by a governance unit on top of the hierarchy, but is seen rather as a central process of 'Strategic Renewal', that links and stimulates interaction between the different functions of the enterprise. Leadership is understood in a lateral and serving sense and contains a strong ethical component. The 'leader' is one who serves others to make a transformational difference in the organisation.

For each of the five functions we propose a transformational process, based on our GENE spiral that we introduced earlier (⇨4, 5).

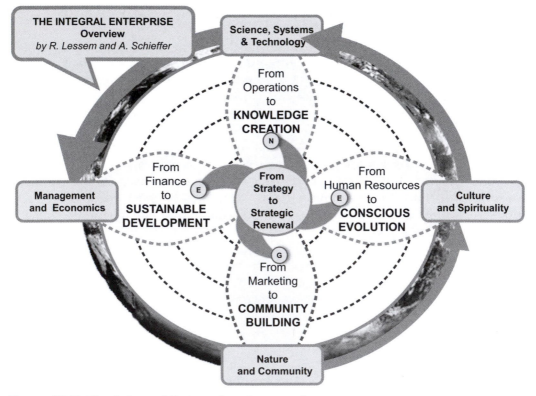

Figure 20.3 The Integral Enterprise: An overview

Figure 20.3 provides an overview on the Integral Enterprise, its transformed functions and the transformational GENE spiral in its centre.

We maintain that any reconfiguration of the enterprise would need to come with an inbuilt transformation process, enabling each enterprise to continuously evolve its own theoretical base and organisational practice. With this challenge, we conclude this chapter.

20.4   Integration

In summarising this 'Western' organisational perspective, we can say the following: A number of recently emergent enterprise, management and leadership concepts – like for example social and societal entrepreneurship, social business and corporate social responsibility – play an important role in promoting all round sustainability. None of them, however, has transformed the overall structure and functioning of the management processes that underlie the enterprise. That is where our work on the Integral Enterprise comes in. We emphasise the need for a transformation of the organisational functions and a subsequent reintegration so vehemently, as we regard a truly Integral Enterprise as a powerful developmental agent within society.

In our work on *Transformation Management*, we have illustrated the enormous development potential of an Integral Enterprise with the practical cases of Sekem in Egypt, Canon in Japan, Linux in Finland/USA and Visa in the USA.

Given the lead role that enterprise has anyway taken in society, its redefinition, along integral lines, would provide the whole of humanity with a fundamental leverage. An enterprise that is simultaneously a community builder, grounded in society's needs ('South'), a conscious evolver, tapping into the cultural creativity of itself and society ('East'), a knowledge creator, releasing its innovation potential ('North'), a sustainable developer, turning finance into a sustaining and restorative medium ('West') and an overall understanding of strategy as a central unit for strategic and moral renewal (Centre) makes a powerful 'force for good'.

Such reconception of the enterprise functions would make corporate social responsibility – the current primary instrument of private enterprise to engage in development – irrelevant, as it would be built genetically into the organisational design. Of course, such a reinterpretation of enterprise and organisation can't happen in isolation with the macroeconomic environment in which it is embedded. But as we shall illustrate in Integral Economics in Round 3 in this realm (⇨21), some rare cases of Integral Enterprises have already demonstrated in practice that they can have an enormous impact on rebuilding local economies. We are now ready to move to the level of societal development, where we will also review such macroeconomic implications.

Before we move on, let us engage again – through reflection and prospective action – with the guiding questions and theory presented in this chapter, as well as with the major development challenges derived thereof. If you are not yet associated with a particular organisation or community, now – in this action-driven 'Western' realm – you may want to found one, together with others. If your primary association is one with a university – be it as member of its faculty or as participant in an educational or research programme – you may want to consider using this as your core transformational context.

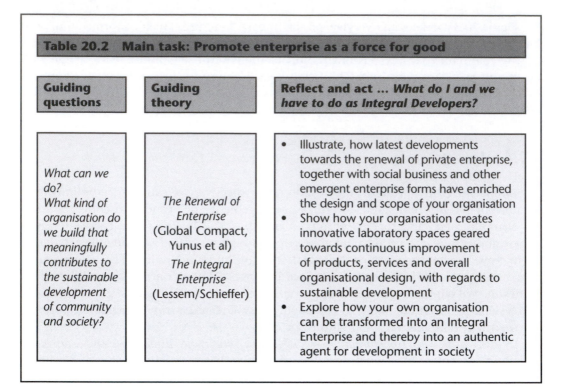

Table 20.2   Main task: Promote enterprise as a force for good

Guiding questions	Guiding theory	Reflect and act ... *What do I and we have to do as Integral Developers?*
What can we do? *What kind of organisation do we build that meaningfully contributes to the sustainable development of community and society?*	*The Renewal of Enterprise* (Global Compact, Yunus et al) *The Integral Enterprise* (Lessem/Schieffer)	• Illustrate, how latest developments towards the renewal of private enterprise, together with social business and other emergent enterprise forms have enriched the design and scope of your organisation • Show how your organisation creates innovative laboratory spaces geared towards continuous improvement of products, services and overall organisational design, with regards to sustainable development • Explore how your own organisation can be transformed into an Integral Enterprise and thereby into an authentic agent for development in society

We now turn, in 'Western' integral guise, from individual and organisation to economy and society as a whole.

References

1   Tennyson, R. and IBLF (1998). *Managing Partnerships: Tools for Mobilising the Public Sector, Business and Civil Society as Partners in Development*. London: IBLF.

2   Cescau, P. (2007). *Beyond Corporate Social Responsibility: Social Innovation and Sustainable Development as Drivers of Business Growth*. Speech given at INSEAD Fontainebleau campus on 25 May 2007.

3   UN Global Compact website: www.unglobalcompact.org / Accessed: 8 February 2012.

4   Melford, C. (2012). On: IBLF Website (www.iblf.org) / Accessed: 8 February 2012.

5   Virgin Unite website: www.virginunite.com / Accessed: 2 March 2012.

6   The Elders website: www.theelders.org / Accessed: 3 March 2012.

7   Virgin Unite website: www.virginunite.com / Accessed: 2 March 2012.

8   Leadbetter, C. (2002). *Up the Down Escalator*. London: Viking.

9   Gavell, M., Johannisson, B. and Lundqvist, M. (2009). *Entrepreneurship in the Name of Society*. Stockholm: Knowledge Foundation.

10   Lundqvist, M.A. and Williams Middleton, K.L. (2010). Promises of Societal Entrepreneurship: Sweden and Beyond. In: *Journal of Enterprising Communities: People and Places in the Global Community*, Vol. 4, Issue 1.

11   Bradley, T. (3 September 2012). Beyond Social Enterprise: The Emergence of Societal Entrepreneurship. In: *The 3rdimagazine* (www.the3rdimagazine.co.uk).

12 Yunus, M. (2006). *Creating a World without Poverty*. New York: Public Affairs.
13 Yunus, M. (2010). *Building Social Business: The New Kind of Capitalism that Serves Humanity's Most Pressing Needs*. New York: Public Affairs.
14 Yunus, M. (2010). *Building Social Business: The New Kind of Capitalism that Serves Humanity's Most Pressing Needs*. New York: Public Affairs.
15 Campbell, C. (2006). Women, Mother Earth and the Business of Living. In: Steyart, C. and Hjorth, D. *Entrepreneurship as Social Change*. Northants: Edward Elgar.
16 McGinnis, M.V. (1998). *Bioregionalism*. London: Routledge.
17 Holmgren, D. (2010). *Permaculture: Principles and Pathways beyond Sustainability*. Petersfield, Hants: Hyden House.
18 Hopkins, R. (2008). *The Transition Handbook: From Oil Dependency to Local Resilience*. Totnes, Devon: Green Books.
19 Hjorth, D. and Bjerke, B. (2006). Public Entrepreneurship: Moving from Social/Consumer to Public/Citizen. In: Steyart, C. and Hjorth, D. *Entrepreneurship as Social Change*. Northants: Edward Elgar.
20 The Partnering Initiative website: www.thepartneringinitiative.org / Accessed: 1 October 2012.
21 Lessem, R. and Schieffer, A. (2009). *Transformation Management: Towards the Integral Enterprise*. Farnham: Gower.

21 *Societal Wealth and Well-being: A Western Societal Perspective*

Guiding Question: What kind of economic frameworks do we implement, that serve to foster the sustainable development of our society and of the world at large?

21.1   Orientation

The 'Western' economic and societal development level we are now entering, following in the footsteps of individual and organisational development, is the most complex of all. It is on this level where not only the most efforts of established development work are directed, it is also a highly contested field with the greatest political and financial interests at stake. It is, conventionally speaking, about economic wealth and about defending it. It is about political power and about securing such power. In addition, this is a terrain where convictions and ideologies are particularly strong. It is here then where our integral perspective usually faces its own strongest critics.

Our attempt throughout this book has been to build a new foundation for this third societal round. As Integral Developers – and in particularly as Integral Development agencies – we are now asked to come up with new societal and macroeconomic designs that are able to complement, evolve and even replace existing approaches to economic development. Thus, we now review the following questions:

- What kind of economic frameworks and systems do we implement, that build purposefully on the three other realms of Integral Development, and that serve to foster the sustainable development of our society and of the world at large?
- What can such new and evolved economic and societal frameworks learn from the organisational and individual levels, so that they are designed to nurture and scale up those innovative impulses in Round 1 and Round 2 that are already making significant contributions to the co-creation of equitable and sustainable livelihoods?
- How can an Integral Economy thereby be built upon an Integral Enterprise and upon a fully Integral Life?

In the beginning of this book (⇨2), we had felt the need to first review the conventional 'Western' wisdom in economic development theory as well as analysing the most influential 'economic development mechanism' that has operated in the past three decades: the so-called Washington Consensus. In so doing, we found that none of these conventional approaches to economic development draws purposefully on developmental approaches to individual life and organisational enterprise.

In reviewing economic development theory, we also found that the theories of Karl Marx have been completely sidelined and regarded as a digression, in particular after the collapse of Communism. However, given the social downsides of mainstream capitalism, his work is gradually coming back into the discussion.

While we agree that much of the Marxian theory and practice got somehow distorted, often abused and all too often seemed to fail in developmental intent, by banning Marx from the discussion capitalists have thrown out an important baby with the bathwater. We have thereby been deprived of an enormous wealth of critical and relevant thinking that can indeed help us to advance our own theory and practice with regards to the current economic system.

As Integral Developers we are open enough to have a thorough look at Marx, to see what kind of lessons we can take from his work for Integral Development. David Harvey, an internationally renowned economic geographer from the UK, now based at City University in New York, provides us with key insights into Marx and his relevance for our times. The reflections on Marx are followed by our own work. With *Integral Economics* we introduce a new economic model that transcends the unresolved dialectic between capitalism and Communism, and opens ourselves to an understanding of economics, that builds on the most innovative economic thought and practice of all worlds. Embedded in Integral Economics, we also present a dynamic approach to rebuild our economies in an integral manner. We end this 'Western' review of societal development with American complexity scientist Sally Goerner's groundbreaking work on the new science of sustainability, through which she leads the way towards an Integral Society, with an Integral Economy as one of its core components.

21.2   Does Marx still Matter? Evolving Capitalism with Marx

THE ECONOMIC WITHOUT THE SOCIAL IS UNSUSTAINABLE

In common economic parlance, capitalism and communism are unlikely bedfellows. Adam Smith and Karl Marx are rather enemies than friends, even though Marx drew prolifically on Ricardo, Smith's successor, to derive his labour theory of value. Moreover, and as is fairly well known, Adam Smith's *Theory of Moral Sentiments* which was his counterpart to *The Wealth of Nations,* had a certain resonance with where the humanist Marx was coming from.

We argue that the success of the Western European economies, most especially the German and Scandinavian 'social economies' after World War II was due to a marriage of the social and the economic. They anticipated some, though not all, of Marx's arguments. Indeed, the German ordoliberalism, that drove the economic post-war-agenda in Germany, even had a name for such marriage: the 'social market economy'.

However, while especially in the 1960s and 1970s the so-called communitarian Nippo-Rhenish (Japan and Germany) economic approaches, if not also the Scandinavian social democracies, seemed to offer a genuine alternative to the Anglo-Saxon market based, individualistic model, by the 1980s and 1990s this alternative was on the wane. The fall of the Berlin Wall had ultimately ended any real possibility of such a Nippo-Rhenish/Anglo-Saxon developmental dynamic.

As we have revealed in *Integral Economics,* there were some major European economic thinkers, aside from Marx and the German ordoliberals, who conceived of a form of 'social economics' that constituted something of a dialectic between market and society – Sismondi in Switzerland, Ruskin and Hobson in England – but their work barely saw the light of the macroeconomic day. Of course at a micro level cooperative enterprises like Mondragon in Spain (⇨18), and movements like the kibbutz movement in Israel[1] – 260 of them as of 2012 – have been paving the socioeconomic way. It is only in recent years, that Marxian thought is increasingly re-entering the discussion through a small number of serious intellectuals. They intend to break the 'taboo' that is still overshadowing much of today's economic discourse when it comes to Marx. One of these 'taboo-breakers' is David Harvey.

REVISITING MARX' CONVERGENCE OF EUROPEAN PHILOSOPHY: AN INTEGRAL SURPRISE

David Harvey, a contemporary, economic geographer and long-time follower and interpreter of Karl Marx, argues in his *Companion to Capital* that for Marx 'new knowledge arises out of taking radically different conceptual blocs, rubbing them together and making revolutionary fire'.[2] Moreover, he explicitly fused research methodology and social science. In *Das Kapital*, his seminal work, Marx brings together divergent intellectual traditions to create a completely new revolutionary framework for knowledge, thereby drawing on Europe as a whole.

The grand conceptual frameworks that converge are these:

- classical political economy (seventeenth to mid nineteenth century) is mainly British, building in particular on Ricardo;
- philosophical reflection and inquiry originated with the Greeks, especially Aristotle and Epicurus;
- German philosophy, most particularly the dialectical philosophy of Hegel;
- utopian socialism, primarily French, although it was an Englishman, Thomas More, who is generally credited with originating the modern utopian socialist tradition, followed by Robert Owen in the eighteenth century.

Indeed, Marx himself lived for extensive periods in Germany, France and England, and based his doctoral studies on the classical Greek philosopher Epicurus. With the help of David Harvey's work, we looked at the rich diversity in European tradition that Marx draws on. What emerged was a fascinating 'integral surprise':

- *South:* Marx grounded his work in Greek natural philosophy, specifically in Aristotle (use value) and Epicurus, whose philosophy of a tranquil, self-sufficient life may well be seen as a philosophy of being. We position this Greek nature based philosophy in the integral South.
- *East:* Marx' thinking evolved through the German cultural evolutionary perspective, in particular Hegelian dialectics. In our integral logic, this would be his most 'Eastern'

ingredient. Germany and German philosophy, furthermore, is Marx's cultural and philosophical home.

- *North:* Marx developed his thinking further through French Utopian Socialism. Given the strong French inclination for raison and intellect, we can see this element as the northern ingredient of Marx's fusion of European philosophy.
- *West:* Marx ended up by revisiting Ricardo's theory of (socially necessary) labour value. Concluding, his conceptual reference points were wholly European (thereby also largely ignoring the rest of the world), while his practical context was primarily English. The inclination towards pragmatism, entrepreneurship, adventure and play makes this aspect of Marx's thinking the most 'Western' one.

In Figure 21.1 we illustrate how Marx integrated European thought in his own theory.

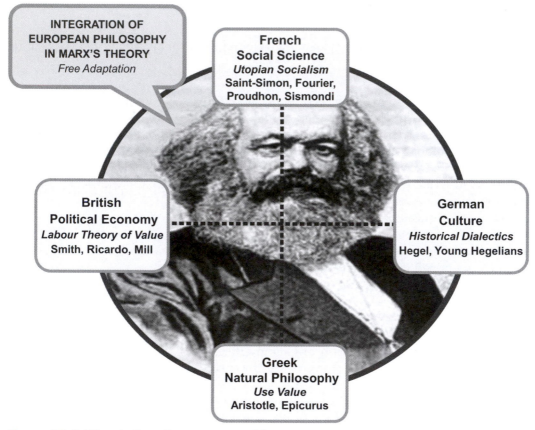

Figure 21.1 Marx's four European worlds

As we can see, Marx felt he had to re-create and reconfigure what social science is all about. Marx's methodology derives from dialectics that had not previously been applied to economics. While his dialectical ideas derive from Hegel, his 'dialectical method' is opposite to his fellow German philosopher. Marx's approach is materially and socially based, Hegel's approach primarily ideational. However, like Hegel, dialectics is to be used to enable us to understand and represent processes of motion, change and transformation.

For example, Marx does not simply talk about labour. He talks about the labour process. Capital, at the same time, is not a thing, but rather a process that exists only in motion. Capitalism is nothing if not on the move. Consequently, many of Marx's concepts are formulated around relations rather than stand-alone principles; they are about transformative activity.

TRANSFORMATIVE ACTIVITY AND THE DEVELOPMENTAL DIALECTIC: EVOLVING DARWIN

Marx clearly envisaged his work as some sort of continuation of Darwin's, with the emphasis on human as well as natural history. In the preface to the first edition of *Capital*, he stated, that its aim is to view 'the development of the economic formation of society' from the standpoint of natural history.

> *Darwin has directed attention to the history of natural technology, that is the formation of the organs of plants and animals, which serve as the instruments of production for sustaining their life. Does not the history of the productive organs of man in society, of organs that are the material of every particular organisation of society, deserve equal attention? And would not such a history be easier to compile, since, as the Italian 18th century philosopher and historian Vico says, human history differs from natural history in that we have made the former but not the latter?*[3]

The idea that there has been a human evolutionary process in which we can discern radical shifts not only in technologies but also in whole modes of social life is clearly very important to Marx. Marx did, however, not read Darwin uncritically 'It is remarkable', he wrote to Engels, 'how Darwin recognises amongst beasts and plants his English society with its competition and division of labour including the Malthusian struggle for existence'. The problem lies, as Marx sees it, in Darwin's ahistorical approach to a purely natural evolution without reference to human action in changing the face of the earth.

UNDERSTANDING THE INTERRELATEDNESS OF THE WHOLE: ELEMENTS CONSTITUTING AN 'INTEGRAL' TOTALITY

But what Marx appreciated was Darwin's approach to evolution as a process open to historical reconstruction and theoretical investigation. He was committed to understanding the human evolutionary process in like fashion. This is where his emphasis on processes comes in. Marx's review of machinery and large-scale industry was an analysis of how the industrial form of capitalism emerged out of handicraft and manufacturing.

For Marx, 'Technology reveals the active relation of man to nature, the direct process of the production of his life, and thereby it also lays bare the process of the production of the social relations of his life and of the mental conceptions that flow from those relations'.[4] Marx here links in one sentence six identifiable conceptual elements: first, technology; second, the relation to nature; third, the actual process of production; fourth, daily life; fifth social relations; and ultimately mental conceptions. These elements are not static but all in motion, linked through 'processes of production that guide human evolution'. Actually, Marx is often depicted as a technological determinist, who thinks that changes in the productive forces determined the course of human history, including

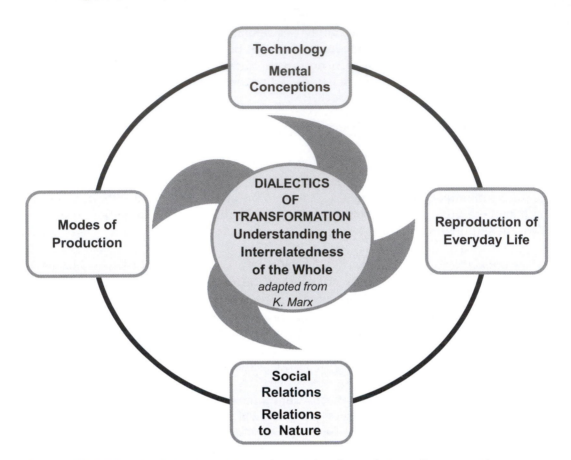

Figure 21.2 Marx's dialectics of transformation in an integral perspective

the evolution of social relations, mental conceptions, the relation to nature and the like. Harvey does not share this interpretation.

Marx generally eschews causal language. Technology, for him, does not 'cause' or 'determine', but it 'reveals' or 'discloses' the relation to nature. What Marx is saying, is that technologies and organisational forms internalise a certain relation to nature as well as mental conceptions and social relations, daily life and labour processes. Conversely all these elements internalise something of what technology is about. A detailed study of daily life under capitalism will, for example, 'reveal' a great deal about our relation to nature, and so on. Similarly, the study of our relation to nature cannot go very far without examining the nature of social relations, our production systems, mental conceptions of the world, the technologies deployed and how social life is conducted. All of these elements constitute a totality, and we have to understand how the mutual interactions between them work. Again, we can illustrate all these core elements identified by Marx that constitute the 'totality', in an integral, dynamic manner (Figure 21.2). Again, we are surprised, how multifaceted and relational Marx's thinking was.

Here's an example of what Marx's interrelated perspective could mean for us. Say, we wanted to build enterprise. Seeking to understand the totality we would want to know:

- What kinds of technologies are going to be embodied?
- What is the relationship to nature?
- What kinds of social relations are envisaged?
- What systems of production and reproduction are going to be incorporated?
- What kind of daily life is envisaged?
- What mental conceptions are going to be involved?

WHERE IT WENT WRONG? WHAT WE CAN LEARN FOR TODAY?

For Harvey, these six elements constitute distinctive moments in the overall process of human evolution understood as a totality. No one moment prevails over the others, even as there exists within each moment the possibility for autonomous development: e.g. nature independently mutates and evolves, as do ideas, social relations and so on. All these elements co-evolve and are subject to perpetual renewal and transformation as dynamic moments within the totality. It is like an ecological totality, which the French philosopher Gilles Deleuze calls an 'assemblage' of moments co-evolving in a dialectical manner.

From such a dialectical perspective, technological determinism (technology) is as wrongheaded as environmental determinism (nature), class-struggle determinism (social relations), idealism (mental conceptions) or determinism arising out of everyday life (cultural). Major transformations such as the movement from feudalism to capitalism occur through a dialectic of transformation across all moments.

Where did it go wrong? This co-evolution has developed unevenly in space and time to produce all manner of local contingencies. Perhaps one of the biggest failures of the conscious attempt to build socialism and Communism on the basis of capitalism was the failure to recognise the need to engage politically across all these moments in a way that was sensitive to geographical and cultural specificities. The temptation of revolutionary Communism was to reduce the dialectic to a simple causal model whereby one or another moment was placed in the vanguard of change. That according to Marx's own thinking inevitably failed, from an overall perspective.

What can we learn as Integral Developers from Marx today? There is certainly a need to overcome any remaining hesitation to bring Marx into the discussion. What we have been trying to demonstrate with this short overview, via David Harvey, is that Marx has enormous value to offer in our shared attempts to actualise Integral Development. His avoidance of simplistic cause-effect explanations, and his emphasis on interrelatedness of all aspects of social change exhibits strong resonance with a systemic, evolutionary and transformational view on systems that has become current currency today, spearheaded by the natural sciences as we have shown (⇨15, 16). Let us bring Marx back into the forum, as one of many voices that can inform us. Let us look at the flaws and strengths of his theory alike. From our observation, it is also the resolute insistence of the business and economic establishment to only acknowledge one possible economic orientation – namely 'capitalism' – that causes the current impasse. Refusing other perspectives makes any system immobile and static. We need to dare to deconstruct and reconstruct our current system to build a sustainable future. It is with this purpose of creating a space for such deconstruction and reconstruction that we have written Integral Economics to which we now turn.

21.3   The Integral Economy: A Roadmap for Economic Transformation

STUCK IN ONE WORLD: THE NEED TO REINVENT AN ECONOMIC SYSTEM THAT WORKS FOR ALL

Years ago, after we had completed our work on the *Integral Enterprise*, that we briefly introduced at the organisational level of this Western realm, we increasingly gained the conviction, that we could not address organisational transformation in isolation of an economic transformation. For micro-organisational transformation is bound to be limited by the macroeconomic context to which organisations are required to adapt. This very macroeconomic system is failing us to such a degree that we are collectively called upon to seek a more viable alternative. To those who claim that the existing system still works and may only have to be tweaked a bit here and there, we argue that it only works for an elite few, and that the time has come for us to develop an economic systems that works for all of us and for the planet. We regard such a system as a crucial prerequisite for our collective survival.

Our painful observation had been, that after the demise of communism we were caught in one economic world (capitalism) – and with it in one particular Western or rather Anglo-Saxon frame of mind. Muhammad Yunus once commented that mainstream free market theory suffers from a conceptualisation failure, a failure to capture the essence of what it is to be human. And indeed this was what some of Britain's leading economists – among them Geoffrey Hodgson, Paul Ormerod and Bridget Rosewell – admitted in an open letter to the Queen of England in August 2009, after the Queen had publicly posed the question, why economists had not foreseen the financial and economic crisis the world was facing. The following excerpt from their letter is most illuminating:

> We believe that the narrow training of economists – which concentrates on mathematical techniques and the building of empirically uncontrolled formal models – has been a major reason for this failure in our profession. This defect is enhanced by the pursuit of mathematical technique for its own sake in many leading academic journals and departments of economics. There is a species of judgment, attainable through immersion in a literature or a history that cannot be adequately expressed in formal mathematical models. It's an essential part of a serious education in economics, but has been stripped out of most leading graduate programs in economics in the world, including in the leading economics departments in the United Kingdom. Models and techniques are important. But given the complexity of the global economy, what is needed is a broader range of models and techniques governed by a far greater respect for substance, and much more attention to historical, institutional, psychological and other highly relevant factors ... As trained economists and United Kingdom citizens we have warned of these problems that beset our profession. Unfortunately, at present, we find ourselves in a minority.[5]

We fully agree with this statement and asked ourselves whether the human mind is indeed not more creative than being restricted to defining economics as an either or between capitalism and communism – another expression of the 'dualistic disease' that we were lamenting at the beginning of the book. Was the world – in past and present, and across all cultures – not more inventive than that? We decided to do a thorough analysis and to use our integral and transcultural approach to analyse the economic situation of the world – in theory and in practice. This was the starting point for our work on *Integral Economics*, a book that we subtitled *Releasing the Economic Genius of Your Society*.[6] For, indeed, the wealth of economic diversity that we encountered made us hopeful that we collectively have the ability to reinvent economics. What is crucial though is that we surface this 'wealth', as it is largely hidden from economic classrooms and textbooks.

TOWARDS AN INTEGRAL UNDERSTANDING OF THE ECONOMY: THREE SURPRISING FINDINGS

Touring the world's economic theory and practice in an integral manner, we had a couple of Eureka moments.

Firstly, we found that if we applied the four integral realms to map economic theory and practice we could clearly see that there was profound economic thinking in each of them. We also noticed that there was an overriding economic theme in each of the four realms, which led us to the following classification (see Figure 21.3):

- The 'Southern' natural and communal realm promotes the 'Self-Sufficient community-based Economy'.
- The 'Eastern' cultural and spiritual realm promotes a 'Developmental culture-based Economy'.
- The 'Northern' scientific and technological realm promotes a 'Social knowledge-based Economy'.
- The 'Western' realm was promoted in the past through a neo-liberal market economy; but below the surface we can recognise the gradual emergence of what we called a 'Living life-based Economy' – which is basically a creative revisiting of the Anglo-Saxon economic model with a strong focus on ecology and sustainability.

Secondly, while such rich economic diversity in theory and practice is arising, the mainstream Western model is not only disconnected from this diversity, but is superimposing its model as a universal approach. Such domination of one world over the others leads from an integral perspective to an imbalance of the entire system. That is exactly what we are experiencing in this day and age. The superimposition of the Western model, however, also leads to a total sidelining of all other approaches, which often don't even find their way into the consciousness of seasoned economists. As a consequence, these approaches are not sufficiently interconnected to mutually inform and strengthen each other.

Thirdly, we found a wealth of new economic thinking emerging from the field of 'religion and humanity'. We placed it in the centre of our model (see Figure 21.3 on the next page), as it provided something like a moral core of economic thought and practice. More precisely, we found a wealth of literature on Indigenous economic thinking, Catholic economics, Islamic economics, Buddhist economics, and on more generally humanistically oriented approaches to economics, among others. Given that present day debates on a required reorientation of economics often focus only on a 'need for new values', we tend to overlook that most of our societies are profoundly rooted in religious or humanistic philosophies that go far beyond an articulation of singular values.

The religious rooting is even significantly stronger in the so-called developing world than in the more secular geographic North-West of the world. Indeed, we find that

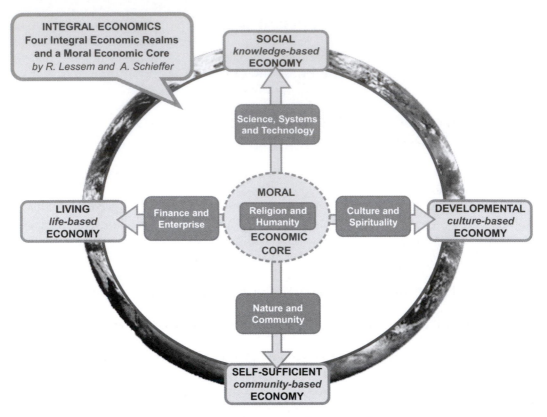

Figure 21.3 The Integral Economy: Overview framework

the common (Western) understanding of economics has effectively banned religion, humanistic philosophy or spirituality from its territory, unaware of the close original link between market economics and Protestantism. One may well make the point that the current economic system is footloose and lacks anchoring in cultural and societal layers that are deeper than moral codices, a set of values or outer regulations based on them. Furthermore, all of the latter seem to have little effect on overcoming the downsides of the current system. Any fundamental revisiting of economics, so we argue, would need to revisit the relationship between the economy and the moral core of a society, to enable the necessary alignment between the philosophical and ethical inner substance of a society and its practical, outer economic systems and activities.

BUILDING AN INTEGRAL ECONOMY

The integral and transcultural approach enabled us to provide sufficient space for the rich diversity of innovative economic theory from all four integral realms – as well as from the moral core – that can now help us to gradually rebuild our economies as well as a global economic system. This space is not a closed one, as the body of the theory and practice is continuously evolving. We certainly were also not able to put every approach and their multiple variations on the integral map. Also, we are certainly aware, that any model – and so also ours – has inbuilt structuring principles around which its components are ordered. We thus emphasise, that the map is not the territory. But for the first time, to

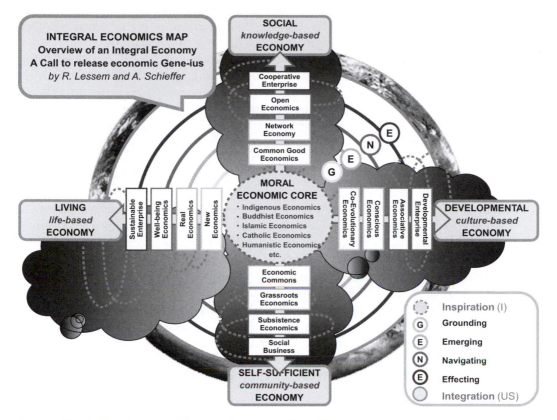

INTEGRAL ECONOMICS MAP
Overview of an Integral Economy
A Call to release economic Gene-ius
by R. Lessem and A. Schieffer

SOCIAL
knowledge-based
ECONOMY

Cooperative Enterprise
Open Economics
Network Economy
Common Good Economics

MORAL
ECONOMIC CORE
• Indigenous Economics
• Buddhist Economics
• Islamic Economics
• Catholic Economics
• Humanistic Economics
  etc.

LIVING
life-based
ECONOMY

Sustainable Enterprise
Well-being Economics
Real Economics
New Economics

Co-Evolutionary Economics
Conscious Economics
Associative Economics
Developmental Enterprise

DEVELOPMENTAL
culture-based
ECONOMY

Economic Commons
Grassroots Economics
Subsistence Economics
Social Business

SELF-SUFFICIENT
community-based
ECONOMY

Inspiration (I)
G Grounding
E Emerging
N Navigating
E Effecting
Integration (US)

Figure 21.4 The Integral Economics map: Detailed overview

our mind, a map had been developed that surfaced a huge quantity of the economic variety that the world as a whole had to offer. This transdisciplinary and transcultural economic map allows economic students and social innovators to engage with a rich picture of the economic landscape – a landscape that is designed to stimulate comparison, critique, evolution and innovation as well as to encourage a purposeful rebuilding of our economies. In Figure 21.4 we provide a detailed overview of the Integral Economics map.

The map that we developed is not static. Rather we have developed a transformative rhythm that provides guidance in concretely rebuilding an economy. This so-called GENE-rhythm (see Figure 21.4) follows the fourfold transformational rhythm of grounding, emerging, navigating and effecting, designed to release economic gene-ius and is similar to the one we apply in Integral Development. In Integral Economics we illustrate that if we work purposefully through each of the four economic realms and gradually through all of them in a South-East-North-West fashion – informed by the wealth of the moral economic core – we arrive in each realm at practical applications that help us to translate new economic thinking into transformative practice. Here is an illustration of what we mean:

• *South:* Working through the gene-ius of the 'Southern' realm of a community-based self-sufficient economy we evolve 'from profits to profiting society', and we actively revisit the extent to which our own community or enterprise is participating in building a self-sufficient economy, and thereby contributing locally to alleviate poverty.[7] The role model we surfaced in the 'Southern' realm is the 'social business' and self-sufficiency movement, embodied by Grameen in Bangladesh.

- *East:* Working through the gene-ius of the 'Eastern' realm of a culture-based developmental economy we evolve 'from survival to co-evolution', and we actively revisit the extent to which our community or enterprise is co-evolving with its multiple stakeholders, thereby becoming an agent for a developmental economy.[8] The role model we surfaced in the 'Eastern' realm is the developmental enterprise, embodied by Canon in Japan as well as the development movement Sarvodaya in Sri Lanka (⇨14).
- *North:* Working through the gene-ius of the 'Northern' realm of a knowledge-based social economy, we evolve 'from hierarchy to democracy', and we actively revisit the extent to which our community or enterprise responds to continuous technological change and social challenges in a cooperative and democratic manner?[9] The role model we surfaced in the 'Northern' realm is the cooperative enterprise, embodied by Mondragon in Spain (⇨18), the world's largest worker's cooperative and a leader in the social-economic cooperative movement.
- *West:* Working through the gene-ius of the 'Western' realm of a life-based living economy we evolve 'from growth to sustainability', and we actively revisit the extent to which our community or enterprise is modelled upon nature, thereby sustainable and restorative, building up human, natural and financial capital in parallel.[10] The role model we surfaced in the 'Western' realm is the 'sustainable enterprise', embodied by the case of Interface in the USA (⇨22), a corporate leader within the sustainability movement.

BUILDING ON PRACTICE: THE FUTURE HAS ALREADY BEGUN

Each of the four Integral Economic realms helps us to revisit our own practice (the final 'E' of the GENE), building on the other three components (G + E + N) of our transformational rhythm.

We present case stories of organisations that integrally embody each particular realm. In our research into relevant practice, we found another astonishing fact. All of the organisations that embodied such new economic practice, engaged simultaneously in developing new theory and realising a new practice. We called them 'mesa-organisations' as we see them somewhere in between the micro and the macro economy. They provide powerful orientation for the design of whole new macroeconomic systems. It is for that reason that we believe that the future is already in the making, and it is crucial that we simultaneously consult innovative theory and practice. All of the cases we introduce can be seen as developmental agents for society. It is for that reason that we briefly introduce them also in Integral Development, opening thereby the border between economics and development.

BUILDING THE INTEGRAL ECONOMY: FIVE RECOMMENDATIONS

Rebuilding local economies – and in the wake contributing to rebuilding the global economy – remains a tall order of immense proportions. In an attempt to provide further guidance to local developmental agents we concluded Integral Economics with five critical success factors:[11]

1. Implement an Integral Economic Laboratory as a Local Catalyst: This laboratory is at the centre of economic renewal. Its task is to contribute to an integral understanding of economics and to engage itself with the rich diversity of economic theory and practice from all over the world (using the Integral Economics map). It articulates the particular economic challenges of the specific society it is based in, and it needs to be interlinked with other similar laboratories from all over the world, to stimulate cross-fertilisation.
2. Focus on a Real Burning Issue and Decide on the Most Relevant of the Four Realms to Start with.
3. Maintain Interconnected Focus: The economy does not work mechanically and in linear fashion, but resembles a highly complex living system. Hence, any approach towards economic renewal requires us to build and navigate within an interconnected web of macro and micro, local and global, individual and communal, academic and practical, elements.
4. Build an Economic Ecosystem: It is important not to act in isolation, but to involve co-creators. It is recommended to build communities of co-creators around burning issues. These communities should be built up so that they form innovation ecosystems, providing the necessary 'support structure' for social and economic transformation. In Integral Economics we show, that such an ecosystem is comprised of stewards, catalysts, researchers and facilitators, as well as, what we called a 'soul force'.
5. Join Existing Local and Global Movements for Socioeconomic Transformation: This final success factor involves leveraging our individual, organisational and communal efforts by linking up with local and global movements that are relevant for the particular burning issues on which we are focusing. Such movements provide an important 'energetic wave' that we can build on in our efforts.

We notice, how the Integral Economy purposefully integrates the three levels of self, organisation and society: on the level of the self it invites individual transformation agents to concretely engage in the rebuilding of local economies; on the level of the organisation, it acknowledges the existence of so-called mesa-organisations (the cases mentioned above), that serve as living intimations of future economic models; and, on the level of society, it seeks to initiate and articulate new economic frameworks.

OUTLOOK ON THE INTEGRAL ECONOMY

Ultimately, we are required to renew our prevailing macroeconomic system. Integral Economics can be regarded as a blueprint for such an endeavour. What makes it 'practical' is that the work of rebuilding the economy starts in our own particular contexts. From there we begin our engagement, from there we seek to transform locally and to contribute globally. With the practical cases we demonstrated that we do not need to start from scratch, but that almost all societies hold locally relevant impulses for economic renewal, on which we can build. Integral Economics is designed in that it interconnects innovative theory and practice in a manner that enables us to locally revisit our own theoretical and practical economic foundations, and to engage in a process of gradually releasing the economic gene-ius of our own community and society. Thereby it brings the task of rebuilding our global economy to each of our doorsteps.

This task, however, is only manageable if we locally set up the necessary infrastructure, such as an Integral Economic Laboratory, supportive ecosystems and strong links with local-global movements as well as similar laboratories. If our local engagements are interconnected and if a growing number of people contribute to a new integral theory and practice, we have indeed an opportunity to transform the existing macroeconomic system. The initial map that Integral Economics provides is not the territory, but the more of us apply and evolve it, the more the creative interplay of the rich diversity of the world's most innovative economic theory and practice can catalyse true change. Then, an Integral Economy can serve to bring about an Integral Society, to which we now turn.

21.4   Towards the Integral Society: The New Science of Sustainability

TOWARDS AN INTEGRAL SOCIETY

Most people think of sustainability mainly in terms of saving the planet. However, Sally Goerner maintains in her *New Science of Sustainability* that sustainability is actually about saving civilisation by changing our societal dream from a late-modern nightmare of untrammelled greed to an integral prophecy of sustainable vitality achieved by following nature's own plan for healthy development.[12]

She and her colleagues show how today's shift from a modern to an Integral Society mirrors the last shifts from the Renaissance, Reformation, Scientific Revolution and Enlightenment already under way. Goerner thereby takes on from where Marx has left off, though adding a good dose of complexity theory to Marx's dialectical approach.

Where sustainability activists originally focused on environmental degradation, the Gordian knot of disasters we now face, according to Goerner, is pushing more and more people to realise that unsustainability springs from systemic problems in modern culture itself. For her, the Integral Age that we introduced earlier (⇨4) is working towards a networked, partnership culture linking a newly Integral Society. Economically, it is bringing the Internet, the information age, and, with them, a tremendous leap in collective, learning accompanied by:

- An Integral Economy.
- Holistic alternatives to health.
- A renewed concern for community.
- A renewed sense of spirituality based on an appreciation of the oneness of the universal force that created, enfolds and guides all things.
- Efforts toward more integrated and empowered education.
- The sustainability movement seeing the global civilisation, economy, and biosphere as one entwined ecosystem.

CO-DEVELOPMENT IN A LEARNING UNIVERSE

For Goerner, who is also founder and director of the Integral Science Institute, the Integral Age is a time when human beings reconnect, heal schisms, and begin reweaving civilisation in harmony with the natural world and its principles. It isn't that economies work like ecosystems so much as economies and ecosystems are both examples of deeper principles at work. In fact, since 'eco' means 'house', and 'logos' means 'rules', one could say that what emerges is a rigorous, new understanding of 'the rules of the human house', as well as our planetary home. Here civilisation is a knowledge ecology, a wisdom-making web that follows certain universal principles of growth and development.

Taken together, a new understanding of energy and web dynamics leads to a dynamic theory of evolution, which suggests that all growth and development arises from a universal self-organising process that is driven by energy flow and given shape by the invisible ordering properties of web dynamics. Instead of a cosmic accident governed by 'selfish genes' evolution becomes a co-evolving energy process that gives rise to, sculpts, and embraces all things. If we take such dynamic evolution to its fullest, it is only logical that (see also Table 21.1):

- *Evolution* is a universal, self-organising process of growth and co-development whose patterns are seen from the origins of matter to the latest cycles of civilisation. It is not the chance outcome of random mutations acting on selfish genes.
- *Life* is a naturally integrated, mind-body learning system, not an accident.
- *Humanity* is a collaborative learning species, not a self-serving beast.
- *Civilisation* is an organic learning ecosystem that adapts by changing its collective mind, not an empire-building system seeking ever-bigger conquests.

Thus, in dynamic evolution, societal fitness comes from individual and societal wholes that:

- Foster diversity: needed to fill niches and find new ways.
- Distribute empowerment and intelligence: every cell in the body, for example, has its own intelligence, and decisions are made at the lowest possible level.
- Facilitate effective communication throughout the whole: different parts of the living system can't do their job properly without such.
- Circulate nourishment throughout the whole: deterioration of tissues in one part spreads illness and possibly death throughout.
- Promote synergetic exchanges: to improve the health of individual and community at the same time.

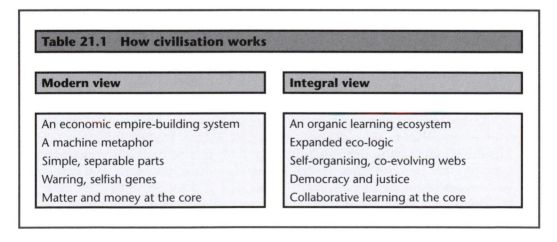

Table 21.1   How civilisation works

Modern view	Integral view
An economic empire-building system	An organic learning ecosystem
A machine metaphor	Expanded eco-logic
Simple, separable parts	Self-organising, co-evolving webs
Warring, selfish genes	Democracy and justice
Matter and money at the core	Collaborative learning at the core

The new science of sustainable-integral development thereby shows that stable jobs, long-term prosperity, social vitality, and environmental health are all byproducts of a human ecosystem that follows nature's laws of life and learning. Such an eco-logic, for Goerner, would restore the connection between social justice and economic health.

A NEW VISION OF LIFE

Goerner argues that today's dynamic view of evolution replaces the old vision of life. This new perspective offers a rigorous explanation of how all things rise from and are still part of an awesomely ordered, co-evolving energy flow web:

- The cosmos is highly ordered and everything is part of the design.
- Body and mind (organisation and intelligence) are intertwined.
- Diverse talents in cooperation are central to biological evolution.
- Collaborative learning is humanity's main survival strategy.

Therefore, while the scientific detail behind this worldview is new, a little thought suggests that the same basic vision was described 3,000 years ago and has remained tucked in civilisation's bosom for the entire time. As part of a 'philosophia perennis' the following remains to be valid:

- Humanity is brought into being by a creative force in the cosmos.
- An obligation to live in harmony with each other and the greater design.
- The value of each individual and the importance of weaving diverse talents into a community partnership that increases the vitality of all.

THREE CORE LESSONS TO REALISE THE NEW VISION OF LIFE: SELF-ORGANISATION, DEVELOPMENT CYCLES, INTRICACY

Therefore, a combative struggle for selfish interest makes less and less sense as a basis for economics or for evolution. Instead we need to learn from three core lessons.

Lesson 1 – Self-Organisation Requires Three Basic Elements: These are (a) pressure caused by an energy build-up, or gradient towards certain behaviour (b) natural diversity that forms a seed-crystal that opens a new path of flow and (c) a whole path or complete circuit through which energy can move. An example: in economics, demand for a new product creates pressure. The energy build-up implicit in the demand may light up some inventor whose new gadget (diversity) is capable of channelling (tapping) that demand. If diversity and demand link up with a whole path – a network that aligns people to develop, produce, market and distribute the product – then economic energy will pour into that organisation, making it grow.

Lesson 2 – Systems Move through Development Cycles: When the system reaches its limits, some quirk of natural diversity seeds a new, more intricate system of organisation to move energy faster. Living organisms, ecosystems and economies all become more developmentally advanced as it does. So while a business, for Goerner, may grow bigger and more complex, no matter how sophisticated it becomes, it will periodically have to find a new, more effective form of organisation.

Lesson 3 – Evolution Leans towards Higher Intricacy: Most scientists describe evolution as increasing 'complexity', but from an energy perspective the goal is actually intricacy. Like a lace tablecloth a system's strength and resilience comes from keeping energy flowing through thousands of small circles bound in an ever-growing meshwork of connective tissue.

COLLABORATION: THE MOST RESPONSIBLE PATTERN FOR INCREASING COMPLEXITY IN LIFE

Once intelligence entered the picture, evolution also ceased to be a completely passive event. Living organisms make choices that directly affect survival. Free will, Goerner argues, exists because we can process information and select our own paths. So, while energy laws still operate in the background, we choose to go with one flow or another. Despite our current emphasis on warlike competition, the pattern of collaborative community is most responsible for increasing complexity in life.

Hence such multi-cellular collaborations probably started out of necessity, not altruism. Yet the results led to the complex organisms we know today. For billions of years cells learned to invent new occupations. Each new profession off-loaded work from others and opened new possibilities. Gut cells, lung cells, and nerve cells were all specialists whose efforts proved very complex functional wholes. Member cells also became more mutually dependent.

EVOLUTIONARY DYNAMICS: THE EVOLUTIONARY BRAID OF CULTURE, ECONOMICS AND ORGANISATION STRUCTURE

Goerner organises evolutionary dynamics into three key threads, each of which is essential to the survival of a collaborative whole:

- *Collaboration:* Healthy patterns of cooperation are needed to keep diverse members of the human ecosystem working smoothly together.
- *Intelligence and Learning:* A society's survival depends on its ability to act appropriately and change rapidly in response to signals coming from in- and outside.
- *Organisation Structure:* If a society's human infrastructure is frayed, malnourished or insufficiently intricate for the size, the organisational structure falls apart.

Social evolution then involves a kind of mutually affecting ballet along these three threads, which is most easily seen as a complex interaction amongst culture, economy and organisation structure:

- *Culture:* Culture reflects the 'mind' aspect of society because the meshwork of values, beliefs, customs, scientific theories and overarching worldviews represent a vast reservoir of experience that human groups have accumulated over a long time.
- *Economic Systems:* They form a core 'body' aspect of civilisation; they form the societal equivalent of metabolism, the system by which the social organism processes resources and grows and revitalises itself by circulating energy and information to all parts of the social body. Money, like blood, is a form of information flow that triggers

resource processing and flow while allowing the economy to expand beyond face-to-face bonds.

- *Organisation Structure:* It consists of formal arrangements and informal social ties such as trust, competence and friendship.

THE EVOLUTION OF CIVILISATION: READY FOR THE NEXT STAGE

Over the eons, the above combination has pushed human societies, for Goerner, through four major stages of social, structural and economic co-development. We are now, she says, poised for a fifth. Spanning over a million years of evolution, these stages are:

1. Foraging pods.
2. Prganised hunter-gatherer tribes.
3. Agrarian trading villages.
4. War-based hierarchical civilisation.
5. Global, networked, learning civilisation.

We are still in the age of war-based, hierarchical civilisation and, though 'dominator'-logic is much mollified, it is still around. However, a variety of factors suggest that command-and-control hierarchies can no longer effectively handle global civilisation's burgeoning complexity. The following Table 21.2 illustrates few of the core characteristics that distinguish the still prevailing modern view to the emergent integral view.

Table 21.2 Comparative worldviews		
	Exclusively modern view	**Inclusively integral view**
Life	Struggle	Learning
Prosperity	Money and material means	Healthy human webs
People	Self-centred	Complex
Civilisation	Empire-building machine	Knowledge ecology

WHAT WE ARE BOUND TO BECOME: LEARNING COMMUNITIES IN A LEARNING UNIVERSE

Where modernists saw learning as an individual act of mental gymnastics, integral thinkers see it as a multidimensional, communitarian ripple that takes place within individuals as well as across societies and the globe. Culture takes on new value as we appreciate what it represents: a vast reservoir of past lessons and future dreams organised into a roadmap for how to live, which then guides all we do. Since the stories we tell ourselves about how the world works form our greatest survival tool, to degrade culture is to degrade our ability to endure. Collective intelligence is crucial because a society's health depends on the ability to learn as a whole. Social structures must be well knit because the rich, connective tissue of warm, productive, daily relationships holds a society together while helping information flow. A healthy society must have:

- Harmonious collaboration.
- Responsive social intelligence.
- Resilient structure.
- Harmonious relationships with the environment.

From the integral perspective, global civilisation is also undergoing a growth crisis. We are actually waiting for civilisation both to learn and recognise itself with more intricacy, more collaborative coherence and social intelligence. In this context, the word 'sustainability' takes on a very literal meaning. It is not just about the long-term preservation of the world's resources, nor is it just about creating a more equitable and participatory society. For Goerner, 'sustainability' means the ability of global civilisation to evolve intelligently and appropriately within itself and with the world. Only through widespread collaborative learning can we hope to do this not only today, but far into the future.

OUTLOOK ON THE INTEGRAL SOCIETY

Goerner's fresh take on sustainability and our Integral Development fit neatly within a larger tale of developmentally co-evolving societal cycles and radically revised worldviews. Her ability to simultaneously emphasise and interlink scientific thinking, cultural perspective and nature's evolutionary principles and to carry over these combined lessons to all levels of self, organisation, economy and society makes her approach a powerful final perspective in this Western chapter. In pragmatic Western terms, Goerner is able to link the natural and communal South with the cultural and spiritual East, as well as the scientific and technological North, and integrate them altogether into 'Western' practice.

She thus closes the circle between nature and economics, and – by connecting the necessities of tomorrow with the ancient knowledge of yesterday – the circle between past and future. Her institute is a role model of an organisation of the future. The vision of the Integral Institute may serve as an inspirational closing statement to Goerner's perspective:

> *The Integral Science Institute is a collaborative learning organisation whose mission it to develop the scientific foundation, intellectual vision and fractal social organisation needed to support a robust, sustainable and collaborative learning civilisation. This mission is founded in the belief that a collaborative learning civilisation – that is, having a world who's citizens are equal partners in improving and sustaining our global life conditions – is the key to solving society's most threatening problems.*[13]

21.5   Integration

In this penultimate 'Western' chapter, set within the realm of enterprise and economics, we have come a long way from conventional development economics that we briefly revisited in the beginning of this book (⇨2).

In a perhaps surprising first step we have engaged with Karl Marx, whose theories, with the apparent collapse of mainstream economics, have recently appeared back on the international scene, now in a less dogmatic manner. We discovered that parts of his thinking are highly relevant in advancing to a more holistic perspective of economics and society.

With Integral Economics (societal), following from Integral Enterprise (organisational) and an Integral Life (individual) that came before, we have then introduced a fully integral perspective to economics that allows us not only to understand economics from a whole world perspective, but also to engage in processes to rebuild the economy, locally and globally. Such an integral approach to economics builds on the particularities of diverse cultures.

An integral perspective to economics finds increasing resonance in global economic theory and practice. The theoretical work of the German economist Christian Arnsberger on *Full-Spectrum Economics*[14] is just one example. Arnsberger, whose approach redefines economics based on Ken Wilber's integral approach (⇨19), explains that the increasingly influential post-classical paradigm drawing on systems science, evolutionary game theory, complexity economics and neuroeconomics, as well as behavioural-experimental economics, is a major advance. However, he argues, it remains fundamentally flawed when it comes to saying anything about interior notions such as personal affectivity or collective culture. Arnsberger maintains that to build a genuinely full-spectrum paradigm, consciousness and culture, as well as the idea of evolutionary development, need to be introduced. For him, part of the full-spectrum economics is the economist's introspective study of him or herself and his or her context. Agreeing with Arnsberger's claims, we would add, however, that catalytic processes as introduced by Integral Development are needed, enabling individuals, organisations and communities to actively build such new economic systems.

Then, and only then, can a newly Integral Economy be brought about, fully embedded in an Integral Society – an inspiring perspective, which we introduced through the work of the US transdisciplinary scientist Sally Goerner towards the end of this chapter.

Before we move on to the fourth level of this 'Western' realm, we pause to engage – through reflection and prospective action – with the guiding question and theory presented in this chapter. This includes the major development challenges derived thereof. At this stage it is of primary importance to identify, how you and your organisation or community can reach out into society at large, thereby becoming a veritable agent for societal development. For this to happen, you and your organisation or community are challenged to articulate and conceptualise your own learnings and findings with regards to development, based on your experiences in Round 1 (the formative grounding of your own self) and in Round 2 (the reformative response of your organisation or community). Hence, this normative Round 3 is very much about coming up with new development norms that can inform – large-scale – the learning and development of your society at large.

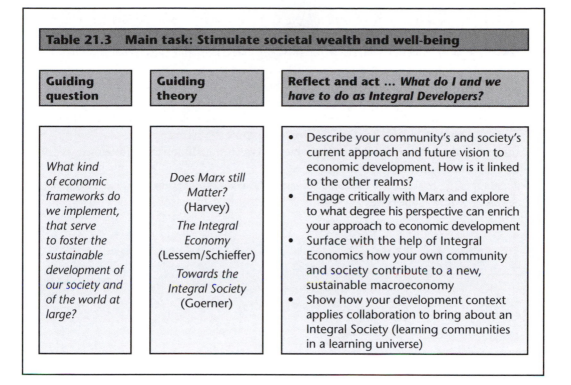

Table 21.3 Main task: Stimulate societal wealth and well-being

Guiding question	Guiding theory	Reflect and act ... What do I and we have to do as Integral Developers?
What kind of economic frameworks do we implement, that serve to foster the sustainable development of our society and of the world at large?	Does Marx still Matter? (Harvey) The Integral Economy (Lessem/Schieffer) Towards the Integral Society (Goerner)	• Describe your community's and society's current approach and future vision to economic development. How is it linked to the other realms? • Engage critically with Marx and explore to what degree his perspective can enrich your approach to economic development • Surface with the help of Integral Economics how your own community and society contribute to a new, sustainable macroeconomy • Show how your development context applies collaboration to bring about an Integral Society (learning communities in a learning universe)

We are now ready to turn to the culminating, transformative effect of this 'Western' realm. This effect will be first illustrated by Interface in the USA, and secondly by the internationally active TIGE–Initiative. Both cases will be complemented by a multitude of global experiments that is increasingly visible. Altogether, they pave the way for integrating the levels of individual, organisational and societal development, through an exciting new educational-developmental institution that we called 'University of Life'.

References

1   Palgi, M. and Reinharz, S. (eds) (2011). *One Hundred Years of Kibbutz Life: A Century of Crisis and Reinvention*. London: Transaction Publishers.
2   Harvey, D. (2009). *A Companion to Marx's Capital*. London: Verso.
3   Marx, K. (1990). *Capital: A Critique of Political Economy*. Vol. 1. London: Penguin.
4   Marx, K. (1990). *Capital: A Critique of Political Economy*. Vol. 1. London: Penguin.
5   Hodgson, G. et al. (10 August 2009). *Letter to the Queen of England*. http://www.feed-charity.org/user/image/queen2009b.pdf.
6   Lessem, R. and Schieffer, A. (2010). *Integral Economics: Releasing the Economic Genius of your Society*. Farnham: Gower.
7   Lessem, R. and Schieffer, A. (2010). *Integral Economics: Releasing the Economic Genius of your Society*. Farnham: Gower, p. 328.
8   Lessem, R. and Schieffer, A. (2010). *Integral Economics: Releasing the Economic Genius of your Society*. Farnham: Gower, p. 330.

9   Lessem, R. and Schieffer, A. (2010). *Integral Economics: Releasing the Economic Genius of your Society*. Farnham: Gower, p. 333.

10   Lessem, R. and Schieffer, A. (2010). *Integral Economics: Releasing the Economic Genius of your Society*. Farnham: Gower, p. 335.

11   Lessem, R. and Schieffer, A. (2010). *Integral Economics: Releasing the Economic Genius of your Society*. Farnham: Gower, p. 344.

12   Goerner, S. et al. (2008). *The New Science of Sustainability: Building Foundations for Great Change*. Chapel Hill, NC: Triangle Centre for Complex Systems.

13   Integral Science Institute website. Available at: www.integralscienceinstitute.org / Accessed: 18 February 2012.

14   Arnsberger, C. (2012). *Full-Spectrum Economics: Toward an Inclusive and Emancipatory Social Science*. London: Routledge.

CHAPTER **22** *Western Integration via a University of Life: The Cases of Interface, TIGE and Global Creative Experimentation*

Guiding Question: How can we sustainably actualise the Western realm of Integral Development, rooted in enterprise and economics?

22.1   Orientation

In this final chapter of the 'Western' realm, we come to its culminating and integrating round of self, enterprise and economic actualisation, ultimately brought about through a University of Life. As in the final 'Southern' (⇨10), 'Eastern' (⇨14) and 'Northern' (⇨18) chapters before, we illustrate through practical cases, not only how the first three rounds of individual, organisational and societal can be meaningfully integrated in theory and practice, but also how they can altogether be further actualised through an educational institution, regenerating the existing approach to education. Again, we need to be aware of the fact that this culminating 'Western' perspective needs to build to a significant degree on what has come before.

In this 'Western' realm, with its core theme of 'Rebuilding Infrastructure and Institutions via Enterprise and Economics', the actualising educational institution is a *'University of Life'*. Being an enabling space to co-create 'equitable and sustainable livelihoods' as the core 'Western' value, such a university type focuses on capacity building and individual realisation. Individual realisation, then, is not to be understood as an isolated personal journey, but rather as a co-evolutionary endeavour that enables each individual to bring about his or her best qualities in the service of society. Hence, key defining terms of the University of Life are 'capacity', 'co-creation' and 'contribution'.

One may want to add 'courage', as this 'Western' realm requires the Integral Developer to 'do things differently', and to engage in creative experimentation that challenges the status quo. Such new modes of actions inevitably shake existing systems and invariably provoke resistance. But the very essence of a 'University of Life' is its being in direct, practical touch with 'life' and addressing core developmental issues in an action-learning experimental style.

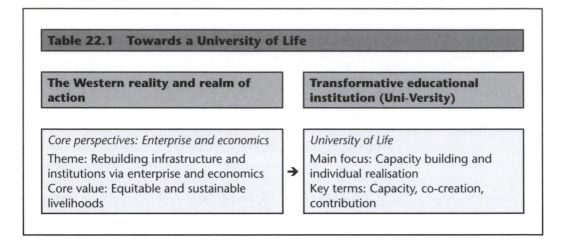

Table 22.1   Towards a University of Life

The Western reality and realm of action	Transformative educational institution (Uni-Versity)
Core perspectives: Enterprise and economics Theme: Rebuilding infrastructure and institutions via enterprise and economics Core value: Equitable and sustainable livelihoods	*University of Life* Main focus: Capacity building and individual realisation Key terms: Capacity, co-creation, contribution

As in the other three realms, so we also build up 'Universities of Life' in a bottom-up fashion, evolving them progressively through the four rounds of Integral Development. That does not mean to necessarily start from scratch, but it does mean that the Integral Developer needs to understand for him or herself how sustainable livelihood can be co-created. In other words, skills and will – capacity and character – are required from the Integral Developer to manifest sustainable livelihood in his or her own life. Furthermore, as we have seen earlier (⇨19), such Integral Development on an individual level has not only economic dimensions, but integrates ecological, spiritual, technological-scientific as well as economic-enterprise aspects.

We personally maintain that the 'Western' economic-entrepreneurial articulation (of an individual, an organisation and a society) should follow (rather than lead) the natural-communal ('South'), cultural-spiritual ('East') and scientific-technological ('North') articulation of a living system. An economic system disconnected from nature, community, culture and science is footloose and ultimately destructive, a fact that we can experience all too good these days. In short, the 'West' needs to 'follow the rest', rather than the other way round.

On an individual level, that requires us to strive for a 'full life perspective' (⇨19). Action then flows out of a connectedness to all aspects of life. In other words, one's 'doing', entrepreneurial activities and so forth are in touch with natural and communal life, cultural and spiritual life as well as scientific and technological life. Active 'Western doing' (in the material world) is then seen as only *one* mode of human expression, aligned with 'Southern being' (in relationship with nature and other beings), 'Eastern becoming' (in quiet reflection or even total stillness) and 'Northern thinking' (in pursuit of thoughts, learning, and knowledge creation). Such a balanced view on human life transcends the current overemphasis on action in isolation, which has proven to be destructive for individual, organisational and societal life.

On an individual level, this fact is increasingly understood. The challenge we collectively face is to translate this insight into new, viable life practices, resulting in sustainable livelihood, nurturing all aspects of life.

Such new individual integral life practices (Round 1) then need to be brought forward into sustainable, integral enterprises (Round 2), and from there onto an integral economy (Round 3). The University of Life (Round 4) needs to serve as a practical, experimental space to enable, test and implement such new frameworks and practices in an integrated way.

While the requirements of a University of Life sound like a tall order (and indeed they are), you will notice in the following cases that such innovative educational spaces are already emerging, at least to some significant degree. What is necessary, though, is to bring such emergent, new universities to collective consciousness and to create and evolve them much more purposefully. Then they can help bringing about the necessary changes on the economic and political level on a large scale, gradually turning enterprise and economics into enabling forces for sustainable livelihoods. Universities of Life are then new forms of educational-developmental spaces that can literally emerge anywhere, as the two following cases will show. In addition, they would also have to influence the transformation of existing educational systems, and be influenced, in turn, by them. Indian-French political scientist Rama Mani rightfully critiques that 'Achieving the Millennium Development Goal of education will be pointless if all it produces is uncritical, unreflective, uncreative computer-literate and commercially savvy clones who can staff corporate and government offices capably but could never discern societal divisions ...'.[1]

What you will notice in the cases to come – from Interface Corporation in the USA, to TIGE as a global initiative, to the stories of creative experimentation – all of them have a strong emphasis on the individual contribution to a larger cause. Therefore, personal creativity, individual initiative and skill-sets are much more in the foreground than in the other realms. This realm is about 'making things happen', 'co-creating new realities' and 'bringing out the best in every person' (in terms of capacities and character), and, above all, 'learning from life experiences'. Noticeably, there is also a growing sense of community. But it is different from the communal orientation promoted by the cases of Chinyika and First Peoples Worldwide (⇨10), the overall individual to societal awakening process promoted by Sarvodaya (⇨14), or indeed the systematised knowledge creation promoted by an authentic 'Mode 2 University' (⇨18). In short, we are engaging here with a renewed 'Western' perspective – as a response to the increasing realisation that the overemphasis on the individual in today's modern society has primarily resulted in egocentric political and economic practices that have damaged social cohesion and the well-being of society as a whole.

In this evolved 'Western' guise, the individual is seeking to reconnect to community, to enhance his or her individuality. That allows us to gradually re-establish the link between the 'communal South' and the more 'individual West' – though not in linear fashion, but cyclically via the 'East' and 'North'. In other words, a heightened consciousness ('East') and a deepened knowledge ('North') of the interconnectedness of all life, is helping to bring the hitherto footloose 'West' back into the integral fold. Naturally, this is a continuously co-evolving process – a process that has no end. Its core purpose is to permanently strive towards dynamic balance, towards healthy co-creation between all realms.

We shall now introduce our main 'Western' cases, beginning with Interface Corporation in the USA.

22.2 Integrated Western Practice: Interface in the USA, the Global TIGE Initiative, and Creative Experimentation Worldwide

THE CASE OF INTERFACE IN THE USA: TOWARDS REDESIGNING COMMERCE

Introduction

We have been following Interface for many years. As the world's largest manufacturer of modular carpets and as a global icon for being one of the most advanced American enterprises in terms of sustainable development, we have introduced its remarkable story also in one of our earlier books.[2] The case of Interface is particular striking, because it is, at one and the same time, highly successful in conventional economic terms, while spearheading a movement of enterprises in America committed towards sustainability, far beyond state imposed regulations. In the process, it has deliberately set out to 'learn from life'.

For the first 21 years of its existence, Interface was merely focused on economic and technological excellence. It required a metaphorical 'spear in the chest' of its founder, Ray Anderson, to dramatically shift the course of the enterprise. We shall now tell the Anderson-Interface story through the four rounds of Integral Development, whereby the fourth round is an intimation of a University of Life, which takes nature as its core source of inspiration.

Round 1 – Self: Ray Anderson's 'spear in the chest' and his daring mid-course correction towards a full life

Born in 1934, Ray Anderson is a product of the Great Depression of World War II, as well as of the post-war era, the latter being a period of enormous prosperity and economic opportunity in America. His father had quit school after only his eighth grade and gone to work to enable his sisters to eventually go to college. That awareness shaped his father's determination not to let his sons waste their lives. As a result, one of Anderson's brothers became a doctor, the other a teacher, and he, Ray, an industrial engineer by profession.

Anderson grew up with a book in one hand and a ball in the other. While he earned a football scholarship to get him into Georgia Tech, it was his friendship with books that served to transform the scholarship opportunity into an excellent education. Working hard at university he graduated in 1956 with the highest honours, earning a bachelor's degree in Industrial Engineering. He spent the next 17 years climbing the corporate ladder and preparing himself by gaining broad business experience. In 1973, aged 38, enjoying an excellent position with a major corporation, he cut the corporate umbilical cord to found a new company to produce free-lay carpet tiles. At the time carpet tiles were just beginning to be used in American office buildings. The timing and the product concept were seemingly perfect.

Twenty-five years later the company had become global. As of 2011, it produced in 10 manufacturing sites located in the US, UK, the Netherlands, Australia, Thailand and China. Sales in 2007 topped $1.1 billion. Yet, as successful as Interface seemed to be, for Anderson it was flawed. It took him, though, a very long time to realise it. For the first 21 years of the company's existence, he never gave a thought to the fact that the company was taking from the earth. He had very little environmental awareness, until 1994.

It was then, when some of the people in Interface Research Corporation, the company's research arm, received questions from customers about what the company was doing for the environment. At that stage Anderson had no environmental vision whatsoever. Then, through sheer serendipity, someone sent him Paul Hawken's book *The Ecology of Commerce*.[3] He read it and it changed his life. It was an epiphany, a 'spear in the chest', as he called it. A powerful sense of urgency emerged. Anderson was particularly taken by Hawken's central thesis: that business and industry must take the lead in directing the earth away from the route it is on toward the abyss of man-made collapse.

Instigated by Anderson's psychological and environmental 'mid-course correction',[4] Interface started its dramatic transformation towards sustainability. In parallel, Anderson changed his personal life style. He built an off-the-grid private home, exchanged his luxury limousine with a low-emission car and turned increasingly towards spirituality.

In the beginning of this change in course, Anderson returned to books, with a vengeance – and he took a number of his colleagues at Interface with him on that journey. There was much to learn on sustainable development. He and his colleagues read, among many others, Rachel Carson's seminal *Silent Spring*,[5] then Al Gore's *Earth in Balance*,[6] and Donella Meadows' *Beyond the Limits*.[7] He devoured Daly and Cobb's *For the Common Good*,[8] trying to get to grips with the economics of sustainability.

How then did Anderson's new thinking transform the organisation he led? We return briefly to the origins of Interface, before we describe in more detail this remarkable shift of direction.

Round 2 – Organisation: Turning Interface into a force for good

The Interface model of a sustainable enterprise and its founder Ray Anderson have achieved iconic status in the US, at least from the mid 1990s onwards. Anderson's 'first life', as he terms it, spanned the initial 38 years of his sojourn on earth, during which he prepared himself, in his own words, to be the entrepreneur who would found the company that came to be called Interface Inc. His 'second life' began with the act of creation of Interface Carpets, founded to produce and sell carpet tiles for American office buildings. Surviving its start-up phase it then prospered beyond Anderson's dreams. By 2007, Interface provided 40 per cent of all the carpet tiles used in commercial buildings in the world. Since its founding, it has grown into a billion-dollar corporation, named by *Fortune Magazine* as one of the 'Most Admired Companies in America' and the '100 Best Companies to Work For'. It has diversified and globalised its businesses, with sales in 110 countries and manufacturing facilities on four continents and is now the world's leading producer of soft-surfaced modular floor coverings.

However, in 1994, after a sequence of events, Anderson discovered an urgent and unexpectedly rewarding new calling for himself. Thus began his 'third life', with a new vision of what he wanted Interface to become: the spearhead of the next industrial revolution.[9]

Anderson became determined to make Interface the first name in industrial ecology. His mission was to convert the organisation into a restorative enterprise, first to reach sustainability, then to become restorative – to put back more than it takes out from the

Earth and to do good to the Earth, not just no harm. And he suggested a strategy: 'reduce, reuse, reclaim, recycle' – later he added 'redesign'. Quickly it became clear that the company would require a systems perspective, or, in Interface's term, a 'whole company approach'.

Interface began making carpets with lower pile heights and higher densities, utilising carpet face constructions that wear better in high traffic, but use less material – a tiny, but important step in de-materialising business and industry, and an intriguing aspect of what has been termed the next industrial revolution. The embodied energy not used in the nylon not consumed was enough, according to Anderson, to power his whole factory making the redesigned products – twice. Already then, Interface was preparing to provide a cyclical service to its customers, to be involved with them beyond the life of the company's products, into the next product reincarnation, and the next. The distribution system would, through 'reverse logistics', become a collection and recycling system, keeping those precious carpet molecules moving through successive product life cycles. Interface was thereby practicing what the US architect William McDonough and the German chemist Michael Braungart would coin 'cradle-to-cradle'[10] – a revolutionary new perspective that suggests to model the 'metabolism' of technology and industry on the metabolism of nature – hence making a positive, rather than a negative, environmental impact by redesigning industrial production.

Perhaps Interface's most impressive product development in such 'cradle-to-cradle-spirit', was Evergreen Lease, its perpetual lease carpet. Evergreen Lease has become a manifestation of the future, for a wide range of durable manufacturing goods. It is one example of how commerce can be redesigned for the twenty-first century to reduce dependence on diminishing virgin resources, and to increase efficiency in resource usage.

In 2009, Anderson estimated that Interface was more than halfway towards its goal to sustainability.[11] In July 2012, Interface announced the following figures[12] as per the end of 2011:

> *Energy intensity used at manufacturing facilities – per unit of product – is down 47 percent since 1996. Thirty-one percent of Interface's total energy use comes from renewable sources. Actual greenhouse gas emissions at manufacturing facilities have been reduced by 32 percent from a 1996 baseline. Waste sent to landfill per unit of product decreased by 88 percent since 1996. Water intake per unit of product has reduced by 84 percent since 1996.*[13]

At the core of Interface's progression towards sustainability are two systems called 'EcoMetrics' (a term coined by Ray Anderson himself) and 'SocioMetrics'. Annually, all of Interface's manufacturing facilities are assessed. It is noteworthy that the organisation is 'simultaneously taking three paths on this journey – defined by reductions in its environmental footprint, dedication to product innovation and commitment to culture'.[14] While the first two paths are readily understood, Interface's commitment to culture – as a factor on the journey to sustainability requires further explanation. Primarily it is about creating a culture of 'inspired thinkers' that continue to find innovative solutions that change the business. Via SocioMetrics, data are collected 'in several key areas that track the company's social capital and investment in people, including the company's employees and local community members'.[15] Examples (for the year 2011) are 10.000 hours of time that Interface's employees volunteered in communities with a view to creating environmental awareness. The most recent initiative is Interface's commitment to the:

> *Green Apple Day of Service, where the company will encourage its employees, customers and suppliers to volunteer towards school sustainability projects in the communities where it operates around the world. The company will identify schools and school districts globally for service projects that can have a meaningful impact on the environments in which children and young adults learn.*[16]

We begin to see more clearly how Interface is expanding its outreach into society.

Round 3 – Society: Showing businesses a pathway to sustainability and engaged in enhancing societal well-being

For Interface, sustainability does not stop at the organisational level. Already in its organisational mission it articulates its leadership role with regards to becoming a role model for sustainable development, and its responsibility towards its customers and multiple stakeholders as well as for environment and society as a whole:

> *Interface will become the first name in commercial and institutional interiors worldwide through its commitment to people, process, product, place and profits. We will strive to create an organisation wherein all people are accorded unconditional respect and dignity; one that allows each person to continuously learn and develop. We will focus on product (which includes service) through constant emphasis on process quality and engineering, which we will combine with careful attention to our customers' needs so as always to deliver superior value to our customers, thereby maximising all stakeholders' satisfaction. We will honour the places where we do business by endeavouring to become the first name in industrial ecology, a corporation that cherishes nature and restores the environment. Interface will lead by example and validate by results, including profits, leaving the world a better place than when we began, and we will be restorative through the power of our influence in the world.*[17]

Interface is aware, that in order to reach the ambitious sustainability goals, ultimately commerce itself needs to be redesigned (see Round 4). That requires, according to Anderson, the acceptance of entirely new notions of economics. Working towards that goal, the organisation engages relentlessly in increasing awareness for sustainability issues.

In 2001, Anderson handed over the executive helm of the company to Dan Hendrix, remaining its chairman and CEO. From then on, Anderson focused almost exclusively on promoting the case for sustainable business all over the world. He gave over a thousand speeches, wrote further books and columns.

Anderson saw Interface's role in showing businesses a pathway to sustainability. In that sense, he saw himself and Interface almost, in our terms, as a University of Life (see below), though he was under no illusion that this process would take time: The Environmental Leader, a leading sustainability magazine, quotes him:

I also believe that it doesn't happen quickly … it happens one mind at a time, one organisation at a time, one building, one company, one community, one region, one new, clean technology, one industry, one supply chain at a time … until the entire industrial system has been transformed into a sustainable system, existing ethically in balance with Earth's natural systems, upon which every living thing is utterly dependent.[18]

Toward the turn of the century Anderson was appointed to President Clinton's Council on Sustainable Development. That led to him co-chairing the Presidential Climate Action Plan in 2008, a team that presented the Obama Administration with a 100-day action plan on climate. These are just two cases through which Anderson actively engaged in changing the (sustainable) development policies of his country, as well as influencing corresponding infrastructure and systems.

Anderson looked also beyond ecological sustainability. As he approached his seventies, Anderson had come to believe that the growing field of spirituality in business is a cornerstone of the next industrial revolution.[19] He also had come to recognise that the ascendancy of women in business is coming at the nick of time. It is their instinctive, nurturing nature – also of course found in some men – that will elevate genuine caring in business. Caring for human and natural capital as much as the business world has traditionally cared for financial capital will give social equity and environmental stewardship their natural places alongside economic progress, and move society to reinvent the means of achieving economic progress itself.

Having researched Interface, we see the organisation as an example for an emergent University of Life. In what way? While the story of Interface has not – as in the cases Chinyika (⇨10) or Mondragon (⇨18) – been translated in full-fledged research and educational programmes, the organisation has created, in the spirit of what we coin a University of Life, a living space of experimenting and action-learning. Clearly, as Round 4 reveals, nature itself has become the central source of learning for Interface and its followers.

Round 4 – Interface as a University of Life inspired by nature

Learning from the nature-university: Towards new product and business designs

Anderson was increasingly looking for a new business design for Interface. However, there was no blueprint for this kind of organisation in business. But there was in nature. If nature designed an industrial process, what might it look like? How could Interface translate the operations of nature into a model for a business?

Nature, for Anderson, has a set of fundamental operating principles:[20] it runs on sunlight and other renewable energy sources, it fits form to function, it recycles everything and it is extremely efficient – never creating excess or wasting – and, finally, it rewards cooperation. Interface's job was to translate these principles into a new model for business. To begin with, it meant that it would become a business that runs on renewable energy. The company would carefully eliminate waste from all areas of its operations and recycle and then reuse the materials from its products and those that support its business. It would find a use for everything it uses and waste nothing. And finally, it, too, would reward cooperation – with suppliers, customers, investors and with communities.

Anderson told a group of his people at a design workshop: 'Go, and see how nature would design a floor covering. And don't come back with leaf designs; that's not what I mean. Come back with design principles. What are nature's design principles?' His people subsequently spent a day in the forest, looking at the forest floor, looking at the streambed, and finally it dawned on them: there are no two things alike on the forest floor. Each stick and every leaf is different. Yet, there is a uniformity to that chaos; a sort of organised chaos. 'You can pick up a stick here and drop it there, and you can't tell you've changed anything'. They came back realising that nature's design principle is basically organised chaos and total diversity. And they designed a carpet tile where no two were alike. Aside from being a very pleasant aesthetic that emulates the forest floor, it turned out to be practically waste-free in the production process. One could not find a defect – if there was indeed a defect, it was camouflaged by the design. The installation process has practically no waste. When the installer gets to the edge of the room and cuts the last piece to fit, the scrap from the last piece can be used somewhere else, and it could not be recognised as a cut carpet tile.

Inspiration from biomimicry: More from nature's university

Anderson continued his personal learning journey, and turned Interface increasingly into a learning organisation. When he read Janine Benyus's famous book, *Biomimicry: Innovation inspired by Nature*,[21] he found many of Benyus' suggestions of how to model an industrial enterprise after nature, already reflected in Interface, such as the idea of cyclical processes, doing no harm to the biosphere, taking nothing from the earth that is not naturally and rapidly renewable, and producing no waste.

Anderson wanted to drive the whole company with sunlight, renewable energy, closing the loop on material flows so that one has not only the basic organic cycle – the dust-to-dust cycle – but in an analogous way, a technical cycle that takes used-up products and gives them life-after-life through the recycling process, so that no molecules are lost; everything stays in the material loop. All of that is basically emulating nature in an industrial system, and that remains the company goal. This represents a total transformation. It was a burst of insight, followed by a couple of years of studying the literature and thinking.

Out then came the plan for pursuing sustainability. Using the natural metaphor of a mountain, Interface called this plan 'Climbing Mount Sustainability' (Figure 22.1). The seven fronts of the mountain were identified, and the organisation explored how to climb each of those fronts to meet at the top, at that point where the ecological footprint is zero.

Climbing 'Mount Sustainability': Towards the restoration of the Earth

Front 1 – *Eliminate Waste:* Interface was pursuing the goal of creating a prototypical company of the twenty-first century on seven fronts. Though Interface was at different stages with each, Anderson hoped all would meet at the top. The first goal was that of 'Zero Waste'. In pursuit of zero waste, unwanted linkages in the biosphere were attacked. Furthermore, the Interface Quest programme (an acronym signifying: Quality

Utilising Employee Suggestions and Teamwork) engaged all employees in identifying and eliminating waste throughout all of the organisation's operations and processes.

Front 2 – *Benign Emissions:* The second front was so-called 'Benign Emissions' to attack another unwanted linkage in the biosphere. The company had inventoried every stack and every outlet pipe at Interface, and it was reducing its emissions daily. But Anderson knew that to prevent toxic emissions altogether the company had to go upstream and prevent toxic substances from entering its factories in the first place.

Front 3 – *Renewable Energy:* This third front meant eventually harnessing renewable energy. Interface had declared all fossil fuel derived energy to be waste and targeted for its elimination. Its first application of photovoltaic power was in its North Carolina factory. In Canada the company had contracted with Ontario Hydro for 'green power' (solar and wind), even though it costs more.

Front 4 – *Closing the Loop:* The fourth front was to introduce closed loop recycling. The supply of recycled rather than virgin molecules in the technical loop was analogous to the supply of money in an economic system (the multiplier effect), affecting directly the resource-efficiency of the enterprise.

Front 5 – *Resource-Efficient Transportation:* This front was least within the company's control, and yet, difficult to achieve. Yet, Anderson maintained, that the organisation's

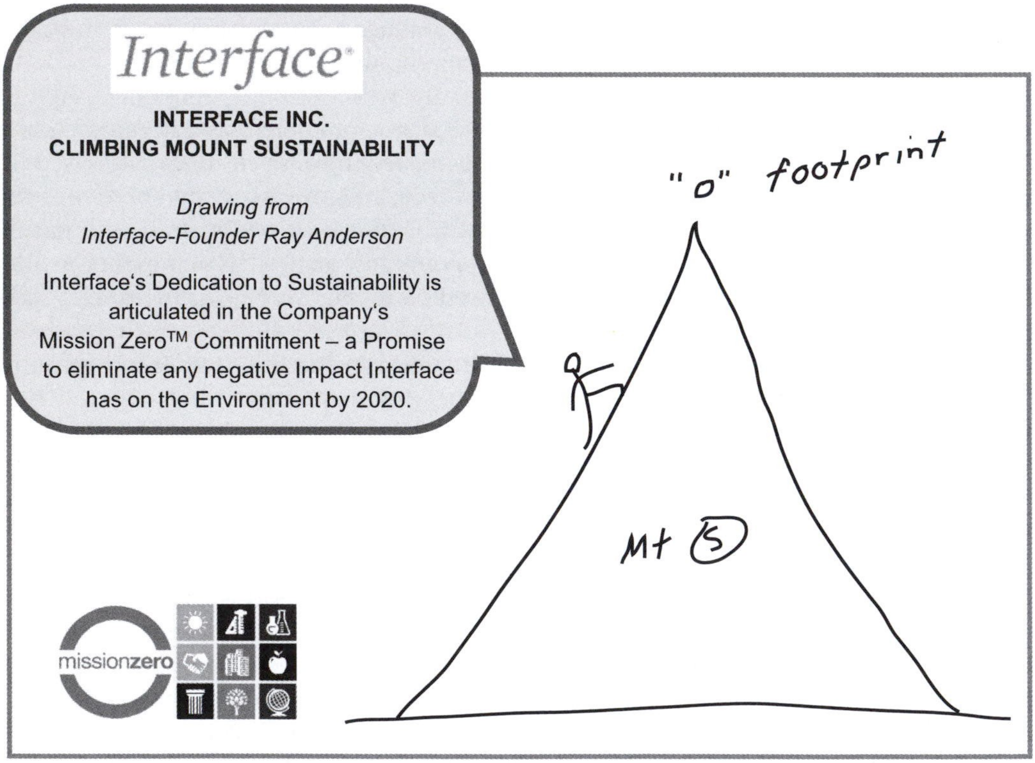

Figure 22.1 Interface: Climbing 'Mount Sustainability'

responsibility would need to be extended to this front, if full sustainability was to be achieved.

Front 6 – *Sensitivity Hookup:* This front spawned numerous desirable connections: service to the community, closer relations amongst the company's own people, as well as with suppliers and customers.

Front 7 – *The Redesign of Commerce:* This seventh and final front called for the redesign of commerce itself. Redesigning commerce probably hinges, more than anything else for Anderson, on the acceptance of entirely new notions of economics, especially prices that reflect full costs. To Interface, it meant shifting emphasis from simply selling products to providing services. Thus, its investment in downstream distribution, installation, maintenance and recycling had to all aim at forming cradle-to-cradle relationships with customers and suppliers.

The roadmap to 'Mount Sustainability' and the underlying concept base were developed over the course of a year or two. Interface had to go through a total cultural transformation, a process that is still continuing. Anderson imagined the kinds of initiatives that would be necessary to make it to the top of each of those fronts, to become the prototypical, sustainable company of the twenty-first century: strongly service oriented, resource-efficient, wasting nothing, solar-driven, cyclical, strongly connected to its customers and suppliers, building social equity with and through them.

The new mindset – mapped out by Mount Sustainability – was beginning to permeate everything that the company did, especially product design and development.

Focus on continuous discovery and action-learning: From a band of scouts to an eco-dream team, from one world learning to a global learning network

Anderson' life journey was one of continuous learning and discovery as well as putting his learnings immediately into action. Increasingly he reached out to influence the learning journeys of others, within and beyond Interface.

The process of turning Interface in an authentic learning organisation, had, however, despite many successes, also many failures. We find the typical patterns of a University of Life – continuous experimentation, implementing of successful experiments into practice, acknowledging failures, retrial. Honesty and openness about when things work and when they do not work was practised. That became also evident in our own dialogue with Interface. The following excerpt of a recent conversation with Interface's Vice President of Sustainability, Erin Meezan, mirrors that attitude and provides a good sense for the difficult and ongoing process of living a 'learning Interface':

> *In our attempt to become a learning organisation, we have had an interesting series of tries with different structures. In the early days – after Ray Anderson introduced the new vision for the company and challenged us to accept these new values and come up with a way to apply it to our manufacturing enterprise – we did a lot of learning! It was a time of exploration and several folks in the company were doing this rapid learning. We call them now 'a band of scouts'. It was a small group of executives working closely with Ray Anderson to make the vision apply*

to a manufacturing model. They read a lot, went to outside conferences, started talking to environmental thought leaders like David Brower, the founder of Friends of the Earth and Amory Lovins, founder of the Rocky Mountains Institute. Then we recruited the 'Dream Team'.[22]

This so-called 'Eco-Dream Team' comprised of major environmental thinkers and practitioners of our time: from Amory Lovins, L. Hunter Lovins, Janine Benyus, Karl-Henrik Robèrt, Paul Hawken, Walter Stahel and others. In the early days of Interface's transformation process it was this Dream Team that helped the organisation understand conceptually what sustainable development is about, how it could be translated into a modern manufacturing process and what the overall strategic process towards sustainability might look like. Over time, the interaction became less frequent, as relevant knowledge got distributed within the organisation. Up to this day, members of the Dream Team are involved in accompanying Interface in its challenging journey, now primarily engaged on a project basis. Meezan describes how the learning process further evolved within the organisation:

As the framework was developed, the need for learning grew and we started to do a couple of things formally to take that framework and try to embed it into our global companies. That required more training and learning with a much bigger group of global employees. We hired a company that did experiential learning – and it was so successful with the US business that we brought them into the company as 'One World Learning'. We asked the OWL-team to start working with all of our global businesses. It also had a mission to work with outside firms as well. I think this was an early misstep – giving them the charge to create learning experiences for our internal teams and to sell their services externally caused a lot of pressure and ultimately was not an achievable goal.[23]

Though One World Learning was ultimately abandoned, Meezan affirms that it had delivered a number of essential experiences that, in her words, 'are still acknowledged as life changing, or at a minimum, perspective changing by our global associates'.[24] The original mission of One World Learning had been to help Interface learn the 'Natural Step' developed by the Swedish cancer scientist Karl-Henrik Robèrt in Sweden – a sustainability framework that has been adopted by leading corporations worldwide, such as IKEA, Starbucks and Nike.[25] Designed as a unifying framework for sustainable development – rooted in the natural sciences and continuously aligning business practices with the sustainability goal – it supported Interface's ultimate aim for sustainability.

Later, Interface established a sustainability consulting arm called InterfaceRAISE – in particular, after other leading US companies, such as retail giant Wal-Mart approached Interface to help them develop their own sustainability standpoints and strategies. Though the company enjoyed some success, it was ultimately closed down, for a set of complex structural, strategic and leadership reasons.[26] Once that decision was made, Interface immediately hired an external organisation to extract – with the input of Interface employees – the core learnings from this experiment.

Having gone through this exercise, Interface experimented for a number of years with appointing so-called 'learning leaders' within its various global businesses. It did not take Interface long, though, to acknowledge, that these leaders on their own – with relatively little resource and network – could not achieve much in a highly decentralised organisation such as Interface.

Currently, a global team of Interface associates is in the process of defining what new structure would best enable the organisation to harness and grow its learning capabilities through an adequate network model. For Meezan:

We started by acknowledging that we learn daily, that we are decentralised, that we have passionate people – but we need to connect them, increase their skill set and let them work in a network model to develop and deliver a global strategy to take us to the next level in terms of development. Ultimately, we want to establish a Global Learning Network.[27]

For Interface, such a Global Learning Network is not to be confined to its organisational boundaries. Rather, it encourages and supports its employees to actively transport their 'sustainability learnings' into their own communities. Interface has begun to trace and evaluate such private initiatives of its staff members, with the intention of reflecting on them in an internal project called 'I am Mission Zero'. Additionally, Interface is attempting to calculate the value of the people in the organisation through a human capital value assessment. Here, they are guided by the 'Present Value of Future Earnings Approach'[28] by Baruch Lev and Aba Schwartz, an approach also employed by India's Infosys that ranks among the world's most progressive corporations with regards to sustainability.

As this process of internal experimentation goes on, Interface remains active, on many levels, to spur societal learning. The company sponsors, for example, a chair at the Industrial and Systems Engineering (ISyE) School at Ray Anderson's old university, Georgia Tech, that became known as the Anderson-Interface Chair of Natural Systems. Interestingly enough, the internal 'Interface-University-of-Life' – as a veritable learning organisation – and the external 'Chair of Natural Systems', have not yet been integrated. This indeed reflects the remaining divide between industry and academe.

Outlook

In its strong orientation towards nature, the (in our terms) 'Interface-University-of-Life' seems to almost follow in the footsteps of the great American philosopher Ralph Waldo Emerson. His book *Nature*,[29] published in 1836 became the spiritual and intellectual headwater of one branch of American environmentalism. In his time, the university was a place to wrestle with big ideas. The campus was not a factory creating specialists for the job market. He did not dwell on the loss of nature and its resources at the hands of agriculture and industry, but concentrated instead on the ways nature informed ideas and truth. In a 1833 lecture he concluded:

Nature is a language and every new fact one learns is a new word; but it is not a language taken to pieces and dead in a dictionary, but the language put together into a most significant and universal sense. I wish to learn this language not that I may know a new grammar, but that I may read the great book which is written in that tongue.[30]

Interface is a powerful example to illustrate, how nature and its underlying design patterns could indeed be employed as the central inspiration for a genuine University of Life – transforming the organisation towards sustainability and in the course – as the

Interface case has shown – providing inspiration, new knowledge and societal leadership for many organisations.

Such an action-learning-driven university type can be designed in and around organisations, helping them to adapt and evolve innovatively on an ongoing basis.

In 2011, Ray Anderson died of cancer, at the age of 77. Interface, as a company stays committed to its vision and its promise to eliminate any negative impact the organisation has on the environment by 2020.

In 2012, the Ray C. Anderson Foundation – an entity separate from Interface, managed by the Anderson family – had changed its original focus on philanthropic activities to become a custodian of Anderson's legacy. In a self-description that the foundation offers, we find the notion of 'business as a force for good' (our Round 2) and its aspired impact on societal well-being:

> *The Ray C. Anderson Foundation was created in honour of the late Ray C. Anderson (1934–2011), founder of Interface, Inc. During his time at Interface, Ray championed the notion of businesses doing well by doing good. It's these noble qualities of advancing knowledge and innovation around environmental stewardship and sustainability that recognised Ray as a pioneer in industrial ecology.*[31]

The purpose of the foundation is to continue what Ray Anderson started: harmonising society, business and environment; supporting a sustainable society; and contributing to create a better world for future generations. It seeks to achieve that through research und funding, as well as through educational and project-based initiatives that 'advance the revolution in sustainable production and consumption'.[32]

The Interface-University-of-Life, as we see it, continues, on many levels. Table 22.2 below summarises the four levels of the Interface case.

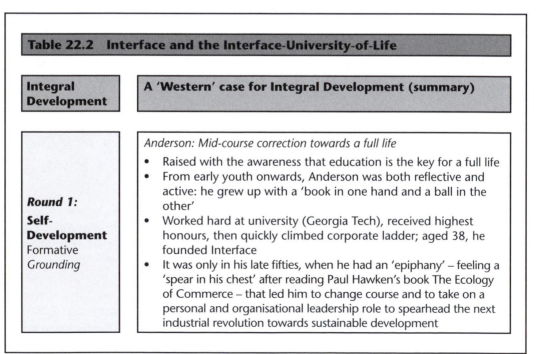

Table 22.2   Interface and the Interface-University-of-Life

Integral Development	A 'Western' case for Integral Development (summary)
Round 1: **Self-Development** Formative *Grounding*	*Anderson: Mid-course correction towards a full life* • Raised with the awareness that education is the key for a full life • From early youth onwards, Anderson was both reflective and active: he grew up with a 'book in one hand and a ball in the other' • Worked hard at university (Georgia Tech), received highest honours, then quickly climbed corporate ladder; aged 38, he founded Interface • It was only in his late fifties, when he had an 'epiphany' – feeling a 'spear in his chest' after reading Paul Hawken's book The Ecology of Commerce – that led him to change course and to take on a personal and organisational leadership role to spearhead the next industrial revolution towards sustainable development

Table 22.2	Continued

Integral Development	A 'Western' case for Integral Development (summary)
Round 2: **Organisational Development** Reformative *Emergence*	*Interface: Turning the organisation into a force for good* • Determined to make Interface the first name in industrial ecology • The mission was to convert the organisation into a restorative enterprise, first to reach sustainability, then to become restorative – to put back more than its takes out from the earth. the strategy was: 'reduce, reuse, reclaim, recycle, redesign' • Commitment to mission zero: no more negative impact by 2020
Round 3: **Societal Development** Newly normative *Navigation*	*Beyond Interface: Promoting societal well-being* • Interface articulated early its leadership role with regards to becoming a role model for sustainable development, and its responsibility towards its customers and multiple stakeholders as well as for environment and society as a whole • From 2001, Anderson focused on promoting the case for sustainable business. He gave over a 1,000 speeches, wrote books and columns, joined President Clinton' Council on Sustainable Development, and presented President Obama with a climate action plan • Interface supports its employees to actively transport their 'sustainability learnings' into their own communities. The company has begun to trace and evaluate such private initiatives of its staff members, with the intention of reflecting on them in an internal project called 'I am Mission Zero'. • Interface is aware, that in order to reach the ambitious sustainability goals, ultimately commerce itself needs to be redesigned. that requires the acceptance of entirely new notions of economics
Round 4: **Integrating Uni-Versity** Full transformative *Effect*	*Interface-University-of-Life: Nature as university core* • Following Anderson's mid-course-Correction, and determined to reach Mission Zero by 2020, Interface was turned into a space for continuous action-learning and discovery • Nature (life itself!) became the greatest teacher: following natural patterns of self-organisation, complexity, cradle-to-cradle-cycles, and incorporating concepts such as biomimicry and the natural step, Interface continues to develop new products, sustainability frameworks (e.g. 'Mount Sustainability') and explore new organisational designs. • Close cooperation instigated with the Anderson-Interface Chair in Natural Systems (sponsored by Ray Anderson) at Georgia Tech. • After Anderson's death, Interface's commitment remains: harmonising society, business and environment; supporting a sustainable society; and contributing to create a better world for future generations

We now turn from a corporate example to a civic one, but we shall soon see where the common notion of a University of Life appears, notwithstanding their differences.

THE CASE OF INITIATIVES OF CHANGE AND OF TRUST AND INTEGRITY IN THE GLOBAL ECONOMY (TIGE)

Overview

The story of the global initiative of Trust and Integrity in the Global Economy (TIGE) cannot be told without first telling the story of Initiatives of Change (IofC) out of which the former grew. Both intertwined cases illustrate an interconnected self-organisation-society journey, with a real potential to institutionalise such an approach through what we call in this 'Western' realm, a University for Life.

Prelude to TIGE – Initiatives of change

As the main emphasis in this case will be on TIGE, this prelude serves to condense the (almost) 'integrally-rounded' journey of IofC, a 'diverse, global network committed to building trust across the world's divides'.[33] For many of its members, IofC is much more than a network, but rather 'a way of life'.

Initiatives of Change evolved out of the so-called Oxford Group that was initiated by university students in the late 1920s. In 1938, in the wake of impending World War II, its founder Frank Buchman, an American Christian missionary born in 1878, called for a 'moral and spiritual re-armament to work towards a "hate-free, fear-free, greed-free world"'.[34] A crucial moment for Buchman's relentless commitment for what became later known as Moral Re-Armament was a life changing spiritual experience that he underwent during a visit to England in 1908. In his own words:

> I began to see myself as God saw me, which was a very different picture than the one I had of myself ... I realised how my sin, my pride, my selfishness, had eclipsed me from God. I was the centre of my own life. That big 'I' had to be crossed out ... It produced a vibrant feeling, as though a strong current of life had suddenly been poured into me.[35]

That moment changed the course of his life, and led, in the aftermath to the foundation of Moral Re-Armament (MRA). After World War II, this programme of moral and spiritual reconstruction contributed immensely to reconcile former enemies in war torn Europe, in particular France and Germany. Renowned heads of business and government have been historically associated with MRA. From the very beginning, MRA saw itself as a space for dialogue and honest conversations.

Though a global network, it has a strong 'Western' action-driven emphasis on addressing global predicaments. The core constituencies of its name – 'initiative' and 'change' – underline its pragmatic orientation on making a tangible impact on society.

Furthermore, inspired by Buchman's own spiritual experiences, IofC – as it has more recently been called – attributes vital importance to individual transformation as the starting point of societal change. According to IofC sources, Buchman was often quoted with: 'Human nature can be changed. That is the root of the answer. National economies can be changed. That is the fruit of the answer. World history can be changed. That is the destiny of our age'.[36] In the spirit of this 'destiny', IofC has become a platform for grooming individual change makers, each of them active in his or her given context.

Originally IofC was primarily rooted in Christian spirituality, with its 'mantra' being 'up', 'in' and 'out'. It thereby followed a pattern of Christian discipleship, with 'up' meaning God-wards, 'in' refers to the development of the inner self and 'out' encourages outward engagement in society. In particular over the past years, IofC's approach to spirituality has transcended a primarily Christian perspective and become more universal, providing space for all faiths and none. IofC's so-called 'four absolute standards' – honesty, purity, love and unselfishness – seek to point to the essence of all major faiths.

Over time, the initiative expanded its work towards reconciliation and human security around the world, and gradually took on also a range of other burning issues, related to human progress as well as economic and social well-being. As it widened its scope, the network also changed its original name, and constitutes, since 2001, as 'Initiatives of Change'. With programmes running all over the world, the network continues to make significant positive contributions to societies.

The movement recognised, in fact since the 1970s, that without dealing with the economic aspects of the world, peace between nations could not prevail. It was in 1973 – at the time of the first oil crisis and global inflation and the Vietnam War at its height – when the first Caux Conference for Business took place. Business leaders associated with Caux conceived of the idea of an annual conference at Caux to address how industry could take up such a task, as well as the kind of global changes that were needed. Their conviction was that industry, rightly led and motivated, should be an agent of the kind of changes needed in the world. Their vision included the great themes of business, industry and the economy, combined with the personal search for the role each individual can play. With the environmental challenges of industry emerging within the world's consciousness, so also IofC began to address these issues.

Early speakers at conferences included industrial and trade union leaders, and also pioneers of new economic thinking such as Umberto Colombo of the Club of Rome and world-renowned economist E.F. Schumacher. They addressed themes ahead of their time such as 'Industry's New Responsibilities' (1977), 'How Can Industry Meet the Needs of People?' (1979) and 'Tomorrow's Technology – Fear or Hope?' (1980).

One regular participant was Shoji Takase, Senior Managing Director of the Toshiba Electric Co. For 15 years Toshiba sent joint labour-management delegations to Caux. They took home the idea that 'it's not who is right but what is right' that counts, and used it as a foundation for an era of improved labour relations in Japan.

Such was the respect for Caux in Japanese industry that when in 1985 Frits Philips, former president of Philips, invited a number of top Japanese industrial leaders to a private session at Caux to discuss with European and American colleagues how a trade war might be averted, they came in strength. This was the beginning of the Caux Round Table, now an independent worldwide group.

Between 1990 and 2000 a new development dramatically changed the nature of industry, business and services. The Information Technology revolution had begun to transform work places and subsequently private homes and society as a whole. This was regarded as the next great engine of progress that was to drive the work place and working practices, creating new jobs that did not exist before and creating a shift in the balance that existed in the world. The whole definition of the work place, which used to be a geographically located site with regular working hours was transformed into to borderless global workspace.

With the IT revolution came the new term 'globalisation' – symbolising the rapid transition that was taking place in the world economy. In 1997, Bill Jordan, then General Secretary of the International Confederation of Free Trade Unions, addressed the Caux conference on the theme 'The Morality of Globalisation'. Since then the search for how to humanise the process of globalisation, and honest dialogue between its supporters and opponents, became an increasingly important theme at Caux.

Between 2001 and 2005 the three major, illustrious individual driving forces of the Caux Business and Industry conferences retired from their positions: Ryuzaburo Kaku, Chairman and Chief Executive of Canon (⇨12) and champion of *kyosei* (business-societal co-evolution), Neville Cooper, founder of Britain's Institute of Business Ethics, and Frits Philips, of the Dutch multinational Phillips. It was a time when IofC was confronted with having to rethink its own stance towards a global economy that, despite many well-meant individual efforts, seemed to dramatically increase the gap between the rich and the poor.

IofC felt the urge to respond creatively to such a global predicament and it looked for someone who could act as chief coordinator for this new venture. In 2006, the Caux Foundation Initiatives of Change Switzerland contacted Mohan Bhagwandas who responded to the call. It has here that the story of TIGE starts.

We shall now follow the TIGE story as it moves through the three rounds of individual, organisational and societal development, and explore, finally in Round 4 its next evolutionary step.

Round 1 – Self: Mohan Bhagwandas – Responding to the call of economic renewal

Mohan Bhagwandas, an Australian resident with Sri Lankan origins, had been associated with IofC since the 1970s At the age of 21, he joined the movement, attracted by its guiding motto 'first transform yourself, then transform society'.

Experiences of poverty that he witnessed around him during his childhood left an indelible print in his heart. Seeing people living in unbearable circumstances in the slums of Colombo, and observing the hardship of people working in unimaginable conditions in Sri Lanka's factories, seeded his passion to dedicate his own life to uplifting such people. IofC was for him the place to put this passion into reality.

After 15 years of professional work as an IT consultant in Asia and Australia and an equal time spent committing himself on a voluntary basis to the IofC network, Bhagwandas felt prepared to respond to IofC's call to develop an active engagement platform to contribute to the moral renewal of global economics. It was out of that spirit that TIGE was born.

Bhagwandas can well be described as one of these rare, mature personalities where a strong inner moral compass is matched with a persistent, calm dedication to service through action. Guided by a strong rootedness in values and a deep spirituality, combined with a strong sense of duty and pragmatism, he brings clarity to the people and contexts he engages with. Frantic pace and agitation are alien for him, as much as the need to push himself to the front rows of life. Equipped with a strong presence, he acts more in the background, nurturing and mentoring the people working with him. In terms of Robert Greenleaf, Bhagwandas is a prototype of a 'servant leader'.[37]

Having worked in the ICT industry and as a business consultant for many years, Bhagwandas understands the implications of ICT on the economy, and in particular on the financial industry. For him, money, which originally was a means towards an end, has increasingly become a mere 'product' to be traded with, on newly created and rapidly expanding financial markets. He argues that the commoditisation of money may well be one of the core root causes of the crisis we face today. Responding to this crisis is for him a matter of moral renewal. For him, the biggest global challenge is a question of 'Trust and Integrity' at the core of the world's micro- and macroeconomic institutions.

Bhagwandas is convinced that processes of inner renewal on the individual if not also institutional level is so crucial, because the technological revolution allows not only for widespread participation in economic processes, but also gives individuals and small institutions enormous leverage. The more power is distributed into networks (politically and economically), the more important, so maintains Bhagwandas, becomes trust and integrity on an individual level. Thus 'Trust and Integrity in the Global Economy' came into being as a theme of a conference, platform and programme – inaugurated in the summer of 2007. Since its inception it has attracted, unlike usual business conferences and networks, not only corporate participants, but also students, academics, not-for-profit organisations, and simply people representing many walks of life – altogether interested in bringing about renewed or alternative economic practice.

Round 2 – Organisation: TIGE – Designed as a collaborative 'force for good' with regards to global economic renewal

It is important to see Bhagwandas not as an isolated driving force behind TIGE. He is supported by a team of energetic, young social innovators, by other Caux veterans, as well as by his wife Daya, an educator dedicated to the development of children with a profound interest in organisational and societal change. Bhagwandas and his wife first met at Caux and share the overall value base of IofC that gave rise to TIGE.

The collaborative design for the team behind TIGE was also a recognition that leadership would not any longer come primarily from few individuals likes Kaku, Philips and others, but would need to be understood in much more co-creative and collaborative terms.

Hence, from the beginnings of TIGE, the aim was to enlist and engage a new generation of young professionals and activists who would take leadership in a world that had been transformed by social networks and the information revolution.

It was equally clear from the outset that the focus could not only be on the industrial economy. For Bhagwandas and his team, there was no option but to move into a much more broad based focus on the global economy. Thus the initiative was launched to bring change around the interdependent issues of economy, environment, sustainability, food security and social enterprise – all based on inner transformation and personal commitment to core moral values.

But TIGE is not only a force for outer renewal. It also plays an important role in shifting existing boundaries within the larger IofC network. At a time in which many of the issues hitherto addressed by IofC are now addressed by a multitude of NGOs and other organisations, networks and initiatives all over the world, and in which the format of annual conferences alone became increasingly inadequate to deal with dynamically evolving burning issues, the overall organisational structure of IofC has become ripe for a new lease of life. A core challenge that IofC faces, from our integral perspective, is that of overcoming a still relatively centralised global structure, and an implicitly inbuilt 'Eurocentrism' within the movement, rooted in its historical legacy and which is still tangible despite its members' nationalities increasingly reflecting all corners of the world. IofC's current leadership is consciously working on these issues, but is facing, as occurs in any transformation process, also massive internal challenges. Thus, TIGE can also be seen as a spark of renewal within the overall IofC-world. As such, it actively deals with typical transformation patterns of resistance, frustration and transitional pain – a process that has not yet been concluded.

From its origins, TIGE saw itself as much more than a conference. It was its intention to also build a network of people with a passion for change, who can network with each other at a professional and personal level. The value proposition has been to create a core group across continents who share the same dream and belief that 'together we can make a difference to the world'. It seeks to provide a creative space for exploration, dialogue and positive action across all sectors of the global economy. And to a significant degree it has succeeded in doing so.

For Bhagwandas, TIGE aims to engage business people and decision-influencers in 'honest conversations' on the issues of globalisation and in relation to the human face of economics. With what purpose? TIGE's mission is to 'strengthen the motivations of care and moral commitment in economic life and thinking, in order to create jobs, correct economic and environmental imbalances and tackle the root causes of poverty'. It aims to encourage 'conscience-based decision-making leading to organisational change in business and economic life, at a time when integrity and trust are more than ever needed following the global banking and economic crises'.[38]

During the first five years of its existence, TIGE has exposed conference participants to a large number of enterprises, who are dedicated to act within society as a 'Force for Good' (⇨20) and to contribute to societal well-being at large. Much of TIGE's work was happening on an individual and organisational level. But gradually, TIGE also reached out to the societal level.

Round 3 – Society: Catalysing new macroeconomic thinking that foster societal wealth and well-being

Increasingly TIGE grew into a platform of change for society at large and various initiatives have been catalysed, shaped, evolved or initiated at TIGE. To name just three of the most recent examples that occurred at TIGE 2012; firstly, the celebration of the World Values Day, initiated during the conference by a group of Swedish social entrepreneurs; secondly, the birth of an Initiative on Integral Economy and Society in Slovenia; and thirdly, the launch of the New Wilberforce Alliance which seeks to 'free the world from the modern-day slavery caused by the culture of greed' by British banker Paul Moore. Though most of the initiatives are still at an early and fragile state, it is nevertheless remarkable to witness the level of activism coming out of TIGE.

Underlying its impact and future potential, Moore described TIGE as the real founder and mother of this emerging activist movement 'to free the world from the slavery of greed, with its addiction to excessive growth and consumption for the few and the consequential human misery and environmental destruction, that inequality causes, for the many'.[39]

Encouraging as these initiatives are, TIGE is increasingly conscious, that, after having laid a solid foundation over the first five years of its existence, that it needs to grow beyond conferences and networked processes in order to have a more sustainable impact on the moral climate of the global economy.

Our (Trans4m's) own cooperation with TIGE began exactly on this societal level at a time when the initiative became more intensely engaged with thinking about veritable alternatives to the current mainstream macroeconomic framework. Bringing our macroeconomic approach to Integral Economics (⇨21) as well as our prior work on the Integral Enterprise (⇨20) to the 'TIGE-Table', we discovered a natural 'match' between TIGE's focus on 'integrity' and our own integral work that allowed to conceptually articulate integrity within micro- and macroeconomic frameworks, content-bases and processes. As we began to cooperate, we became jointly aware that an authentic engagement with new macroeconomic theory and practice, including a substantiation of TIGE's work with regards to the impact of 'integrity' would require much more intense action-learning and action-research driven process. That brings us to the University of Life.

Round 4 – University of Life: Towards actualising TIGE's full potential

The challenge ahead, for TIGE, will be to fully actualise its potential to create a sustainable developmental-educational space – that enables individual growth as well as the theoretical and practical engagement with new macroeconomic frameworks on an ongoing basis.

In that regard, TIGE has taken encouraging steps. Through ever growing networks – supported by so-called 'meshworks', a social technology that promotes connections between individuals, ideas, interests, people groupings, structures, etc.[40] – TIGE seeks to create more permanent processes of change. Thereby, the initiative attempts to mimic the complex ecosystem of the global economy and to apply nature's way of creating in the human society (social biomimicry).

At the very heart of these more permanent processes is a young generation of social-innovators-to-be from all over the world. Four such leaders from the first batch of TIGE social innovators are: Joe Swann from UK, who went on to establish 'My Social Innovation' (MySI), a social enterprise that enables young people to set up and sustain their own social enterprises; Genevieve LeBaron, now a Postdoctoral Research Fellow at the University of British Columbia, passionate about bringing social transformation in the political economy; George Katito, a Zimbabwean researcher, committed to developing social frameworks based on African knowledge systems; and Tehmina Siganporia, now Head of Legal Department at the Karnataka High Court, India, seeking to address the social contradictions of Indian society through the integrity of Law.

Under the mentorship of Bhagwandas and other IofC veterans like Don de Silva, Head of Programmes of IofC UK, and others, the now second batch of young leaders co-creatively design and orchestrate the meshwork spaces and seek to stimulate an expanded and growing network of social entrepreneurs all over the world. Mexican social architect Juan-Carlos Kaiten, Indian developmental economist Rishab Khanna, Russian developmental economist Tatiana Sokolova, Swedish social entrepreneur Fredrik Hallberg and Australian environmental scientist, urban planner and film director Tom Duncan are just few of the major drivers from within the younger generation. Each of them pursues his or her own developmental projects in their respective countries: Kaiten as a developer of a 'Social Alchemy'-tool and orchestrator for dialogue spaces for sustainable development in Mexico; Khanna as an organisational innovator helping to bring about integral organisations – such as Om Creations and Sadhana School in Mumbai (⇨14) and applying the knowledge derived from TIGE to the Indian Youth Climate Network IYCN;[41] Solokova, who is currently completing her Masters in Sustainable Development at University of Uppsala, Sweden, has become the main person in charge of handling design and logistics for the annual TIGE conference from 2013 onwards; Hallberg is engaged in establishing ethical leadership in Sweden; and Duncan is driving the development of an ecovillage in Australia's New South Wales and simultaneously works on a film on 'Australia's Carbon Farmers'. Focusing on individual projects, and yet intensely connected across space and over the year, they see themselves as conveners of a physical-virtual 'University of Life', kept 'alive' through large-scale collaboration around major themes and across continents.

In the words of Kaiten:

> As humanity transitions towards a global society, opportunities and challenges have grown in equal magnitude. Severe, global depletion of ecosystems and social turmoil have initiated a widespread public response. If the many small actions were to connect and collaborate strategically, then a greater impact could be made on the system to move towards sustainability. Along with continuous technological and scientific development, society is discovering new ways of organising itself for a more just, sustainable and harmonious world. This is giving birth to a large social body that is becoming aware of its own existence and is learning to take its first baby footsteps.[42]

What seems to be important, though, is to significantly strengthen the action-research foundation on which these relatively loosely operating networks are working. They would enable TIGE to engage in processes that lead to new knowledge that can then authentically inform alternative economic realities. As in the case of Interface presented earlier in this chapter, such systematic and continuous action-learning-action-research-processes have the potential to frame conceptually new realities and develop new economic patterns. TIGE's task would be to enable such processes and link through them social innovators-to-be with enterprise that are on the cutting edge of creating new economic realities.

Catalysed through TIGE, we ourselves, through Trans4m, began to gradually engage in such processes. Initially, we interacted intensely with a small group of macroeconomic transformation agents that we met through TIGE. One of these transformation agents is educational specialist Darja Piciga – a member of the former Government Office of Climate Change, now senior expert at the Ministry of Agriculture and the Environment – who is employing an integral economic approach to national policy planning in Slovenia as well as to educational programmes that focus on sustainable economic development. At this stage, she is pursuing the application of the framework of Integral Economics to an 'Integral Green Economy in Slovenia'. In September 2011, her office submitted a strategy for the transition of Slovenia to a Low-Carbon Society by 2050 to public consultation. It provides a vision of Slovenia in 2050 as a highly integrated and inclusive society with business focusing on promoting sustainability through an enhanced quality of life and natural environment. The holistic feature of the Slovenian Low-Carbon Strategy is the result of several integrative processes in general policy planning and implementation as well as in relevant sectoral and cross-sectoral policies promoted over the past decade – linked to the strategic and programming exercises on EU (e.g. Lisbon strategy, EU 2020 strategy) and international levels (e.g. OECD Green Growth Strategy).[43] It is too early to say, whether this integral strategy finds acceptance – be it as a stand-alone document or by being incorporated into Slovenia's Development Strategy for the 2014 to 2020 period. However, it is being purposefully evolved as an 'Exit for Austerity' – in particular for Slovenia, but also as a role model for other relevant EU countries. Overall, it is an impressive example of aspired societal change, catalysed, at least in its initial phase, by TIGE.

Growing TIGE into a permanent developmental-educational, research and action space will be necessary to increase its future impact. The overall notion of such a University of Life – as a potential to be actualised by TIGE – could then also well inform the future evolution of IofC in general. When Egyptian paediatrician and educational reformer Omnia Marzouk became the new president of IofC International in 2011, she expressed the view: 'Nothing lasting can be built without a desire by people to live differently and exemplify the changes they want to see in society'.[44] This is truly the language of a University of Life.

Together with TIGE, we are currently experimenting with bringing university students, dedicated to transforming the global economy and the educational system underlying it, to TIGE – as an embedded part of their studies. In the summer of 2012, in cooperation with Da Vinci Institute in South Africa and TIGE, we brought a group of five of Da Vinci's South African Bachelor of Commerce students for two weeks to Switzerland. In the first week the students worked intensely with Trans4m on the Integral Economy and Integral Enterprise. In the process they developed a vision for transformational economic education in South Africa – calling it *Ithemba Lezwe*, a Zulu term meaning 'Hope of the Nation' – that they are now taking forward as a shared action-research project within their studies and into their local communities in South Africa. In the second week the students joined the TIGE conference, presenting their vision to participants and enriching it in the process. Da Vinci, TIGE and Trans4m now plan to deepen their cooperation, and bring students on a regular basis to TIGE. In such a networked fashion, TIGE actively influences educational processes in a transformative way – the South African case could well be developed into a role model for cooperation with other universities in future.

There remains a lot to do. But the case illustrates the potential that network-spaces like TIGE have, in particular when they are embedded in a supportive global network. Both, TIGE and IofC, if they actualised their full potential of driving widespread societal change, could grow – together with likeminded organisations – into catalytic forces for a fundamentally different economy. What is required though, from our integral perspective, is the enrichment of its value orientation ('East') and pragmatic strength ('West') with processes of knowledge creation ('North'), altogether rooted and responding to burning issues in local communities ('South'). That would make, as we see it, the ingredients of a veritable University of Life.

The concluding Table 22.3 sums up the Integral Development journey of TIGE, on its way towards such a University of Life.

Table 22.3   TIGE Trust and Integrity in the Global Economy

Integral Development	Towards a University of Life (summary)
Round 1: **Self-Development** Formative *Grounding*	*Mohandas Bhagwandas: Responding to the call of economic renewal* • Deeply influenced by early childhood experience of poverty • Uplifting people became his passion. He joined IofC, attracted by its motto 'first transform yourself, then transform society' • Guided by a strong rootedness in values and a deep spirituality, combined with a strong sense of duty and pragmatism, he brings clarity to the people and contexts he engages with • For him, the biggest global challenge is to infuse 'trust & integrity' at the core of the world's micro- and macroeconomic institutions
Round 2: **Organisational Development** Reformative *Emergence*	*TIGE: Designed as a collaborative 'force for good' with regards to global economic renewal* • 'Trust and integrity in the global economy' came into being (2008) as a theme of a conference, platform and programme • From the beginnings, the aim was to engage a new generation of young professionals and activists who would take leadership in a world transformed by social networks and the information revolution • It was TIGE's intention to build a network of people with a passion for change. The value proposition has been to create a core group across continents who share the same dream and belief that 'together we can make a difference to the world'. TIGE seeks to provide a creative space for exploration, dialogue and positive action across all sectors of the global economy
Round 3: **Societal Development** Newly normative *Navigation*	*Beyond TIGE: Catalysing new macroeconomic thinking that fosters societal wealth and well-being* • TIGE grew into a platform of change for society at large and many initiatives have been enabled or initiated by TIGE. Strong emphasis is given to issues related to ecology and sustainability – infusing the economy with life-affirming rather than life-destroying principles • TIGE was described as the real founder and mother of an emerging activist movement 'to free the world from the slavery of greed' • Encouraging as these Initiatives are, TIGE is conscious, that, after having laid a solid foundation, that it now needs to grow beyond conferences and networked processes in order to have a more sustainable impact on the moral climate of the global economy

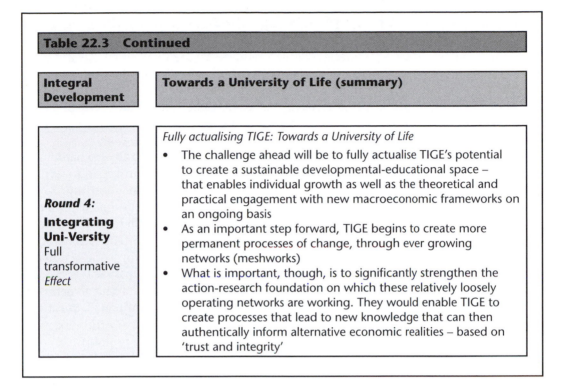

Table 22.3 Continued

Integral Development	Towards a University of Life (summary)
Round 4: **Integrating Uni-Versity** Full transformative *Effect*	*Fully actualising TIGE: Towards a University of Life* • The challenge ahead will be to fully actualise TIGE's potential to create a sustainable developmental-educational space – that enables individual growth as well as the theoretical and practical engagement with new macroeconomic frameworks on an ongoing basis • As an important step forward, TIGE begins to create more permanent processes of change, through ever growing networks (meshworks) • What is important, though, is to significantly strengthen the action-research foundation on which these relatively loosely operating networks are working. They would enable TIGE to create processes that lead to new knowledge that can then authentically inform alternative economic realities – based on 'trust and integrity'

We now turn to some other, briefer cases of global experimentation that not only add further flavour and scope to our would-be Universities of Life, but that only illustrate the wide range of global activities with regards to engaging with alternative, positive futures. Management philosopher Margaret Wheatley and her colleague Deborah Frieze call such creative new engagement in *Walk Out Walk On* 'life-affirming' actions;[45] for ecologist-activist Paul Hawken, these are the signs of what he coined *Blessed Unrest* – a growing collective of global initiatives and movements actively shaping a new world.[46]

SHORT WESTERN CASES OF CREATIVE EXPERIMENTATION TO SEED PRACTICAL POSITIVE CHANGE

Overview

Having read the prior two cases, you will have rightfully noticed, that by now there are many cases of creative experimentation taking place all over the world. Perhaps they are not always as systematic and impactful as Interface, or as globally oriented as the TIGE Initiative. But increasingly, we come across inspiring examples of new action-learning oriented experimental organisations, initiatives or movements that engage in testing and implementing new economic and political practices. As of now, many of such experiments happen almost spontaneously, often they are short-lived. There is a clear need to understand such attempts to create social laboratories better, in order to bring about social and economic change more widespread and more sustainably.

It is quite noticeable, that much of such experimentation has taken place in so-called 'Western' countries – from the US to Australia to Europe. Often, it has an individual touch to it, with one or few key entrepreneurial personalities driving the agenda. Also, regular, it has a focus on the development of new capacities, on co-creation with others or within networks and on making a tangible contribution. Often, we find a strong ecological orientation – or, in other words, a focus on 'life'. We could witness such a dual 'South-Western' orientation at Interface and at TIGE, and it is recognisable also in some of the short cases presented in the following.

In a few cases, such initiatives have resulted in the set-up of a new kind of experimental universities or in attempts for innovation from within existing universities. Typical changes that can be witnessed in such new or reformed educational institutions are related to, among other characteristics: a closer link of teaching to the pressing problems of our time; an interest of students to contribute to solving such problems; a redefinition of the teacher–student relationship into co-learners; more participatory educational style; and more transdisciplinary curricula. In rare cases, such as in classes of world-renowned integral philosopher and founder of the Global Dialogue Institute, Ashok Gangadean, based at Haverford College in the US, students are asked to explore and experiment with new ways of thinking. Gangadean, in promoting what he calls 'integral education', creates co-learning spaces in which participants learn to 'step back from the egocentric boxes of our discourse and thinking to become attuned to reality and to flourish'.[47]

Gangadean is also a leading exponent for an inner, more integral renewal of Liberal Arts education, dedicated to help building character and to raise consciousness on an individual level. Such a Liberal Arts education would then serve as individual foundation for collective transformation processes on a societal level. That requires, in the terms of Cardinal John Henry Newman and his educational classic on *The Idea of a University* (first published in 1873), the university to be a true 'Alma Mater' (from latin 'nourishing mother'), knowing her children one by one, rather than being a foundry, mint or treadmill.[48] Though liberal arts education has its roots in Europe, it had in the past decades almost exclusively associated with liberal arts colleges in the USA, Gangadeans's Haverford College being one of them.

Since the 1990s, however, we witness a gradual revival of liberal arts education in Europe, usually offered by so-called university colleges. Frontrunners were, together with the University College of Dublin, a couple of university colleges in the Netherlands, the first being the University College of Utrecht and the Roosevelt Academy Middelburg. Others followed, such as the Amsterdam University College and, in 2013, the Erasmus University College in Rotterdam. The Dutch impulse for revitalising liberal arts education was spearheaded by educational reformer and sociologist Hans Adriaansens who was frustrated with the large-scale climate of university education in the Netherlands, and sought to complement it through small scale and academically intensive undergraduate colleges.[49]

More recently, other university colleges or specific liberal arts bachelor programmes started to mushroom all over Europe, among them the University College of London, the University of Manchester, the ECLA European College for Liberal Arts (now fused with the American liberal arts college Bard) in Berlin and the University College of Freiburg.

In a nutshell, we can recognise many instances of such developments of the conventional notion of education – in the case of higher education traditionally hosted by universities – into a much more creative and experimental function of, simultaneously, education *and* development. In the course of that transformation, the conventional university is either required to reform itself accordingly (which for the time being does not happen), or – in the integral logic we are following – is complemented, perhaps long-term even substituted, by such new Universities of Life that are lodged in and deal with real life issues.

In that respect it is noticeable that Harvard Business School Professor Clayton Christensen, the world's foremost thinker on 'disruptive innovation', recently advocated in an article titled 'School of Life' the crucial importance of treating life as a school, a school which is more important than the formal educational achievements we gather:

> *The challenges your children will face serve an important purpose: they help them hone and develop their capabilities they need to succeed throughout their lives ... It's tempting for us to judge success by just looking at the nouns on a resume – it's like the scoreboard of what we have achieved. But much more important in the long run are the verbs in the resume – the courses we have taken as we go through the various schools of experience.*[50]

In the following we present a number of snapshots of how the increasing need for creative experimentation in order to bring about social innovation is increasingly articulated throughout society.

Gaia University: An 'un/learning' educational-developmental institution promoting an ecosocial economy

Gaia University, founded by Liora Adler and Andrew Langford, is a good showcase for a recently emerged educational laboratory. A 'decentralised university', it sees itself as 'an un/learning community for liberating intelligences and knowledge-making systems for the benefit of life on Earth'.

Its decision to be internationally rather than nationally accredited (by the International Management Centres Association), is a reflection of the university's belief that the core socioeconomic-environmental issues it is seeking to address, can't be confined to national borders and are of general interest for all humanity.

Strongly employing virtual communication tools and having established a vibrant e-learning environment, Gaia offers courses and diplomas, primarily geared to provide mentorship and guidance to students for their particular learning and action projects. To enable collaboration among associates, they are grouped in 'learning guilds' of three to five peers, for the time of their studies. Major themes within Gaia University's curricula range from Permaculture, Ecovillage Design, Peace Studies, Ecocities, Appropriate Technology, Traditional Wisdom, Eco-Health, Sustainable Economics, Bioregionalism, Life Transitions, Natural Building, Social Communication and the Art for Social Change[51] – all relevant for 'rebuilding infrastructure and institutions' as our core theme in this realm.

The university's mission mirrors not only the attempt to break down the institutional design of conventional universities, but also its aspiration to create new language, thinking and consequently new practice through developmental-educational processes:

Gaia University was founded to contribute significantly to growing a coherent global worknet of action-learning, open professionals working in full-spectrum guilds as integrative ecosocial designers, facilitators, and managers who are leaderfully engaged in a supported, synergistic web of all-scale, all-quadrant projects designed for human transformation towards ecological regeneration and social justice.[52]

As a self-declared 'un-institution', Gaia University seeks to support its students – called 'associates' – in realising their own projects with regards to bringing about positive social change. Primary focus on this journey is to unlock the transformation potential of the individual. As associates it attracts those who:

are likely to have a strong sense that learning and unlearning are critical activities in this liberation process and, if they are not already vigorous, confident, emotionally literate, self-directed and engaged learners who are also capable of designing and delivering effective world-changing action they are intent on developing these capacities as a priority'.[53]

Once associates have graduated, they are welcome to initiate their own 'unlearning school' – in association with Gaia University. Thereby, in 'open source' style, the university seeks to grow organically.

Gaia University derives its names from the British natural scientist James Lovelock's 'Gaia Theory'[54] that holds that planet Earth is a living organism, functioning on the principles of interconnectedness and interdependence. *Gaia* itself is an ancient name for 'Mother Nature' or the 'Nature Goddess' that can be traced back to the Minoan culture 7000 BC.

Building on this simultaneously ancient and modern concept of Gaia, the university's core objective is to drive the co-creation of sustainable livelihood. In its own words: 'A primary goal for Gaia University is to co-create, with myriad partners, a thriving ecosocial economy in which millions can make their livings independent of the current ecosocially destructive dominant culture'.[55]

Giordano Bruno Global Shift University: Promoting a whole life educational experience

Another example for a recently set up University of Life is the Giordano Bruno Global Shift University that seeks to promote a 'world renaissance' through 'whole life educational experiences'. Founded in 2011 by internationally renowned systems thinker and integral theorist Ervin Laszlo in close cooperation with the Club of Budapest, it regards itself as 'a humanistic online institution, committed to creating informed and ethical agents of change who bring a new consciousness, a fresh voice and up-to-date thinking to the global community, transforming obsolete paradigms and empowering the co-creation of an equitable, responsible and sustainable world'.[56]

Laszlo, one of the pre-eminent protagonists for a new integral, global paradigm, is, among about 75 other books, also the author of *World Shift 2012: Making Green Business, New Politics and Global Consciousness Work Together*[57] – a passionate plea for renewing global enterprise, economics and politics. He looks back on an impressive life story as a scientist and social philosopher, as well as an outstanding record of personal activism in response to major challenges of our time. In 1993, Laszlo, Hungarian by birt the Club of Budapest as an 'international association dedicated to developing of thinking and a new ethics that will help resolve the social, political, eco ecological challenges of the 21st century'.[58] In 2008, the Club of Budapest – a veritable 'Force for Good' – became integrated in the World Shift Network that continues to work for new ways for societal well-being. It is out of the individual initiative of Laszlo, and the supportive organisational environment of the Club of Budapest and the World Shift Network, that the Giordano Bruno University emerged. In a nutshell, hence, we can observe here the four-level trajectory that underlies this new university.

The university offers bachelor programmes in Business Administration, International Relations, Education, Psychology and History of Arts, among others, and a master's programme in International Business and in Human Rights. Students, however, who seek to enrol in any of the university's academic programmes, need to undertake first a three-months certificate course called 'Our World' – focusing on knowing the world, knowing oneself, and, finally, changing the world.

The holistic approach and laboratory character of the Giordano Bruno University is evident in particular in its approach to education:

> The University focuses not on traditional methods of education, but on a new pedagogy for this century that preserves cultural heritage and develops comprehensive knowledge. It also serves as a permanent laboratory to examine and update human thinking in order to produce professionals who are capable of transforming outdated dysfunctional structures. This vision requires building new and ever-evolving curricula and educational delivery systems that leverage the power and reach of digital tools to engage learners in self-learning through interdisciplinary collaboration in the framework of a horizontally integrated learning environment.[59]

Its innovative educational system, employing the most up-to-date pedagogical theories, is called 'Whole Life Educational Experience'. The approach is based on two primary philosophical and pedagogical pillars: inward (introspection) and outward (facing the world).

This Whole Life Education Experience is regarded as:

> the centrepiece of the operating system of the Giordano Bruno Global Shift University, because it will allow unifying and synthesising all of our educational fundaments, such as: a) General knowledge acquisition; b) Learning; c) Methodology; d) Professional Training; e) Specialisation; along with avant-garde ideas … in the framework of holistic and critical thinking.[60]

Facilitated through its Whole Life Education Experience Tool it aspires 'to generate social networks which engage students in dynamic interaction which promotes life-long connections across space and cultures'.[61] Like the Gaia University, the Giordano Bruno Global Shift University has a planetary perspective, reaching out to all humanity. Like Gaia University, it focuses on building capacity and character of individual 'change accelerators', though, like Gaia, collaboration among students and within wider networks is highly encouraged and facilitate. This focus on a global perspective, as well as the dual rhythm of 'individual initiative with a communal orientation' is a typical feature within this 'Western' realm.

Findhorn, Global Ecovillage Network, Gaia Education and beyond: Inspiring constellations promoting holistic education for sustainable living

The Findhorn Foundation, an ecovillage founded in 1962 by Peter and Eileen Caddy and their friend Dorothy Maclean on the north-eastern coast of Scotland, is one of the finest examples within Europe of a centre for practically based, holistic education, that grew organically out of a co-creative community experiment in conscious and sustainable living. According to our colleague Robin Alfred, CEO of Findhorn Consultancy Service, the Findhorn Foundation remains, 50 years after its founding, a thriving community and network:

> Recognised by the UN as an NGO in 1997, and awarded Best Practice designation by the UN Centre for Human Settlements in 1998, it welcomes over 2000 people a year to residential training courses, has developed into a bustling community of over 500 people and numerous small businesses, and is one of only 9 UN CIFAL centres worldwide – centres that train urban designers, planners, politicians and others in ways to build resilient communities.[62]

The by-now over 30 businesses that are part of the New Findhorn Association seek to apply Findhorn's sustainability principles into organisational practice.

The Findhorn Foundation College moreover, established in 2001, promotes a holistic and pragmatic approach to accredited training programmes that aspires to combine 'the best of mainstream education with experiential learning'.[63] Aiming to link inner growth with outer action, the College develops and offers a variety of courses in further and higher education and professional development that focus simultaneously on personal and spiritual development as well as on valuable life and work skills. Curricula draw directly on the experiential learnings from within the Findhorn community.

Findhorn is also an active member of the Global Ecovillage Network (GEN)[64] – a network to which also our cases Sarvodaya in Sri Lanka (⇨14) and Sekem in Egypt (⇨24) belong. The Findhorn College collaborates with GEN and Gaia Education, an internationally renowned designer and provider of education for sustainable development, in offering a 'Design for Sustainability' programme. This programme is based on Gaia Education's 'Ecovillage Design Curriculum' – an officially recognised contribution to the United Nations Decade of Education for Sustainable Development. Linking theory and practice, it draws 'on the experience and expertise developed in a network of some of the most successful ecovillages, community projects and research centres for carbon-constrained lifestyles across the Earth'.[65] The programme's guiding framework, developed by Gaia Education, is a sophisticated Mandala-shaped, holistic education model, centred around four core dimensions of sustainability: ecological, worldview, social and economic. At the centre of the Mandala lies 'Integral and Participatory Design'. This model is geared to promote 'healthful planetary evolution, as well as the well-being and quality of life of individuals and their communities everywhere' and is geared to 'exploring and expanding the perceived limits of human potential'.[66]

The cooperation of Findhorn, GEN, and Gaia Education, for us, is another impressive example that illustrates the increasing influence of such Universities of Life – designed as action-learning spaces that seek an immediate integration of sustainable principles into individual and organisational lives – hence promoting 'learning from life'.

The Integral Institute: Enabling humanity to live an integrated, good life

Ken Wilber, the foremost integral philosopher of our time (⇨19), has set up with a large number of eminent scientists and scholars the Integral Institute that takes forward the integral theory he has developed into a vast array of disciplines. 'The Institute's vision is that humanity lives with the awareness necessary to compassionately integrate the fragmented and partial perspectives of differing pursuits of the good life'.[67] The Integral Institute has a clear orientation to contribute to the solution of the world's most complex problems, primarily through research and educational programmes:

> Among the primary goals of the Institute are research and cultivation of leadership of complex, global issues facing humanity in the 21st century, and in particular, those issues that can only be solved with a comprehensive, Integral and non-partial approach to the complex interdependencies that tend to characterise these issues. Global warming; evolutionary forms of capitalism; and the culture wars in political, religious, and scientific domains are all examples of problems to which the Institute hopes to bring new clarity.[68]

The Institute has also made inroads into the conventional university arena, seeking to bring about change from within established institutions. By now, the John F. Kennedy University as well as the Fielding Graduate University, both based in California, offer Graduate Certificates and Master of Art Degrees, the first of its kind, fully dedicated to Integral theory and practice.

UN Decade for Education for Sustainable Development

Worthwhile to mention, on a global level, are certainly also the efforts of UNESCO as lead agency of the DESD 'UN Decade for Education for Sustainable Development' (2005 to 2014), seeking to mobilise the world's educational resources to build a sustainable future. For UNESCO (United Nations Educational, Scientific and Cultural Organisation), such education for sustainable development 'allows every human being to acquire the knowledge, skills, attitudes and values necessary to shape a sustainable future. Education for sustainable development means including key sustainable development issues into teaching and learning; for example, climate change, disaster risk reduction, biodiversity, poverty reduction, and sustainable consumption'.[69] A particular emphasis is given on 'participatory teaching and learning methods that motivate and empower learners to change their behaviour and take action for sustainable development'.[70] The clear intention is visible to turn educational programmes into catalytic seedbeds for active, positive change.

Much more experimentation on the global horizon

The Gaia University, the Giordano Bruno Global Shift University and the Integral Institute are just few remarkable examples of newly emerging Universities of Life. Looking closely, there are many other similar impulses around, many in a more emergent stage. These cases, together with our lead stories of Interface and TIGE enable us to distil now some core defining patterns of a University of Life.

22.3   Actualising the University of Life: Laboratory for Active Change

These newly emergent trends signal dramatic changes in the conventional university world. One development, that we are likely to witness much more in the near future, is a push to make universities more relevant for today's burning issues. Creative variations of the University of Life are likely to show up in multiple forms – focusing on new skills, relevant for our time, and on the evolution of ethical codes, that are resonant with sustainable life on the planet. Such Universities of Life will become important platforms to bring about new practices, large scale.

Universities of Life are of utmost significance. However, they are likely to primarily address the still relatively small 'species' of the 'global citizen' – inspired individuals with a global perspective who look for opportunities to learn and apply new skills for societal betterment. Universities of Life, hence, as a culmination of this 'Western' realm need to be complemented by 'Southern' Communiversities, 'Eastern' Developmental Universities as well as renewed 'Northern' Research Universities.

Why this is necessary, we have illustrated throughout this book. In the final chapters that follow, we shall summarise our core arguments, and introduce, as the climax of this book, the Integral University, which seeks to integrate all the above-mentioned new Uni-Versity types.

The University of Life itself can be described as a laboratory for creative experimentation and as an innovative, conducive space in which new individual, organisational and societal practices can be conceived of, tested and implemented.

Anyone advocating more balanced development processes is acutely aware of the difficulties involved in changing established living patterns – however harmful the existing ones may be. The still dominant modernist worldview is so all-pervasive that it requires enormous inner strength and outer efforts to develop alternative frameworks and implement new practices. What is needed, hence, are spaces of creative imagination and experimentation where we can systematically test, evolve and share new life practices.

As we have seen in the cases introduced, such a University of Life is not necessarily a formal entity. It can be anywhere, embedded in groups, initiatives, and organisations that feel the commitment to try out and practice new forms of life (of doing business, of doing politics, of living with nature, etc.) in a systematic way. It can, of course, but rather seldom is, also be part of a real university – as we witnessed in the examples of Gaia University or the Giordano Bruno Global Shift University.

We chose the term 'University of Life' for many reasons:

- It is embedded in the middle of 'real life' (such as, for example, within an enterprise or a movement).
- It is linked to a sincere and systematic attempt to study and understand what life is about, how it works, what we can learn from nature, and how we live in nature – as a part of it – without harming it. In that process, it takes life – and its natural patterns – as its principal teacher.
- It explores the particularity of human life, and how sustainable human systems can be created – from healthy relationships to living enterprises, from a life-affirming economy to a balanced political system.

- It enables 'whole life experiences' – equally valuing inner and outer experiences. It sees the human being and human systems holistically.
- Like nature, it is thriving on interconnectedness, co-creation and co-evolution. It sees itself as part of a living network of learning and action.
- It is – like nature – a space for experimentation and evolution. It is a social laboratory, active as a transformative force in society.

Though most of the cases we used would not consciously call themselves Universities of Life, we consider them qualified, based on the above-mentioned criteria. It is crucial that the experimental and transformational laboratories that they represent are studied in more detail, in order to be able to drive development processes more effectively. They are of enormous value not only for organisational learning, but for the sustainable development of entire societies.

While in natural sciences the laboratory is common currency, in the social sciences it is not. Rather, we notice a tremendous lack of such laboratories. This is hard to understand, given the daunting social and economic challenges we are facing worldwide, seemingly with ever increasing speed. We clearly need to find ways to embed such action-learning-driven social laboratories widely in society. They are spaces of intense learning and conscious evolution.

Of course, there are no standard designs or recipes to build them. As diverse, as the expressions of life are in general, so is the variety of this educational entity. And yet, based on the theory and practice shared in this 'Western' realm, we can extract useful patterns. The Table 22.4 below summarises core steps, highlighting how we can work towards the establishment of Universities of Life.

Table 22.4   Integral Development rhythm of the 'Western' realm

Main theme: Rebuilding infrastructure and institutions via enterprise and economics
Core value: Equitable and sustainable livelihoods

Round 1: **Self-Development** Formative *Grounding*	*Lead a full Life* As Integral Developer you seek to engage with the full reality of your development context. You are thereby not only concerned with outer Practice, but also with underlying institutional realities and knowledge disciplines, as well as philosophies, worldviews and deeply rooted cultural images – knowing that reality is created within and between these various reality-layers. You actively revisit and shape your own Life practice, seeking to embrace all aspects of a full, integrated life. You do so with the awareness that new organisational and societal realities need to be modelled and embodied by individuals that lead a fully integrated, sustainable life

Table 22.4   Continued

Main theme: Rebuilding infrastructure and institutions via enterprise and economics
Core value: Equitable and sustainable livelihoods

Round 2: **Organisational Development** Reformative Emergence	*Promote enterprise as a force for good* Continually, you explore how existing organisational designs can be evolved in order to turn your own organisation into a force for good. You are familiar with the most evolved enterprise designs – from social and societal enterprise, to social business, from eco-enterprise to integral enterprise. You contribute in turning the organisation into a creative laboratory, enabling it to become a thought and action leader with regards to social and technological Innovation, fostering sustainable development
Round 3: **Societal Development** Newly normative *Navigation*	*Enhance societal wealth and well-being* Fully aware of the history of conventional economic and political development, you and your organisation (or community) have derived tangible clues for a new approach to socioeconomic development – based on your own formative-individual and your enterprise's reformative-organisational experiences. Such a new approach goes beyond mere economic growth, but is oriented towards overall societal wealth and well-being. You and your organisation (or community) practically contribute to the evolution of alternative approaches to healthy economic and political practices, and see yourself as well your organisation and community as active development agents to bring about an Integral Society.
Round 4: **Integrating Uni-Versity** Full transformative *Effect*	*Fully actualise the 'Western' realm through a University of Life* These new developmental norms and practices are institutionalised via a veritable social laboratory that enables their systematic testing, evolution and implementation. Such a 'University of Life' is lodged in the very heart of 'real life' and is embedded within your organisation, movement, community, or initiative. It focuses on action-learning, builds capacities and forms and requires character and courage. New processes, products, services and practices are continuously developed and tried out – all with a view to societal betterment. Courses for individual students are not in the foreground: rather, the University of Life provides a continuous platform for interactive processes that result in the co-creation of equitable and sustainable livelihoods Thereby existing economic and political infrastructure and institutions are gradually transformed, bottom-up

22.4   Integration: Integral Development as Equitable and Sustainable Livelihoods

INTEGRATING THE 'WESTERN' ROUND 4

We have learned in this final round about the need to evolve a potent 'developmental vehicle' out of the first three rounds, that facilitates the interconnection of the development journeys experienced for self, organisation and society. In this 'Western' case we called such a transformational entity a 'University of Life'. Use the following summarising Table 22.5 to reflect back on this fourth and final round of the 'Western' realm and note your own thoughts and prospective actions in order to bring about a University of Life.

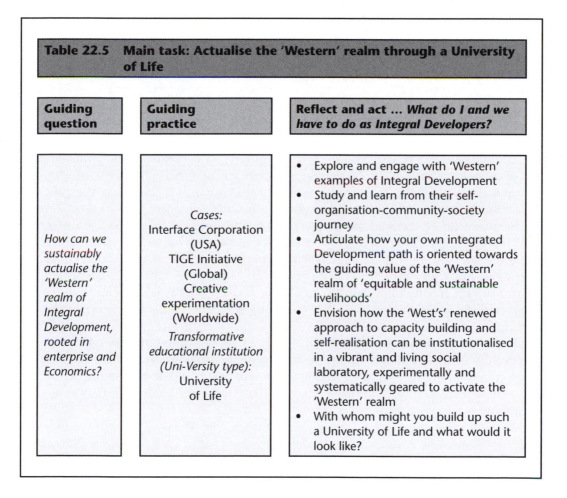

Table 22.5   Main task: Actualise the 'Western' realm through a University of Life

Guiding question	Guiding practice	Reflect and act ... *What do I and we have to do as Integral Developers?*
How can we sustainably actualise the 'Western' realm of Integral Development, rooted in enterprise and Economics?	*Cases:* Interface Corporation (USA) TIGE Initiative (Global) Creative experimentation (Worldwide) *Transformative educational institution (Uni-Versity type):* University of Life	• Explore and engage with 'Western' examples of Integral Development • Study and learn from their self-organisation-community-society journey • Articulate how your own integrated Development path is oriented towards the guiding value of the 'Western' realm of 'equitable and sustainable livelihoods' • Envision how the 'West's' renewed approach to capacity building and self-realisation can be institutionalised in a vibrant and living social laboratory, experimentally and systematically geared to activate the 'Western' realm • With whom might you build up such a University of Life and what would it look like?

INTEGRATING THE FULL 'WESTERN' REALM

We are now ready to conclude this 'Western' realm of Integral Development. Over the course of the past four chapters you have worked yourself progressively through the four levels of self (Round 1), organisation (Round 2), community-and-society (Round 3), and, finally, through integrated educational-and-developmental practice (Round 4). In the fourth round, you were presented with the case stories of Interface Corporation in the USA and the TIGE Initiative that operates globally, as well as with an array of short cases embodying the creative experimentation that takes place in order to practically renew this 'Western' realm, through, ultimately, a University of Life.

We have started out this 'Western' realm – in the introduction of Chapter 19 (Round 1) – with an explanation that we approach enterprise and economics and the realm's core developmental theme of 'Rebuilding Infrastructure and Institutions' in a totally new way. We have not, as it is conventionally the case in development theory and practice, started out on the macro, societal level. Rather, we have reconfigured enterprise and economics from the bottom-up. Enterprise and economics are the most outwardly oriented dimensions in development, and we maintain that fundamental changes on the societal level (Round 3) require, for and foremost, new approaches to individual (Round 1) and organisational (Round 2) life practice. Changes in Round 1 and 2 can then, as we have shown, influence new business practices and economic frameworks and policies on a societal level. All cases presented emphasised the highly experimental nature of this journey through the three rounds. Hence, we have argued that there is a need to create spaces for experimentation within society – embodied in, what we call, 'Universities of Life'. Such universities would then act as action-learning oriented social laboratories and as invaluable seedbeds for widespread societal transformation.

The image of the University of Life requires us to dramatically broaden any conventional understanding of a university that we may still cling to – though the Communiversity (⇨10), the Developmental University (⇨14) and even the renewed Research University (⇨18) have already significantly widened our take on how a university could and should function. The University of Life now takes the university fully out of the conventional logic of buildings, classrooms, courses and exams, but takes the individual and organisational challenges that we face in real life in the very centre for our learning and action. A University of Life is learning from life, it is seeking to affirm, sustain, nurture and contribute to life; and it is designed for continuous 'life-long' learning and development – always linking reflection and action, always open for experimentation and co-evolution.

In the concluding Figure 22.2 we take you once more through the full journey of the 'Western' realm: we indicate the main developmental tasks of each round; we provide an overview of the core thinkers and practitioners that illustrate the nature of each of the four rounds; and we summarise the core developmental challenges that you, your organisation and your community face in each round.

As in all of the four realms, the journey through this 'Western' integral realm is not to be understood in linear fashion. However, the composite view on the four successive rounds, and the large variety of relevant thinkers and practitioners, is designed to help us as Integral Developers to build, step by step, new (individual, organisational and societal) infrastructure and institutions strong enough to implement sustainable micro- and macroeconomic as well as balanced sociopolitical practices.

Having journeyed together through the 'Southern', 'Eastern', 'Northern' and, now, the 'Western' realm – with each realm culminating in an educational institution that is designed to leverage that realm's particular development contribution – we are arriving at our final destination. In the following, concluding chapters we seek to pull all the threads

REBUILDING INFRASTRUCTURE AND INSTITUTIONS VIA ENTERPRISE & ECONOMICS
Releasing the Gene-ius of the 'western' integral Realm of Action

Your Development Calling & Challenge	MAIN TASK	GUIDING THEORY GUIDING PRACTICE	LEARNING AND DEVELOPMENT PROCESSES FOR INTEGRAL DEVELOPMENT – AGENT & AGENCY
Round 1: Self Development *Formative Grounding*	**LEAD A FULL LIFE**	**Co-Creating Full Realities** (Lessem / Schieffer) **The Integral Life** (Wilber et al)	• Surface the full Reality of your Development Context: from Images to Ideologies, from Institutions to Inclinations and explore how you can simultaneously work with all four Levels of the Development Topography • Map yourself, your Context, Issue(s) and Capacities in Wilber's integral Quadrants and discover Development Possibilities, Tasks and Obstacles • On a personal Level, engage with Integral Life Practice, and name your Development Tasks towards an Integral Life (Sustainable Livelihood)
Round 2: Organisational Development *Reformative Emergence*	**PROMOTE ENTERPRISE AS A FORCE FOR GOOD**	**The Renewal of Enterprise** (Global Compact, Yunus et al) **The Integral Enterprise** (Lessem / Schieffer)	• Illustrate, how latest Developments towards the Renewal of private Enterprise, together with Social Business and other emergent Enterprise Forms have enriched the Design and Scope of your Organisation • Show how your Organisation creates innovative Laboratory Spaces geared towards continuous Improvement of Products, Services and overall organisational Design, with regards to Sustainable Development • Explore how your own Organisation can be transformed into an Integral Enterprise and thereby into an authentic Agent for Development in Society
Round 3: Societal Development *Normative Navigation*	**STIMULATE SOCIETAL WEALTH AND WELL-BEING**	**Does Marx Still Matter?** (Harvey) **The Integral Economy** (Lessem / Schieffer) **Towards the Integral Society** (Goerner)	• Describe your Community's and Society's current Approach and Future Vision to economic Development. How is it linked to the other Realms? • Engage critically with Marx and explore to what Degree his Perspective can enrich your Approach to Economic Development • Surface with the help of Integral Economics how your own Community and Society contribute to a new, sustainable Macro-Economy • Show how your Development Context applies Collaboration to bring about an Integral Society (Learning Communities in a Learning Universe)
Round 4: Integrating Uni-Versity *Transformative Effect*	**GIVE RISE TO A UNIVERSITY OF LIFE**	**Cases:** Interface Corporation (USA) TIGE-Initiative (Global) Creative Experimentation (Worldwide) **UNIVERSITY OF LIFE**	• Explore & engage with 'western' Examples of Integral Development • Study and learn from their self-organisation-community-society Journey • Articulate how your Development Path is oriented towards the guiding Value of the 'western' Realm of 'equitable & sustainable Livelihood'? • Envision how the 'West's' renewed Approach to Capacity Building and Self Realisation can be institutionalised in a vibrant and living social Laboratory, experimentally and systematically geared to activate the 'western' Realm? With whom might you build up such a 'University of Life' and how would it look like in your Case?

G E N E

Figure 22.2 Releasing the gene-ius of the 'Western' realm

of Integral Development together, culminating in the Integral University as the main institutional vehicle for full-fledged Integral Development (⇨25).

References

1   Mani, R. (2011). Creation amidst Destruction: Southern Aesthetics and R2P. In: Mani, R. and Weiss, T.G. (eds), (2011). *Responsibility to Protect: Cultural Perspectives in the Global South*. London: Routledge, p. 122.

2   Lessem, R. and Schieffer, A. (2010). *Integral Economics: Releasing the Economic Genius of Your Society*. Farnham: Gower.

3   Hawken, P. (1994). *The Ecology of Commerce: A Declaration of Sustainability*. New York: HarperBusiness.

4   Anderson, R. (1998). *Mid-Course Correction: Toward a Sustainable Enterprise: The Interface Model*. White River Junction, VT: Chelsea Green.

5   Carson, R. (2002). *Silent Spring*. Boston, MA: Mariner.

6   Gore, A. (2006). *Earth in the Balance: Ecology and the Human Spirit*. Emmaus, PA: Rodale.

7   Meadows, D. (1993). *Beyond the Limits: Confronting Global Collapse, Envisioning a Sustainable*. White River Junction, VT: Chelsea Green.

8   Daly, H. and Cobb, J. (1994). *For the Common Good: Redirecting the Economy toward Community, the Environment, and a Sustainable Future*. Boston, MA: Beacon.

9   Anderson, R. (1998). *Mid-Course Correction: Toward a Sustainable Enterprise: The Interface Model*. White River Junction, VT: Chelsea Green.

10 McDonough, W. and Braungart, M. (2009). *Cradle to Cradle: Remaking the Way We Make Things*. New York: Vintage.

11 Hymas, L. (2009). Green-biz pioneer Ray Anderson says Sustainability literally pays for itself. In: *GRIST* (www.grist.org), 19 October 2009.

12 Ray C. Anderson Foundation website. Available at: www.raycandersonfoundation.org / Accessed: 2 October 2012.

13 Interface press release (July 2012). *Interface Backgrounder: EcoMetrics® and SocioMetrics™ at the Core of Tracking Interface, Inc.'s Advancement toward Sustainability*. Atlanta, GA: Interface.

14 Interface Backgrounder (2011). *EcoMetrics® and SocioMetrics™ at the Core of Tracking Interface Inc.'s Advancement towards Sustainability*. Internal Document (accessible through Interface's Sustainability Unit), p. 1.

15 Interface Press Release (July 2012). *Interface Backgrounder: EcoMetrics® and SocioMetrics™ at the Core of Tracking Interface, Inc.'s Advancement toward Sustainability*. Atlanta, GA: Interface.

16 Interface Backgrounder (2011). *EcoMetrics® and SocioMetrics™ at the Core of Tracking Interface Inc.'s Advancement towards Sustainability*. Internal document (accessible through Interface's Sustainability Unit), p. 2.

17 Interface Corporation website. Available at: www.interfaceglobal.com / Accessed: 2 October 2012.

18 Ray Anderson, Interface Chairman and Sustainability Leader Dies at 77. In: *Environmental Leader* (www.environmentalleader.com), 9 August 2011.

19 Anderson, R. (2009). *Confessions of a Radical Industrialist – Profit, People Purpose: Doing Business by Respecting the Earth*. New York: St. Martin's Press.

20 Anderson, R. (Spring 2004). Nature and the Industrial Enterprise. In: *Engineering Enterprise*. Alumni Magazine for IsyE. Atlanta, GA: Georgia Institute of Technology.

21 Benyus, J. (2002). *Biomimicry: Innovation Inspired by Nature.* New York: Harper Perennial.

22 Meezan, E. (2012). Conversation with Erin Meezan (15 October 2012).

23 Meezan, E. (2012). Conversation with Erin Meezan (15 October 2012).

24 Meezan, E. (2012). Conversation with Erin Meezan (15 October 2012).

25 Robèrt, K.-H. (2002). *The Natural Step: Seeding a Quiet Revolution.* Gabriola Island, BC: New Society Publishers.

26 Toffles, M., Eccles, R. and Taylor, C. (2011). *InterfaceRAISE: Sustainability Consulting.* Internal Case Study (N9-611-069). Boston, MA: Harvard Business School.

27 Meezan, E. (2012). Conversation with Erin Meezan (15 October 2012).

28 Lev, B. and Schwartz, A. (1971). On the Use of the Economic Concept of Human Capital in Financial Statements. In: *The Accounting Review*, Vol. 46, Issue 1.

29 Emerson, R.W. (1836). *Nature.* Boston, MA: James Munroe and Company.

30 Richardson, R.D. (1995). *Emerson: The Mind on Fire.* Berkeley, CA: University of California Press, p. 155.

31 Ray C. Anderson Foundation website. Available at: www.raycandersonfoundation.org / Accessed: 27 September 2012.

32 Ray C. Anderson Foundation website. Available at: www.raycandersonfoundation.org / Accessed: 27 September 2012.

33 Initiatives of Change International website. Available at: http://www.iofc.org/en / Accessed: 5 November 2012.

34 Initiatives of Change website. Available at: http://www.caux.iofc.org/en/network-history / Accessed: 4 November 2012.

35 Lean, G. (1988). *Frank Buchman.* London: Fount, pp. 30f.

36 Initiatives of Change website. Available at: http://www.caux.iofc.org/en/node/61706 / Accessed: 5 November 2012.

37 Greenleaf, R. (2002). *Servant Leadership: A Journey into the Nature of Legitimate Power and Greatness.* 25th Anniversary Edition. Mahwah, NJ: Paulist Press.

38 Caux Initiatives for Business (2012). *Report on the Fifth Annual Conference on Trust and Integrity in the Global Economy.* Caux: Initiatives of Change, p. 3.

39 Caux Initiatives for Business (2012). *Report on the Fifth Annual Conference on Trust and Integrity in the Global Economy.* Caux: Initiatives of Change, p. 11.

40 Beck, D. (2000). *Meshworks – A 2nd Tier Perspective and Process.* Available at: http://www.integratedsociopsychology.net/meshworks-perspective-process.html / Accessed: 4 November 2012.

41 Khanna, R. (2010). *Trust and Integrity in the Global Economy: How Can It Be Applied?* TIGE internal document. 15 October 2010. Caux: Initiatives of Change.

42 Kaiten, J.C., Niederhumer, S. and Stonehouse, K. (2010). *Large Scale Collaboration towards Strategic Sustainable Development.* Karlskrona: School of Engineering Blekinge Institute of Technology, p. 1.

43 Piciga Darja website. Available at: www.dpiciga.com/trajno1.html / Accessed: 4 November 2012.

44 Initiatives of Change International website. Available at: http://www.iofc.org/en / Accessed: 5 November 2012.

45 Wheatley, M.J. and Frieze, D. (2011). *Walk Out Walk On: A Learning Journey into Community Daring to Live the Future Now.* San Francisco, CA: Berret-Koehler.

46 Hawken, P. (2008). *Blessed Unrest: How the Largest Social Movement in History Restores Grace, Justice and Beauty to the World.* London: Penguin.

47   Bronson, M.C. and Gangadean, A. (2012). Circling the Square: Redesigning Integral Education Discourse through Deep Dialogue. In: *ReVision*, Vol. 18, Issue 2, p. 2.

48   Newman, J.H. (1996). *The Idea of a University*. Republished within Rethinking the Western Tradition series. New Haven, CT: Yale University Press.

49   Tak, H. and Oomen, B. (eds) (2012). *De Disciplines Voorbij: De Colleges van Hans Adriaansens*. Liber Amicorum voor Hans Adriaansens. Middelburg: Roosevelt Academy.

50   Christensen, C. (2012). School of Life. In: *HBS Alumni Bulletin*, September 2012, p. 49–51.

51   Brunk, T. (2012). An Educational Paradigm for Global Regeneration: Gaia University. In: *Permaculture Activist*. Available at: www.permacultureactivist.net / Accessed: 6 October 2012.

52   Gaia University website. Available at: www.gaiauniversity.org / Accessed: 5 October 2012.

53   Gaia University website. Available at: www.gaiauniversity.org / Accessed: 5 October 2012.

54   Lovelock, J. (2000). *Gaia: A New Look at Life on Earth*. Oxford: Oxford Paperback.

55   Gaia University website. Available at: www.gaiauniversity.org / Accessed: 5 October 2012.

56   Giordano Bruno University website. Available at: www.giordanobrunouniversity.com / Accessed: 5 October 2012.

57   Laszlo, E. (2009). *World Shift 2012: Making Green Business, New Politics and Global Consciousness Work Together*. Rochester, VT: Inner Traditions Bear and Company.

58   Club of Budapest website. Available at: www.club-of-budapest.org/ Accessed: 5 October 2012.

59   Giordano Bruno University website. Available at: www.giordanobrunouniversity.com / Accessed: 5 October 2012.

60   Giordano Bruno University website. Available at: www.giordanobrunouniversity.com / Accessed: 5 October 2012.

61   Giordano Bruno University website. Available at: www.giordanobrunouniversity.com / Accessed: 5 October 2012.

62   Alfred, R. (2012). *Holistic Leadership*. Unpublished paper. Findhorn: Findhorn Consultancy Service.

63   Findhorn Foundation website. Available at: www.findhorn.org/workshops/college / Accessed: 15 October 2012.

64   Global Ecovillage Network website. Available at: http://gen.ecovillage.org / Accessed: 16 October 2012.

65   Findhorn Foundation website. Available at: www.findhorn.org/workshops/college / Accessed: 15 October 2012.

66   Gaia Education website. Available at: www.gaiaeducation.org / Accessed: 15 October 2012.

67   Integral Institute website. Available at: www.integralinstitute.org / Accessed: 7 October 2012.

68   Integral Institute website. Available at: www.integralinstitute.org / Accessed: 7 October 2012.

69   UNESCO website. Available at: www.unesco.org / Accessed: 6 October 2012.

70   UNESCO website. Available at: www.unesco.org / Accessed: 6 October 2012.

PART VII

Unity in Diversity: Fully actualising Integral Development via the Integral University

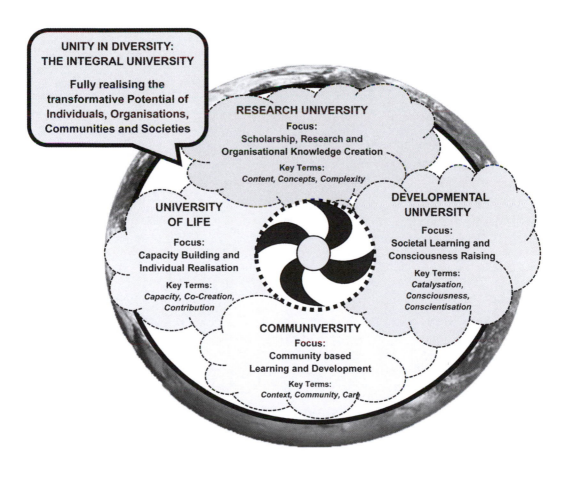

23 We Have Come a Long Way!: Reviewing the Integral Development Journey

Guiding Question: What are the main learnings from the Integral Development journey?

23.1   Orientation: The Grounds Covered

We have come a long way!

We have travelled the entire Integral Development terrain. We have covered all four realities and realms. We have rhythmically journeyed through individual, organisational and societal development. And we have engaged with new types of universities, each actualising one of the four realms.

We have understood the terrain of Integral Development. But we have yet, in this final part of the book, to co-create a new entity that is able to fully institutionalise Integral Development.

Before we come to this culminating task, we need to consolidate, in this review, upon the Integral Development journey.

23.2   The Integral Development Journey: A Full Review

RETRACING OUR STEPS: BUILDING UP INTEGRAL DEVELOPMENT

We began our journey by arguing that the current development crisis is not only a crisis within the discipline of so-called development studies and/or in the political and economic practice of development (⇨1). Rather, the overall ineffectiveness of current development theory and practice, as lamented by a large number of renowned international development thinkers and practitioners, is merely one of many symptoms of a profound civilisational crisis humanity as a whole is facing. We illustrated with the help of those critical thinkers and practitioners that humanity is in a transition phase from a modernist, rational, monocultural, capitalist paradigm towards a new evolutionary stage. During this transition time – which, according to the leading American sociologist Immanuel Wallerstein, may well last for another few decades – humanity will have to deal with massive disruptions, on all levels. While some thinkers hold that the direction and outcome of such a new evolution is totally unknown, there are a growing number of social philosophers articulating the rise of an Integral Age. Indeed, all over the world, we can notice attempts to develop more integrated, holistic and balanced perspectives – within scientific disciplines, within various domains of life and within organisations. Local and global movements are promoting ecological balance, sustainable development, gender equality, social justice, cultural unity in diversity, religious dialogue within and in between religious (and non-religious) belief systems, equitable livelihoods, inter- and transdisciplinary forms of knowledge creation, peaceful co-evolution of nations and civilisations and more. All these initiatives seek to bring about a more integrated approach, overcoming the highly fragmented and unequal state of our current world.

In the process, the predominant dualistic thought-and-action pattern of the modernist era – which also underlies the distinction between 'developed' and 'developing' societies – begins to dissolve. We can witness globally a rising awareness that this current evolutionary phase is not any more engaged in 'tweaking' existing systems, but rather points towards something fundamentally new.

In a thorough analysis of past and present development discourses (⇨2) we surfaced major disintegrating patterns. We subsequently (⇨3) suggested a set of integrative orientations that would need to be included in a new more integrated approach to development, serving to overcome the destructive impact of the existing one. In doing so, we laid the foundation for our approach to Integral Development, building on our prior work on Integral Community, Enterprise, and Economics, Integral Research and Dynamics.

We then shared with you the above integral body of work we have evolved over the past decades, following in the footsteps of the founding mothers and fathers of integral thinking. At the core of our work, which we see contributing to this new era, is our so-called 'Integral Worlds' model (⇨4). The particular contribution we make through it lies in its overall transformative approach to specific cultural contexts. Thereby we work transculturally with diverse reality perspectives, bring a wide range of knowledge fields to the transdisciplinary table, and engage, transpersonally, individuals, organisations, communities and societies. Together with a growing international network of co-researchers, as well as with educational and research institutions, we continue to evolve the Integral Worlds approach, as well as its numerous local and global applications across many social science disciplines.

The generic Integral Worlds approach, as we then illustrated, is also the foundation of the specific approach to Integral Development introduced in this book. We demonstrated its ability to address major shortcomings of past and current development work (⇨5).

The four main elements of the Integral Development approach, drawing from our overall 'Integral Worlds' approach, are what we called the '4Rs': Realities, Realms, Rounds and Rhythms. These four constituents are dynamically and interactively interwoven. Their meaning is recapitulated in Table 23.1 below.

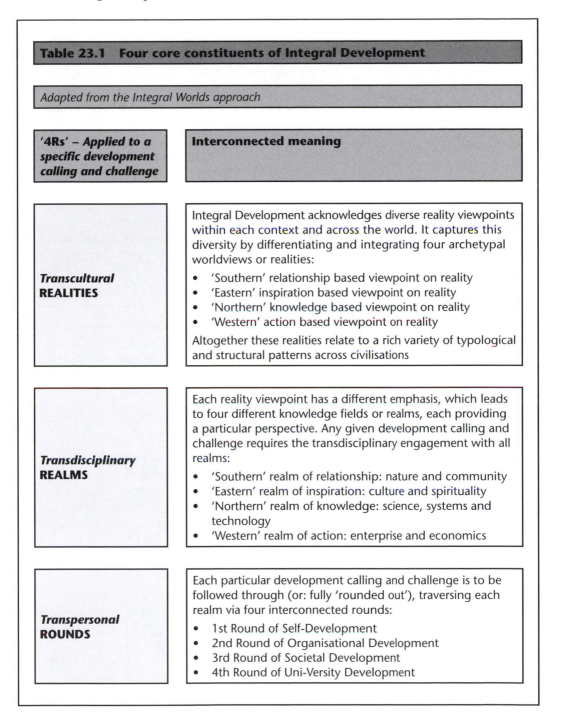

Table 23.1 Four core constituents of Integral Development

Adapted from the Integral Worlds approach

'4Rs' – Applied to a specific development calling and challenge	Interconnected meaning
Transcultural REALITIES	Integral Development acknowledges diverse reality viewpoints within each context and across the world. It captures this diversity by differentiating and integrating four archetypal worldviews or realities: • 'Southern' relationship based viewpoint on reality • 'Eastern' inspiration based viewpoint on reality • 'Northern' knowledge based viewpoint on reality • 'Western' action based viewpoint on reality Altogether these realities relate to a rich variety of typological and structural patterns across civilisations
Transdisciplinary REALMS	Each reality viewpoint has a different emphasis, which leads to four different knowledge fields or realms, each providing a particular perspective. Any given development calling and challenge requires the transdisciplinary engagement with all realms: • 'Southern' realm of relationship: nature and community • 'Eastern' realm of inspiration: culture and spirituality • 'Northern' realm of knowledge: science, systems and technology • 'Western' realm of action: enterprise and economics
Transpersonal ROUNDS	Each particular development calling and challenge is to be followed through (or: fully 'rounded out'), traversing each realm via four interconnected rounds: • 1st Round of Self-Development • 2nd Round of Organisational Development • 3rd Round of Societal Development • 4th Round of Uni-Versity Development

Table 23.1	Continued

Adapted from the Integral Worlds approach

'4Rs' – Applied to a specific development calling and challenge	Interconnected meaning
Transformational RHYTHMS	Realities (worldviews), realms and rounds are altogether aligned with and are hence subject to fourfold transformational rhythms: • 'Southern' formative and grounding (G) • 'Eastern' reformative and emerging (E) • 'Northern' (newly) normative and navigational (N) • 'Western' (fully) transformative and effecting (E) These rhythms stimulate and enable dynamic and interactive processes towards authentically addressing the development calling and challenge at hand. They are designed to release the GENE-ius of a particular self, organisation, community and society

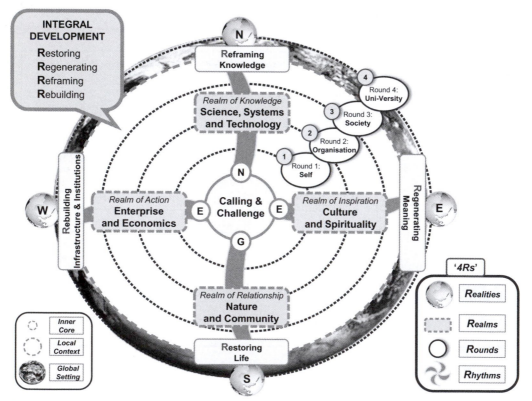

Figure 23.1 The Integral Development model

The interactive and dynamic engagement of all '4Rs' with a specific, central development calling and challenge, lodged within a particular local context and global setting, is reflected in the circular, integral framework of Integral Development (Figure 23.1).

Having laid out the full architecture of the Integral Development model, we then introduced (⇨6) you to the full terrain of Integral Development, including compass and travel maps. We now briefly revisit the Integral Development terrain.

THE INTEGRAL DEVELOPMENT TERRAIN

Each reality viewpoint informs a specific realm or knowledge field. Each of the four realms is underpinned by a particular theme. For example, the main development theme underlying the 'Southern' realm of relationship with its perspectives of nature and community is expressed as 'restoring life in nature and community'. Then, each realm contributes to the realisation of a specific guiding value reflecting the full potential of the realm. For example, the 'Northern' realm of knowledge with its perspectives of science, systems and technology is underpinned by the value of 'open and transparent knowledge creation'. These main themes and core values, summarised in the following Table 23.2, inform the integral journey.

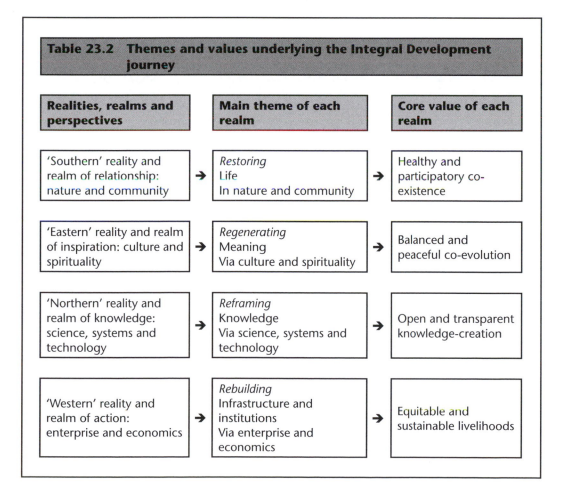

Table 23.2 Themes and values underlying the Integral Development journey

Realities, realms and perspectives	Main theme of each realm	Core value of each realm
'Southern' reality and realm of relationship: nature and community	*Restoring* Life In nature and community	Healthy and participatory co-existence
'Eastern' reality and realm of inspiration: culture and spirituality	*Regenerating* Meaning Via culture and spirituality	Balanced and peaceful co-evolution
'Northern' reality and realm of knowledge: science, systems and technology	*Reframing* Knowledge Via science, systems and technology	Open and transparent knowledge-creation
'Western' reality and realm of action: enterprise and economics	*Rebuilding* Infrastructure and institutions Via enterprise and economics	Equitable and sustainable livelihoods

In order to fully actualise the potential of the four realities and realms, we as Integral Developers need to gradually engage with all four rounds of individual, organisational, societal, and Uni-Versity development, dynamically led by the Integral Development rhythms that we introduced earlier.

With these four rounds (self-organisation-society-Uni-Versity) rhythmically associated with each of the four ('Southern', 'Eastern', 'Northern' and 'Western') realities and realms, we came up with a travel map in a matrix form that encompasses 16 fields, that is four rounds and rhythms for each of the four reality viewpoints and realms (⇨6). We subsequently engaged with each field through a separate chapter in this book (⇨7 to 22). In each of the 16 chapters we introduced a guiding question, stimulating reflection and action around the particular development calling and challenge at hand. At the end of each chapter we provided a table, summarising the guiding question, core thoughts or cases, together with a set of developmental tasks, designed to spur further reflection and action.

As we jointly moved through the Integral Development terrain, the developmental tasks in each realm always started with your individual round, to then successively round out, as it were, organisation, society and Uni-Versity in turn. While you may have started this journey on your own, you would thereby be guided to gradually engage your particular context – concretely with a group, organisation, community and society.

Your Development Calling & Challenge	SOUTH Restoring Life in Nature & Community	EAST Regenerating Meaning via Culture & Spirituality	NORTH Reframing Knowledge via Science, Systems & Technology	WEST Rebuilding Infrastructure and Institutions via Enterprise & Economics
G Round 1: Self Development *Formative Grounding*	KNOW YOUR SELF AND YOUR CONTEXT	EMBARK ON THE JOURNEY OF THE SELF	ENGAGE IN TRANSDISCIPLINARY LEARNING AND RESEARCH	LEAD A FULL LIFE
E Round 2: Organisational Development *Reformative Emergence*	BUILD AN ECO-SYSTEMIC ORGANISATION	FOSTER ORGANISATIONAL CO-EVOLUTION	BRING ABOUT ORGANISATIONAL KNOWLEDGE CREATION	PROMOTE ENTERPRISE AS A FORCE FOR GOOD
N Round 3: Societal Development *Normative Navigation*	EMBED DEVELOPMENT IN COMMUNITY AND SOCIETY	CATALYSE EVOLUTIONARY STAGES IN SOCIETY	BUILD A KNOWLEDGE AND NETWORK SOCIETY	STIMULATE SOCIETAL WEALTH AND WELL-BEING
E Round 4: Integrating Uni-Versity *Transformative Effect*	GIVE BIRTH TO A COMMUNIVERSITY	ENABLE THE EMERGENCE OF A DEVELOPMENTAL UNIVERSITY	ESTABLISH A REFRAMED RESEARCH UNIVERSITY	GIVE RISE TO A UNIVERSITY OF LIFE

Figure 23.2 Integral Development: Summary of main tasks

Furthermore, in each realm we linked theory and practice. While on the first three rounds (self, organisation and society) we focused primarily on relevant theory, in the final round we emphasised the integration of that theory through new practice. We illustrated such new practice through inspiring case stories from all over the world. Each of these cases, however, embodies not only an integrated organisation or community, it also represents a new educational-developmental space, that we coined a 'Uni-Versity'. We argued, that for each integral reality and realm to be fully actualised, such new Uni-Versities would need to be established. Why? Because such institutionalisation would then promote the development of new Integral Development theory and practice in a way that it can be 'universally' shared, while at the same time being lodged in a particular context. Without such a conscious articulation through a Uni-Versity, the danger is that the particular knowledge and consciousness generated in a given case as well as its practice would not developmentally inform and transform society at large. That has been our repeated experience.

Figure 23.2, on the previous page, shows the Integral Development Map with its 16 fields. While at the beginning of the journey, when we introduced the travel maps (⇨6), the fields were filled with specific questions and with an indication of the guiding theory and practice provided in the underlying chapters, at this summary stage of our journey we present the major developmental task in each field. Thereby, this culminating map provides you with the core challenges of the full Integral Development journey.

How then do we travel through the Integral Development terrain, engaging with its major tasks, ultimately actualising the transformative potential of self, organisation and society?

TRAVELLING FROM SELF TO UNI-VERSITY AND FROM SOUTH TO WEST, BOTTOM-UP AND INSIDE-OUT, FOREVER SPIRALLING AND CYCLING

In journeying through the integral terrain, we cannot help but notice the complementarity along horizontal lines (e.g. the line of organisational development from a 'Southern', 'Eastern', 'Northern' and 'Western' perspective) as well as along vertical columns (e.g. 'Eastern' individual, organisational, societal and ultimately Uni-Versity development). Though development per se is far from being linear, we propose, however, a gradual purposeful evolution from self to society and then Uni-Versity, as well as from 'South' to 'West'. Why?

Firstly, because we see Integral Development as a means of 'empowering' you to engage meaningfully and effectively with development, following your own calling and challenge. Such 'empowerment' involves first getting to know yourself and to deeply understand the personal developmental tasks and capacities on Round 1. We thereby seek to avoid projecting our own development needs on others. Then, having a better understanding for ourselves – including our true callings and challenges, our development capacities and needs – we gradually transcend the individual perspective and begin a journey of co-development with relevant others, including a relevant group, organisation, community and society. We thereby take personal responsibility for Integral Development and take to heart the famous quote attributed to Mahatma Gandhi: 'Be the Change you want to see in the World'.

Secondly, by pursuing the four rounds from self to Uni-Versity, we also contribute to rebuilding organisations, community and societies, bottom-up. From the very beginning, you are invited to make a tangible contribution, within your concrete context, around your calling and challenge. The starting point of development is no longer a development policy but a shift of consciousness on the individual level, that 'trickles up' – as opposed to the much evoked but never realised 'trickling down' of global wealth into local contexts. Conventional development is thereby literally turned on its head. It is not delegated any longer to remote governments or anonymous development institutions. Rather it begins, 'here and now', with 'you and me'. At the same time, we recognise that 'you' without 'me', and abstracted from a particular cultural and societal context, will never lead to Integral Development.

Thirdly, by moving 'South' to 'West', we avoid overlooking the hitherto much neglected relational and inspirational dimensions of development. In more precise terms, local nature and community and local-global culture and spirituality have often been sidelined as intangible, and hence irrelevant. In Integral Development we not only acknowledge the relevance of the more intangible, inner and implicit dimension of development embodied in the 'South' and 'East', we even make it the starting point of the development journey. That may not always be necessary, but with the 'South' and 'East' being excluded for so long, we see the need to make purposeful efforts to strongly emphasise these two reality viewpoints, until we have arrived at a healthy, dynamic balance between these two worlds and the more tangible, outer and explicit worlds of the 'North' and the 'West'. In that sense, we suggest we travel purposefully 'inside-out', from self to society, and from 'South' to 'West'. From our experience, such 'inside-out' development also serves to strengthen the first point of getting to know ourselves (from within) before engaging with outer development.

Fourthly, such bottom-up and inside-out Integral Development orientations provide a useful structure for consciously engaging with development – at least initially. The more you individually and collectively know your terrain, the more you can then design your very own travel paths within – and beyond – it.

That brings us to a final point. Ultimately, the development journey is to be understood as a cyclical and forever spiralling process. Though, for reasons of communication, we have translated the Integral Development terrain into a two-dimensional matrix, we invite you to always refer back to the original cyclical model (Figure 23.1) which provides a much better sense for the co-evolutionary, dynamic, cyclical, spiralling and networked patterns that underlie every natural and human system – and hence also every development process. The matrix map is a helpful tool for us to consciously engage with the multitude of development tasks. But it is certainly not to be understood in a static and linear manner.

To fully actualise Integral Development we now turn to the new educational-development entities we have marked out. These are the spaces where an ever-deeper understanding of how Integral Development works needs to be cultivated – in theory and practice. We see these Uni-Versity spaces as immensely important, as we see them as the loci of authentic development. Case stories on their own may inspire and certainly do some good. But they usually don't provide the crucial educational and developmental real-life contexts and consciousness, structures and processes that we need to bring about the new. It is for this reason that we now turn in some more detail to these Uni-Versities that ultimately embody our journey.

23.3 Towards Actualising Integral Development: Four New Uni-Versities

EDUCATION AS THE ULTIMATE STARTING POINT IN ALL CASES: AN IMPORTANT OBSERVATION TO BEGIN WITH

All cases introduced in this book serve not only to illustrate the more integrated forms of development in theory and in practice. They have also created new types of educational-developmental entities that we call Uni-Versities. In analysing these cases, we have made an interesting observation. In literally all of them we discovered already in the first individual round of the developing self a profound affinity to learning and education that then, in turn, strongly informed the organisational and societal rounds that followed, albeit not necessarily consciously. Almost all of them experimented in the course of their 'all-round' development journey with various forms of education. For example:

- Paul Chidara Muchineripi (PhD) and Steve Kada (PhD) from Chinyika, Zimbabwe, joined our master's programme on Social and Economic Transformation and subsequently our PhD programme on Integral Development. In the course of this programme, they brought food security (master's programme) and an alternative community economic development approach (PhD programme) to Chinyika and other Zimbabwean Communities (⇨10). Both of them had been in education before, Chidara as a management developer, Steve as a school teacher, social worker and organisational developer.
- A.T. Ariyaratne (PhD), the founder of Sarvodaya, is a former high school teacher who invented the Shramadana Process as a new form of participatory action learning and designed Sarvodaya as a whole as a learning initiative. His son Vinya Ariyaratne (PhD), a medical doctor and passionate teacher, now heads up the initative and strongly supports the evolution of the Sarvodaya Institution for Higher Learning into a full-fledged Uni-Versity (⇨14).
- Radhike Khanna, the founder of Om Creations, laid the foundation for her learning organisation for mentally challenged women in a PhD on Special Education (⇨14).
- Father Don Jose Maria Arizmendi, an avid learner and philosopher himself, started first a Polytechnic School that then became the seedbed for the Mondragon Corporation and later for Mondragon University (⇨18).
- Ray Anderson, the founder of Interface, who loved sports and learning from early childhood (he grew up 'with a ball in one hand, and a book in the other'), turned his entire enterprise into an experimental learning organisation, recruited a so-called 'Dream Team' of internally renowned learning guides assisting the organisational transformation towards sustainability and founded a university chair of Natural Systems (⇨22).

What we are coming around to, is that the Uni-Versities they originated had already implicitly been seeded at a relatively early age. This seed had then, in the course of their particular development journeys, been further nurtured. We argue that this particular 'educational and research seed' is often overlooked. There is a tendency to distinguish between thinkers and doers, between academics and practical innovators. Many of us like to think that the people behind outstanding entrepreneurial or developmental cases are rather those who dismiss education and turn solely to practice.

Back to 'either/or'? While such cases certainly exist, we argue that behind profound social innovations are people that managed to bring both worlds together. Hence: 'both/and', if not 'both and more'!

This is an important insight. The fact that many of today's systems (enterprise, economics, finance, development, etc.) have become dysfunctional may contribute to the fact, that fundamental renewal requires the simultaneous development of new theory and new practice. As today's conventional universities are not fulfilling this crucial task – by being often hopelessly out of touch with their society's most burning issues – there is an urgent need to bring about new forms of universities and to transform existing ones. That is exactly what we have done in the fourth round of Integral Development.

However, we have to say that there is a bit of a twist to this developmental-educational tale. In revisiting the journeys undertaken by the visionary leaders and educators in our model cases, there is one major limiting factor. While most of them simultaneously inaugurated development together with research and educational activities, they did so without conscious awareness of how the latter processes were antithetical to those they themselves underwent as part of their prior, formal education. So by the time they came to play an instrumental part in developing such Uni-Versities out of their prior developmental enterprises, they all too often fell educationally back on old, tried and tested ways, which at least in part undermined their developmental objectives.

It is here where Integral Development purposefully takes their journey on, in articulating four new types of universities that are able to institutionalise such new development theory and practice more purposefully. Given the important role that they have to play in the future, we shall now revisit them in some more detail.

RENEWING OUR UNDERSTANDING OF UNIVERSITIES: FOUR NEW UNI-VERSITIES AS CRUCIAL CATALYSTS FOR INTEGRAL DEVELOPMENT

Overview

Throughout the book we have illustrated that each of the four realities and realms culminates in one particular Uni-Versity type, after having progressively covered the rounds of individual, organisational and societal development. Such a Uni-Versity is designed to institutionalise diverse self-organisational-societal developmental impulses through an educational institution that can then serve to make the newly derived development theory and practice universally accessible. The gradual local build-up of such Uni-Versities could then result in a global network of such institutions. Together, they can have a powerfully integral developmental impact on the world at large, with each staying in touch with the particular community and society it is serving. Each Uni-Versity is:

- a 'uni-que' educational-developmental expression of an actualised developmental journey;
- 'uni-ting' individual, organisational and societal development;

- 'uni-versalising' new development theory and practice through making it institutionally accessible for the world – though remaining in 'uni-on' with its particular local and societal ground out of which it emerged;
- responding in a locally relevant and resonant way to particular developmental callings and challenges, while simultaneously contributing to global development – thereby nurturing a world of 'uni-ty' in 'di-versity', locally and globally.

Each of these four Uni-Versities actualises the full potential of a particular realm, and hence serves to contribute significantly to the realisation of the realm's core value. Table 23.3 shows all four Uni-Versity types in an overview.

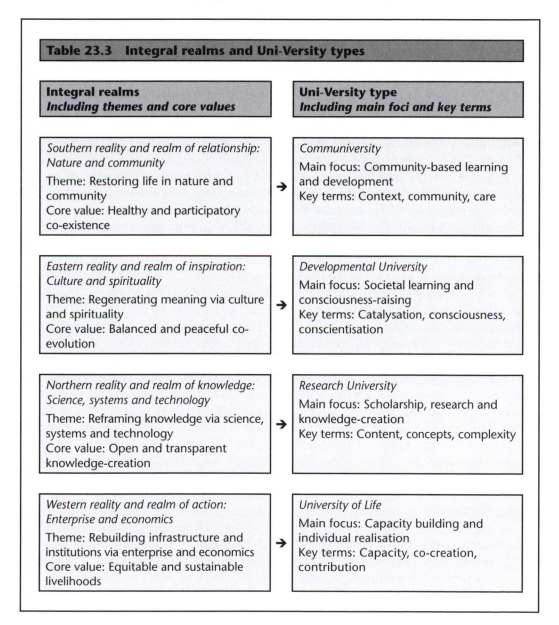

Table 23.3   Integral realms and Uni-Versity types

Integral realms *Including themes and core values*	Uni-Versity type *Including main foci and key terms*
Southern reality and realm of relationship: *Nature and community* Theme: Restoring life in nature and community Core value: Healthy and participatory co-existence	*Communiversity* Main focus: Community-based learning and development Key terms: Context, community, care
Eastern reality and realm of inspiration: *Culture and spirituality* Theme: Regenerating meaning via culture and spirituality Core value: Balanced and peaceful co-evolution	*Developmental University* Main focus: Societal learning and consciousness-raising Key terms: Catalysation, consciousness, conscientisation
Northern reality and realm of knowledge: *Science, systems and technology* Theme: Reframing knowledge via science, systems and technology Core value: Open and transparent knowledge-creation	*Research University* Main focus: Scholarship, research and knowledge-creation Key terms: Content, concepts, complexity
Western reality and realm of action: *Enterprise and economics* Theme: Rebuilding infrastructure and institutions via enterprise and economics Core value: Equitable and sustainable livelihoods	*University of Life* Main focus: Capacity building and individual realisation Key terms: Capacity, co-creation, contribution

As you engaged with all of them in the course of the book, you have noticed that only one of the four types shows strong similarities with the conventional university, as we know it, which is the 'Northern' Research University. However, we maintain that even such a Research University needs to be fundamentally reframed in order to fully actualise the 'Northern' realm and to authentically embody 'open and transparent knowledge creation' – as opposed to mere knowledge assimilation. Such 'reframing' takes scholarship, research and knowledge creation out of their rather narrow, abstract perspectives and links them to relevant communal and societal development needs and capacities. Indeed, this is the very essence of the research and educational programmes we at Trans4m have developed; these programmes are underpinned by developmental trajectories spanning fundamental research and transformative action.

Moreover, we discovered that for each Uni-Versity to be fully actualised it not only needs to build on the three prior – individual, organisational and societal development – rounds within its own realm; it also needed at least some connection to the three other Uni-Versity types.

With this in mind, we now turn to each one of them to distil its major features.

Southern Communiversity: Focus on community-based learning and development

The 'Communiversity' (community + university) represents the culmination of the 'Southern' realm of relationship. It is a deeply contextualised research-and-education platform with a primary focus on communal learning and development, both within the institution and outside it. This platform serves to catalyse intensive processes of communal learning, through which communities reclaim their full problem-solving potential. The cases of Chinyika in Zimbabwe as well as globally operating First Peoples Worldwide (⇨10) have been the prominent 'Southern' cases introduced. A Communiversity can be articulated as 'village learning centres' or as community-based programmes that draw purposefully on local, indigenous knowledge systems and build on the 'vitality' of a particular place to activate the full potential of a given community.

At the heart of the Communiversity is a 'healing component' to restore the relational fabric within a community – required to release its participatory potential – and of the community to its natural environment. Chinyika's revitalisation started with a community gathering on Chinyika rock, a place of great ancestral significance, and it focused, at least in its initial phase almost exclusively on the re-introduction of finger millet as the core source of nourishment. In the case of First Peoples Worldwide, we are reminded of its 'Keepers of the Earth Program' that evokes the important role that indigenous people have to play as guardians of our natural habitat and of wisdom sources, enabling humanity to engage in 'healthy and participatory co-existence' between people and with the planet. The restoration of relationship in all its connotations – to oneself, among members of community, to other communities, to nature, to 'inner nature', etc. – is crucial to tap the developmental potential of a community and all its members. We argue, that such 'restoration of life in nature and community' as the central theme of the 'Southern' realm is equally relevant for a Zimbabwean rural community like Chinyika, as for a Greek urban community in Athens. Table 23.4 below provides an overview on core aspects of the Communiversity.

Table 23.4 'Southern' Communiversity

Restores life in nature and community
Contributes to healthy and participatory co-existence

- Focus:
  - Deeply contextualised research-and-education platform with a primary focus on communal learning and Development/serves to catalyse intensive processes of communal learning, through which communities reclaim their full problem-solving potential
- Structures and Processes:
  - Institutional form: community learning centre
  - Research and learning programmes: ongoing participatory programmes building on Indigenous knowledge systems
  - Socioeconomic foundation: community-based enterprises and livelihoods
  - Governance structures: community-based governance systems
  - Accreditation processes: community-based procedures, ceremonies, rituals
- Atmosphere and Ambience:
  - Attribute: heart/emotional intelligence/interpersonal and intrapersonal intelligences
  - Sound/music: heartbeat/strong earthy rhythms/Indigenous music
  - Instrument: drums/human body
- Required Qualities of Integral Developer:
  - Ability to observe, empathise and care
  - Ability to face reality: to describe things as they are, not as one wants them to be
  - Ability to deeply immerse oneself in a particular natural and communal context
  - Ability to relate to other human beings/ability to tune into the relational level of existence (including relationship to yourself; relationship with others, in groups, organisations and communities)
  - Ability to strongly relate to and care for nature and to see relationship and interrelatedness as core principles in nature
  - Ability to 'look deep' underneath the Surface, to see the generative grounds of a particular context
  - Trust and love
- Suggested Symbol:
  - Web of life within a circle – representing life and the interdependency of all life, framed in one huge web/the circle alludes to the original oneness of all life, underlying all of creation

Eastern Developmental University: Focus on societal learning and consciousness-raising

The Developmental University embodies the culmination of the 'Eastern' realm of inspiration and its cultural and spiritual perspectives. A Developmental University transcends the level of an individual, organisation and community and has its main focus on societal learning and consciousness-raising. Indeed, it acts as a veritable catalyst for the evolution of societal consciousness, and thereby taps strongly into the cultural and spiritual sources of a society. In that process it renews the cultural grounds of a society and contributes to the 'regeneration of meaning' as the main theme of the 'Eastern' realm. For our case studies, we drew on Sarvodaya in Sri Lanka as well as on Om Creations and Aravind in India (⇨14). Sarvodaya is the case with the largest scope. Over the past 50 years it engaged in 'the awakening of all' (the translation of the term *Sarvodaya*), which comprised individual and community, societal and global development. While it has not yet set up tangible university structures and systems, it is, however, embodying in an impressive manner a Developmental University, being embedded in about 15,000 villages within Sri Lanka. While Sarvodaya deals with a wide range of developmental issues, Om Creations and Aravind in India each focus on one core issue: Om Creations on mentally challenged women and their inclusion in India's society, and Aravind on overcoming 'unnecessary blindness' and the integration of blind people into society. Through their respective engagement with hitherto excluded minorities into society – be it poor rural dwellers, ethnic minorities, mentally challenged women, or blind people – all these three Developmental Universities catalytically contribute to raise consciousness, or, in Paulo Freire's term, to *conszientise* society. Addressing imbalances, they foster a more 'balanced and peaceful co-evolution', the core 'Eastern' value, in between the diverse groupings of society. In all of three cases we found, despite their large-scale outreach into society, a strong rootedness in one or more particular communities, thereby exhibiting also strong elements of a Communiversity. Indeed, we argue that such a link needs to be present, at least to some degree, to ensure the sustained relevance of a Developmental University for local communities. Table 23.5 below provides an overview on core aspects of the Developmental University.

Table 23.5   'Eastern' Developmental University

Regenerates meaning via culture and spirituality
Contributes to balanced and peaceful co-evolution

- Focus:
  - Catalyst for societal learning and consciousness-raising/taps strongly into and renews the cultural and spiritual sources of a society
- Structures and Processes:
  - Institutional form: community education infrastructure and institutionalised community network (e.g. Sarvodaya)
  - Research and learning programmes: serving to interconnect individual, organisational, communal and societal development
  - Socioeconomic foundation: social rehabilitation, employment creation, community finance and social innovation centres
  - Governance structure: energising hub and self-governing communities
  - Accreditation: model villages and/or communities/community evaluation schemes

Table 23.5   Continued

Regenerates meaning via culture and spirituality
Contributes to balanced and peaceful co-evolution

- Atmosphere and Ambience:
  - Attribute: spirit (supported by heart)/spiritual intelligence
  - Sound/music: stillness or spherical sounds/sounds of emergence/contemplative music
  - Instrument: harp/flute/bell
- Required Qualities of Integral Developer:
  - Listening (picking up the implicit messages behind the explicit ones)
  - Reflective, intuitive and pattern-seeking mind
  - Will and ability to grow in consciousness
  - Ability to enter unknown, unfamiliar spaces
  - Ability to engage with the cultural and spiritual dynamics of a particular place
  - Ability to question and to let go of some of one's own convictions and beliefs
  - Openness for surprising Insights and for emerging patterns of culture
  - Ability to co-evolve with others, and to be a catalyst for the evolution of others
  - Ability to envision and to imagine the new, emerging dialectically out of the old
  - Faith in oneself and in others
- Suggested Symbol:
  - Spiral of conscious co-evolution – represents regeneration and renewal of the cultural and spiritual dimension in humans and society

Northern reframed Research University: Focus on scholarship, research and knowledge creation

The integrally reframed Research University represents the culmination of the 'Northern' realm of knowledge. It is focused on scholarship, research and knowledge creation aiming – simultaneously – for social and technological innovation. Natural sciences are neither dominating, nor are they subordinated to the social sciences – and humanities are restored to their rightful place alongside social and natural sciences. For such a resurrected Research University reconnects to Humboldt's original vision and appreciates education as 'inner-directed' and as a process of constant personal –as well as, in our case, organisational – (trans)formation. Knowledge is not regarded as static, but as continuously and dynamically unfolding. Research is seen as an 'art form' fostering the originality of the researcher (and hence his/her potential to innovate).

The cases in point that we introduced in this book are firstly Mondragon University that grew out of the Polytechnic School founded by Arizmendi, which then became the seedbed of Mondragon Corporation. Constituted as a cooperative, Mondragon University serves the members' cooperatives of Mondragon, and aspires to be a catalyst for social innovation, alongside technological innovation. Our second case, the prospective foundation of a new University for Africa – in which we ourselves are involved alongside co-researchers from Nigeria, Zimbabwe and South Africa – illustrates how a transdisciplinary and transformational PhD process (analogous to Arizmendi's Polytechnic School) can serve as the seedbed for a new type of Research University. Such a reframed Research University, then, is not to be seen as an isolated innovation in the education and research field. Rather, with their particular orientation towards content, concepts and complexity, they are to be understood as complementary forces to the 'Southern' Communiversity and the 'Eastern' Developmental University. Table 23.6 below provides an overview on core aspects of a reframed Research University.

Table 23.6 'Northern' Research University

Reframes knowledge via science, systems and technology
Contributes to open and transparent knowledge creation

- Focus:
  - Focused on scholarship, research and knowledge creation aiming – simultaneously – for social and technological Innovation/understands education as 'inner-directed', and as a process of constant personal (trans)formation/knowledge is not regarded as static, but as continuously and dynamically unfolding/research is seen as an 'art form' fostering the originality of the researcher
- Structures and Processes:
  - Institutional form: knowledge-creating university
  - Research and learning programmes: transdisciplinary programmes combining social sciences, natural sciences and the humanities to promote innovation
  - Socioeconomic foundation: public and private research funding/student fees
  - Governance structures: academic departments/innovation networks
  - Accreditation: individual achievement awards (e.g. academic degree, scientific ladder)/centres of excellence
- Atmosphere and Ambience:
  - Human organism/attribute: mind/intelligence (supported by spirit and heart)
  - Sound: symphony/complex, highly structured music
  - Core instruments: symphony orchestra
- Required Qualities of Integral Developer:
  - Conceptual and analytical strength
  - Ability to share knowledge in the context of teamwork
  - Ability to translate strong cultural images into concepts and theories
  - Ability to deal with complexity
  - Some playfulness/ability to let go of useless thoughts
  - Intellectual explorer, adventurer of the mind
  - Ability to articulate and communicate new thoughts
- Suggested Symbol:
  - Grid of knowledge – represents intelligent, structure-seeking and organising processes of knowledge creation

The University of Life: Focus on capacity building and individual realisation

The University of Life embodies the culmination of the 'Western' realm of action. The University of Life itself can be described as a laboratory for creative experimentation, and as an innovative, conducive space in which new individual, organisational and societal practices can be conceived of, tested and implemented. It represents new ways of learning and mirrors the growing desire for developmental-educational spaces that deal, hands-on, through action learning and action research with the burning issues societies are facing.

Universities of Life are:

- embedded in the middle of 'real life' (such as, for example, within an enterprise or a movement);
- linked to a sincere and systematic attempt to study and understand what life is about, how it works, what we can learn from nature, and how we live in nature – as a part of it – without harming it;
- enablers of 'whole life experiences' – equally valuing inner and outer experiences, seeing the human being and human systems holistically;
- thriving, like nature, on interconnectedness, co-creation and co-evolution. They see themselves as part of a living network of learning and action;
- like nature, spaces for experimentation and evolution. They are social laboratories, active as transformative forces in society.

With Interface in the USA and the global initiative TIGE, we introduced two cases that illustrated the diverse expression a University of Life can take (⇨22). In both cases though – the one an enterprise dedicated to sustainable development, the other a conference-initiative-movement focusing on re-establishing trust and integrity in the global economy – we could sense the urgency and immediacy to deal with their respective issues of concern, hands-on, life-centred.

Creative variations of the University of Life are likely to show up in multiple forms – focusing on new skills, relevant for our time, and on the evolution of ethical codes, that are resonant with sustainable life on the planet. Such Universities of Life will become important platforms to bring about new practices, on a large scale.

Such a University of Life is not necessarily a formal entity. It can be anywhere, embedded in groups, initiatives, and organisations that feel the commitment to try out and practice new forms of life (of doing business, of doing politics, of living with nature, etc.) in a systematic way. It can, of course, but rather seldom does, express itself as a real university – as we have seen in the examples of Gaia University or the Giordano Bruno Global Shift University (⇨22).

Universities of Life are therefore richly variegated in nature and scope. However, as we illustrated, they are likely to primarily address the still relatively small 'species' of the 'global citizen' – inspired individuals with a global perspective who look for opportunities to learn and apply new skills for societal betterment. Universities of Life, hence, need to be complemented by 'Southern' Communiversities, 'Eastern' Developmental Universities as well as renewed 'Northern' Research Universities. Table 23.7, on the next page, provides an overview of core aspects of a University of Life.

Table 23.7 'Western' University of Life

Rebuilds (human) infrastructure and institutions via enterprise and economics
Contributes to equitable and sustainable livelihoods

- Focus:
  - Laboratory for creative experimentation/an innovative, conducive space in which new individual, organisational and societal practices can be conceived of, tested and implemented/represents new ways of learning and enables to deal, hands-on, through action learning and action research with the burning issues societies are facing
- Structures and Processes:
  - Institutional form: experimental and network- and/or enterprise based living laboratory (e.g. Interface)
  - Research and learning programmes: action-learning-action-research processes
  - Socioeconomic foundation: self-financing/volunteerism
  - Governance structures: initiative-driven learning-and-enterprise-networks
  - Accreditation: project-based evaluation of business-and-community-impact
- Atmosphere and Ambience:
  - Human organism/attributes: hand (supported by mind, spirit and heart)
  - Sound/music: jazz (exploring new patterns; co-creating new structures)
  - Instrument: jazz combo (clarinet, saxophone, cello, etc.)
- Required Qualities of Integral Developer:
  - Ability to team up with others
  - Ability to translate knowledge into capacities, and capacities into action
  - Strong project management skills
  - Ability to construct an appropriate form to fulfil a specified Function
  - Focus and determination to make a tangible contribution
  - Stamina and willingness to face and overcome obstacles on the way
  - Strong communication skills
  - Humility to see one's own work share as a contribution to a larger project
- Suggested Symbol:
  - Arrow of integrated action: represents focus, goal-oriented, co-creative realisation of a new Development impulse through actively building new infrastructure and institutions

Outlook: Where do we go from here?

For all of the Uni-Versity types that we introduced in this book, the following applies:

- Each can serve to complement, if not altogether reform, the existing educational system of a society.
- Each is primarily an authentic articulation of one particular reality and realm, applied to successive rounds, following an integral rhythm.
- Each thereby carries to some degree the other realms within itself (e.g. Sarvodaya with its strong emphasis on evolution derived out of its cultural-spiritual perspective, is also strongly focusing on community needs). Hardly any of the cases we introduced is

purely and only representing one particular type, but they each embody a particular emphasis.

The final point alludes to a 'holographic representation' whereby each Uni-Versity type carries already in embryonic form the totality of all other types. If we look at it from an evolutionary perspective, we see all four Uni-Versities as authentic, but partial expressions of a larger, not yet fully visible totality. In other words, we envision the full integration of the Communiversity, Developmental University, Research University and the University of Life into an 'Integral University'.

23.4   Integration: A Final Major Task Ahead

We have come to the end of our Integral Development journey. Almost!

Almost – because this chapter served not only to pull together all the threads of the entire journey but also to introduce you to a final task that lies ahead of us. We call this culminating task the 'co-creation of an Integral University'. It arises, as we interconnect the Uni-Versity types of each of the four realms: the 'Southern' Communiversity, the 'Eastern' Developmental University, the 'Northern' Research University and the 'Western' University of Life.

Such a synthesis is not a mere alignment of these four types in a coherent framework. Much more, it is about creating a new, now fully integral entity that is brought about through the creative and dynamic interaction of the four individual Uni-Versities.

It is about fully institutionalising Integral Development through a potent developmental-educational platform that can drive the Integral Development agenda in the most effective way.

Such an entity does not yet exist in practice. However, in the following penultimate chapter we introduce you to a recently founded university in Egypt that we regard as an early pioneer on the way towards an Integral University. The case of Sekem and Heliopolis University does not yet represent a full-fledged Integral University, but it provides us with crucial insights in how an Integral University may look like in practice.

24 *Integral University Pioneer: Sekem and Heliopolis University for Sustainable Development*

Guiding Question: How can Integral Development be institutionalised in practice?

24.1   Orientation: A New Uni-Versity Beginning

In this penultimate chapter, we share the Integral Development case story of Sekem in Egypt that culminates in the origination of Heliopolis University. Altogether, we see this new university as a pioneering example for what we call an Integral University. There is still a lot to do, and Heliopolis University is facing challenging years ahead in growing into a truly Integral University. Yet, we can see a number of highly promising ingredients touching on all integral realms introduced in this book.

The Sekem-Heliopolis case is followed by a critical evaluation that may help all of us to build on this pioneering case and to make further headway towards a fully Integral University.

24.2   Pioneering Steps towards an Integral University: Sekem and Heliopolis University for Sustainable Development in Egypt

INTRODUCTION

The case of Sekem in Egypt represents perhaps one of the finest articulations of an integrated individual-organisational-societal development model in the world, which launched its Heliopolis University for Sustainable Development in October 2012. It is a story about the continuous evolution of human beings, an organisation and a community, that is infused with a remarkable capacity to include multiple perspectives: ecological, pedagogical, philosophical, spiritual, artistic, cultural, technological, entrepreneurial, economic and political. For Swiss pedagogue Daniel Baumgartner, who studied Sekem over many years – including our integral interpretation of its enterprise model – Sekem can only be understood as a 'holistic synthesis' of many interwoven components.[1] Furthermore, the Heliopolis University for Sustainable Development that recently evolved out of Sekem, represents an inspiring attempt to ultimately actualise an integrated approach to human development, albeit in a challenging educational environment, massively constrained by Egyptian regulatory authorities and the conventions of academe.

On the surface, Sekem is a remarkable enterprise that has won international recognition for its future-oriented, sustainable business model. Awarded with the Right Livelihood Award in 2003, its founder Ibrahim Abouleish has also been selected in the same year as one of the world's most 'Outstanding Social Entrepreneurs' by the Schwab Foundation for Social Entrepreneurship, and has received the 'Business for Peace Award' in 2012. As we take a closer look, one discovers that Sekem is much more than a business, but a whole societal microcosm in itself, comprised of economic, cultural, societal and ecological institutions and endeavours, set within a very particular society and community.

For many years we have been working closely with Sekem, in particular in relation to its latest evolutionary step: the design and establishment of its Heliopolis University for Sustainable Development. We have done extensive research on its uniquely integrated enterprise design[2] and its approach towards an Integral Economy.[3] What interests us here is the self-organisation-society journey it underwent in the past and is continuing in the present, culminating now in Heliopolis University for Sustainable Development. We begin with the story of Dr Ibrahim Abouleish, before we turn to the emergence of Sekem itself and finally to its interaction with and impact on society, in Egypt and the world. This interaction represents indeed a new means of navigation toward sustainable development, which itself gave rise to the final effect: one of the world's first universities with a full-fledged focus on sustainable development.

ROUND 1 – SELF: IBRAHIM ABOULEISH'S FORMATIVE PERSONAL GROUNDING – CREATIVE TENSION AND DYNAMIC BALANCE BETWEEN POLARITIES

From his youth Ibrahim Abouleish carried a formative vision deep in his heart, a vision larger than himself. Upon completion of school, he left Egypt in 1956 against the will of his father to study in Austria; before his departure he wrote a letter to his father, in which he expressed in most picturesque language his vision of renewing the village that he loved most in his childhood. This vision contains many of the elements – from enterprises to schools, from hospitals to theatres – that he was to realise through Sekem.[4] When Abouleish much later, after a visit to Egypt in 1975, developed his full-fledged vision of developing a flourishing community in the middle of the Egyptian desert, he responded also to his childhood experiences of an Egypt that lived far below its potential, disconnected from the knowledge and wisdom of the ancient civilisation that was slumbering in its own past. It was an Egypt that had lost its creative impulse, its vitality. Sekem, the organisation that he and his family were to found after their return to Egypt in 1977, was seen, from the very outset, as a catalyst to restore Egypt to its former vitality. It carries this task in its name, *Sekem* being the transliteration of an Egyptian hieroglyph meaning 'vitality of the sun'.

For Ibrahim Abouleish, this restorative task, had to begin with his adult development. Searching for impulses of revitalisation, he discovered them through the juxtaposition of two crucial 're-sources': the first source he revisited within himself, consciously awakening to the mysteries of life, rooted in his own Islamic faith and Egyptian cultural background; the second source he was to recognise outside himself, in interaction with other, most especially European cultures and philosophies.

As he pursued his studies of chemistry, physics, mathematics and geology and later during his successful career with a leading pharmaceutical laboratory in Austria, he immersed himself in European thinkers and philosophies. It was in particular the German philosopher-poet Johann Wolfgang von Goethe's natural philosophy and the Austrian polymath Rudolf Steiner's anthroposophical orientation that inspired the mind of the young Abouleish. However, he never lost contact with his Egyptian and Islamic heritage, and indeed was able to employ the cross-cultural impulses to catalyse his personal vitalisation and conscious evolution. For Abouleish it was this fusion of inner and outer, local and global horizons that helped him co-evolve how he himself could contribute to a renaissance of his country. He began to develop a fundamentally new, natural and cultural, as well as technological and economic approach to sustainable human development. This approach would draw simultaneously on the best of his own and of other cultures, and would link valuable insights of Egypt's Middle Eastern cultural achievements over the millennia with the best that Western and Northern philosophy and technology had to offer. It was out of this amalgam of the inner and the outer, of the local and the global, of tradition and modernity that Sekem as an idea, and later as an organisation emerged.

The degree to which Abouleish himself is acutely conscious of the creative tension between the '*East*' and the '*West*' within himself, is reflected in the German subtitle of his book on Sekem, translated 'How an Encounter of Orient and Occident transformed Egypt'.[5] It is also illustrated in the following personal experience: in the summer of 2010 we were invited to run a workshop on the design of Sekem's envisioned university. In his typical networking style, Abouleish had invited not only local staff members and experts (a fine fusion of Egyptians and Europeans, primarily Germans) to this workshop, but also a group of potential contributors from all over the world. Abouleish probed continuously and simultaneously into both the inner philosophical and spiritual rooting of the university, as well as into its intellectual design and practical validity. At one stage he abruptly addressed one of us across the room: 'Alexander, what do you think of the term "sustainable development"? Should it be part of the university's name?' The surprised response was:

> I have my doubts. Sustainable Development is a term coined in the West and has become fashionable in the past thirty years, with little overall result, and this at a time when the world is at the brink of destruction. Ancient Egypt, however, had the principle of sustainable development, moderation and balance embodied in one of its goddesses, Maat, and that civilisation lived for over 3,500 years. Being in Egypt, is there no better philosophy we can draw on, one that is coming out of its ancient civilisation?

The room turned silent, as Abouleish did not respond. Instead, he stood up and left the room. After two long minutes he returned with a statue of the Ancient Egyptian goddess Maat in his hands. He held it up and said: 'For all important decisions I try to keep the principles in mind that the goddess embodies: balance, justice and truth'.

He added that even if the term 'sustainable development' was to be kept in the university's name, one would need to ensure that the principles that sustained and guided ancient Egypt for thousands of years would remain part of it. Abouleish was convinced that tradition and modernity, the local and the global had to be held in a fine balance. In this regard it is fascinating to see that 'balance' is also seen by many Islamic scholars as the central value in Muslim faith. The Qur'an states: 'And the heaven He raised and imposed the balance. That you not transgress within the balance. And establish weight in justice and do not make deficient the balance'.[6]

Abouleish, by now in his mid seventies, embodies within himself a rare balance between the Middle East and Europe, as well as between a love for soil and nature on the one hand and for scholarship, philosophy and intellect on the other. He alternates between a powerful masculine and entrepreneurial will force and feminine warmth and caring for people. He has both a spiritual inclination to continuously raise the consciousness of himself and others and a material orientation to 'make things happen'. He fluctuates between at times an almost pharaonic management style, imposing his will on his environment, and modern democratic man, serving to build up relationships and communities, visible when he convenes his staff and people from outside Sekem in circles of equality and fruitful interaction. He is a carrier of timeless wisdom sourced in ancient civilisations and a visionary of the future, almost a seer, able to anticipate sustainable pathways for humanity. Abouleish has integrated this wide range of qualities within himself to a large degree. At times, they clash as opposing forces, resulting in a leadership style that is not without its paradoxes.

Yet, he embodies a relentless energy to continue the journey of individual and collective evolution and a purposeful orientation to transcend the creative tension that occasionally arises out of this complex bouquet of remarkable characteristics. At the core of his being, Abouleish states in his own words, is unlimited enthusiasm and love:

> The enthusiasm for my work, the boundless love which fills my heart for all around me, brings forth a vision of the community: A community in which people of all nations and cultures work and learn in peace, and resonate together in harmony as a symphony; a community in which vocations from all walks of life, from all age groups, from all levels of consciousness, acknowledge, nurture and love the divine world and strive towards noble ideals; a living, ever regenerating community maintaining its dynamism by reaching towards the science of the spirit … a community pursuing truth and tolerance, generously offering its understanding in the service of the earth and man; a people where modesty and diligence prevails over vanity and comfort, and all endeavours are blessed.[7]

Abouleish's life tells the story of relentless personal development, never letting go of his vision. During the time when he built up Sekem, together with his Austrian wife Gudrun, later with his daughter Mona and his son Helmy, who is now becoming the major force within Sekem in his own visionary-ecological light, Helmy's wife Konstanze and a whole group of loyal community members, they jointly believed in making the impossible happen. It all started in the middle of the Egyptian desert at a location no one believed could be transformed into the flourishing oasis it later became and that, up to today, constitutes the vibrant heart of the Sekem Group of Companies and the cultural activities of Sekem.

ROUND 2 – ORGANISATION: THE ORGANISATION SEKEM – EMERGENT REFORMATION OF ECONOMIC, CULTURAL AND SOCIETAL ENDEAVOURS, BASED ON HARMONY WITH NATURE

The ability of Ibrahim Abouleish to integrate the polarities of human existence constitutes the foundation of the integrated organisational model that Sekem was to become. This model was not carved in stone from the very beginning, but it evolved and still continues to emerge in an organic process. Its evolution is nurtured by an ever-deeper understanding of 'outer nature', including the ecological principles of nature and sustainable agriculture, as much as the dynamics of the inner human nature. This alternating rhythm of engaging with outer and inner nature is tangible almost instantly for every visitor of Sekem: the former embodied in Sekem's origin as an organic farm and in its companies processing the natural products of the by now over 600 farms connected to Sekem; the latter embodied in the rich variety of cultural activities taking place at Sekem on a daily basis. In that sense the Sekem Group of Companies and the Sekem Development Foundation are the Yang and Yin of Sekem as a whole; the creative dance between them seems to be a key source for Sekem's overall 'vitality'. This vitality is oriented towards the overriding vision of Sekem to enable the sustainable development of individuals, society and the environment.

Founded in 1977 in the Egyptian desert some 60 km north-east of Cairo, Sekem's 'origin myth' tells the story of desert land being turned into fertile soils through the practices of biodynamic agriculture. Such reclaimed soils provided the basis for the cultivation of herbs, fruits and vegetables that were further processed into high-quality food and phyto-pharmaceutical medicines. A whole range of companies, consolidated within the Sekem Group, emerged over time: from Isis focusing on organic foods to Atos manufacturing phyto-pharmaceuticals, from Nature-Tex producing organic cotton textiles to Libra dealing with organic cultivation, from Lotus processing organic herbs and spices to Hator packaging fresh produce for local and international markets. The objectives that the Sekem Group of Companies is striving to accomplish reflect its overall orientation towards sustainable development:[8]

- Healing the environment through the application of biodynamic agriculture methods.
- Developing solutions, providing services, and manufacturing a variety of products that meet the consumers' true needs and conform to the highest quality standards.
- Marketing and distributing products in partnership with farmers, producers, vendors and consumers.

Shortly after Sekem had started to engage in its first business projects, the organisation embarked upon its cultural-educational activities. Already in 1984, the Sekem Development Foundation was established as an umbrella organisation, with the objective to 'contribute to the development goals of the Egyptian people and to facilitate the realisation of Egypt's unique contribution to global advancement and progress'[9] From a kindergarten to primary and secondary school, from education for children with special needs to vocational training, from a hospital, that provides health services for about 30,000 patients a year to community outreach programmes, from the Academy of Applied Arts and Sciences and the Sekem Environmental Science Center (SESC) to, finally, its latest brainchild, the Heliopolis University for Sustainable Development: the cultural-educational activities of Sekem are manifold and continuously growing.

Sekem's societal activities are represented by the Cooperative of Sekem Employees, an association of its almost 2,000 employees, that:

> seeks to develop work models that ensure respect for the dignity of humankind and guarantee the equality of everybody in the community. It aims to raise consciousness of the concepts of humanity and sustainability and the importance of sharing and mutual trust among the employees of all Sekem companies.[10]

How then do these three levels (or indeed interconnected 'rounds') of self, organisation and society interlink? We observed that Sekem continuously creates spaces composed of an inner, reflective and inspirational dimension (the cultural field) and an outer, more active and ultimately transformational dimension (the economic field), interlinked by the social dimension (societal field), that is seeking not only to ensure equal participation and rights of every employee in the co-creative process but also to translate such processes into viable working models for organisations and the economy. The cultural, economic

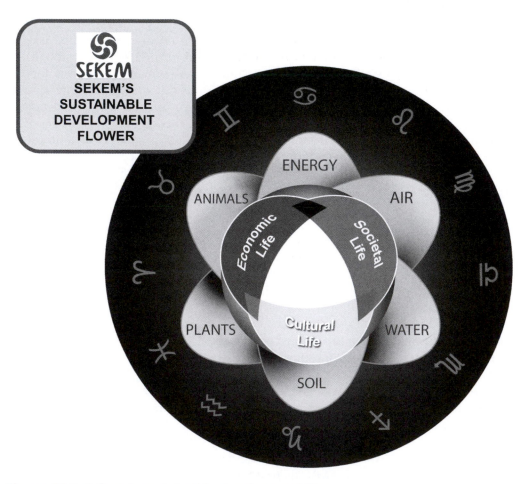

Figure 24.1 Sekem's sustainable development flower

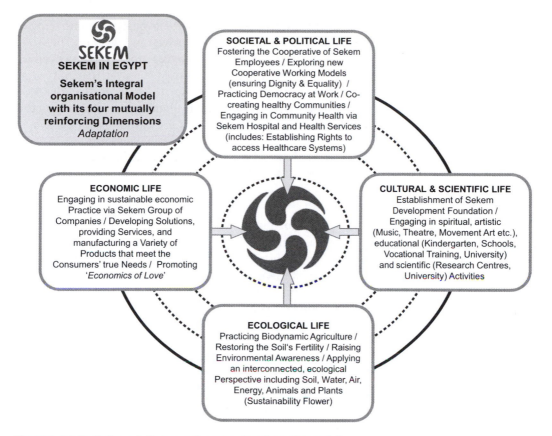

Figure 24.2 Sekem's integral organisational model

and social fields are altogether embedded in a fourth dimension, the natural environment. The 'rootedness' of Sekem's economic, cultural and societal activities in Egyptian soil and nature, provides for organic, evolutionary metaphors for its organisational self-understanding (Sekem's logo is a circular, dynamically revolving sun-symbol, representing vitality) as well as for its overall orientation towards sustainable development, captured in Sekem's so-called 'sustainable development flower'.[11]

The latest version of Sekem's sustainable development flower (Figure 24.1) pictures not only the interconnected dimensions of Sekem's economic, cultural (which includes here spiritual, artistic, educational and scientific) and societal (including political and juridicial) life – but also their overall 'embeddedness' within the earth's natural biosphere, as well as within a larger cosmic order, symbolised by the signs of the zodiac.

In cooperation with Sekem, we have translated these four realms into an integral perspective (see Figure 24.2) that – together with the dynamic evolution of self and organisation, community and society – has become the guiding model for the development of Heliopolis University for Sustainable Development. In Ibrahim Abouleish terms, all these four dimensions are brought into creative interplay, thereby becoming mutually invigorating. The Sekem logo in the centre of the model – internally coined 'the wheel of balance' – symbolises this dynamic, ever-evolving interaction of all dimensions.

It is important to bring to our attention, that the integral perspective is deeply resonant with the two core guiding philosophies of Abouleish and Sekem: Islam and

Anthroposophy. Rudolf Steiner's 'threefolding' framework for a healthy society[12] with economics, politics and culture as the three core pillars of society and with brotherhood (economics), justice (politics) and freedom (culture) as the main values of these three pillars, is well reflected in Sekem's economic, societal and cultural dimensions. Furthermore, core Islamic values such as unity (*Tawheed*), justice (*Adl*), balance (*Mizan*), and moderation (*Zuhd*) are deeply embedded in Sekem's holistic, balancing organisational model. How then is Sekem impacting society?

ROUND 3 – COMMUNITY-SOCIETY: SEKEM IN SOCIETY – BECOMING A NAVIGATIONAL FORCE FOR A NEW NORMATIVE SUSTAINABLE DEVELOPMENT IN EGYPT AND THE WORLD

Sekem's past contributions to society are immense, and have been, from the outset, built into the organisational design of Sekem. They have literally 'grown' out of the organisation. Sekem's dynamic vitality and its focus on sustainable development, have flowered within the Egyptian society and beyond in many ways. In parts, Sekem's societal influence has been institutionalised, e.g. through the foundation of the Egyptian Biodynamic Association (EBDA), promoting biodynamic farming in Egypt and through the set-up of the International Association of Partnership in Ecology and Trade (IAP), together with several European partners 'to create a dynamic interaction between farmers, producers and traders to provide consumers with the highest quality of organic products at the fairest price'[13] In other instances, Sekem's societal engagement has been translated in national environmental policies: here, the national banning of aerial spraying of pesticides on cotton as a consequence of Sekem's own research on more sustainable ways of pest control stands out. Sekem's greatest local, national and international impact on society, however, is its providing the world with a living role model not only for a sustainable enterprise, but also, as we have intimated in our work *Integral Economics*, for paving the way for an alternative approach to economics as a whole.

However, the societal upheavals during and in the aftermath of the 2011 Egyptian uprising and the Arab Spring within the wider region resulted also in turbulence within Sekem, which led to a somewhat painful process of self-reflection, re-orientation and consolidation. During that time, Ibrahim Abouleish battled with a serious disease, and his son Helmy was charged with ultimately groundless allegations, that kept him in custody for a similar period of 100 days. Both, father and son, underwent profound processes of self-scrutiny and inner transformation, ultimately emerging with regained inner strength and a new sense of direction. While roles in the past were clearly distinguished – Helmy Abouleish acted as CEO of the Sekem Group of Companies while Ibrahim Abouleish focused primarily on the Sekem Development Foundation – they seemed to have grown closer together, uniting forces to now build up Heliopolis University for Sustainable Development, which had in fact been brewing for over 10 years. This was, and is, to be a culmination of Sekem's engagement with society, reaching out to those young Egyptians, who are motivated to actively contribute to the renewal of Egyptian society. Finally, parts of the third generation of the Abouleish family, now in their twenties, are increasingly making their mark within Sekem and Heliopolis University.

ROUND 4 – INTEGRATING UNIVERSITY: HELIOPOLIS UNIVERSITY – EFFECTING SUSTAINABLE DEVELOPMENT OF SELF, ORGANISATION, COMMUNITY AND SOCIETY

Heliopolis University follows in the wake of all that has come before, now with a pre-emphasis on passing on the Sekem legacy, thereby interconnecting its story with that of the larger Egyptian society, via its young people. It aims not to follow the road of conventional universities that merely focus on providing degrees for individual students, educated to fit the existing job requirements of society. Instead – as its ultimate objective – it seeks to educate individuals, to create new organisational knowledge, to promote learning communities, and ultimately develop Egyptian society. Aspiring to outgrow the conventional approach to education, it is determined to become a space for transformation, in which faculty and students are developed and research is undertaken in holistic fashion: thus, education and research shall serve to cultivate the transformational knowledge, skills and attitudes to deal with Egypt's most burning socioeconomic issues and to purposefully contribute to bringing about sustainable organisations and a sustainable society. Rather than education fitting students merely into existing job schemes, such transformational approach to education and research, altogether underpinned by sustainable development, will lead to not only the creation of new kinds of integral enterprises, like Sekem, but also to new kinds of livelihoods – following the kind of life and vocational trajectory that the Abouleishs' themselves have done.

The university's overall programmes and curricula reflect the integrated inner-outer rhythm of Sekem. Students and faculty are simultaneously exposed to a humanistic core programme, focusing on the inner development of the individual self in the context of group and community, and to initial specialists programmes – on sustainable approaches to Business and Economics, Pharmacy, and Engineering. Learners and researchers, individually and collectively, are supposed to make a tangible outer contribution in their particular field, thereby engaging in the sustainable development of Egypt as a whole.

This is achieved through its enriched educational curricula as well as learning and research processes, that shall interactively link students to four interconnected areas, evolved out of the integral approach:

- *Context:* Engaging with relevant context.
- *Consciousness:* Raising of human consciousness.
- *Content:* Assimilating inspiring content.
- *Contribution:* Making a significant contribution.

The university as a whole becomes thereby fully embedded in society, dealing concretely with its most burning socioeconomic issues and innovating viable sustainable futures.

In Figure 24.3 we provide an overview of the integral design that is at the heart of Heliopolis University. This design constitutes a whole new perspective on a university, and will require intensive faculty, as well as ongoing curriculum, development. It is a process of discovering and implementing a new, holistic approach to learning, researching and innovating, in the context of a particular society. Part of this process is to navigate the difficult political and educational environment that the university is facing. The conservative Egyptian education authorities, not to mention also some of the faculty – eager to follow established Western standards rather than developing their own

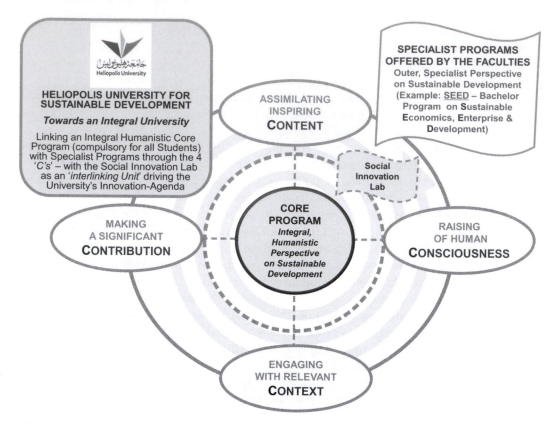

Figure 24.3 Heliopolis University: Applying an integral design

– have only partially bought into Heliopolis University's new approach to curriculum content and educational design. However, notwithstanding the above, as the university has opened its doors in autumn 2012, it did so as one of world's first universities with an exclusive thematic focus on sustainable development.

Furthermore, it will be a university that has not been conceived of in typical top-down fashion (per governmental decree or through isolated private initiative), but it has grown, organically, out of the life of Ibrahim Abouleish, his wife, son and other close allies, as well as out of an organisational role model, that stood the test of time over 30 years, and that we have identified as an integral one, promoting now through the university Integral Development.

CHALLENGES AHEAD

Of course, we know that the university will continue to face major challenges on its way. In the beginning, the major focus will still be on individual education, albeit an enriched form of it, as its focus on the '4Cs' (Context, Consciousness, Content, Contribution) – rather than on exclusively content – reveals. The potential focus on organisational knowledge creation, communal learning, and societal innovation, is more characteristic of Sekem itself than it is, at the moment, of the university. According to the vision of the Abouleishs, this will, however, evolve in time.

A crucial element in the successful realisation of this integral vision is Heliopolis University's 'Social Innovation Lab'. This lab has been established with a focus on four major interconnected areas of activities, altogether designed to make sustainable development 'REAL':

1. R: research on social innovation to create a unique research-to-innovation process as the 'inner nucleus' of the lab.
2. E: education for social innovation by co-developing education curricula together with the faculties as well as teaching and learning processes serving Heliopolis University internally and externally.
3. A: action of social innovation by facilitating concrete social innovation projects, bringing together faculty, students, business, and external partners.
4. L: leveraging social innovation in order to upscale and/or transfer the solutions found to address societal burning issues.

In our latest conceptual evolution we changed "REAL" to "CARE", an acronym representing Catalysation, Activation, Research and Education (whereby the former term Leveraging has been replaced by Catalysation). As much as Sekem itself is a role model of and enabler for 'sustainable communities', so Heliopolis University aspires to become a catalyst for developing sustainable communities, thereby building a CARE-ing Egyptian society and contributing to a CARE-ing world. As declared in the University's vision: 'Heliopolis University strives for the sustainable development of individuals, communities and nature in Egypt and the world'.[14] For us, Heliopolis University has all the potential to grow into a full-fledged Integral University. A possible way for its further evolution in a truly integral fashion includes the following:

- building into its research and educational design the 'enabling of sustainable communities' over and above merely individual educational processes;
- evolving its capacity – led by the Social Innovation Lab – to influence societal and global consciousness with regards to sustainable development;
- altogether linked with the transdisciplinary creation of original knowledge through research that leads to social innovation on the ground (including the gradual evolution of its curricula);
- the integration of all of this within evolved educational processes, that build (a) individual capacities in relation to the field of studies *and* with regards to societal transformation, (b) the ability for co-creation among students, faculty and communities (to match the complex challenges society is facing), and (c) enabling students and faculty, thereby, to make tangible contributions to Egyptian communities, society and beyond.

In summarising the case of Sekem and Heliopolis University, we have devised Table 24.1.

Table 24.1   Towards an Integral University

Integral Development	The Practical Case of Sekem and Heliopolis University
Round 1: **Self-Development** Formative *Grounding*	*Ibrahim Abouleish: Knowing his vision, developing his self* • From his Youth, Abouleish carried a vision deep in his heart, a vision to renew nature and community in the Egyptian desert • For Abouleish, this restorative task had to begin with his personal development and self-knowledge. Searching for impulses of revitalisation, he turned to two sources: an inner source (rooted in his own Islamic faith and Egyptian cultural background); an outer source (e.g. European cultures and philosophies)
Round 2: **Organisational Development** Reformative *Emergence*	*Sekem: Ecosystem for a sustainable enterprise-community and a 'force for good' in Egyptian society* • Sekem's integrated economic, cultural and societal activities are rooted in Egyptian soil and nature, as well as in its communities • Sekem continuously creates spaces composed of an inner, reflective and inspirational dimension (the cultural field) and an outer, more active and ultimately transformational dimension (the economic field), interlinked by the societal dimension, that is seeking not only to ensure equal participation and rights of every employee in the co-creative process but also to translate such processes into viable working models for organisations and the economy
Round 3: **Societal Development** Newly normative *Navigation*	*Beyond Sekem: Embedding Development in Egyptian society and contributing to societal well-being* • Sekem Development Foundation was established to contribute to the development goals of Egypt and to facilitate the realisation of Egypt's unique contribution to global advancement and progress • Sekem's societal influence has been institutionalised, e.g. through the foundation of the Egyptian Biodynamic Association (EBDA), promoting biodynamic farming in Egypt and through the set-up of the International Association of Partnership (IAP), together with several international partners to create a dynamic interaction between farmers, producers and traders to provide consumers with the highest quality of organic products at the fairest price • In some Instances, Sekem's societal engagement has been translated in national environmental policies

Table 24.1 Continued	
Integral Development	**The Practical Case of Sekem and Heliopolis University**
Round 4: **Integrating Uni-Versity** Full transformative *Effect*	*Heliopolis University for Sustainable Development: Towards an Integral University* • The original Sekem Vision is mirrored in Heliopolis University's Vision, striving for the sustainable development of individuals, communities and nature in Egypt and the world • Equally reflected in the design of the university are Sekem's integrated enterprise-approach and the orientation of Sekem Development Foundation to contribute to the development goals of the Egyptian people and promote Egypt's unique contribution to global advancement and progress • Aspiring to outgrow the conventional approach to education, HU is determined to become a space for transformation, in which students are developed and research is undertaken in holistic fashion: thus, education and research shall serve to cultivate the transformational knowledge, skills and attitudes to deal with Egypt's most burning socioeconomic issues and to purposefully contribute to bringing about sustainable organisations, communities and society

24.3   Integration: Almost!

The story of Sekem and Heliopolis University for Sustainable Development is one of truly remarkable achievements.

In this concluding part of the chapter we seek, however, to cast a critical eye on the combined story of Sekem and Heliopolis University.

Such a critical evaluation is necessary to avoid the danger of lapsing back into a conventional university design. This danger is imminent, given not only the conservative educational landscape within which Heliopolis University is operating within Egypt, but also the global mindset of what a university is, and what it is not.

Throughout this book, we have challenged the conventional notion of a university, and introduced four new types of so-called Uni-Versities, only one of which – the 'Northern' Research University – somehow resembles the mainstream understanding of a university.

Looking closely at these four Uni-Versity types, we see all of them mirrored, to some degree, within Sekem-Heliopolis University – yet with potential for much fuller integration to be realised in the years to come. What do we mean? Let us examine, for this existing case, all four components of a fully Integral University (in brackets you find the corresponding CARE functions):

- *Communiversity* (A = Activation of Community): Originally, Sekem has started out as what we term a Communiversity. Building up a 'Sustainable Community in the Egyptian Desert', it had developed from the beginning, a kind of Community Learning Centre. Such a centre, though not called as such, is active still today in various articulations – from philosophical-practical morning meetings to all kinds of participatory educational and research programmes embedded within Sekem. This educational-research impulse located in the original Sekem community is relatively disconnected from the actual Heliopolis University. To give one example: while Sekem has become an international icon for a sustainable enterprise and economic model, the respective curricula of Heliopolis University hardly build on this new theory and practice; nor is Heliopolis University purposefully feeding back – through newly generated knowledge – into the original Sekem community.

- *Developmental University* (C = Catalysing Societal Consciousness): Sekem has developed over time hundreds of Egyptian farms, as well as local and national communities, altogether becoming a large network for sustainable development in Egypt and beyond. In this regard, the Sekem Initiative can be interpreted as a Developmental University, fostering societal learning and consciousness-raising in relation to sustainable development. This Uni-Versity dimension of Sekem is, however, not yet fully articulated, and it is also not sufficiently linked up with the newly founded Heliopolis University. Therefore Heliopolis University sees itself still primarily as a provider of individual education, rather than being (in addition) a catalyst for community development (Communiversity) and subsequently one of societal development (Developmental University). While in aspiration it seeks to embrace these two Uni-Versity types, this is not yet sufficiently reflected in its curricula and learning designs. An important issue for Heliopolis University to explore, from our point of view, would be how the university – through its programmes, processes and projects – might actively serve this network of communities and organisations by responding to their developmental needs and capacities.

- *Research University* (R = Innovation Driven Institutional Research): Facing conservative higher-education authorities, Heliopolis University is obliged to infuse its curricula with mainstream educational content (e.g. conventional finance, economics) with relatively little flexibility to explore alternative paradigms. Efforts have been undertaken to focus evaluation schemes more on group and social learning (through new knowledge and new practice) rather than individual learning, The numerous partnerships with communities and organisations resulting from existing research projects provide a good basis for Heliopolis University to concretely contribute to the sustainable development of Egyptian communities (as per its mission) and organisations. More emphasis can be put on making the university a catalyst for collective knowledge creation.

- *University of Life* (E = Transformative Individual Education): Incorporating the principles of a University of Life would mean that Heliopolis University engages students and faculty much more strongly (from the outset, and as per design) in concrete projects, addressing burning issues in Egyptian society through action-learning-action-research processes.

Knowing the existing Sekem-Heliopolis University environment, we are aware that most of these aspects do exist in pockets, but have not yet been integrated through mutually reinforcing processes. Faculty, at this stage, is naturally concerned with getting the educational show on the university road, focusing on content, programmes and courses. It hence requires an enormous conscious effort driven by key representatives of Sekem and Heliopolis University to use the promising ingredients to become a 'different' university that does not follow the mainstream model. This is the kind of 'mission impossible', familiar to those who were involved in setting up Sekem and Heliopolis University in the past.

A major role in coordinating and continuously reinforcing such conscious efforts lies with the Social Innovation Lab that is embedded in Heliopolis University, and that is supposed to work as a force for integration and innovation. In this early stage of Heliopolis University, the role of this lab has, however, not yet been fully fleshed out.

In that regard we are working together with Maximilian Abouleish-Boes who has been engaged for many years together with his wife Soraya – granddaughter of Ibrahim and daughter of Helmy Abouleish – within the Sekem Initiative. Abouleish-Boes, who has joined our PhD programme on Integral Development, has long been working within Sekem on sustainable development matters. In 2011, Abouleish-Boes and his wife lived and worked for almost one year on the Green Waadi farm near Minya in Upper Egypt that is part of a Sekem company in charge for Land Reclamation. Both of them are determined to build on what has been learnt by the Sekem Group as a whole, and to understand how the original Sekem model can be replicated and upscaled in an authentic manner. In the process they seek to team up with an interdisciplinary and multicultural group of people that share this vision.

From the very outset, they see their work intimately connected with the Sekem Initiative as well as with Heliopolis University. Abouleish-Boes continues to participate in the evolution of Sekem as a manager for sustainable development activities and in 2012 took on a key role within the Social Innovation Lab. With his multiple responsibilities within the larger network of Sekem and Heliopolis University, he is thereby uniquely positioned to contribute substantially to the much-needed further integration of the various Uni-Versity impulses within Heliopolis University. In his eyes, the core challenge, especially in this initial phase, lies in the purposeful integration of the existing initiatives within the Sekem-Heliopolis University ecosystem and the foundation of a shared identity among the people involved.

As mentioned, the Social Innovation Lab would play a crucial role in supporting and facilitating the kind of community-based and society-related research described earlier. These processes can then also feed into the development of the University of Life dimension within the emergent Integral University, whereby a project driven action-learning-and-action-research-space is developed, in which students, university faculty, Sekem employees, civil society and partners from all over the world can address burning issues on multiple levels through new practice. Abouleish-Boes' dissertation will be purposefully designed around this task and Trans4m is dedicated to play a co-evolutionary role in this process.

Throughout this critical evaluation, we are acutely aware of the difficulties Sekem and Heliopolis University deal with on a daily basis. We therefore present these reflections the light of the long-term vision that we share with the founders and core team within Heliopolis University – to create a new form of a university that can indeed become a force for Integral Development within society and the world at large.

It is in this spirit that we now turn to the final chapter, in which we map out the core features of an Integral University.

References

1   Baumgartner, D. (2012). *Der Arabische Frühling zwischen Zorn und Zukunft*. Basel: Futurum, pp. 85ff.
2   Lessem, R. and Schieffer, A. (2009). *Transformation Management: Towards the Integral Enterprise*. Farnham: Gower, pp. 308ff.
3   Lessem, R. and Schieffer, A. (2010). *Integral Economics: Releasing the Economic Genius of Your Society*. Farnham: Gower, pp. 75ff.
4   Abouleish, I. (2005). *Sekem: A Sustainable Community in the Egyptian Desert*. Edinburgh: Floris.
5   Abouleish, I. (2005). *Die Sekem Vision: Eine Begegnung von Orient und Okzident verändert Ägypten*. Stuttgart: Johannes M. Mayer.
6   Qur'an 55:7–9.
7   Abouleish, I. (2010). In: *Sekem – An Image Brochure*. Internal document.
8   Sekem (2010). *Sekem – An Image Brochure*. Internal document.
9   Sekem (2010). *Sekem – An Image Brochure*. Internal document.
10 Sekem (2010). *Sekem – An Image Brochure*. Internal document.
11 *Sekem Report on Sustainable Development 2011*. Available at: http://www.sekem.com/node/162.
12 Steiner, R. (2003). *Threefold Commonwealth*. Whitefish: Kessinger.
13 Sekem (2010). *Sekem – An Image Brochure*. Internal document.
14 Heliopolis University website. Available at: www.hu.edu.eg/HUvision / Accessed: 4 September 2012.

CHAPTER 25

Co-Creating the Integral University: Fully Realising the Transformative Potential of Individuals, Organisations and Societies

Guiding Question: How can we fully actualise Integral Development through an Integral University?

25.1   Orientation: Getting Real! Fully CARE-ing!

And now 'for real'! Having reviewed the entire Integral Development journey (⇨23), and having subsequently been inspired by the case of Sekem and Heliopolis University (⇨24), we learned that in order to fully institutionalise Integral Development, there is still much work to be done.

The most significant challenge is to integrate the four Uni-Versity types, and their respective CARE functions, each of them embodying the actualisation of one of the four realities and realms. In that process we seek to create a fundamentally new educational-development entity – the Integral University.

As we shall show in this chapter, such an Integral University has the potential to contribute substantially to the holistic renewal of individuals, organisations, communities and societies.

Based on what we have learnt about the framework, processes and underlying theory and practice of Integral Development, we introduce in this culminating chapter the major design principles for the Integral University.

We conclude this book by sharing, in a nutshell, some of the latest developments out of our own practice, geared to lead to the establishment of an Integral University.

25.2   The Integral University: Integrating Communiversity, Developmental University, Research University and University of Life

OVERVIEW

The problem with which we are faced is that the image of a 'university' as an entity that is oriented primarily toward the education (often not even 'development') of the individual is so hard-wired into our consciousness that the notion of an Integral University is very difficult to take on board. For by an Integral University we mean an entity that integrates, in a new way, the four types of Uni-Versities that we have introduced in the course of this book. Figure 25.1 provides an overview of the Integral University.

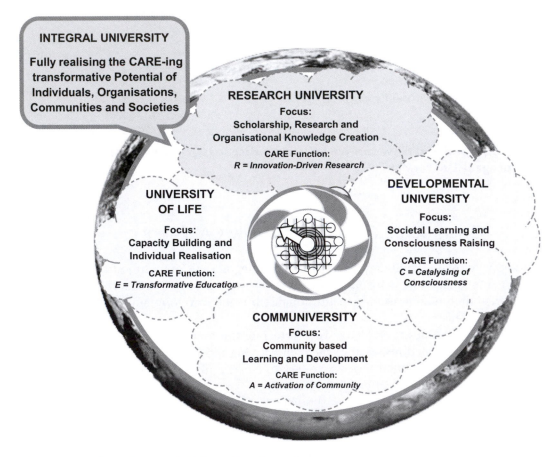

Figure 25.1 The Integral University: Overview

The figure illustrates the interdependent, overlapping nature of all four Uni-Versity types within the Integral University. The 'turbine' in its centre conveys the dynamism within this integral entity. The symbol within it is a combination of the four individual Uni-Versity symbols whereby the 'Western' arrow of Integrated action is underlain by the 'Northern' grid of knowledge, the 'Eastern' spiral of conscious co-evolution and the 'Southern' web of life.

With the case of Sekem and Heliopolis University for Sustainable Development in Egypt we introduced in the previous chapter a fascinating educational-developmental venture that seems to be on the way towards an Integral University. As we are entering here largely unchartered waters, this pioneering case has understandably still a long way to go.

And indeed, integrating all four Uni-Versity types is a tall order. We argue, however, that it is not an impossible one. For as we have shown in the latter part of the book, the 'holographic design' of Integral Development makes each individual Uni-Versity type mirror, at least to some degree, the integral whole. If we purposefully build on these 'integral ingredients', we see a good chance to arrive at our goal to build a fully Integral University.

In these final pages of our book, we sketch out the most significant components for the actualisation of an Integral University, as we can see it now.

Of particular importance are the following three tasks:

1. Integrate two revitalised existing and two newly invented university modes.
2. Integrate the structures and processes of all four Uni-Versity types.
3. Embed and maintain a research and development centre as integrating force.

TASK 1: INTEGRATING TWO REVITALISED EXISTING AND TWO NEWLY INVENTED UNIVERSITY MODES

In the process of purposefully building an Integral University, we begin to revisit the existing and known university modes. Earlier in this book (⇨18), we have introduced the two officially recognised modes:

- *Mode 1:* Conventional (most common) university-type pursuing education and research, focusing on the individual
- *Mode 2:* Additional (less common) university-type pursuing knowledge production, focusing on organisations.

Of course, we have no problem in identifying a pre-eminent Mode 1 institution – usually focusing on individual education and research – but often our imagination stops there. Looking back, we notice that many of the pre-eminent Mode 1 universities such as Harvard, MIT, Oxford or Cambridge, emerged originally out of a liberal arts heritage. We have illustrated that most of these institutions initially carried a strong societal vision and saw themselves as a seedbed for individual capacity building and learning for the common good. In that respect, they are the 'predecessors' of what we coined in this book the University of Life. Unfortunately, as we have argued, this original impulse has been lost in most cases. Hence, most of today's Mode 1 universities have become largely irrelevant to contributing to society's most burning issues. The University of Life seeks to 'revitalise' Mode 1.

When we turn to Mode 2 universities, we maintain that they are equally inhibited as are most Mode 1 institutions. Why? Because, once we move onto organisational knowledge creation – which Nonaka and Takeuchi have so astutely identified in such institutions as Canon and Sharp, Toyota and Toshiba[1] – we tend to look rather to manufacturing corporations than to universities. However, we see a real opportunity to align such organisational knowledge creation with an authentic Mode 2 university – a potential that has hitherto been hardly realised. Hence, the rather rare forms of Mode 2 universities, like Da Vinci in South Africa or Warwick University in the UK, are very much a halfway house between individual and organisation, because the 'workplace challenges' that they focus on remain primarily individual rather than group or organisational challenges. They thereby remain somewhat removed from a 'knowledge-creating organisation'. The reframed Research University, as introduced in this book, seeks to renew Mode 2. With such renewed Mode 1 and Mode 2 universities we can then move to what we call Mode 3 universities, focusing on community development and learning. Here, however, we face a lot of trouble.

There seems so far to be a tendency to lose touch with the university world, once we move onto community development or societal learning. Take, for example, Chinyika in Zimbabwe. In itself it is an extraordinary case of communal development (⇨10), led by Chidara Muchineripi and Steve Kada; however, once an educational programme had been offered by Muchineripi's company BTD, Da Vinci and Trans4m, the link with such community development almost disappeared, despite the prior intention to use the programme to leverage Chinyika's initial community impact. As for Sarvodaya (⇨14), probably the world's most unique example of societal learning, once they sought to establish a Sarvodaya Rural University and confronted the higher educational accrediting authorities in Sri Lanka, they were dragged back to the individual arena, where the societal, the communal and even the organisational are lost.

The same has applied to Heliopolis University for Sustainable Development (⇨24). Here, the national Egyptian accrediting authorities and the faculty are all attuned primarily to the education of individuals. At the same time, Ibrahim Abouleish himself faces the divide between his own experience of his individual education in Austria and the approach to organisational knowledge creation, community development and societal learning, in which the Sekem Group that he founded has been significantly engaged in Egypt.

However, each of these cases is close to a breakthrough. As a first step to creating Integral Universities, there was a need to become aware of the multiplicity of potential university modes, to then gradually begin to transcend the existing focus on (primarily) Mode 1 and (secondarily) Mode 2 Universities. Further evolution is required, as we have shown, for both modes – Mode 1 to be aligned more closely with a more contemporary University of Life and Mode 2 with a renewed Research University. Then, we suggest adding two additional modes (Mode 3 and Mode 4) that reflect the alternative forms of communal and societal learning that we have introduced. We have illustrated earlier that Mode 3 is already intimated through the rise of the Communiversity (⇨10), and Mode 4 is preceded by the emergence of the Developmental University (⇨14). In that sense, all four modes are building on somehow established grounds. Figure 25.2 illustrates these four – individual, organisational, communal and societal – Uni-Versity modes altogether and provides clues for the design and outcomes of each.

In time, what is required are accrediting structures to accredit all four modes in integral combination to legitimise the processes of individual and organisational, communal and societal learning and innovation altogether. To prepare this ground, we shall now come to an Integrated perspective on the underlying structures and processes of the Integral University.

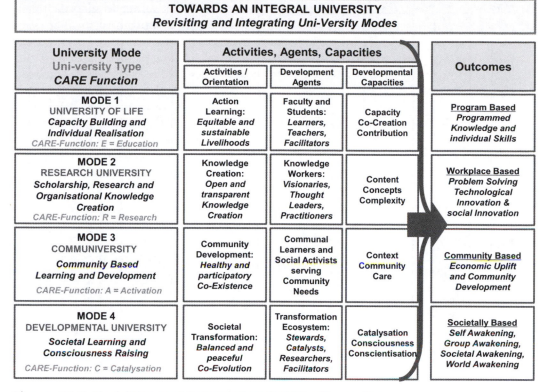

TOWARDS AN INTEGRAL UNIVERSITY
Revisiting and Integrating Uni-Versity Modes

University Mode Uni-versity Type CARE Function	Activities, Agents, Capacities			Outcomes
	Activities / Orientation	Development Agents	Developmental Capacities	
MODE 1 UNIVERSITY OF LIFE *Capacity Building and Individual Realisation* CARE-Function: E = Education	Action Learning: *Equitable and sustainable Livelihoods*	Faculty and Students: *Learners, Teachers, Facilitators*	Capacity Co-Creation Contribution	Program Based *Programmed Knowledge and individual Skills*
MODE 2 RESEARCH UNIVERSITY *Scholarship, Research and Organisational Knowledge Creation* CARE-Function: R = Research	Knowledge Creation: *Open and transparent Knowledge Creation*	Knowledge Workers: *Visionaries, Thought Leaders, Practitioners*	Content Concepts Complexity	Workplace Based *Problem Solving Technological Innovation & social Innovation*
MODE 3 COMMUNIVERSITY *Community Based Learning and Development* CARE-Function: A = Activation	Community Development: *Healthy and participatory Co-Existence*	Communal Learners and Social Activists serving Community Needs	Context Community Care	Community Based *Economic Uplift and Community Development*
MODE 4 DEVELOPMENTAL UNIVERSITY *Societal Learning and Consciousness Raising* CARE-Function: C = Catalysation	Societal Transformation: *Balanced and peaceful Co-Evolution*	Transformation Ecosystem: *Stewards, Catalysts, Researchers, Facilitators*	Catalysation Consciousness Conscientisation	Societally Based *Self Awakening, Group Awakening, Societal Awakening, World Awakening*

Figure 25.2 Revisiting and integrating Uni-Versity modes

TASK 2: INTEGRATING STRUCTURES AND PROCESSES OF ALL FOUR NEW UNI-VERSITY TYPES

We now connect major structural and processal elements of the four Uni-Versity types, as derived earlier in this chapter, to build an overall design for an Integral University. Table 25.1 integrates these aspects and illustrates the distinctiveness as well as the strong complementarities of all four types. As you engage with the table, note that to build up an Integral University, you are likely to begin in the '*South*' within a particular community, setting up a community learning centre.

From there you move to the 'East', evolving a community education infrastructure within a growing community network. It is from that basis that you then advance to the 'North' building up a knowledge creating university, firmly rooted in one or more communities and within a particular society. Such a 'Northern' knowledge creating university has a strong organisational orientation that can then also feed into the 'West': the University of Life with its specific laboratory character. Taken together, the four Uni-Versity types provide the final articulation of the Integral University.

As Table 25.1 illustrates, the same complementarities that we find with regards to the institutional forms of the four Uni-Versity types, we can also identify for the research and learning programmes, the socioeconomic foundations, governance structures, and approaches to accreditation.

Table 25.1 Towards an Integral University: Structures and processes

	Southern Communiversity	Eastern Developmental University	Northern Research University	Western University of Life
Institutional Form	Community learning centre	Community education infrastructure and community network	Knowledge-creating university	Experimental network- (and/or) enterprise-based living laboratory
Research and learning programmes	Ongoing participatory programmes building on indigenous knowledge systems	Processes serving to interconnect individual, organisational, communal and societal Development	Transdisciplinary programmes combining social and natural sciences and humanities to promote innovation	Combined action-learning-action-research processes
Socioeconomic foundation	Community-based enterprises and livelihoods	Social rehabilitation, employment creation, community finance and social innovation centres	Public and private research funding, student fees	Self-financing, volunteerism
Governance structures	Community-based governance systems	Energising hub and self-governing communities	Academic departments, innovation networks	Initiative-driven learning- and-enterprise-networks
Accreditation	Community-based procedures, ceremonies, rituals	Model villages and/or communities, community evaluation schemes	Individual achievement awards, centres of excellence	Project-based evaluation of business-and-community-impact

Of course, only in rare cases will an Integral University be built up from scratch in a more linear 'South-East-North-West' fashion. In reality, we need to start with who we are and what we have at hand: be it a rural or urban community, an enterprise, an existing Mode 1 or Mode 2 university and so on. From there, we progressively evolve our existing Uni-Versity type and integrate the remaining three, step by step. Whatever the situation is, with which we are faced, this template can provide us with orientation for the overall design. To enact this design though, we need an institutional 'integrating force', set within the emergent Integral University, to stimulate the development process on an ongoing basis.

TASK 3: EMBEDDING AND MAINTAINING A RESEARCH AND DEVELOPMENT CENTRE AS INTEGRATING FORCE

The challenge at hand is complex and difficult. Building an Integral University requires more than an overall vision: it requires as well an institutional driving force and sustained process to give continuous attention to this task. In our terms, it requires an embedded research-to-innovation centre, placed in the heart of the emergent university.

This aspect is often underestimated in attempts to build up new types of Uni-Versities. Without such ongoing research-to-innovation processes, the new entity is likely to be shaped according to conventional standards.

As we have seen in the case of Sekem and Heliopolis University (⇨24), the overall process to bring about an Integral University can only be successful, if such ongoing research and development is taken on by its Social Innovation Lab.

What then do we see as the core functions of such a research and development centre? Here is an overview:

- Mapping, evolving and ultimately actualising all four university modes, and their corresponding CARE functions, introduced.
- Mapping, evolving and actualising the structure and processes underlying the Integral University at hand.
- Orchestrating and guiding the process for actualising the institutional form of the Integral University which (ideally) begins in a specific community ('South') with a Community Learning Centre; continues then to develop a community educational infrastructure and community network ('East'), thereby reaching out into society at large; builds up from there a concrete knowledge creating University ('North') with a focus on primarily organisational knowledge creation; culminating with experimental and network-and-enterprise-based living laboratories that focus on primarily individual capacity building.
- Ensuring thereby that context ('South'), consciousness ('East'), content ('North') and contribution ('West') are interactively aligned within the emergent Integral University.
- Developing educational and research programmes, processes and curricula based on the overall Integral Development framework and trajectory, which need to be locally evolved and assimilated, making them an authentic expression of the particular context.
- Linking the emergent Integral University with a global network of likeminded impulses, thereby fostering co-learning and co-research.

- Gradually building up a transdisciplinary and transcultural knowledge base and faculty, engaging and linking both in continuous networked research and development processes.

With this responsibility to bring about such fundamentally new university design, structure and processes, the role of this Research and Development Centre within the Integral University cannot be overestimated.

Having dealt with the major tasks with regards to establishing an Integral University, we shall now turn to the final conclusion.

25.3 Full Integration: Realising our Transformative Potential via the Integral University – A Vision to Strive For! Together!!

REALISING OUR TRANSFORMATIVE POTENTIAL

We begin this final part of the book by sharing with you our own practical engagement with the Integral Development journey.

Over the past several years, we have developed together with participants of our current PhD programme on Integral Development – that we run in partnership with Da Vinci in South Africa – the vision to co-create an Integral University. That is supported by the particular design of the research-to-innovation process, underlying our programmes. It follows a 4C-storyline, designed to support each Integral Developer, together with what we term his or her innovation ecosystem, to make a significant contribution to his or her societal context and to become a co-evolver of an Integral University. Table 25.2 introduces this journey from call to contribution.

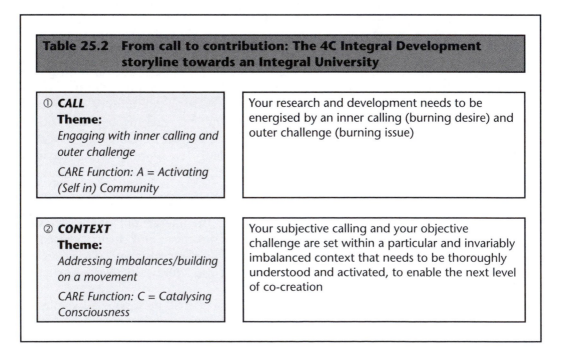

Table 25.2 From call to contribution: The 4C Integral Development storyline towards an Integral University

① **CALL** **Theme:** *Engaging with inner calling and outer challenge* *CARE Function: A = Activating (Self in) Community*	Your research and development needs to be energised by an inner calling (burning desire) and outer challenge (burning issue)
② **CONTEXT** **Theme:** *Addressing imbalances/building on a movement* *CARE Function: C = Catalysing Consciousness*	Your subjective calling and your objective challenge are set within a particular and invariably imbalanced context that needs to be thoroughly understood and activated, to enable the next level of co-creation

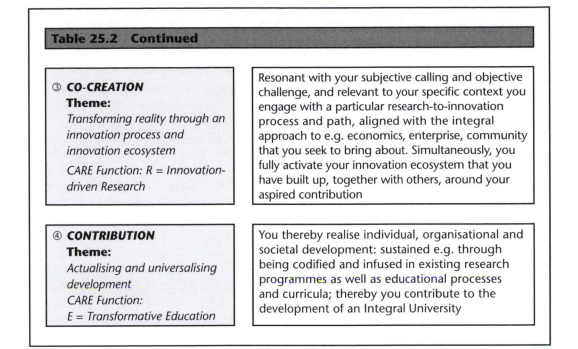

Table 25.2   Continued

③ **CO-CREATION** **Theme:** *Transforming reality through an innovation process and innovation ecosystem* *CARE Function: R = Innovation-driven Research*	Resonant with your subjective calling and objective challenge, and relevant to your specific context you engage with a particular research-to-innovation process and path, aligned with the integral approach to e.g. economics, enterprise, community that you seek to bring about. Simultaneously, you fully activate your innovation ecosystem that you have built up, together with others, around your aspired contribution
④ **CONTRIBUTION** **Theme:** *Actualising and universalising development* *CARE Function:* *E = Transformative Education*	You thereby realise individual, organisational and societal development: sustained e.g. through being codified and infused in existing research programmes as well as educational processes and curricula; thereby you contribute to the development of an Integral University

With all members of our doctoral community embarking – individually and collectively, personally and institutionally – on their particular call-to-contribution journeys, we have a tangible opportunity to bring about, jointly, new forms of Uni-Versities, and ultimately an Integral University.

With many participants currently coming from Southern (South Africa, Zimbabwe), Western (Nigeria) and Northern (Egypt) Africa, and prospectively from East Africa as well, such a new Integral University would fully bring Africa to the Integral University table. Our vision is fuelled by the desire that for Africa to rise out of its current predicament, it requires new forms of universities that are designed and built for Africa. Such an Integral University builds on home-grown knowledge (indigenous) in conjunction with knowledge from abroad (exogenous), and its educational and research processes deal concretely – through theory and action – with the most burning issues African societies are facing. Moreover, it is aimed at communities, organisations and whole societies, not just at individuals.

This vision is not limited to Africa alone. The vision carried by our group includes a global perspective, and sees such a new Integral University as a contribution to the world at large.

At the time of concluding this book, the following distinct and interconnected impulses are taking place within our doctoral and postdoctoral community of Integral Developers, altogether contributing to the co-evolution of an Integral University:

- *TRANS4M (Center for Integral Development) Switzerland, Together with All Participants:* to provide an integral knowledge base, currently focused on economics, enterprise and community, as well as research and development processes to serve as a shared platform for all participating individuals, organisations and societies.

- *Social Innovation Lab at Heliopolis University for Sustainable Development, Egypt:* to develop the overall trajectory for the establishment of an Integral University, using Heliopolis University as a platform to gradually integrate Communiversity (at Sekem and within local communities), Developmental University (Sekem Network of Communities), Research University (the institutional research core of Heliopolis University) and University of Life (action-learning-action-research driven educational programmes, processes and projects linked to Heliopolis University and also to Sekem companies), altogether facilitated by the Social Innovation Lab.
- *CISER (Centre for Integral Social and Economic Research) Nigeria:* to develop the theme of 'Inclusive Finance and Economics for Africa' as a means to renew the Nigerian and African economy, thereby gradually evolving CISER Nigeria to a renewed Research University; to surface and expand the holistic business and community development model underlying Pax Herbals in Ewu (Edo State) thereby bringing about community health and well-being, and evolving Pax Herbals gradually into a Communiversity, in a first phase, and a Developmental University in the second phase.
- *Pundutso Center for Integral Develoment and CISER (Centre for Integral Social and Economic Research) Zimbabwe:* to develop the theme of 'Empowering Communities' in particular through 'Community Economic Development' and through new forms of African entrepreneurship in and for Zimbabwe and Africa at large; Pundutso and CISER Zimbabwe are focusing on bringing about Communiversities in rural and urban Zimbabwe, thereby building on and expanding the role model of the Chinyika Communiversity. The ultimate vision is to bring about an Integral University in Zimbabwe.
- *IGSE Integral Green Economy in Slovenia:* to employ an integral economic approach to national policy planning in Slovenia as well as to educational programmes that focus on sustainable economic development; to support the building up of an Integral University through creating a synergetic knowledge 'network of networks', thereby connecting existing programmes and networks; such an Integral University would engage in individual, organisational and local community development, stimulating the integral, sustainable development of Slovenia as a whole.
- *SEED Centre, Hope University, Liverpool, UK:* to further develop the SEED (Social and Ethical Enterprise Development) Centre into a 'seedbed' for new integral, social enterprise and societal entrepreneurship designs and into a driver for the establishment of a new, complementary community currency (Liverpool Pound). SEED is geared towards supporting the sustainable development of Liverpool and its city region, but is, also, engaged in various national and international networks to help co-create the process of social entrepreneurship to social enterprise development, into the formation of more resilient social (and solidarity) economies, culminating in the evolution of ecosystems for societal entrepreneurship and transformation. The background for SEED is that it has originated out of a spiritual movement for developing social and ethical business, looking to strengthen the emergence of societal entrepreneurship through a new educational programme (preliminary title: 'Master's in Integral & Societal Entrepreneurship and Economics'); to ultimately spearhead the evolution of Hope University into a renewed Research University, serving the Integral Development of both the wider Liverpool city region and co-creating SEED centres across the world.

Other concrete impulses in India, Sri Lanka, Zambia and the US complement the current picture. We shall continue this journey over the years to come.

INTEGRAL DEVELOPMENT: TOGETHER – WITH YOU!

With Integral Development we have introduced an approach that is designed to contribute to a more healthy and participatory, balanced and peaceful, open and transparent as well as equitable and sustainable outcome of our collective development efforts – be it on an individual, organisational, communal, societal or global level. While we attempted to offer a coherent framework and process to engage in such Integral Development, we believe that the impact of the integral framework and processes on their own is rather limited.

What is required is an institutional anchoring of Integral Development through developmental-educational spaces that we coined Uni-Versities. We differentiated between a 'Southern' Communiversity, an 'Eastern' Developmental University, a 'Northern' Research University and a 'Western' University of Life.

Each of these Uni-Versities represents an actualisation of one of the four Realities and Realms, achieved through the application of transformative Rhythms to the four developmental Rounds.

The interactive application of the '4Rs' of Realities, Realms, Rhythms and Rounds around a central development calling and challenge, set within a particular context, is the key we offered to release the Integral Development genius.

The final conceptual and institutional culmination of Integral Development is the Integral University, integrating all four Uni-Versity types, and their corresponding CARE functions. We see such an Integral University as perhaps one of the most potent vehicles that we can co-create to assist us in purposefully engaging with the fundamental, evolutionary shift that humanity is collectively facing and which we described in depth in the opening chapters.

Integral Development invites us to fundamentally review and renew our conventional take on what a university is about. By introducing four new Uni-Versity types, culminating in the Integral University, the university is placed right in the centre of society. It is newly designed to play its role as society's core development agent, addressing its most burning issues, by involving individuals, organisations, and communities. It is designed to integrally activate the rich diversity within each individual, organisation, community and society and in between all of them. It is designed to bring about 'Unity in Diversity', hence: Uni-Versity.

We are fully aware that our work remains in constant evolution. In other words: Integral Development, as it is presented here, is not the final answer. As an approach it is meant to assist you, your organisation, community and society in your own development work. It invites you to evolve it further, within your context, with your own colleagues and network, and, of course, also together with us.

Let us travel together. Integral Development is a shared journey towards a more positive, wholesome future to which each one of us can contribute. It is a journey to integrally develop our selves, our organisations, communities and societies.

It is the journey to fully realise the transformative potential in all of us!

Reference

1   Nonaka, I. and Takeuchi, H. (1995). *The Knowledge-Creating Company: How Japanese Companies Create the Dynamics of Innovation.* Oxford: Oxford University Press.

Index

Note: **Bold** page numbers indicate figures, *italic* numbers indicate tables.

If you have found this book useful you may be interested in other titles in this series

TRANSCULTURAL FOCUS

Transformation Management
Towards the Integral Enterprise
Ronnie Lessem and Alexander Schieffer
ISBN 978-0-566-08896-4

Integral Research and Innovation
Transforming Enterprise and Society
Ronnie Lessem and Alexander Schieffer
ISBN 978-0-566-08918-3

Integral Economics
Releasing the Economic Genius of Your Society
Ronnie Lessem and Alexander Schieffer
ISBN 978-0-566-09247-3

Integral Dynamics
Political Economy, Cultural Dynamics and the Future of the University
Ronnie Lessem with Alexander Schieffer, Junie T. Tong and Samuel D. Rima
ISBN 978-1-4094-5103-7

AFRICAN FOCUS

Inclusive Organizational Transformation
Rica Viljoen
ISBN 978-1-4724-2300-9

Integral Community
Political Economy to Social Commons
Ronnie Lessem, Paul Chidara Muchineripi and Steve Kada
ISBN 978-1-4094-4679-8

An Integral Approach to Development Economics
Islamic Finance in an African Context
Basheer A. Oshodi
ISBN 978-1-4724-1125-9

GOWER

MIDDLE EASTERN FOCUS

Islamic Values and Management Practices
Quality and Transformation in the Arab World
Maqbouleh M. Hammoudeh
ISBN 978-1-4094-0752-2

Islam and Sustainable Development
New Worldviews
Odeh Rashed Al-Jayyousi
ISBN 978-1-4094-2901-2

ASIAN FOCUS

Remaking Ourselves, Enterprise and Society
An Indian Approach to Human Values in Management
G.P. Rao

Culture and Economics in the Global Community
A Framework for Socioeconomic Development
Kensei Hiwaki
ISBN 978-1-4094-0412-5

Finance and Society in 21st Century China
Chinese Culture versus Western Markets
Junie T. Tong
ISBN 978-1-4094-0129-2

EUROPEAN FOCUS

Finance at the Threshold
Rethinking the Real and Financial Economies
Christopher Houghton Budd
ISBN 978-0-566-09211-4

Crafting an Integral Enterprise
Towards a Sustainable Telecommunications Sector
Reza Moussavian
ISBN 978-1-4094-6310-8

NORTH AMERICAN FOCUS

Spiritual Capital
A Moral Core for Social and Economic Justice
Samuel D. Rima
ISBN 978-1-4094-0484-2

GOWER